Informal Assessment and Instruction in Written Language: A Practitioner's Guide for Students with Learning Disabilities

Nancy Mather
and
Rhia Roberts
University of Arizona

John Wiley & Sons, Inc.

New York • Chichester • Brisbane • Toronto
Singapore • Weinheim

Library of Congress Cataloging-in-Publication Data
Mather, Nancy.
      Informal assessment and instruction in written language: a practitioner's guide
for students with learning disabilities / Nancy Mather, Rhia Roberts.
          p.   cm.
      Includes bibliographical references and index.
      ISBN 0-471-16208-6
      1. Learning disabled children—Education—Language arts.   2. English language—
Composition and exercises—Study and teaching (Elementary)   3. English
language—Composition and exercises—Ability testing.   I. Roberts, Rhia, 1959–
II. Title.
LC4704.85.M38   1995
372.6′23—dc20   94-29759

Printed in the United States of America

10 9 8 7 6 5 4

ACKNOWLEDGMENTS

The process of writing a book is infinitely more important than the book that is completed as a result of the writing, let alone the success or failure that book may have after it is written . . . the book is merely a symbol of the writing. In writing the book, I am living. I am growing. I am tapping myself. I am changing. The process is the product.

—Theodore Isaac Rubin

We would like to thank many people for helping us with the process of creating this book. First, several teachers contributed writing samples. Vesta Udall provided numerous writing samples from students in her classes. Melissa Moffett King, Sherry Maher, Susan Edgecombe, Barbara Falwell, Sonya Miller, Linda Nathanson, Jane Sadowsky, Cathy Orzechowski, Nalan Babur, and Janet Tesch also provided samples. We also wish to express our appreciation to all of the students who contributed their writing to this book, both knowingly and unknowingly. Throughout the book, all names have been changed.

Wendy Randall Wall made several contributions to the book: developing the first draft of questions to ask about a student's knowledge of the writing process approach, summarizing several strategies, contributing samples from her students, and preparing the first drafts of the appendices. Nancy Slavick Robertson and Joan Scully contributed an analysis. Dr. Pat Tomlan assisted with the writing of Chapter 4 and helped us keep up-to-date with legal issues. Brenda Hanna helped us review the cases and select a few to eliminate.

Some recommendations in the analyses were excerpted or adapted from *Woodcock-Johnson Psycho-Educational Battery—Revised: Recommendations and Reports* (Mather & Jaffe, 1992). Thank you to Dr. Lynne Jaffe for her efforts on this previous publication.

Several people assisted with preparation of the manuscript. Special thanks is expressed to Nancy Neveln for her assistance and preparation of several figures, her help with printing, and her remarkable attention to detail. She was always willing to move over from her computer to let us print. Rich Frost and Brian Grove provided invaluable assistance and salvaging of text when the computer crashed. Thank you, in particular, for helping us not have to rewrite all of Chapter 3. Ironically, the lost chapter was on the writing process approach, so we revisited the drafting stage.

Jane Todorski, the production editor, was very patient with us. Even though we wanted always to add "just one more thing," she kept her sense of humor. We appreciate her assistance and careful readings and rereadings of the text. As a final note, we would both like to express special thanks to our parents, brothers, and sisters for their continuing support, encouragement, and love throughout our lives and to Benjamin and Daniel for providing welcomed distractions.

CONTENTS

LIST OF FIGURES AND TABLES

Figures

Tables

1

INTRODUCTION: VERY GENTLY WITH NO RED MARKS

Writing is easy:
All you do is sit staring at the blank sheet of paper,
until the drops of blood form on your forehead.

— Gene Fowler

For many students, acquiring writing skills is not easy. Writing is the most complex language task (Lerner, 1993; Morris & Crump, 1982) and many students have severe and persistent problems developing writing skill. Although many students with writing difficulties have language or learning disabilities, others do not. Whatever the reason for the difficulty, the important consideration is that effective writing is essential to school success (Stewart, 1992). The skills needed are multifaceted, ranging from the production of legible handwriting to the production of organized discourse.

Some students have difficulty with handwriting or with basic writing skills such as spelling, whereas others have difficulty expressing and organizing their ideas or taking notes. Vogel (1987) described the problems faced by students with learning disabilities when they are required to integrate all the skills necessary to take lecture notes:

> . . . the task of taking notes in lectures is overwhelming, nor is it any wonder. Note-taking requires simultaneous listening, comprehending, and synthesizing and/or extracting main ideas while retaining them long enough to formulate a synopsis and write it down. The writing act, in turn, requires automaticity and speed in letter formation and sufficient legibility and spelling ability to decipher what has been written at a later time. (p. 523)

Clearly, the components of writing are interwoven; difficulty in one aspect of writing, such as spelling, often contributes to difficulty in another aspect of writing, such as taking notes or expressing ideas. Writing is a complex process that requires the linking of language, thought, and motor skills (Outhred, 1989). No other school task requires as much synchronization (Levine, 1994). Unfortunately, problems with any aspect of written language may affect a student's ability to communicate effectively (Lerner, 1993).

Too often students with writing difficulties develop counterproductive coping strategies, such as only writing words they know how to spell, avoiding complex ideas, and writing as little as they can to get by (Outhred, 1989). Consider the following example of a student with limited spelling skill. Mike, a third-grade student with strong oral language skill but difficulty with writing, currently produces short, simple stories. In answer to the question of how he chooses a topic for writing, Mike replied: "I look at the words on the board and on the walls, then I make up a story using those words and the extra ones I know how to spell like *the*." He further noted that many of his stories feature the police because he now knows how to spell that word. Figure 1–1 illustrates one of Mike's stories involving the "police." Clearly, poor spelling skills can place a limitation on word choice (Morris & Crump, 1982).

The writing of Greg, a fourth-grade student, provides another example of the impact of limited spelling skill on writing. As part of a writing assessment, Greg was asked to write responses to several items on the Woodcock-Johnson-Revised Writing Samples test (Woodcock & Johnson, 1989). On item number 7, Greg was given the following prompt: "This woman is a queen. Write a good sentence that tells what this man is."

While contemplating the task, Greg mused aloud: "The man is a king. Oh boy! Hard words! I can't

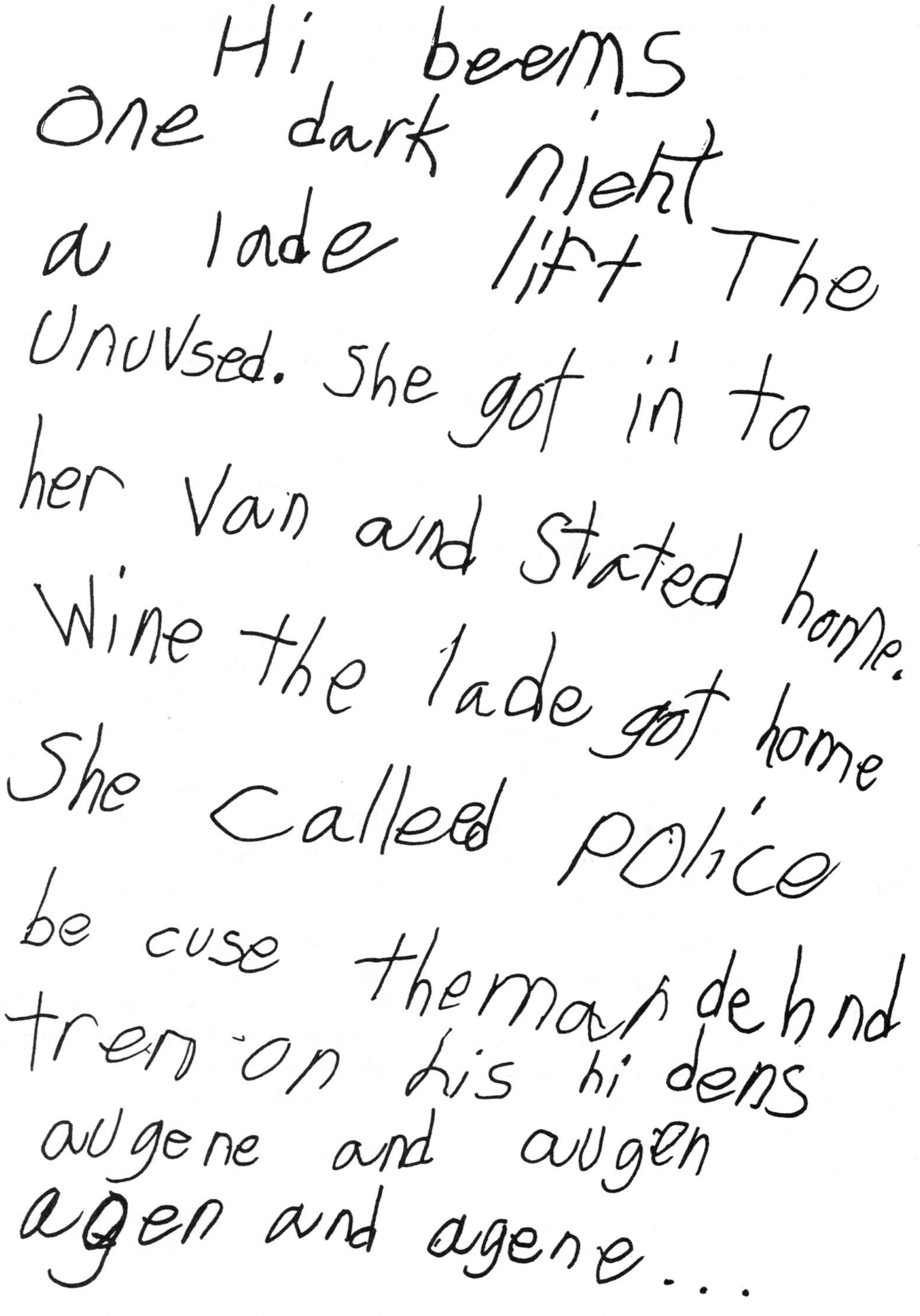

Hi beems
One dark night
a lade lift The
UnuVsed. She got in to
her van and Stated home.
Wine the lade got home
She called police
be cuse the man dehind
trem on his hi dens
augene and augen
agen and agene...

Translation:

High Beams

One dark night a lady left the university. She got into her van and started home. When the lady got home she called the police because the man behind her turned on his high beams again and again.

Figure 1-1. A story about the police by Mike, a third-grade student.

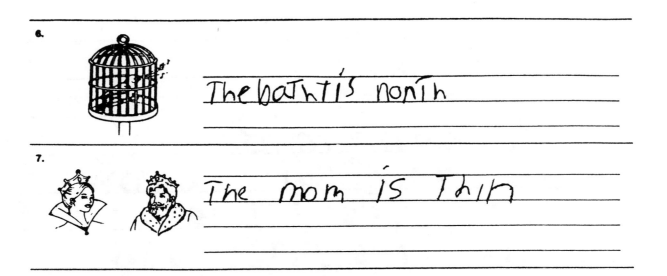

Figure 1-2. Written responses on the WJ-R Writing Samples test by Greg, a fourth-grade student. This sample was provided to Dr. Pat Tomlan by Joyce Charbonneau, a special education teacher in Carbondale, CO.

spell those words. The man is rich. Another hard word! What can I spell? I can spell mom and dad. Can I use mom in my sentence? The mom is rich. I don't know how to spell rich. What do I know how to spell? Thin! I can spell thin." Following this dialogue, Greg produced the following sentence, presented in Figure 1-2: *The mom is thin.* Presently, Greg's expression is hampered severely by his limited spelling skill. Without knowledge of Greg's thought processes, one may surmise that his problem is with language and/or conceptualization, rather than with spelling.

Unfortunately, it is difficult for students such as Mike and Greg to focus upon the construction of meaning if their attention is directed toward letter formation, spelling, or neatness (Graves, 1983). The important question then becomes: How can Greg's teacher help him? One common complaint we have heard from teachers around the country is that they know a student has trouble with writing but do not know why or, more important, what to do about it.

Some teachers do not receive enough training on how to help students improve their writing. Although university programs should train teachers in both the comprehensiveness of the written language process as well as in diagnostic procedures (Roit & McKenzie, 1985), many teachers received their train-ing at a time when written language instruction was not emphasized. In other instances, beginning teachers enrolled in preservice training programs did receive information about writing instruction in their coursework, but did not have enough practical experience analyzing written products and implementing instruction (Mosenthal & Englert, 1987). Similarly, school psychologists are usually not well prepared to understand the nature, prevalence, and needs of children with writing disabilities (Kulberg, 1993). The writing problems of students with learning disabilities are so severe and extensive, it is surprising that writing has been such a low priority (Zaragoza & Vaughn, 1992).

Without training in how to assist students with writing difficulties, teachers become frustrated. For example, during the first week of school Ms. Hall, a third-grade teacher, entered the teacher's lounge with a story written by Ann. Although Ann was using invented spelling, a necessary stage through which children progress, Ms. Hall was concerned about Ann's present level of development in writing skill. After showing her colleagues the paper, presented in Figure 1-3, Ms. Hall asked: "What should I do?"

She had written a comment on Ann's paper noting the failure to comply with the assignment of writing

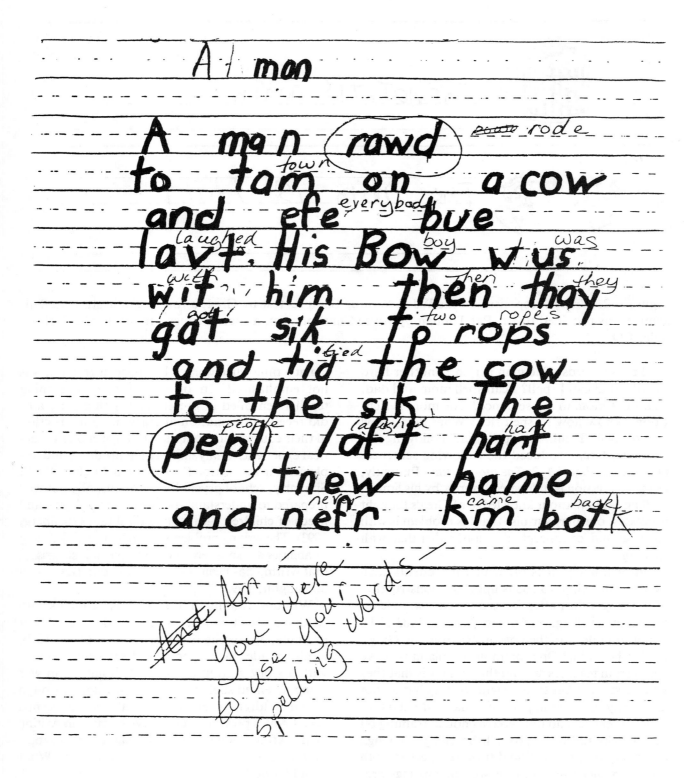

Figure 1-3. A story using her spelling words written by Ann, a third-grade student.

a story incorporating the week's spelling words. Although failure to complete the assignment was the least of her concerns, Ms. Hall did not know what else to say.

Often, teachers recognize the problem, but are unsure of how to intervene. Intervention is imperative because failure to progress in writing can be devastating. For example, during the first week of an eighth-grade English class, Ms. Downing asked the students to write something about themselves that they would like to share with her. She provided several examples: "Perhaps you have a special pet or you took an exciting trip this summer; or you could discuss your family or an activity that you really enjoy. The main requirement is to let me know something about you." At the end of the 50-minute period, Tom handed her the essay presented in Figure 1–4.

Semi-Translation:

Like me I have a disability. I had it since third grade. I am . . . my disability. For example I know how hard it is. I can't spell right. . . . For all my life I know I am afraid to write a note to my girl friend. She doesn't know that I have but I don't know how to tell her because I don't know how she is going to act. I don't know why I am telling you but I know I am not stupid.

Figure 1–4. An essay written to his teacher by Tom, an eighth-grade student.

Tom's difficulty with writing is readily apparent, as is his desire to communicate to the audience, his teacher. If students cannot write, they are deprived of an important tool for both expression and the organization of thought (Graves, 1978). So how do we start? *Very gently with no red marks*. Ms. Downing acknowledged his message and responded to his writing with the following comment: "Thank you for telling me about your struggle with writing. Writing is hard to learn, but I would like to help you write a letter to your girlfriend." Clearly, students such as Tom require intensive, systematic instructional programs to increase their writing skill.

Effective writing teachers are able to: (a) analyze written products and (b) develop specific instructional plans to help students succeed in writing. In order to select appropriate interventions, one must identify and prioritize the areas of concern. Prior to developing instructional objectives, a teacher must determine a student's educational needs (Hasbrouck, Tindal, & Parker, 1994) and identify the strengths on which to build. With careful analysis of a student's present performance level, instructional programs can be designed to increase writing competence.

The purpose of this book is to help educators increase their proficiency in analyzing and teaching writing to students with learning disabilities. Presently, a trend exists to describe students with learning disabilities with a more generic label, such as students with learning problems or learning differences. The authors decided to maintain the focus on students with learning disabilities because of the existence of an extensive research base and the many intervention strategies that have been developed for use with these students. Furthermore, the authors believe that individuals with learning disabilities do exist and that these students often require specific interventions. The majority of accommodations and instructional strategies described in this text, however, are applicable to all students with writing difficulties, regardless of etiology.

The text is organized into nine chapters. Following the introductory chapter, the second chapter provides a review of the various components of written language and the types of difficulties students may have with handwriting, spelling, usage, vocabulary, and text structure. The third chapter provides an overview of the writing process approach. The fourth chapter reviews the legal protections and the various accommodations to which students are entitled. Chapters 5, 6, and 7 contain summaries of instructional strategies that may be used to enhance student performance in the areas of handwriting, basic skills, and written expression. The eighth chapter presents analyses of 20 writing samples from students in first- through eighth-grade levels. The writing assignments are reviewed within a diagnostic-prescriptive format. The ninth chapter contains 15 writing samples, 10 of which have guided questions. These samples may be used for independent study assignments or in-class discussions. The appendixes provide lists of educational software, instructional programs, books on writing assessment and instruction, and the addresses of publishers. This book is appropriate for use in university courses that include writing assessment and instruction, or as a reference for practicing elementary or middle-school teachers, special education teachers, speech-language therapists, and/or school psychologists.

2

COMPONENTS OF WRITTEN LANGUAGE

We need only try to imagine the enormous changes in the cultural development of children that occur as a result of mastery of written language and the ability to read — and of thus becoming aware of everything that human genius has created in the realm of the written word.

— Vygotsky, 1978, p.116

Many students with learning disabilities have severe and persistent difficulties developing writing skill. The difficulties often continue into adulthood and are more prevalent than reading problems in older students (Vogel, 1985). In general, research findings support low abilities on all aspects of written language for students with learning disabilities at every age (Myklebust, 1965, 1973; Nodine, Barenbaum, & Newcomer, 1985; Vogel, 1985; Vogel & Moran, 1982). These students make minimal improvement in writing across the grades, and every year the gap between writers with and without learning disabilities widens (Houck & Billingsley, 1989; Newcomer & Barenbaum, 1991; Poplin, Gray, Larsen, Banikowski, & Mehring, 1980; Tomlan, 1986). In many instances, the writing performance of students with learning disabilities may appear similar to that of students 3 to 6 years younger (Tomlan, 1986) and, subsequently, instruction must be geared to their developmental levels.

Writing is a multidimensional process and students vary in regard to skill level as well as with respect to the aspects of writing that cause difficulty (Berninger & Hooper, 1993; Berninger & Whitaker, 1993). Consequently, educators can increase their diagnostic skill by understanding the various components of writing. The purpose of this chapter is to review the major components of written language depicted in Figure 2–1, including: (a) handwriting, (b) spelling, (c) usage, (d) vocabulary, and (e) text structure. In addition, the various types of difficulties experienced by writers with learning disabilities and the role of technology are discussed. The final section presents an orientation to instructional strategies.

Handwriting

Handwriting is a fine-motor skill that enables individuals to communicate their thoughts in writing. Although presently few people pay attention to handwriting instruction, rapid, legible, and comfortable writing is important for school success (Graham, 1992; Graham & Miller, 1980; King, 1985) as our society still places great value on the appearance of handwriting (Sampson, Van Allen, & Sampson, 1991). Even though a passage may be well composed, if a reader cannot decipher a student's handwriting, the meaning is lost (Larsen, 1987). As noted by Isaacson (1994): "A family member receiving a letter cannot appreciate the rich context and social interaction that accompanied the writing process if he or she cannot read the letter" (p. 53). An individual who cannot produce legible script or write quickly and easily is severely hampered in communicative capability (Hamstra-Bletz & Blote, 1993). Legible handwriting is fundamental to other writing skills (Hoy & Gregg, 1994).

In addition, clear, consistent, legible handwriting is important and rewarding to the student (Arena, 1970). Students often feel frustrated in regard to their handwriting skill. Figure 2–2 presents a report written by Taylor, a third-grade student. Although Taylor has several ideas that he wishes to express, he has difficulty with the size of his letters and spacing. On an average, he writes two words per line. In an interview, Taylor comments that he has a lot to say, but he finds it hard to fit the words on the paper. Writing requires such effort that Taylor has trouble concentrating on the content of his assignments.

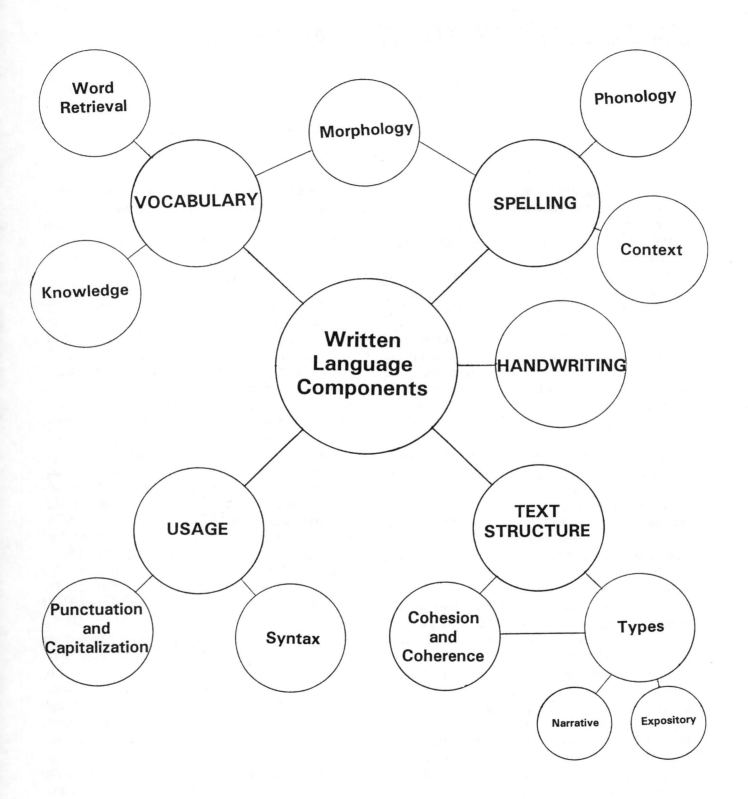

Figure 2–1. The various components of writing skill.

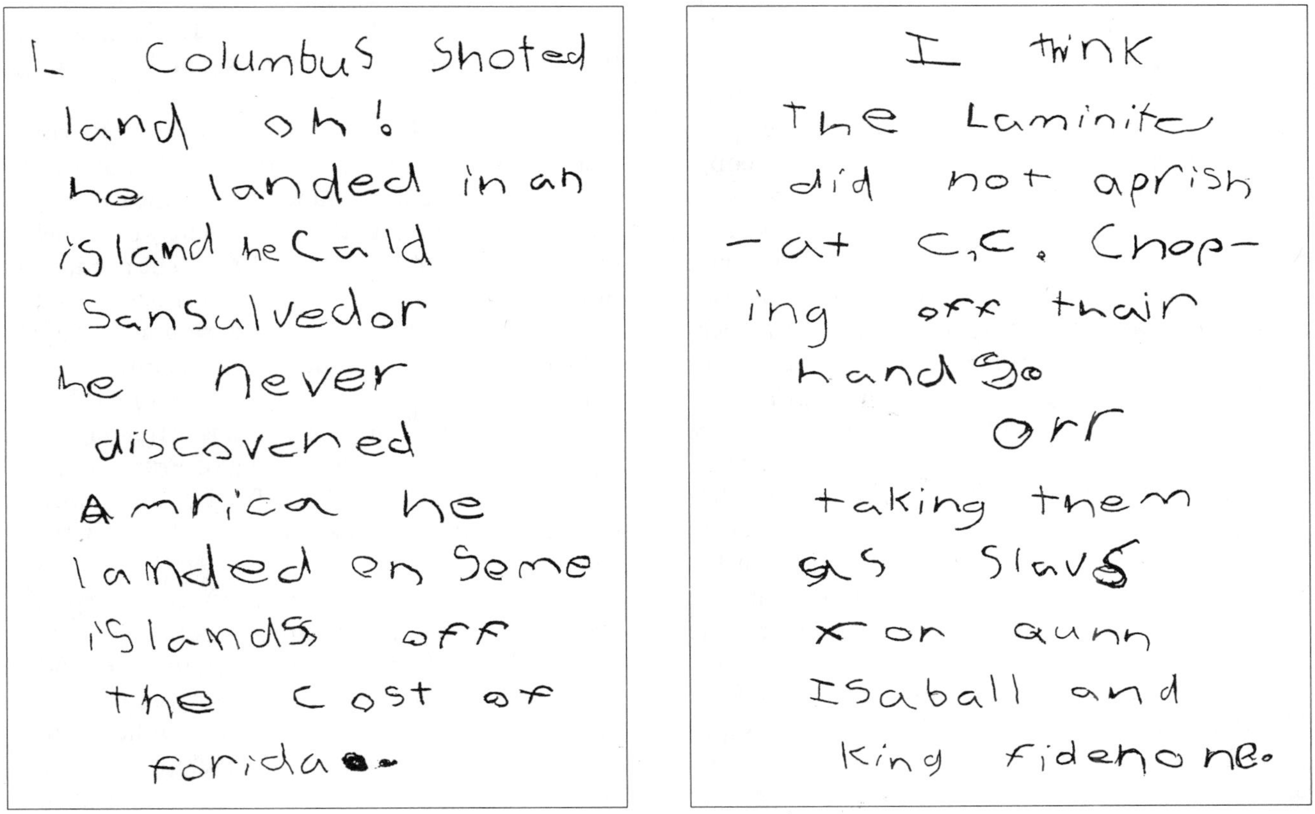
I. Columbus shoted
land oh!
he landed in an
island he cald
Sansulvedor
he never
discoverd
Amrica he
landed on some
islands off
the cost of
forida.

I think
The Laminite
did not aprish
-at C.C. Chop-
ing off thair
hands so
orr
taking them
as slavs
or qunn
Isaball and
king fidenone.

Figure 2–2. Report written by Taylor, a third-grade student.

Components of Handwriting

Handwriting requires a multiplicity of skills. To write legibly, students must produce graphic images and recall the motor patterns for manuscript and/or cursive letters (Silverman, Zigmond, Zimmerman, & Vallecorsa, 1981). The individual must be able to recognize and discriminate letters, judge the spacing of letters and words, and recall and reproduce letter forms. To produce effective handwriting, students need to develop both legibility and fluency. Legibility refers to the clarity and correctness of letter formation, whereas fluency refers to production speed (Salend, 1994).

Legible handwriting includes six, interrelated characteristics: (a) letter formation, or the composition of the stroke; (b) size and proportion, or the size of the letters and the proportional size between capital and lowercase letters; (c) spacing, or the amount of spacing between letters and words; (d) slant, or the consistency in direction of the writing; (e) alignment, or uniformity of size and consistency on the writing line; and (f) line quality, or the steadiness and thickness of the line (Barbe, Wasylyk, Hackney, & Braun, 1984). These characteristics can be evaluated by analyzing student performance within a composition, on dictated sentences, and on tasks involving near- and far-point copy. In addition, the evaluator may ask students to copy sentences using their fastest writing, then their typical writing, and then their neatest writing.

Factors Affecting Performance

Some students with learning disabilities have extreme difficulty developing legible handwriting. The individual has difficulty transferring information from the visual to the motor system (Hamstra-Bletz & Blote, 1993; Johnson & Myklebust, 1967). These students may be diagnosed as having dysgraphia, or a disturbance in visual-motor integration. Although little is written with regard to the behaviors of students with handwriting difficulties, Bain (1991) summarizes four common characteristics:

an unconventional pencil grip, fingers too near the pencil point, trouble with erasing, and difficulty with letter alignment.

Poor handwriting is often reflective of underlying deficits. A student may have difficulty executing the motor movements needed to write or copy, transferring visual input into fine-motor movement, and/or performing activities that require visual or motor judgments (Lerner, 1993). Some students have difficulty with both handwriting and copying tasks because of poor visual memory for letter sequences or poor eye-muscle control (Bain, 1991; Kurtz, 1994).

Bryan, an eighth-grade student with poor handwriting skill, discussed with Mr. Marcus, his science teacher, the difficulty he was having copying classnotes from the chalkboard. Bryan explained that he did not have enough time to copy the lecture notes because he had to look back and forth for every single letter. He further noted that each time he looked back up at the board, he had trouble locating his place.

In addition to having difficulty copying, students like Bryan are often prone to letter reversals and letter transpositions. For most students, reversals are resolved by the end of first grade (Tompkins,

1994). Even in eighth grade, Bryan's writing still contains occasional *b* and *d* reversals. Reversals and transpositions are often more persistent in individuals with learning disabilities.

For other students, difficulty with handwriting increases as they attempt to compose. Simultaneous attention to spelling, punctuation, ideation, and sentence generation results in a seemingly overwhelming task (Bain, 1991; Graham, 1992). The production of letters requires so much conscious attention that the writer's ability to record and examine thoughts is disrupted (Graham & Harris, 1988; Graves, 1983).

In some cases, the actual task of writing is laborious and the speed of production is extremely slow. Figure 2–3 illustrates the writing of Frank, a third-grade student. Although the final product may be judged as legible, Frank spent over 1 hour writing his response.

In other cases, handwriting is affected by specific illegibilities. Figure 2–4 illustrates a paragraph written by Jill, an eighth-grade student. Although the other letters are formed correctly, Jill's reversed formation of the letter *e* affects the legibility of her writing.

Although handwriting skill develops as students progress through school, some secondary and post-

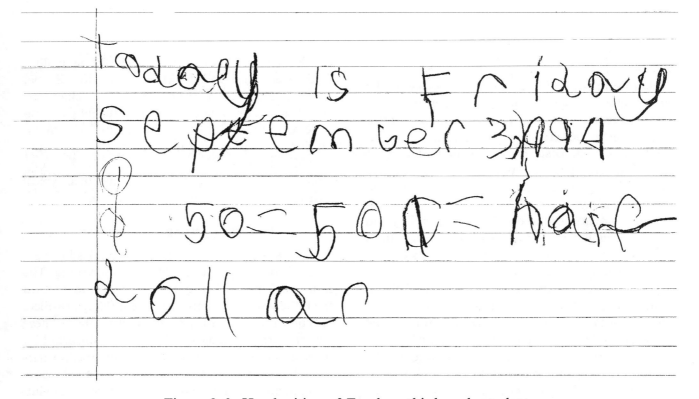

Figure 2–3. Handwriting of Frank, a third-grade student.

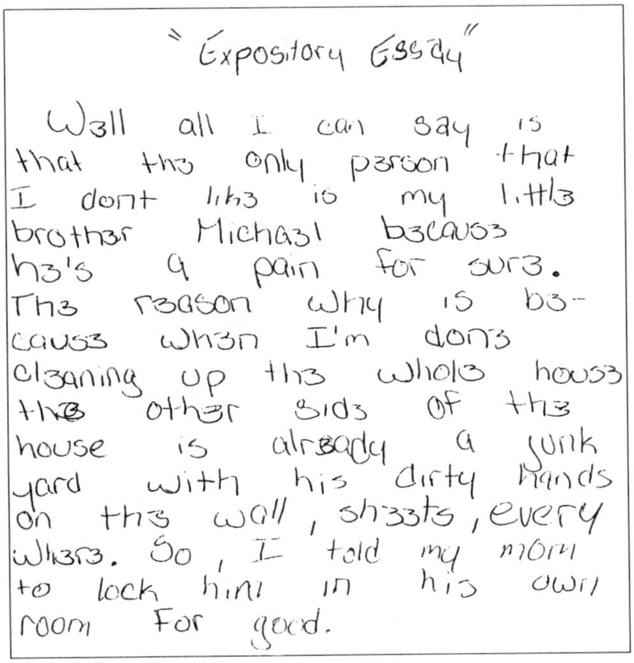

Figure 2–4. Handwriting of Jill, an eighth-grade student.

secondary students have yet to develop legible writing styles (Hughes & Smith, 1990). In addition, many university students with learning disabilities do not write as fast as the general population (Hughes & Suritsky, 1994). For individuals with learning disabilities, therefore, handwriting problems often persist throughout the school years. In a longitudinal study, Hamstra-Bletz and Blote (1993) found that second-grade students with dysgraphia still had writing problems in the higher grades.

Figure 2–5 illustrates the writing of Jeremy, a college senior, who was enrolled in an introductory course on learning disabilities. Jeremy was diagnosed as having dysgraphia in third grade. These samples are excerpts from his classnotes and include a definition of dysgraphia. Throughout his college career, Jeremy's instructors complained that his printing was practically illegible.

As a general rule, students with poor handwriting skill require a great deal of overteaching and practice (Bain, 1991). Jeremy notes, however, that he had 6 years of intensive handwriting instruction in elementary school. When discussing his instructional history, he laughs and states: "A lot of good it did me." Perhaps Jeremy practiced forming letters but received little direct instruction.

Historically, individuals with poor handwriting received assistance from others with more talent. In the 1500s one could employ a writing master who would transform one's poor efforts into a writing style beautiful to behold (Hanna, Hodges, & Hanna, 1971). Some students today would love the opportunity to hire a scribe to recopy their writing. Fortunately, many students are able to take advantage of technology, such as laptop computers, to complete their assignments.

Handwriting and Technology

Using computers, legibility is the rule rather than the exception (Hunt-Berg, Rankin, & Beukelman, 1994). Many students find writing on a computer easier than with paper and pencil (Lewis, 1993). In addition, the use of word processors eliminates the need to recopy. Students can use computers and not worry about handwriting or messy written documents (Lerner, 1993). Consequently, their writing is easier to read. In addition, because of the legible product, teachers can respond more readily to content rather than handwriting quality (Hunt-Berg et al., 1994). The question may then arise: "Why should we care about handwriting skill in the age of computers?" Conceivably, the time may come when handwriting skill decreases in value as computers with word processing programs become standard equipment in elementary classrooms (Tompkins, 1994). Presently, however, the information processing age is here, but the resources are not. Computers are not standard equipment in the majority of homes or elementary classrooms.

Furthermore, even if a time comes when each elementary child has a laptop computer, handwriting will still be a necessary skill. Situations will always exist in and out of school where an individual's knowledge, competency, and attitude will be judged through handwriting (Bain, 1991). As noted by Smith (1994): "Despite the availability of word processors, handwriting difficulties still will interfere with productivity in note taking and essay exams and negatively influence the judgment of teachers when grading exams or an employer when reading a job application. Therefore, every effort must be made to help the student's handwriting become as fluent and legible as possible" (p. 442).

In addition, people will always find themselves in places where computers are impractical, unavail-

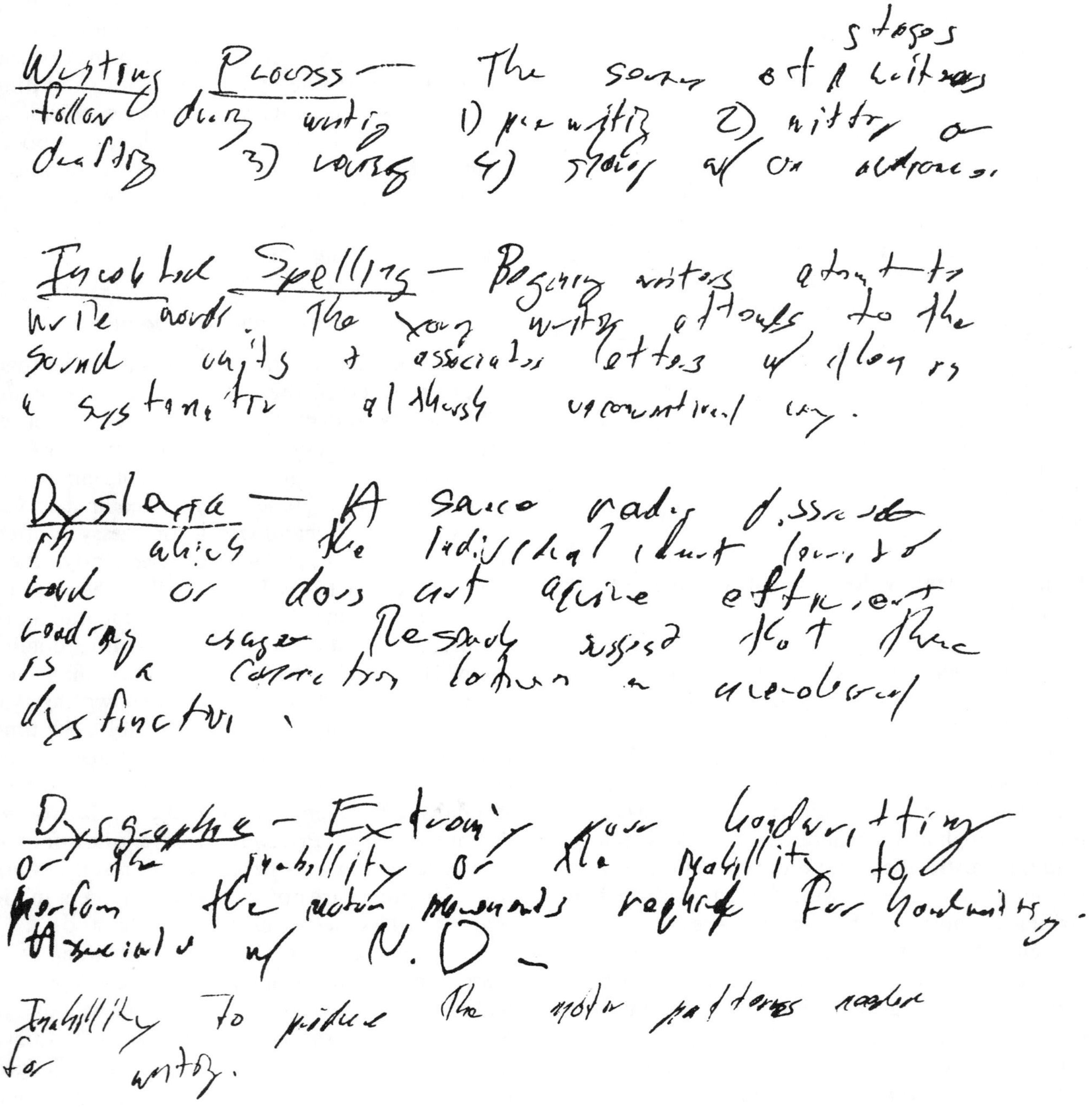

Figure 2–5. Handwriting of Jeremy, a college student.

able, or unnecessary. For example, many people will still, at times, prefer to use handwriting for: (a) writing letters to friends and relatives, (b) writing short notes to others, (c) filling out forms, (d) taking notes in classes, or (e) recording messages and ideas when away from school or the workplace. Although technological advances have impacted the daily use of handwriting for some people, competencies in this skill are definitely still important (Polloway & Smith, 1992).

The problems and effects of illegible handwriting are further illustrated in the article "Getting it Write," presented in Figure 2-6. Even in the information processing age, legible, fluent handwriting will still remain an important skill (Bos & Vaughn, 1994).

Spelling

Of all the basic skill areas, acquisition of spelling skill is the most difficult for some students. When compared to normally achieving peers, individuals with learning disabilities score significantly lower in most areas of written expression, but particularly on measures of spelling (Adelman & Vogel, 1990; Cordoni, 1979; Poplin et al., 1980; Wong, Wong, & Blenkinsop, 1989).

For individuals with learning disabilities, spelling difficulties often persist even after reading skill is acquired (Seidenberg, 1989). These students exhibit serious spelling problems that emerge early and continue into secondary school and college (Adelman & Vogel, 1990; Bruck, 1993; Cone, Wilson, Bradley, & Reese, 1985; Cordoni, 1979; Dalke, 1988; Leuenberger & Morris, 1990; Poplin et al., 1980; Vogel, 1989; Vogel & Moran, 1982). Figure 2-7 presents a letter written by Denny, a college senior, to his professor. The note explains the tardiness of his assignment. Although his excuses are well documented, difficulties with both spelling and handwriting are apparent.

Even though the most critical aspect of written language performance is the ability to express ideas, basic skills, such as spelling, are also important as they affect the judgment of writing quality (Brown, 1981), the clarity of the ideas, and an individual's ability to communicate. Problems in spelling can interfere with communication, fluency, and self-confidence (Scheuermann et al., 1994; Wilde, 1990). As noted by Gearheart and Gearheart (1989): "There are students who can express themselves unusually well in writing despite inadequate spelling and handwriting, but these are the exceptions. Often their lack of ability in these other two areas 'masks' their potential ability in written expression" (p. 404). Unfortunately, poor spelling may contribute to lowered grades across academic areas (Scheuermann, Jacobs, McCall, & Knies, 1994).

Figures 2-8 and 2-9 illustrate the thoughts of two fourth-grade students, Jerry and Marge, writing about pollution. Jerry writes: "Clean Air. Good to smell, good air. We can stop pollution now. Please

When learning the three R's in grade school it seems a lot of us weren't paying much attention, at least to one big *R*—Writing. Illegible handwriting is becoming a troublesome problem in many areas.

For starters, sloppy script costs businesses $200 million a year, according to the Writing Instrument Manufacturers Association of Marlton, New Jersey. Film developer Eastman Kodak is stuck with nearly 400,000 unreturnable rolls of film a year due to illegible addresses. And the U.S. Postal Service routes 38 million pieces of illegible mail to its dead letter office every year at a cost of $4 million. Some post offices even hire skilled handwriting experts to try to decipher hundreds of letters each day.

In the workplace, only 10 percent of executives say their employees' handwriting is legible. Forty-one percent say that handwriting is getting worse.

"Secretaries say they spend more time trying to figure out what the boss intended for them to do than doing the chore itself," says Barbara Getty, handwriting and calligraphy instructor at Portland State University and coauthor of *Write Now: A Complete Self-Teaching Program for Better Handwriting.*

But while clear handwriting is on the decline, studies found that handwritten *personal* notes are still preferred over typewritten ones.

Figure 2-6. "Getting it Write" newsclipping.

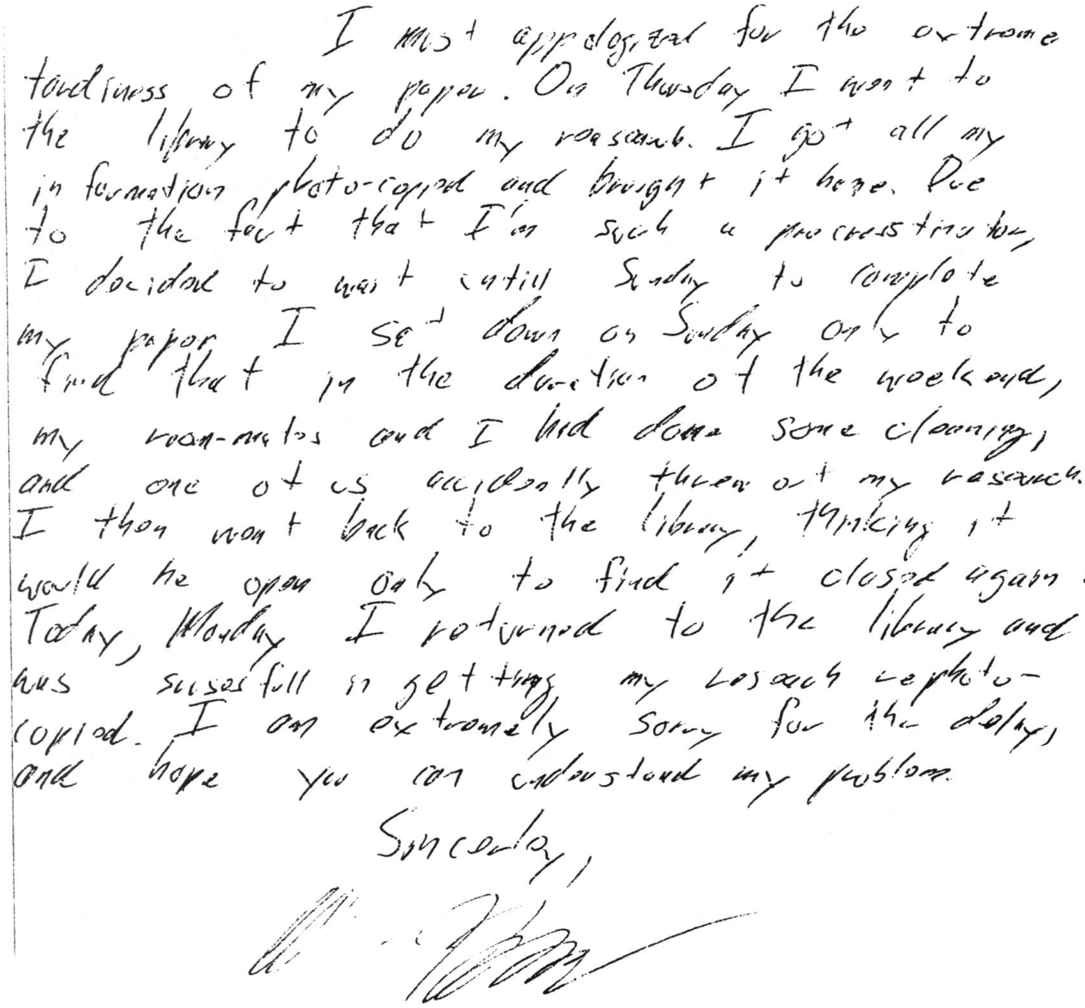
I most appologized for the extreme tardiness of my paper. On Thursday I went to the library to do my research. I got all my information photo-copied and brought it home. Due to the fact that I'm such a procrastinator, I decided to wait until Sunday to complete my paper. I sat down on Sunday only to find that in the duration of the weekend, my room-mates and I had done some cleaning, and one of us accidently threw out my research. I then went back to the library, thinking it would be open only to find it closed again! Today, Monday I returned to the library and was sucsesfull in getting my research rephoto-copied. I am extremely sorry for the delay, and hope you can understand my problem.

Sincerely,

Figure 2–7. A letter to his professor by Denny, a college senior.

keep our air clean." Marge writes: "Save the Earth. Keep the air clean here. Don't go in the car, just walk. We can pick up trash." Unfortunately, the ideas of both students are lost in poor spelling.

Students with spelling problems are often embarrassed by their limited spelling skill. For example, Dennis, a third-grade gifted student with a learning disability, commented that he would do his utmost to ensure that nobody saw his written assignments. On being asked why, Dennis replied, "I know I'm intelligent, but my writing makes me look so dumb."

Similarly, Cleary (1993) reported the following account written by Jason, a 14-year-old student:

One day the home room had a spelling bee and we were sent to watch or pretispiat. I chose not to and the other kids did but the other two took a chanch of hilmiatoin [humiliation]. *I wasn't in it and I was still hilmiatolined! I bent over my desk and asked how to spell "home" to a girl. She giggled and whispered to her friend. In five minutes every one was laughing.*

Many students with learning disabilities are good writers but poor spellers, who persist with writing despite their intense frustration with spelling. Amanda, a fourth-grade student, wrote the letter presented in Figure 2–10. Although the letter contains

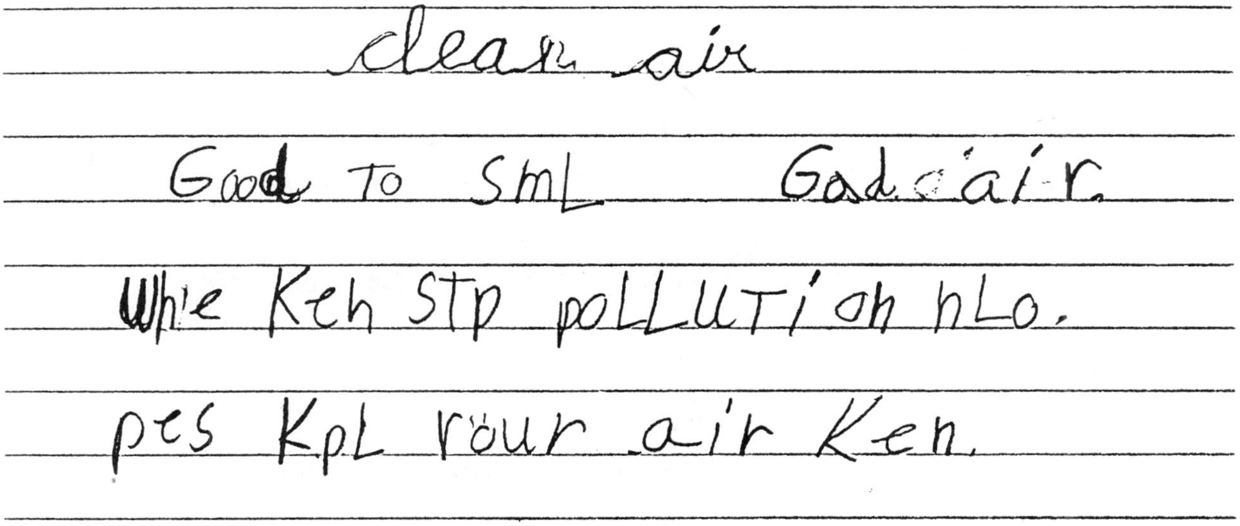

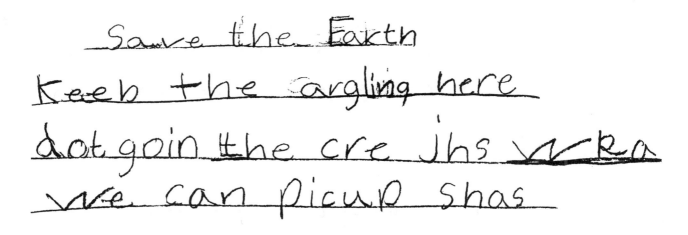

clean air

Good To Sml   Gadsair.

Whe Keh Stp poLLuTi on nLo.

pes KpL rour air Ken.

Figure 2-8. A passage written by Jerry, a fourth-grade student.

Save the Eaxtn

Keeb the argling here

dot goin the cre Jhs wcRn

wce can picup shas

Figure 2-9. A passage written by Marge, a fourth-grade student.

many errors in spelling and punctuation, the content is carefully sequenced and persuasive.

Despite poor spelling, Amanda was able to communicate her wishes to her grandmother. For some students, however, spelling difficulties thwart their communicative attempts. For example, the paragraph illustrated in Figure 2-11 is an excerpt from a story written by Joyce, a sixth-grade student. In this example, the student's poor spelling interferes with her ability to communicate.

One important consideration is that neat, legible handwriting can reduce negative attention to spelling difficulties. As can be observed in Figure 2-12, Rich, a sixth-grade student, has difficulty with spelling. Despite having a heavy line quality, his writing has an attractive appearance. In addition to neat, legible letter formation, Rich indents paragraphs and observes margins. His spelling problems are not as readily apparent and his teachers appreciate and reinforce his effort.

Components of Spelling

Accurate spelling requires knowledge of our writing system and the structure of orthography.

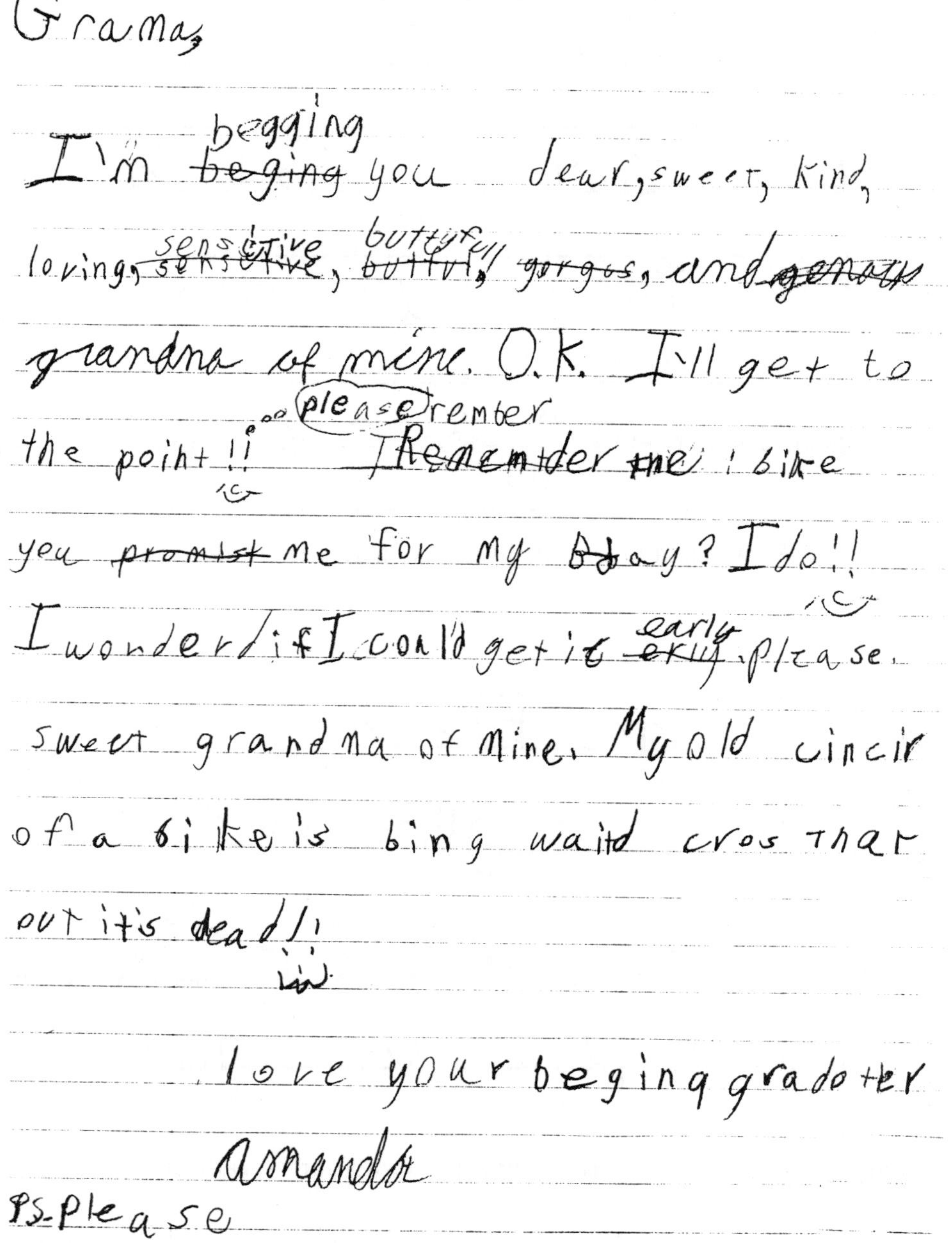

Grama,

I'm ~~beging~~ begging you dear, sweet, kind, loving, ~~sensitive~~, ~~butifl~~ gorgos, and ~~genrous~~ grandma of mine. O.K. I'll get to the point!! ~~I Remember the~~ please rember i bike you ~~promisk~~ me for my ~~bday~~? I do!! I wonder if I could get it ~~early~~ please. sweet grandma of mine. My old cincir of a bike is bing waitd cros thar out it's dead!!

love your beging grado ter
Amanda
P.S. Please.

Translation:

Grandma,
I'm begging you dear, sweet, kind, loving, sensitive, beautiful, gorgeous, and generous grandma of mine. O.K. I'll get right to the point. Please remember the bike you promised me for my birthday? I do!! I wonder if I could get it early, please, sweet grandma of mine. My old clunker of a bike is dying. Wait cross that out. It's dead.

Love your begging granddaughter,
Amanda

P.S. Please.

Figure 2-10. A letter to her grandmother by Amanda, a fourth-grade student.

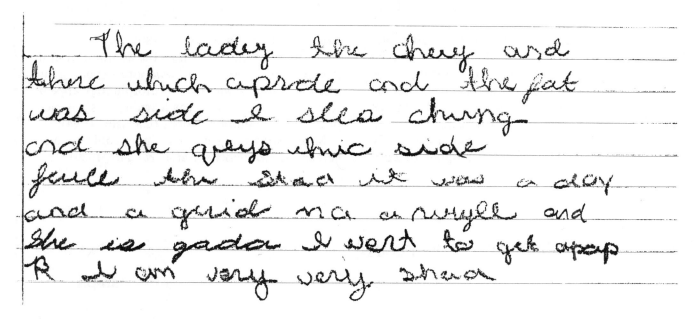

Figure 2-11. A paragraph written by Joyce, a sixth-grade student.

Three aspects of language have particular relevance to spelling: phonology, morphology, and context (Hanna et al., 1971). These aspects can be particularly problematic for students with learning disabilities.

Phonology

Phonology, or knowledge of the sounds and sound sequences, plays the most important role. Initially, students must acquire knowledge of the sound-to-letter principles that govern English spellings or what is known as the alphabetic principle. English orthography can be used to represent over 40 phonemes, the smallest units of language sounds. Although phonemes have no meaning in and of themselves, spelling requires the accurate sequencing of phonemes to create a meaningful word.

Morphology

In addition to learning the spelling of phonemes, children must also learn to spell morphemes (Carlisle, 1994). Morphemes, the components of basic word structure, are the smallest meaningful units of language and include both roots and affixes. Roots are free morphemes that can stand alone. In some words, two root words are combined together to form a compound word, such as combining the words *rain* and *coat* to form the word *raincoat*. Affixes (prefixes and suffixes) are bound morphemes

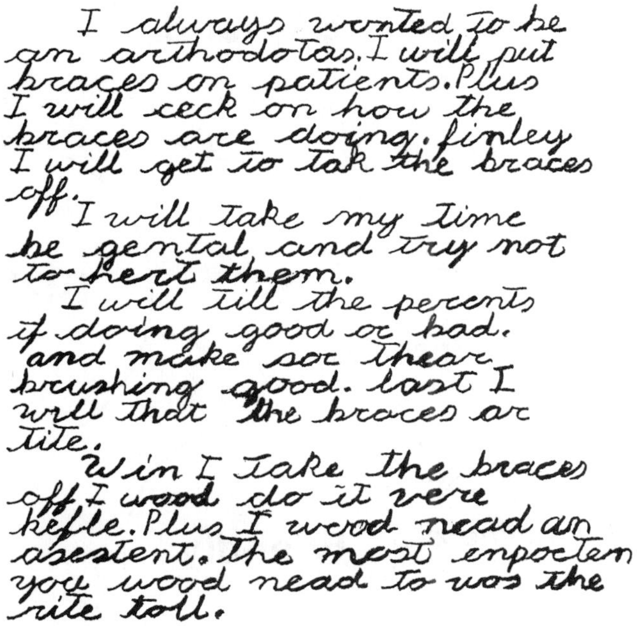

Figure 2-12. An assignment produced by Rich, a sixth-grade student.

that, when attached to root words, change their meaning (Mercer & Mercer, 1993). An understanding of morphology enables a student to form plurals, show possession, or change a verb to past tense. A student's phonological knowledge is then combined with understanding of morphological principles in order to spell words correctly.

Although the spellings of many English words do not adhere to regular phoneme-grapheme correspondence patterns, regularity is often apparent at a deeper, morphological level (Bailet, 1990; Chomsky, 1970; Hodges, 1977; Stubbs, 1980). Spelling proficiency involves the identification and application of linguistic rules (Bailet, 1990). Knowledge of the morphological principles of English, therefore, makes possible the spelling of thousands of words (Hanna et al., 1971) as a small number of correspondences combine in various ways to produce a large number of words (Dixon, 1991; Dixon & Engelmann, 1979; Stubbs, 1980).

Figure 2–13 illustrates how the addition of morphemes to the root word *friend* alters spelling and word meaning. Awareness of morphology appears to be a crucial element for learning to spell morphologically complex words (Carlisle, 1994).

Many students with learning problems have language-based deficits (Kamhi & Catts, 1989). They

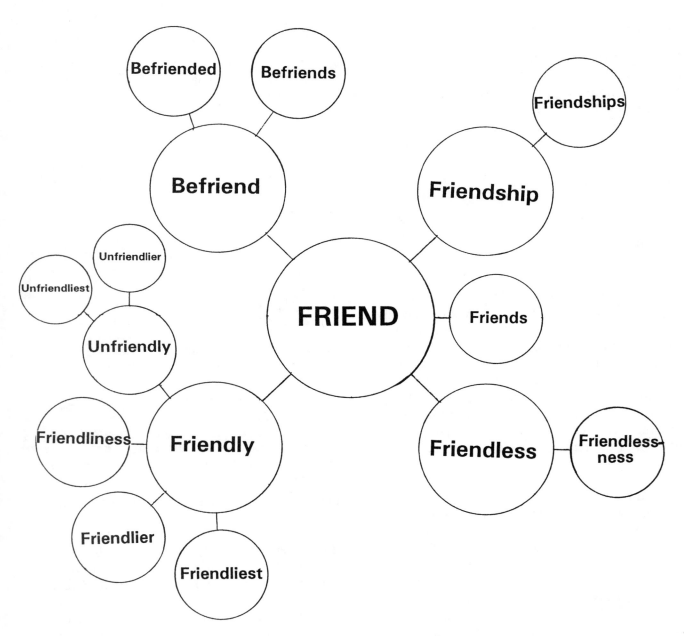

Figure 2–13. How the addition of morphemes alters spelling and word meaning.

are not as proficient as their peers in applying morphological knowledge to spelling (Bailet, 1990; Carlisle, 1987). When attempting to spell, these students have difficulty with formation of noun plurals, noun possessives, and verb tenses (Wiig & Semel, 1984). One general finding is that students with morphological deficits often omit word endings (Bailet, 1990; Hux & Stogsdill, 1993; Roth & Spekman, 1989; Vogel, 1974). For example, Carlisle (1987) found that ninth-grade students with learning disabilities showed less evidence of using morphological knowledge in spelling than normally achieving fourth graders. They have difficulty in learning rule-based linguistic systems and fail to integrate higher-level linguistic information into their spelling rule system (Bailet, 1990; Carlisle, 1994). Some of the students who repeatedly omit word endings when writing do not have difficulty with oral syntax and morphology (Johnson, 1993).

Other students have problems that are more pervasive and involve many aspects of language. Figure 2–14 illustrates a descriptive paragraph written by Fiona, an eighth-grade student. Her difficulties with morphology and usage are readily apparent.

Context

Contextual knowledge aids a writer in word choice and in the spelling of homonyms or words that differ in meaning but not in sound. The overall meaning of the words preceding and/or following a given word helps a student to determine the correct spelling (Hanna et al., 1971). Students with learning disabilities often have difficulties producing the correct spellings of homonyms and require considerable practice to master the words. Figure 2–15 illustrates a partial retelling of "The Night before Christmas" by Cathie, a fifth-grade student. Her confusion with regard to homonyms is evident in the sample.

A Developmental Process

Knowledge of linguistic principles related to spelling increases developmentally. Because many students with learning disabilities develop more slowly

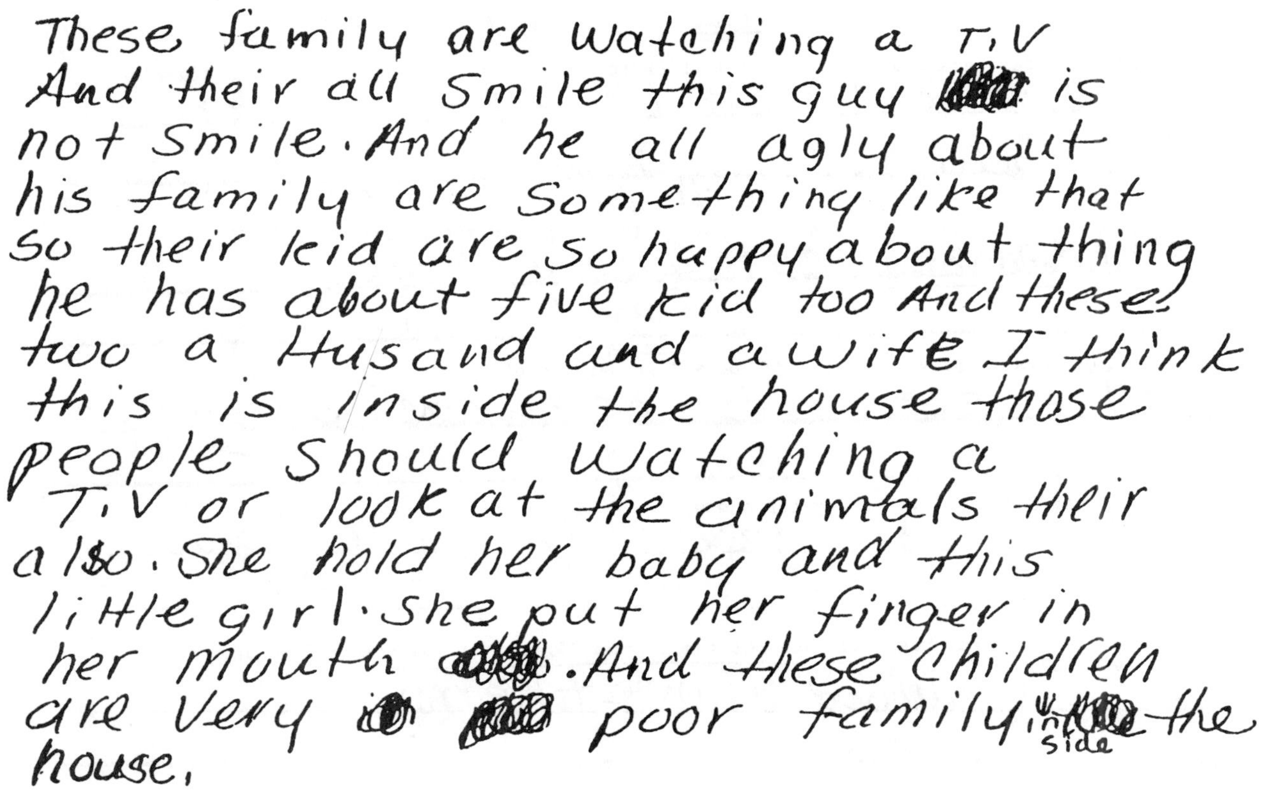
These family are watching a T.V
And their all Smile this guy is
not Smile. And he all agly about
his family are something like that
so their kid are so happy about thing
he has about five kid too And these
two a Husand and a wife I think
this is inside the house those
people Should watching a
T.V or look at the animals their
also. She hold her baby and this
litHe girl. She put her finger in
her mouth. And these Children
are very poor family in side the
house.

Figure 2–14. A descriptive paragraph written by Fiona, an eighth-grade student.

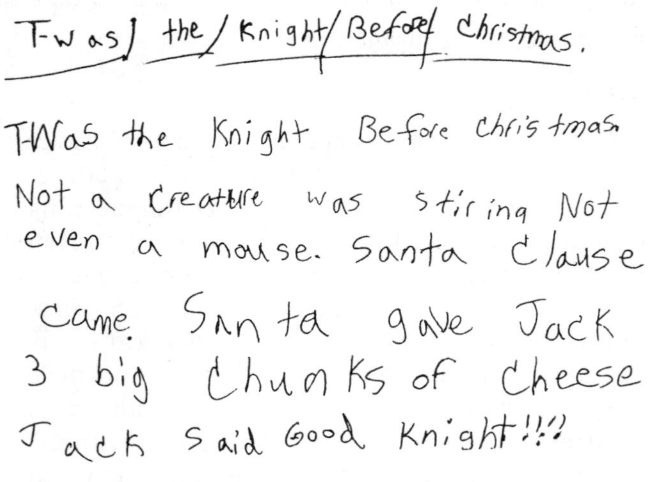

T-was] the / Knight / Before] Christmas.

TWas the Knight Before Christmas
Not a Creature was stiring Not
even a mouse. Santa Clause
came. Santa gave Jack
3 big Chunks of Cheese
Jack said Good Knight!!!!

Figure 2-15. A retelling by Cathie, a fifth-grade student.

in spelling skill than peers without disabilities, they also have more difficulty detecting their spelling errors (Deshler, Ferrell, & Kass, 1978; Espin & Sindelar, 1988; MacArthur, Graham, & Skarvoed, 1986). Bradley, a fourth-grade student, completed the worksheet presented in Figure 2-16. He was asked to answer questions about the story in complete sentences. Although he received credit for most of his responses, the teacher wrote the comment; *Please spell words correctly.*

Although one can empathize with the teacher's frustration in regard to Bradley's spelling performance, the important consideration is that students spell the best they can given their present level of knowledge. Asking them to spell correctly will not change their ability to spell. Spelling is a learned behavior (Hanna et al., 1971). Over time, children's

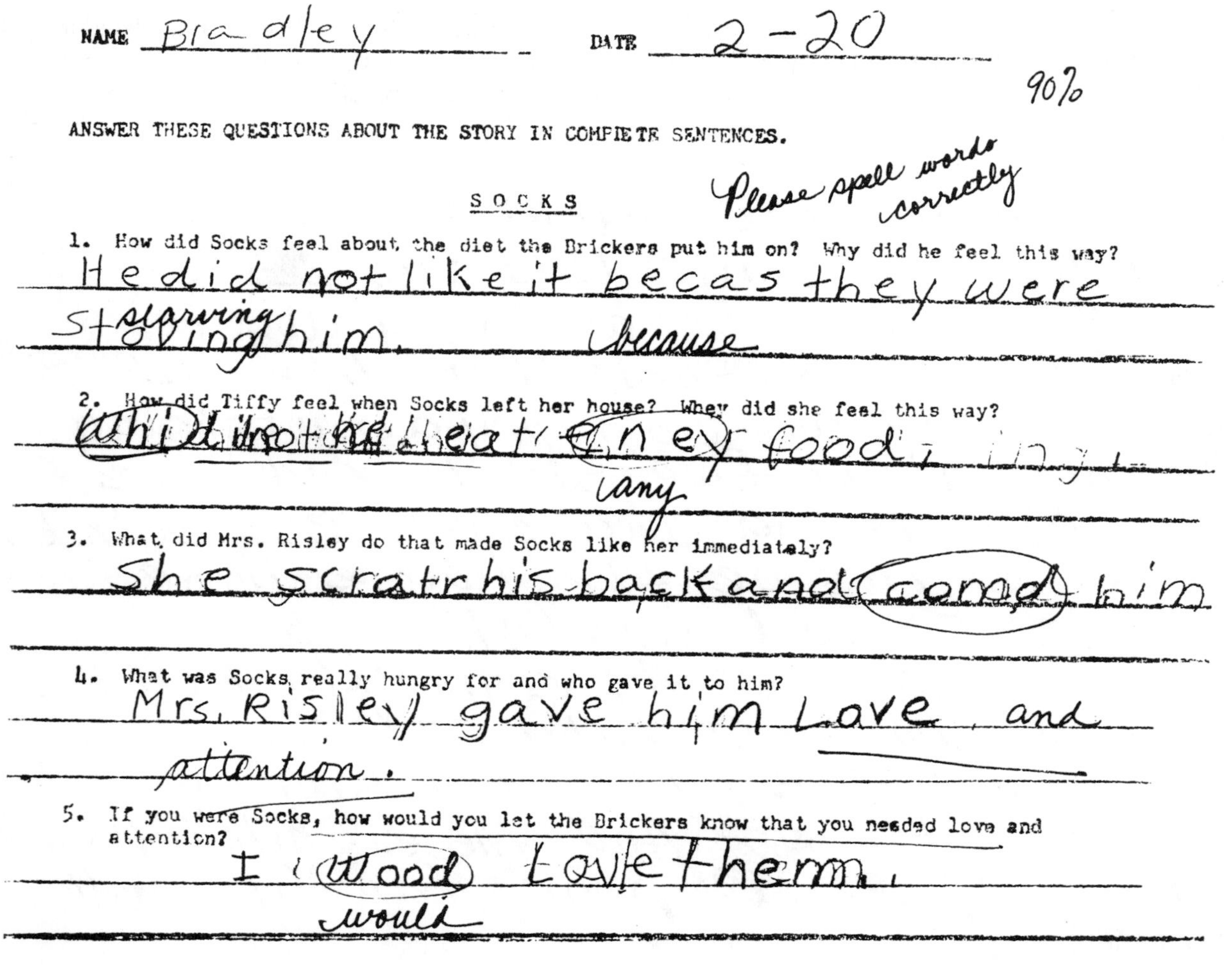

NAME Bradley   DATE 2-20

90%

ANSWER THESE QUESTIONS ABOUT THE STORY IN COMPLETE SENTENCES.

S O C K S   Please spell words correctly

1. How did Socks feel about the diet the Brickers put him on? Why did he feel this way?
He did not like it becas they were
starving him.   because

2. How did Tiffy feel when Socks left her house? Why did she feel this way?
(whild not) he eaten ey food;   any

3. What did Mrs. Risley do that made Socks like her immediately?
She scratr his back and (comd) him

4. What was Socks really hungry for and who gave it to him?
Mrs. Risley gave him Love, and
attention.

5. If you were Socks, how would you let the Brickers know that you needed love and attention?
I (wood) tayke themm.   would

Figure 2-16. Worksheet by Bradley, a fourth-grade student.

writings reflect their increasing knowledge of the letters and sounds of the English language.

Invented Spelling

When first learning to write, children use the articulatory features of spoken language to guide their spelling attempts (Bailet, 1991). In many classrooms, beginning writers are encouraged to write words the way they sound or to "invent" their spellings. These invented spellings reveal a child's active search for the rules that govern our writing system (Sampson et al., 1991) and provide powerful indicators of a writer's developing knowledge of sound-symbol relationships (Adams, 1990; Beers & Henderson, 1977; Cunningham & Cunningham, 1992; Read, 1986). Encouraging kindergarten and first-grade students to engage in invented spelling during writing increases both their reading and spelling skill (Adams, 1990; Chomsky, 1971; Cunningham & Cunningham, 1992).

Beginning writers draw and scribble, attempting to create forms that resemble symbols (Bernstein, 1989). As knowledge of the English spelling system develops and students become more familiar with print, they exhibit increasing sensitivity to English spelling patterns (Bailet, 1991) and their attempted inventive spellings evolve systematically toward more standard forms. This evolving knowledge of our spelling system appears to be reflected in several developmental stages.

Stages

Based upon research of spelling errors, children appear to progress through several developmental stages when learning to spell (Ehri, 1986, 1989; Gentry, 1982a, 1982b, 1984; Reid, 1988; Weiner, 1994). Although theorists vary somewhat in stage enumeration and description, the belief is that students move through a series of stages in their acquisition of spelling skill (Weiner, 1994). Although many students with learning disabilities progress through the same stages, the rate is slower than that of peers without learning disabilities. The invented spellings of some individuals with learning disabilities, however, deviate significantly from normal developmental patterns (Bailet, 1991).

Prephonetic or prephonemic. In the initial stages of learning to spell, a child will combine a string of unrelated letters to communicate a message. Figure 2–17 presents a story with illustrations by Ben, a first-grade student with prephonetic spelling. Ben understands that written symbols convey meaning, but he does not understand that letters represent sounds.

A few older students also still exhibit prephonetic spelling. Joey, a sixth-grade student was asked to write several responses to questions by his teacher, Mr. Steen. Figure 2–18 presents Mr. Steen's questions, Joey's responses, and Joey's oral explanation of his responses.

Semi-phonetic. At the semi-phonetic stage, letters are used to represent sounds, but only a few sounds in words are represented. In some instances, students will use the names of letters, rather than the letter sounds (Adams, 1990). For example, the word "while" may be written as *yl*. During this stage, although spellings may follow logical linguistic patterns, very few correct spellings are known. A student may know consonant sounds, long vowel sounds, and an occasional sight word. Figure 2–19 illustrates the writing of Andy, a third-grade student with semiphonetic spelling.

Phonetic. At the phonetic stage, students produce spellings that demonstrate sound-symbol correspondence. When writing, they attempt to record all of the sounds within a word and present them in the correct sound sequence. Figure 2–20 illustrates the writing of June, a fourth-grade student with phonetic spelling.

Transitional. At the transitional stage, the writer demonstrates awareness of many of the conventions of English orthography. For example, the student spells the past tense of a verb as -*ed* even when the ending sounds like a \t\, such as in the word "trapped."

Correct. At this stage, the writer possesses multiple strategies for determining standard spelling. Although not all words are spelled correctly, the writer regularly employs the word-specific features and orthographic patterns of English spelling (Rhodes & Dudley-Marling, 1988).

Factors Affecting Performance

Someone once said two kinds of people exist in this world: good spellers and poor spellers. Poor spellers want to become good spellers but, most of the time, they cannot. Often, poor spellers' performances do not improve by exposure to correct spellings through reading. Instead, each word has to

Figure 2–17. A story and illustrations by Ben, a first-grade student.

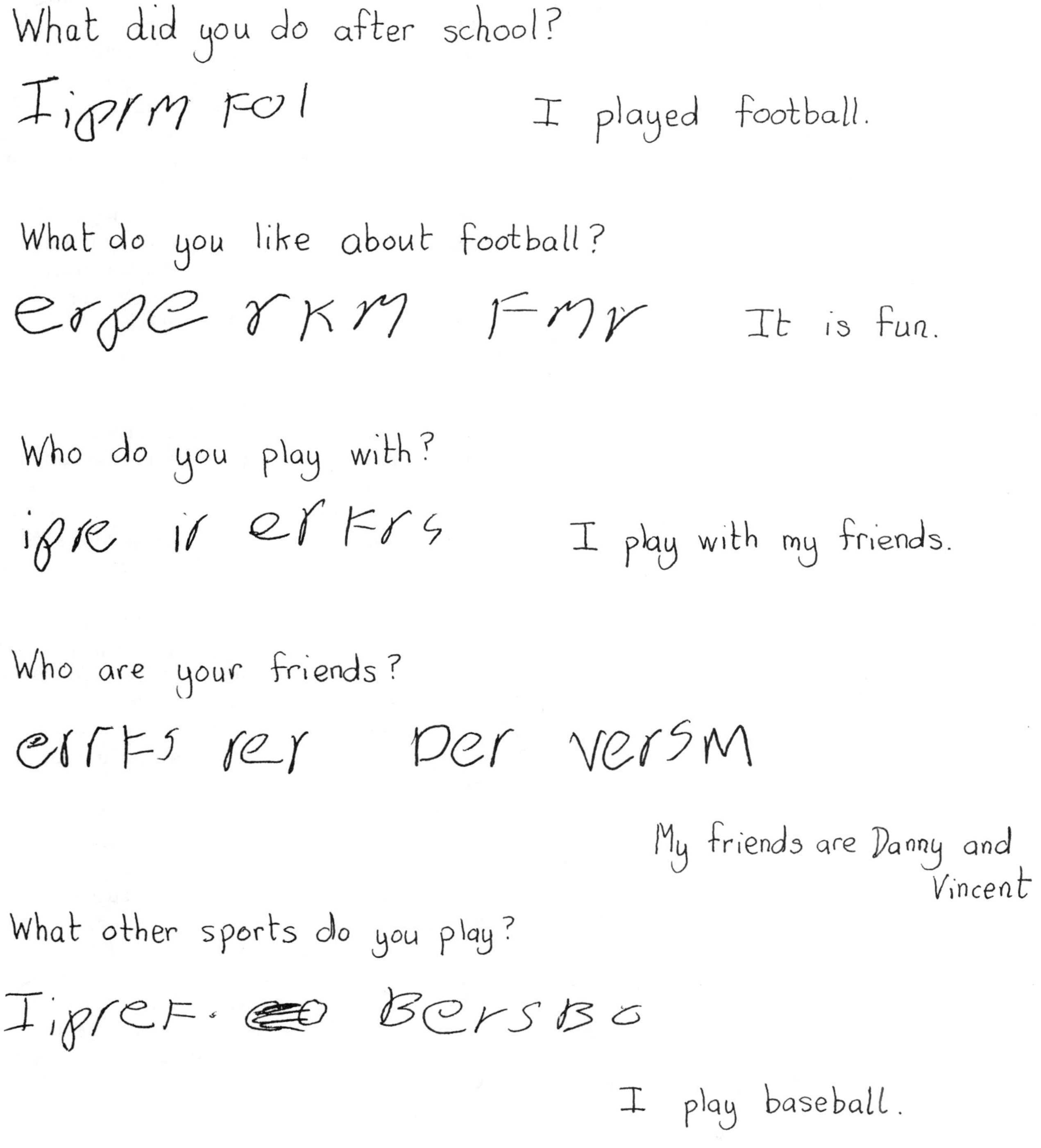

What did you do after school?

I iprm Fol   I played football.

What do you like about football?

erpe rKM FMr   It is fun.

Who do you play with?

ipe ir erFrs   I play with my friends.

Who are your friends?

errFs rer   Der versm

My friends are Danny and
Vincent

What other sports do you play?

I iprer. Bersbo

I play baseball.

Figure 2–18. Responses to questions by Joey, a sixth-grade student.

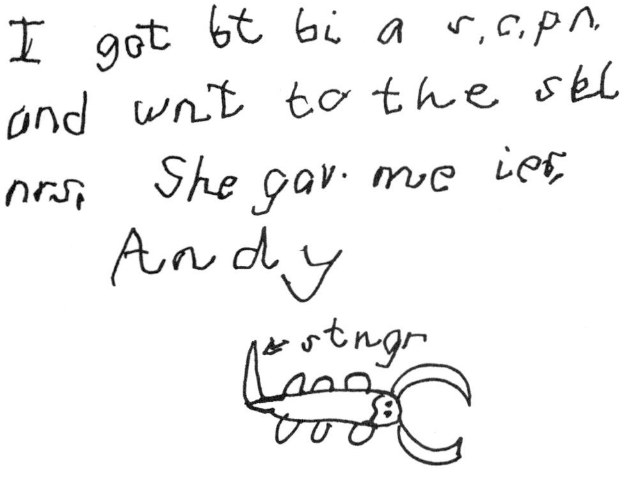

I got bt bi a r,c,pn and wnt to the skl nrs. She gav. me ice

Andy

Figure 2–19. A story by Andy, a third-grade student with semi-phonetic spelling.

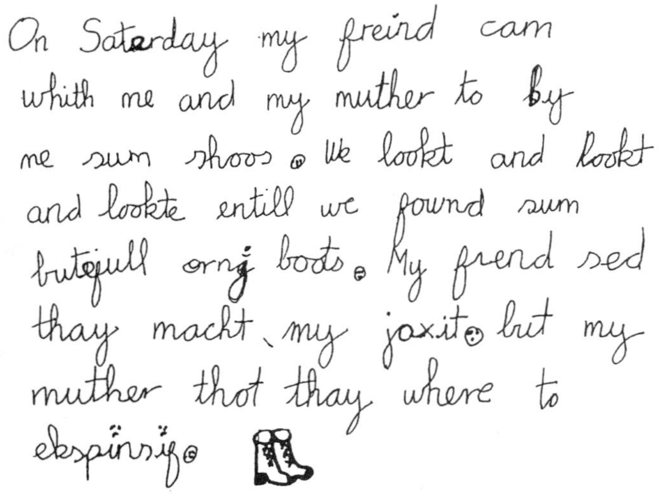

On Saterday my freird cam whith me and my muther to by me sum shoos. We lookt and lookt and lookte entill we found sum butejull ornj boots. My frend sed thay macht my joxit but my muther thot thay where to ekspinsiy.

Figure 2–20. A story by June, a fourth-grade student with phonetic spelling.

be learned by rote. Consider Kevin, an eighth-grade student, who is a good reader but a poor speller. When writing his book report on *Tom Sawyer*, he spelled the name "Becky" as: *Beacy, Beckey, Becky, Becy, Beecy,* and *Beacey.* Despite numerous exposures to the word, Kevin did not retain the correct spelling.

Good spellers, in contrast, seem to learn to spell easily. They note spellings when reading and quickly acquire a substantial spelling vocabulary. For them, progress in spelling is rapid. Fortunately, spelling skill is not highly related to general verbal competence.

Numerous cognitive and linguistic factors affect spelling competence (Bailet & Lyon, 1985). Some students may have trouble progressing from the semi-phonetic to phonetic stage because of poor phonological awareness, or from the phonetic to transitional stage because of poor visual-orthographic memory. Both phonological and orthographic coding skills have been identified as factors that contribute to poor spelling (Bailet & Lyon, 1985; Berninger & Whitaker, 1993; Moats, 1991b). To spell correctly, students must be able to recall both the spoken pattern or the sequence of phonemes, as well as the visual letter sequences (Seidenberg, 1989). These problems may exist together or in isolation (Berninger & Whitaker, 1993).

Phonological Awareness

Phonological awareness refers to knowledge of sounds in spoken words. This awareness is often measured by tasks such as rhyming words, matching initial consonants, isolating single sounds from words, deleting phonemes, and counting the number of phonemes or syllables in spoken words (Stahl & Murray, 1994). Awareness of sounds is necessary for learning how to spell.

Many students with learning disabilities have particular difficulty with blending (pushing sounds together) and retrieving phonological information from memory (Bruck, 1990, 1992; Kamhi & Catts, 1986). They do not realize that words can be segmented into syllables, syllables into distinct phonemes, and that specific letters are placed in sequence to represent these sounds (Seidenberg, 1989). Students with this type of difficulty often have trouble progressing from the semi-phonetic to the phonetic stage of spelling because they lack the ability to manipulate the sound structure of spoken words (Ehri, 1989). As a result, they have limited knowledge of sound-symbol relationships.

Figure 2–21 presents the writing of Kirsten, a second-grade girl. The title of the assignment, taken from a popular children's book, was written on the board. Although Kirsten has specific ideas with regard to her horrible day, deciphering the meaning of her passage is difficult.

Phonological processes are critical for spelling development in the early school years (Bailet, 1991). Awareness of the internal structure of words facilitates success in learning how to spell (Blachman, 1994). Conversely, poor phonological awareness

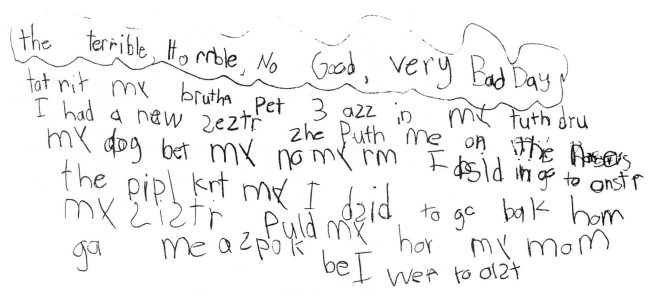

Figure 2–21. A story by Kirsten, a second-grade girl with limited phonological knowledge.

impairs ability to segment, analyze, and synthesize speech sounds (Stanovich 1982a, 1982b). These simple phonological skills are related significantly to spelling performance through high school (Calfee, Lindamood, & Lindamood, 1973). Even spelling problems in young adults often reflect specific deficits in the phonological processing of language (Moats, 1991b). For example, Bruck (1993) found that although college students with the childhood diagnosis of dyslexia attempted to preserve the phonological structure of words, they had poorer knowledge of the associations between sounds and spellings.

In some cases, the problem is severe. Figure 2–22 illustrates a dictated paragraph written by Mark, a 16-year-old with extreme difficulty translating English sounds into symbols. Although Mark knew what he was trying to write, his response is impossible to read.

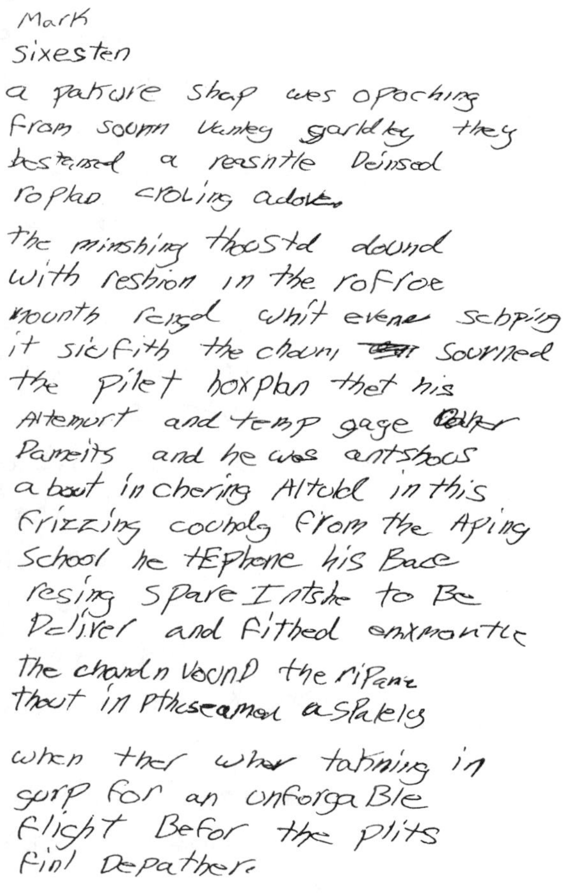

Visual-Orthographic or Graphemic Memory

Competence at the correct spelling stage may be most dependent upon rote visual memory (Frith, 1980). Some children with learning disabilities have difficulty progressing from the phonetic to the transitional stage of spelling because they have trouble recalling orthographic patterns. Vellutino, Scanlon, and Tanzman (1994) define orthographic coding as: " . . . the ability to represent the unique array of letters that defines a printed word, as well

Figure 2–22. A dictated story written by Mark, a 16-year-old with limited phonological knowledge.

as general attributes of the writing system such as sequential dependencies, structural redundancies, and letter position frequencies" (p. 314). The clinician may note that the spellings of this type of student often "don't look like English" (Willows & Terepocki, 1993). With this type of difficulty, the writer has good knowledge of sound-symbol relationships, but poor memory for letter sequences. As a result, the student tends to produce phonetic spellings even for high-frequency words; the recall of "how words look" continues as a serious problem (Willows & Terepocki, 1993). In general, poor spellers rely primarily on sound/symbol knowledge, whereas good spellers use orthographic knowledge and visual memory as well (Weiner, 1994).

Figure 2–23 presents the writing of Felicia, a seventh-grade student with a severe spelling disability. Analysis of Felicia's spelling reveals her insensitivity to and difficulty with retention of English orthographic patterns. Because she has trouble remembering letter sequences in words for spelling, she relies primarily on the way words sound.

Joseph, a fifth-grade student, has similar difficulties. Four of his journal entries are presented

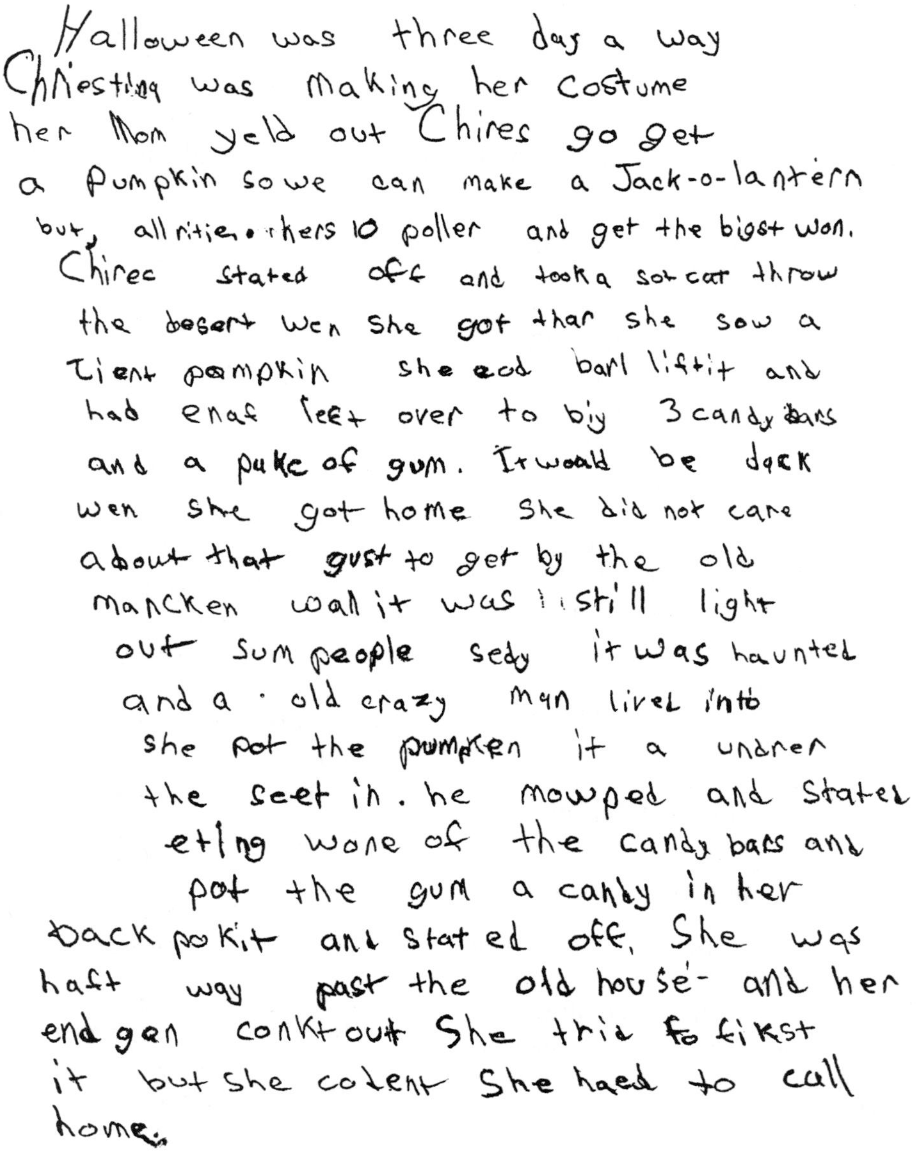
Halloween was three day a way
Chriestina was making her costume
her Mom yeld out Chires go get
a pumpkin so we can make a Jack-o-lantern
but, all nitie others 10 poller and get the bigst won.
Chiree stated off and took a sot cat throw
the besert wen she got thar she sow a
Tient pampkin she cod barl liftit and
had enaf leet over to biy 3 candy bars
and a puke of gum. It would be dark
wen she got home she did not care
about that gust to get by the old
mancken wall it was still light
out sum people sedy it was haunted
and a old crazy man lived into
she pot the pumpken it a undner
the seet in. he mowped and stated
eting wone of the candy bars and
pot the gum a candy in her
back pokit and stated off. She was
haft way past the old house and her
endgen conkt out She tria to fikst
it but she cotent She haed to call
home.

Figure 2–23. First page of a story written by Felicia, a seventh-grade student with spelling difficulty.

in Figure 2-24. Within the same page of his journal, he spelled the word "yesterday" three different ways. He also reversed the letters *b* and *d* several times.

As can be seen from the writings of Felicia and Joseph, spelling can be a significant, persistent problem. Students with learning disabilities often have chronic, intractable spelling problems (Moats, 1991b). Acquisition of spelling skill is an arduous task for many writers, but particularly those with learning disabilities. As noted by Meyer, Pisha, and Rose (1991): "The thousands of patterns that comprise the correct spellings of English words present a daunting challenge to students with learning disabilities" (p. 118). Unfortunately, markedly impaired spelling skill can affect the development of other aspects of writing skill.

I got noting to rite
Adout Begse I Didnt Do
a tin Ersday

EstDay me and my Boutreing
wet to the river Jongms
I sasd Bri'd

Satre Day I uen to the Inden
rens and I went hunting

esat beay I went suming
at rive m

Figure 2-24. Four journal entries by Joseph, a fifth-grade student.

Spelling and Technology

Spelling difficulties can be partly reduced through the use of electronic aids. As is true for students with handwriting difficulties, students with spelling difficulties can benefit from the use of word processors and spell checkers. Although these programs differ in size and content, most have high-frequency lists to which other words can be added (Hunt-Berg et al., 1994). If a speech synthesizer is used, the student can have the words read aloud to assist in selecting the correct option.

Sometimes people assume, however, that poor spellers can resolve their difficulties by simply using a computer or spell checker. Many students with

severe spelling problems have not developed sufficient skill to use these compensations independently. In order to use a spell checker, an individual must be able to spell phonetically; otherwise, the computer will not recognize the entry. The computer may mark the questionable pattern, but not generate the correct spelling. In many instances, the student must be able to select the correct spelling from a list of words, and some students have difficulty choosing the correct option.

In addition, spell checkers have two common weaknesses: (a) the inability to recognize any words that have not been programmed into them and (b) the inability to interpret language (Meyer et al., 1991). Because the computer operates at the letter pattern level, it cannot detect errors in meaning such as common homonyms. Consequently, words that are misspelled within the context in which they are used are missed by the computer (Lewis, 1993). The important point to realize is that one must be a fairly proficient speller to operate a spell checker independently.

Figure 2-25 illustrates a paragraph written by Melissa, a seventh-grader with poor spelling skill. She comments that she loves writing but hates spelling. She hopes that someday she will have a computer to help her spell or, if not, she will hire people to write for kids. Unfortunately, Melissa's spelling skill is not yet good enough for her to use a spell checker to aid in making corrections.

As noted by Meyer et al. (1991): "No existing spelling checker will enable a student with learning disabilities to be fully independent as a speller"

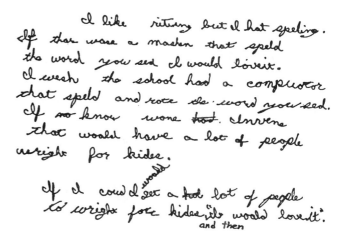

Figure 2-25. Melissa, a seventh-grade student with poor spelling skill.

(p. 122). Spell checkers can, however, relieve students of attention devoted to basic skills and help them concentrate on the author's role (Lewis, 1993).

Usage

Written language is more rule-governed than spoken language and is different from conversation in its form (Isaacson, 1994). To communicate in writing with clarity, students must master rules involving capitalization, punctuation, and syntax. Both recollection and application of these English composition skills require knowledge of language structure.

Components of Usage

Usage includes the conventions of composition: punctuation, capitalization, and syntax. Mastery of these written language conventions requires conscious attention to learn and apply the principles (Meyer et al., 1991). Knowledge of these rules becomes particularly important when students attempt to edit their assignments. The removal of usage errors provides the polishing touch to written expression (McCoy & Prehm, 1987).

Punctuation and Capitalization

Correct use of punctuation and capitalization is a matter of courtesy to the reader (Van Allen, 1976). The appropriate use of capital letters and punctuation marks can make the difference between writing that is understandable and writing that is confusing (Hanna et al., 1971). These grammatical rules can aid in clarifying the writer's intent (Poteet, 1987). Figure 2–26 presents a paragraph written by Laurie,

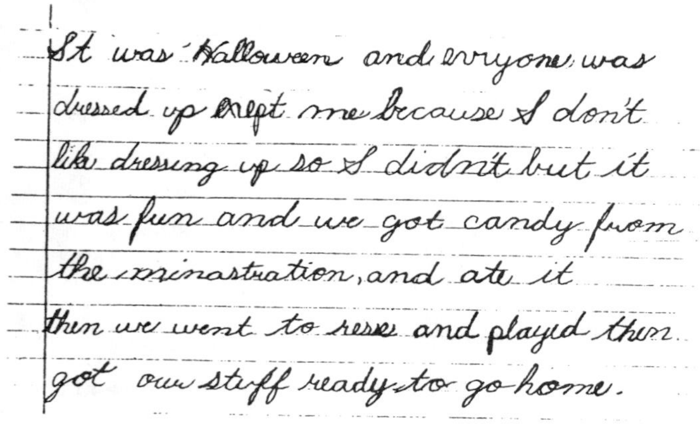
It was Halloween and evryone was dressed up exept me because I don't like dressing up so I didn't but it was fun and we got candy from the minastration, and ate it then we went to resse and played then got our stuff ready to go home.

Figure 2–26. A paragraph written by Laurie, a fifth-grade student.

a fifth-grade girl. Her run-on sentences detract from her message.

Syntax

Syntax, frequently referred to as a component of grammar, represents the structure of a language and includes the rules for combining words into sentences and identifying the relationships among the various words of a sentence. Syntax includes knowledge of: (a) clause structure, or noun phrases and verb phrases within clauses, and (b) the rules for forming negatives, questions, and complex sentences through embedding and conjoining (James, 1989). More simply put, syntax refers to the predictable patterns found in sentence. As Gould (1991) described: "Even in a nonsense sentence, 'The iggle oggled the uggle,' the actor, action and recipient are known as are the patterns for changing the form of the sentence to a negative or a question" (p. 134). The selection and use of syntactic structures are writing components essential for clarity (Gould, 1991; Gregg, 1991). In addition, skill in manipulating, expanding, and altering syntactic patterns makes a writer's style more interesting (Gould, 1991). Knowledge of morphology is also important for understanding sentence structure. As morphological knowledge increases, a student's ability to produce more complex language structures evolves.

Figure 2–27 illustrates the writing of George, an eighth-grade student. His assignment was to write a paragraph about his favorite sports. In this paragraph, George overuses the conjunction *and* and he writes the phrase *I like* six times. As is apparent in this sample, failure to expand and alter syntactic patterns results in uninteresting writing.

Factors Affecting Performance

Unlike their peers without disabilities, students with learning disabilities have difficulty internalizing syntactic rules for effective use (Anderson, 1982). As with other areas of written language, these writers lack proficiency in syntax (Myklebust, 1973; Poteet, 1978), and have difficulty applying punctuation and capitalization rules (Anderson, 1982; Houck & Billingsley, 1989; Poteet, 1978, 1980; Thomas, Englert, & Gregg, 1987).

The application of punctuation and capitalization rules is particularly problematic for students

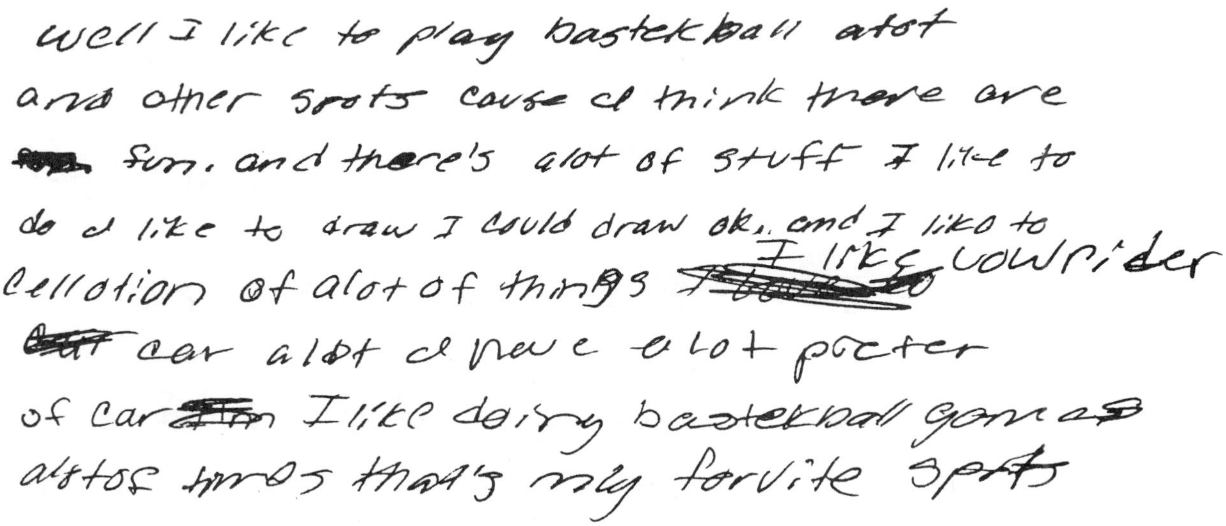

Well I like to play bastekball alot
and other spots cause I think there are
~~fun~~ fun. and there's alot of stuff I like to
do I like to draw I could draw ok. and I like to
collotion of alot of things ~~I like to~~ lowrider
~~car~~ car alot I have a lot poster
of car ~~car~~ I like doing bastekball games
alsos times that's my forvite spts

Figure 2-27. A paragraph written by George, an eighth-grade student.

with learning disabilities (Poplin et al., 1980; Vogel & Moran, 1982). Examination of their assignments shows that one third or more of the sentences contain errors in capitalization or punctuation (MacArthur & Graham, 1987; Moran, 1981). Houck and Billingsley (1989) found that the level of accuracy in capitalization obtained by eleventh-grade students with learning disabilities was similar to that obtained by normally achieving fourth-grade students.

Application of punctuation rules has also been identified as a particular problem (Newcomer & Barenbaum, 1991; Vogel, 1985). Students with learning disabilities have trouble determining sentence boundaries and applying the correct punctuation (Moran, 1988). For some students, these errors may be more indicative of difficulty with syntax rather than poor, or limited, instruction in punctuation (Gregg, 1991).

Difficulties with syntax are also common in the written expression of these students (Anderson, 1982). Some common usage problems involve the use of pronouns, subject-verb agreement, consistency of verb tense, and dangling modifiers (Rhodes & Dudley-Marling, 1988). In a review of the written composing abilities of students with learning disabilities, Newcomer and Barenbaum (1991) described the depressed performance in syntactic skills that did not diminish with age. In general, students with syntactic delays produce sentences that lack the length or complexity of those produced by peers (Mercer & Mercer, 1993). Characteristically,

the students have difficulty producing complex, embedded forms and their sentences lack variety (Gould, 1991). In addition, these students often are delayed in their ability to transform sentences into negative, interrogative, or passive forms (Seidenberg, 1989). Furthermore, they tend to write run-on sentences that link too many clauses together using words such as *and*, *but*, or *then* (Hasbrouck, Tindal, & Parker, 1994). Figure 2-28 presents a paragraph written by Tyrone, a seventh-grade student. Similar to the writing of Laurie and George presented in Figures 2-26 and 2-27, Tyrone's sentences lack complexity and are joined together with too many conjunctions.

Poor syntax may be indicative of a variety of language disorders (Anderson, 1982). In reviewing clinical findings, Gregg (1991) identified the following types of syntactic errors made by writers with learning disabilities: (a) word omissions, (b) word order errors, (c) incorrect verb and pronoun use, (d) word ending errors, (e) lack of punctuation, (f) lack of capitalization, (g) discrepancy between oral and written language, (h) metalinguistic problems, and (i) problems in cohesion (p. 74). Children and adolescents with learning disabilities tend to use fewer modifiers such as adjectives, adverbs, and prepositional phrases (Moran, 1988). As noted, they also tend to omit word endings. For some students, however, omission of word endings may be the result of oversight rather than lack of knowledge (Goodman, Casciato, & Price, 1987).

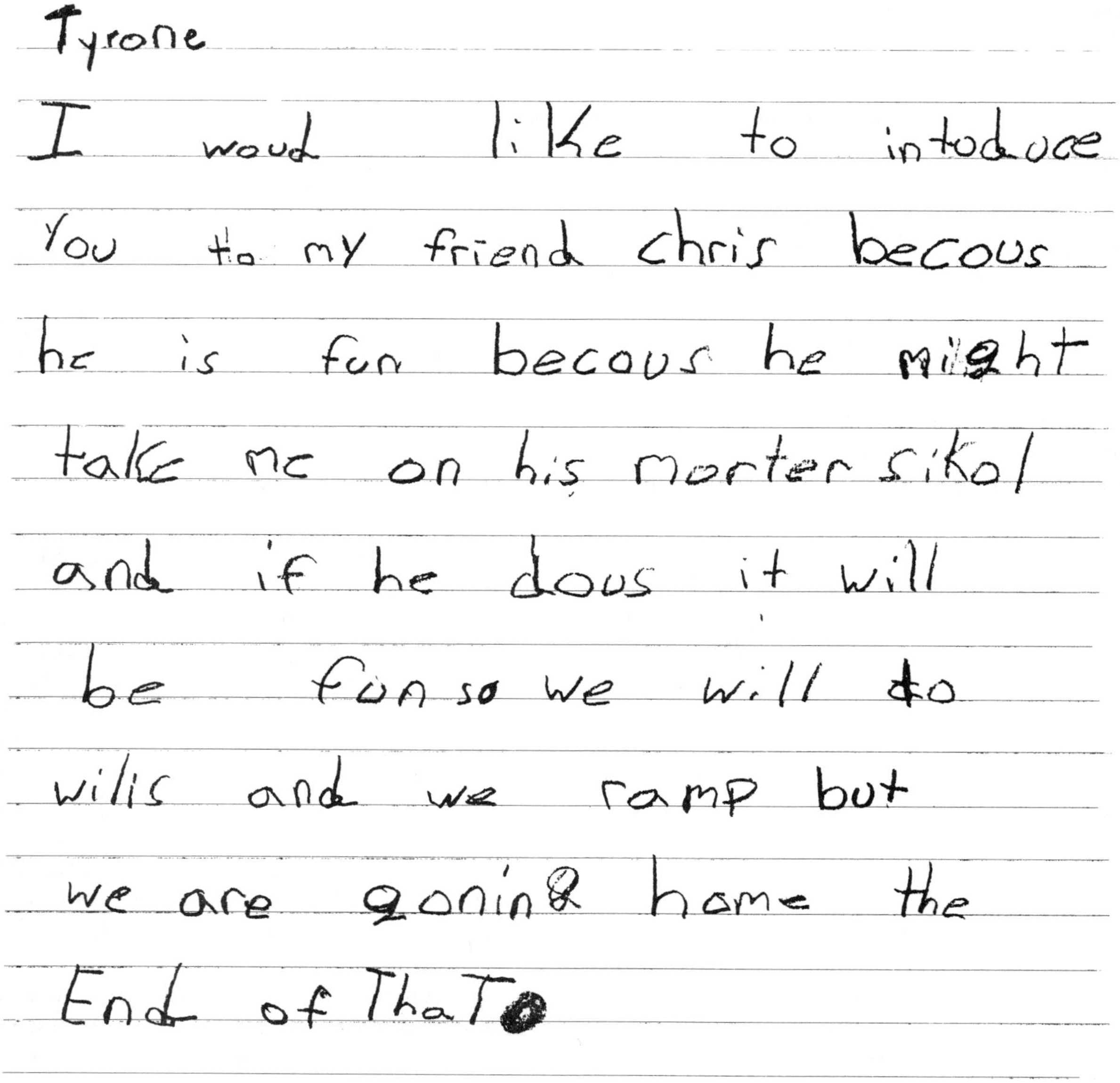

Tyrone

I woud like to intoduce you to my friend chris becous he is fun becous he might take me on his morter sikol and if he dous it will be fun so we will to wilis and we ramp but we are goning home the End of ThaT

Figure 2-28. A paragraph written by Tyrone, a seventh-grade student.

The literature in regard to the written language usage errors made by students with learning disabilities is, at present, limited both in quantity and quality (Gregg, 1991). Some students who experience delays in their ability to generate and use a variety of sentence patterns require oral language intervention. The purpose of this intervention is to help the student develop a conceptual base that can be reinforced and expanded upon through writing (Gould, 1991). Other students have adequate oral syntactic development, but have trouble formulating written sentences. In either case, intervention is necessary because the ability to vary syntactic structures by altering, expanding, and manipulating words and phrases adds variety and interest to an individual's writing (Gould, 1991).

Usage and Technology

Several grammar programs exist that are designed to help students correct usage errors in their compositions. After students enter text, they can check their work for grammatical errors such as subject-verb disagreement and incomplete or run-on sentences, as well as for capitalization and punctuation errors. In addition, students can vary syntactic structure by manipulating and expanding sentences.

With some of the existing grammar programs, students can either proofread a document as it is being written or wait until the first draft is finished (Lewis, 1993). Grammar-check programs are not as widely used as spell checkers. Presently, many teachers feel that these types of programs are not very useful (Tompkins, 1994). It is likely, however, that the utility of grammar-check programs will increase as more talking versions are developed. In addition, new applications, such as grammatically based word cueing, will help students increase their syntactic competence. This type of program applies the syntactic rules of English to determine what words to offer a student for choices. For example, when the student types in a noun, a list of verbs appears; or, if the student types in a word such as "yesterday," a list of past tense verbs will appear (Hunt-Berg et al., 1994).

Vocabulary

A critical aspect of good writing is selecting correct and effective words (Isaacson, 1987). A discrepancy often exists between the oral and written vocabulary of many students with learning disabilities with their oral vocabulary being far superior to the vocabulary that they select when writing. Their dictated stories are often better than what they produce by hand or on a word processor (Graham, 1990; Lane, 1994; MacArthur & Graham, 1987) and when interviewed they have much more knowledge about a topic than is reflected in their writing (Englert et al., 1988).

As an example, Tom, a fifth-grade student, related to his teacher his favorite experience on his trip to Ohio:

"Well, we went to see my grandma and my favorite part of all was that we spent two whole days at Cedar Point. It's like a big carnival. We rode the roller coaster, the ferris wheel, and they had this rocket ship that really could spin you around. I even won a goldfish at one booth, but it took me three tries. My dad said that it probably would have been cheaper to buy one. It really was neat and even my grandma went on the rides. Well, all of them except the rocket ship. She was kidding but she said that one would make her even more dizzy than she already is."

Figure 2–29 presents Tom's written summary of this experience.

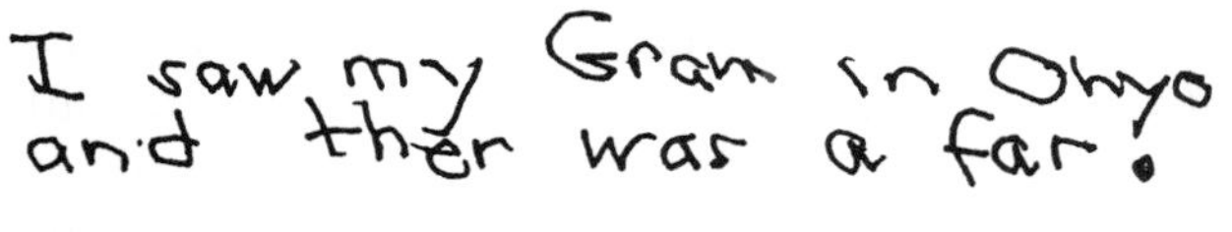

Figure 2–29. A story about his trip written by Tom, a fifth-grade student.

Components of Vocabulary

The importance of vocabulary knowledge has been the focus of considerable research in recent years (Beck, Perfetti, & McKeown, 1982; Enright, Duran, & Peirce, 1986; Kameenui, Carnine, & Freschi, 1982; Stahl, 1983). The vocabulary available to writers is determined by their familiarity with words, their conceptual understanding of words, and their ability to retrieve words as needed (Gould, 1991). In planning writing, one consciously selects appropriate words to place in the context of sentences (Israel, 1984). A skilled writer attempts to use precise word choices, varied vocabulary, and colorful descriptive language (Vogel, 1985).

A teacher should attempt to identify a student's difficulties with vocabulary by analyzing several writing samples. In reviewing writing, one should consider a student's (a) word-retrieval ability, (b) knowledge of morphology, and (c) breadth and depth of word knowledge.

Word Retrieval

Word retrieval involves the rapid recovery of individual words that are stored in memory. When students have difficulty with word retrieval, the problem is not the lack of intact word knowledge, but rather accessibility to the words (Gerber, 1993). Even when students know specific words, they may fail to recall them (Gould, 1991).

As he was turning in his essay, Howard, a sixth-grade student, was trying to recall the word "staple."

He explained to his teacher: "It's the thing that holds the papers together, but not the one you take off easy. The one that is stuck." Brad often has trouble retrieving words that are a part of his oral vocabulary. He can often explain the function of the object but has trouble producing the specific name.

Morphology

One major influence on the development of vocabulary is the awareness of morphological rules (Carlisle, 1993; Wysocki & Jenkins, 1987). Students' knowledge of morphology helps them to gain meaning by recognizing how prefixes, roots, and suffixes contribute to word meaning (Nagy, Diakidoy, & Anderson, 1993). These rules function as the cueing system that allows students to discriminate parts of speech from the function of words in sentences.

Nagy et al. (1993) reviewed the various distinctions among affixes. Affixes include both prefixes and suffixes. Suffixes may be inflectional or derivational. When added to a word, an inflectional suffix creates a different form of the same word and changes the meaning. For example, the suffix -ed is added to the verb *walk* to demonstrate past tense. When added to a word, a derivational suffix generally makes a new word and changes the part of speech. For example, the suffix -ness is added to the adjective *happy* to form the noun *happiness*. For most students, knowledge of the meanings of common English suffixes undergoes significant development between fourth grade and high school, with most of the growth occurring between the fourth and seventh grades (Nagy et al., 1993). In general, derivational suffixes are the most abstract and difficult concept of morphology that students are asked to learn; this may be because derivational suffixes are associated more with the complex syntax of written language, rather than with everyday conversation (Nagy et al., 1993).

Understanding both the meaning of root words and affixes increases vocabulary knowledge (Carlisle, 1993). Figure 2–13, presented in the section on spelling, illustrates how the addition of morphemes to the word *friend* alters both spelling and word meaning.

Word Knowledge

Semantics includes both knowledge of word meanings and the various shades of meaning a word may have. Semantic knowledge helps one to differentiate between words that have shared, yet different, meanings such as the difference between "dusk" and "night" or "sympathy" and "empathy." In addition to knowledge of individual words, semantic development also includes the understanding of both the literal and figurative meaning of sentences (Gerber, 1993).

Factors Affecting Performance

Vocabulary deficits are frequently exhibited by individuals with language and learning disabilities throughout their school years (Israel, 1984; Wiig, 1981). Students with learning disabilities often have difficulty expressing themselves because they do not seem to know the right words to use (Johnson & Myklebust, 1967; Simmons & Kameenui, 1990; Wiig, 1981). The difficulty may be due to limited understanding of morphological principles or, in some instances, a student may have difficulty with word retrieval (German, 1979, 1982; Perfetti & Hogaboam, 1975). In other instances, a student has trouble producing the right word because of limited depth and breadth of word knowledge or limited semantic associations (Johnson & Myklebust, 1967). Unfortunately, difficulties with vocabulary persist into adulthood and can hinder educational performance at all levels (Israel, 1984; Strominger & Bashir, 1977; Vogel & Moran, 1982).

Morphology

Students with morphological delays do not acquire the rules for word formation at the same rate and complexity as normally achieving peers (Mercer & Mercer, 1993). After an extensive review of literature, Gerber (1993) summarized the syntactic/morphological problems of students with learning disabilities. When compared to individuals without disabilities, these students demonstrate less mastery of morphological inflections for verb tense, plurality, and possession. They have difficulty with both the comprehension and use of affixes (Wiig & Semel, 1984). Limited understanding of morphological principles affects their ability to produce meaningful written discourse.

Word Retrieval

In addition to delayed morphological development, individuals with learning disabilities also tend to have word- retrieval difficulties (Denckla & Rudel,

1976; German, 1979; Johnson & Myklebust, 1967; Kail & Leonard, 1986; Perfetti & Hogaboam, 1975; White, 1979; Wiig & Semel, 1975, 1984; Wiig, Semel, & Nystrom, 1982; Wolf, 1986). On all word-retrieval tasks, individuals with learning disabilities make more substitution, association, and circumlocution errors than do their normally achieving peers. In addition, these students are often slower to respond in both conversation and writing than their peers.

Characteristics of students with word-retrieval difficulties include: (a) a delay in producing words, including common objects, letters, colors, or numbers; (b) omission and substitution of words; (c) circumlocutions (e.g., "the thingamajig you use after washing your hands so you can wipe your hands [towel]"); and (d) use of gesture, pantomime, or nonverbal vocalizations (Gerber, 1993). Students also may have trouble writing words in the appropriate order, recalling verbal opposites, naming associated members of a semantic category, and defining words (Denckla & Rudel, 1976; Gerber, 1993; Simmons & Kameenui, 1990; Wiig & Semel, 1975; Wiig et al., 1982; Wolf, 1986). These problems may be apparent in both spoken and written language (Wiig & Semel, 1984). Figure 2–30 illustrates a paragraph written by Rebecca, a third-grade

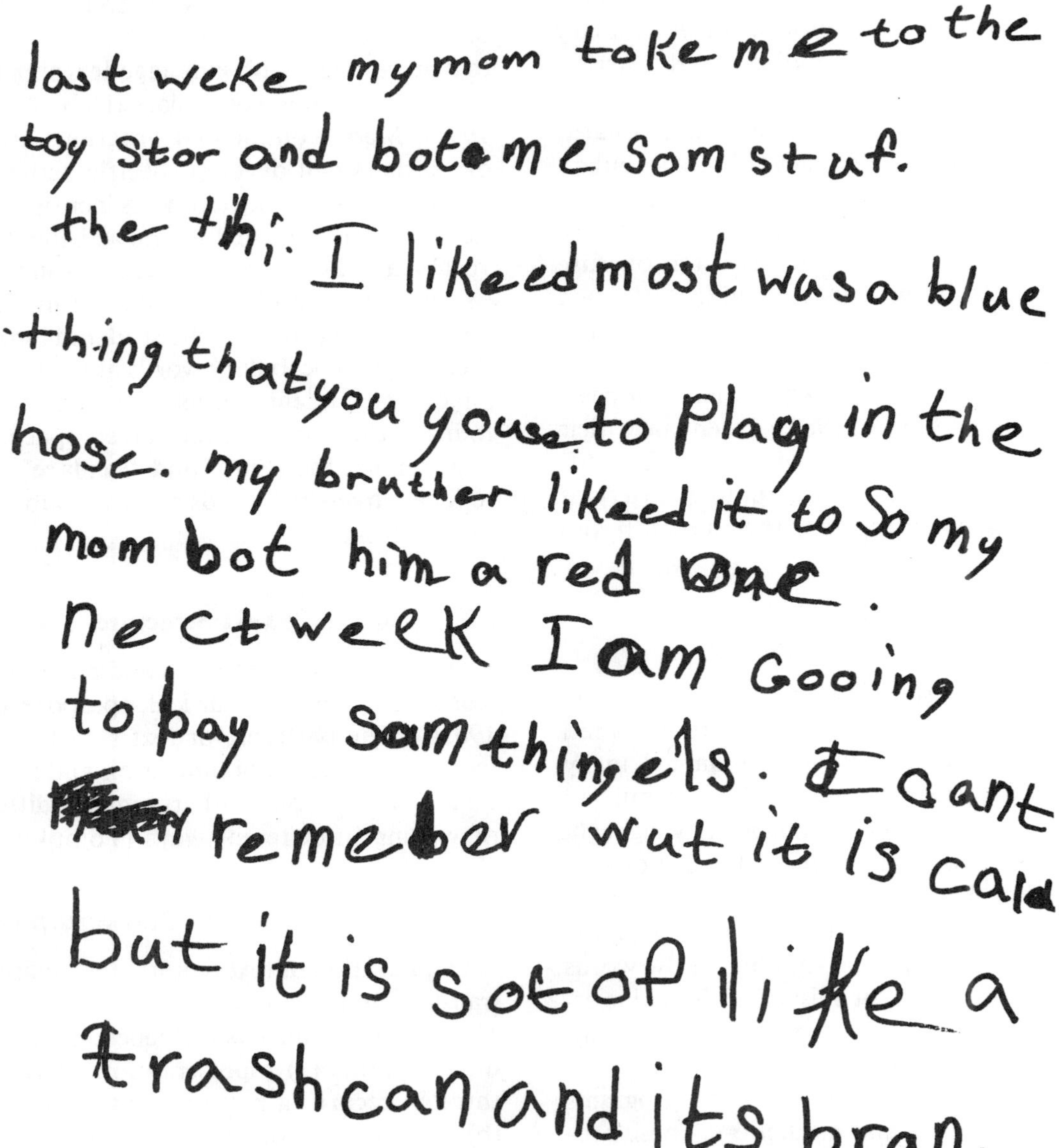

last weke my mom toke me to the toy stor and bote me som stuf. the thi. I likeed most was a blue thing that you youse to play in the hose. my bruther likeed it to so my mom bot him a red one. nect week I am gooing to bay sam thing els. I oant remeber wut it is cald but it is sot of like a trashcan and its bran.

Figure 2–30. A paragraph written by Rebecca, a third-grade student.

student. In both speaking and writing, Rebecca has difficulty using precise vocabulary.

Different subtypes of word retrieval problems may exist (Donahue, 1986). One type may be characterized by increased errors and/or slower retrieval speed of less familiar words; another may be characterized by a longer time to retrieve highly familiar words (Gerber, 1993). Unfortunately, many word retrieval problems persist into adulthood (Israel, 1984).

Word Knowledge

When compared to age-mates, students with learning disabilities often display significant differences between the breadth and depth of the vocabulary and knowledge they store (Vallecorsa & Garriss, 1990). These students may have inadequate representation of words in memory (Kail & Leonard, 1986). Although they are not devoid of vocabulary knowledge, they are less able to demonstrate their knowledge than peers (Simmons & Kameenui, 1990). Students with learning disabilities often overuse general, nondescriptive words (Gould, 1991) such as *thing*, and their writing lacks specificity and elaboration. Even college students with learning disabilities use fewer different words than their peers without disabilities (Gajar, 1989). To enhance their writing performance, students with vocabulary difficulties need to receive instruction in a variety of strategies designed to increase their breadth and depth of word knowledge.

Vocabulary and Technology

Computers can also be used to help students expand their vocabulary. Although some teachers feel that the usefulness of these programs is limited, many word processing programs welcome with a built-in thesaurus (Tompkins, 1994). A student may highlight a word and the program will provide a list of synonyms and sometimes antonyms. To replace a word, the student selects the desired alternative from the list. If further choices are desired, one of the words provided can be targeted for a list of additional selections. The student can then replace the word with a more precise synonym.

Hunt-Berg et al. (1994) describe several programs involving word cueing and prediction. These programs provide users with choices of words or phrases to select when composing. The word choices are typically presented in a small window on the screen, and the writer selects a word by typing its number or a predesignated function key. All word-cueing programs allow writers to use the initial letters of words to obtain an array of choices. Hunt-Berg et al. note that the most sophisticated application of word cueing is word prediction. These prediction programs are able to suggest words based on frequency, recency of use, grammatical correctness, or commonly associated words and phrases. Hunt-Berg et al. observe that these programs can provide writers with opportunities to use words that are more specific, varied, and richer in meaning.

Computer-assisted instruction with synthesized or digitized speech also seems to be an efficient way to help students with language-learning disabilities acquire and retain vocabulary (Hebert & Murdock, 1994). Many commercial programs are available or teachers can develop specific activities on the word processor to help students increase vocabulary. Lerner (1993) suggested several activities for building vocabulary. For example, a teacher can write a series of sentences with blanks inserted in place of the vocabulary words that the student is studying and then list the vocabulary words at the bottom of the page. The student can use the "Move" command to insert the word into the correct space. Or, a student can use the "Find" and "Replace" commands to locate overused words and then substitute more precise terms.

Text Structure

Written texts are designed and patterned to represent ideas and achieve particular purposes (Horowitz, 1985a). The patterns, or text structures, selected by writers enhance organization and the presentation of information. Authors organize different kinds of writing in different ways (Tompkins, 1994).

Components of Text Structure

Organization of text requires the abilities to plan, translate, and review what has been written (Stewart, 1992). Performance is influenced by two kinds of organization: (a) representation of relationships through recurring patterns or text structures and (b) employment of strategies specific to writing (Englert & Mariage, 1991). In considering a writer's ability to organize and structure text, the cohesiveness of a student's writing must first be examined. Next, the student's knowledge of narrative and expository writing must be determined.

Cohesion and Coherence

As noted by Kerrigan (1979), a writer's business is to show connections. A writer must attend to both the transitions from one sentence to the next, as well as the overall, logical development of ideas (Vogel, 1985). In other words, text organization requires attention to both cohesion and coherence. Cohesion involves the specific ways sentences are linked together and the transitions within and between sentences, whereas coherence refers to the organization of a text and how the ideas are linked together (Witte & Faigley, 1981). A writer must then consider both the between-sentences relationships or cohesion, as well as the total form or coherence of the composition (Gregg, 1991).

A guiding rule when writing is to decide what the relationship between a sentence and a preceding sentence is and then, if possible, add a connective that indicates that relationship (Kerrigan, 1979). Relationships between sentences are often established with cohesive ties. Cohesive ties function similarly to highway marks and road signs, helping the reader to recognize relationships (Horowitz, 1985a). Gregg (1985) discussed three types of cohesive ties: grammatical, transitional, and lexical. Grammatical ties include words that refer to a noun in another sentence or paragraph (Gregg, 1991). An example of a grammatical tie is the use of a pronoun to refer to a noun in a previous sentence. Transitional ties are words or phrases that illustrate the relationships between sentences, such as *for example* or *consequently*. Lexical ties are established through the selection of vocabulary, such as repeating a word more than once within a text or using a synonym. Good writers pay careful attention to these cohesive devices so that the content and structure of their writing interact to create meaning (Tindal & Hasbrouck, 1991).

In contrast, students with learning disabilities often have difficulty using connective words that signal temporal and causal relationships (Weaver & Dickinson, 1982). These writers tend to use fewer cohesive conjunctions than writers without disabilities (Moran, 1988). Figure 2–31 illustrates the first draft of a descriptive paragraph about Christmas written by Myrna, a third-grade student. Myrna attempts to unite her ideas by using the connective *and*.

In contrast, Figure 2–32 illustrates a descriptive paragraph written by Sandra, a sixth-grade student, who was asked to describe a favorite place. Arrows were added to illustrate Sandra's use of cohesive ties to sequence her text.

Text coherence, therefore, relies both upon topic maintenance and the careful sequencing of ideas. Coherence and cohesion in writing also involve consideration of the audience and sensitivity to the reader's needs (Gregg, 1991). Thus, the text structure or the underlying organizational schema allows the writer and the reader to communicate more easily because what has been written reflects an anticipated organization. For instance, the structure for a descriptive paragraph is different from the schema for a chapter in a book. Similarly, narrative texts have different syntactic patterns and cohesive characteristics than expository text (Westby, 1994). Consequently, another factor that influences textual organization is competence in the genre (Gregg, 1991) or knowledge of the recurring patterns or structures in text (Englert & Mariage, 1991).

Types of Text Structure

Englert and Mariage (1991) noted that " . . . text structure can be used to promote a dialogue in the classroom that creates shared understandings about the organization and meaning of texts. In essence, it provides students with a common language for interpreting and negotiating the meaning of their texts, as well as for making themselves understood by others" (p. 331). The two major types of text structure are narrative or story writing and expository or essay writing (Britton, Burgess, Martin, McLeod, & Rosen, 1975).

Narrative. To succeed in school, students must be able to produce a topic-centered narrative (Westby, 1994). Knowledge and understanding of the underlying framework or set of rules associated with narrative structure have been referred to as story schema and story grammar (Laughton & Morris, 1989; Montague, Maddux, & Dereshiwsky, 1990; Nezworski; Stein, & Trabasso, 1982). Story schema refers to the mental representations an individual has of story parts and their relationships, whereas story grammar describes the rules and regularities found in text and their temporal and causal relations (Mandler & Johnson, 1977; Montague et al., 1990; Stein & Glenn, 1979; Stein &

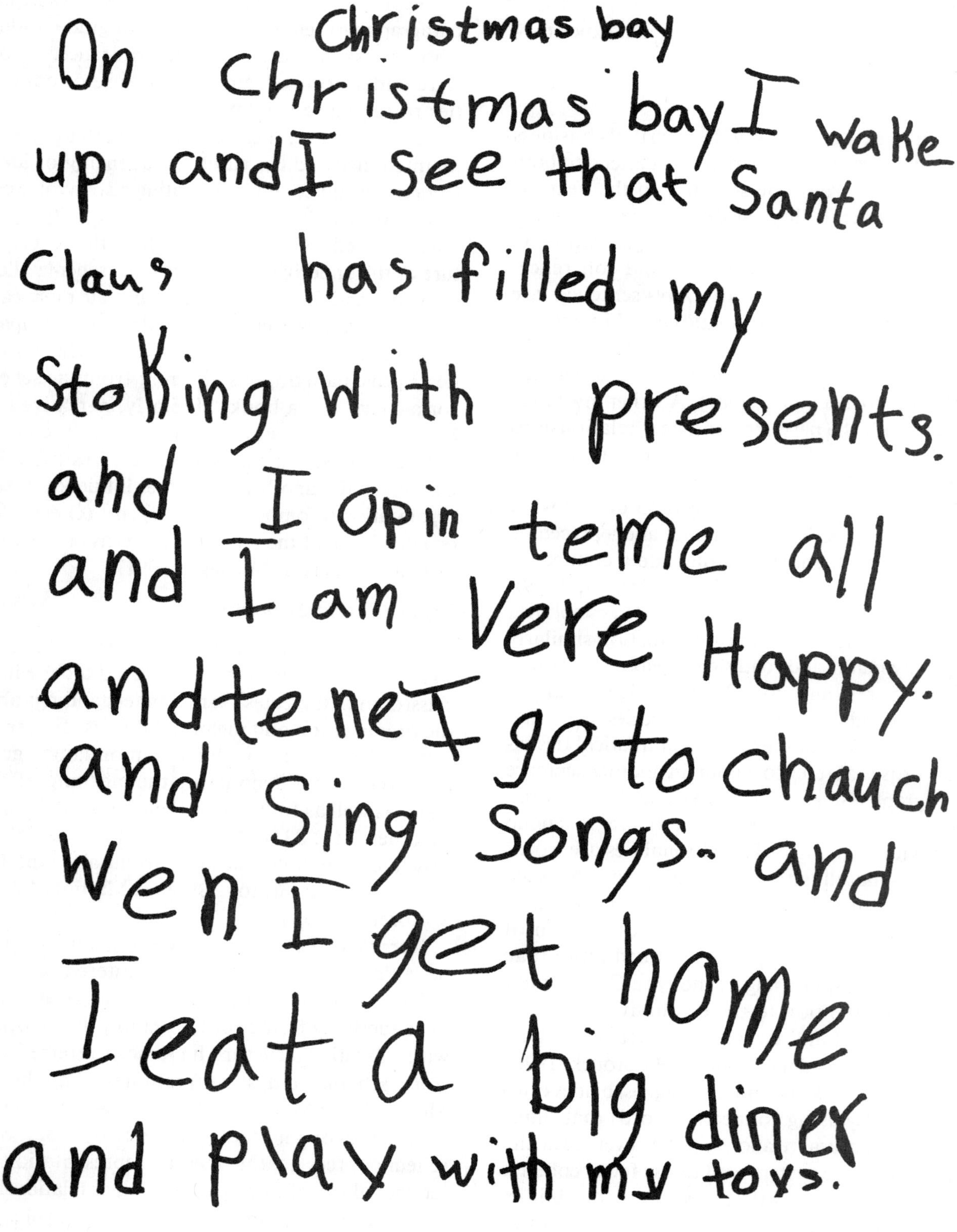

On Christmas bay
Christmas bay I wake
up and I see that Santa
Claus has filled my
stoking with presents.
and I opin teme all
and I am vere Happy.
and tene I go to chauch
and Sing Songs. and
Wen I get home
I eat a big diner
and play with my toys.

Figure 2–31. A descriptive paragraph written by Myrna, a third-grade student.

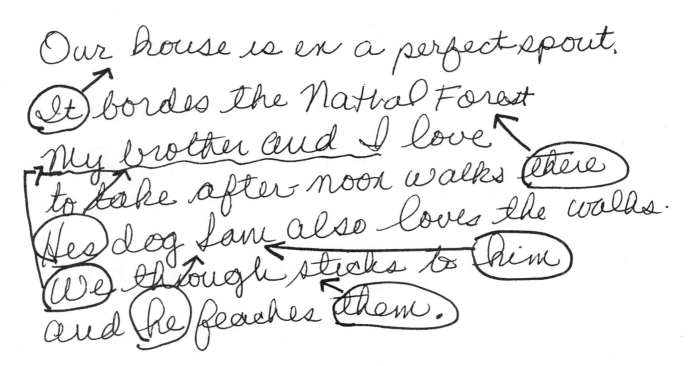

Figure 2–32. A descriptive paragraph written by Sandra, a sixth-grade student.

Trabasso, 1982). Story grammar provides students with a hierarchical framework that guides comprehension and production of narrative text (Montague & Leavell, 1994).

Story grammar elements include: (a) setting, or the main characters, time, and place; (b) beginning, or the event that triggers the story; (c) reaction, or what the main characters do; (d) attempt, or what effort is made to attain the goal; (e) outcome, or the results of the attempt to reach the goal; and (f) ending, or the consequences and final response of the main characters (Mandler & Johnson, 1977). A more simplified story grammar could include four major story parts: (a) setting, or the introduction of the characters, time, and place; (b) problem, or a predicament that confronts the main characters; (c) goal, or the character's attempts to solve the problem; and (d) outcome, or the success or failure of the characters to accomplish the goal (Thomas, Englert, & Morsink, 1984).

Some students with learning disabilities have good understanding of story grammar. The first drafts of their narratives contain all of the story elements. For example, Luke, a fifth-grade student, wrote a horror story, presented in Figure 2–33. Although a teacher may have concerns in regard to his spell-ing and handwriting, Luke has established a setting, presented the main characters, created a problem, and provided a resolution and ending.

Figure 2–34 illustrates an analytic scale developed by Tindal and Hasbrouck (1991) for evaluating narrative stories. This scale can help a teacher evaluate three specific dimensions of writing: story-idea, organization-cohesion, and conventions-mechanics.

Expository. The writer of expository text explains or provides information about a topic (Newcomer & Barenbaum, 1991). In this genre, an author writes to share information with readers (Tompkins, 1994). Many elementary-age children have trouble understanding the nonfiction that they read and then reconstructing the information into an appropriate written form (Lewis, Wray, & Rospigliosi, 1994). In general, expository writing is more complex than story writing because students must search for content, find ways to organize material, and consider the reader's knowledge of the topic (MacArthur, Schwartz, & Graham, 1991). Consequently, many students with learning disabilities have more difficulty writing expository than narrative text (Gerber, 1993).

A number of expository text structures exist. The structures are pertinent to four aspects of

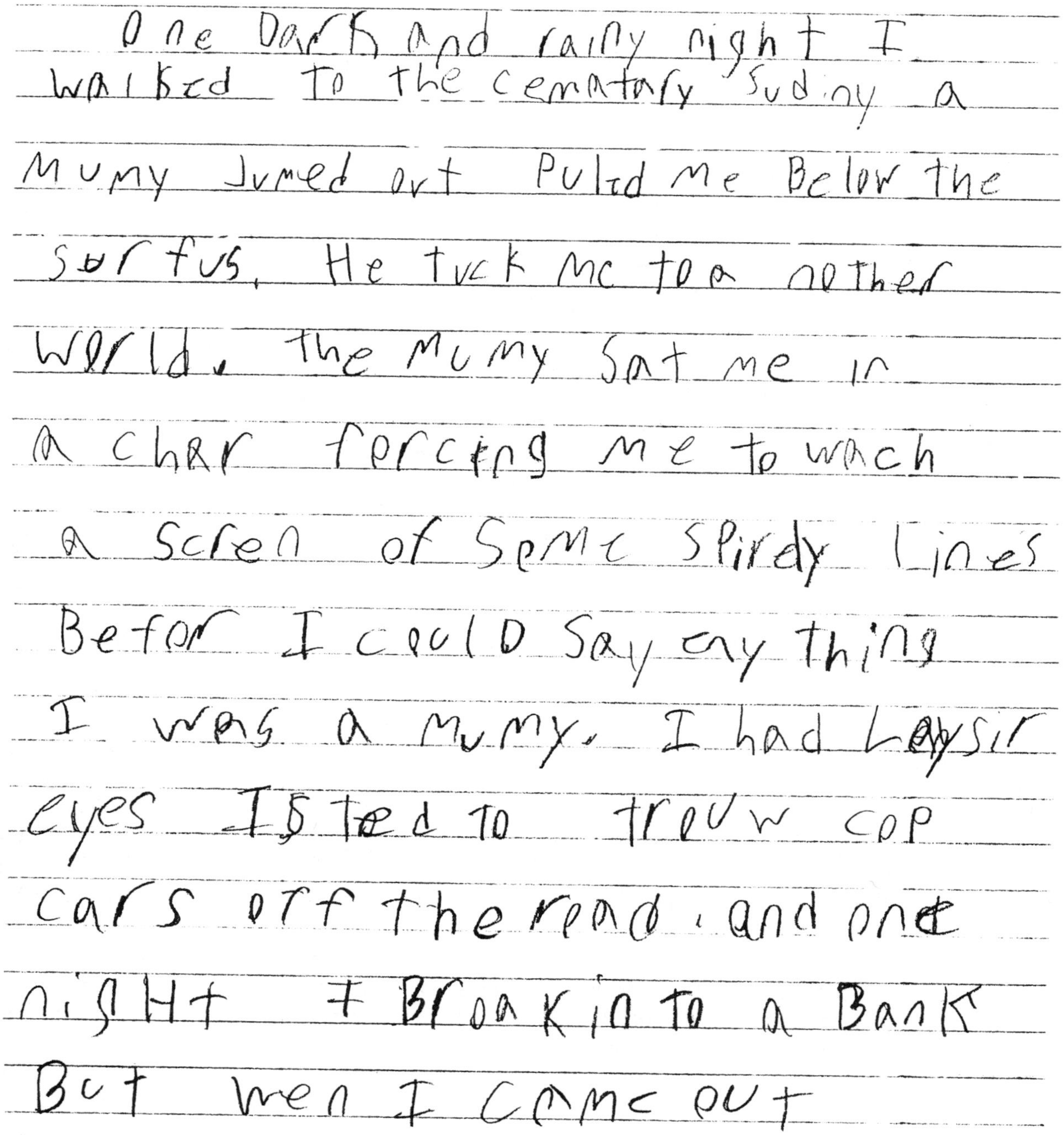

One Dark and rainy night I
walked to the cematary suddny a
mumy jumed out Puled me Below the
surfus. He tuck me to a nether
world. The mumy sat me in
a chair forceing me to wach
a scren of some spirdy lines
befor I could say anything
I was a mumy. I had laysir
eyes I stred to trouw cop
cars off the road, and one
night I broak into a Bank
But wen I came out

Figure 2–33. A horror story by Luke, a fifth-grade student.

informational texts: (a) planning, (b) organizing, (c) drafting, and (d) monitoring (Englert & Mariage, 1991). These text structures can be applied to answer different text structure questions. Examples of text structure include: comparison/contrast, explanation, problem/solution, and thesis/statement (Meyer, 1975; Meyer, Brandt, & Bluth, 1980).

Similarly, Horowitz (1985a) identified five types of text patterns that have been found in school texts: temporal order (time order), attribution (list structure), adversative (compare-contrast), covariance (cause-effect), and response (problem-solution). Each structure is signaled by various semantic and syntactic techniques (Englert & Mariage, 1991). Figure

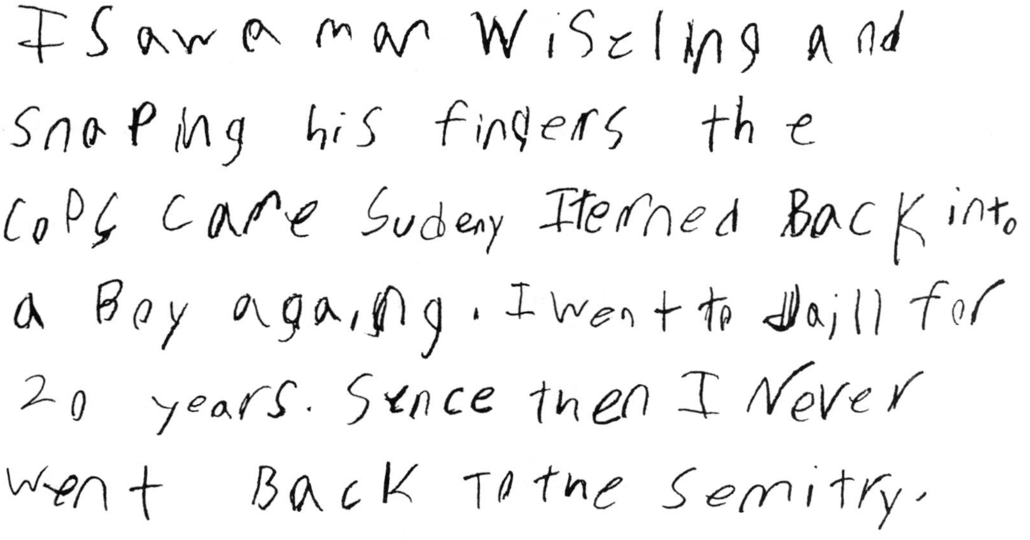

I saw a man Wiseling and snaping his fingers the cops came sudeny iterned Back into a Boy againg. I went to Jaill for 20 years. Sence then I Never went Back To the semitry.

Figure 2-33 (cont). A horror story by Luke, a fifth-grade student.

7-11 in Chapter 7 presents the most common types of expository text structures. This figure provides a brief description of each text structure and a sample sentence that may be used as a model for the informal evaluation of student writing.

In reality, texts usually contain multiple text structures, rather than a single structure (Englert & Mariage, 1991). For example, an author may develop an argumentative essay by comparing and contrasting various opinions and then discussing sequentially the reasons that support his or her viewpoint.

Figures, 2-35, 2-36, 2-37, illustrate three student drafts of different types of text structure. Casey, an eighth-grade student wrote a descriptive paragraph about his cat. Carl, a sixth-grade student, wrote a sequential paragraph on how to construct a snowman. Marnie, a seventh-grade student, was instructed to write a compare-contrast paragraph reflecting traditional and modern views on family and marriage in Japan.

Factors Affecting Performance

Text organization poses problems for writers with learning disabilities (Gould, 1991). The compositions of students with learning disabilities are often characterized by irrelevancies, redundancies, early terminations, and limited organization and coherence (Newcomer & Barenbaum, 1991).

As an example of incorporating irrelevant details into an assignment, Figure 2-38 illustrates the writing of Jane, a seventh-grade student. Jane was asked to write an opinion paper expressing how she liked the assigned literature book. After commenting that she liked the book, Jane writes a series of unrelated details. Her writing is characterized by irrelevancies, mechanical errors, and poor organization. She did not attempt to integrate information from prior knowledge or experience. Rather than plan her composition, Jane appears to have included any ideas that came to mind without regard to their relevance to her composition.

In contrast, Erik, an eighth-grade student, was asked to write an opinion paragraph on his feelings about guns. His first draft is presented in Figure 2-39. Erik attempts to introduce his topic by describing the function of guns. He then goes on to incorporate his personal experiences and reveal his concerns. Although revisions and edits are needed, Erik includes relevant details and personal experience.

Knowledge of expository text structures is important to successful writing (Englert & Mariage, 1991) and increases as students progress through school (Stewart, 1992). Although text structure knowledge increases with maturation (Laughton & Morris, 1989), students with learning disabilities have rudimentary knowledge of text structure and the strategies that might facilitate idea generation

Story-Idea	Organiz.-Cohesion	Conven.-Mechan.
5	**5**	**5**
—includes characters —delineates a plot —contains original ideas —contains some detail —word choice —contains descriptors (adverbs and adjectives) and colorful, infrequently used, and/or some long words.	—overall story is organized into a beginning, middle, and an end. —events are linked and cohesive —sentences are linked, often containing some transitions to help with organization (finally, then, next, etc.)	—sentence structure generally is accurate —spelling does not hinder readability —sometimes contain dialogue —handwriting is legible —punctuation does not effect readability too much —word usage generally is correct (s,v,o/homophone/s-v agreement)
4	**4**	**4**
—includes characters, but they are not original, often coming from movies —delineates a plot, although it is not as clear as 5 —contains some orignial ideas but is fairly predictable —contains some detail —includes descriptors (adverbs and adjectives) —word choice: contains some descriptors (adverbs and adjectives) and some colorful, infrequently used, and/or long words	—story has somewhat of a beginning, middle, and an end. —events appear somewhat random, but some organization exists —sample may contain some transitions to help with organization: finally, then, next etc.) —story often contains too many events, disrupting cohesion	—sentence structure generally is accurate but not as good as 5 —spelling does not hinder readability too much —sometimes contains dialogue —handwriting is legible —punctuation does not effect readability too much —word usage generally is correct (s,v,o/homophone/s-v agreement)
3	**3**	**3**
—characters are predictable and undeveloped —plot is somewhat haphazard —may or may not contain original ideas —lacks detail —word choice is somewhat predictable only sometimes contains descriptors (adverbs and adjectives)	—somewhat of a plot exists but story may still lack a beginning, middle or an end. —events are somewhat random —often lacks transitions —sometimes lacks referents	—sentence structure has a few problems —spelling is somewhat of a problem —may use dialogue but does not punctuate it correctly —handwriting is legible —punctuation is fair —problems sometimes occur with word usage (s,v,o/homophone/s-v agreement)
2	**2**	**2**
—includes few if any characters —plot is not developed or apparent —contains virtually no original ideas —detail is significantly absent —events are very predictable —word choice is predictable, lacking descriptors (adverbs and adjectives)	—plot lacks organization into a beginning, middle and an end —events are random, lacking in cohesion —lacks transitions —often lacks referents	—sentence structure makes story difficult to read —spelling makes it difficult to read —may use dialogue but does not punctuate it correctly —handwriting is not very legible —punctuation is inconsistent and problematic —word usage is problematic (s,v,o/homophone/s-v agreement)
1	**1**	**1**
—includes few if any characters —plot is non-existent —contains no original ideas —detail is significantly absent —events are few and predictable —lacks descriptors (adverbs and adjectives)	—plot is virtually nonexistent —events are few and random —lacks transitions —lacks referents	—sentence structure is problematic —spelling makes it extremely difficult to read —handwriting is illegible, making it extremely difficult to decode —punctuation is virtually nonexistent —word usage is problematic (s,v,o/homophone/s-v agreement)

Figure 2-34. An analytic scale for evaluating narrative stories.

Note. From "Analyzing Student Writing to Develop Instructional Strategies," by G. Tindal & G. J. Hasbrouck, 1991, *Learning Disabilities: Research and Practice, 6*, p. 239. Copyright 1991 by Lawrence Erlbaum Associates. Reprinted by permission.

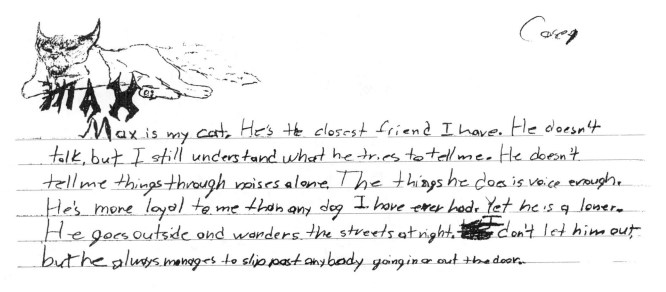

Max is my cat. He's the closest friend I have. He doesn't talk, but I still understand what he tries to tell me. He doesn't tell me things through noises alone. The things he does is voice enough. He's more loyal to me than any dog I have ever had. Yet he is a loner. He goes outside and wanders the streets at night. I don't let him out, but he always manages to slip past anybody going in or out the door.

Figure 2–35. A descriptive paragraph by Casey, an eighth-grade student.

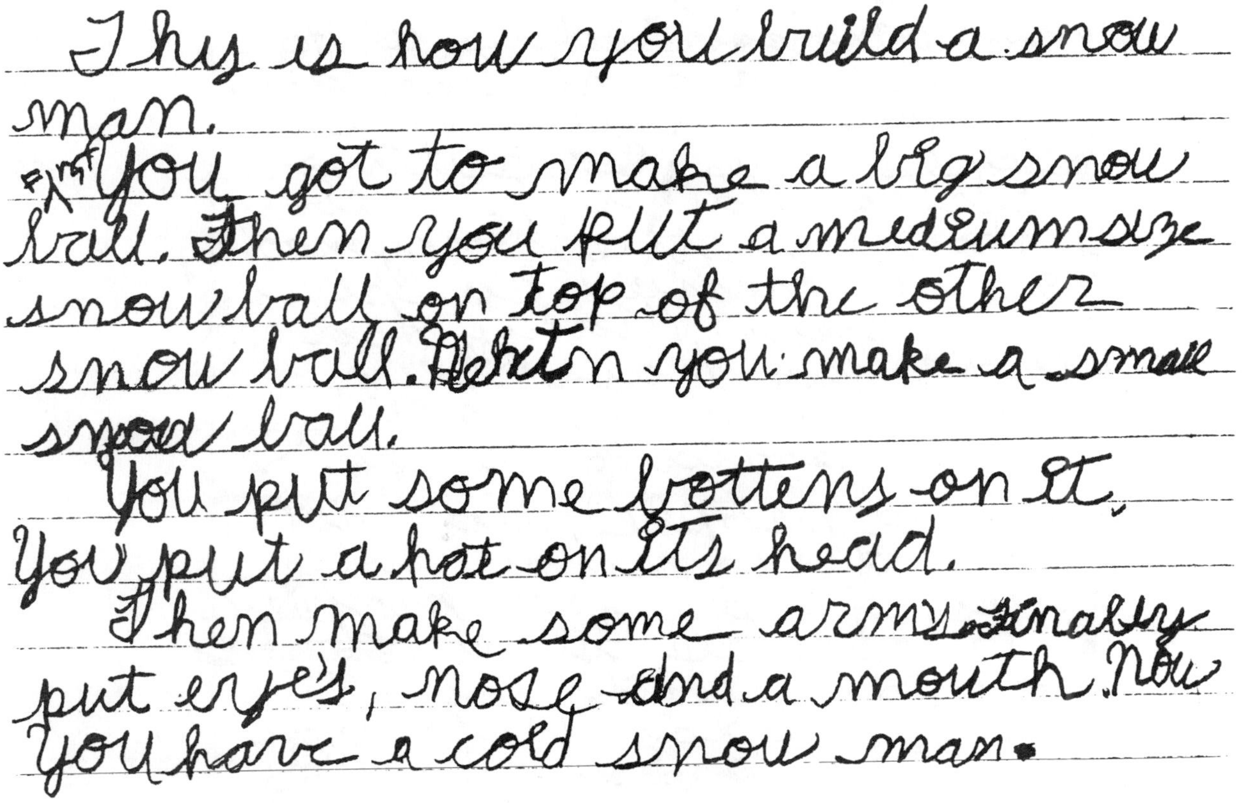

This is how you build a snow man.

You got to make a big snow ball. Then you put a medeum size snowball on top of the other snow ball. Then you make a small snow ball.

You put some bottens on it. You put a hat on its head.

Then make some arms. Finally put eye's, nose and a mouth. Now you have a cold snow man.

Figure 2–36. A sequential paragraph by Carl, a sixth-grade student.

Marriage and family life have changed from the past to the present in Japan. Although family is still the center of life, there is more of a chance to be an individual. In the past the father ruled the family. Today the fathers rule is not as strong and the wife or mother is more involved because the father works so much. In the past parents arranged the marriages. Today 60% of the marriages are still arranged. Today people are getting married latter. A new custom is the honeymoon, 98% of married couples take them. Many old traditions have been saved. Weddings are still important events. Before people did not have that much when they first got married. Now people start their marriage with more things. Today weddings are big business and cost a lot of money.

Figure 2–37. A compare-contrast paragraph by Marnie, a seventh-grade student.

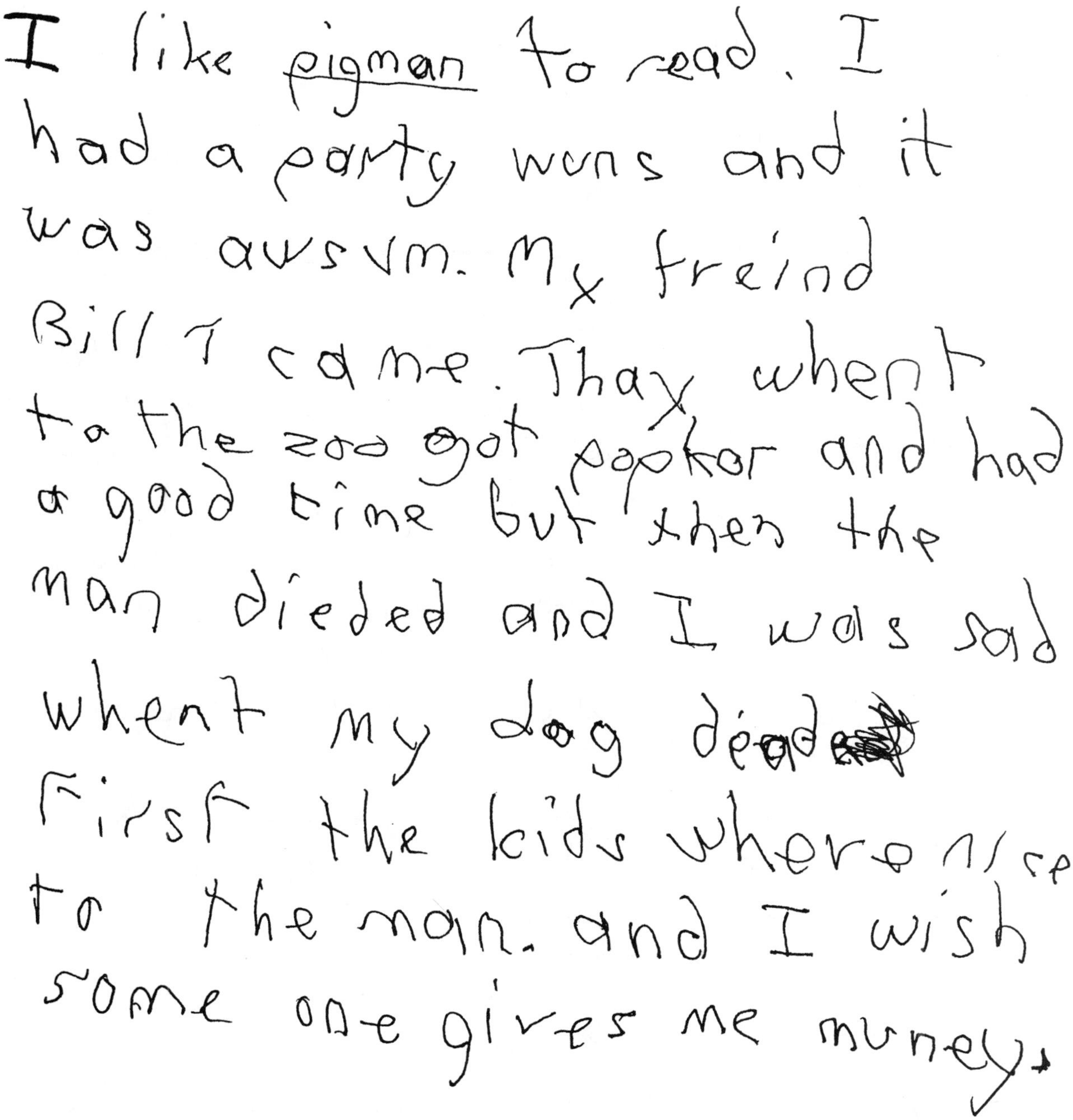

I like pigman to read. I
had a party wuns and it
was awsvm. My freind
Billy came. Thay whent
to the zoo got popkor and had
a good time but then the
man dieded and I was sad
whent my dog deaded
First the kids where nice
to the man. and I wish
some one gives me muney.

Figure 2–38. An opinion paper by Jane, a seventh-grade student.

and organization (Barenbaum, Newcomer, & Nodine, 1987; Englert & Hiebert, 1984; Montague et al., 1990; Newcomer & Barenbaum, 1991; Nodine et al., 1985; Stewart, 1992; Wong et al., 1989).

Knowledge of Narrative Structure

For many students with learning disabilities, knowledge of narrative structure of the major story elements is not fully developed (Laughton & Morris, 1989; Montague & Graves, 1993; Newcomer & Barenbaum, 1991; Nodine et al., 1985; Worden, 1986). These students tend to have ineffective strategies for creating and composing stories (Crealock, 1993; Montague et al., 1990; Nodine et al., 1985). Although schematic knowledge of stories is acquired by individuals with learning disabilities

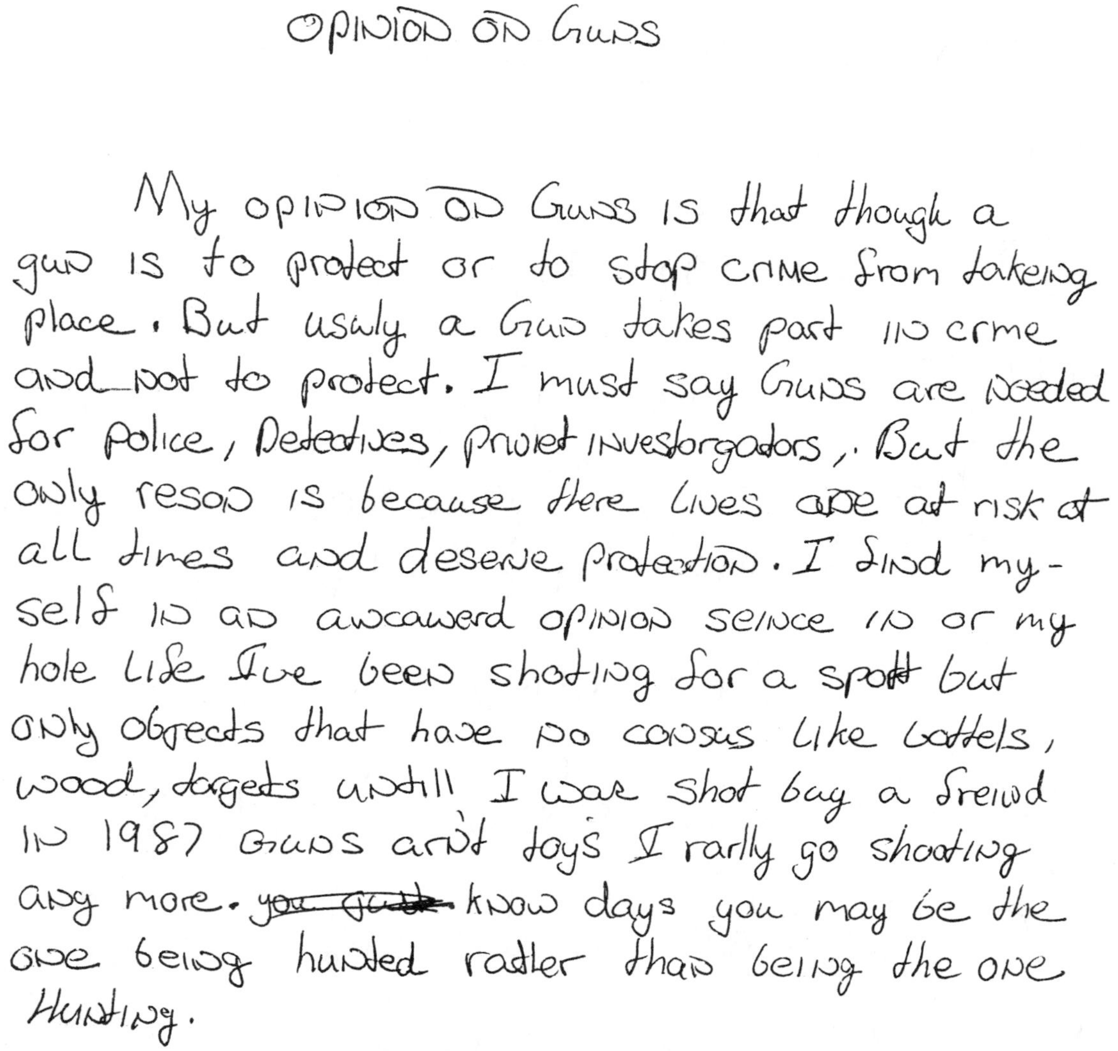

OPINION ON GUNS

My opinion on Guns is that though a gun is to protect or to stop crime from takeing place. But usuly a Gun takes part in crime and not to protect. I must say Guns are needed for Police, Detectives, Privet Investorgators, . But the only reson is because there Lives are at risk at all times and desene Protection. I find my-self in an awcawerd opinion seince in or my hole Life I've been shoting for a sport but only objects that have no consus Like bottels, wood, targets untill I was shot bay a freind in 1987 Guns arnt toys I rarlly go shooting any more. ~~you guess~~ know days you may be the one being hunted radter than being the one Hunting.

Figure 2–39. An opinion paragraph by Erik, an eighth-grade student.

(Laughton & Morris, 1989; Worden, 1986), deficiencies exist in activation of prior knowledge, conceptual knowledge, and strategic knowledge (Torgesen, 1986). Examination of the written narratives of students with learning disabilities revealed that nearly half of the students wrote compositions with no story line (Nodine et al., 1985). In addition, the majority of stories written by students with learning disabilities did not include explicit goals, starting events, and/or the characters' emotional reactions. In general, when compared to peers without disabilities, elementary-age students with learning disabilities include fewer story components when writing narratives (Laughton & Morris, 1989), write briefer descriptions, and include unrelated, idiosyncratic responses (Nodine et al., 1985).

Students' differing abilities to use text structure are often apparent in their use of story grammar as a framework for story writing (Stewart, 1992). Figure 2–40 presents the initial draft of the beginning of a story by Hefina, a sixth-grade student. Although Hefina has described the setting, she has not determined the major problem or problems that the main characters will encounter. Consequently, the story line does not progress and the presented ideas are disjointed. In addition to direct instruction in story grammar, Hefina would benefit from instruction designed to increase organization of narrative text.

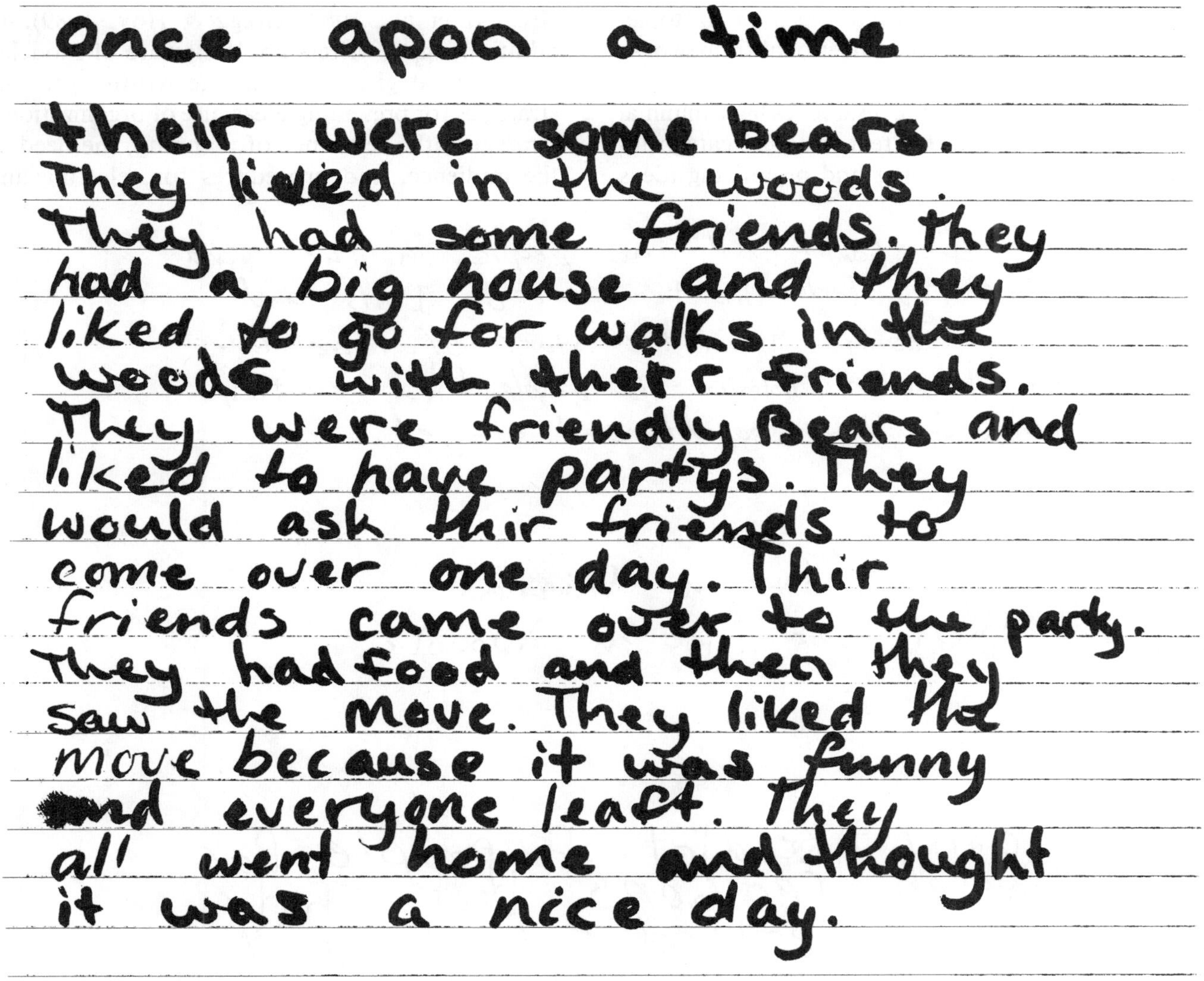

Once apon a time their were some bears. They lived in the woods. They had some friends. They had a big house and they liked to go for walks in the woods with their friends. They were friendly Bears and liked to have partys. They would ask thir friends to come over one day. Thir friends came over to the party. They had food and then they saw the move. They liked the move because it was funny and everyone leaft. They all went home and thought it was a nice day.

Figure 2–40. The beginning of a story by Hefina, a sixth-grade student.

Knowledge of Expository Structure

Students with learning disabilities also have difficulty understanding and using expository text structures (Englert & Mariage, 1991; Englert, Raphael, Anderson, Gregg, & Anthony, 1989; Englert & Thomas, 1987; Stewart, 1992; Thomas et al., 1987; Tindal & Hasbrouck, 1991). Their writing is less organized and includes fewer ideas (Englert & Mariage, 1991; Gregg, 1983; Gregg & Hoy, 1989), particularly with the compare/contrast category of expository writing (Thomas et al., 1987). In general, their compositions contain unclear introductions, few details, and inadequate summaries or conclusions (Stewart, 1992). In addition, writers with learning disabilities possess incomplete knowledge with

regard to processes related to organizing, monitoring, and revising text on the basis of text structure (Englert et al., 1989; Englert, Raphael, Fear, & Anderson, 1988). Their processes are linear; information is unrelated and generated sentence-to-sentence rather than including sections of related information in which main ideas are stated first followed by supporting facts and details (Scardamalia & Bereiter, 1986; Stewart, 1992; Thomas et al., 1987). Finally, these students have difficulty detecting problems within compositions such as poor organization and insufficient content (Stewart, 1992).

Figure 2–41 illustrates first drafts of opinion essays written by seven different eighth-grade students from an English class. Their assignment was to write an essay about a person whom they admired. Although several of the students have a few ideas on the topic, their failure to develop organizational frameworks for their writing is apparent.

Individuals with learning disabilities have minimal strategic awareness of the text structure categories that may aid in generating and organizing ideas

(Englert et al., 1989; Gregg & Hoy, 1989). In addition, these writers are less aware of modeled writing strategies, steps in the writing process, strategies for presenting ideas, use of organizational strategies, the relevance of planning, the need of the audience, and procedures for selecting and

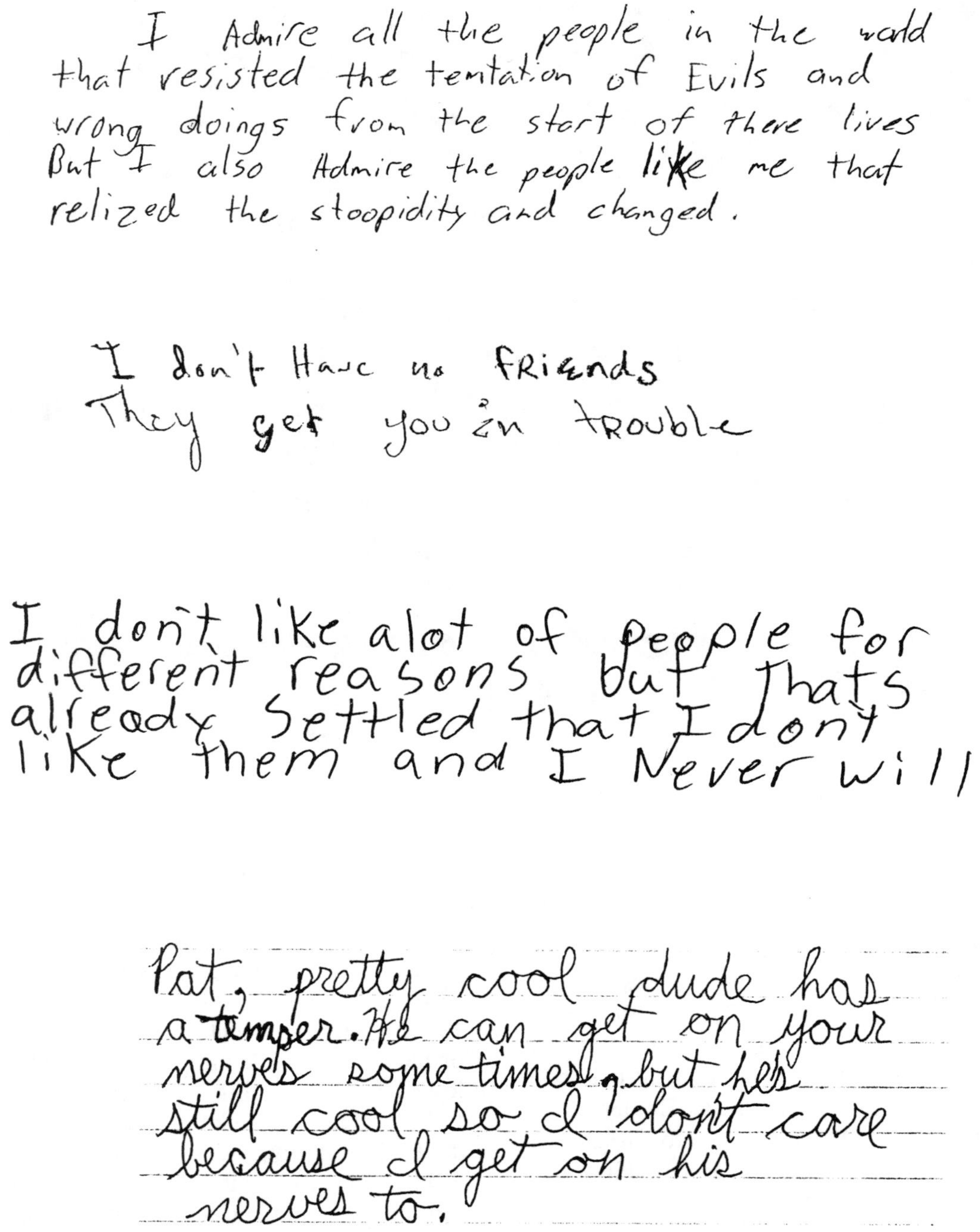

I Admire all the people in the world that resisted the temtation of Evils and wrong doings from the start of there lives But I also Admire the people like me that relized the stoopidity and changed.

I don't Have no FRiends They get you in trouble

I don't like alot of peeple for different reasons but Thats already settled that I don't like them and I Never will

Pat, pretty cool dude has a temper. He can get on your nerves some times, but he's still cool, so I don't care because I get on his nerves to.

Figure 2-41. Opinion essays written by seven different eighth-grade students.

a person I admire

The person I admire is my friend Juan
because I've known him forever. we've been friends
and enimes in the past but we alyse see it
trogh so thats who I admire

Description about a Parent,
My mom is cool, but I
really don't talk to her to
much. And my dad lives in P.A.
so oh well. I try to look
out for my self,

Well let see, well I guess
you could say that I don't
like nobody in this class
and theirs 3 girls I don't like
So for them to improve is for
them to tech them self about
improveing them self and how
to act right and not stupid.

Figure 2-41 (cont.). Opinion essays written by seven different eighth-grade students.

integrating information from multiple sources (Englert et al., 1988; Wong et al., 1989).

Text Structure and Technology

Students with learning disabilities can also benefit from the use of word processors for writing stories and essays. Although teachers see the benefit of the use of computers in most subjects, they are most excited about the improvement they see in students' written language (Smith & Luckasson, 1992). In general, the quality of writing is enhanced when students use computers (Messerer & Lerner, 1989; Outhred, 1989; Snyder, 1993).

Many computer software programs are available to help students develop their skills in both narrative and expository writing. Several examples are presented in Appendix A. Many of these programs are available that integrate text and graphics. For writing narratives, students often begin the program by developing pictures to illustrate their compositions. Programs with graphics are often effective in motivating both beginning and reluctant writers to write text to accompany their illustrations (Lewis, 1993). Students can also use the word processor to complete story starters, keep a diary or journal, or send electronic mail (Lerner, 1993).

Desktop publishing programs can help students to produce their own reports, newsletters, and newspapers (Lewis, 1993). These programs permit students to arrange the layout in one or two columns, insert headings and captions, and add graphics to illustrate the text. In addition, students can use electronic encyclopedias to gather information for their essays and reports.

Several new software programs combine word processing with speech synthesis. This feature allows students to enter text as the synthesizer reads it back to them by repeating a word or an entire line. Many times when students hear the text that they have written, they go back to revise it to make it "sound right" (Sampson et al., 1991).

Computer-supported writing provides new hope for students who have experienced repeated failures in writing (Hunt-Berg et al., 1994). Computers may also contribute to the development of a positive teaching/learning environment that has a productive balance between formal teacher input and individualized instruction and between teacher-centered and peer-mediated learning (Snyder, 1993).

Orientation to Instructional Strategies

Writers with learning disabilities often require instructional techniques that differ from those provided to normally achieving peers (Gregg & Hoy, 1989). Assessment and treatment of written language difficulties, therefore, require an understanding of the different components of written language (Gregg, 1991). Learning to write involves the mastery of numerous skills, and students with learning disabilities often show extreme variation in these skills (Meyer et al., 1991). In attempting to increase writing competence, individuals with learning disabilities often encounter obstacles that seem insurmountable.

Even though these students attempt to produce coherent prose, their writing is often marred by poor handwriting, spelling, or usage and/or organizational problems. Perhaps the most distinguishing characteristic of these writers is their difficulty learning the skills of symbolization or composition through incidental exposure (Moats, 1991a). In many instances, student writing skill could be improved if holistic approaches to writing were supplemented with more explicit, direct instructions (Borkowski, 1992). For at-risk primary students intensive, explicit instruction does work (Pressley & Rankin, 1994). At present, the real culprit for some students is inadequate instruction (Ehri, 1989). These students are not taught the skills that normally achieving peers acquire and apply automatically; consequently, their initial difficulties are compounded over the years and across the curriculum (Roit & McKenzie, 1985).

Writing instruction for students with learning disabilities, therefore, involves balancing process and product as well as acknowledging both the author and secretary roles (Isaacson, 1989, 1994; Smith, 1982). A product-oriented approach emphasizes the skills students need to become proficient writers, such as handwriting and basic writing skills; a process-oriented approach is geared toward effective communication of ideas and focuses upon the student's own ideas and interests (Meyer et al., 1991). Both types of approaches are needed to teach individuals with learning disabilities.

Comprehensive writing programs include instruction to help students develop: (a) procedural knowledge of the process of writing; (b) declarative knowledge about the purposes, text structures, and mechanical aspects of writing; and (c) conditional knowledge in regard to when to use the strategies (Isaacson, 1994). Table 2–1, prepared by Issacson, presents

Summary of Facts about the Writing Task and the Learner and Their Implications for Instruction

Knowledge about the task	Facts about the learner (common characteristics)	Implications for instruction	
		What we should teach	How we should teach
General Understandings			
Writing is communication with a reader.	Poor perspective-taking abilities	How to listen and give feedback about another's writing	Provide an audience for the author's work
			Provide opportunities for discourse with peers about writing
The language of writing is more formal than conversational speech.		How to differentiate good from less effective writing in its ability to communicate	Read to students (to familiarize them with the language of books)
			Provide examples of effective and ineffective writing
Writing requires thinking.	Deficient metacognitive skills	How to use self-evaluation, self-monitoring, and self-reinforcement strategies	Model thinking processes required in writing
			Provide opportunities for collaborative problem-solving with peers
Specific Knowledge			
Procedural knowledge (the process of writing)	Deficient repertoire of strategies	Steps in the writing process: planning, drafting, and revising	Model process
			Prompt (procedural facilitation) e.g., think sheets
	Poor selective attention		Teach explicitly: Focus students' attention on separate parts and critical aspects of process
Declarative knowledge			
The author's role		The text structures related to the different purposes of writing	
		The vocabulary and language of writing	Provide opportunities for discourse with peers about writing
	Specific memory deficits		Provide meaningfully organized information (conceptual models)
The secretary's role	Lack of automaticity in hand-writing and spelling	Spelling	Provide systematic (vs. seren-dipitous) instruction
		Handwriting	
		Capitalization and punctuation rules	Provide opportunities for application through use of editing strategies
			Precue spelling of topic-related words during planning stage
			Encourage invented spelling during drafting stage
	Poor reading abilities	Reading instruction	Have students read compositions aloud
			Have students collaborate with peers who read better
Conditional knowledge		Different purposes for writing	Teach knowledge and skills in problem sets related to purposes for writing

Table 2–1. Summary of Facts About the Writing Task and the Learner and Their Implications for Instruction.

Note. From "Integrating Process, Product, and Purpose: The Role of Instruction," by S. L. Isaacson, 1994, *Reading & Writing Quarterly, 10*, pp. 39–62. Copyright 1994 by Taylor & Francis. Reprinted by permission.

an overview of task knowledge, common learner characteristics, and implications for instruction across the writing domain. Accomplished teachers support the development of skills necessary for successful expression of ideas (Meyer et al.,1991). Instruction is directed to the social and creative aspects of writing, as well as the organizational and mechanical (Isaacson, 1994). As noted by Pressley and Rankin (1994), there is value in doing authentic tasks, as well as practicing the components.

To become effective, independent writers, students with learning disabilities require intensive, systematic writing programs. For many of these students, explicit instruction is imperative if they are going to learn to read and write (Pressley & Rankin, 1994). Chapters 5, 6, and 7 discuss instructional programs and present a variety of strategies, both product- and process-oriented, for teaching handwriting, basic writing skills, and written expression. The decisions in regard to which writing strategies to use are made through consideration of the student's development (Rhodes & Dudley-Marling, 1988). Based upon each writer's needs, instruction is diversified (Tindal & Hasbrouck, 1991).

When problems appear in any component of written language, difficulties with other aspects of writing skill often develop. Teachers often feel overwhelmed about how to incorporate all of the components when planning writing instruction (Isaacson, 1994). Fortunately, when skills are assessed and specific instruction is provided, students increase their writing proficiency.

3

WRITING PROCESS APPROACH

Small wonder then that the writing process works best with the disenfranchised, who become a bit giddy at the prospect of seeing their words on paper affecting the thinking of others.

—Graves, 1985, p. 37

As noted by many authors, writing is a recursive process that requires extensive time for planning, composing and revising (Bos, 1988; Bos & Vaughn, 1994; Calkins, 1986; Flower & Hayes, 1980; Graves, 1983, 1985; Murray, 1980; Vogel, 1985). The art of writing is never mastered; even competent writers move back and forth through the various stages in a constant interchange of self-expression and self-evaluation. The challenge is present to a second-grader in writing a sentence, as well as to an adult in writing a book (Dagenais & Beadle, 1984). As noted by Dagenais and Beadle, the challenge is even greater for students with language and learning disabilities. When compared to competent writers, these students have difficulties with all stages of the process (Stewart, 1992).

Many students with learning disabilities struggle with writing because attention must be directed to a wide range of skills and processes simultaneously (MacArthur, Schwartz, & Graham, 1991; Newcomer & Barenbaum, 1991). Kerchner and Kistinger (1984) described a picture of a student with learning disabilities: "That portrait depicts a child awkwardly grasping a pencil and much-used eraser, attempting to fulfill an assignment by writing words on paper. We might entitle this portrait 'Personification of Frustration'" (p. 329). They further suggested that, as educators, we have unwittingly added many of the brush strokes to create this portrait by subscribing to the theory that children must first learn to spell and punctuate before attempting to write.

In the past, emphasis on written language instruction was product oriented and prescriptive; students wrote on topics assigned by the teacher and then turned in their papers for grades (Tompkins & Friend, 1988). In fact, in many special education classrooms, instruction in writing conventions was the major, if not the exclusive, focus of instruction (Bos, 1988). In recent years, attention has shifted away from a focus on the written product and form of writing toward viewing writing as a process of thinking, formulating, drafting, rejecting, revising, and refining (McCarthey, 1994; Meyer et al., 1991). Students must develop their plans and review their texts even as they put words on the page (McCutchen, Covill, Hoyne, & Mildes, 1994). Research on both the composing process and teaching methods indicates that writing involves stop, review, start-again processes (Hillocks, 1987) and most experts recommend that it should be taught as such (Tompkins & Friend, 1988).

The purpose of this chapter is to review the process approach to writing instruction. This approach places emphasis on what students do and think as they write, rather than on the finished product (Tompkins, 1994). Because students with learning disabilities are less familiar with writing tasks, less knowledgeable about the importance of planning, and less aware of the intended audience than their peers (Newcomer & Barenbaum, 1991), the writing process approach to instruction is particularly effective for them. Use of this approach enables many students with learning disabilities to participate in supportive classrooms and receive quality instruction and guidance from their teachers.

Stages in the Writing Process

Instructional activities associated with process-oriented approaches typically include: brainstorming, focusing on students' ideas and interests, conducting small-group activities, holding conferences, emphasizing multiple drafts, and postponing editing skills until the final draft (Applebee, 1986). To initiate a writing process approach and encourage student independence in writing, Graves (1985) recommended that a teacher employ the following procedures: (a) provide opportunities for daily writing for a minimum of 30 minutes; (b) work to establish each student's areas of expertise; (c) compile writing in folders; (d) participate in the program by sharing writing, moving through the classroom, and responding in a predictable fashion to students' writing; and (e) end each period with students responding to each others' writing.

Through the use of process approaches, students are encouraged to examine and participate in each step of a writing task (Lapp & Flood, 1993). Typically, the task is divided into several stages: (a) prewriting activities, (b) drafting, (c) revising, (d) editing, and (e) publishing (Flower & Hayes, 1980; Graves, 1983, 1985; Murray, 1980; Tompkins, 1994). Or, as Ellis (1994b) described, writing is a process that involves thinking ahead (prewriting), thinking during (production), and thinking back (editing and revising). Within these stages, the starting or ending points of writing are not fixed (Lapp & Flood, 1993). The model is interactive, and a writer may drop back to an earlier stage at any time. For example, a student may realize when drafting an essay that she does not have enough information on the topic. Subsequently, she would return to a prewriting activity, such as going to the library to research specific facts. Prior to engaging in prewriting activities, however, a student must be motivated to write.

Fostering Motivation

An important goal of writing instruction is to help students develop a positive attitude toward writing activities (Graham & Harris, 1993; Phelps-Gunn & Phelps-Terasaki, 1982). When interviewed, students with learning disabilities indicate that poor motivation contributes to their writing difficulties (Graham, Schwartz, & MacArthur, 1993). These students are often discouraged about their lack of success in writing and their perceived inability to succeed often results in a withdrawal of effort from writing tasks (Meyer et al., 1991). Some students dread the task of writing and comment when faced

with a writing assignment: "Do I have to?" "How long does it have to be?" In one instance, a student may refuse to complete an assignment. In another instance, a student will do the least amount of writing that is needed to fulfill the assignment. In other words, the primary motivating force for the student is failure avoidance through task compliance, rather than a desire to communicate through writing (Ellis, 1994b).

Students with writing difficulties often paralyze their own creative impulses by censoring themselves (Landsman, 1993). They become frustrated when others are unable to understand the message because of poor legibility, spelling, or organization. For example, Figure 3–1 illustrates an assignment completed by Marcos, a fourth-grade student. Marcos was asked to write several math word problems for a peer to solve. Although Marcos completed the assignment, his peer informed him that he was unable to read, and, consequently, could not solve the word problems. In response, Marcos grabbed his paper back and commented that it was a "dumb assignment" anyway. Perhaps Marcos' behavior is somewhat reminiscent of the words of Graves (1985): "If I arrive at the blank page with a writing history filled with problems, I am already predisposed to run from what I see. I try to hide my paper, throw it away, or mumble to myself, 'This is stupid'" (p. 38).

Many individuals with writing disabilities have good ideas, but have become disenfranchised by the number of red marks on their papers or the rather intimidating comments from teachers. As an illustration, Mike, a fourth-grade student, was asked to write five sentences that would be considered a "fact" and five sentences that would be considered an "opinion." Figure 3–2 presents his paper and his teacher's feedback that was written in bright red ink.

Because of negative feedback from others, some students perceive that their problems with writing are actually greater than they really are. Figure 3–3 illustrates the first draft of a seventh-grade student, Bertha, who is concerned about her poor spelling skill. Although her spelling is not perfect, she succeeds in communicating through writing. Somehow through her experiences, Bertha has come to perceive that spelling is a major problem in her life. Bertha needs to regain confidence in herself and her skills as a writer.

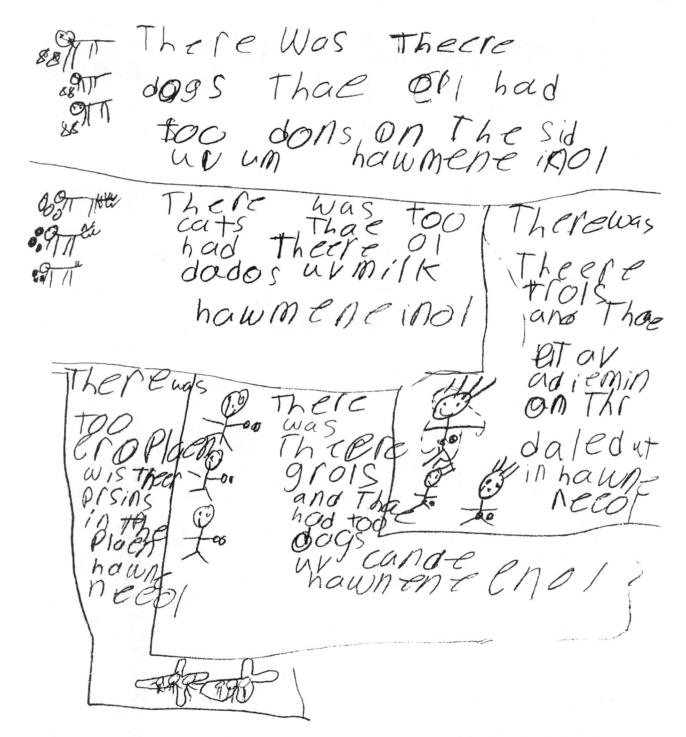

Figure 3-1. Math word problems written by Marcos, a fourth-grade student.

Similarly, in his journal, Bryan, a fifth-grade student, expresses his dislike of the class spelling book. Two journal entries are presented in Figure 3-4. After discussing a daily accomplishment, he expresses his disdain for the book.

Before beginning a writing program with students like Marcos, Mike, Bertha, and Bryan, a major hurdle to overcome is their attitude toward writing and reluctance to write. Motivation theories help to explain why one student is motivated to write, whereas

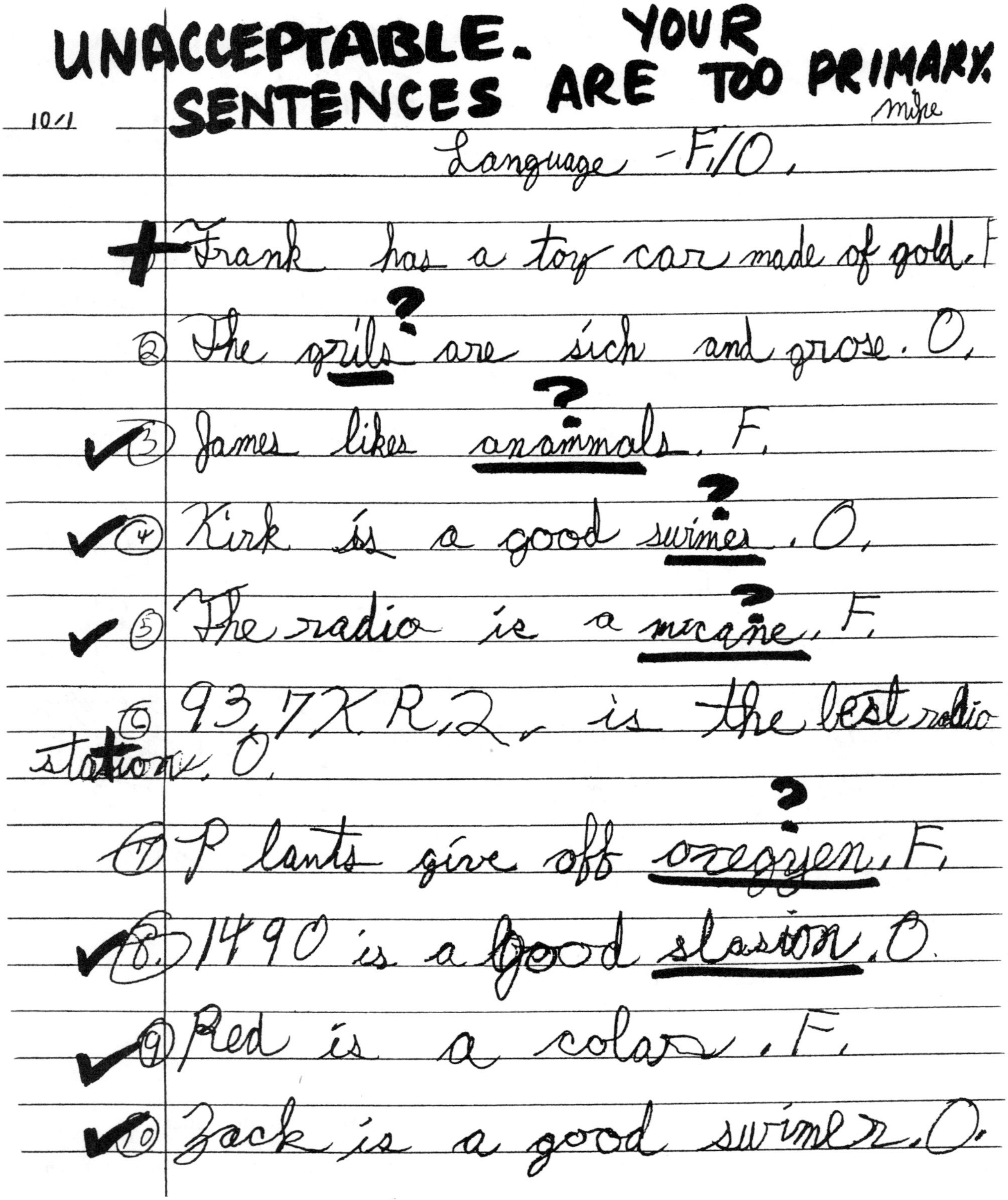

UNACCEPTABLE. YOUR SENTENCES ARE TOO PRIMARY. *Mike*

10/1

Language - F/O.

+ Frank has a toy car made of gold. F

② The girls are rich and prose. O.

✓③ James likes animals. F.

✓④ Kirk is a good swimer. O.

✓⑤ The radio is a mecane. F.

⑥ 93.7 KRZ is the best radio station. O.

⑦ Plants give off oxygen. F.

✓⑧ 1490 is a good staion. O.

✓⑨ Red is a color. F.

✓⑩ Zack is a good swimer. O.

Figure 3–2. Fact and opinion sentences by Mike, a fourth-grade student.

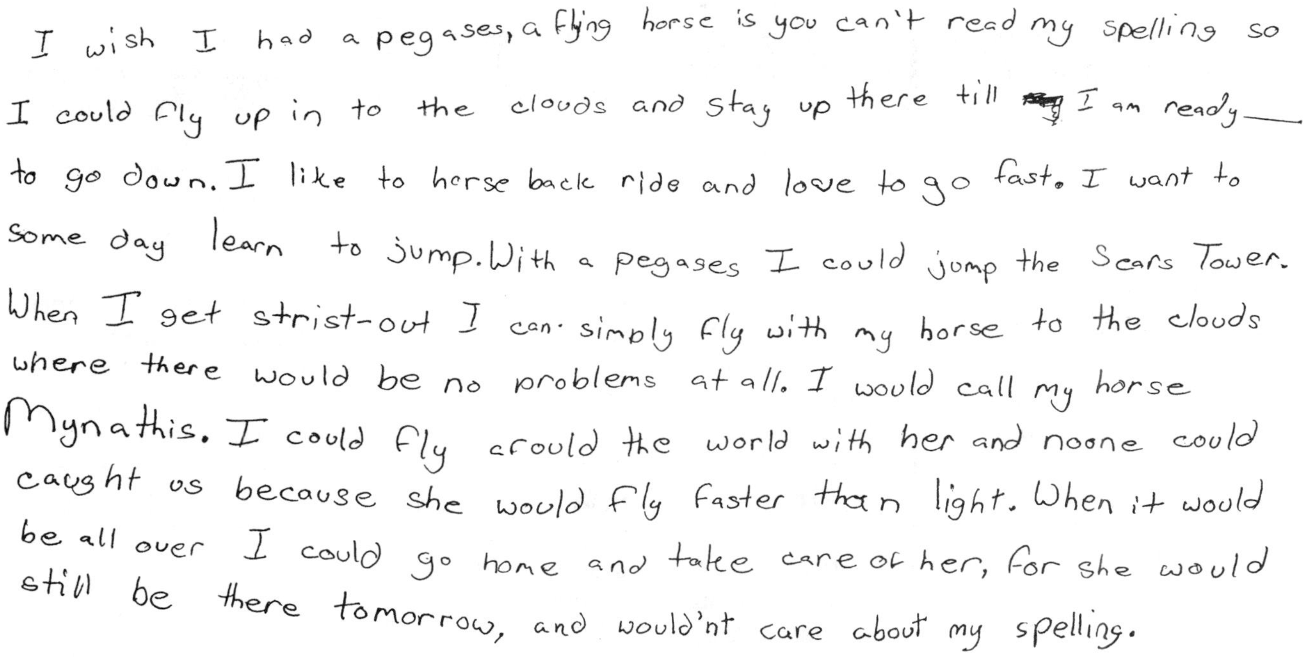

I wish I had a pegases, a flying horse is you can't read my spelling so I could fly up in to the clouds and stay up there till I am ready to go down. I like to horse back ride and love to go fast. I want to some day learn to jump. With a pegases I could jump the Sears Tower. When I get strist-out I can simply fly with my horse to the clouds where there would be no problems at all. I would call my horse Mynathis. I could fly arould the world with her and noone could caught us because she would fly faster than light. When it would be all over I could go home and take care of her, for she would still be there tomorrow, and would'nt care about my spelling.

Figure 3–3. First draft of a story written by Bertha, a seventh-grade student.

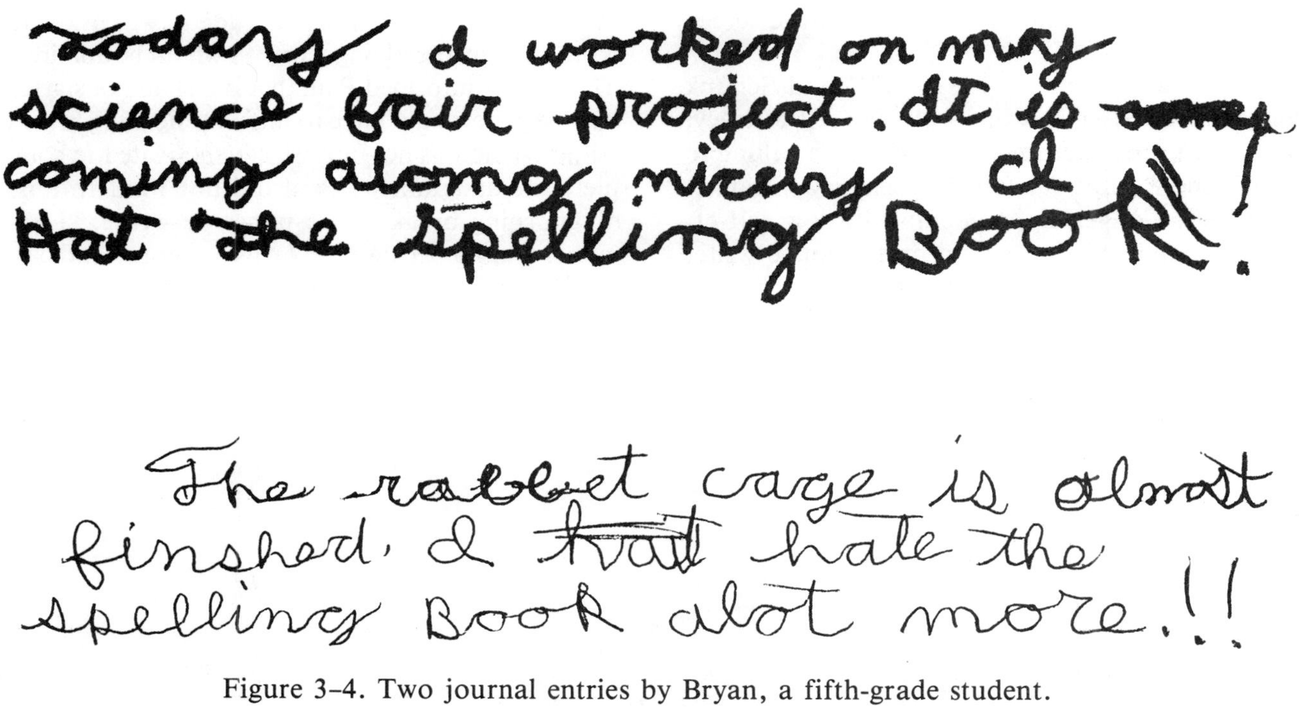

Today I worked on my science fair project. It is coming along nicely I hat the spelling Book!

The rabbet cage is almost finshed. I hate the spelling Book alot more.!!

Figure 3–4. Two journal entries by Bryan, a fifth-grade student.

another is not (Cohen, 1986). To understand the effect of motivation on performance, both intrinsic and extrinsic motivators must be considered.

Intrinsic Motivation

Intrinsic motivation comes from within the individual and is based upon a person's experiences, perceptions, and emotions. A facet of intrinsic motivation is self-efficacy. Self-efficacy refers to one's beliefs regarding his or her abilities to complete tasks at designated levels (Schunk, 1989; Schunk & Swartz, 1993). These elements can combine to become a motivator in themselves (Cohen, 1986). For example, Matthew, an efficient and effective writer, may complete his writing assignments because he enjoys writing and has a past history of success on similar assignments.

Conversely, Sheila, a fifth-grade student with learning disabilities, has not been successful on writing assignments, does not enjoy these tasks, and, consequently, is not intrinsically motivated. Figure 3–5 illustrates a paragraph written by Sheila about her dog. She spent over 1 hour producing the four sentences: "I love my dog. I have fun with my dog. She is smart. She knows how to open the screen door."

As noted by Schunk (1989, 1991) and Schunk and Swartz (1993), students with high self-efficacy, such as Matthew, enjoy writing and are willing to expend more effort than others when they encounter difficulty. Conversely, students with low self efficacy, such as Sheila, would prefer not to write.

To encourage participation, a teacher must attempt to eliminate threats and demands to perform and conform, and, instead, to explore learning activities that are relevant and interesting to the student (Adelman & Taylor, 1990). Fortunately, direct instruction in the use of strategies for writing helps students to form positive attitudes about writing (Danoff, Harris, & Graham, 1993; Graham & Harris, 1993). Subsequent success on writing tasks enhances self-efficacy, and high self-efficacy helps a student to be goal directed and intrinsically motivated. Individuals who are intrinsically motivated are then able to seek out, confront, and conquer challenges (Deci, 1978). Unfortunately, many individuals with learning disabilities are unlikely, at least initially, to seek out such challenges in writing activities. Consequently, they often require extrinsic incentives and motivators to engage in writing tasks.

Extrinsic Motivation

Extrinsic motivation originates from sources outside the individual and is fostered by external rewards. These incentives often help students who avoid challenges to put forth more effort (Smith, 1994). Paul, an eighth-grade student, was asked to write an essay describing a person whom he admired. The teacher informed Paul that if he had not started his essay, he would have to miss his morning break. Although he was not intrinsically motivated to complete the assignment, Paul did not want to miss his morning break. In response he wrote: "I admire my mom because she owns her house and car.

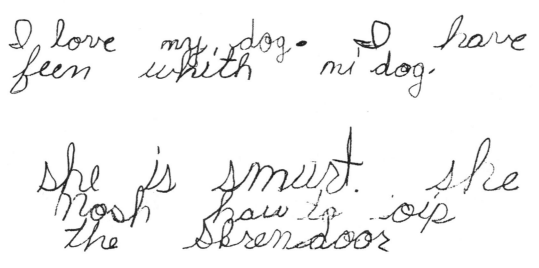

Figure 3–5. A paragraph written by Sheila, a fifth-grade student.

Everything is paid for. I didn't know what to write about but I did it anyway so I can go on break."

External motivators have been central to special education programs for the past decade (Cohen, 1986) and have played an important role in the education of individuals with learning disabilities (Hewitt, 1967). The traditional behaviorist approach to external motivators is that tasks are broken down into component parts. Reinforcement programs are then implemented so that extrinsic incentives are earned for either successful approximations or completion of a task. Depending upon the needs of the student, the type and frequency of the rewards will vary. The goal of these programs is to fade the reinforcement gradually as the student assumes more responsibility for completing tasks independently. Teachers often guide their students from being extrinsically to intrinsically motivated.

Components of Motivation

Individuals with learning disabilities depend, to a large degree, on their teachers to foster motivation and to create a program for change when necessary. A motivation change program should include the following four components (Cohen, 1986; deCharms, 1971, 1976): (a) self-study, (b) goal setting, (c) personal responsibility, and (d) transfer.

Self-study is similar to self-awareness and is essential to all components. Although students with learning disabilities tend to have less positive attitudes toward writing than their peers, they may have unrealistically high expectations regarding their abilities to complete writing tasks (Graham et al., 1993). Through self-study, individuals with writing difficulties can be encouraged to recognize their unique strengths, weaknesses, motives, and individuality.

Goal setting helps these individuals to set realistic goals for writing assignments and to plan activities in order to accomplish their goals. Personal responsibility refers to recognition and interpretation of one's role in completion of writing activities. Individuals who take responsibility for their accomplishments are able to: (a) monitor their actions, (b) set realistic goals, (c) organize and sequence activities to attain goals, and (d) assume responsibility for the outcomes of their actions.

The last of the four concepts, transfer, enables the individual to accomplish other personal and social goals in both academic and nonacademic settings. For example, Craig realizes the importance of writing for the successful completion of a task and makes a list of the materials he needs to repair his bicycle. Rosalie decides independently to write a letter to her best friend and a thank-you note to her grandmother for her birthday gift. An important component for motivational change is encouraging students to engage in activities outside the classroom that facilitate maintenance, generalization and expansion of learning (Adelman & Taylor, 1990).

All individuals can be guided toward increased autonomy in writing through promoting ownership and providing choices to guarantee investment in activities (Cohen, 1986). Carefully planned writing programs are essential for teaching students that writing is a valuable learning tool for all (Raimes, 1983). In general, the most effective writing programs are those that are inventive, relevant, and exciting and are founded upon several points: (a) the commitment, motivation, and enthusiasm of the teacher; (b) the selection of curricular activities that are interesting, original, and capture attention; and (c) the provision of positive feedback on writing assignments (Phelps-Gunn & Phelps-Terasaki, 1982). As students begin to have fun with writing, their motivation increases (Graves & Hauge, 1993).

Students who can express themselves in writing are able to share their major concerns in regard to their experiences and emotions. Writing thus becomes a vehicle for expanding and clarifying one's own thoughts and voice. Teachers must encourage all students to share their thoughts, particularly those for whom writing is difficult. Ken, a sixth-grade student, wrote a paragraph, presented in Figure 3–6, in regard to how he wished people would view him. Although the writing is difficult to read because of poor spelling, his ideas and feelings about his situation are clear.

Fortunately, Ken's teacher provided positive feedback on his first draft. For students with writing difficulties like Ken, implementation of the process approach will help them become more motivated, cooperative, and confident about their writing skill (Whitt, Paul, & Reynolds, 1988). The process approach provides a contextual, highly motivating framework where the goal of writing for communication is emphasized from the first day (Meyer et al., 1991). This supportive, social context provides the motivation for engaging in meaningful writing activities (MacArthur et al., 1991).

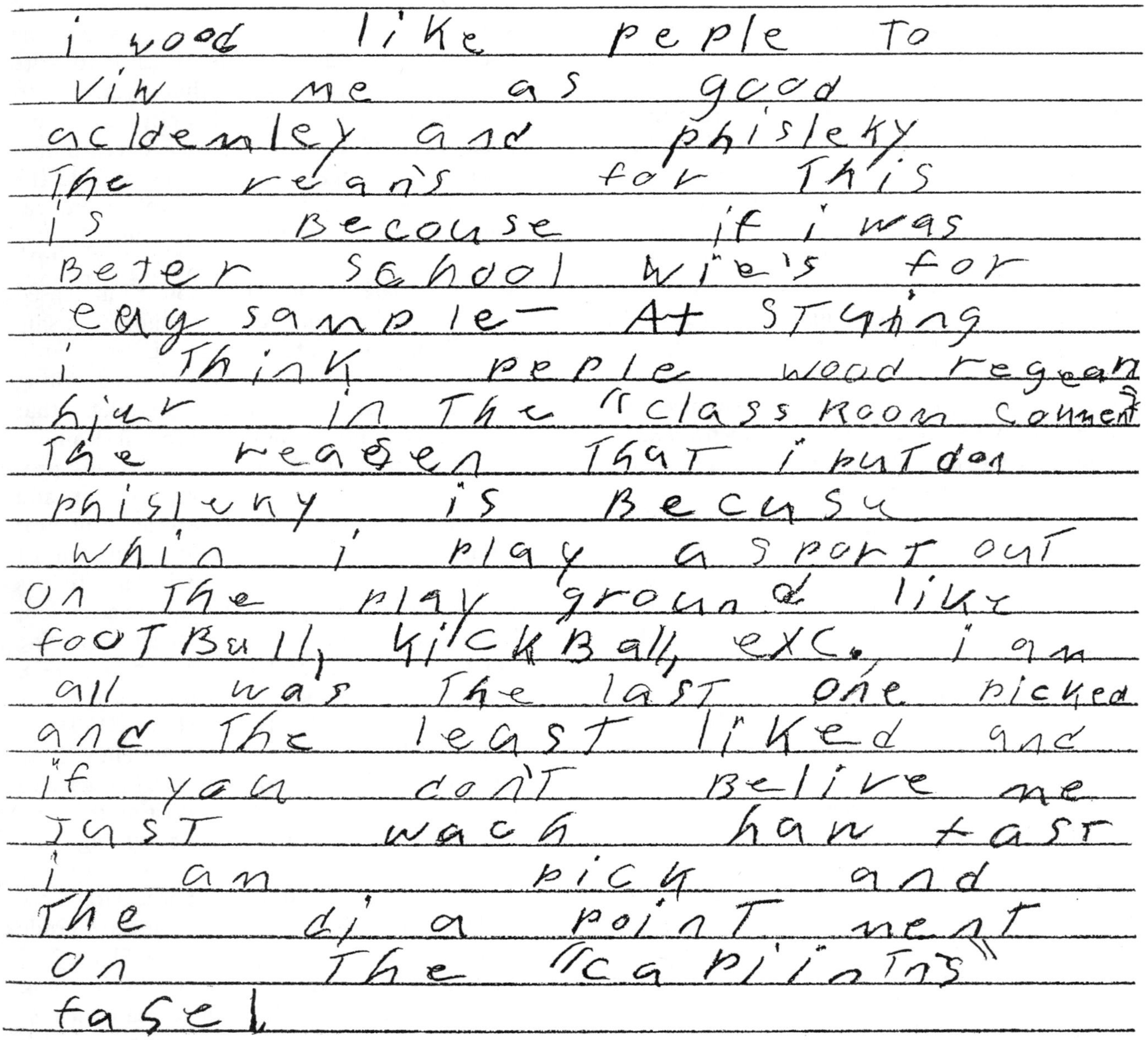

i wood like peple To
viw me as good
acldemley and phisleky
The rean's for This
Is Becouse if i was
Beter school wie's for
eag sample— At STuting
i Think peple wood reggean
hjur in The "class Room comment
The reaøen That i putdon
phisleky is Becusu
whin i play a sport out
on The play ground like
fooTBall, kickBall, exc, i am
all was The last one picked
and The least liked and
if you donT Belive me
JusT wach han tasT
i am pick and
The di a poinT neat
on The "capiïnTs"
fasel

Translation:

I would like people to view me as good academically and physically. The reason for this is because if I was better school wise for example, at studying. I think people would regret their in the classroom comment. The reason that I am put down physically is because when I play a sport out on the playground like football, kickball, etc. I am always the last one picked and the least liked and if you don't believe me just watch how fast I am picked and the disappointment on the captain's face.

Figure 3-6. A paragraph by Ken, a sixth-grade student.

Figure 3–7 presents two paragraphs written by Derek, a seventh-grade student. The first paragraph was an initial draft, whereas on the second, he received feedback from his teacher in regard to both ideas and mechanical errors. Clearly, his writing has improved with the support and assistance provided by his teacher. When writing to trusted teachers, students know that the response will be sympathetic, and that initial discussion will focus upon what is written, not how it is written (Tompkins, 1994).

In summary, positive feedback and discussion help students improve their attitude toward writing (Polloway, Patton, & Cohen, 1981). Assignments must also be purposeful, meaningful, and interesting (Ediger, 1993). Once students are motivated to write, the process begins.

Prewriting

Prewriting activities encourage a writer to think and develop ideas prior to writing the first draft of a composition. These activities precede written assignments, whether the mode of writing is descriptive, narrative, persuasive, or comparative (Whitt et al., 1988). The ideas are generated in a rich environment with a multitude of input (Vogel, 1985) and the writer uses various strategies and activities to choose a topic, generate ideas, identify the audience, and devise an outline (Whitt et al., 1988).

This stage may include techniques such as brainstorming, mentally rehearsing what one wants to write, semantic webbing and mapping, or conducting research. Semantic webbing and mapping provide concrete pictures of the outline (Tompkins

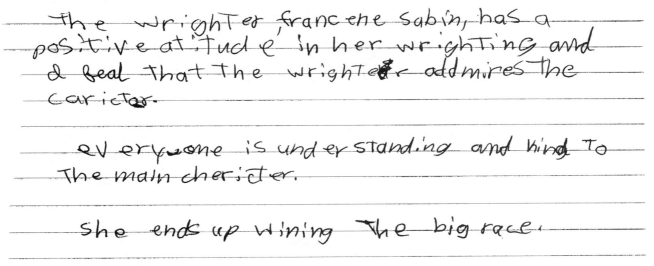

Figure 3–7. Two paragraphs by Derek, a seventh-grade student.

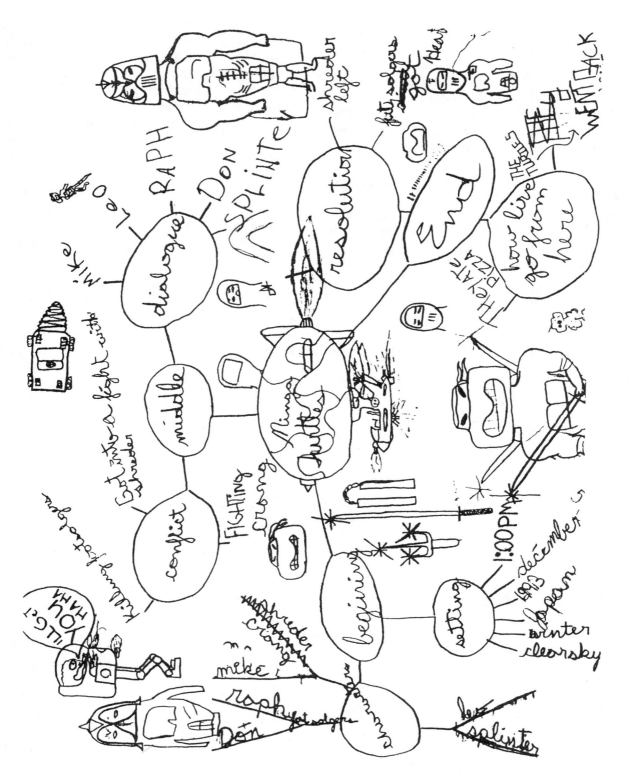

Figure 3-8. A semantic map by William, a sixth-grade student.

& Friend, 1986) and can be used as an individual, a group, or a class activity (Whitt et al., 1988). During this stage, teachers help students to realize that writing is an active, exploratory process that requires thinking about and organizing ideas prior to writing (Isaacson, 1994; Roit & McKenzie, 1985). Some students become quite creative in their use of prewriting strategies. William, a sixth-grade student, created the semantic map illustrated in Figure 3-8 prior to writing a story about the Ninja Turtles.

Similarly, Thomas, a fourth-grade student with good ideas but spelling difficulties, has generated lists of nouns, adjectives, and verbs (presented in Figure 3-9) to help him create horror stories. From this strategy, he prepares the beginning of two stories illustrated in Figure 3-10.

Even college students benefit from activities during the prewriting stage that emphasize thinking, planning, discussing, and outlining (Vogel & Moran, 1982). In general, the major purposes of these activities are to: (a) provide students with rich experiences, (b) assist students in generating ideas for writing, and (c) aid in the structuring of the content that students have gathered (Tompkins & Friend, 1986).

Oral discussion of the general idea encourages rehearsal of the writing (Kerchner & Kistinger, 1984) and can help students organize information, increase background knowledge, and plan their writing. Some students may benefit from telling the story to a classmate and getting feedback through questions and suggestions (Moulton & Bader, 1986). As noted by Silverman et al. (1981), prewriting activities that involve time to think, to experience, to discuss, and to interact with language are likely to have a positive effect on written language achievement. Effective writing programs provide opportunities for students to discuss their ideas with others prior to writing and to write in a variety of modes for different audiences and purposes.

Ellis (1994b) identified the following three phases of the prewriting or thinking ahead stage: preview, review, and predict. To preview, writers consider their own knowledge of the topic, identify the reader, and think about what the reader already knows and will want to know about the topic. To review, writers develop a graphic organizer in order to identify main ideas and details. To predict, writers consider the needs of the reader and then decide how the ideas should be organized.

Many students recognize that they need help with the thinking ahead stage of generating and organizing their ideas. The written comment by Bonnie, a sixth-grade student, presented in Figure 3-11, reveals her desire for prewriting assistance. Many students benefit from keeping lists of possible topics or perusing a teacher's card file that is filled with topic suggestions. As examples, 50 journal starters, 25 story starters, and 25 story enders are included in Chapter 7.

Planning Content and Organization

Planning, an important aspect of the composing process, refers to generating and organizing ideas, setting goals, and determining strategies to reach those goals (Montague, Graves, & Leavell, 1991). In many instances, students have trouble with production because not enough time has been devoted to planning activities. Figure 3-12 illustrates journal entries for Melinda, a third-grade student. Although the teacher provides some feedback about her ideas, the message reminds us that students need help generating, planning, and organizing their thoughts.

Similarly, when Mark, an eighth-grade student, was asked to write an essay on his opinion in regard to the importance of education, he eventually produced the sentence presented in Figure 3-13.

Mark's attempt to write an essay illustrates lack of planning at the prewriting stage. As noted by Landsman (1993): " . . . I have met so many students who never get started in the first place, who have very little material to shape or craft or 'spell check,' who are actually stopped dead in their tracks because they are afraid to put pen to paper" (p. 2).

In other instances, students produce more writing, but the initial drafts reveal little preplanning of content and poor organization. Instead of systematically organizing their ideas, they start writing as soon as an idea arises (Stewart, 1992). When asked to write a story, Robbie, a fourth-grade student, wrote the following draft illustrated in Figure 3-14. Although he begins the story naming several characters and students from his class, the remaining sentences seem unrelated. Two of the sentences were prompted by environmental stimuli: He looked at the "Say No to Drugs" poster on the classroom wall and observed another student writing about a Sega Genesis.

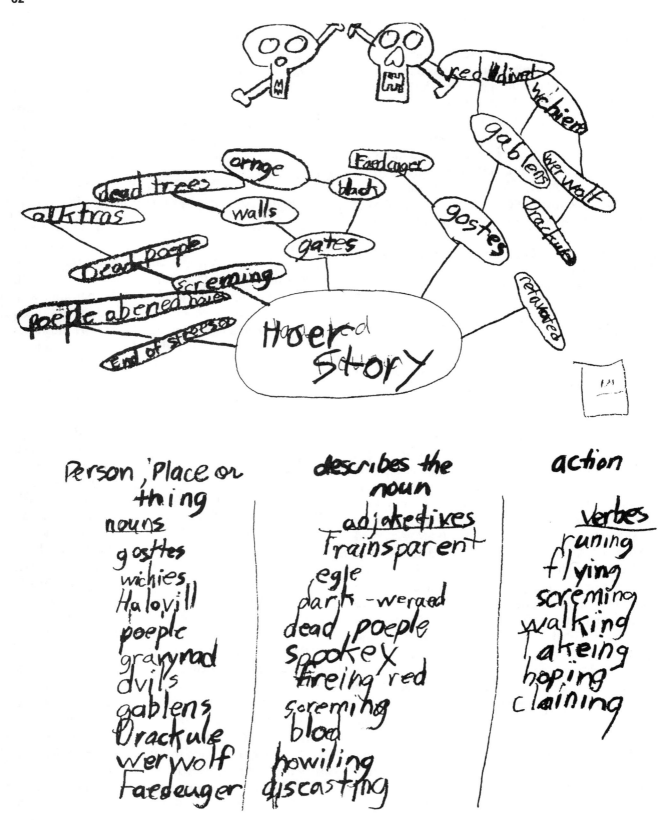

Figure 3–9. Use of a prewriting strategy by Thomas, a fourth-grade student.

One dark night where a house sits! A dark man walks to the dark house, sitting upon, Tucson. RREEE! Crash! aahhahgh shoooed pllop! pllop! Reer, Reerooo "ahah gottahied!" said the fugitive. "You in there come out with your hands up" said the police, BANG! "What the" said the fugitive "hocuspocus turn, thiseevel duer into a black blobe" said the wiche

One dark night were a dark howes sites!!... a dark man walkes to the dark howes siting open Tucson. RREEEEEE!! crash! aah hhahah! shoodd! pllop! pllop! pllop! pllop! pllop! Reer, Reeroo "ahahah got hied! got hied! got hied! poosh you in therr come out with your hardes up! said polees. eetete "what the" said the F! "whoo weispoock teurn thise evel doquer in to a balck blobe" said the wiche. The trainsparent gostes toach the Evel dour away, to the dead poeple to eat, his slimy stency slicet up guts. What the said, the poeles offerers "sir lookit sir" said offecer cliff. "It is bounes" said cliff!....

Figure 3-10. Two beginnings of stories by Thomas, a fourth-grade student.

I am haveing truble thinking of some thing ~~II~~ to wright.

Figure 3–11. A comment written by Bonnie, a sixth-grade student.

Dec. 15.

The other therd grad room got fldd.

Iqnll
I got nothing to rite

Did you get up this morning?

THIS PAPER IS BEING REVIEWED
☑ IDEAS
☐ SPELLING
☐ HANDWRITING

How did you feel about coming to school today?

I fel Happy to day I playd with because I got in mischief.

Figure 3–12. Journal entries written by Melinda, a third-grade student.

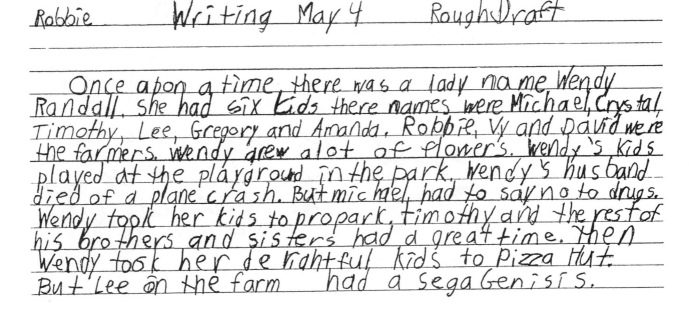

People need education, I guess,
I just dont know how to explain
why.

Figure 3-13. A sentence written by Mark, an eighth-grade student.

Robbie   Writing May 4   Rough Draft

Once upon a time, there was a lady name Wendy Randall. She had six kids there names were Michael, Crystal, Timothy, Lee, Gregory and Amanda. Robbie, Vy and David were the farmers. Wendy grew a lot of flowers. Wendy's kids played at the playground in the park. Wendy's husband died of a plane crash. But michael had to say no to drugs. Wendy took her kids to propark. timothy and the rest of his brothers and sisters had a great time. Then Wendy took her delrightful kids to Pizza Hut. But Lee on the farm had a Sega Genisis.

Figure 3-14. The initial draft of Robbie, a fourth-grade student.

Fortunately, when time and structure for planning are provided, students with learning disabilities produce narrative compositions that are comparable to normally achieving peers (Montague et al., 1991). Doris, a fifth-grade student, has received instruction in how to write a sequential paragraph. Prior to writing, the class brainstormed different topics that could be adapted to this format and discussed and listed cohesive ties on the board. Doris decided to write on the steps involved in brushing teeth. As part of a prewriting activity, she wrote each step in a different box on her paper. Doris then used this paper, presented in Figure 3-15, to write the first draft of her paragraph.

Audience

Another important aspect of the prewriting process is identifying the intended audience. Too often students write without any sense of a real audience who wish to read what they have to say (Gage, 1986). Writing is a process of developing an idea and sharing that idea with others. Whereas the decisions may change as students rewrite, prior to composing a first draft, writers must have a tentative concept of purpose, audience, and form (Tompkins, 1994).

Drafting

In the drafting stage, the writer records ideas on paper. Typically, students write on one side of the paper and skip every other line to facilitate revision (Tompkins, 1994). At this stage, attention is directed to the generation of ideas, rather than to mechanical concerns. Correct spelling is deemphasized because it is difficult to focus on both content and spelling simultaneously (Tompkins &

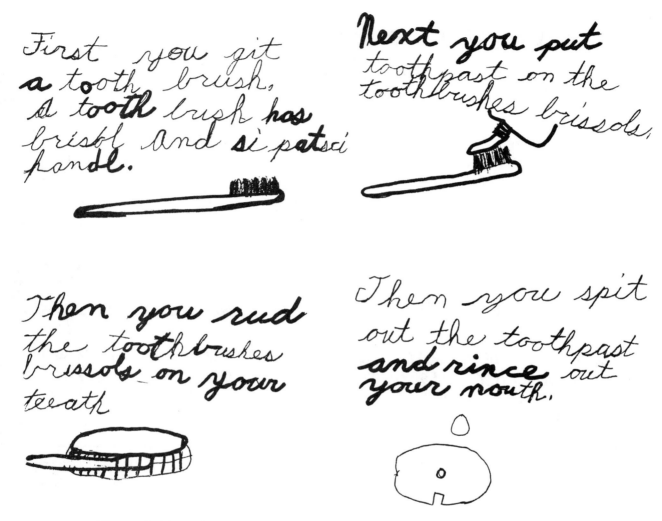

Figure 3-15. Use of a prewriting strategy by Doris, a fifth-grade student.

Friend, 1988). In addition, reinforcing that spelling is not a concern in the original draft of written work will encourage students to stop avoiding words that they do not know how to spell (Polloway et al., 1981). Furthermore, an early emphasis on basic skills frustrates students and reduces their enthusiasm for writing (Montague & Leavell, 1994). Students are encouraged to keep their pencils moving in order to promote fluency (Whitt et al., 1988). As a result, they are able to concentrate on one aspect of writing, rather than being overwhelmed by all aspects of the process (Zaragoza & Vaughn, 1992).

In most instances, students should not be graded on first drafts, but rather receive constructive feedback that will guide them in the revising stage. For his English class, Bart, an eighth-grade student, was asked to write a paragraph that provided support for his opinion on a topic. After being given several sample paragraphs to read, he selected the topic: Mondays are boring. His first draft is presented in Figure 3-16. Although one can empathize with the teacher's concerns, the assigned grade is unlikely to motivate Bart to revise his paragraph.

Revising

When I was 90, I was asked to single out my finest work. My answer was: "My next one."

—Frank Lloyd Wright

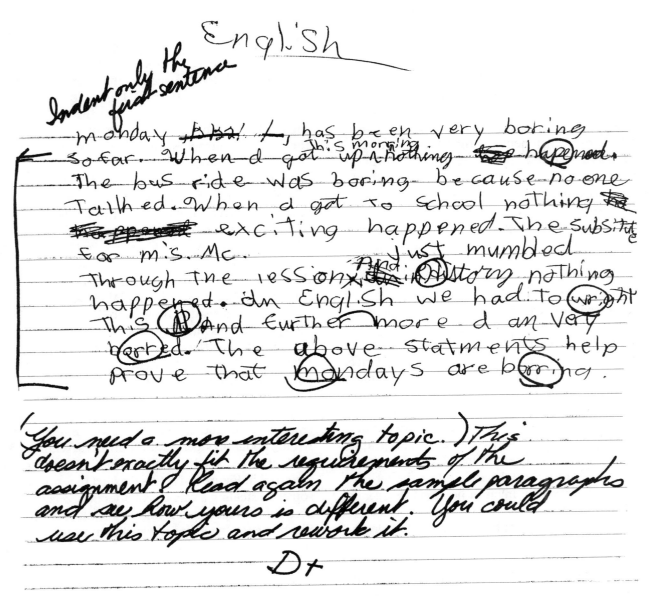

Indent only the
first sentence

English

Monday, [Blah], has been very boring
so far. When I got up this morning nothing happened.
The bus ride was boring because no one
talked. When I got to school nothing
happened exciting happened. The substitute
for m.s. Mc. just mumbled
through the lesson. And in history nothing
happened. In English we had to write
this. And further more I am very
bored. The above statments help
prove that mondays are boring.

You need a more interesting topic. This
doesn't exactly fit the requirements of the
assignment. Read again the sample paragraphs
and see how yours is different. You could
use this topic and rework it.

D+

Figure 3–16. First draft of a paragraph by Bart, an eighth-grade student.

When revising, writers evaluate what they have written and then make changes in meaning depending on their writing goals. Feedback is provided by a more knowledgeable other who makes suggestions with regard to how the writer can clarify organization and ideas. Peers and teachers ask questions to help the writer clarify content and sequence ideas. In this stage, primary emphasis is placed on communication and content, rather than on form. The purpose of revising is to improve, not perfect, a piece of writing (Moulton & Bader, 1986).

Although the importance of revision is widely recognized, many writers do not revise much (Fitzgerald & Stamm, 1992). Revising is difficult for all writers, but particularly for beginning writers and students with learning disabilities (Beal, 1993; Bos & Vaughn, 1994). In the past, many students with learning disabilities have considered their writing assignments to be finished when they have completed their first drafts (Tompkins & Friend, 1988). If they do revise their papers, they tend to approach it like cleaning a house: They tidy up only a few words to make it appear neater (Graham et al., 1993). Gage (1986) described how students often feel about revision:

> Revision is ordinarily perceived by students as a perfunctory exercise in cosmetic editing: correcting only the surface faults that the teacher has marked. When students revise in this way, they are responding to revision as a kind of punishment for their errors, rather than as a further opportunity to rethink what they have to say and their reasons for saying it. Revision cannot be a penalty for crimes against grammar; it must be an occasion for reassessing every aspect of the writing after having had the opportunity to see how others respond to it. (p. 27)

Through active modeling and discussion of writing, teachers can help students become more adept at using revision strategies and revising their own writing. In general, word changes are considered to be low-level changes, whereas phrase, sentence, and multisentence changes are considered to be more sophisticated (Tompkins & Friend, 1988). By crossing out, drawing arrows, and writing in the space above the lines, students learn to add words, move phrases, alter sentences, and rewrite or delete paragraphs (Tompkins, 1994). These macro-level changes of text require more thought and reflect the writer's ability to plan revisions in his or her mind (Fitzgerald & Stamm, 1992).

In summary, students benefit from strategy instruction that is aimed at detecting and revising unclear writing (Beal, 1993; Wong et al., 1994). As noted by Schwartz (1977): "Rewriting is not just recopying neatly, minus a few punctuation errors. It is not just fixing what is wrong. Rewriting is finding the best way to give your newly discovered ideas to others, it's a finishing, a polishing up, and it should be creative and satisfying as any job well done" (p. 736). Experienced writers understand that the real writing begins at the revising stage (Tompkins & Friend, 1988).

Audience Needs

One theory of literature states that what is written is only fully realized when a reader reconstructs what is on the page (Willis, 1993). Thus, when drafting and revising, writers need to attend to the relationship between the information presented in the text and the reader's comprehension; if the text is unclear, the reader will not understand the message (Beal, 1993). A sense of audience requires the writer to make adjustments and choices while writing by considering the intended reader and then taking the reader's perspective (Gregg, 1991; Hoy & Gregg, 1994). A dialogue exists between the author and the reader and the reader acts as an interpreter of the author's purposes and meanings (Silliman & Wilkinson, 1994).

Unfortunately, individuals with learning disabilities often fail to take the perspective of the reader into account when writing (Gerber, 1993). They often do not elaborate or provide the reader with enough information to understand the meaning of the written text (Hoy & Gregg, 1994). They have difficulty considering what information is new to the audience and must be explained and what information is already known and does not need to be repeated. This interplay between writer and reader is referred to as the given-new principle (Clark & Clark, 1977). Because the reader is often not present, the writer must make frequent assessments and judgments to monitor the clarity of the message.

Many times students erroneously assume that the teacher is the audience and knows what they are writing about (Cooper, 1988). Carol, a seventh-grade student, was asked to write an opinion paper, illustrated in Figure 3–17. She decided to write about someone stealing a car. Carol does not consider the needs of the reader as she fails to introduce her topic. She presents "new" information without explanation and makes erroneous assumptions in regard to the reader's "given" information. Any other audience would be required to infer the student's referents (Cooper, 1988).

Similarly, Ian, an eighth-grade student, was asked to write a paragraph, illustrated in Figure 3–18, that presented the reasons why teenagers would use alcohol or drugs. Although Ian has several ideas about the topic, he does not begin by explaining the topic. Consequently, his message becomes restricted to his teacher. As noted by Gage (1986), students must know that they do not write exclusively for their teachers, but for other inquiring minds who share their concerns for finding answers.

In general, students with learning disabilities appear to have difficulty predicting which parts of their essays will confuse readers (Wong, Wong,

I think that guy is pretty stupid for something like that (and I bet he feels it too). I think he deserves everything he gets just for being such an idiot in the first place. If your stupid enough to do something like that, then you deserve to get caught.

Figure 3–17. An opinion paper by Carol, a seventh-grade student.

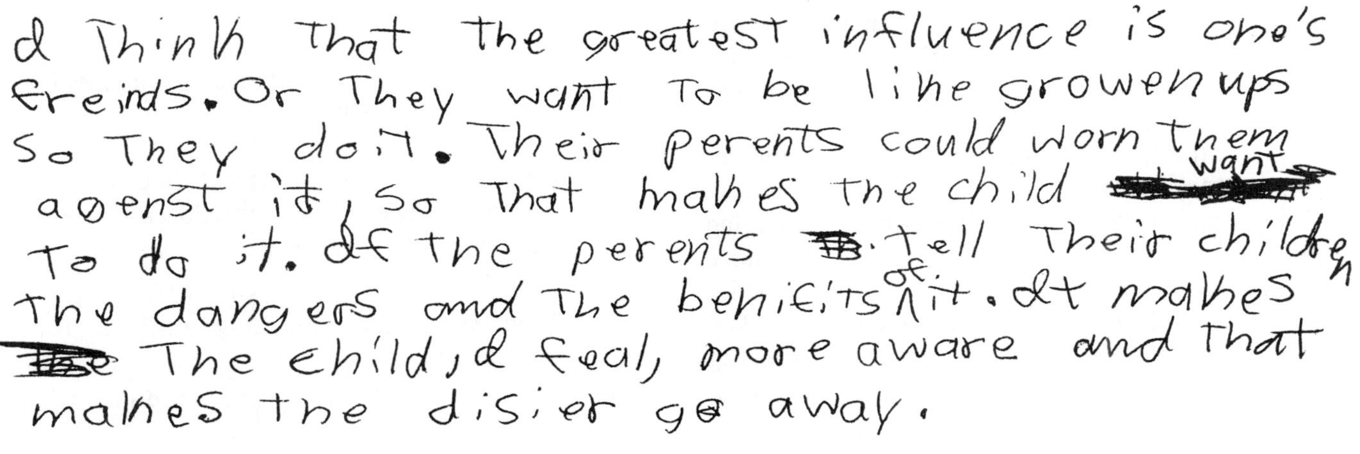

I Think that the greatest influence is one's freinds. Or They want To be like growen ups So They do it. Their perents could worn them agenst it, so That makes the child want to do it. If the perents tell Their children the dangers and The benifits of it. It makes The child, I feal, more aware and that makes the disier ge away.

Figure 3–18. An enumerative paragraph by Ian, an eighth-grade student.

Darlington, & Jones, 1991). They are less inclined to identify reader needs (Isaacson, 1994) and tend to assume that others will interpret text in the same way as they did (Beal, 1993). Wong et al. noted that students failed to develop adequate metacognition about audience needs and lacked reflectiveness about their own writing. Transforming one's inner language to written text requires one to enter the social context of the reader (Vygotsky, 1962). The need for explicitness is increased when speakers are not face to face (Silliman & Wilkinson, 1994).

Only when the writer can step from self and address the reader, can he or she begin to use the skills of logic, reasoning, objectivity, and analysis to communicate with the reader (Phelps-Gunn & Phelps-Terasaki, 1982). When students revise, strategies can be used to help them increase sensitivity to the readers' needs.

As a final note, one may wonder when the revising process should be considered complete. Willis (1993) observed that for a 6- or 7-year-old, *finished* is when he or she is done writing, whereas for a mature writer, it is often difficult to decide when to stop making changes. Obviously, the amount of revision depends upon the purpose of the writing, but the process itself can be exhilarating. As Willis described: "Our lives are full of revision, conscious and unconscious. Revision is a form of learning; it pushes us farther into experience, which alters how we perceive the past and prepares us for the future" (p. 1).

Editing

Revising and editing are conducted separately so that neither is neglected (Tompkins, 1994). In most instances, a teacher will want to focus on mechanical errors after the revisions have been completed. In the editing stage, the writer proofreads a piece to detect and correct errors in spelling, punctuation, capitalization, and usage. As noted in Chapter 2, many students with learning disabilities have extreme difficulty with basic writing skills, such as spelling or producing legible handwriting. In some instances, these severe production difficulties can undermine the strong motivational benefits of a process approach (Meyer et al., 1991) as some teachers respond more to the mechanics of writing than to content and form (DeGroff, 1992).

The majority of students with learning disabilities require specific assistance to recognize and correct their errors in basic skills. Students with poor spelling skill cannot edit without the assistance of a more knowledgeable other. Otis, a third-grader, provides an example presented in Figure 3–19. On being asked to edit his story, Otis corrects some of his spelling errors with different errors and, in some instances, alters correct spellings.

On occasion, a teacher may fail to acknowledge or provide the type of support a student needs to succeed. Figure 3–20 illustrates a paragraph written by Jeanne, a fourth-grade student. For an in-class assignment, Jeanne was asked to write a paragraph on the benefits of being healthy. Students worked independently on their paragraphs. Jeanne's paper was returned the next day. In this instance, Jeanne's teacher failed to acknowledge that a student's proofreading can only be as accurate as his or her prior knowledge (Archer, 1988).

The most effective way to teach basic skills is during the editing stage (Tompkins, 1994). In many instances, particularly for students with learning

disabilities, a teacher will want to focus on one or two skills during editing, rather than reviewing all of the errors. Concentrating on a few skills helps the student learn to use those skills effectively and not become overwhelmed by all the errors (Dowis & Schloss, 1992). During this meeting, attention may be directed to a particular difficulty (e.g., subject-verb agreement, verb tense). Later, practice can be provided to facilitate generalization. As a general rule, teachers should avoid the "red pencil treatment." Intensive marking of student papers is ineffective and costly in terms of teacher time (Phelps-Gunn & Phelps-Terasaki, 1982).

Feedback on mechanical errors. Simms (1983) outlined several practices to avoid when giving feedback on written assignments:

1. Applying the "red pencil treatment" based solely on mechanics.
2. Marking an excessive number of errors.
3. Correcting errors in areas not yet taught.
4. Presenting isolated pattern practice or formal instruction in grammar.

In addition, Simms outlined several practices for giving appropriate feedback:

1. Maintaining a positive attitude in evaluation and providing constructive feedback involving strengths as well as correction of weaknesses.
2. Offering feedback at the prewriting stage.
3. Identifying and marking only a few mechanical errors.
4. Providing feedback on an individual basis.

As noted, a teacher should begin by praising the positive attributes of a student's paper and not marking all of the errors. Some students have difficulty with many aspects of writing skill. A paragraph written by Keisha, a fifth-grade student, is presented in Figure 3–21. Although Keisha has difficulties with ideation, usage, and spelling, her teacher's first comment was a compliment about the neat handwriting.

The teacher must always be aware of, and teach to, the student's present writing performance level. Students are not expected to correct errors that are beyond their present performance level (Archer, 1988), and skills that a student is not ready to incorporate into writing should not be taught (Mather,

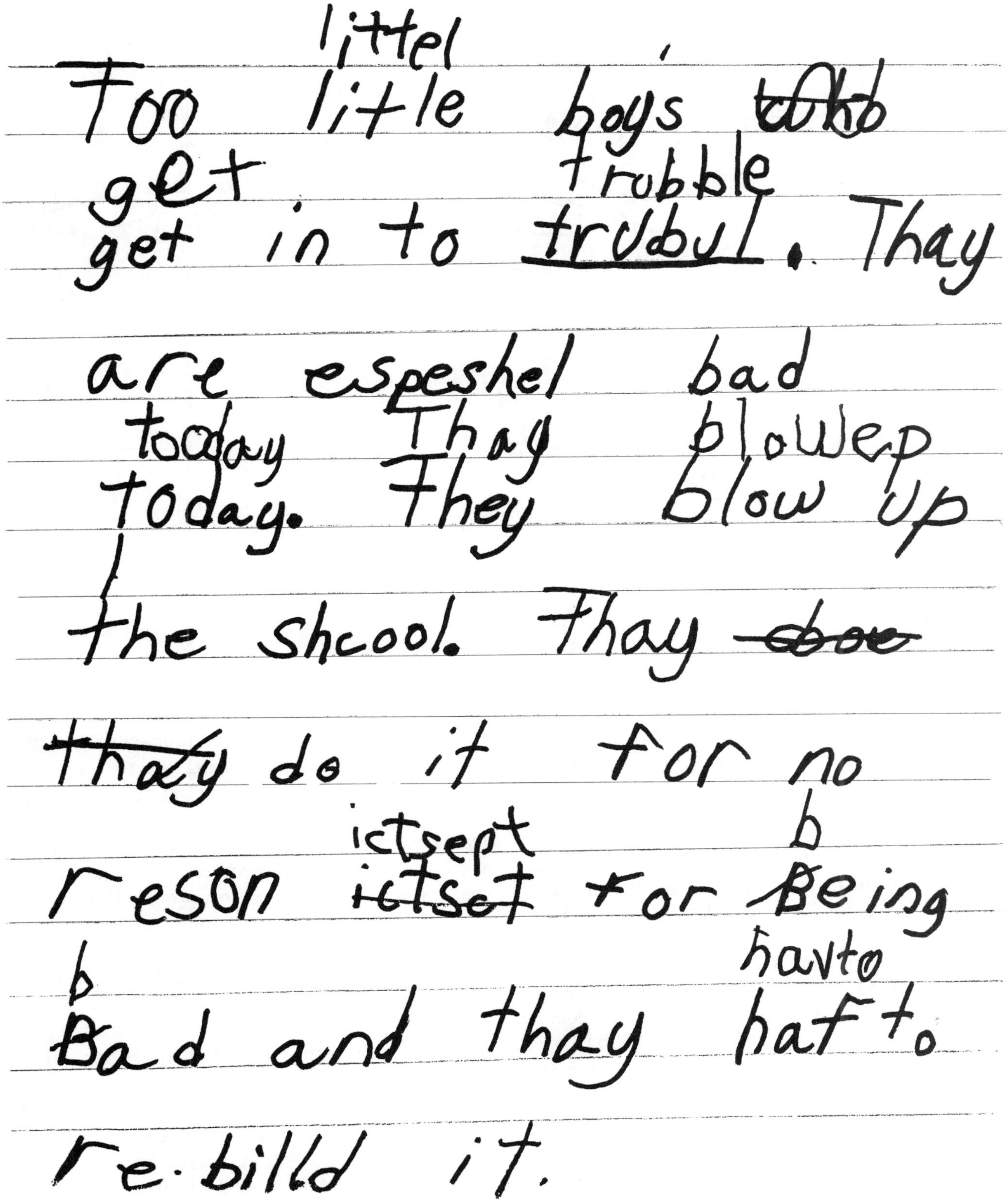

Too little boys ~~who~~
get trubble
get in to trubul. Thay

are espeshel bad
today. Thay blow up
the shcool. Thay ~~doo~~

~~thay~~ do it for no
reson ictsept for Being
Bad and thay hafto
re·billd it.

little (above "lite")
trubble (above "trubul")
today (above "today")
blowep (above "blow up")
ictsept (above "ictset")
b (above "Being")
havto (above "hafto")
b (beside "Bad")

Figure 3–19. A story written and edited by Otis, a third-grade student.

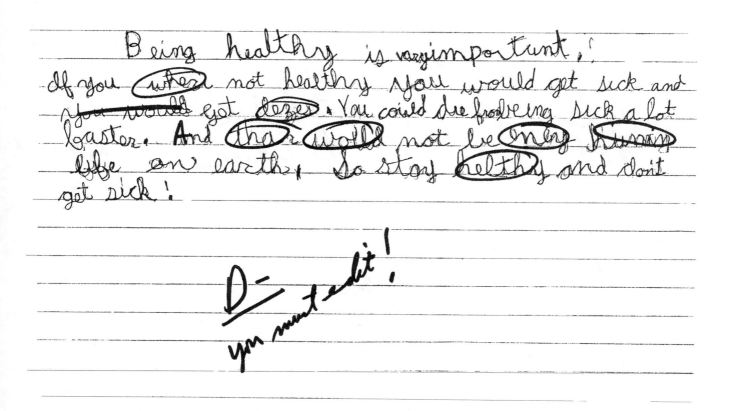

Figure 3-20. A paragraph on the benefits of being healthy written by Jeanne, a fourth-grade student.

1991). A skill should be taught, however, as soon as the student attempts to use it in writing (Poteet, 1987).

Perhaps the most important component for providing feedback is maintaining a positive tone in writing evaluations. Unfortunately, teachers' use of language is influenced by writing achievement; results from a recent study demonstrated that elementary teachers were more positive in their evaluations of students with high writing achievement than those with low writing achievement (DeGroff, 1992). As further noted by Applebee, Langer, Jenkins, Mullis, and Foertsch (1990), better writers are more likely to receive positive comments on their papers than poorer writers.

Conferences

Writers aren't exactly people, they're a whole lot of people trying to be one person.

—F. Scott Fitzgerald

Mini-conferences can be conducted to provide individualized feedback during the revising and editing stages. A critical element of both the revising and editing stage is receiving feedback from the teacher and/or a small group of peers. Although writers' responses vary, conferences appear to assist many students in the revision process (Fitzgerald & Stamm, 1992). Through peer or teacher conferencing, students may receive help editing their work. Conferencing may be considered the heart of the writing procedure (Bos & Vaughn, 1994) as young writers may learn more about writing through collaborating with other authors than by any other method (Sampson et al., 1991). Conference discussions help writers identify reader expectations and increase understanding of the reader's needs (Fitzgerald & Stamm, 1992; Isaacson, 1994).

During collaboration, students often talk about an activity, hear the perspectives of others, and examine their thoughts in a social context (Daiute &

The mean Tiger

Keisha

That tiger was very very mean.
The maen tiger wit to sleppy he had
to give him some medicne to yoto
slopep we had some equipment on his
head he was dream about killing
pepole and eatng tham and nawing some
of the pepole of slaves that we his
dream but it well have naver some
of the ners was goin. I was wer
thert cit that Tiger is os os os
mean. That Tiger is going to
get very very meaer and meare
he will not eat my for he
biffen or he lunch that tiger is os mere
The End
of the Tiger

Dow you No wut the
tiger did to the Mus he
Killing her.
The End

Figure 3-21. A paragraph written by Keisha, a fifth-grade student.

Dalton, 1993). Collaboration links learning and higher level thinking. As noted by Daiute and Dalton (1993): "... collaboration encourages children to express and reflect on thinking that might otherwise remain unexamined or unelaborated. Writing is a skill that requires much generative and reflective thinking and action. Experienced writers actively control the writing process, planning and forming their ideas through their interactions with others" (p. 293).

Some students need specific instruction in how to conference and benefit from a guide or checklist to indicate what they are to look for in the writing of others. With instruction and encouragement from both their teacher and peers, students with learning disabilities begin to view themselves as capable writers (MacArthur et al., 1991).

Peer Conference

Peer feedback is a significant component of a process-oriented writing program. Students have diverse experiences and knowledge they can share during a collaboration (Daiute & Dalton, 1993). As noted by Daiute and Dalton, the relationship between expert and novice shifts during the composing process as different skills become relevant and students can look to each other for support on performance in complementary domains.

For example, Jim has lots of ideas for writing and an excellent vocabulary, but has trouble spelling. Daniel has more expertise with spelling and punctuation and capitalization rules, but has trouble generating ideas and writing complex sentences. Together they are able to assist each other and increase their writing skill.

A teacher may also provide input to the peer conference by demonstrating how to ask questions and make comments and by encouraging students to rephrase and clarify their comments (Rhodes & Dudley-Marling, 1988). Although the majority of students appear to profit from group conferences, a few students may prefer individual conferences with the teacher (Fitzgerald & Stamm, 1992).

Teacher Conference

Teachers often meet independently with students to help them address a specific problem in their writing at various times in the writing process. During these meetings, it is important that the teacher does not dominate the interaction. Through expert-novice collaboration, the teacher guides the student as they work on activities and solve problems together (Daiute & Dalton, 1993). The conference involves active negotiation by teacher and student and mutual control of topic and structure (McCarthey, 1994).

Purpose of the conference. The teacher conference provides an opportunity for the teacher and student to learn from each other. The most important factor is that individual conferences should focus on one or two elements the student needs for writing (Rhodes & Dudley-Marling, 1988). The teacher's feedback should be explanatory, specific, and include suggestions for making corrections (Graham & Harris, 1988). For example, a student can explain the problems encountered during the drafting stage, and how the problems were addressed (Whitt et al., 1988). The teacher can reinforce any concepts, rules, or strategies that were taught during the writing process, and then discuss specific content. In addition, more advanced composition skills such as the use of descriptive adjectives or compound sentences may be taught. Furthermore, conferences provide teachers and students the opportunity to reflect on their writing competencies and to set goals for future writing assignments (Tompkins, 1994).

Brief conferences. Frequent, brief conferences are usually more effective than lengthy, in-depth conferences (Bos & Vaughn, 1994; Rhodes & Dudley-Marling, 1988). Tompkins (1994) provided the following illustrations of short informal conferences: (a) on-the-spot conference—a brief visit to monitor some aspect of the assignment; (b) prewriting conference—a discussion to aid in gathering and organizing information; (c) drafting conference—a discussion of specific trouble spots; (d) revising conference—a meeting to formulate specific suggestions for revision; (e) editing conference—a discussion to assist in the identification and correction of mechanical errors; (f) instructional mini-lesson conference—a meeting to provide special instruction on a strategy or skill; (g) assessment conference—a review of a student's growth in writing and plans for future writing; and (h) portfolio conference—a review of writing samples and materials a student has placed in a writing folder.

Revision conference. If students are unaware of the ambiguities in their own writing, they are unlikely to revise and clarify their stories (Wong et al., 1991). Consequently, a revision conference becomes particularly important for helping students to improve the content of their story. During this conference, the teacher seeks to understand and clarify what the writer has said (Applebee, 1986). Unfortunately, too often papers are graded independently by a teacher and then returned to the student; what is missing from this scenario is meaningful feedback through discussion with the teacher (Ellis, 1994b).

Figure 3–22 presents the first draft of a fairy tale written by Andy, a fourth-grade student. In a revision conference, the teacher praises Andy for his creative first draft and makes specific comments about his use of metaphors. She then notes specific areas in the story that require clarification. As Andy's story progresses, confusion exists in regard to who is the prince and who is the princess. In one sentence, the princess is referred to with a masculine pronoun. With the guidance and questioning of his teacher, Andy identified ways to resolve the ambiguities and clarify his story. After Andy had revised his story, the teacher met with him in regard to his errors in basic skills.

Similarly, Ms. Adrien, an eighth-grade English teacher, conducts daily, individualized revision conferences with her students. Samples of first drafts of descriptive paragraphs of five of her students, Bart, Pearl, Craig, Jeremy, and Ethan, are presented in Figure 3–23.

The assignment was to write paragraphs describing their perfect homes. Ms. Adrien reviewed the samples and then presented both positive comments and suggestions to her students in a revision conference. She provided suggestions for their topics, but helped them to expand upon their own ideas.

Bart. Bart wrote three sentences. In this short sample, his vocabulary is imprecise and he does not appear to have much to say. After looking at Bart's paragraph, Ms. Adrien notes that he would have benefitted from increased time devoted to prewriting activities. These activities would have helped him develop a plan to sequence his description prior to writing. He does not introduce the topic, and the details describing his perfect house are not presented sequentially. In the opening sentence, he notes that his house is very large and the carpet is plush. He then writes that the house is in the country. The closing thought appears only tangentially related to the topic (*I have cows and pigs so I could eat them*). In their meeting, Bart and his teacher brainstorm other observations he could include and develop a framework for sequencing his ideas. They also discuss possibilities for a concluding statement.

Pearl. Pearl begins by writing the title for her paragraph: *My Perfect home.* She then informs the reader of the location of the house. She wants her house to be in California with a view of the beach. She then loses the focus of the assignment and fails to maintain the topic. She shifts to a discussion about the merits of living in California. The focus becomes egocentric as she reports the opinion of her friends and her own personal thoughts. She discusses that she's never going to live there and concludes that she will never know what it is like.

Her vocabulary is imprecise and simplistic. Although she appears to have some knowledge of meaning of the word "camouflaged," the usage is incorrect as she writes: *Most of my friends say that place is camoflashed to what going on around every one.*

As with Bart, Ms. Adrien notes that Pearl would have benefitted from increased planning prior to writing. Her failure to maintain the topic suggests that she really did not have a plan in regard to the information she needed to describe her perfect home. In the conference, her teacher reviews with her the structure of a paragraph and helps her to identify her topic, develop her ideas, and consider a concluding sentence.

Craig. Craig begins his paragraph by introducing his reader to the topic and writes, *My perfect home would be a nice, big beach house in California.* He uses humor by concluding that until he is settled with a family, he would have big parties all the time. Although descriptions are included, Craig's sentence patterns lack variety. The majority begin with: *It would have . . .* In addition, one sentence is incomplete.

During a revision conference, the discussion centers upon ways several sentences could be rewritten and elaborated upon to increase interest. In addition, Craig and Ms. Adrien discuss ways that he could correct the incomplete sentence.

Jeremy. Jeremy begins with an interesting topic sentence, noting that he'll have to win the lottery to afford his perfect house. The organization of his paragraph is logical. He uses two cohesive ties (*first, second*) to connect his thoughts. He describes two improvements and then uses humor in his ending by describing his ideal roommate.

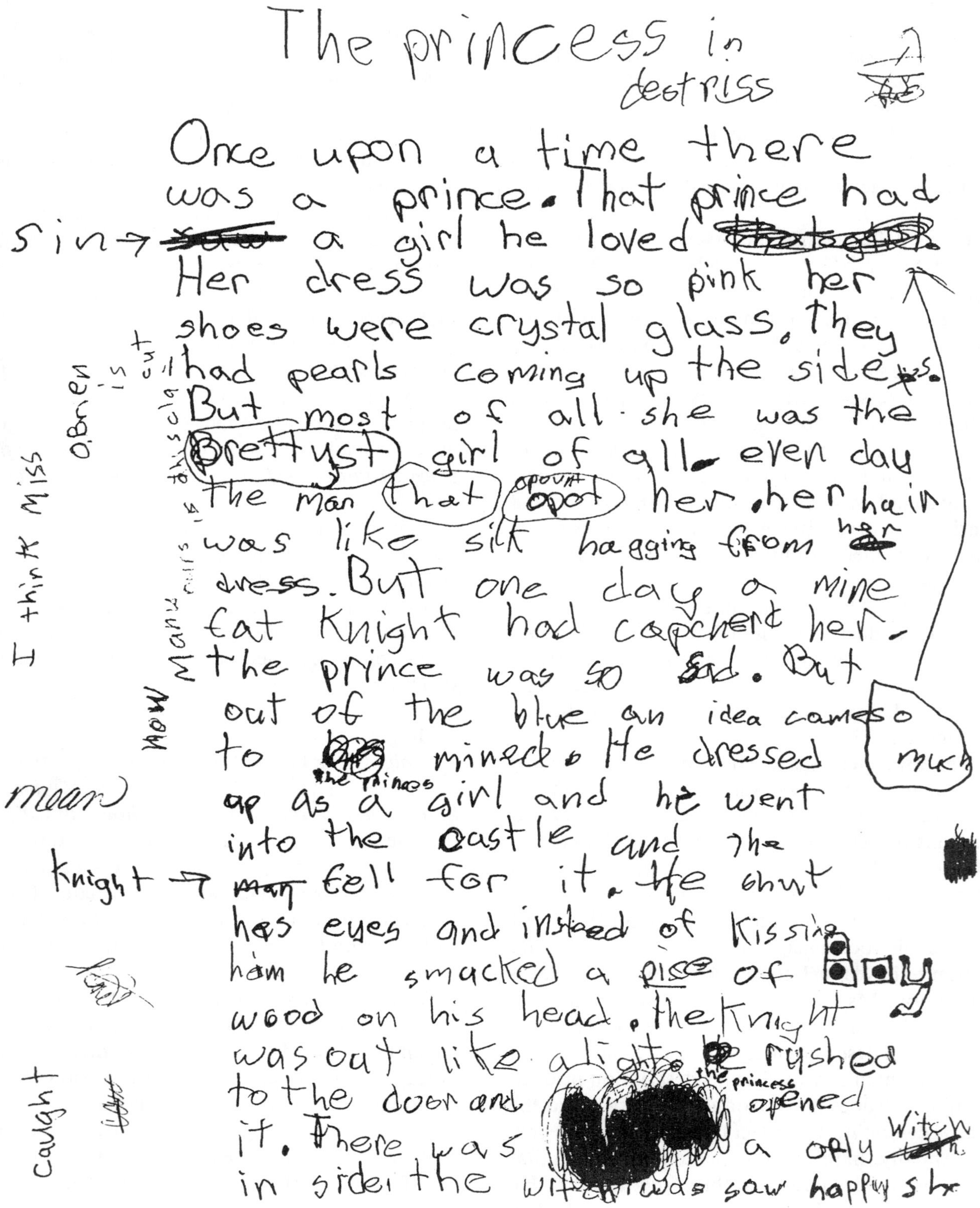

The princess in
destriss

Once upon a time there
was a prince. That prince had
sin→ saw a girl he loved that togther.
Her dress was so pink her
shoes were crystal glass, They
had pearls coming up the sides.
But most of all she was the
Brettyst girl of all. even day
the man that opot her. her hair
was like silk hagging from her
dress. But one day a mine
eat Knight had capchert her.
the prince was so Sad. But
out of the blue an idea comes o
to his mineck. He dressed much
up as a girl and he went
into the castle and The
Knight→ man fell for it. He shut
has eyes and insteed of Kissing
him he smacked a piec of boy
wood on his head. the Knight
was out like a light. he ryshed
to the door and the princess opened
it. There was a only Witch
in side. the witch was saw happly she

Teacher annotations in margins:

I think Miss O.Brien is vulld desciple

How Many error's how

mean)

Knight →

caught

piect

Figure 3–22. First draft of a fairy tale by Andy, a fourth-grade student.

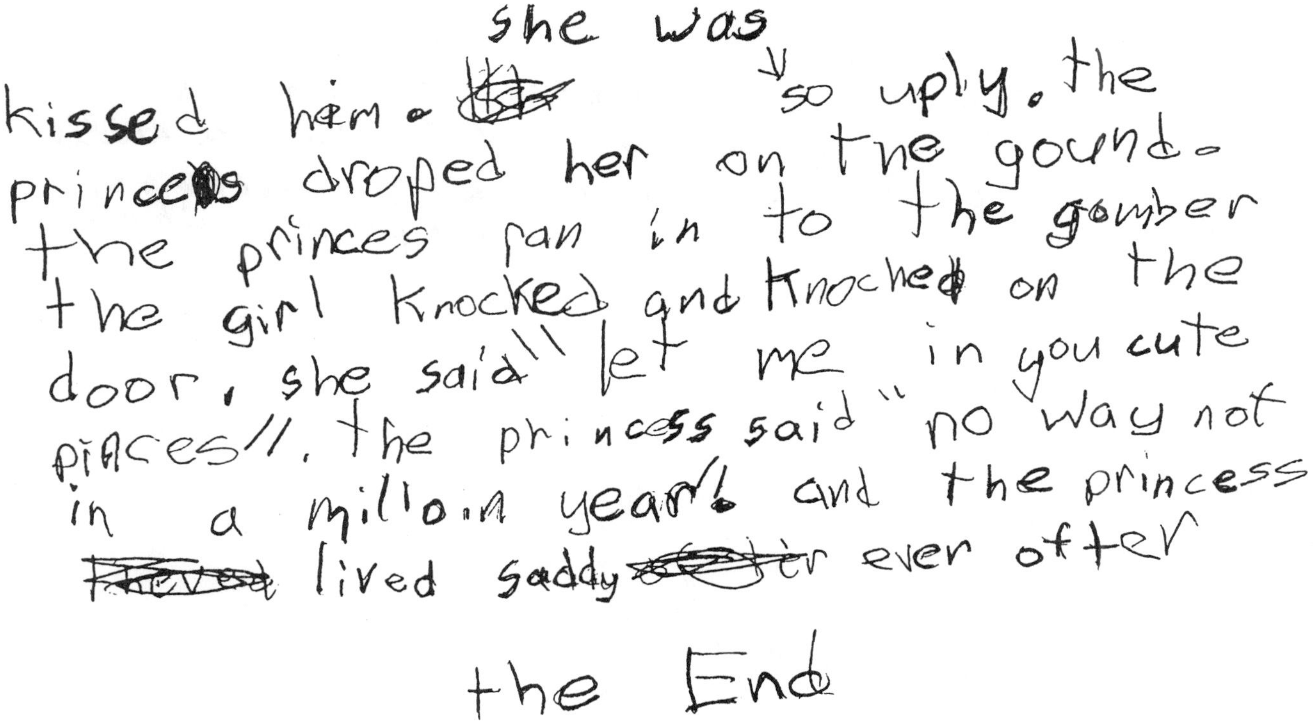

kissed him. ~~the~~ she was
princess dropped her on the gound.
so ugly. the
the princes ran in to the gomber
the girl knocked and knocked on the
door, she said "let me in you cute
piAces//. the princess said "no way not
in a milloin year"/ and the princess
~~Preves~~ lived saddy ~~after~~ ever ofter

the End

Figure 3–22 (cont). First draft of a fairy tale by Andy, a fourth-grade student.

The first sentence consists of two sentences joined without a conjunction. Near the end of the paragraph, Jeremy has written two incomplete sentences. The appearance of Jeremy's essay is unattractive. Jeremy's handwriting is small and difficult to read. He writes in the middle of the paper, rather than observing the margins.

As with Craig, Jeremy has a good start on his paragraph. In the revision conference, Ms. Adrien and Jeremy discuss the presentation of his ideas. Although he maintains the topic he is writing about, it is not a description of his perfect home, but rather the improvements he would make to an existing home. Ms. Adrien encourages Jeremy to clarify this in his topic sentence and to strengthen the paragraph by including one more home improvement.

Ethan. The overall appearance of Ethan's writing is attractive, particularly for a first draft. His handwriting is neat and easy to read. He indents the first paragraph and uses margins. Although Ethan's paragraph is written as one long sentence, his introductory statements about his lazy rich man's home capture the reader's attention. His vocabulary is precise and his vivid descriptions enable the reader to create a visual image of the surroundings. For example, he notes that his house will contain black lacquer and black leather furniture and that his big water bed will have silk sheets.

In the revision conference, Ms. Adrien and Ethan determine what parts of the paragraph may confuse the reader and how these sections could be clarified. To begin, they identify where his sentences begin and end. Next they discuss a few of the thoughts that seem unclear. For example, when describing the "voice command" in the kitchen, he writes: . . . *everything to be cooked would just have to be told what to do,* and in the concluding thought he writes: . . . *to relax in this would be the somewhat modernly explained lazy home.*

The five descriptive paragraphs on "My Perfect Home" illustrate the variability that exists among students on any assignment. Although each of the students has written the first draft of a paragraph, the writings differ both in ideation and organization. In addition, a teacher would have different, specific comments for each student in a revision conference.

Bart

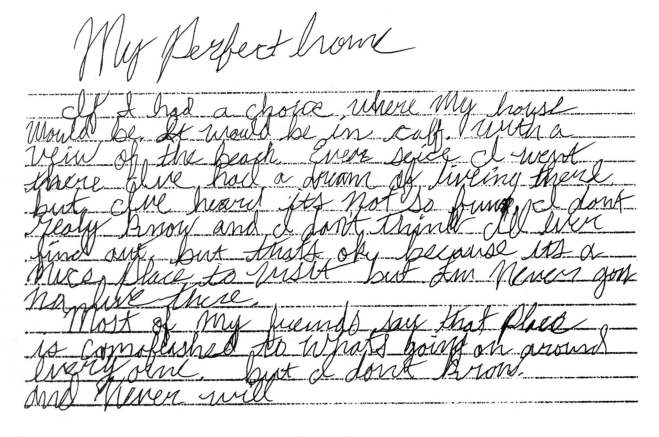

Pearl

Figure 3-23. First drafts of descriptive paragraphs written by five students.

Craig

My perfect home would be a nice big beach house in California. It would have alot of windows in the back so it would be easy to see the ocean from almost anywhere in the house. It would have a 3 car garage. A basement made made into a game room with a pool table and a stereo. And a pool on the side of the house. It would have a exercise room. It would have atleast 3 bed rooms one for me and my future wife, and the others for my future kids. But untill then I would have big partyies all the time.

Jeremy

My perfect home would call for me to win the lottery it would cost so much. I would first take the second to bigest room and totally sound proof it for my band. Second I would tear out the floor thru one one the front room and put on indoor pool in. With a bridge leading down the hall. That is pretty much all I would do. Except for a 22 year old blont model for a maid.

Figure 3-23 (cont.) First drafts of descriptive paragraphs written by five students.

Ethan

"My perfact Home"

My perfact home would be most defenitly more suitable to be called a lazey richmans home because it would be furnished with black laqure furniture and Leather furniture evrywere I thought nessisary and a big screen tv w/ remote 4 head vcr in sterro and not to mention a very loud sterro system w/ cd plyer and spekers all over the place and a big water bed w/ silk sheets in my room w/more spekers and evry thing I have can be controld by voice comand in any room even out side and the kittchen would also be voice comand evry thing to be cooked would just have to be told what to do and it would get it done and also a large wieght room and a pool table and a spa, pool to relix in sthis would be the some what moderly explaned lazy Home.

Figure 3-23 (cont.) First drafts of descriptive paragraphs written by five students.

Publishing

In the publishing stage, the writer prepares the final draft to be shared with others. This may involve preparing illustrations, recopying or typing the work, or making final corrections with a word processor. Neat handwriting and correct spelling are only important for the final draft, when the written work is prepared to share with others (Walmsly, 1984). In this final stage of the writing process, students come to view themselves as authors (Tompkins, 1994).

Instruction in the Writing Process

Written expression provides a visual representation of one's thoughts, feelings, and ideas (Poteet, 1980). Viewed within this framework, Vygotsky's (1978) work has important implications for instruction in the writing process. As summarized by Englert and Mariage (1991): "Vygotsky's work suggests that higher cognitive processes are first learned in social interactions with more knowledgeable language users who model the process and the inner talk that directs the process. These language users have an important responsibility to model writing strategies as they think aloud to make visible the normally invisible cognitive processes related to planning, drafting, and monitoring their drafts" (p. 340).

The Teacher's Role

Although the transition is not easy for many, teaching writing as a process requires valuing processes over products (DeGroff, 1992). Accomplished writing teachers provide inspiration and encouragement to students by helping them develop their ideas and the skills necessary to express those ideas (Meyer et al., 1991). The teacher provides a highly structured classroom that is carefully designed for developing student independence (Graves, 1985).

Within this supportive classroom environment, children feel free to experiment and risk error, allowing for maximum exploration of the processes of literacy (Dobson, 1985). The teacher acts as both instructor and coach (MacArthur et al., 1991), but not as a judge who evaluates assignments and assigns grades (Tompkins, 1994). The teacher encourages the student to extend his or her thinking by building upon ideas and providing support through questions and suggestions (McCarthey, 1994). The teacher provides responses to the young writer that demonstrate respect for the student's ideas (Willis, 1993). Campione, Rutherford, Gordon, Walker, and Brown (1994) use the term "guided discovery," an approach midway between pure discovery learning and direct instruction, to describe the teacher's role of furnishing guidance while fostering self-direction.

Tonya, an eighth-grade student, wrote an essay on the topic of the "Perfect Teacher." Her opening sentence stated: "The perfect teacher knows when to push a student and when to leave the student alone." As Tonya has observed, both guidance and experience are important to the development of writing skill (Carlisle, 1994).

The teacher, therefore, is a collaborator rather than evaluator (Applebee, 1986). As collaborator, the teacher guides students in their knowledge development while working with them on academic problems (Daiute & Dalton, 1993). His or her roles are then to: (a) model the self-talk needed to perform the task, (b) provide opportunities for students to collaborate with more skilled language users, (c) encourage students to participate in discussions of

writing, and (d) help students internalize the language and strategies they need to direct their own writing activities (Englert & Mariage, 1991). Students often learn these strategies by observing more competent writers and receiving guidance from teachers in writing conferences (MacArthur et al., 1991). The teacher models to students what happens inside the mind of a writer, focusing upon the critical overt or covert behaviors associated with each step (Ellis, 1994b; Frager, 1994). In other words, effective teachers teach by thinking aloud, showing each student how he or she learns, and making frequent assessments of the student's understanding (Graves, 1985).

The teacher possesses the ability to engage students in meaningful tasks, use effective strategies, and assess the students' progress dynamically (Daiute & Dalton, 1993). A first step is to ascertain a student's present level of understanding of the writing process. Figure 3–24 illustrates questions that a teacher may ask a student in order to evaluate knowledge and application of the writing process.

Instructional Procedures

The purpose of process activities is to teach students particular strategies to resolve difficulties in their writing (Applebee, 1986). As Applebee described:

In a given classroom, the kinds and extent of process-oriented activities would vary from task to task in response to the difficulties posed by each task. Some tasks would require extensive prewriting activities; some would involve help with drafting; some would go through a variety of revisions; some would be edited to share with others; some would emphasize competent first-and-final draft performance. Running through all of these variations would be an awareness, on the part of the teachers and students alike, that there are many different strategies for approaching each task; and both tasks and strategies would be varied in a principled way. (p. 107)

In general, strategies that are taught in the context within which they will be applied are more likely to be maintained and generalized (Graham & Harris, 1993).

General
>
> Does the student understand the purpose of the writing process approach?
>
> What is the student's attitude toward the writing process approach?
>
> Does the student take pride in his/her writing at the various stages?

Prewriting
>
> Does the student understand the purpose of prewriting strategies?
>
> What is the student's attitude toward prewriting?
>
> What prewriting strategies does the student use?
>
> Is information gathered from various sources?
>
> Is the information adequate?
>
> Does the student generate enough ideas?
>
> Does the student define the topic and purpose?
>
> Is there evidence of sufficient planning?
>
> Does the student consider the intended audience?
>
> What prewriting skills need attention?

First Draft
>
> Does the student understand the purpose of writing a draft?
>
> What is the student's attitude toward writing a draft?
>
> Is the information from the prewriting activities used?
>
> Is the focus on the main idea?
>
> Does the student place more emphasis on content than mechanics?
>
> Does the student take time to think while composing?
>
> What skills in composing a first draft need attention?

Revision
>
> Does the student understand the purpose of revision?
>
> What is the student's attitude toward revision?
>
> Does the student respond positively to advice and feedback from others?
>
> Does the student use a variety of sentence constructions, such as simple, compound, and complex?
>
> Does the student attempt to select more precise vocabulary?
>
> Is the student able to add, delete, and/or move sections?
>
> Does the student read the draft to ensure clarity and logic?
>
> Are new ideas and information added to the main and sub-topics?
>
> Does the student consider the audience while revising?
>
> Are specific revision strategies used?
>
> Does the student make changes to reflect the suggestions from both the teacher and peers?
>
> Can the student explain how the revisions have improved his/her composition?
>
> What revision skills need attention?

Editing
>
> Does the student understand the purpose of editing?
>
> What is the student's attitude toward editing?

Figure 3-24. Questions for evaluating knowledge and application of the writing process.

Editing (continued)

> Does the student identify many of his/her own errors?
> What types of errors does the student identify?
> Does the student:
>> write in complete sentences?
>> use conjunctions correctly (e.g., but, because, and)?
>> use correct subject-verb agreement?
>> use correct verb tense?
>> form plurals correctly?
>> use possessives appropriately?
>> use pronouns appropriately?
>> use homonyms appropriately?
>> use comparatives/superlatives appropriately (e.g., bigger, biggest)?
>> use word endings correctly (e.g., ed, ing, ly)?
>> apply correct punctuation rules?
>> apply correct capitalization rules?
>> use correct spelling?
> Does the student successfully correct identified errors?
> What editing strategies does the student use?
> Does the student use available resources (e.g., teacher/peer suggestions; dictionary/thesaurus)?
> Can the student explain why the changes are necessary?
> What editing skills need attention?

Final draft

> Does the student understand the purpose of writing a final draft?
> What is the student's attitude toward writing a final draft?
> Have all previous comments and feedback been taken into consideration?
> Is the structure and sequence of the final draft appropriate?
> Is the purpose of the writing clear?
> Has the perspective of the reader been considered?
> Were the majority of grammatical and spelling errors corrected?
> What final draft skills need attention?

Sharing

> Does the student understand the reason for sharing his/her work?
> What is the student's attitude toward sharing his/her work with peers?
> How does the student prefer to share his/her work (e.g., reading, displaying)?
> Can the student suggest different ways in which s/he would like to share his/her work?
> Does the student participate when other students share their work?

Figure 3-24 (cont). Questions for evaluating knowledge and application of the writing process.

Zaragoza and Vaughn (1992) summarized the elements of the writing process approach that correspond with recommended instructional procedures: (a) provision of adequate time for writing and a range of writing tasks, (b) creation of a social climate that fosters and encourages writing, (c) integration of writing with other academic subjects, (d) attention to the processes of writing with emphasis on composition during writing and to spelling and punctuation after writing, (e) instruction in the characteristics of good writing, and (f) involvement by encouraging students to generate their own goals for improving their writing.

Students with learning disabilities do not understand the process of composing as well as their normally achieving peers (Graham et al., 1993). Consequently, within a process approach to writing, they may benefit from more intensive, structured, and explicit instruction in the processes central to effective writing than they typically receive (Sawyer, Graham, & Harris, 1992). Students with learning disabilities require specific strategy instruction that focuses on both content and skills (Danoff et al., 1993; Isaacson, 1989; Montague & Leavell, 1994). Mini-lessons during the writing process that involve active participation and modeling can increase their writing skills (Dowis & Schloss, 1992). Students can also benefit from the use of a word processor.

Word Processing

Word processors are an invaluable aid when students compose. They are useful at all stages of the writing process and are a natural complement to the writing process approach (Meyer et al., 1991). As noted by Tompkins (1994), word processors can be used for note taking, shaping ideas in the drafting stage, revising and refining during the editing stage, and printing out final copies. When students use word processors, teachers can devote more attention to their papers' content, rather than form (Lewis, 1993). Based upon the visibility of the writing process, word processing provides opportunities for increased collaboration and communication between a student and teacher (Mather & Bos, 1994). This public scrutiny enhances students' writing development and increases collaborative and cooperative behavior (Snyder, 1993).

Students with learning disabilities particularly benefit from the use of word processors during the revising stage. Edits and suggestions may be incorporated easily without the need for tedious recopying. When refining their writing, students can move text easily from one place in the document to another. As noted by Lewis (1993): "This flexibility simplifies editing, thereby making it more likely that students will approach writing as a process, rather than as a dreaded task to be completed as quickly as possible" (p. 280). Elimination of the need to recopy makes the task less laborious and more enjoyable, and, subsequently, promotes thinking (Snyder, 1993). in addition, the final products produced by the students look professional when they are printed.

Conclusion

Effective writers employ strategic behaviors to complete the subprocesses of planning, writing, and revision (Welch, 1992). As children learn to write, they must develop a variety of cognitive and metacognitive strategies for planning, writing, and revising (MacArthur, Graham, & Schwartz, 1993). The central goals of writing programs are then to develop writers who possess: (a) a wide range of cognitive and metacognitive strategies for planning, writing, and revision; (b) adequate basic writing skills; and (c) the ability and motivation to use writing to achieve a variety of purposes throughout their lives (MacArthur et al., 1991). The procedures selected to teach writing should help students become more adept at solving new problems, making sense of what they have learned, and defending and elaborating their own ideas (Applebee, 1986). Writing often helps students to clarify their ideas and values.

As teachers, a major responsibility is to help students improve their writing skill. Usually they are thankful. Figure 3–25 presents a note written by Peter, a sixth-grade student. After apologizing for referring to his teacher as an "old goat," he expresses his gratitude for her assistance with writing.

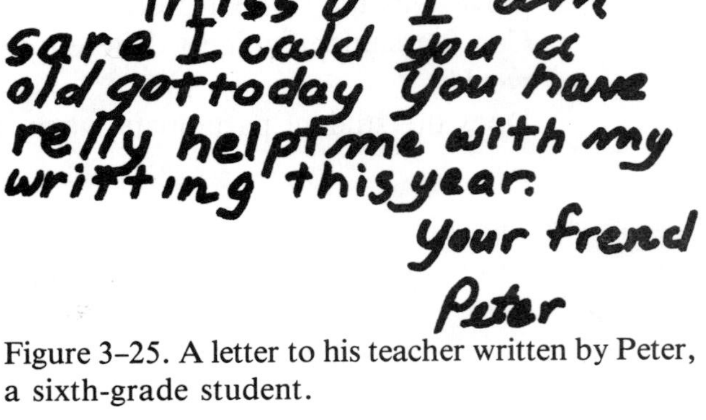

Figure 3–25. A letter to his teacher written by Peter, a sixth-grade student.

4

ACCOMMODATIONS AND MODIFICATIONS

The essence of our effort to see that every
child has a chance
must be to assure each an equal opportunity
not to become equal,
but to become different
to realize whatever unique
potential of body, mind and spirit
he or she possesses.

— John Fischer

Greater emphasis is placed on writing than any other skill in our schools (Gajar, 1989; Stewart, 1992; Vogel, 1987). Unfortunately, many individuals with learning disabilities, particularly at secondary levels, fail courses in the mainstream due to the heavy demands on writing (Donahoe & Zigmond, 1990). These students are at a tremendous disadvantage if curricular adjustments and accommodations are not made throughout their school careers. Consequently, the continued difficulties experienced by students with learning disabilities justify the employment of classroom accommodations that are unnecessary for most students (Moats, 1991a). Special accommodations, such as extra time to complete exams and written assignments and permission to take a reduced load, help students attain their goals (Van Ness, 1989).

The purpose of this chapter is to consider: (a) the definition of accommodations and compensatory strategies, (b) the determination of the amount of support, (c) the selection of appropriate accommodations, (d) the legal requirements related to provision of accommodations, and (e) the specific accommodations that may be implemented for writers with disabilities.

Definition of Accommodations and Compensatory Strategies

Accommodations are not substitutes for a carefully designed remedial program (Bain, 1991), but rather are adjustments in curricular demands that allow a student to succeed. These changes in the school environment result in the provision of equal opportunity and equal access to all students. The changes may be procedural or attitudinal, may involve environmental access, or may include the use of assistive equipment or technology. Figure 4–1 depicts the four types of accommodations available.

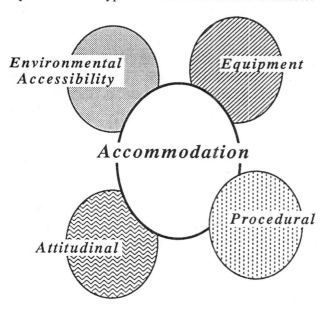

Figure 4–1. Four types of accommodations available to individuals with disabilities.

Accommodations differ from compensatory strategies. Compensatory strategies are the tactics students use to help themselves perform tasks. These strategies may be developed instinctively by the student, using his or her ingenuity, or taught by a teacher familiar with the student's learning style and the task demands. The ultimate goal of instruction in compensatory strategies is that students develop the skills to complete challenging tasks independently. For some students, the use of compensatory strategies allows them to meet the regular classroom expectations without leaving the mainstream (Masters, Mori, & Mori, 1993).

Consider the following example. Ryan, a seventh-grade student, required both compensatory strategies and accommodations to succeed in his regular classes. Ryan's decoding, reading comprehension, and written syntax were age appropriate. In contrast, he demonstrated significant word-retrieval problems and visual-motor difficulties. When he tried to write down his ideas, he couldn't generate the words he needed and his handwriting speed was unusually slow. For Ryan, compensatory strategies included the use of a pencil grip and the development of keyboarding and word processing skills.

In addition to compensatory strategies, Ryan required both procedural and attitudinal accommodations. Procedural accommodations impact the policies and practices teachers use in managing their classrooms. For Ryan the procedural accommodations necessary included permission to use a computer for all written assignments and acceptance of in-class written assignments as homework.

Attitudinal accommodations involve alterations in one's belief system. In Ryan's case, attitudinal accommodation was necessary on the part of one of his teachers who initially rejected altering classroom/curricular expectations and would not allow the use of a laptop computer. Through staff development efforts, the teacher began to understand Ryan's need for accommodation in order to have equal opportunity to learn.

Determination of the Amount of Support

Unfortunately, a universal, standard compensatory or accommodation plan does not exist. Little information exists in regard to how to judge whether an accommodation for a particular student with learning disabilities is either appropriate or reasonable (Scott, 1994). The types of writing difficulties experienced by individuals are varied and, therefore, the accommodations must be unique. In planning a program, the strengths and educational needs of a student must be analyzed carefully to determine appropriate educational support within a specific context (Applebee & Langer, 1983; Bain, 1991). Determination of the amount of support involves consideration of two student-related factors: (a) the

zone of proximal development and (b) the need for instructional scaffolding.

Zone of Proximal Development

A major determinant in selecting modifications involves consideration of a student's present performance level. Vygotsky (1978) distinguished between two developmental levels: the actual level of development and the level of potential development. The distance between a student's present level of performance and his or her level of potential performance is called the zone of proximal development. Potential performance is defined as that which could be obtained with adult guidance or in collaboration with more knowledgeable peers. Vygotsky recognized that good instruction is one step beyond present performance or slightly in advance of development.

Two implications are inherent in this concept. When making curricular adjustments for a student, a teacher should: (a) ascertain that the student is working within his or her instructional level and (b) attempt to create situations that involve purposeful pairing with more knowledgeable others. Students are able to perform at a higher level when paired with partners with more extensive knowledge who can model the accepted way of performing the task (Daiute & Dalton, 1993).

Instructional Scaffolding

With the correct support or "scaffolding" (Bruner, 1978; Cazden, 1980), every individual can experience success. The concept of scaffolding can be used with individual students or in group instruction. Building on the work of Vygotsky (1962, 1978), Applebee and Langer (1983) developed the concept of instructional scaffolding. Learning is seen as a process of gradual internalization of procedures (Applebee, 1986; Applebee & Langer, 1983) and allows for the exploration of effective instruction within the context of a more collaborative role between the student and the teacher (Applebee, 1984).

Instructional scaffolding, therefore, allows for collaboration in tasks that would be too difficult for the individual to undertake alone, but at which he or she can succeed with adult interaction (Applebee, 1986). The intent of scaffolding is to reduce the number of components that a student must manage. Three steps are involved: (a) the difficulties posed by a new task must be determined, (b) specific strategies that can overcome the anticipated problems must be selected, and (c) the activity must be structured so that the strategies are explicit and appropriate (Applebee & Langer, 1983).

The particular tasks requiring instructional scaffolding will vary from grade to grade and from course to course (Applebee & Langer, 1983). For example, Figure 4-2 presents a poem written by Helen, a second-grade student. Helen's ideas are good but she has some difficulty with spelling. Her teacher must encourage Helen to continue writing and not penalize her for spelling.

Jessica, however, requires a different accommodation. As depicted in Figure 4-3, Jessica, an eighth-grade student, has trouble with handwriting. Her teachers complain constantly that her poor handwriting creates problems for them when grading her work. Jessica, therefore, requires the accommodation of a word processor or a peer transcriber for some written assignments.

In addition, the amount and type of scaffolding will vary with regard to the intensity of an individual's needs (Applebee, 1984; Applebee & Langer, 1983). Scaffolding may be needed in the instructional materials (e.g., textbooks, assignments, direct in-

struction), as well as in teacher-student interaction (Applebee, 1986).

Effective instructional scaffolding incorporates a number of principles that provide a new way to approach familiar teaching tasks (Applebee, 1984; Applebee & Langer, 1983; Langer, 1984). Some of the features are; (a) student ownership of the learning event, (b) appropriateness of the instructional task, (c) a structured learning environment, (d) shared responsibility, and (e) transfer of control. An instructional approach incorporating these principles encourages students to select their own topics and write their own opinions and solutions. In addition, the role of the teacher would shift from evaluator of quality or the judge of success to an interested reader and skilled editor (Applebee, 1986). When instruction is scaffolded, any teaching technique is appropriate provided that the technique is seen as only one of a variety of ways to address the problem (Applebee, 1986).

The provided supports or scaffolds must be evaluated periodically to determine their effectiveness in meeting an individual's needs. Supports are withdrawn gradually as the individual is able to assume more responsibility for learning (Applebee & Langer, 1983; Conway & Gow, 1988). The teacher models the activity, coaches the student, and fades

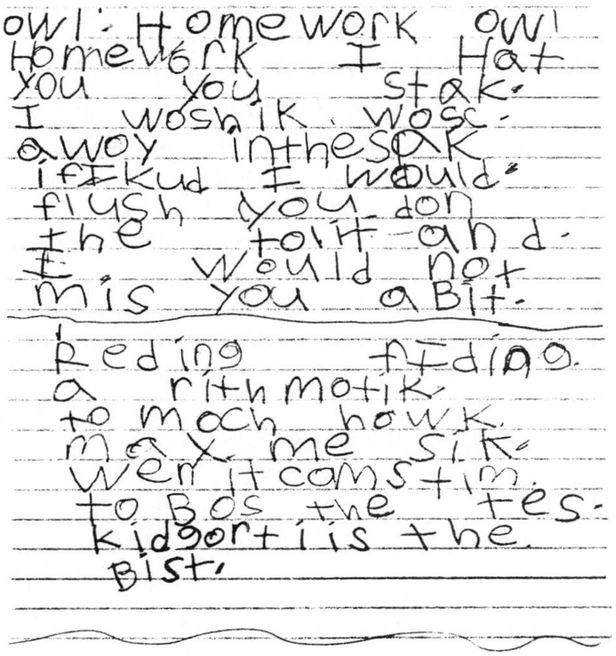

Translation:

Oh homework, oh homework
I hate you. You stink.
I wish I could wash you
Away in the sink.
If I could, I would flush you down the toilet
And I would not miss you a bit

— — — — — — — — — —

Reading, writing, arithmetic -
Too much homework makes me sick
When it comes to pass the test
Kindergarten is the best.

Figure 4-2. A poem written by Helen, a second-grade student.

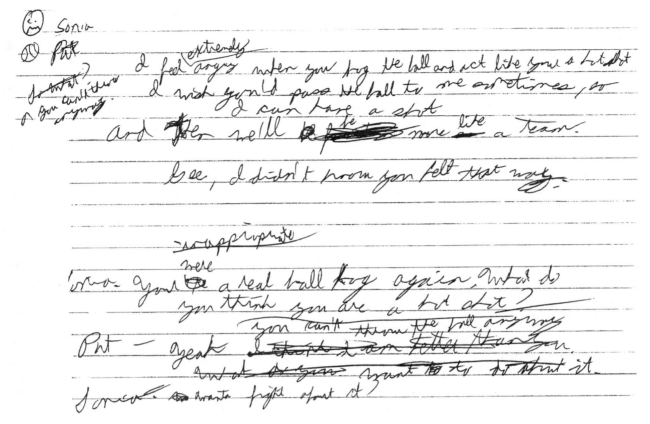

Figure 4-3. A note written by Jessica, an eighth-grade student.

all support by continuously assessing the student's ability to perform independently (Daiute & Dalton, 1993).

In the dictionary, the word *scaffold* has two distinct meanings:

1. a temporary supporting structure, usually made of wood or metal, put up for workers when they are building.
2. a high platform used for execution, usually by hanging.

Unfortunately, for many students with writing difficulties, the education system has afforded them academic experiences reminiscent of the second definition. Standards and competencies are set out of reach and the students fail. One future goal for all classroom teachers is to provide individuals with the support they need to achieve success.

Selection of Appropriate Accommodations

Teachers often assume the responsibility of determining when certain accommodations are and are not appropriate. In some cases, accommodations are necessary if the student is to have academic success; in other cases, accommodations are a disservice as the student is capable of managing the task without assistance. How does a teacher determine what accommodations are necessary for a student? In order to make this judgment, a teacher must have information relative to a student's present performance level (Bain, 1991), as well as an idea of the amount of time and effort the student expends completing the assigned tasks.

In some instances, accommodations are critical. Ben, an eighth-grade student, failed his first spelling test. Figure 4–4 illustrates his performance. After scoring his test, the teacher wrote on the top: *Study to take over.* When Ben met with the special education teacher, he informed her that he had studied for over 4 hours. She then determined that Ben could not read any of the spelling words. Clearly, the selected spelling words were too difficult for Ben. Without an accommodation, such as a shorter or an easier list of spelling words, Ben will be unable to succeed.

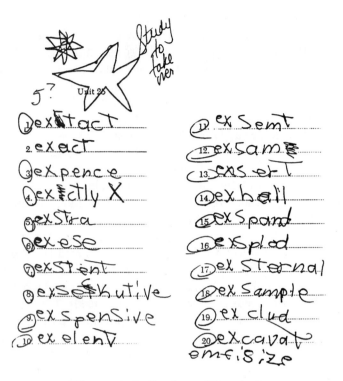

Figure 4–4. Ben's spelling test.

Several years later when Ben enrolled in college, his English professor informed him that he would not pass the course with "spelling like that." When Ben told his instructor that he had a learning disability that made it difficult for him to spell, she was unsympathetic. After failing several in-class essays, Ben dropped his English course and, subsequently, left college. In this instance, Ben did not receive appropriate accommodations (i.e., permission to complete in-class assignments out of class), nor did he take responsibility for the use of appropriate compensatory strategies (i.e., the use of a spell checker).

In many instances, accommodations are the key to success for students with written language difficulties. Ted, a sixth-grade student, was receiving failing grades due to his incomplete work. During the first grading period, his behavior and attitude toward school deteriorated. On one occasion, the class was given an assignment to conduct library research for a report. Ted used the card catalogue and located the books. He then read everything about Henry VIII that he needed for his report. When asked, Ted could describe all of Henry's wives and how they died. Ted refused, however, to write notecards and would not begin a first draft. The

teacher, annoyed with Ted, sent him to the office. Instead of going to the office, Ted hid in the boys' bathroom. When he was discovered, the principal called his parents to inform them of Ted's actions.

After multiple meetings at school, Ted's parents sought psychological counseling. The psychologist suggested an evaluation for learning disabilities. Results of the evaluation indicated that Ted had an extensive vocabulary but limited knowledge of sentence syntax, poor visual-spatial perception, and slow visual-motor speed. With diagnostic information in hand, the parents returned to the school seeking, not special education services, but appropriate accommodations. Ted was soon allowed to use a computer for his written assignments. Instead of illegible printing, Ted was able to produce neat typewritten text. In addition, the printed copy allowed his teacher to provide direct instruction on sentence syntax. Within 4 months, Ted was turning in quality work on time and his grades and self-concept improved dramatically.

On occasion, unnecessary accommodations are made that actually inhibit student progress. Ian, a fifth-grade student with a mild hearing impairment, had made limited progress in writing. In an initial interview, Ian's mother commented that the hardest accomplishment for a child with a hearing impairment was learning to write. The results of an educational evaluation indicated that although Ian had reading skills at grade level, his writing performance was significantly below average. He had difficulty with speed of production and letter formation. The examiner noted further that Ian could hear sounds easily and had minimal difficulty pronouncing phonically regular nonsense words. Because Ian had no difficulty hearing English language sounds, one would predict that Ian would be able to learn to translate sounds into words and learn to spell.

When asked about his school writing program, Ian noted that for the last 2 years he had a peer transcriber who did all of his writing. He further explained that the hardest thing for a child with a hearing impairment was to learn how to write. In this situation, expectations communicated from others, as well as the specific accommodations that were made for Ian, adversely affected his skill development. As Johnson (1991) commented: "All too often, poor readers and writers are permitted to listen to tapes or give oral responses in class. While these temporary accommodations may be necessary for students to obtain and convey knowledge, we should not deprive them of a valuable form of communication for themselves and others" (p. ix). As a general rule, the selected accommodations should not interfere with instruction, be a substitute for remedial programs, or inhibit student progress in writing.

The Negotiation Process

Often the process of determining appropriate accommodations involves negotiation. Sometimes the negotiation occurs between teacher and student, at other times between teacher and teacher. Teachers should involve students when determining appropriate accommodations. Otherwise, students may feel that adjustments are being forced upon them. Figure 4–5 illustrates a note written by a fourth-grade student after the teacher had tried to help the student position his paper by placing a piece of tape diagonally across his desk (Maniet, 1986). One can see from the student's written response that he found this adjustment to be both unnecessary and a little insulting.

Resistance to curricular adjustments by the student and/or teacher may prove problematic initially. For example, some students may reject the idea of altering assignments or requirements. At the beginning of the school year, Ms. Turnbull, Matthew's fifth-grade teacher, noticed that he was struggling with mastery of the 20 words on the weekly spelling test. After 2 weeks of poor grades, Ms. Turnbull met with Matthew to discuss possible adjustments in the spelling program. She began by commenting about Matthew's neat handwriting and then noted Matthew's difficulty on the two final tests. Ms. Turnbull asked Matthew his opinion in regard to his performance. Matthew informed her that he had studied for the tests but the words were too hard and he just could not remember them all. In response, Ms. Turnbull suggested that Matthew's weekly list be reduced to 10 words. At this suggestion, Matthew responded that he wanted his list to have 20 words, just like all the other kids. Ms. Turnbull then suggested that Matthew take the 20-word spelling test, but that she would grade only the 10 words that they had preselected. Matthew commented that this adjustment would be "just great."

Although many regular education teachers are receptive and quite accustomed to making adjustments, a few may initially resist changing standards for certain individual students. They may feel that the requests to modify instruction for one or two students ask them to abandon highly valued practices (Margolis & McGettigan, 1988). When asked to reduce the number of spelling words for Matthew, Ms. Turnbull could have responded: "If I alter the expectations and assignments for Matthew, it would not be fair to the other children."

In the video *How Difficult Can This Be?*, Lavoie (1990) makes two important points with regard to this type of argument: (a) Matthew's needs have nothing to do with the other children and (b) the word *fair* has been misinterpreted. *Fair* does not mean equal, but instead that every student gets what he or she needs to succeed. Matthew needs 10 words to be successful, whereas Jonathan, his classmate, can handle all 20.

On rare occasions, a teacher may be unwilling to make specific accommodations for a student. Todd, an eighth-grade student with a learning disability, requested oral examinations from his science teacher, Mr. Janus. Mr. Russell, the special education teacher, also spoke to Mr. Janus regarding the need for alternative methods of assessment for Todd. Mr. Janus responded to both that he was unwilling to make this adjustment. Fortunately, Mr. Janus is obligated legally to make classroom accommodations for Todd; individuals who have been diagnosed as having learning disabilities and have qualified under the IDEA or Section 504 have certain legal protections relative to appropriate school accommodations.

Legal Requirements for Individuals with Learning Disabilities

Provision of services in school settings for individuals with specific learning disabilities has been problematic. A major source of confusion involves the interpretation of legal requirements and protections afforded to these individuals. The following sections provide brief reviews of the general legal requirements pertaining to learning disabilities. The first section discusses requirements under the Individuals with Disabilities Education Act of 1990 (IDEA, PL 101–476), the reenactment of the Education for All Handicapped Children Act of 1975

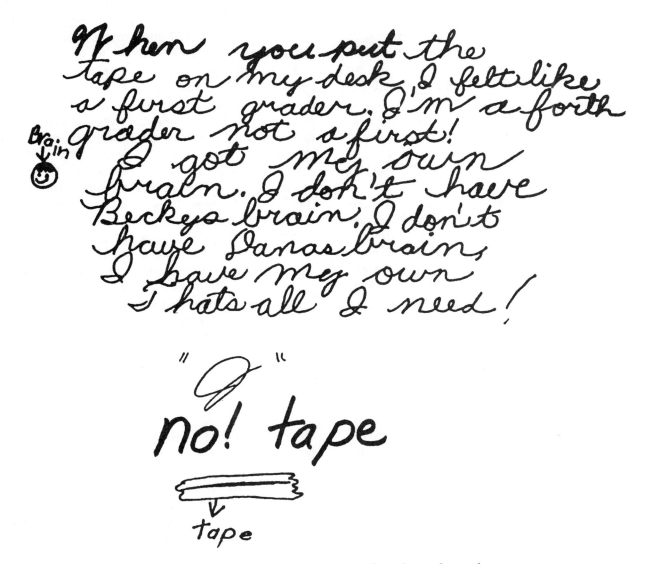

Figure 4–5. A note written by a fourth-grade student.

Note. From *Mainstreaming Children with Learning Disabilities: A Guide to Accompany: "L.D." Does Not Mean Learning Dumd!* (p. 25) by P. Maniet, 1986, South Orange, NJ: Maniet Bellermann Foundation. Copyright 1986 by Pamela J. Maniet. Reprinted by permission.

(EHA, PL 94–142). The next section discusses requirements under Section 504 of the 1973 Rehabilitation Act (PL 93–112) and the Americans with Disabilities Act of 1990 (ADA, PL 101–336).

Eligibility Under the IDEA

Among the various disability areas, the most controversy exists with regard to the eligibility criteria for learning disabilities services. One problem stems from the lack of agreement about the definition of learning disabilities as no general consensus exists with regard to who should be served (Hammill, 1990).

To be diagnosed as having a specific learning disability under the IDEA, an individual must: (a) be identified by a multidisciplinary evaluation team, (b) not achieve commensurate with his or her ability level in at least one of seven areas when provided with age- and ability-appropriate experiences, and (c) evidence a significant discrepancy between achievement and intellectual ability in one or more of seven areas. The seven areas include:

oral expression, listening comprehension, written expression, basic reading skill, reading comprehension, mathematics calculation, and mathematics reasoning [34 CFR Section 300.541(a)]. The multidisciplinary evaluation team may not identify an individual as having a specific learning disability if the severe discrepancy between ability and achievement is primarily the result of: a visual, hearing, or motor impairment; mental retardation; emotional disturbance; or environmental, cultural, or economic disadvantage [34 CFR Sections 300.7(b)(10), 300.541(b)].

Most states have developed discrepancy formulas to resolve the classification dilemma (Frankenberger & Harper, 1987). For most discrepancy formulas, results from an individually administered intelligence test are compared to results from a standardized achievement test (Frankenberger & Harper, 1987; Martin, 1992a; Mather & Healey, 1990). Despite increasing dissatisfaction with this criterion (Kavale, 1987; Mather & Healey, 1990), the majority of states currently employ discrepancy formulas (Frankenberger & Fronzaglio, 1991; Frankenberger & Harper, 1987). This practice continues even though many of the formulas are complicated and mathematically incorrect (Mastropieri, 1987; Reynolds, 1984–1985).

The discrepancy concept is the most controversial, yet most widely accepted, component of the definition (Hammill, 1990). Unfortunately, to many people, the concept of a specific learning disability has become synonymous with an aptitude-achievement discrepancy. In addition, personnel in some school districts believe that determination of an aptitude-achievement discrepancy is more important than development of an accommodation and/or intervention plan.

Eligibility under Section 504 and the ADA

Eligibility for services under Section 504 differs from the IDEA qualification criteria. As the law mandates equal access and equal opportunity, a severe discrepancy is not required for accommodations. Eligibility procedures are not clearly addressed in Section 504, but have been clarified to some extent by the Office of Civil Rights (OCR) rulings and by Hakola (1992), an education law expert.

The regulations governing implementation of Section 504 (1988) provide a broader definition of a disability than can be found in the IDEA regulations (Jacob-Timm & Hartshorne, 1994; Martin, 1992b). In Section 504, a disability is defined as any physical or mental impairment that substantially limits a major life activity [34 CFR Section 104.3(j)]. Because learning is a major life activity, educators are mandated to make reasonable accommodations for students with learning disabilities. In order for a student to receive accommodations, however, the disability must be currently affecting learning (*OCR Senior Staff Memorandum*, 1992).

Compliance with the IDEA mandates is enforced by the Office of Special Education Programs (OSEP). As Section 504 is a civil rights act for individuals with disabilities, compliance is enforced by OCR and applies to agencies and schools that receive any federal financial assistance (i.e., all public schools and some private institutions). The law states:

> No otherwise qualified individual with a disability in the United States . . . shall, solely by reason of his disability, be excluded from the participation in, be denied the benefits of, or be subjected to discrimination under any program or activity receiving Federal financial assistance [34 CFR Section 104.4(a)].

Section 504 bars discrimination by mandating the awareness of an individual's abilities and disabilities (Jacob-Timm & Hartshorne, 1994; Scott, 1990). Unlike anti-racial or anti-sex discrimination acts that mandate equal treatment, Section 504 recognizes that discrimination on the basis of a disability may be caused by identical treatment or neutrality (Scott, 1990).

The wording is the same in the ADA (1990) as in Section 504 and the two acts are identical in regard to the accommodations mandated for individuals with disabilities. The ADA, however, extends the mandates to private institutions with 15 or more employees. The schools specifically mentioned in the ADA are nursery, elementary, secondary, undergraduate or postgraduate private school, or other places of education.

As a result of the ADA, individuals with learning disabilities in most private schools are now afforded the same legal protections that their counterparts in public schools have been provided for over two decades. Individuals in some private institutions, however, continue to be protected by Section 504 rather than the ADA. For example, a private school that receives any federal funding (e.g., funding in order provide federal loans to students) is responsible for providing accommodations whenever necessary under Section 504. Only private institutions that are independent and self-supporting are regulated solely by the ADA.

One exception exists to the extension of the legal mandates to private schools. An exemption was granted to schools directly affiliated with religious organizations. If a student in a parochial school, therefore, is not being provided with appropriate accommodations, the parents may not have the recourse mandated by Section 504 and the ADA (Martin, 1994).

Although both laws mandate that reasonable accommodations be made, much latitude exists in the interpretation of "reasonable." For example, in the case of *Southeastern Community College v. Davis* (1979), the Supreme Court ruled that a university did not have to modify the clinical nursing program into an academic instructional program in order to accommodate a woman with a hearing impairment because a "fundamental alteration" of the program would be entailed.

A similar decision was reached in *Doherty v. Southern College of Optometry* (1987) when the judge ruled that Section 504 does not require that educational institutes lower or substantially change program standards to accommodate individuals whose disabilities prevent them from meeting the standards. In addition, the elimination of a course requirement that is necessary to the completion of the degree was ruled an unreasonable accommodation. Although the decision was appealed, it was upheld (*Doherty v. Southern College of Optometry*, 1988). In general, court decisions suggest that waiving a course requirement is not expected under Section 504 as long as: (a) a variety of academic adjustments and accommodations are provided, and (b) the school can demonstrate that such requirements are essential to the program (*City University of New York [NY]*, 1992). If these two requirements cannot be met, however, the laws stipulate that changes in policies, procedures, and practices and/or the provision of auxiliary aids must be made unless they would impose fundamental alterations in a program's requirements, or impose undue financial or administrative burden on the institution (Scott, 1990).

Reasonable accommodations must be determined for the student on an individual basis (*D'Amico v.*

New York State Board of Law Examiners, 1993). Some confusion exists, however, in regard to compliance standards for reasonable accommodations. For example, Subpart B of the Section 504 regulations (covering employment) and Subpart E (covering postsecondary and vocational education) contain a reasonable accommodation limitation. In contrast, OCR interprets Subpart D (covering elementary and secondary education) as not containing such a limitation. To date, there has been no legal action requiring OCR to clarify reasonable accommodation compliance standards in elementary and secondary schools [Digest of Response, 20 IDELR 134, 1993]. As a guideline for determining the provision of necessary accommodations, OCR has developed the following four-part test (Kincaid, 1994): (a) when necessary, adequate documentation of the disability has been provided; (b) accommodations are necessary; (c) accommodations are provided; and (d) accommodations are adequate and effective.

Under Section 504 mandates, services are provided primarily in the general education classroom (Katsiyannis & Conderman, 1994). Unfortunately, although accommodations place minimal demands upon teacher time or school funds, some classroom teachers perceive these adjustments as being inherently problematic. One of the concerns is that providing accommodations for one student is inherently unfair to the others. Cases exist whereby the OCR found this concern to violate Section 504. For example, a student with a learning disability requested additional time to take chemistry tests and was refused on the basis that the additional time would have to be given to all. The OCR found the practice to violate Section 504 (*Big Bend Community College [WA]*, 1991). In *Dinsmore v. Pugh and the Regents of the University of California at Berkeley* (1989), a faculty member refused to provide a student with extended time on an examination. In an out-of-court settlement, the college was required to clarify its accommodation policies and the faculty member was deemed personally liable and forced to pay monetary damages (Scott, 1994).

Similarly, a college in Iowa was found to be out of compliance due to the refusal of an instructor to modify test-taking procedures (*Eastern Iowa Community College District [IO]*, 1991). The college was also determined to be out of compliance in another instance when an instructor refused to allow a student to tape-record a class, deeming the recording as "disruptive."

The documentation of litigation involving violation of legal mandates emphasizes the important role played by advocates of individuals with disabilities. In an effort to encourage parents to become advocates for their children, Section 504 mandates that, when requested, schools must provide written notice of parental rights and the protocol for lodging a complaint (Jacob-Timm & Hartshorne, 1994; Martin, 1994). This mandate, like many others, has been in effect since the introduction of Section 504 in 1973, but schools have been forced to comply only since the introduction of the ADA. Although no funding is available for service provision to students who qualify under Section 504 or the ADA, both laws provide for enforcement of mandates by authorizing OCR to remove the federal financing of schools found to be out of compliance (Jacob-Timm & Hartshorne, 1994; Katsiyannis & Conderman, 1994).

Both the ADA and Section 504, therefore, bar discrimination; the spirit of the laws, ensuring equal educational opportunity, however, far exceeds this. Achieving equity for individuals with disabilities depends not only on avoiding discrimination, but also on removing subtle attitudinal barriers. Many barriers are not architectural but are due to prejudice, attitude, and ignorance (Grubb, 1993).

Some school personnel may complain that the accommodations mandated by law give individuals with disabilities an unfair advantage. The intent of Section 504 is not to award high grades to everyone, but to provide equal opportunity to students with disabilities (Gamble, 1993; Jacob-Timm & Hartshorne, 1994). Individuals with disabilities often require adjustments or accommodations such as untimed tests, or access to a spell checker to have equal access, as nondiscrimination requires an accommodation of the individual learning process (Scott, 1990).

Accommodations should not, however, be discriminatory in favor of individuals with disabilities (Gamble, 1993). For example, modifications on examinations should not alter the measurement of skills or knowledge that the exam is supposed to test (Grubb, 1993). The purpose of the law is to accommodate a disability by providing equal opportunity, not to favor an individual.

Section 504 expands protection to students with learning disabilities who were, in the past, deemed ineligible for special education services by their public or private school (Jacob-Timm & Hartshorne, 1994; Martin, 1992b). This protection is most relevant to: (a) students who have deficits in areas such as attention, reasoning, processing, memory, coordination, social competency, and emotional maturity (Jones, 1991); and (b) those who have moderate to severe needs (Lillie, 1992, Martin, 1992b) and documentation of a learning disability from an outside agency. Students with writing difficulties may fall into either of these two groups.

Misinterpretation of Legal Mandates

Section 504 has often been ignored or misinterpreted by school personnel (Martin, 1992b). For example, confusion has stemmed from school districts equating the phrase "substantially limits" (Section 504) with severe discrepancy (PL 94–142, IDEA) (Jones, 1991; Martin, 1992a) despite evidence that the two are not interchangeable (Martin, 1992a).

In addition, for many years school districts have mistakenly operated under the premise that they are forbidden by law to provide services to a student who has failed to qualify under the IDEA eligibility criterion (Martin, 1991). In reality, schools are obligated to provide appropriate accommodations to students if they qualify under Section 504.

Interpretation and implementation of Section 504 have proven troublesome to many school districts due to the lack of information and clarification. One major misconception is that compliance with the IDEA is equivalent to compliance with Section 504 (Katsiyannis & Conderman, 1994; Martin, 1991). This is not so: Every student covered by the IDEA is also covered by Section 504, but the reverse is not true. A student could fail to qualify for services under the IDEA, yet still qualify for services and procedural safeguards under Section 504 (Toombs, 1990). Although Section 504 does not provide a school district with financial support toward the education of the student, the act mandates that the student be granted any necessary accommodations. Although the limited financial resources available for staff development may not foster positive attitudes toward the mandate, individuals should not be left to fend for themselves in classrooms designed for others.

The mandates of Section 504 do not cease with high school graduation. Section 504 requires that postsecondary institutions (from technical training schools to private 4-year universities) make reasonable accommodations for the physical and mental limitations of individuals. Individuals with written language disabilities, therefore, are entitled to accommodation not only as children but also as adults.

In addition to educational institutions, the law pertains to businesses. For example, employable adults may require accommodation in testing (i.e., a transcriber to take the Bar Exam) or other certification/licensure requirements, or they may need specific accommodations to meet the essential functions of a job. The law mandates that accommodations be made for an individual to succeed despite his or her disability, providing the individual is "otherwise qualified" and can perform the essential aspects of the job. This legislation provides the opportunity for individuals with writing disabiliities to succeed.

Staff at public institutions have long known their responsibilities under Section 504 with regard to individuals with physical impairments. In the last decade, programs have expanded to include services for students with learning disabilities. Personnel in private schools are currently learning about their responsibilities to individuals with learning disabilities under Section 504 and the ADA.

Responsibility for accommodation is shared equally by the individual student and the school. Unlike students in elementary and secondary education, postsecondary students are obligated to notify the institution of the disability and the necessary academic adjustments and auxiliary aids (Kincaid, 1994). The student has the responsibility to self-disclose; each individual needs to inform the appropriate personnel and provide documentation as to the nature and severity of the disability, as well as the recommended accommodations. The school has the responsibility to provide equal opportunity to all individuals through appropriate, reasonable accommodations. The need for accommodations, however, must be documented by a qualified individual (*California State University-Long Beach*, 1992).

Scott (1994) prepared an accommodation decision chart for college students, presented in Figure 4–6, that is applicable to students of all ages with learning disabilities. As noted, prior to mandatory provision of an accommodation, it must be determined that: (a) a student has a learning disability, (b) the documentation is adequate, (c) the student is qualified, and (d) the accommodation is reasonable.

The true interpretation of the law evolves through the courts. As more court complaints are filed and resolved, institutions will receive further guidance in this evolving legal arena (Kincaid, 1994). Accommodations that have been suggested either explicitly or implicitly in litigation vary in terms of the time and effort necessary for successful implementation. Often they are no more complex than arranging for extended time on tests, providing computer access in a central location, or not penalizing for spelling on in-class assignments.

Specific Accommodations for Writers with Disabilities

What accommodations should then be selected for a student? The answer is whichever and however many are necessary to give the individual an equal opportunity to achieve in the specific setting. Depending upon the nature and severity of the writing problem, students will vary in the type and number of accommodations required (Jacob-Timm & Hartshorne, 1994). Some individuals may need to present assignments orally or on tape; others may need extended time on tests. As with teaching strategies, curricular adjustments are tailored to unique individual needs.

Once the need for specific accommodations has been determined, the question then becomes what accommodations are available and viable to the ecology of the classroom. In many school districts, a team meets to identify appropriate student accommodations. Figure 4–7 presents a Student Accommodation Plan written for Frank, an eighth-grade student with a learning disability. This plan was developed by Frank, his special education teacher, and his regular classroom English teacher. In addition to receiving these specific accommodations, Frank enrolled in a typing class to improve his keyboarding skills.

Figure 4–8 presents a sample Accommodation Plan form that may be duplicated. This sample form is a suggestion only. School districts are encouraged to modify and develop specific forms to meet their documentation needs.

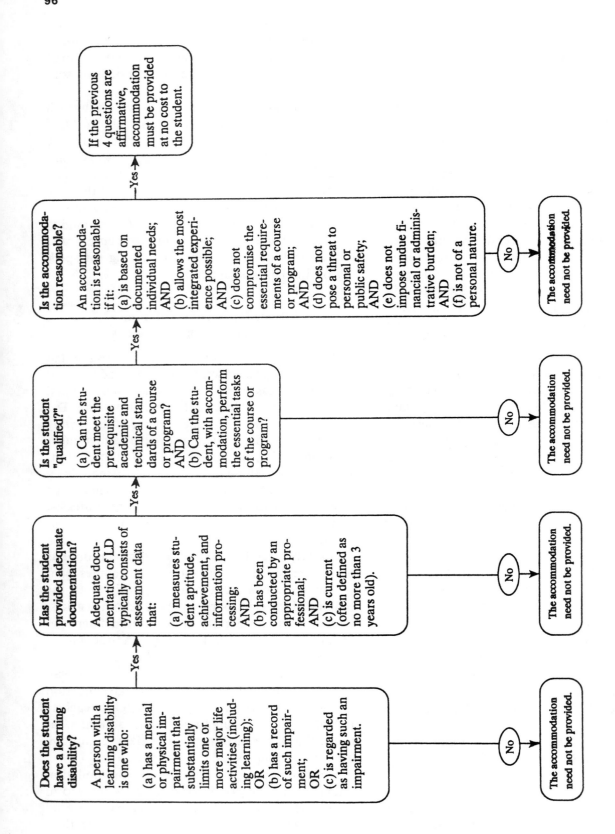

Figure 4–6. An accommodation decision chart.

Note. From "Determining Reasonable Academic Adjustments for College Students with Learning Disabilities" by S. S. Scott, 1994, *Journal of Learning Disabilities*, 23, p. 409. Copyright 1994 by PRO-ED. Reprinted by permission.

Student Accommodation Plan

NAME: Frank Kellogg   DATE OF MEETING: February 4, 1994

DATE OF BIRTH: 1/15/80   SCHOOL: Foster High school

                             GRADE: 9

1.   Describe the present concerns:

Slow writing speed.
Low spelling skill.

2.   Describe the type of disability:

Learning Disability.
Poor visual-motor skill.
Slow handwriting speed.

3.   List the reasonable accommodations that are necessary:

1) Provide untimed examination for all tests that require writing.
2) Permit the use of a laptop with a spell checker for all assignments and exams.

4.   Designate in which classes accommodation will be provided:

All.

Review/Reassessment Date: 5/2

Participants:

_____

_____

cc: Student's Cumulative File
Attachment: Information Regarding Section 504 of the Rehabilitation Act of 1973.

Figure 4-7. A Student Accommodation Plan for Frank, an eighth-grade student.

Student Accommodation Plan

NAME:_____   DATE OF MEETING: _____

DATE OF BIRTH:_____   SCHOOL: _____

GRADE: _____

1.   Describe the present concerns:

2.   Describe the type of disability:

3.   List the reasonable accommodations that are necessary:

4.   Designate in which classes accommodation will be provided:

Review/Reassessment Date: _____

Participants:

_____

_____

_____

_____

_____

cc: Student's Cumulative File
Attachment: Information Regarding Section 504 of the Rehabilitation Act of 1973.

Figure 4–8. A sample Student Accommodation Plan.

Although Section 504 mandates that reasonable accommodations be made, an official list of acceptable accommodations does not exist. The following academic adjustments, however, are noted specifically in the law: (a) modifications to the method of instruction, (b) extended exam time, (c) alternative testing formats, and (d) increased time in which to complete a course [34 CFR Sections 104.44 (a)(b)(c)]. In general, the primary accommodation for students with moderate to severe writing difficulties is to permit them to express themselves in ways that require limited or no writing (Masters et al., 1993). These students often require specific auxiliary aids, such as the use of tape recorders. In addition, students with severe spelling problems or handwriting problems often benefit from the use of a word processor (Outhred, 1989).

Some school personnel have questioned whether or not educational institutions must purchase computers and calculators for students who require these aids. The ADA codifies that institutions may not charge individuals with disabilities for the provision of necessary auxiliary aids and services [28CFR Sections 35.130(f), 36.301(c)] and this mandate has been upheld in court (*State University of New York*, 1993). The regulations to Section 504 and the ADA clarify, however, that institutions are not mandated to provide services of a personal nature, such as individualized tutoring [34 CFR Section 104.44(d)(2); 28 CFR Sections 35.135, 36.306].

Specific accommodations relevant to written language are presented in several sources (Dagenais & Beadle, 1984; Masters et al., 1993; Mather & Jaffe, 1992; McCarney & Cummins, 1988). The following list provides examples of adjustments that may be needed by an individual with writing difficulties:

- Provide direct instruction in writing with one-to-one tutorials.
- Adjust the difficulty level of in-class writing assignments.
- Reduce the number of written assignments.
- Reduce the length of assignments both in the classroom and at home. For example, assign a shorter spelling list or accept a paragraph of writing instead of several pages.
- Tailor homework assignments that involve writing to the individual's skill level.
- Provide extended time on writing assignments and in-class exams.

- Administer exams orally. Give exams individually or the student may dictate responses into a tape recorder for grading at a later time.
- Allow alternative methods for displaying content mastery, such as allowing oral presentations or special projects.
- Permit dictation of written assignments to a transcriber, such as a teacher, parent, or peer.
- Provide the student with classnotes from the instructor or peer.
- Provide tape recordings of the class lectures rather than requiring the student to take notes.
- Limit or eliminate copying requirements from both the blackboard and textbooks.
- Teach the student how to use a tape recorder to complete specific assignments. For example, provide practice preparing and orally dictating an essay for an English class.
- Accept tape-recorded assignments as an alternative to written assignments.
- Grade on individualized, pre-established criteria. A particular writing assignment may be graded on content only, whereas another may focus on form, such as the use of capitalization.
- Provide many ungraded opportunities for skill development.
- Provide opportunities for the student to work on assignments in small groups.
- Provide the student with a cross-age tutor to help with writing tasks.
- Encourage the student to participate in some aspect of the writing.
- Modify the grading system for writing assignments. Grades can be weighted to reflect effort or assigned on the basis of individualized progress.
- Modify the grading system for the student by placing greater emphasis on special projects, rather than on performance on written assignments.
- Grade the student on improvement of writing skill, rather than performance as compared to peers.
- Provide alternative exam formats that do not require extensive writing, such as multiple-choice, short answer, or fill-in the blank.
- Divide written exams into several sections that can be administered over several days.
- Provide structured assistance with editing.

- When grading assignments, do not penalize for errors in basic skills, such as punctuation errors, misspellings, or poor handwriting.
- Allow the student to write all exam responses on a computer.
- Encourage the student to use an electronic spell checker when editing papers.
- Encourage the use of technology, such as a word processor or electric typewriter.
- Encourage the student to use spelling and grammar correction word processing programs before turning in assignments.
- Permit the use of spell checkers, tape recorders, and other electronic aids during exams.

Conclusion

Many individuals with writing disabilities can succeed in regular classrooms provided that specific accommodations and curricular adjustments are made. The type and amount of support necessary will vary from individual to individual, as well as from grade to grade and course to course (Applebee & Langer, 1983). The amount of scaffolding provided will decrease as the student becomes more proficient in the task.

The provision of support for individuals with writing disabilities is mandated in federal and state laws. Personnel in both public and private schools are expected to conform with these laws. Legal policies protect the needs of individuals with writing disabilities; educators must now ensure that these policies be turned into practice.

Teachers are responsible for providing environments where students can succeed. To provide for success, teachers must believe that: (a) all students can learn, (b) success breeds success, and (c) schools control the conditions of success (Garcia, 1992). Most accommodations and modifications are not expensive or time-consuming; they simply involve looking at the situation in a different way (Gamble, 1993). For many students with learning disabilities, provision of appropriate accommodations is the only way that equal educational opportunity will be achieved (Scott, 1994).

5

HANDWRITING

One thing only is certain—that the written language of children develops in this fashion, shifting from drawings of things to drawing of words.

—Vygotsky, 1978, p. 115

Even though many children exhibit poor handwriting, handwriting has been identified as the "neglected R," or the ignored stepchild of written language, because few teacher education programs train teachers how to teach handwriting (Bain, 1991; Graham, 1986; Milone, Wilhide, & Wasylyk, 1984). Handwriting is often thought to be the least important subject in the school curriculum (Bos & Vaughn, 1994). Although students should not be required to demonstrate neat handwriting every time they pick up a pencil or a pen (Tompkins, 1994), handwriting instruction needs to be an integral part of the school curriculum (Salend, 1994).

Handwriting

This chapter begins with a review of handwriting principles. Next, various writing styles, the instructional needs of left-handed writers, and the use of word processing are discussed briefly. Specific instructional strategies are then provided for the areas of: (a) readiness, (b) letter formation, (c) reversals, (d) copying skill, (e) fluency, (f) self-evaluation, and (g) appearance.

Principles

Graham and Madan (1981) noted that an effective program for teaching letter formation is based upon the following four principles: (a) overlearning letters in isolation and then applying them in a written context; (b) forming letters with external cues, such as verbalizing and tracing until they become automatic; (c) encouraging students to evaluate their own handwriting; and (d) providing students with assistance in maintaining a consistent and legible writing style.

Important elements of handwriting instruction, therefore, include: teacher modeling and describing letter formation, discussing critical attributes, tracing, self-verbalizing, writing from memory, feedback, and reinforcement (Graham & Madan, 1981; Graham & Miller, 1980). Many students require explicit and direct help to establish the patterns needed for legible, fluent writing (Graham, 1983). Skills are overlearned in isolation and then applied in meaningful assignments (Graham & Madan, 1981; Graham & Miller, 1980). In general, students benefit from supervised practice with immediate reinforcement and correction (Meese, 1994). As skill progresses, students can improve their handwriting as they write meaningful text, such as copying the final drafts of their own compositions for publication (Rhodes & Dudley-Marling, 1988).

On rare occasions, handwriting improves without direct intervention. Figures 5–1 and 5–2 illustrate two writing samples from Esther, a third-grade student. The second sample was written 2 weeks after the first sample. When the second sample was written, Esther had started receiving medication for Attention Deficit Hyperactivity Disorder (ADHD). Clearly, her difficulties with handwriting were related to ADHD, as the appearance of her writing improved substantially with this treatment. Medication alone, however, does not usually cure the handwriting problem. It may facilitate the process for a few students, but most will also need explicit instruction.

The numerous instructional programs for handwriting have many common elements. Many of the

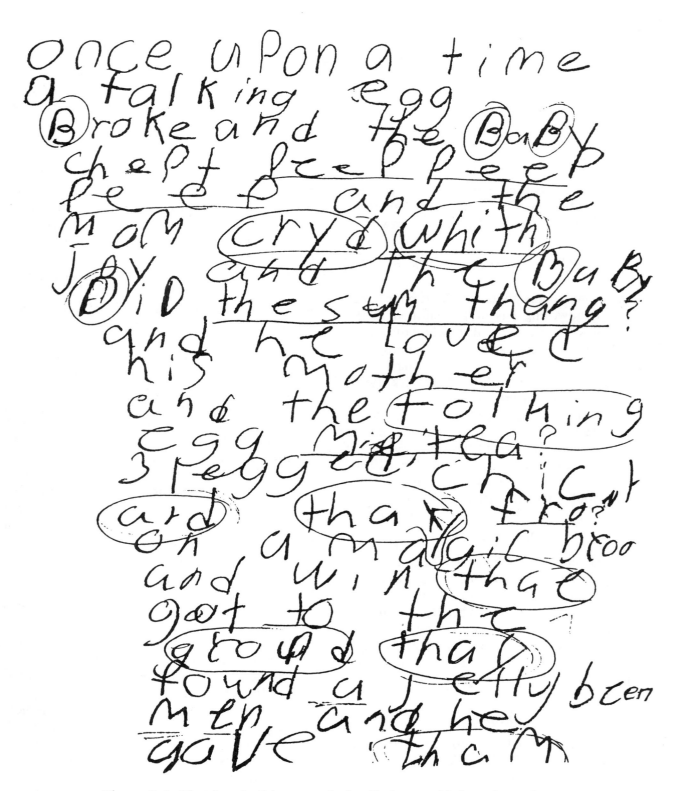

Figure 5-1. First handwriting sample for Esther, a third-grade student.

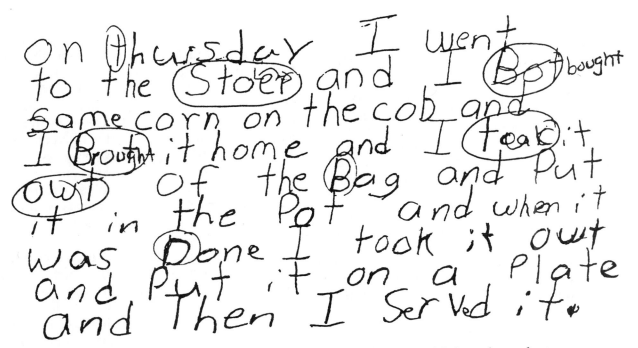

Figure 5–2. Second handwriting sample for Esther, a third-grade student.

common elements are contained in the following general procedures for improving handwriting skill, described by McCarney and Cummins (1988):

1. Provide the student with ample opportunities to practice handwriting skill.
2. Model neat and correct handwriting at all times.
3. Have the student trace over models. As skill develops, slowly fade the models.
4. Initially, provide the student with primary paper with a middle line in order to foster the correct size of letters. As skill develops, have the student use standard paper.
5. Provide the student with wide-ruled paper. As skill improves, gradually reduce the width of the lines.
6. If spacing is problematic, provide the student with paper that has both horizontal and vertical lines. Teach the student to write one symbol in each box, to leave one box empty after a comma, and two empty boxes after a period.
7. If the student's handwriting is affected by poor positioning of the pencil, provide the student with a triangular pencil grip.

8. When teaching handwriting to older students, provide them with functional opportunities to practice handwriting (e.g., filling out job application, bank forms, etc.).
9. Ensure that consistent expectations are maintained by all school personnel involved with the student.
10. Recognize and reinforce improvement.

Writing Styles

In many programs, handwriting instruction begins with manuscript writing and then progresses to cursive handwriting instruction at the end of the second or beginning of the third grade (Wood, 1993). Some controversy exists, however, in regard to whether children with handwriting difficulties should be taught manuscript or cursive writing first (Smith, 1994).

Manuscript or Cursive

Some students appear to profit from early instruction in cursive writing (Fernald, 1943). There are several advantages to teaching students cursive rather than manuscript writing in first grade. First, the students are not confounded by another writing system. Second, because all cursive letters are made from left to right, a student may not make as many letter reversals. Third, the continuous writing rhythm can help with spacing and speed (Smith, 1994).

Some individuals, however, believe that manuscript is an easier style and the method of preference for young children to learn. Because the letter forms are composed of simple sticks and circles, they may be easier to form than cursive letters and they are similar to the print style that children see in books (Barbe, Milone, & Wasylyk, 1983). In addition, cursive writing can pose problems for some young children as they do not have the fine-motor coordination to make the required continuous strokes (Wood, 1993).

This problem is not always limited to young children as, in some instances, an older student has such difficulty learning cursive writing that learning a new style becomes counterproductive. For example, Frank, a third-grade student, had extreme difficulty developing a legible manuscript style. Fortunately, his teacher realized that it was more important to spend time on authentic writing activities than to insist that Frank spend time learning cursive writing.

Learning a new writing style appears to be particularly problematic for students with learning disabilities (Thurber, 1983). When new writing styles are introduced, other aspects of writing performance often deteriorate. For example, when a student changes from manuscript to cursive, spelling and sentence structure may regress (Bernstein, 1989). Even when cursive writing has been practiced enough to become semi-automatic, some individuals with learning disabilities may continue to see a deterioration in spelling and punctuation when writing in cursive. For example, Jesse, a fourth-grade student, enjoys writing in cursive and is proud of the neat and legible work that he produces. He makes twice as many spelling and punctuation errors, however, when using cursive than he does when printing.

Jesse explained to his teacher: "It's like my brain's a battery and it has enough energy to make nice handwriting or to spell right, but not enough to do both." Jesse and his teacher agreed that every first draft would be printed so that his attention could be used for expressing his ideas. During the editing stage, his errors in basic skills would be corrected. The final draft would be copied in cursive so that Jesse could continue to be proud of his work.

Manu-Cursive/D'Nealian

One way to avoid having to teach a new style is to begin instruction with a manu-cursive style. Manu-cursive is a writing style that combines manuscript and cursive letter formation. The most well known example of a manu-cursive writing style is D'Nealian (Thurber, 1983). In this method, the majority of letters are formed with a continuous motion, thus providing a natural progression from manuscript to cursive letter formation. Letters are connected by adding joining strokes. Manu-cursive approaches are effective for students with learning disabilities for several reasons. First, in using this writing style, students make fewer reversals and transpositions. Second, they do not need to learn two different methods for writing, and third, letters are formed in a single, continuous motion. In addition, D'Nealian offers visual, auditory, and tactile-kinesthetic clues to aid in the memory process. Figure 5–3 presents D'Nealian manuscript and cursive letters with the suggested audio directions.

Depending upon a student's age, ability, and interest, instructional training in a particular writing style may be recommended (Mather, 1991). As a general principle, permit variation in handwriting styles and allow students to use the style that they prefer. If a student is producing legible work at an adequate speed, ignore small irregularities in style that do not detract from communication by requiring unusual effort from readers (Meese, 1994; Rhodes & Dudley-Marling, 1988). Some students will always prefer to use manuscript writing, whereas others will prefer a manu-cursive or cursive writing style. One conclusion from a decade of research on handwriting instruction is that the switch from manuscript to cursive writing is not necessary (Askov, Otto, & Askov, 1970). The important point to remember is that in designing an instructional program for handwriting, the goal is to help students develop fluent, legible handwriting so that they can communicate effectively in writing (Tompkins, 1994). Although most individuals will master a legible handwriting style, a few will not. These students will write the majority of their assignments on word processors.

Word Processing

Word processors can help students bypass handwriting difficulties, allowing all students to produce

Number Descriptions

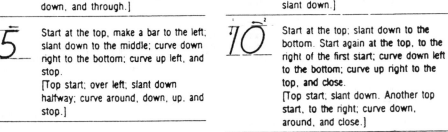

1	Start at the top; slant down to the bottom. [Top start; slant down.]
2	Start a little below the top; curve up right to the top, curve down right to the middle, slant down left to the bottom, make a bar to the right. [Start below the top; curve up, around; slant down left; and over right.]
3	Start a little below the top; curve up right to the top; curve down right to the middle; curve down right again to the bottom; curve up left, and stop. [Start below the top; curve up, around halfway; around again, up, and stop.]
4	Start at the top; slant down to the middle; make a bar to the right. Start again at the top, to the right of the first start, slant down through the bar to the bottom. [Top start; down halfway; over right. Another top start, to the right; slant down, and through.]
5	Start at the top, make a bar to the left; slant down to the middle; curve down right to the bottom; curve up left, and stop. [Top start; over left; slant down halfway; curve around, down, up, and stop.]
6	Start at the top; slant down left to the middle, curve down left to the bottom; curve up right to the middle; curve left, and close. [Top start; slant down, and curve around, up, and close.]
7	Start at the top; make a bar to the right; slant down left to the bottom. [Top start; over right; slant down left.]
8	Start a little below the top; curve up left to the top and down left to the middle; curve down right to the bottom; curve up left; slant up right, through the middle, to the beginning, and touch. [Start below the top; curve up, around, down; a snake tail; slant up right; through; and touch.]
9	Start at the top; curve down left to the middle; curve up right to the beginning, and close; slant down to the bottom. [Top start; curve down, around, close; slant down.]
10	Start at the top; slant down to the bottom. Start again at the top, to the right of the first start; curve down left to the bottom; curve up right to the top, and close. [Top start; slant down. Another top start, to the right; curve down, around, and close.]

Figure 5-3. D'Nealian Numbers and Letters.

Note. From D'Nealian ® Handwriting by Donald Neal Thurber. Copyright ©1987 by Scott, Foresman and Company. Reprinted by permission.

a neat, clean copy of written work. Because of severe difficulties with handwriting or their difficulties focusing upon handwriting, spelling, syntax, and ideation simultaneously, some students need to begin word processing instruction as early as second or third grade. To become efficient at word processing, students require instruction in both keyboarding skills and in the operation of the word processing program. Students should learn how to enter, save, edit, and print text. As noted by MacArthur (1988): "If computers are to contribute to better writing, they must be integrated with an effective instructional program" (p. 541).

Many students could benefit from instruction in both handwriting and word processing. Consider the journal entry of Philip, a third-grade student, presented in Figure 5-4. He has written his name and the sentence: *Boo went in the water.* Philip's rate of production is extremely slow. He spent 20 minutes on this journal entry.

Based upon the severity of his fine-motor difficulties, Philip's teacher developed a program that included a structured, multisensory method for handwriting as well as instruction in keyboarding skills. In addition, the teacher implemented some specific accommodations because of Philip's extreme

Lowercase Manuscript Letter Descriptions

a — Start in the middle; curve down left to the bottom; curve up right to the beginning, and close; retrace down, and swing up.
[Middle start; around down, close up, down, and a monkey tail.]

b — Start at the top; slant down to the bottom; curve up right to the middle; curve left, and close.
[Top start; slant down, around, up, and a tummy.]

c — Start a little below the middle; curve up left to the middle, curve down left to the bottom; curve up right, and stop.
[Start below the middle; curve up, around, down, up, and stop.]

d — Start in the middle, curve down left to the bottom; curve up right to the beginning; touch, and keep going up to the top; retrace down, and swing up.
[Middle start; around down, touch, up high, down, and a monkey tail.]

e — Start between the middle and the bottom; curve up right to the middle; curve down left; touch, and keep going down to the bottom; curve up right, and stop.
[Start between the middle and bottom; curve up, around, touch, down, up, and stop.]

f — Start a little below the top; curve up left to the top; slant down to the bottom. Make a crossbar in the middle.
[Start below the top; curve up, around, and slant down. Cross.]

g — Start in the middle; curve down left to the bottom; curve up right to the beginning, and close; retrace down to halfway below the bottom, and hook left.
[Middle start; around down, close up, down under water, and a fishhook.]

h — Start at the top; slant down to the bottom; retrace up halfway; make a hill to the right, and swing up.
[Top start; slant down, up over the hill, and a monkey tail.]

i — Start in the middle; slant down to the bottom, and swing up. Make a dot above the letter.
[Middle start; slant down, and a monkey tail. Add a dot.]

j — Start in the middle; slant down to halfway below the bottom, and hook left. Make a dot above the letter.
[Middle start; slant down under water, and a fishhook. Add a dot.]

k — Start at the top; slant down to the bottom; retrace up halfway; curve right; make a small loop left, and close; slant down right to the bottom, and swing up.
[Top start; slant down, up into a little tummy, and a monkey tail.]

l — Start at the top; slant down to the bottom, and swing up.
[Top start; slant down, and a monkey tail.]

m — Start in the middle; slant down to the bottom; retrace up, and make a hill to the right; retrace up; make another hill to the right, and swing up.
[Middle start; slant down, up over the hill, up over the hill again, and a monkey tail.]

n — Start in the middle; slant down to the bottom; retrace up; make a hill to the right, and swing up.
[Middle start; slant down, up over the hill, and a monkey tail.]

o — Start in the middle; curve down left to the bottom; curve up right to the beginning, and close.
[Middle start; around down, and close up.]

p — Start in the middle; slant down to halfway below the bottom; retrace up; curve down right to the bottom; curve left, and close.
[Middle start; slant down under water, up, around, and a tummy.]

q — Start in the middle; curve down left to the bottom; curve up right to the beginning, and close; retrace down to halfway below the bottom, and hook right.
[Middle start; around down, close up, down under water, and a backwards fishhook.]

r — Start in the middle; slant down to the bottom; retrace up; curve right, and stop.
[Middle start; slant down, up, and a roof.]

s — Start a little below the middle; curve up left to the middle and down left halfway; curve down right to the bottom; curve up left, and stop.
[Start below the middle; curve up, around, down, and a snake tail.]

t — Start at the top; slant down to the bottom, and swing up. Make a crossbar in the middle.
[Top start; slant down, and a monkey tail. Cross.]

u — Start in the middle; slant down to the bottom, and curve right; slant up to the middle; retrace down, and swing up.
[Middle start; down, around, up, down, and a monkey tail.]

v — Start in the middle; slant down right to the bottom; slant up right to the middle.
[Middle start; slant down right, and slant up right.]

w — Start in the middle; slant down to the bottom, and curve right; slant up to the middle; retrace down, and curve right; slant up to the middle.
[Middle start; down, around, up, and down, around, up again.]

x — Start in the middle; slant down right to the bottom, and swing up. Cross through the letter with a slant down left.
[Middle start; slant down right, and a monkey tail. Cross down left.]

y — Start in the middle; slant down to the bottom, and curve right; slant up to the middle; retrace down to halfway below the bottom, and hook left.
[Middle start; down, around, up, down under water, and a fishhook.]

z — Start in the middle; make a bar to the right; slant down left to the bottom; make a bar to the right.
[Middle start; over right, slant down left, and over right.]

Figure 5–3 (cont). D'Nealian Numbers and Letters

Capital Manuscript Letter Descriptions

 Start at the top; slant down left to the bottom. Start again at the same point; slant down right to the bottom. Make a crossbar in the middle.
[Top start; slant down left. Same start; slant down right. Middle bar across.]

 Start at the top; slant down to the bottom; retrace up; curve down right to the middle; curve left, and close; curve down right to the bottom; curve left, and close.
[Top start; slant down, up, around halfway, close, around again, and close.]

 Start a little below the top; curve up left to the top; curve down left to the bottom; curve up right, and stop.
[Start below the top; curve up, around, down, up, and stop.]

 Start at the top; slant down to the bottom; retrace up; curve down right to the bottom; curve left, and close.
[Top start; slant down, up, around, and close.]

 Start at the top; make a bar to the left; slant down to the bottom; make a bar to the right. Make a bar to the right in the middle.
[Top start; over left, slant down, and over right. Middle bar across.]

 Start at the top; make a bar to the left; slant down to the bottom. Make a bar to the right in the middle.
[Top start; over left, and slant down. Middle bar across.]

 Start a little below the top; curve up left to the top; curve down left to the bottom; curve up right to the middle; make a bar to the left.
[Start below the top; curve up, around, down, up, and over left.]

 Start at the top; slant down to the bottom. Start again at the top, to the right of the first start; slant down to the bottom. Make a crossbar in the middle.
[Top start; slant down. Another top start, to the right; slant down. Middle bar across.]

 Start at the top; slant down to the bottom. Make a small crossbar at the top, and another at the bottom.
[Top start; slant down. Cross the top and the bottom.]

 Start at the top; slant down to the bottom; curve up left, and stop.
[Top start; slant down, and curve up left.]

 Start at the top; slant down to the bottom. Start again at the top, to the right of the first start; slant down left to the middle, and touch; slant down right to the bottom, and swing up.
[Top start; slant down. Another top start, to the right; slant down left, touch, slant down right, and a monkey tail.]

 Start at the top; slant down to the bottom; make a bar to the right.
[Top start; slant down, and over right.]

 Start at the top; slant down to the bottom. Start again at the same point; slant down right to the middle; slant up right to the top; slant down to the bottom.
[Top start; slant down. Same start; slant down right halfway, slant up right, and slant down.]

 Start at the top; slant down to the bottom. Start again at the same point; slant down right to the bottom; slant up to the top.
[Top start; slant down. Same start; slant down right, and slant up.]

 Start at the top; curve down left to the bottom; curve up right to the beginning, and close.
[Top start; around down, and close up.]

 Start at the top; slant down to the bottom; retrace up; curve down right to the middle; curve left, and close.
[Top start; slant down, up, around halfway, and close.]

Start at the top; curve down left to the bottom; curve up right to the beginning, and close. Cross through the bottom of the letter with a curve down right.
[Top start; around down, and close up. Cross with a curve down right.]

Start at the top; slant down to the bottom; retrace up; curve down right to the middle; curve left, and close; slant down right to the bottom, and swing up.
[Top start; slant down, up, around halfway, close, slant down right, and a monkey tail.]

 Start a little below the top; curve up left to the top and down left to the middle; curve down right to the bottom, curve up left, and stop.
[Start below the top, curve up, around, down, and a snake tail.

 Start at the top, slant down to the bottom. Make a crossbar at the top.
[Top start, slant down. Cross the top.

 Start at the top; slant down to the bottom, and curve right; slant up to the top; retrace down, and swing up.
[Top start; down, around, up, down, and a monkey tail.]

 Start at the top; slant down right to the bottom; slant up right to the top.
[Top start; slant down right, and slant up right.]

 Start at the top; slant down right to the bottom; slant up right to the top; slant down right to the bottom; slant up right to the top.
[Top start; slant down right, slant up right, slant down right, and slant up right again.]

 Start at the top; slant down right to the bottom, and swing up. Cross through the letter with a slant down left.
[Top start; slant down right, and a monkey tail. Cross down left.]

 Start at the top; slant down right to the middle. Start again at the top, to the right of the first start; slant down left to the middle; touch, and keep going down to the bottom.
[Top start; slant down right halfway. Another top start, to the right; slant down left, and touch on the way.]

 Start at the top; make a bar to the right; slant down left to the bottom; make a bar to the right.
[Top start; over right, slant down left, and over right.]

Figure 5-3 (cont.). D'Nealian Numbers and Letters.

Lowercase Cursive Letter Descriptions

a — Go overhill; retrace halfway; curve down to the bottom; curve up right to the middle, and close; retrace down, and swing up.
[Overhill; back, around down, close up, down, and up.]

b — Go uphill to the top; loop left down to the bottom; curve up right to the middle; curve left; and sidestroke right.
[Uphill high; loop down, around, up, and sidestroke.]

c — Go overhill; retrace halfway; curve down to the bottom, and swing up.
[Overhill; back, around, down, and up.]

d — Go overhill; retrace halfway; curve down to the bottom; curve up right to the middle; touch, and keep going up to the top; retrace down, and swing up.
[Overhill; back, around down, touch, up high, down, and up.]

e — Go uphill to the middle; loop left down to the bottom, and swing up.
[Uphill; loop down, through, and up.]

f — Go uphill to the top; loop left down to halfway below the bottom; loop right up to the bottom line; close; and swing up.
[Uphill high; loop down under water, loop up right, touch, and up.]

g — Go overhill; retrace halfway; curve down to the bottom; curve up right to the middle, and close; retrace down to halfway below the bottom; and loop left up through the bottom line.
[Overhill; back, around down, close up, down under water, loop up left, and through.]

h — Go uphill to the top; loop left down to the bottom; retrace up halfway; make a hill to the right, and swing up.
[Uphill high; loop down, up over the hill, and up.]

i — Go uphill to the middle; retrace down, and swing up. Make a dot above the letter.
[Uphill; down, and up. Add a dot.]

j — Go uphill to the middle; retrace down to halfway below the bottom; and loop left up through the bottom line. Make a dot above the letter.
[Uphill; down under water, loop up left, and through. Add a dot.]

k — Go uphill to the top; loop left down to the bottom; retrace up halfway; curve right; make a small loop left, and close; slant down right to the bottom, and swing up.
[Uphill high; loop down, up into a little tummy, slant down right, and up.]

l — Go uphill to the top; loop left down to the bottom, and swing up.
[Uphill high; loop down, and up.]

m — Go overhill; slant down to the bottom; retrace up, and make a hill to the right; retrace up; make another hill to the right, and swing up.
[Overhill; down, up over the hill, up over the hill again, and up.]

n — Go overhill; slant down to the bottom; retrace up; make a hill to the right, and swing up.
[Overhill; down, up over the hill, and up.]

o — Go overhill; retrace halfway; curve down to the bottom; curve up right to the middle; close; and sidestroke right.
[Overhill; back, around down, close up, and sidestroke.]

p — Go uphill to the middle; retrace down to halfway below the bottom; retrace up; curve down right to the bottom; curve left; close; and swing up.
[Uphill; down under water, up, around into a tummy, and up.]

q — Go overhill; retrace halfway; curve down to the bottom; curve up right to the middle, and close; retrace down to halfway below the bottom; loop right up to the bottom line; close; and swing up.
[Overhill; back, around down, close up, down under water, loop up right, touch, and up.]

r — Go uphill to the middle; sidestroke right; slant down to the bottom, and swing up.
[Uphill; sidestroke, down, and up.]

s — Go uphill to the middle; slant down to the bottom; curve left, and close; retrace to the bottom, and swing up.
[Uphill; down, around, close, and up.]

t — Go uphill to the top; retrace down, and swing up. Make a crossbar in the middle.
[Uphill high; down, and up. Cross.]

u — Go uphill to the middle; retrace down, and curve right; slant up to the middle; retrace down, and swing up.
[Uphill; down, around, up, down, and up.]

v — Go overhill; slant down to the bottom, and curve right; slant up to the middle; and sidestroke right.
[Overhill; down, around, up, and sidestroke.]

w — Go uphill to the middle; retrace down, and curve right; slant up to the middle; retrace down, and curve right; slant up to the middle; and sidestroke right.
[Uphill; down, around, up, down, around, up again, and sidestroke.]

x — Go overhill; slant down right to the bottom, and swing up. Cross through the letter with a slant down left.
[Overhill; slant down right, and up. Cross down left.]

y — Go overhill; slant down to the bottom, and curve right; slant up to the middle; retrace down to halfway below the bottom; and loop left up through the bottom line.
[Overhill; down, around, up, down under water, loop up left, and through.]

z — Go overhill; curve down right to the bottom; curve down right again to halfway below the bottom; and loop left up through the bottom line.
[Overhill; around down, around again, and down under water, loop up left, and through.]

Figure 5–3 (cont.). D'Nealian Numbers and Letters.

Capital Cursive Letter Descriptions

Start at the top; curve down left to the bottom; curve up right to the beginning, and close; retrace down, and swing up.
[Top start; around down, close up, down, and up.]

Start at the top; slant down to the bottom, retrace up; curve down right to the middle; curve down right again to the bottom; curve up left; touch; sidestroke right, and stop.
[Top start; down, up, around halfway, around again, touch, sidestroke, and stop.]

Start a little below the top; curve up left to the top; curve down left to the bottom; and curve up right.
[Start below the top; curve up, around, down, and up.]

Start at the top; slant down to the bottom; curve left, and loop right; curve up right to the beginning; close; loop right, swing up, and stop.
[Top start; down, loop right, curve up, around, close, loop right, through, and stop.]

Start a little below the top; curve up left to the top; curve down left to the middle; curve down left again to the bottom; and curve up right.
[Start below the top; curve up, around to the middle, around again to the bottom, and up.]

Start a little below the top; slant down to the bottom, and curve up left; sidestroke right. Make an overhill-underhill crossbar at the top; and a straight crossbar in the middle.
[Start below the top; down, around, up, and sidestroke. Wavy cross and a straight cross.]

Start at the bottom; go uphill to the top; loop left down to the middle, and swing up; slant down to the bottom; curve up left, across the uphill; sidestroke right, and stop.
[Bottom start; uphill high, loop through the middle, up, curve down, around, through the uphill, sidestroke, and stop.]

Start a little below the top; curve up right to the top; slant down to the bottom. Start again at the top, to the right of the first start; slant down to the bottom; retrace up halfway; curve left, touch, loop right, swing up, and stop.
[Start below the top; make a cane. Top start, to the right; down, up, left, touch, loop right, through, and stop.]

Start a little below the middle; sidestroke left; curve down right to the bottom; go uphill to the top; loop left down to the bottom, and swing up.
[Start below the middle; sidestroke left, curve down, around, uphill high, loop down, and up.]

Start at the bottom; curve up left to the top; loop right down to halfway below the bottom line; loop up left, and through.
[Bottom start; curve up, around, touch on the way down under water, loop up left, and through.]

Start a little below the top; curve up right to the top; slant down to the bottom. Start again at the top, to the right of the first start; slant down left to the middle, and touch; slant down right to the bottom, and swing up.
[Start below the top; make a cane. Top start, to the right; slant down left, touch, slant down right, and up.]

Start a little below the top; curve up right to the top; loop left, and keep going down to the bottom; curve left; loop right, and swing up.
[Start below the top; uphill; loop down, loop right, and up.]

Start a little below the top; curve up right to the top; slant down to the bottom; retrace up, and make a hill to the right; retrace up; make another hill to the right, and swing up.
[Start below the top; make a cane, up over the hill, up over the hill again, and up.]

Start a little below the top; curve up right to the top; slant down to the bottom; retrace up; make a hill to the right, and swing up.
[Start below the top; make a cane, up over the hill, and up.]

Start at the top; curve down left to the bottom; curve up right to the beginning, and close; loop right, swing up, and stop.
[Top start; around down, close up, loop right, through, and stop.]

Start at the top; slant down to the bottom; retrace up; curve down right to the middle; curve left, and close.
[Top start; down, up, around halfway, and close.]

Start a little below the top; curve up right to the top; curve down right to the bottom; loop right, and swing up.
[Start below the top; curve up, around, down, loop right, and up.]

Start at the top; slant down to the bottom; retrace up; curve down right to the middle; curve left, and close; slant down right to the bottom, and swing up.
[Top start; down, up, around halfway, close, slant down right, and up.]

Start at the bottom; go uphill to the top; loop left down to the middle, curve down right to the bottom; curve up left, across the uphill, sidestroke right, and stop.
[Bottom start; uphill high, loop through the middle, curve down, around, through the uphill, sidestroke, and stop.]

Start a little below the top; slant down to the bottom, and curve up left; sidestroke right. Make an overhill-underhill crossbar at the top.
[Start below the top; down, around, up, and sidestroke. Wavy cross.]

Start a little below the top; curve up right to the top; slant down to the bottom, and curve right; slant up to the top; retrace down, and swing up.
[Start below the top; make a cane, around, up, down, and up.]

Start a little below the top; curve up right to the top; slant down to the bottom, and curve right; slant up right to the top; sidestroke right, and stop.
[Start below the top; make a cane, around, slant up right, sidestroke, and stop.]

Start a little below the top; curve up right to the top; slant down to the bottom, and curve right; slant up to the top; retrace down, and curve right; slant up to the top; sidestroke right, and stop.
[Start below the top; make a cane, around, up, down, around, up again, sidestroke, and stop.]

Start a little below the top; curve up right to the top; slant down right to the bottom, and swing up. Cross through the letter with a slant down left.
[Start below the top; curve up, slant down right, and up. Cross down left.]

Start a little below the top; curve up right to the top; slant down to the bottom, and curve right; slant up to the top, retrace down to halfway below the bottom line; loop up left, and through.
[Start below the top; make a cane, around, up, down under water, loop up left, and through.]

Start a little below the top; curve up right to the top; curve down right to the bottom; curve down right again to halfway below the bottom line; loop up left, and through.
[Start below the top; curve up, around, down, around again, and down under water, loop up left, and through.]

Figure 5-3 (cont.). D'Nealian Numbers and Letters.

Figure 5-4. Journal entry of Philip, a third-grade student.

difficulties in handwriting. For example, on occasion the teacher substituted oral book reports for written ones and encouraged Philip to work on assignments with a peer who did the majority of the writing. Although laptop computers can be vital for the success of students like Philip, compensatory devices are not substitutes for carefully designed handwriting programs (Bain, 1991).

Left-Handed Writers

Students who write with their left hand often require some special adjustments. Howell (1978) presented the following three instructional considerations. First, have students who write with their left hand hold the pencil about an inch farther back than right-handed writers do. Do not encourage them to hook the wrist when writing, but if they write successfully in this fashion, do not attempt to reeducate them (Polloway & Patton, 1993). Second, have students slant their papers slightly to the right when writing with cursive. Finally, permit these writers to slant their letters in a way that allows for comfortable writing. As noted by Tompkins (1994), many left-handed writers write letters vertically or with a slight backward slant.

Readiness Activities

Some young children may not have developed the prerequisite motor skills needed for handwriting. For these students, provide activities that focus upon the development of necessary fine-motor and visual-motor skills. Readiness skills can be developed through activities such as cutting, tracing, coloring, and copying shapes (Salend, 1994). Mercer and

Mercer (1993) suggested that prior to formal handwriting instruction a student should be able to: (a) trace geometric shapes and lines; (b) connect dots on paper; (c) draw horizontal and vertical lines; (d) draw a backward circle, a curved line, and a forward circle; (e) draw slanted lines; (f) copy simple shapes; and (g) note likenesses and differences in letter forms. For most students, however, it may be argued that focusing on readiness activities simply takes away time from direct instruction in handwriting (Polloway & Patton, 1993) as the prerequisite skills can actually be developed within drawing and writing activities.

Simply encouraging children to color and draw can help them develop the motor skills necessary for handwriting. Errol, a first-grade student, was resistant to writing, although he liked to draw. Initially, his teacher allowed him to work on his drawings during writing time. After 1 month, Errol began to want to place a title on his pictures, and soon thereafter he began to put his thoughts on paper. Figure 5-5 illustrates Errol's portrayal of his superheroes. For this illustration, he wanted to label each character.

Several readiness exercises that involve writing have been described by Giordano (1983a, 1983b, 1984). These activities can be used with students with handwriting difficulties, as well as with reluctant writers.

1. Scribbling. Prepare a student for the motor movements needed in handwriting through scribbling. Provide different mediums, such as finger-paints, pencils, and crayons.
2. Imitation. Have the student copy words or part of words in manuscript. Use different sources, including the transcription of some of the student's dialogue.
3. Tracing. Write several sentences that are dictated by the student. Have the student choose one or two words and trace over them with a yellow marker.
4. Completion. While writing a sentence, read the words aloud and pause before the last word. Have the student choose an appropriate response from two or three word cards.
5. Automatic writing. Select a word that can be written automatically by the student. Have the student write the word in different situations such as next to selected items in a list

Figure 5–5. An illustration by Errol, a first-grade student.

or catalogue, or next to a sentence or picture to show preference.

Kurtz (1994) describes several common problems that may interfere with handwriting, including: (a) uncertain hand dominance, (b) immature pencil grasp, (c) posture, (d) poor stability or positioning of the paper, (e) difficulty copying from the chalkboard, and (f) problems with spatial organization. She recommends several instructional strategies, described below, that may help children with motor learning difficulties.

Hand Preference

Prior to formal handwriting instruction, a few students need assistance in establishing hand preference. If a preferred hand has not been identified by first grade, the teacher should determine the hand that is better coordinated. If the more skilled hand is not readily identified, the teacher may consult with an occupational therapist. Initially, the child may wear jewelry on that hand as a reminder of which hand to use when writing. Because many children with delayed hand dominance have trouble crossing the midline of the body, papers should be placed on the same side of the desk as the preferred hand.

Pencil Grasp

Some students with low muscle tone often persist in using ineffective pencil grips. They use their shoulders and elbows to control the pencil, rather than their fingers. In general, these children benefit from a variety of sensorimotor activities and exercises. Examples of activities include: (a) tracing around stencils or templates, (b) drawing in clay with a stylus, (c) drawing on sand or carbon paper, or (d) writing while standing at a chalkboard. Kurtz notes that one of the best chalkboard activities for encouraging proper hand position is to present students with work that is slightly below eye level.

Two pencil grips have been found effective. The pencil may be held lightly between the thumb and first two fingers, with the index finger placed on top of the pencil. The pencil rests upon the first knuckle of the middle finger. Or, as an alternative, a student may prefer the D'Nealian pencil grip. For this grip, the pencil is held between the index and middle fingers with about a 25-degree slant. The two fingers and thumb grip the pencil about one half inch above the point.

Posture

Poor posture can also contribute to handwriting difficulties. Posture can often be improved by providing the child with the proper size chair and desk. The child should have a chair that has a flat back and seat so that he or she may maintain a symmetrical body position. The child's feet should rest flat on the floor and the desk height should be slightly above the elbows so that both forearms can rest comfortably on the desk. As a rule, the child should be able to move his or her writing arm smoothly and easily across the paper.

Paper Positioning

The position of the paper can also affect legibility. Some students have difficulty positioning their papers on their desks. These students may benefit from taping the paper in the correct position or using a clipboard until they learn to position the paper at the correct angle automatically. If the student has trouble stablilizing the paper, a large sheet of construction paper can be taped on the desk to keep the paper from slipping. Students who avoid crossing the midline may be helped by slanting the paper toward the dominant hand or placing the paper to the side of their midline. When writing cursive, right-handed students typically slant the paper to the left, whereas left-handed students slant the paper to the right.

Copying from the Chalkboard

In general, students who have difficulty copying from the chalkboard should not be required to copy large amounts of material. When copying is necessary, they should be seated as close to the material to be copied as possible. For some students, teachers may: (a) reduce the amount of material to be copied from the board, (b) use colored chalk to highlight certain words or phrases, (c) provide a printed copy of the assignment on their desk to copy from near point, or (d) have a peer provide a carbon copy of the assignment.

Spatial Organization

Students with problems in spatial organization may have difficulty writing letters on the appropriate lines. They often have trouble organizing their writing neatly on the paper. These students may benefit from highlighting the lines on the paper with colored markers or, in some instances, using paper with raised lines. Students with severe difficulties may benefit from use of a cardboard frame that forces the pencil to stop when it hits the top or bottom of the line. For students who fail to observe margins, a piece of clear tape may be placed along the sides of the paper as a reminder to stop writing.

Letter Formation

This writing business. Pencils and what-not. Over-rated, if you ask me. Silly stuff. Nothing in it.

— A. A. Milne

Many workbooks exist that provide students with practice in letter formation. These exercises, however, often do not provide sufficient instruction to result in fluent, legible handwriting (Smith, 1994). For teaching letter formation, use of a combination of instructional methods appears to be superior to any one technique (Graham, 1983). With these techniques, direct instruction includes modeling, practice, self-evaluation, and provision of feedback.

Instructional methods typically begin with letter forms, and then gradually progress to writing words, short phrases, and finally sentences (Smith, 1994). All of the methods contain a number of systematic steps and many of them are multisensory. Multisensory (visual-auditory-kinesthetic-tactile) strategies may be most effective for teaching correct letter formation (Kurtz, 1994). The major instructional goal of these methods is to help children form letters easily and automatically.

Fauke Approach

Some students with learning disabilities need more intensive instruction when learning to form letters than do their peers without disabilities. Fauke, Burnett, Powers, and Sulzer-Azaroff (1973) described a procedure for teaching beginning writers how to form letters that has built-in systematic instruction. The procedure consists of the following steps:

1. Model correct letter formation.
2. Discuss formation and the production of the letter with the student.
3. Have the student name the letter.
4. Have the student trace the letter with his or her finger.

5. Have the student trace the letter with a pencil.
6. Have the student trace the letter with a magic marker.
7. Make the letter form from yarn.
8. Have the student trace the yarn letter with his or her finger.
9. Ask the student to write the letter while looking at the model.
10. Have the student write the letter from memory.
11. Reward the student for correctly formed letters.
12. Have the student repeat all steps as necessary.

Progressive Approximation Approach

Even when a student has mastered the majority of letter formations, some letters continue to be problematic for some individuals. Hofmeister (1973) described a procedure designed to help the student recognize and correct errors in letter formation. The following steps are used:

1. Have the student copy the letter with a pencil.
2. Examine the letter and correct any errors by marking over the error with a highlighter.
3. Have the student erase any incorrect lines.
4. Tell the student to trace over the correctly formed letter.
5. Ensure that the student repeats all steps until the letter is correctly formed on the initial try.

Self-Guided Symbol Formation Strategy

Graham and Madan (1981) described an intensive remedial method for helping a student master the formation of a particular letter. The procedure is practiced on lined paper and can be used with either cursive or manuscript writing. The strategy consists of the following five steps:

1. Identify the letter that the student typically forms incorrectly. Ask the student to write a sample sentence that contains all of the letters, such as: *The quick brown fox jumps over the lazy dog.*
2. Select one letter that the student has trouble forming. Model the correct letter formation

with a crayon, marker, or chalk. Write the letter again while verbally describing the process. Continue until the student can repeat the verbal description with the teacher.

3. Have the student trace the letter until he or she can verbalize the steps alone. If needed, guide the student's tracing through the use of arrows or colored dots. Encourage the student to act as his or her own instructor, by defining the task, correcting errors, and praising accurate letter formation. Continue with step 3 until the student can copy the letter five times correctly.

4. Describe the formation of the target letter while the student attempts to visualize and write the letter. Provide corrective feedback. Continue until the student can write the letter five times from memory.

5. Have the student practice the target letter in meaningful contexts. Begin with practice of single words, phrases, and then sentences.

Furner Approach

An alternative multisensory approach was described by Furner (1969). The following steps are used:

1. Establish a purpose for the lesson and involve the student in the activity.
2. Provide numerous guided exposures to the letter.
3. Have the student write the letter while describing the process.
4. Have the student visualize the letter as you write it and describe the process.
5. Teach the letter form by simultaneously having the student focus on the letter, state aloud the letter formation process, and write the letter.
6. Have the student compare the written letter with a model provided by you.

Fernald Method

A widely used approach that has proven successful for numerous students was described by Fernald in 1943. This multisensory method for teaching letter formation reinforces learning through tracing. To use the method, the teacher follows these steps:

1. Ask the student to watch you as you write the letter in crayon on an index card.
2. Have the student trace the letter numerous times, while saying the letter name.
3. When the student feels ready, ask him or her to turn over the card and form the letter properly from memory.

Gillingham and Stillman

Some students enjoy writing on a chalkboard and the kinesthetic feedback from the movement of the chalk on the board may help with memory. Gillingham and Stillman (1973) incorporated a chalkboard into their multisensory approach that involves tracing, writing, and saying the letter name. The following steps are used:

1. Write a letter on the chalkboard. Model correct letter formation as you say the letter name.
2. Have the student trace the letter while saying the letter name. Have the student continue to trace until he or she is comfortable with formation and knows the letter name.
3. Have the student copy the letter while saying the letter name.
4. Have the student write the letter from memory while saying the name.

VAKT Approach

Students need varying amounts of repetition when learning letter forms. Choosing a method must, therefore, be dictated by individual needs. The best method will be the one that provides sufficient practice for learning to occur but not so much that the student becomes bored. For individuals in need of more support, Graham and Miller (1980) described a multisensory approach, similar to the Fernald method, that involves systematic repetition and practice. The following steps are used:

1. Write the letter with a crayon while the student observes.
2. Say the name of the letter with the student.
3. Have the student say the name of the letter while tracing it with his or her index finger.
4. Repeat step 3 until the student is successful on five consecutive trials.

5. Have the student write the letter while looking at the model.
6. Repeat step 5 until the student copies the letter successfully three times.
7. Have the student say the name of the letter while writing it from memory.
8. Repeat step 7 until the student has written the letter successfully three times.

Niedermeyer Approach

An alternative approach involving systematic repetition was described by Niedermeyer (1973). Before initiating the method, the teacher prepares a dotted representation of the letter to be learned. These steps are then followed:

1. Give the student a dotted representation of the target letter.
2. Have the student trace over the dots.
3. Repeat steps 1 and 2 with the student 12 times.
4. Have the student copy the letter.
5. Repeat step 4 with the student 12 times.
6. Pronounce the letter name while the student writes the letter.

D'Nealian

Not all methods are geared toward manuscript letters. For example, Thurber (1983) described a six-step procedure for teaching letter formation using manu-cursive or D'Nealian letters, presented in Figure 5–3. This method introduces letters in groups of similar formation and incorporates visual, auditory, tactile, and kinesthetic modalities. The following steps are used:

Step 1:
  a. Tell the student what letter will be formed (e.g., "Now, we will make the letter _____.").
Step 2:
  a. Make eye contact with the student.
  b. Orally state the directions (e.g., "up," "around," "down," etc.) for writing the letter while simultaneously writing the word in the air. If facing the student, write the word backwards, so that the child can see the correct formation of the letter.

Step 3:
  a. Have the student repeat the directions while you trace the letter in the air.
Step 4:
  a. When letter formation is mastered, have the student practice writing the letters on paper with a marker or pencil.
  b. Have the student write the letter with a few other letters in groups of three; two or three different groups may be needed for learning the correct formation.
  c. Have the student repeat the directions for the letter when writing.

At this point, ask the student not to erase but simply to cross out errors and practice again so that progress can be seen. Students should know that when they practice something, new mistakes are expected as part of the learning process.

Step 5:
  a. Trace the letter on the student's arm, hand, or back with a finger while saying the directions. Repeat this step if necessary.
Step 6:
  a. Have the student trace the letter on your hand and say the directions.
  b. When the student succeeds, check to see if he or she has memorized the letter's formation. Do this by saying the directions and tracing the letter inaccurately on the child's hand. Encourage the student to indicate the error.

Self-Instructional Procedure

Some students learn easier and faster when a visual method of teaching is used. Other students excel with a kinesthetic method. Still others prefer to rely upon their memorization of the oral directions of letter formation. Graham (1983) described a procedure that emphasizes the audio directions. The following steps are used:

1. Based on the student's needs, select a letter.
2. Write the letter as the student watches closely.
3. Describe the movements that are made when the letter is formed.
3. Have the student repeat the verbalization of the steps of letter formation.

4. Repeat steps 1–3 two more times.
5. Form the letter while describing the mechanics of the process.
6. Repeat step 5 until the student can verbalize the movements of the process in unison with the teacher.
7. Have the student trace the letter with his or her index finger while verbalizing the process with the teacher.
8. Repeat step 7 until the student can trace the letter and verbalize the steps simultaneously.
9. Trace the letter with a pencil while:
   —defining the task ("I have to write the letter 'a'")
   —verbally directing the process ("I have to start on the midline")—correcting errors as they occur ("No, that's not on the midline")
   —self-reinforcing ("That's a good curve").
10. Model step 9 both with and without errors.
11. Continue until the student can imitate the steps of the strategy successfully.
12. Have the student continue to use the procedure until the process is repeated successfully three times.
13. Describe the steps of the letter formation while the student writes it.
14. Repeat step 13 until the student can write the letter from memory successfully three times.

Hanover Cursive Writing Method

Even though no rule exists about the order for introducing letters, some type of consistent sequence is likely to benefit students with learning disabilities. Hanover (1983) believed that cursive letters are learned easier and faster when similarly formed letters are presented and practiced in the following order:

1. e, l, h, f, b, k
2. b, o, v, w
3. n, s, y
4. c, a, d, o, q, g
5. n, m, v, y, x
6. f, q
7. g, p, y, z

Some letters are included in more than one letter family. Once one group has been mastered, instruction progresses to the next. Once the lowercase letters are learned, uppercase letters are introduced in groups.

Sequence for Instruction in Manuscript and Cursive Letters

Polloway and Patton (1993) described sequential groupings for introducing both lowercase and uppercase manuscript and cursive forms. The letters are grouped by common features:

Manuscript lowercase.
1. o a d g q
2. b p
3. c e
4. t l i k
5. r n m h
6. v w
7. x y
8. f j
9. u
10. z
11. s

Manuscript uppercase.
1. L H T E F I
2. J U
3. P R B D K
4. A M N V W X Y Z
5. S
6. O Q C G

Cursive lowercase.
1. i u w t j
2. a d g q
3. n m x y v
4. r s p
5. c e
6. o z
7. b f h k l

Cursive uppercase.
1. N M H K U V Y W X Q Z
2. P B R
3. T F
4. C E

5. A
6. D
7. G
8. I
9. L
10. O
11. S
12. J

Polloway and Patton further suggest that teachers be consistent in their use of terminology, using "lowercase" and "uppercase" to describe letters.

Handwriting without Tears

Several commercial programs are available to assist students with the development of handwriting skill. One example is Handwriting without Tears (Olsen, 1994). The program is comprehensive, relatively inexpensive, and provides instruction in readiness, printing, and cursive. Readiness activities are presented using wood pieces that represent big and little curves and big and little lines. The program is developmentally based and can assist students who have difficulty with legibility, spacing, or reversals. The materials for printing and cursive instruction include both teacher guides and student workbooks.

Reversals

Although reversals are common before the age of 6 or 7, a few students continue to reverse letters beyond these ages. When second- and third-grade students still reverse letters in writing, efforts should be made to remedy the problem (Gearheart & Gearheart, 1989). If the problem is persistent or interrupts the student's train of thought, a variety of instructional strategies may be used to help a student reduce or eliminate reversals. In general, avoid excessive attention to reversals so that students do not become overanxious (Rhodes & Dudley-Marling, 1988). Treat reversals as minor spelling errors that will be corrected during the editing stage.

General Strategies

Students who reverse letters benefit from direct intervention (Bos & Vaughn, 1994). The following list of principles and strategies has been adapted from several sources (Gearheart & Gearheart, 1989; Kampwirth, 1983; Mather & Jaffe, 1992; McCarney & Cummins, 1988; Meese, 1994):

1. Do not emphasize timed writing activities, as reversals are more frequent in this type of activity.
2. Help the student create a list of the more common words containing the reversal(s).
3. Teach common words that contain the problematic letters though a VAKT approach. Have the student vocalize the individual letter sounds instead of the whole word.
4. Encourage the student to use the list of common words as a reference during every writing assignment.
5. Draw directional arrows under letters or words that tend to be reversed.
6. For a younger student, print the words frequently reversed in two colors: the first letter in green, and the rest of the word in red. Remind the student to observe the traffic sign colors.
7. Write the commonly reversed letters or words on a transparency. Put a green dot where the student is to begin forming the letter or word, directional arrows throughout, and a red dot at where to stop. Project the image onto the chalkboard and have the student trace over it. On a daily basis, have the student trace over the stimulus several times.
8. Use a multisensory method to overteach a simple, common word beginning with one of the problematic letters. For example, if a student reverses *b* and *d*, teach *dad* and point out that all three letters are formed in the same way. Encourage the student to think of the word (e.g., "dad") when uncertain as to letter formation.
9. Use visual clues for teaching the student the forms of frequently confused letters. For example, show the student that the letter *b* can be formed with the fingers of the left hand and *d* with the right. Tell the student that because the alphabet is written from left to right and *b* comes first in the alphabet, *b* is the letter made with the left hand. Because the letter *d* comes after *b*, it is made with the right hand.
10. Have the student trace problematic words. Provide different surfaces (e.g., sandpaper, jello, fur).

11. Encourage the student to use cursive, not manuscript, as reversals appear less frequently in cursive.

12. Do not penalize the student for reversals, but reinforce the correct letter formations.

13. During the editing stage, give the student an index card with the problematic letter or word written on it. Have the student check formation.

14. Help the student recall the orientation of letters by using language clues. For example, remind the student that a lowercase "b" is just an uppercase "B" that lost its top.

15. To reduce reversals, have the student name the letter and state aloud the movement pattern made when writing a frequently reversed letter. For example, when forming the letter *b*, the student may say: "start high, line down, back up and around."

16. Place a manuscript alphabet at the student's desk so that the child may self-check letters when editing.

17. Provide separate instruction for frequently reversed letters. Practice *b* and *d* on different occasions.

18. Show the student how to trace confusing letters by writing the cursive form of the letter over the manuscript form. A cursive *b* will fit nicely over a printed *b* but not a printed *d*.

19. Teach the student that the letter *b* has a hump on its right side, the letter *d* has a hump on its left side, and the letter *p* has a tail that goes down.

20. Write a cue word and provide an illustration for any commonly reversed letters, such the letter *b* with a picture of a boy, and the letter *d* with a picture of a dog. Have the student keep the words on the corner of his or her desk or in a spelling dictionary.

Single-Symbol Procedure

Some students only have difficulty remembering the orientation of a few letters. The single-symbol procedure, adapted from Heydorn (1984), may be used to practice single symbols. The following steps are used:

1. Write very large letters or symbols on a piece of paper or the chalkboard.

2. Have the student trace over the letter or symbol 5 to 10 times while saying the letter or number and tracing. Monitor the tracing, correcting any errors as they occur.

3. Present the student with a jumbled number of letters/symbols in various orientations on a piece of paper.

4. Have the student circle the correct form of the letter or number.

5. Have a small group of children participate in a game whereby one student writes a problematic letter or number and another names it. When an error is made, ask one student to identify and correct the error.

6. Use a mnemonic device to distinguish between difficult-to-remember letters or numbers (e.g., teach that the upward strokes in *b* and *d* form the headboards in the word *bed*).

Whole-Word Procedure

In addition to reversing letters, some students form words incorrectly due to a tendency to transpose letters in words. Common examples include writing *saw* for "was" or *on* for "no." A multisensory procedure, adapted from Heydorn (1984), may be used to help students eliminate transpositions of common words. With this method, the following steps are used:

1. Have the student write the problematic word on a flash card.

2. Have the student say the word while finger-tracing it.

3. When the student feels comfortable, remove the card and ask the student to write the word from memory.

4. If the word is spelled incorrectly, repeat steps 1–3 until the correct formation has been mastered.

Copying Skill

Students who have a tendency to reverse letters often have trouble copying work from the board or from their books. Consider the four short usage assignments written by Josh, a third-grade student, presented in Figure 5–6. Josh was asked to copy sentences directly from his grammar book and to select the correct form. In addition to experiencing trouble when copying, Josh apparently did not understand the intent of the assignment. For example, instead of writing "I am angry," he wrote: *I am i are angry*. Similarly, instead of writing "These dogs," he wrote: *These Those Them Dogs*.

Josh makes four errors, despite the fact that the assignments were copied directly from his book and did not require spontaneous writing. He writes *dramed* for "drawed," inverting the "m." He reverses the "s" in "Mrs," and he omits an "i" in "visit" and the apostrophe from "my uncle's farm." In addition to difficulty with copying tasks, Josh has letter reversals and misspellings of common words in his spontaneous writing samples.

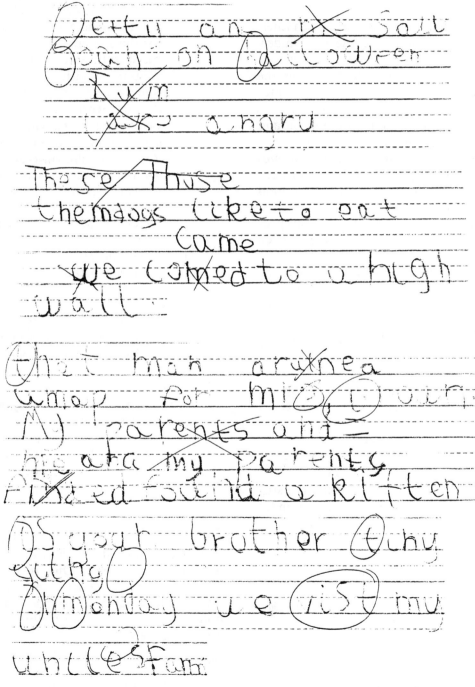

Figure 5–6. A copying exercise by Josh, a third-grade student.

Several strategies may be used to help students improve their copying skills. Kovitz (1982) presented the following strategies:

Paper-to-Paper

Level I

1. Write a sentence with enough space in between each letter so that a small button may fit underneath.
2. Draw a colored dot underneath each letter.
3. Ask the student to copy the word underneath (or to the right) of the text.
4. Have the student put the button on the dot under the first letter, say the letter aloud and copy it.
5. Have the student touch the button and say the letter aloud once more.
6. Have the student move the button onto the next dot (located under the next letter).
7. Have the student say the letter out loud and copy it.
8. Have the student continue with this procedure until the whole word has been completed.
9. Have the student slide the button into the space between two words and say "big space" as a reminder to leave a space before copying the next word.
10. Repeat the steps with the next word.

Level II

1. Eliminate the button, instructing the student to place his or her index finger on the dots to point to the letters.
2. Repeat level I procedures.

Level III

1. Eliminate the dots, instructing the student to place his or her index finger under the letter to be copied.
2. Repeat level I procedures.

Level IV

1. Eliminate the pointing.
2. Repeat level I procedures without the tactile aids.

Chalkboard-to-Paper

Level I

1. Write a sentence on the chalkboard.

2. Draw a colored dot underneath each letter.
3. Tell the student to copy the sentence on paper.
4. Point to and pronounce the first letter.
5. Have the student look at the first letter and pronounce it with the teacher.
6. Have the student copy the letter onto paper. If the activity is being conducted as a group activity, provide enough time for the student with the slowest writing speed to finish copying the letter before continuing with the next letter.
7. Repeat the procedure with each letter of the first word.
8. Before continuing with the second word, point to the space and say "big space."
9. Repeat the steps with each word until the complete sentence has been copied.
10. Repeat steps 1–9 with a new sentence. Have the student remain seated and read each letter aloud while the teacher points to it.
11. Have students repeat step 10 without teacher assistance.

Level II

1. Working independently, have the student copy each letter in sequence from the chalkboard while subvocalizing the letter.

Level III

1. When sufficient fluency and speed are achieved copying individual letters, have students repeat the procedure with two (or more) letters, followed by words, phrases, and sentences.

Fluency

As increased writing demands are placed upon students, handwriting fluency increases in importance (Larsen, 1987). One instructional goal, therefore, is to help students develop a fluid, rapid style. Practice contributes to automaticity as the motor patterns needed for legible writing become more firmly established.

Timed Writings

One technique that may be used to improve writing rate and fluency and to encourage reluctant writers to increase their productivity is daily timed writings. Several variations have been suggested.

Variation I. The first variation has been adapted from Houten, Morrison, Jarvis, and MacDonald (1974). The following steps are used:

1. Write a topic on the board.
2. Have students write about the topic for 10 minutes, trying to write more words than they did on the previous day.
3. At the end of the time period, have students count the number of words, and record the word count on the top of the paper. Do not count words from repetitious or incomplete sentences.
4. Verify the scores and record the word count on a chart.
5. If desired, rate the papers on mechanical aspects, vocabulary, number of ideas, development of ideas, and internal consistency.
6. Return the compositions with feedback.

Variation II. The second variation has been adapted from Alvarez (1983). This method may be more motivating as students choose their own topics. Sufficient knowledge of the topic will help students feel more comfortable in writing. For this procedure, the following steps are used:

1. Have students select their own topics (although the teacher may choose to select the topic occasionally as a variation).
2. Have students write on their topics for 6 minutes, during which time the teacher spells words as requested.
3. At the end of the time period, have the student count the number of words.
4. Have the student record the number of words on the top of the paper and on individual graphs.

Variation III. The motivational aspect included in the second variation of timed writing is also present in this variation, suggested by Douglass (1984). In the method, the teacher writes along with the students. Teacher participation will increase the motivation of some individuals. The following procedure is followed:

1. Have students select their own topics.
2. Spend 5 minutes writing on a topic of your choice while the students do the same.
3. Encourage the students to share their writing.

Variation IV. The following variation was adapted from several sources (Brigham, Graubard, & Stans, 1972; Rumsey & Ballard, 1985; Seabaugh & Schumaker, 1981) and incorporates some behavior modification techniques. For this procedure, the following steps are used:

1. Have students write daily for an assigned time.
2. Have them count and record the number of letters, words, or sentences.
3. Provide individual reinforcements contingent upon performance, such as points for an assigned number of letters, words, or sentences.
4. Provide students with opportunities to trade the reinforcements for various predetermined privileges.

Self-Evaluation

Self-evaluation can help students during the handwriting process. Because self-appraisal is important to all learning, teachers should encourage students to ask questions to assess their handwriting and evaluate their own skill development (Graham & Madan, 1981). These questions can be posted in the classroom or provided to students on cards where they can record their answers.

Self-Evaluation Strategy

Blandford and Lloyd (1987) described an easy-to-follow self-evaluation strategy. The following steps are used:

1. Am I sitting properly for handwriting?
2. Do I have my paper positioned properly?
3. Do I have a correct pencil grip?
4. Do all my letters seem to be on the line?
5. Do all my tall letters seem to touch or come close to touching the top line?
6. Do my short letters take up only half the space between lines?
7. Do I have the right amount of space between words?

Where necessary, or when preferred, this strategy may be expanded as follows:

1. Have the student use a card to guide handwriting.
   Add two reminders to the bottom of the card:
   a. Consult the letter chart affixed to the desk when forgetting how to form a letter.
   b. Strive for neat handwriting.
2. Read the statements and questions on the task card to the student.
3. Model how to perform each of the activities referred to in the questions:
   a. Am I sitting in the correct position?
   b. Is my paper in the correct position?
   c. Am I holding my pencil correctly?
   d. Are all my letters sitting on the line?
   e. Are all my tall letters touching, or nearly touching, the top line?
   f. Are my short letters filling only half of the space in between the lines?
   g. Am I leaving the right amount of space between words?
4. In a grid to the right of the questions, model the recording of student performance:
   a. place a check by each question followed.
   b. place an 'X' by those not followed.
5. Provide the student with practice using the task card with teacher guidance and feedback.
6. Have the student read the task card before attempting any written assignment.
7. During all written assignments, have the student follow the self-instructional questions and record performance on the grid.

Self-Evaluation Checklist

Some students prefer to use a checklist to evaluate their handwriting. Students are asked to read the questions and check a yes or no response next to each question. Figure 5–7 presents a sample handwriting evaluation scale. If desired, a more detailed checklist can be used, such as the one developed by Ruedy (1983).

Appearance

Because the appearance of assignments may influence a teacher's grading, all students can benefit from knowing what factors help to make a paper more attractive. Teachers can help students acquire this knowledge by discussing why papers should have a neat appearance, providing examples of good papers, and encouraging students to evaluate their own papers for appearance.

HOW Strategy

One strategy for evaluating the appearance of finished products is HOW (Archer, 1988). The mnemonic HOW helps students determine: HOW should your paper look? To use this strategy, students review the following elements:

H = Heading provided
1. Write your name on the paper.
2. Write the date.
3. Name the subject.
4. Write a page number if necessary.
O = Organized
1. Use only the front side of the paper.
2. Write within the left margin.
3. Write within the right margin.
4. Leave at least one blank line at the top.
5. Leave at least one blank line at the bottom.
6. Check for spacing.
W = Written Neatly
1. Check that words and/or numbers are written on the lines.
2. Write words and/or numbers neatly.
3. Check that erasures and crossed out words or numbers are neat.

Graphic Organizer

Some students may benefit from a visual depiction that illustrates how a paper should look, such as the one presented in Figure 5–8. Students can actually write drafts into this type of frame.

Conclusion

Development of legible, fluent handwriting is an important goal. Students who have trouble writing legibly often require specific remedial strategies that provide enough practice to make the actions automatic (Masters et al., 1993; Wood, 1993). In many instances, handwriting difficulties are related to inadequate instruction (Graham, 1992; Graham & Miller, 1980) as students do not engage in regular,

Name: _____

Handwriting Evaluation Scale

		YES	NO
1.	I prefer to print rather than write in cursive.		
2.	I combine print and cursive when I write.		
3.	I would like my writing to look better.		
4.	It takes a lot of energy for me to write.		
5.	Writing is hard for me.		
6.	Teachers think my writing is neat.		
7.	I have to think about handwriting too much when I write.		
8.	I write lowercase letters correctly.		
9.	I write uppercase letters correctly.		
10.	I hold my pencil too tightly.		
11.	My hand gets tired when I write.		
12.	My letters have the same slant.		
13.	My letters are formed correctly.		
14.	My letters are consistent in size.		
15.	Letters are crossed and dotted properly.		
16.	I usually like the appearance of my papers.		
17.	Writing is difficult when I use paper without lines.		
18.	I feel proud of my handwriting.		
19.	I leave the right amount of space between letters & words.		
20.	I would rather write on a computer than on paper.		

Figure 5-7. Handwriting Evaluation Scale.

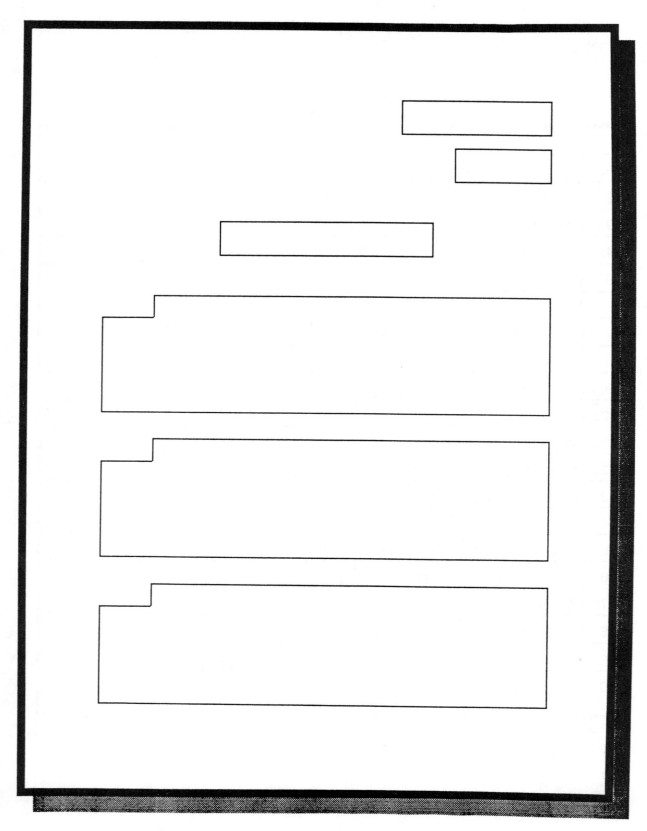

Figure 5–8. Graphic depiction of how a paper should look.

systematic practice with supervision (Hofmeister, 1973). Instructional procedures that promote proficiency and maintenance are needed for teaching all writing styles (Polloway & Patton, 1993). In general, effective handwriting programs provide repetition, review, reinforcement, and feedback.

Students with handwriting difficulties need a great deal of appropriate practice and review (Bain, 1991). Fortunately, with practice, the majority of children learn to produce a script that is in accordance with the conventions of their culture (Hamstra-Bletz & Blote, 1993).

6

BASIC SKILLS

It is a damn poor mind indeed which can think of only one way to spell a word.

—Andrew Jackson, 1833

As noted in Chapter 2, many students with learning disabilities have particular difficulties mastering basic writing skills and, consequently, require systematic interventions. With the present-day emphasis on holistic, process-oriented teaching approaches in schools, the importance of basic skills has been questioned. Many feel that any instruction in basic skills should be accomplished within natural writing tasks, whereas others believe that skill instruction is accomplished more easily out of context.

As a general rule, writing instruction is more meaningful when it is provided within a student's own written communications. Writing experience coupled with direct feedback on the types of errors made enable students to increase their writing proficiency. Students should learn to view the correction of basic skill errors, such as spelling and usage, as a courtesy to the reader (Tompkins, 1994).

This chapter discusses educational interventions for the areas of spelling, usage, and proofreading. Each section begins with a review of general instructional principles and then provides descriptions of specific instructional strategies. Although the majority of the strategies are not presented within the context of writing activities, they can be incorporated easily into the editing stage of the process approach or used as supplementary study techniques.

Spelling

'You ought to write "A Happy Birthday" on it.' '*That* was what I wanted to ask you,' said Pooh. 'Because my spelling is Wobbly. It's good spelling but it Wobbles, and the letters get in the wrong places. Would you write "A Happy Birthday" on it for me?'

—A. A. Milne

The public still places a high value on correct spelling (Krashen, 1993). Consequently, for students with severe learning disabilities, problems with mechanics cannot be disregarded (Meyer et al., 1991). Because of the pervasiveness of spelling problems among students with learning disabilities, quality spelling instruction needs to be a critical concern (Gordon, Vaughn, & Schumm, 1993).

For many students, spelling difficulty is indicative of arrest in one of the stages in spelling development (Moats, 1991b). Therefore, teachers must gear instruction to the appropriate developmental stage. As a general rule, the correction of spelling errors should be done in accordance with the student's functional level in spelling (Ariel, 1992). A student cannot move from pre-phonetic or semi-phonetic spelling to conventional spelling without going through the phonetic and transitional stages.

To become competent spellers, students must learn about the phonological segments represented in English orthography. Fortunately, many children discover the internal structure of words by experiencing numerous opportunities to interact with print (Tangel & Blachman, 1992). For these individuals, Gentry (1984, 1987) provided the following research-based recommendations for spelling instruction:

1. Do not limit spelling to formal instruction. Spelling is a language-based activity best achieved in an environment that emphasizes the functional use of language.

2. Encourage children to write. Provide opportunities for them to create and invent spellings.

3. Encourage invented spellings and phonemic segmentation, particularly with students in the early stages of learning to spell.

4. Place emphasis on expression and content versus mechanics.

5. Provide daily opportunities for students to observe, verify, and correct spelling mistakes. Make sure that students correct their own spelling tests.

6. Teach children a systematic technique for studying unknown words.

7. Provide 60 to 75 minutes of formal spelling instruction per week.

Principles

As noted previously, the current instructional focus in many classrooms is on holistic writing activities and the natural development of spelling skill. Children are provided with experiences that enable them to spell in meaningful contexts (Opitz & Cooper, 1993). In such environments, students with spelling difficulties are given opportunities to experiment with our writing system in a supportive environment where errors are seen as a natural part of learning to spell (Jimenez & Rumeau, 1989).

This type of approach has numerous benefits for the majority of students. Some students, however, require more intensive intervention. If left alone, they lack the strategies for retaining the spelling of new words (Kearney & Drabman, 1993). For example, many students with learning disabilities do not learn to spell through holistic approaches as they do not acquire spelling generalizations through random experience with word patterns (Weiss & Weiss, 1993). For these students, both traditional approaches to spelling, such as weekly spelling tests, and the idea that spelling will take care of itself if children are encouraged to write, are both fundamentally wrong (Graham, Harris, & Loynachan, 1994; Teale, 1992). Scheuermann, Jacobs, McCall, and Knies (1994) provided four reasons why traditional spelling instruction is ineffective for students who have trouble learning to spell: (a) the words targeted are often out of context and unfamiliar to the students, (b) too many words are presented for students to master, (c) no emphasis is placed on

maintenance, and (d) little emphasis is placed on transfer.

Traditionally, teachers have taught spelling through the use of weekly tests. Ms. Gowan, a second-grade teacher, follows this procedure. On Monday, she gives the entire class a pretest on a list of 10 words presented in the reading series. On Tuesday, each student receives a copy of the list. On Wednesday, students write the words 5 times each. On Thursday, students are asked to study the words at home. On Friday, she gives a posttest. Although this procedure is effective for some of the students, several students have still not mastered the words by Friday. Ms. Gowan decides that these students require a more individualized approach.

Ms. Rollins, a third-grade teacher, decides to incorporate spelling instruction into the process approach in her classroom. She abandons the weekly spelling tests and, instead, assists students with spelling as they edit their writing. She believes that as students write, they will naturally improve their skill in spelling. Although her approach is effective for the majority of students in her classroom, three of them do not appear to be progressing in accordance with her expectations. Mark, Janis, and Errol are not retaining the words reviewed in the mini-skills lesson.

As noted by Ms. Rollins, students with limited spelling skill often require considerable practice to master the spelling of words that they use in their writing. These students often benefit more from daily testing, rather than weekly testing with a list of words. Similar to Ms. Gowan, Ms. Rollins decides to create individualized spelling programs for these students.

In order for spelling skill to improve, many students with learning disabilities require intense, direct, systematic instruction that promotes full knowledge of the spelling system (Ehri, 1989; Graham & Miller, 1979). The spelling instruction can then be combined with meaningful classroom writing experiences (Uhry & Shepherd, 1993). For individuals with learning disabilities that affect spelling, Weiss and Weiss (1993) recommended the following principles for spelling instruction:

1. Require practice to the level of automatic response.
2. Use multisensory instruction.
3. Develop an individualized program.

4. Use a variety of approaches to meet the needs of specific learning styles.
5. Reinforce spelling instruction with word family groupings (e.g., when teaching the word *other*, discuss the words *mother*, *brother*, and *smother*.)
6. Provide students in instruction with specific spelling rules.

The English language is highly irregular in the spelling of words. Diamond (1994) noted that our spelling rules have become more and more archaic as our pronunciation keeps changing. He described: "As I am now rediscovering through my twin sons in the first grade, English spelling is so inconsistent that children who have learned the basic rules (insofar as there are any) still can't pronounce many written words or spell words spoken to them" (p. 108). Despite the inconsistencies, instruction in a few specific spelling rules may help some students. Figure 6–1 presents an overview of the most common English spelling rules, summarized by Weiss and Weiss (1993).

Generalization

Although learning words in isolation facilitates acquisition, to promote maintenance and generalization, students must be encouraged to use the words that they have learned to spell in their writing (Polloway & Patton, 1993). Gettinger (1984) notes teachers may help children transfer what they learn in spelling instruction to their written work by: (a) teaching words that demonstrate specific generalizations systematically, (b) teaching children to examine the words they are learning in terms of their spelling patterns and then relating them to other words with similar phonograms, and (c) providing students with opportunities to practice their spelling words in written contexts such as sentences. In addition, systematic instruction in phonology, morphology, and context will help these students develop their understanding of English orthography. This knowledge then contributes to improved spelling skill.

Feedback on Errors

One important instructional principle is that students should not be penalized for poor spelling on first drafts. Anderson (1992) suggested that after students write an essay test or a reaction paper, they can underline all of the words that they think may

be misspelled. This procedure encourages students to use appropriate vocabulary, rather than just the words they know how to spell. All in-class written products are considered to be rough drafts. As noted in the discussion of the writing process approach, correct spelling is only important on final drafts (Rhodes & Dudley-Marling, 1988). In addition, if correct spelling is not the goal of the assignment, it should not be part of the grading criterion.

Unfortunately, students often are punished for poor spelling on content area assignments. Consider Steven, an eighth-grade student and history expert with poor spelling skills. When asked to explain his failing history grades, he commented that his teacher marked any answer that was not spelled perfectly as incorrect. Examination of his tests confirmed that Steven's failing grades were the result of poor spelling, rather than lack of content knowledge.

Similarly, Jane, a sixth-grade student with spelling difficulties, was graded on her spelling rather than on her knowledge. Jane completed the worksheet presented in Figure 6–2 from her grammar book. For this assignment, she was asked to select whether the verb in the sentence should be "do" or "does." Although only one response was incorrect, she received a failing grade based upon incorrect spelling. Clearly, students such as Steven and Jane have been evaluated unfairly.

Individualized Instruction

Students with learning disabilities often require individualized instruction using specific techniques and ongoing evaluation. A variety of word study strategies and self-questioning strategies may be taught to improve skill (Gordon et al., 1993). By using information gained about a student's spelling performance, techniques can be identified to assist each student increase spelling skill (Graham & Miller, 1979).

Spelling Lists

Flow List

One way to orchestrate an individualized spelling program is to use a flow list, or a list that evolves with mastery, as opposed to a fixed list, or a list that never changes. The purpose of using a spelling flow list is to provide systematic instruction and review in order to promote mastery of spelling words.

Rules of Spelling

Why teach spelling rules?

Because they make language more consistent and predictable. If a student can recall a rule or can remember one word that represents an example how that rule works, it will be easier for him to monitor his spelling errors or avoid them. The young adult can probably learn rules now that he wasn't ready for earlier.

Rules should always be verbalized when they are applied. The process of verbalization helps reinforce recall.

As vocabulary spelling words are introduced, the principles of syllabication and the rules of spelling must be introduced appropriately, not just as a list of rules to be memorized.

Silent -e: Words ending in silent **e**, drop the **e** before a suffix beginning with a vowel, but do not drop the **e** before a suffix beginning with a consonant, e.g., *hope, hoping, hopeful; excite, excited, excitement.*

Regular plurals: The most common way of forming the plural of nouns is to add **s** to the singular: *dog, dogs; elephant, elephants; table, tables.*

Plurals of nouns ending in s, x, z, ch, sh are formed by adding **es** to the singular: *gas, gases; torch, torches; tax, taxes; thrush, thrushes.*

Plural of nouns ending in y after a vowel are formed by adding **s** to the singular: *boy, boys; play, plays.* BUT *nouns ending in y after a consonant* form the plural by changing the **y** to **i** and adding **es**: *lady, ladies; baby, babies.*

Plurals of nouns ending in o, add **s** if the **o** follows a vowel: *studio, studios; shampoo, shampoos. But* add **es** if the **o** follows a consonant: *domino, dominoes; potato, potatoes; tomato, tomatoes.*

Plural of nouns ending in f or fe form their plurals regularly by adding **s**: *roof, roofs; fife, fifes.* BUT some nouns ending in **f** or **fe** form their plurals irregularly by changing the **f** to **v** and adding **es**: *leaf, leaves; knife, knives.*

Figure 6–1. Spelling rules.

Note. From *Formulas to Read and Write* (p. 106), by M. S. Weiss and H. G. Weiss, 1993, Avon, CO: Treehouse Associates. Copyright 1993 by Treehouse Associates. Reprinted by permission.

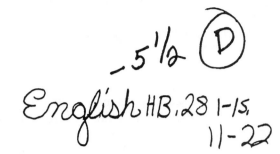

-5½ Ⓓ

English HB. 28 1-15,
11-22

1. Do they always arrive on time?
2. ~~Does~~ She make candy for everyone?
3. ~~Does~~ he want to go with us?
4. Do birds migrate?
5. Do plants need water?
6. ~~Does~~ light help a plant to make food?
7. ~~Does~~ the train stop here every day?
8. Do bears eat both plants and animals?
9. ~~Does~~ rain fall from a ~~cloud~~?
10. ~~Does~~ Patricia go to work every day?
11. Do mice eat cheese?
12. Do Carlos and Zelda ride a bus to school?
13. ~~Does~~ Mother often go to help out in school?
14. ~~Does~~ Jerry and Red like to eat eggs?
15. ~~Does~~ Clarence like to put jelly on his sandwiches?

Figure 6–2. A grammar assignment by Jane, a sixth-grade student.

The spelling list changes as the student learns to spell each word. An example form is presented in Figure 6–3. The following steps have been adapted from McCoy and Prehm (1987):

1. Help the student identify three to six words that he or she uses in writing, but spells incorrectly. Words for the flow list may be taken from a student's writing or from a high-frequency word list, such as those presented in the next section.
2. List the words on the spelling flow list form.
3. Have the student study the words with a strategy and then test the student on the words.
4. Mark each correctly spelled word with a "C" and incorrect words with a check.
5. Provide daily testing and practice with the words.
6. When a word is spelled correctly 3 days in a row, cross it off the list and add a new word.
7. Provide periodic review as needed.
8. Have students file mastered words alphabetically into a word bank. Provide periodic review of the words to ensure retention.

Struthers, Bartlamay, Bell, and McLaughlin (1994) investigated the use of an Add-A-Word spelling program with special education students. In this program, students had individualized words and used flow instead of fixed spelling lists. When a spelling was correct on three consecutive daily tests, the word was replaced by another. The dropped words were retested at a later date, and when mastery was demonstrated they were removed permanently from the list. The results of the study indicated that this type of procedure was more effective for these students than traditional weekly spelling tests.

High-Frequency Lists

Many students with learning disabilities need specific assistance in developing a basic core vocabulary of high-frequency words for writing (Graham et al., 1994). High-frequency word lists contain the most common words used in writing.

Spelling for Writing List. This basic spelling list of 335 words was compiled by Graham et al. (1994). The list, presented in Figure 6–4, includes the words most frequently used by primary-grade children in their writing. It was generated from the most commonly occurring words on four different vocabulary lists. Each word was assigned a grade placement based on difficulty level. This list of high-frequency writing words may be used by poor spellers and students with learning disabilities at both the primary and intermediate grade levels. Although the words are ordered by grade level, they can be reordered to illustrate specific phonics principles (Graham et al., 1994).

Instant Words. The 300 Instant Words list (Fry, 1980), presented in Figure 6–5, contains 60% of the words that make up all of written language. This list may be used to teach students high-frequency spelling words. Identify which words the student knows and does not know how to spell. Establish a program to help the student master the spellings of the unknown words.

An expanded list, containing 1,000 Instant Words (Fry, Polk, & Fountoukidis, 1984) is presented in Figure 6–6. These words make up about 90% of the words used in written material. A space is provided by each word so that it may be checked off after it has been learned.

Personalized Spelling Dictionaries. Many students with spelling difficulties can benefit from keeping an individualized spelling dictionary that contains their own frequently misspelled words. Each letter of the alphabet is written in order on a separate page. Students then write words in their dictionary that they use in their writing, but have difficulty spelling. They may then consult their dictionaries when writing or during the editing stage.

Scheuermann et al. (1994) described the following process for making and using a personal spelling dictionary: (a) obtain a pocket-size notebook, (b) tab the pages in alphabetical order, and (c) if desired, laminate each page. Students may then write words on file folder labels to allow for easy removal once they have been learned. As an alternative, students can use *A Spelling Dictionary for Beginning Writers* (Hurray, 1993). This dictionary contains the words most commonly used by novice writers.

Word Study Methods with a Visual Emphasis

Students who have difficulty with retention of visual orthographic patterns will often benefit from a method that emphasizes the visual features in a word (Mather, 1991). The majority of these techniques

Name _____

Spelling Flow List

Study Words	M	T	W	T	F	M	T	W	T	F	M	T	W	T	F

c = Correct
✓ = Incorrect

Figure 6–3. A chart for spelling flow lists.

Spelling for Writing List

Grade 1 Word List

a	day*	into*	play*
all	did	is	ran
am	do	it*	red
and*	dog*	its*	ride
at	for*	let	run
ball	fun*	like*	see
be	get*	look	she
bed	go	man	so
big	good*	may	stop
book	got*	me*	the*
box	had*	my*	this
boy*	he*	no*	to
but	her*	not	two*
came*	him*	of	up
can*	his*	oh	us
car	home*	old	was*
cat	I*	on*	we*
come*	if	one*	will*
dad	in*	out*	yes
			you*

Grade 2 Word List

about*	door	help	mother*	school*	time*
after	down*	here*	much	sea	today*
an*	each	hit	must	ship	told
any	eat	hope*	myself*	show*	too*
are*	end	horse	name*	sleep	took
as	fast	house*	new*	small	tree
ask	father*	how*	next	snow	try
away	feet	just*	nice*	some*	used
baby*	fell*	keep	night	soon*	very*
back	find	kid	now*	start	walk
bad	fire	know*	off*	stay	want*
been*	first*	land	only	still	way
before*	fish	last	open	store*	week
being	five	left	or*	story	well*
best	food	little*	other	take	went*
black	four	live	our*	talk	were*
boat	from*	long	outside*	tell	what
both	funny	looking	over	than*	when*
brother*	game	lot	park	that	while*
buy*	gave	love	playing	them*	white*
by	girl	mad	put	then*	who
call	give	made*	read	there*	why
candy	going*	make*	room	they*	wish
city	happy	many*	said*	thing	with*
coming*	hard	men	same	think*	work
could	has*	more	saw*	three	your
doing	have*	most	say		

Figure 6–4. Spelling for Writing List.

Grade 3 Word List

again*	ever	I'll*	own	team
air	every*	I'm*	party*	that's*
almost	everyone*	it's*	people*	their*
also	everything*	kind	person	these*
always*	eye	knew*	place	thought*
another*	face	lady	ready	trip
anything*	family*	later	real	trying
around*	few	let's*	right*	turn
because*	found*	life	running*	walking
better	friend*	lunch	says	wasn't
can't*	front	maybe*	should	watch
catch	getting*	might*	sister	water
children*	great	money*	someone*	where*
class	hair	morning*	something*	which
didn't*	half	Mr.*	sometime*	won
dinner	having*	Mrs.*	stopped*	world*
does	head	Ms.	summer*	would*
don't*	heard*	never	talking	year
earth	hour	nothing	teacher*	you're
even	hurt*	once*		

---

*Spelling demons or commonly misspelled words. This list may be photocopied for noncommercial use only. Copyright 1994 by PRO-ED, Inc.

Figure 6–4 (cont.). Spelling for Writing List.

Note. From "The Spelling for Writing List" by S. Graham, K. R. Harris, and C. Loynachan, 1994, *Journal of Learning Disabilities, 27*(4), pp. 210–214. Copyright 1994 by PRO-ED, Inc. Reprinted by permission.

involve three components: (a) multisensory word study, (b) emphasis on visual imagery, and (c) writing the word from memory.

Fernald Method

The Fernald method helps the student develop a visual image of the word and, subsequently, spell the word accurately (Fernald, 1943). Tracing and simultaneously pronouncing a word is an effective study technique for some students. The technique (a) ensures attention to the word, (b) provides an auditory-visual link, and (c) controls the direction of word inspection. The following steps are used:

1. Have the student select the word to be studied.
2. Write the selected word on a chalkboard or on a piece of paper.
3. Pronounce the word clearly and distinctly. Have the student repeat the correct pronunciation while looking at the word.
4. Provide the student with time to develop an image of the word. Place emphasis upon the student's preferred sense: a student who learns visually is encouraged to picture the word; a student who learns auditorily is encouraged to say the word; and the student who learns kinesthetically is encouraged to trace the word with his or her finger.
5. When the student says that the word is known, erase the word or remove it and have the student write the word from memory.
6. If the word is written incorrectly, return to step 3. If the word is written correctly, have the student turn the paper over and write the word another time from memory.
7. Create opportunities for the student to use words in writing.

Modified Adapted Fernald Technique (M-A-F-T)

The M-A-F-T (Sutaria, 1984) is a multisensory technique that allows children to write stories,

Instant Words*

First Hundred

Instant Words*

Second Hundred

Words 1-25	Words 26-50	Words 51-75	Words 76-100	Words 101-125	Words 126-150	Words 150-175	Words 176-200
the	or	will	number	new	great	put	kind
of	one	up	no	sound	where	end	hand
and	had	other	way	take	help	does	picture
a	by	about	could	only	through	another	again
to	word	out	people	little	much	well	change
in	but	many	my	work	before	large	off
is	not	then	than	know	line	must	play
you	what	them	first	place	right	big	spell
that	all	these	water	year	too	even	air
it	were	so	been	live	mean	such	away
he	we	some	call	me	old	because	animal
was	when	her	who	back	any	turn	house
for	your	would	oil	give	same	here	point
on	can	make	now	most	tell	why	page
are	said	like	find	very	boy	ask	letter
as	there	him	long	after	follow	went	mother
with	use	into	down	thing	came	men	answer
his	an	time	day	our	want	read	found
they	each	has	did	just	show	need	study
I	which	look	get	name	also	land	still
at	she	two	come	good	around	different	learn
be	do	more	made	sentence	form	home	should
this	how	write	may	man	three	us	America
have	their	go	part	think	small	move	world
from	if	see	over	say	set	try	high

Common suffixes: -s, -ing, -ed

Common suffixes: -s, -ing, -ed, -er, -ly, -est

Figure 6–5. 300 Instant Words

*The first 100 words make up 50% of all written material. The 300 words make up 65% of all written materials. Note. From "The New Instant Word List" by E. B. Fry, 1980, *The Reading Teacher, 34*, pp. 286–288. Copyright 1980 by Edward B. Fry. Reprinted by permission.

illustrate their stories, and improve their spelling through daily writing. This technique may be used with an entire classroom of students. General and specific guidelines for this technique follow:

General:

1. Have each child write a story daily.
2. Encourage students to have only the materials they need on their desks (e.g., pencils without erasers, file box for word cards, scratch paper, folder for completed stories, drawing paper and crayons).
3. If desired, implement a behavior system, such as a token economy, in conjunction with this technique.
4. Provide opportunities to read stories and discuss new words with the class.

Specific:

1. a. Introduce the method as a new method for writing and spelling.
   b. Distribute the materials.
   c. Ask students to begin writing a story.
2. a. Inform students that if they are unsure of how to spell a word, they should raise a hand.
   b. When a student raises his or her hand, bring an index card and a black crayon to his or her desk and write the word on the card.
   c. Read the word twice slowly, emphasizing the syllable sounds.
   d. Ask the student to trace the word with his or her finger while pronouncing it.

Instant Words*

Third Hundred

Words 201-225	Words 226-250	Words 251-275	Words 276-300
every	left	until	idea
near	don't	children	enough
add	few	side	eat
food	while	feet	face
between	along	car	watch
own	might	mile	far
below	close	night	Indian
country	something	walk	real
plant	seem	white	almost
last	next	sea	let
school	hard	began	above
father	open	grow	girl
keep	example	took	sometimes
tree	begin	river	mountain
never	life	four	cut
start	always	carry	young
city	those	state	talk
earth	both	once	soon
eye	paper	book	list
light	together	hear	song
thought	got	stop	leave
head	group	without	family
under	often	second	body
story	run	late	music
saw	important	miss	color

Common suffixes: -s, -ing, -ed, -er, -ly, -est

Figure 6–5 (cont.) 300 Instant Words.

e. Have the student turn the card over and write the word from memory on paper.

f. Have the student check the spelling by examining the index card.

g. If the word is correctly spelled, have the student write the word into the story. If spelled incorrectly, have the student repeat the procedure.

3. a. When the story is complete, ask the student to read it silently and then orally to the teacher.

b. Review new words using the cards. If a word is not identified, the child may recognize it in the story context.

4. Address misspelled words and usage errors at a later time.

5. The following day, type the student's story. Make corrections, and generate new word cards for the misspelled words in the story.

6. On the next day and every following day, have the student review the word cards from the word box.

7. Select some word cards from the student's box, and initiate teacher-created word analysis games (e.g., "What would this word be if it ended with the _____ sound?" "What other words do you know that have this spelling pattern?").

8. Have each student read the finished story to the class. Encourage students to read previously written stories.

9. If desired, have the students illustrate the story.

10. Repeat the process on another day.

Spelling Stories

Once learned, a word must be practiced and used to be retained. The purpose of spelling stories, an activity adapted from Forte and Pangle (1985), is to provide reinforcement of spelling skills within the context of stories. If necessary, a multisensory component can be added for word study.

The game may be used to practice words from a spelling list, an individualized spelling list, or a high-frequency list. Before starting, write the words to be practiced on index cards or on strips of tagboard. The following steps are used:

1. Pair students together to play the game. Provide students with a pencil and piece of paper. Place the stack of word cards between them.

2. Have the first student select a word card and then write a sentence to begin the story that uses the word. Before writing the spelling word, have the student look at the word, turn over the card, and attempt to write the word from memory on a piece of paper. Have the student check the spelling and continue the procedure until the word is written correctly. Have the student read the sentence aloud.

3. Have the second student select a word card and write the next sentence in the story, writing the spelling word from memory. Have the second student then read the two sentences.

4. Have the players continue to select word cards and write and read the sentences until all cards are used and the story is completed.

1,000 Instant Words

___	1. the	___	51. will	___	101. over	___	151. set
___	2. of	___	52. up	___	102. new	___	152. put
___	3. and	___	53. other	___	103. sound	___	153. end
___	4. a	___	54. about	___	104. take	___	154. does
___	5. to	___	55. out	___	105. only	___	155. another
___	6. in	___	56. many	___	106. little	___	156. well
___	7. is	___	57. then	___	107. work	___	157. large
___	8. you	___	58. them	___	108. know	___	158. must
___	9. that	___	59. these	___	109. place	___	159. big
___	10. it	___	60. so	___	110. years	___	160. even
___	11. he	___	61. some	___	111. live	___	161. such
___	12. was	___	62. her	___	112. me	___	162. because
___	13. for	___	63. would	___	113. back	___	163. turned
___	14. on	___	64. make	___	114. give	___	164. here
___	15. are	___	65. like	___	115. most	___	165. why
___	16. as	___	66. him	___	116. very	___	166. asked
___	17. with	___	67. into	___	117. after	___	167. went
___	18. his	___	68. time	___	118. things	___	168. men
___	19. they	___	69. has	___	119. our	___	169. read
___	20. I	___	70. look	___	120. just	___	170. need
___	21. at	___	71. two	___	121. name	___	171. land
___	22. be	___	72. more	___	122. good	___	172. different
___	23. this	___	73. write	___	123. sentence	___	173. home
___	24. have	___	74. go	___	124. man	___	174. us
___	25. from	___	75. see	___	125. think	___	175. move
___	26. or	___	76. number	___	126. say	___	176. try
___	27. one	___	77. no	___	127. great	___	177. kind
___	28. had	___	78. way	___	128. where	___	178. hand
___	29. by	___	79. could	___	129. help	___	179. picture
___	30. words	___	80. people	___	130. through	___	180. again
___	31. but	___	81. my	___	131. much	___	181. change
___	32. not	___	82. than	___	132. before	___	182. off
___	33. what	___	83. first	___	133. line	___	183. play
___	34. all	___	84. water	___	134. right	___	184. spell
___	35. were	___	85. been	___	135. too	___	185. air
___	36. we	___	86. called	___	136. means	___	186. away
___	37. when	___	87. who	___	137. old	___	187. animals
___	38. your	___	88. oil	___	138. any	___	188. house
___	39. can	___	89. its	___	139. same	___	189. point
___	40. said	___	90. now	___	140. tell	___	190. page
___	41. there	___	91. find	___	141. boy	___	191. letters
___	42. use	___	92. long	___	142. following	___	192. mother
___	43. an	___	93. down	___	143. came	___	193. answer
___	44. each	___	94. day	___	144. want	___	194. found
___	45. which	___	95. did	___	145. show	___	195. study
___	46. she	___	96. get	___	146. also	___	196. still
___	47. do	___	97. come	___	147. around	___	197. learn
___	48. how	___	98. made	___	148. form	___	198. should
___	49. their	___	99. may	___	149. three	___	199. American
___	50. if	___	100. part	___	150. small	___	200. world

Figure 6–6. 1,000 Instant Words.

Note. From *The Teacher's Book of Lists* (pp. 22–28) by E. Fry, J. Polk, and D. Fountoukidis, 1984, Englewood Cliffs, NJ: Prentice-Hall. Copyright by Edward Fry. Reprinted by permission.

___	201. high	___	251. important	___	301. body	___	351. listen
___	202. every	___	252. until	___	302. music	___	352. wind
___	203. near	___	253. children	___	303. color	___	353. rock
___	204. add	___	254. side	___	304. stand	___	354. space
___	205. food	___	255. feet	___	305. sun	___	355. covered
___	206. between	___	256. car	___	306. questions	___	356. fast
___	207. own	___	257. miles	___	307. fish	___	357. several
___	208. below	___	258. night	___	308. area	___	358. hold
___	209. country	___	259. walked	___	309. mark	___	359. himself
___	210. plants	___	260. white	___	310. dog	___	360. toward
___	211. last	___	261. sea	___	311. horse	___	361. five
___	212. school	___	262. began	___	312. birds	___	362. step
___	213. father	___	263. grow	___	313. problem	___	363. morning
___	214. keep	___	264. took	___	314. complete	___	364. passed
___	215. trees	___	265. river	___	315. room	___	365. vowel
___	216. never	___	266. four	___	316. knew	___	366. true
___	217. started	___	267. carry	___	317. since	___	367. hundred
___	218. city	___	268. state	___	318. ever	___	368. against
___	219. earth	___	269. once	___	319. piece	___	369. pattern
___	220. eyes	___	270. book	___	320. told	___	370. numeral
___	221. light	___	271. hear	___	321. usually	___	371. table
___	222. thought	___	272. stop	___	322. didn't	___	372. north
___	223. head	___	273. without	___	323. friends	___	373. slowly
___	224. under	___	274. second	___	324. easy	___	374. money
___	225. story	___	275. later	___	325. heard	___	375. map
___	226. saw	___	276. miss	___	326. order	___	376. farm
___	227. left	___	277. idea	___	327. red	___	377. pulled
___	228. don't	___	278. enough	___	328. door	___	378. draw
___	229. few	___	279. eat	___	329. sure	___	379. voice
___	230. while	___	280. face	___	330. become	___	380. seen
___	231. along	___	281. watch	___	331. top	___	381. cold
___	232. might	___	282. far	___	332. ship	___	382. cried
___	233. close	___	283. Indians	___	333. across	___	383. plan
___	234. something	___	284. really	___	334. today	___	384. notice
___	235. seemed	___	285. almost	___	335. during	___	385. south
___	236. next	___	286. let	___	336. short	___	386. sing
___	237. hard	___	287. above	___	337. better	___	387. war
___	238. open	___	288. girl	___	338. best	___	388. ground
___	239. example	___	289. sometimes	___	339. however	___	389. fall
___	240. beginning	___	290. mountains	___	340. low	___	390. kind
___	241. life	___	291. cut	___	341. hours	___	391. town
___	242. always	___	292. young	___	342. black	___	392. I'll
___	243. those	___	293. talk	___	343. products	___	393. unit
___	244. both	___	294. soon	___	344. happened	___	394. figure
___	245. paper	___	295. list	___	345. whole	___	395. certain
___	246. together	___	296. song	___	346. measure	___	396. field
___	247. got	___	297. being	___	347. remember	___	397. travel
___	248. group	___	298. leave	___	348. early	___	398. wood
___	249. often	___	299. family	___	349. waves	___	399. fire
___	250. run	___	300. it's	___	350. reached	___	400. upon

Figure 6-6 (cont.). 1,000 Instant Words.

___	401. done	___	451. plane	___	501. can't	___	551. legs
___	402. English	___	452. system	___	502. matter	___	552. sat
___	403. road	___	453. behind	___	503. square	___	553. main
___	404. half	___	454. ran	___	504. syllables	___	554. winter
___	405. ten	___	455. round	___	505. perhaps	___	555. wide
___	406. fly	___	456. boat	___	506. bill	___	556. written
___	407. gave	___	457. game	___	507. felt	___	557. length
___	408. box	___	458. force	___	508. suddenly	___	558. reason
___	409. finally	___	459. brought	___	509. test	___	559. kept
___	410. wait	___	460. understand	___	510. direction	___	560. interest
___	411. correct	___	461. warm	___	511. center	___	561. arms
___	412. oh	___	462. common	___	512. farmers	___	562. brother
___	413. quickly	___	463. bring	___	513. ready	___	563. race
___	414. person	___	464. explain	___	514. anything	___	564. present
___	415. became	___	465. dry	___	515. divided	___	565. beautiful
___	416. shown	___	466. though	___	516. general	___	566. store
___	417. minutes	___	467. language	___	517. energy	___	567. job
___	418. strong	___	468. shape	___	518. subject	___	568. edge
___	419. verb	___	469. deep	___	519. Europe	___	569. past
___	420. stars	___	470. thousands	___	520. moon	___	570. sign
___	421. front	___	471. yes	___	521. region	___	571. record
___	422. feel	___	472. clear	___	522. return	___	572. finished
___	423. fact	___	473. equation	___	523. believe	___	573. discovered
___	424. inches	___	474. yet	___	524. dance	___	574. wild
___	425. street	___	475. government	___	525. members	___	575. happy
___	426. decided	___	476. filled	___	526. picked	___	576. beside
___	427. contain	___	477. heat	___	527. simple	___	577. gone
___	428. course	___	478. full	___	528. cells	___	578. sky
___	429. surface	___	479. hot	___	529. paint	___	579. glass
___	430. produce	___	480. check	___	530. mind	___	580. million
___	431. building	___	481. object	___	531. love	___	581. west
___	432. ocean	___	482. am	___	532. cause	___	582. lay
___	433. class	___	483. rule	___	533. rain	___	583. weather
___	434. note	___	484. among	___	534. exercise	___	584. root
___	435. nothing	___	485. noun	___	535. eggs	___	585. instruments
___	436. rest	___	486. power	___	536. train	___	586. meet
___	437. carefully	___	487. cannot	___	537. blue	___	587. third
___	438. scientists	___	488. able	___	538. wish	___	588. months
___	439. inside	___	489. six	___	539. drop	___	589. paragraph
___	440. wheels	___	490. size	___	540. developed	___	590. raise
___	441. stay	___	491. dark	___	541. window	___	591. represent
___	442. green	___	492. ball	___	542. difference	___	592. soft
___	443. known	___	493. material	___	543. distance	___	593. whether
___	444. island	___	494. special	___	544. heart	___	594. clothes
___	445. week	___	495. heavy	___	545. sit	___	595. flowers
___	446. less	___	496. fine	___	546. sum	___	596. shall
___	447. machine	___	497. pair	___	547. summer	___	597. teacher
___	448. base	___	498. circle	___	548. wall	___	598. held
___	449. ago	___	499. include	___	549. forest	___	599. describe
___	450. stood	___	500. built	___	550. probably	___	600. drive

Figure 6-6 (cont.). 1,000 Instant Words.

___	601. cross	___	651. hair	___	701. row	___	751. yourself
___	602. speak	___	652. age	___	702. least	___	752. control
___	603. solve	___	653. amount	___	703. catch	___	753. practice
___	604. appear	___	654. scale	___	704. climbed	___	754. report
___	605. metal	___	655. pounds	___	705. wrote	___	755. straight
___	606. son	___	656. although	___	706. shouted	___	756. rise
___	607. either	___	657. per	___	707. continued	___	757. statement
___	608. ice	___	658. broken	___	708. itself	___	758. stick
___	609. sleep	___	659. moment	___	709. else	___	759. party
___	610. village	___	660. tiny	___	710. plains	___	760. seeds
___	611. factors	___	661. possible	___	711. gas	___	761. suppose
___	612. result	___	662. gold	___	712. England	___	762. woman
___	613. jumped	___	663. mild	___	713. burning	___	763. coast
___	614. snow	___	664. quiet	___	714. design	___	764. bank
___	615. ride	___	665. natural	___	715. joined	___	765. period
___	616. care	___	666. lot	___	716. foot	___	766. wire
___	617. floor	___	667. stone	___	717. law	___	767. choose
___	618. hill	___	668. act	___	718. ears	___	768. clean
___	619. pushed	___	669. build	___	719. grass	___	769. visit
___	620. baby	___	670. middle	___	720. you're	___	770. bit
___	621. buy	___	671. speed	___	721. grew	___	771. whose
___	622. century	___	672. count	___	722. skin	___	772. received
___	623. outside	___	673. cat	___	723. valley	___	773. garden
___	624. everything	___	674. someone	___	724. cents	___	774. please
___	625. tall	___	675. sail	___	725. key	___	775. strange
___	626. already	___	676. rolled	___	726. president	___	776. caught
___	627. instead	___	677. bear	___	727. brown	___	777. fell
___	628. phrase	___	678. wonder	___	728. trouble	___	778. team
___	629. soil	___	679. smiled	___	729. cool	___	779. God
___	630. bed	___	680. angle	_	730. cloud	___	780. captain
___	631. copy	___	681. fraction	___	731. lost	___	781. direct
___	632. free	___	682. Africa	___	732. sent	___	782. ring
___	633. hope	___	683. killed	___	733. symbols	___	783. serve
___	634. spring	___	684. melody	___	734. wear	___	784. child
___	635. case	___	685. bottom	___	735. bad	___	785. desert
___	636. laughed	___	686. trip	___	736. save	___	786. increase
___	637. nation	___	687. hole	___	737. experiment	___	787. history
___	638. quite	___	688. poor	___	738. engine	___	788. cost
___	639. type	___	689. let's	___	739. alone	___	789. maybe
___	640. themselves	___	690. fight	___	740. drawing	___	790. business
___	641. temperature	___	691. surprise	___	741. east	___	791. separate
___	642. bright	___	692. French	___	742. pay	___	792. break
___	643. lead	___	693. died	___	743. single	___	793. uncle
___	644. everyone	___	694. beat	___	744. touch	___	794. hunting
___	645. method	___	695. exactly	___	745. information	___	795. flow
___	646. section	___	696. remain	___	746. express	___	796. lady
___	647. lake	___	697. dress	___	747. mouth	___	797. students
___	648. consonant	___	698. iron	___	748. yard	___	798. human
___	649. within	___	699. couldn't	___	749. equal	___	799. art
___	650. dictionary	___	700. fingers	___	750. decimal	___	800. feeling

Figure 6-6 (cont.). 1,000 Instant Words.

___	801. supply	___	851. thick	___	901. company	___	951. gun
___	802. corner	___	852. blood	___	902. radio	___	952. similar
___	803. electric	___	853. lie	___	903. we'll	___	953. death
___	804. insects	___	854. spot	___	904. action	___	954. score
___	805. crops	___	855. bell	___	905. capital	___	955. forward
___	806. tone	___	856. fun	___	906. factories	___	956. stretched
___	807. hit	___	857. loud	___	907. settled	___	957. experience
___	808. sand	___	858. consider	___	908. yellow	___	958. rose
___	809. doctor	___	859. suggested	___	909. isn't	___	959. allow
___	810. provide	___	860. thin	___	910. southern	___	960. fear
___	811. thus	___	861. thin	___	911. truck	___	961. workers
___	812. won't	___	862. position	___	912. fair	___	962. Washington
___	813. cook	___	863. fruit	___	913. printed	___	963. Greek
___	814. bones	___	864. tied	___	914. wouldn't	___	964. women
___	815. tail	___	865. rich	___	915. ahead	___	965. bought
___	816. board	___	866. dollars	___	916. chance	___	966. led
___	817. modern	___	867. send	___	917. born	___	967. march
___	818. compound	___	868. sight	___	918. level	___	968. northern
___	819. mine	___	869. chief	___	919. triangle	___	969. create
___	820. wasn't	___	870. Japanese	___	920. molecules	___	970. British
___	821. fit	___	871. stream	___	921. France	___	971. difficult
___	822. addition	___	872. planets	___	922. repeated	___	972. match
___	823. belong	___	873. rhythm	___	923. column	___	973. win
___	824. safe	___	874. eight	___	924. western	___	974. doesn't
___	825. soldiers	___	875. science	___	925. church	___	975. steel
___	826. guess	___	876. major	___	926. sister	___	976. total
___	827. silent	___	877. observe	___	927. oxygen	___	977. deal
___	828. trade	___	878. tube	___	928. plural	___	978. determine
___	829. rather	___	879. necessary	___	929. various	___	979. evening
___	830. compare	___	880. weight	___	930. agreed	___	980. nor
___	831. crowd	___	881. meat	___	931. opposite	___	981. rope
___	832. poem	___	882. lifted	___	932. wrong	___	982. cotton
___	833. enjoy	___	883. process	___	933. chart	___	983. apple
___	834. elements	___	884. army	___	934. prepared	___	984. details
___	835. indicate	___	885. hat	___	935. pretty	___	985. entire
___	836. except	___	886. property	___	936. solution	___	986. corn
___	837. expect	___	887. particular	___	937. fresh	___	987. substances
___	838. flat	___	888. swim	___	938. shop	___	988. smell
___	839. seven	___	889. terms	___	939. suffix	___	989. tools
___	840. interesting	___	890. current	___	940. especially	___	990. conditions
___	841. sense	___	891. park	___	941. shoes	___	991. cows
___	842. string	___	892. sell	___	942. actually	___	992. track
___	843. blow	___	893. shoulder	___	943. nose	___	993. arrived
___	844. famous	___	894. industry	___	944. afraid	___	994. located
___	845. value	___	895. wash	___	945. dead	___	995. sir
___	846. wings	___	896. block	___	946. sugar	___	996. seat
___	847. movement	___	897. spread	___	947. adjective	___	997. division
___	848. pole	___	898. cattle	___	948. fig	___	998. effect
___	849. exciting	___	899. wife	___	949. fig	___	999. underline
___	850. branches	___	900. sharp	___	950. huge	___	1000. view

Figure 6-6 (cont.). 1,000 Instant Words.

5. As a final step, have the students edit their stories, illustrate them, and/or read them aloud to the class.

Fitzgerald Method

For some students, visual imagery, or "seeing" words in their minds, helps with retention of spelling patterns. Fitzgerald (1951) described a method to increase visual imagery. The following steps are used:

1. Have the student look at the word carefully while focusing on every aspect of the word.
2. Have the student say the word aloud.
3. Tell the student to close his or her eyes and "see" the word.
4. Ask the student to write the word without looking at the spelling.
5. Help the student to check the spelling against the correct spelling.
6. If the spelling is incorrect, ask the student to repeat steps 1–5.

Cover-Write Method

For individuals who experience difficulty in retrieving word images, the cover-write methods may be useful. The following procedure, described by Kirk and Chalfant (1984), consists of several steps:

1. Select a word for the student to learn; write the word on a card and pronounce it.
2. Have the student look at and pronounce the word.
3. Have the student look at the word and say the letter names or sounds while tracing each letter in the air.
4. Remove the word and have the student pronounce the word while tracing it in the air.
5. If necessary, repeat step 3.
6. Have the student continue to pronounce the word while tracing it in the air until the spelling is known.
7. Have the student pronounce the word while writing it on paper. If the word is spelled incorrectly, repeat from step 3.
8. Follow the same steps to teach a new word.
9. Ask the student to trace the first word in the air and write it from memory.
10. Have the student write the word in a notebook that can be used for review purposes.
11. Encourage the student to use the words in written work whenever possible.

Air-tracing does not produce a distinct visual image, but does provide kinesthetic feedback through large-muscle movement. Some individuals, however, may benefit from a distinct visual image. A modification of this method may be beneficial to these individuals. In the modified version of the strategy, the student is asked to trace over the word on paper or a chalkboard instead of in the air (Mather, 1991).

Alternative Cover-Write Method

Based upon the same principles, Edgington (1967) described a slightly different cover-write approach. In this alternative method, three to five words are presented on individual cards using the following steps:

1. Have the student look at and say the first word.
2. Have the student pronounce the sounds of the word while writing the letters.
3. Have the student compare the written word, letter by letter, with the model.
4. When the word is written correctly, have the student repeat steps 2 and 3 four more times.
5. Cover the word and ask the student to write the word while pronouncing it.
6. Repeat all five steps with the new words.

Weiss and Weiss

Another multisensory technique designed to help students revisualize spelling words was described by Weiss and Weiss (1993). The method was designed as a spelling technique for students who have difficulty learning to spell sight words and words that are similar in visual configuration. The following steps are used:

1. Say the word. Have the student repeat it.
2. Show the word. Have the student trace it with his or her whole arm in the air, spell it subvocally, and then say the word again.
3. Say the word, ask the student to close his or her eyes and attempt to picture the word,

saying it, spelling it subvocally, and tracing it in the air or on the desk.

4. Say the word. Have the student repeat the word, write it from memory, and spell it subvocally.

5. Show the student the word in a group of four look-alikes (e.g., *bought*, *bough*, *brought*, *bout*). Have the student select the correct spelling from the group of look-alikes. If a mistake is made, repeat steps 1–4.

6. Review the word and have the student use the word in a sentence.

Visual-Vocal Method

Vocalization of the spelling of a word helps some students to recall the spelling. For example, Daniel, a third-grade student, experienced many problems when trying to learn his spelling words through visual imagery. Methods with a phonic emphasis also failed. Daniel's teacher decided to try the visual-vocal technique described by Westerman (1971). This method, which focuses upon looking at the word and spelling the word orally, was effective with Daniel. For the first time in his school career, Daniel could not only attempt the whole spelling list, but also could write the correct spellings of about 80% of the words. In using this method, the following steps are used:

1. Ask the student to look at the word.
2. Have the student say the word aloud.
3. Tell the student to spell the word orally using the letter names.
4. Have the student say the word aloud once more.
5. Have the student write the word correctly four times consecutively.
6. Ask the student to repeat steps 1–5 until the goal of four correct spellings in a row has been attained.

Visual Spelling

Some students have difficulties sequencing sounds but have good recall of visual images. Individuals who have poor phonological processing skill but strong visual skills may benefit from the technique described by Glazzard (1982). The following steps are incorporated in this method:

1. Write a sentence on the board incorporating the spelling word in-context. Use a drawing of the word instead of the word itself.
2. Read the sentence aloud with the student.
3. Erase the picture and redraw it under the line.
4. Ask the student to read the sentence, verbally filling in the correct (pictured) word in the blank.
5. Write the correct spelling of the pictured object in the blank, spelling the word aloud while writing it.
6. Have the student read the sentence aloud once again.
7. Give the student a copy of the sentence with the spelling word on the line and a drawing of the word under the line.
8. Have the student copy the spelling word at the front of the sentence, verbalizing the sounds as the word is spelled.
9. Repeat the procedure for all the spelling words.
10. Check the previous day's spelling words using a crossword puzzle format. Use picture clues or a sentence completion exercise.

Horn Method 1

Horn (1919) developed several methods that rely on visual imagery to help students improve their spelling skill. For his first method, the following steps are used:

1. Have the student look at the word.
2. Ask the student to say the word.
3. Tell the student to close his or her eyes and picture the word.
4. Ask the student to look at the word to see if it matches the visualization.
5. If the visualization does not match the correct spelling, have the student repeat steps 1–4 as often as necessary.
6. Have the student write the word without looking at it.
7. Tell the student to check the spelling against the word.
8. If the spelling is incorrect, ask the student to repeat steps 1–7.
9. Have the student repeat steps 6 and 7 twice.

Horn Method 2

Thirty-five years later, Horn (1954) described another effective strategy. The following steps are used:

1. Have the student look at the word.
2. Tell the student to say the word aloud, making certain to pronounce each part.
3. Ask the student to look carefully at each part as it is pronounced.
4. Have the student say the names of the letters in the correct sequence.
5. Ask the student to visualize the word.
6. Ask the student to write the word without looking at the spelling.
7. Help the student check the spelling against the word.
8. If errors exist, help the student note the errors, revisualize the word, and rewrite the word.
9. Have the student check the spelling against the word.
10. Have the student repeat any or all of the steps until the word is spelled correctly.

Whole-Word Approach

The whole-word approach, described by Smith (1975), is similar to the approach described by Horn. For this whole-word approach, use the following steps:

1. Have the student look at the word.
2. Ask the student to close his or her eyes and try to visualize the word.
3. Have the student check the spelling of the word.
4. Have the student copy the word or look at each individual letter.
5. Have the student recheck the spelling.
6. Have the student attempt to write the word from memory.
7. Have the student check the spelling and then repeat steps 6 and 7 until the word has been spelled correctly twice.

TV Spelling

Spelling instruction is not limited to the school setting. For example, TV spelling is a simple pro-cedure designed to be used by parents at home to help youngsters improve their spelling (Peters, 1979). The following steps are used:

1. Have some paper and a pencil on hand when watching TV.
2. Have the child watch the beginning of an advertisement.
3. While encouraging the child not to look up, ask him or her to write the name of the product being advertised.
4. After checking the word, have the child rewrite the name saying the name as it is written.

Parents may help their child by providing feedback on the correct spelling after the advertisement has disappeared from the screen.

Chalkboard Spelling

The large-muscle movement involved in writing on the chalkboard may help some students retain words (Fernald, 1943). In addition, the friction caused by the chalk moving along the chalkboard can also aid in retention. Three slightly different chalkboard strategies are presented.

Chalkboard Spelling I. Hildreth (1955) described the following procedure:

1. Write the word on the chalkboard while pronouncing it.
2. Ask the student to study the word.
3. Erase the word.
4. Ask the student to write the word from memory.

Chalkboard Spelling II. Sisernos and Bullock (1983) suggested these steps:

1. Write the word on the chalkboard with a wet sponge.
2. Have the student copy the word before it evaporates.

Modification of Chalkboard Spelling II. Mather (1991) suggested a modification to the Sisernos and Bullock (1983) strategy. The modification differs from the original procedure in that the student must produce the spelling independently. In the modified version, the following steps are used:

1. Write the word on the chalkboard with a wet sponge.
2. Have the student watch the word until it evaporates.
3. Ask the student to try and write the word from memory.

Whole Person Spelling

Olrich (1983) presented several suggestions for spelling instruction that incorporate a number of different strategies:

1. Introducing the spelling words:
   a. Write the words on the chalkboard.
   b. Pronounce the words and explain the meanings.
2. "Mapping" the words.
   a. Have the students share what they find unique about each word, or note a connection they have with the word (e.g., if the word is "committee," note the number of syllables, the smaller words contained within the word, or an experience as a member of a committee).
3. "Picture taking."
   a. Divide each word into syllables and write them on the chalkboard.
   b. Ask the students to make their minds become cameras and record each syllable in their mind's eye.
   c. Have the students close their eyes and picture each correctly spelled syllable.
   d. Have the students keep their eyes closed and "see" the word in its entirety, letter-by-letter, or syllable-by-syllable.
4. Relaxation.
   a. Have the students relax for several minutes while relaxation music is played in the background.
5. Visualization.
   a. With relaxation music playing, encourage the students to imagine themselves in a pleasant and successful situation (e.g., on a beach). Students are encouraged to see, feel, smell, taste, and hear the situation in as much detail as possible.
   b. Ask the students to remain in this imaginary setting and "write" the spelling words (e.g., with a stick in the sand.)

6. Spelling games.
   a. Use a number of different spelling games to help students memorize the words.
7. Using the words in context.
   a. Write a story and leave a blank for each of the spelling words. Have the students choose the correct word.

Computer Software

Computers can also be used to aid in the effective study of spelling in elementary and secondary school, both in regular and special education classes (Rieth, Polsgrove, & Eckert, 1984). Software programs using a "look and write from memory" approach have been developed by a number of companies. The word is flashed on the screen for a preselected length of time, and then the student types the word from memory. Whenever an error is made, the computer flashes the word again. This continues until mastery is achieved. For some programs, the model can be programmed to disappear after the second letter is typed. This fading option may help the writer recall the word independently in the future (Hunt-Berg et al., 1994). The novelty of practicing words on a computer may motivate some students and, subsequently, aid in retention.

Word Study Methods with an Auditory Emphasis

When a student has difficulty sequencing sounds (seen when misspellings contain many of the correct letters but in the incorrect order), a spelling method that emphasizes word pronunciation will be beneficial (Mather, 1991). For these students, effective spelling programs begin with a study of sounds in words and the letters that represent those sounds (Hanna, Hodges, & Hanna, 1971).

Phonological Awareness

The most effective way for improving the spelling performance of beginning writers is to provide training procedures that involve manipulating visual materials in conjunction with auditory input (Bailet, 1991). Phonological awareness can be trained and will help students improve their spelling skill. Teachers can present activities that involve rhyming words, clapping out and counting the number of syllables in words, and pronouncing words by syllables.

Alphabet blocks, Scrabble tiles, and/or magnetic letters can be used to help students increase specific phonological skills. As skill improves, teachers can move from phonological awareness activities to spelling approaches with an auditory emphasis. Several activities designed to build phonological awareness are described below.

Auditory Sequencing. Bannatyne (1971) discussed a procedure for helping students attend to the sequence of sounds when spelling. The following steps are used:

1. Make small letter cards or use Scrabble tiles.
2. Sound out a word slowly and have the student attempt to place the letter tiles in correct sequence from left to right. When necessary, provide demonstrations on how to arrange the tiles before the child attempts to build the word.
3. After building the word, encourage the student to trace and then print the word.
4. As skill increases, use individual letter tiles to break words into syllables or to build several words around a root.

Bag Game. The Bag Game (Lewkowicz, 1994) is an example of an activity that can be used to promote phonemic awareness in kindergarten or first-grade students. The purpose is to heighten awareness of initial consonant phonemes in spoken words. Before playing the game, provide the students with experiences identifying the initial consonant sounds in words.

Use the following procedure to play the game:

1. Select two colorful containers that are not transparent.
2. Select four pairs of familiar objects, such as: shoes, mittens, pencils, rings, or feathers. The objects must be small enough to fit in the bag and large enough to be seen by the group.
3. Have the group name the four kinds of objects and then put one of each pair into each bag.
4. Select one child to be the Sounder and the other to be the Matcher. Give each student a bag.
5. Ask the Sounder to reach into the bag and grasp one of the four objects, keeping it hidden from view. Have the student say the initial consonant sound so that the group can hear.
6. Ask the Matcher to find the object in his or her own bag that begins with the initial sound given and then to lift it so that class members can see it.
7. Ask the Sounder to raise the object in view.
8. Ask the class if the initial consonant sounds match.
9. Choose other children and repeat the game. Add new objects as needed.

This game could be modified to focus on final consonant sounds or, as skill develops, medial vowel sounds.

Making Words. Cunningham and Cunningham (1992) described a guided invented spelling task called Making Words. The purpose of this procedure is to help students develop phonemic awareness and discover how our alphabetic system works by increasing their understanding of sound-letter relationships. This strategy is to be used along with regular writing activities and is a 15-minute activity. Use the following steps:

1. Give each student 6–8 letters. Each child must have his or her own letters to be used to make into 12 to 15 words.
2. Ask each student to make two-letter words using his or her letters.
3. Ask each student to make three-letter words using his or her letters.
4. Continue the pattern, increasing word length by one letter during each step. The final word, a six-, seven-, or eight-letter word, will include all of the letters the student has for that day.

Tables 6–1 and 6–2 illustrate the steps that may be used in planning and teaching a Making Words lesson.

Making Words activities begin with short, easy words and end with a long word that uses all of the letters. Children manipulate the letters to produce a variety of words. For the first lessons, students are given several consonant letters but only one vowel, which is written in red. Later, students may be given two or more vowels. Emphasis in all activities is placed on how words change when letters are moved and different letters are added.

Table 1
Steps In planning a Making Words lesson

1. Decide what the final word in the lesson will be. In choosing this word, consider its number of vowels, child interest, curriculum tie-ins you can make, and letter-sound patterns you can draw children's attention to through the word sorting at the end.
2. Make a list of shorter words that can be made from the letters of the final word.
3. From all the words you listed, pick 12-15 words that include: (a) words that you can sort for the pattern(s) you want to emphasize; (b) little words and big words so that the lesson is a multilevel lesson; (c) words that can be made with the same letters in different places (e.g., barn, bran) so children are reminded that when spelling words, the order of the letters is crucial; (d) a proper name or two to remind them where we use capital letters; and (e) words that most of the students have in their listening vocabularies.
4. Write all the words on index cards and order them from shortest to longest.
5. Once you have the two-letter, three-letter, etc., words together, order them further so that you can emphasize letter patterns and how changing the position of the letters or changing or adding just one letter results in a different word.
6. Store the cards in an envelope. Write on the envelope the words in order and the patterns you will sort for at the end.

Table 2
Steps in teaching a Making Words lesson

1. Place the large letter cards in a pocket chart or along the chalk ledge.
2. Have designated children give one letter to each child. (Let the passer keep the reclosable bag containing that letter and have the same child collect that letter when the lesson is over.)
3. Hold up and name the letters on the large letter cards, and have the children hold up their matching small letter cards.
4. Write the numeral 2 (or 3, if there are no two-letter words in this lesson) on the board. Tell them to take two letters and make the first word. Use the word in a sentence after you say it.
5. Have a child who has the first word made correctly make the same word with the large letter cards. Encourage anyone who did not make the word correctly at first to fix the word when they see it made correctly.
6. Continue having them make words, erasing and changing the number on the board to indicate the number of letters needed. Use the words in simple sentences to make sure the children understand their meanings. Remember to cue them as to whether they are just changing one letter, changing letters around, or taking all their letters out to make a word from scratch. Cue them when the word you want them to make is a proper name, and send a child who has started that name with a capital letter to make the word with the big letters.
7. Before telling them the last word, ask "Has anyone figured out what word we can make with all our letters?" If so, congratulate them and have one of them make it with the big letters. If not, say something like, "I love it when I can stump you. Use all your letters and make _____."
8. Once all the words have been made, take the index cards on which you have written the words, and place them one at a time (in the same order children made them) along the chalk ledge or in the pocket chart. Have children say and spell the words with you as you do this. Use these words for sorting and pointing out patterns. Pick a word and point out a particular spelling pattern, and ask children to find the others with that same pattern. Line these words up so that the pattern is visible.
9. To get maximum transfer to reading and writing, have the children use the patterns they have sorted to spell a few new words that you say.

Note: Some teachers have chosen to do steps 1-7 on one day and steps 8 and 9 on the following day.

Tables 6–1 and 6–2. Steps for planning and teaching a Making Words Lesson.

Two samples of letters and some words to make in a Making Words lesson are presented below:

Letters for lesson with one vowel: *u k n r s t*
Words to make: *us nut rut run sun sunk runs ruts rust tusk stun stunk trunk trunks*
Letters for lesson with two vowels: *a e h n p r t*
Words to make: *an at hat pat pan pen pet net ate eat heat neat path parent panther*

Finger Spelling. Stein (1983) described a procedure called finger spelling that is taught in conjunction with sound blending. The method reinforces auditory discrimination, auditory sequencing, and phonetic spelling for young children or remedial spellers (Stein, 1983). Before this technique is used, the sound/symbol relationships for the following must be mastered: consonants, short vowels, digraphs (*sh*, *th*, *ch*), short-vowel words with final consonant blends, and short-vowel words with initial consonant blends.

Prior to using finger spelling, the teacher must:

a. Create and display a picture chart for short-vowel sounds. The chart must contain pictures of objects whose names begin with each short-vowel sound. Write the target letter under each picture.

b. Create and display a similar chart for the digraphs.

c. Make sets of index cards for each category (e.g., short vowels, digraphs, final blends). Write a word on one side of the card with the picture of the word on the other.

d. Make sets of sentence strips for each category. The sentences incorporate both the target word and others that are frequently seen in reading materials.

The procedure to be used to finger spell is:

i. Raise one finger for each letter *sound* (not letter name). Raise the thumb first, followed by the index finger, the middle finger, the ring finger, and finally the little finger.

ii. Raise two fingers simultaneously for digraphs.

iii. Raise two to three fingers simultaneously for beginning consonant blends. Do not raise fingers simultaneously for final consonant blends.

To begin the finger spelling method, the teacher demonstrates the following procedure:

1. Introduce the technique.
2. Present the picture of a short word on a card and pronounce the word.
3. Spell the word while raising one finger for each sound.
4. Turn over the card to reveal the correct spelling and pronounce the word again.

The procedure continues as the student and teacher practice spelling the word together:

5. Have the student say the word.
6. Have the student spell the word and raise one finger for each sound.
7. Show the student the correct spelling.
8. Have the student say and finger spell the word again.

Next, the student practices finger spelling independently:

9. Hold up a picture.
10. Have the student say the word.
11. Have the student finger spell the word.
12. Show the correct spelling.
13. Have the student say the word and determine if the word was finger spelled correctly.

Finger spelling can also be used to improve spelling in writing. When writing the word, use the following steps:

1. Say a word.
2. Model how to finger spell the word.
3. Write the word on the chalkboard, matching the sound with the corresponding symbols.
4. Repeat the modeling.
5. Dictate the word.
6. Have the student repeat the word, while finger spelling it.
7. Have the student write the word on paper, saying each sound aloud as the letter is written.
8. Show the student the correct spelling of the word.
9. Have the student proofread what has been written, pointing to each letter/word as it is read.

If preferred, have the student clap or push forward chips or tokens for each syllable or phoneme within a word. As the student's skill improves, the technique may be used with sentences.

Gilstrap Method

Other methods with an auditory emphasis may be used with students with more advanced spelling skill. Gilstrap (1962) described a procedure that may be used for single-syllable or multisyllabic words. The following steps are used:

1. Have the student look at the word.
2. Have the student say the word softly.

For words of one syllable:

3. Ask the student to look at the letters and say the name of each one.
4. Have the student write the word without looking at the spelling.

For words of more than one syllable:

3. Tell the student to repeat the word, syllable by syllable, looking at each syllable as it is pronounced.
4. Have the student look at and say the name of the letters, syllable by syllable.
5. Ask the student to write the word without looking at the spelling.

Bannatyne's System

Bannatyne's spelling system (1971) is similar to the Fernald method, but the primary emphasis is placed upon word pronunciation. The approach helps the student increase grapheme-phoneme awareness, or the relationship between the written symbols and their corresponding sounds. Bannatyne explained that if difficult words were broken into syllables, the student will see the long word as a series of manageable short "bits" that have their own conventional spellings. He further noted that spelling can only be learned by establishing the habit of looking at the individual letters of words for their own sake as unit designs. The following steps are used:

1. Have the student pronounce the word slowly.
2. Have the student repeat the word with the separate phonemes being pronounced individually.

3. Have the student study the visual appearance and note how the graphemes match the phonemes.
4. Point to the graphemes in sequence and ask the student to articulate each phoneme.
5. Have the student write the graphemes as units with spaces in between while articulating the phonemes in rhythmic sequence.
6. Have the student copy and trace the word until it can be recalled easily.

Adaptation of the Glass-Analysis Method

The Glass-Analysis method (Glass, 1973) was developed primarily for teaching decoding skills. This method can be modified, however, to improve spelling skills (Mather, 1991). For example, if a student wanted to learn how to spell the word "consideration," the teacher would use the following steps:

1. Identify and discuss the visual and auditory clusters in the word.
2. Ask the student to write the letter(s) that make the "con" sound, then the "sid" sound, then the "er" sound, then the "a" sound, and finally the "tion" sound.
3. Have the student write the word *consideration* while pronouncing each part slowly: "con-sid-er-a-tion."
4. Have the student turn the paper over and write the word *consideration* from memory while saying the word as it is written.
5. Have the student write the word from memory two more times.

When using the Glass-Analysis method for spelling, emphasis should be placed upon correct sound sequencing. This can be accomplished by presenting and practicing the visual and auditory clusters in the order that they appear in the word.

Adaptation of Simultaneous Oral Spelling

Poor spellers can improve their spelling skill by using an adaptation of Gillingham and Stillman's (1973) Simultaneous Oral Spelling (SOS) procedure (Bradley, 1981, 1983). One positive feature of this method is that the student selects the word for learning. Student selection of spelling words may improve motivation and learning. For the adaptation of SOS, the following steps are used:

1. Have the student select a word to learn.
2. Have the student either write the word or form it with plastic letters.
3. Have the student pronounce the word.
4. Have the student write the word while saying the alphabetic name of each letter as it is written.
5. Have the student pronounce the word once more, then check that the word is written correctly.
6. Have the student repeat steps 2 through 5 twice and then repeat the entire procedure for 6 consecutive school days.

Saying the letter names instead of the sounds is more effective for some poor spellers. The technique helps the student label, discriminate, and recall each letter (Bradley, 1983). In contrast, saying the letter names does not appear to improve the performance of students without spelling difficulties.

Alternative Pronunciation

Mather and Jaffe (1992) adapted Ormrod's (1986) Alternative Pronunciation strategy. The purpose of this spelling strategy is to enable phonetic spellers, weak in visual memory, to recall the correct spelling of difficult words. Many individuals use this type of strategy to recall words that contain unusual spelling patterns. For example, to spell *Wednesday*, one may deliberately articulate three distinct syllables: "Wed-nes-day."

The student using Alternate Pronunciation learns two pronunciations of words that are difficult to recall visually. One pronunciation is how the word is spoken. The other, the invented pronunciation, is how the word is written. The second pronunciation is memorized solely for the purpose of retaining the spelling pattern. A different pronunciation for the same word may be devised, depending upon what the student thinks will provide the best clue to the actual spelling.

Examples:

Actual Spelling	Spoken Pronunciation	Alternate Pronunciation
February	Feb' u ary	Feb' ru ary
ache	ake	a'chee
colonel	ker' nal	col' o nel

The following steps are used:

1. Break the word up into parts so that any letters that may be difficult to visualize will be pronounced.
2. Memorize the alternate pronunciation.
3. Write the word according to the alternate pronunciation without looking at the model. Check the spelling.
4. If correct, repeat step 3 two to four times more.
5. If incorrect, invent a new pronunciation that will help the student correct the error.

Syllable Approach

Children with difficulty sequencing sounds may benefit from a syllable approach to teaching spelling. This type of approach helps students to isolate word parts. This technique is most applicable to words with regular phoneme-grapheme correspondence. Cicci (1980) suggested the following steps:

1. Present syllables on flash cards.
2. Have the student look at the card as you pronounce the syllable.
3. Have the student pronounce the syllable.
4. Present several syllables to form words.
5. After the student has practiced the separate syllables, move them together to form a word.
6. Pronounce the word in syllables while the student looks at the word.
7. Have the student pronounce the word in syllables.
8. Have the student write the word in syllables. If the student is unable at first to divide words, pronounce the word in separate syllables while the student writes the word.

Musical Spelling

Some students appear to benefit from unique instructional techniques. Martin (1983) recommended combining spelling practice with music. The method has proven particularly successful with individuals who have experienced failure and frustration with spelling in the past. The technique can be used to practice words that will be tested. The following steps are used:

1. Review the spelling words and their meanings with the student.
2. Write down the words and their meanings.

3. Have the student review the first two words.
4. Have the student record the first two words on a tape recorder by:
   a. spelling the first word
   b. pronouncing the word
   c. defining the word
   d. following steps a through c with the second word.
5. Repeat step 4 while a tape of pre-classical or baroque music is playing at the same volume as the student's voice.
6. Turn off the two tapes while the student reviews the next two words.
7. Have the student repeat steps 4–6 until all the spelling words have been recorded.
8. Ask the student to listen to the tape every morning and evening until the day of the test.

Spelling Grid

Some students can improve their spellings of multisyllabic words through the use of a spelling grid. The purpose of a spelling grid is to promote structural analysis of words. Wong (1986) recommended the following steps:

1. Write the spelling word in column one and then pronounce the word and discuss its meaning(s).
2. Have the student read the word in column one.
3. In column two, have the student write the number of syllables in the word.
4. In column three, have the student divide the word into syllables.
5. In column four, have the student write the suffix of the word.
6. In column five, have the student write the modified spelling of the root word. A sample spelling grid is presented in Figure 6–7.

Word Study Strategies

Knowledge of word patterns and the linguistic structure of words may be taught to individuals with spelling difficulties using specific strategies. Students can then be encouraged to use the patterns to spell new words (Mather, 1991). If a remedial method is to be effective, a student must continue to receive help in order to attain generalization (Bradley, 1981). Provision of self-questioning strategies and guided practice with dictation exercises can help students improve spelling skills. In addition, specific instruction in morphological rules will benefit students with spelling difficulties.

Analogy Strategy

Englert, Hiebert, and Stewart (1985) presented an analogy strategy to help students notice orthographic similarities among words and then to generalize this information to new words. The following procedure is used:

1. Identify the words that a student misspelled on a pretest.
2. Develop a spelling bank of 15 words. Select words for the spelling bank by their similarity to the misspelled words. For example, the word *other* may be selected if the student misspelled the word *brother*.
3. Explain that the last parts of rhyming words are often spelled the same.
4. Present a list of words. Say one word and ask the students to identify the word in the spelling bank that rhymes with the stimulus word.
5. Based on the rhyming rule, have students identify which letters of the printed and orally presented words would be spelled the same.
6. Have students practice the words by spelling them orally from memory.
7. Have students write the words twice from memory.
8. Have students write the words from memory in a test of delayed recall.

After developing the spelling bank, have students practice the transfer words in a cloze passage. Encourage students to fill in the missing words without looking at the analogous words. Ask students to think of the word from the spelling bank that rhymes with the transfer word.

The analogy strategy may also be used to teach words that have the same phonetic features but do not rhyme (Gerber, 1984). The teacher would first identify the nonphonetic features of the word and the students would practice these features.

Spelling Grid

1 Write the word	2 Write number of syllables	3 Divide into syllables	4 Suffix	5 Modified spelling of Root Word

Figure 6–7. A sample spelling grid.

Five-Step Study Strategy

The five-step study strategy (Graham & Freeman, 1985) has been used effectively with elementary school students. After memorizing the steps and practicing them with a teacher, students use the procedure independently. Due to the simplicity of the procedure, upper-elementary and secondary students could apply the method when studying unknown words. Tracing could be eliminated when unnecessary for word retention. The following steps are used:

1. Have the student say the word.
2. Have the student write, while saying, the word.
3. Have the student check the correctness of the word.
4. Have the student trace and say the word.
5. Have the student write the word from memory and check it.

Repeat all the steps as necessary.

Results from research studies indicate that asking students to predict the accuracy of their spellings aids self-monitoring of spelling accuracy (Harris, Graham, & Freeman, 1988). The improvement in spelling may be due to increased awareness of correct spelling patterns.

Self-Questioning Strategy

Some students may benefit from use of a self-questioning strategy to help improve their spelling skill. When using this strategy, the student is encouraged to read what has actually been written as opposed to what he or she thinks has been written. The improvement may be due, therefore, to increased attention to and awareness of sound-symbol correspondence. To implement self-questioning, Wong (1986) described the following strategy:

1. Read the words aloud.
2. Teach students how to break words into syllables.
3. Show students how to identify root words and suffixes.
4. Point out the changes occurring in the root words when suffixes are added.
5. For self-evaluation, have students ask the following questions:
   a. Is this a word I know?
   b. How many syllables do I hear in this word? (Have each student write the number.)

Alternatively, the following prompts for self-questioning may be written on an index card:

   a. Do I know this word?
   b. Do I have the correct number of syllables?
   c. Is there a part of the word I am not sure how to spell?
6. Each student attempts to spell the word.
7. Students check to see that all syllables are written.
8. Students ask themselves if the word looks correct. If not, they underline the part that seems incorrect and try to spell the word again.
10. If the word does not have the correct number of syllables, the word is pronounced again while trying to identify the missing syllable.
11. Students continue with steps 7–10 until the word is known.
12. Students provide self-reinforcement by acknowledging the attempt to improve spelling.

Dictation Spelling Methods

Scarrozzo (1982) described several dictation activities that can be used to reinforce spelling, capitalization, and punctuation skills. In addition, daily dictations can be incorporated into other academic areas; for example, word problems in mathematics that contain previously studied words can be dictated. Also, dictated sentences can be used to target specific spelling patterns (e.g., "The fat cat is on my hat"). The methods and procedures for Scarrozzo's (1982) dictation method are described below:

1. Make up two sentences for dictation daily.
2. Dictate the first sentence slowly, pausing in between words. Have students write the sentence in their dictation notebooks.
3. When the whole sentence has been completed, reread the sentence.
4. Have students skip a line and repeat steps 2 and 3 for the second sentence.
5. Read the sentences again.
6. Have students correct their own papers using a colored pencil.
7. Have students give themselves points for accurately spelling words and for correct capitalization and punctuation. One point is given for each word spelled correctly, each sentence beginning with a capital letter, and each correct ending punctuation mark. Have them circle correct capital letters and end punctuation marks and underline each correctly spelled word. Without drawing attention to errors, have students record the number of correct points on the top of their paper. If desired, when the scoring system has been mastered, have students score each other's work.
8. Note student errors and provide assistance as needed.
9. As a final step, each word is read and spelled aloud by a student and repeated by the teacher.

Scarrozzo (1982) suggested that five types of sentences may be used to practice spelling in context:

i. Sentences containing a specific sound (e.g., "Mit*ch* will wat*ch* the mat*ch*es burn").
ii. Sentences stating a fact from a reading story (e.g., "The little boy was missing for 5 days").
iii. Sentences reinforcing grammatic rules (e.g., "A noun is a person, place, or thing").
iv. Sentences containing weekly spelling words (e.g., "Ann thought that the *trees* and *flowers* looked *beautiful*").
v. Sentences containing simple math word problems (e.g., "Mary had one red ball and five black balls. How many balls did she have altogether?")

Morphology

Despite considerable support for the benefits of incorporating morphology in spelling instruction, empirical investigation of this topic has been limited (Dixon, 1991). Students who have difficulty with word endings, however, often benefit from direct instruction in morphological rules. When incorporating morphology into spelling instruction, teachers are advised to follow a specific sequence. Mercer and Mercer (1993) suggested the following sequence for teaching the addition of common morphemes:

1. Noun plurals
   a. *-s*, e.g., boy*s*, chair*s*
   b. *-es*, e.g., box*es*, fox*es*
   c. *-ies*, e.g., bab*ies*, hobb*ies*
   d. *vowel changes*, e.g., wom*e*n, m*e*n
   e. *irregular additions*, e.g., ox*en*, child*ren*
2. Noun possessives
   a. *-'s*, e.g., girl*'s*, story*'s*
   b. *-s'*, e.g., boys*'*, bus*'*
3. Third person singular, present tense
   a. *-s*, e.g., journey*s*, score*s*
   b. *-es*, e.g., push*es*, crash*es*
4. Past tense
   a. *-ed*, e.g., punish*ed*, frighten*ed*
   b. *-d*, e.g., hope*d*, eliminate*d*
   c. *double consonant, -ed*, e.g., hop*ped*, slam*med*
   d. *-t*, e.g., burn*t*, spen*t*
   e. *irregular verbs*, e.g., brought, sped
5. Comparative and superlative forms of adjectives
   a. *comparative*, e.g., prettier, more handsome
   b. *superlative*, e,g., cleverest, most intelligent
6. Cross-categorical uses of the morpheme "s"
   a. *-s*, e.g., computer*s*, put*s*
   b. *-'s*, e.g., teacher*'s*, there*'s*
   c. *-s'*, e.g., author*s'*, dress*'*
7. Noun derivation
   a. *er*, e.g., run*ner*, bat*ter*
8. Adverb derivation
   a. *ly*, e.g., quick*ly*, brilliant*ly*
9. Prefixes, for example:
   a. *pre*, e.g., *pre*test, *pre*natal
   b. *post*, e.g., *post*secondary, *post*operation
   c. *pro*, e.g., *pro* golfer, or *pro* choice
   d. *anti*, e.g., *anti*depressant, *anti* choice
   e. *de*, e.g., *de*press, *de*form
   f. *un*, e.g., *un*educated, *un*tidy
   g. *im*, e.g., *im*mortal, *im*moral

Usage

This morning I took out a comma and this afternoon I put it back again.

—Oscar Wilde

Instruction in the use of the conventions of composition often receives a disproportionate amount of critical attention from teachers (McCoy & Prehm, 1987). This is particularly unfortunate for students with learning disabilities as they often require direct instruction and feedback to improve their skill. These students do not detect effectively the mechanical errors in their writing (Deshler, Ferrell, & Kass, 1978) and even when the errors are highlighted, they are often unable to correct them (Espin & Sindelar, 1988; MacArthur et al., 1986).

Using individualized checklists, students with learning disabilities can increase their knowledge and understanding of writing conventions. The best way to help students detect and correct usage errors is to use a problem-solving approach during the editing stage (Tompkins, 1994).

Usage also includes the socially preferred way of using language within a dialect (Tompkins, 1994). Teachers must be particularly careful when teaching standard English to speakers with differing dialects. As a caution, variations in cultural syntax (e.g., Black Dialect) should not be viewed as incorrect. The use of nonstandard or standard dialects is an issue of appropriateness, not correctness (Rhodes & Dudley-Marling, 1988). When helping students make corrections, discuss with them how standard English is used in formal types of writing (Tompkins, 1994), whereas dialects are suitable in other contexts. Both forms are appropriate, therefore, in different situations. For example, the language a student uses in a business letter will differ from the language used in writing a letter to a friend. Or, the use of a dialect may be appropriate in a narrative. By encouraging students to write for different purposes, teachers provide students with the breadth of experiences necessary to communicate effectively with a variety of audiences. Subsequently, every writer requires a "wardrobe of languages" to meet changing social demands (Sampson et al., 1991).

Finally, one must consider that the English language is constantly changing and that some traditionally objectionable forms of expression are now viewed as acceptable. For example, previously, the accepted plural of "curriculum" was "curricula" and the accepted plural of "cactus" was "cacti." Presently, both "curricula" and "curriculums" and "cacti" and "cactuses" are acceptable.

As with other areas of written language, instruction in usage should be sequential. Initially, punctuation and capitalization rules should be taught separately and should not interfere with, or discourage, beginning writers. Teachers should begin with structured materials and then help students to apply the rules to their own work in the editing stage (Isaacson, 1987).

Even though direct instruction with supervised practice in context appears effective for teaching both capitalization and punctuation rules, students who have mastered the rules through direct instruction, may not apply them consistently in their own writing (Meyer et al., 1991). Consequently, attention to both acquisition and generalization of these skills is important. To master both capitalization and punctuation rules, a student should be able to recognize when an element should be used and then apply it in new situations (Cohen & Plaskon, 1980). Meyer et al. (1991) noted that mastery of language conventions requires students to: (a) learn what the principle is, (b) practice examples until they are automatic, and (c) apply the principle in written work. In regard to basic capitalization and punctuation rules, by the end of elementary school, students should be able to start sentences with an uppercase letter, end sentences with a period and questions with a question mark, use commas in a list, and use apostrophes in contractions (Hoy & Gregg, 1994).

Punctuation

Punctuation rules can be taught within the context of a student's writing. Students who have learned punctuation in the context of frequent writing often master and transfer these rules more easily than those who have been taught skills in isolation (Calkins, 1983). The key to successful instruction appears to be mastery of the rule, followed by application in authentic writing activities.

Subskills

Poeet (1987) recommended that punctuation subskills be taught in the following order:

1 Period
  Question mark
  Dash
2 Comma
  Underline
3 Apostrophe
  Exclamation point
  Colon
  Quotation marks
5 Hyphen
6 Parentheses

Cohen and Plaskon (1980) provided a more expanded list, sequenced according to the order of presentation in a writing curriculum. The sequence is as follows:

1. Period
   a. At the end of a sentence
   b. Following a command
   c. After an abbreviation
   d. After numbers in a list
   e. Following an initial
   f. After letters and numbers in an outline
2. Comma
   a. In dates (between the day of the month and the year)
   b. In addresses (between the name of the city and the state)
   c. After the greeting of a friendly letter
   d. After the closing of a friendly letter
   e. Between the words given in a list
   f. To set off appositives
   g. After "yes" and "no" when they are used as parenthetical expressions
   h. After the name of a person being addressed
   i. To separate a quotation from the explanatory part of a sentence
   j. After a person's last name when it is written before the first name
3. Question mark
   a. At the close of a question
4. Quotation marks

a. Before and after the direct words of a speaker
   b. Around the title of a story, poem, or an article
5. Apostrophe
   a. To establish a possessive noun
   b. In a contraction
6. Exclamation point
   a. At the end of an exclamatory sentence
   b. After a word or group of words showing surprise or strong feeling
7. Hyphen
   a. In compound words
   b. In compound numbers (e.g., telephone numbers)
   c. Separating syllables of a word that is divided at the end of the line
8. Colon
   a. Between the hour and minutes in the time of day (e.g., 3:25)
   b. After the salutation in a business letter

Punctuation Strategy

This strategy, adapted from McCarney and Cummins (1988), can be used to teach any type of punctuation mark, from periods to exclamation points to quotation marks. The following steps are used:

1. Teach punctuation marks one at a time.
2. Explain when and how the punctuation mark is used.
3. Initially, have the student learn to use the punctuation mark in out-of-context practice sentences.
4. Highlight all of the specific punctuation marks for a number of pages in the student's reading book.
5. Read the book with the student. Pause at each incidence of the punctuation that is being taught and review the usage rules. For example, when teaching periods, pause at the end of each sentence to discuss the complete thought that was finished by a period.
6. Encourage the student to try to use the punctuation mark correctly in written assignments.
7. If errors are made, do not punish incorrect usage, but spend more time on steps 1–5.

8. Have the student proofread written work for the punctuation mark.
9. Encourage the student to read the work aloud when proofreading.
10. Repeat any or all of the steps as necessary.

Capitalization

Relatively simple procedures, such as peer teaching combined with student letter-writing activities, have been used to teach capitalization skills (Campbell, Brady, & Linehan, 1991). Teachers should begin by identifying which rules have been mastered.

Subskills

Thomas et al. (1984) suggested the following instructional sequences for teaching capitalization subskills:

1. First and last names
2. First word in a sentence
3. The word "I"
4. Days, months, and holidays
5. Proper names: people, schools, parks, rivers
6. Addresses: streets, roads, cities, states, countries
7. Personal titles: Mr., Mrs., Miss., Dr.
8. Commercial product names

A more expanded list, adapted from Poteet (1987), is:

1. Names, titles
2. Days, months
3. First word in a sentence
4. The word "I"
5. Proper nouns
6. Letters
7. Abbreviations
8. Initials
9. Time
10. Places
11. Race and nationality
12. School subjects
13. Quotes
14. Organizations
15. Songs
16. Degrees
17. Documents
18. Proper adjectives

An alternative to the above list, suggested by Cohen and Plaskon (1980), is:

1. A person's first name
2. A person's last name
3. The first word of a sentence
4. The word "I"
5. The date
6. Proper names: holidays, months, places, days of the week
7. Names of streets and cities
8. Titles of compositions and books
9. Title names: Mrs., Ms., Mr., Miss., Dr., President Washington
10. Mother and Father, when used as proper names
11. First word in the salutation of a letter
12. First word in the closing of a letter
13. Names of organizations and clubs
14. Geographical names
15. Names of states
16. Commercial product names
17. First word of a quotation
18. Race and nationality

Cloze Procedure

The cloze procedure can also be used to help students practice and review capitalization rules. A variety of letters, some that require capitalization and others that do not, can be deleted from a short passage. Students would read the passage and then reconstruct it by selecting either lowercase or uppercase letters to appear in the blank. This activity could be scaffolded for students with limited skill by placing both forms of the letter that has been deleted underneath the blank.

Syntax

Students with learning disabilities often benefit from direct instruction in syntax. This does not mean formal grammar instruction. Research over the past decade has demonstrated that traditional instruction in grammar is not effective for improving student writing (Hillocks, 1987). Syntactic competence can be increased, however, through modeling, reinforcement, and explicit instruction (Pressley & Rankin, 1994). Syntactic rules are taught within the context of the students' own writing (Anderson, 1982;

Gould, 1991). Instruction within the context of a student's own language promotes long-term learning (Wiig & Semel, 1984).

A variety of sentence-building strategies exist that help students become more aware of and more proficient with sentence structure. These strategies often begin with simple sentence patterns and then encourage students to expand the basic sentences through elaboration.

CATS Strategy

One simple strategy, described by Giordano (1982), is known by the acronym CATS. The acronym is a reminder to: Copy, Alter, Transform, and Supply. Prior to beginning the strategy, three sentences, with a space in between, are written by the teacher. Subsequently, the following steps are used:

C   Have the student *copy* a favorite sentence. If unable to copy, have the student trace the sentence with a yellow marker pen.
A   Help the student *alter* one word in the copied sentence.
T   Have the student *transform* the sentence into a different form, such as turning a statement into a question.
S   Have the student *supply* a response to the transformation, such as answering the question.

Sentence Guides

Students who have trouble writing simple sentences may benefit from a method like the Phelps Sentence Guide Program (Phelps-Terasaki & Phelps, 1980). In this program, the student learns sentence elements by answering questions. The program progresses from simple sentence patterns based on pictures to paragraph writing. The sentence guide consists of nine columns placed across the top of the sheet, each containing a question. By answering the questions, the student produces and then writes sentences.

This program can be adapted by developing different guides that will produce different sentence patterns. A teacher may write a series of questions across the top of a paper. For example, a modified guide could contain the following three prompts: "Who?" "Did what?" "To whom?" Or, a more complex pattern would be: "Who?" "What doing?"

"When?" "Where?" "Why?" These questions may refer to a picture or a story. A student would answer the questions and then write a sentence.

As skill develops, the order of questions may be reversed. For example, instead of starting the sentence with the word "who," the first question could be "when." Once sentence writing has been mastered, pictures that tell a story in sequence may be used to develop skill in paragraph writing.

Sentence Expansion

Tompkins (1994) described a similar procedure for expanding sentences. The following steps are used:

1. Have students write a basic sentence that contains a subject and a verb.
2. Have students respond to four questions:
   What kind?
   Where?
   Why?
   How?
3. After the questions are answered, have students write the expanded sentence.

An example of this technique follows:

Basic sentence: *The woman swam.*
   What kind? athletic
   Where? in the West River
   Why? she needed some exercise
   How? rapidly
Expanded sentence: *Barb, an athletic woman, swam rapidly in the West River to get some exercise.*

As an alternative, some students may benefit from practice with sentence expansion charts. These charts may be developed to illustrate a variety of sentence types. Two samples are presented in Figures 6–8 and 6–9. As a final step, students then write the expanded sentence.

Sentence Construction

Students may be taught syntactic rules as they learn the specific terminology associated with parts of speech. This procedure, adapted from Kuchinskas and Radencich (1986), involves the following steps:

Article	Noun	Verb			
Article	Adjective	Noun	Verb		
Article	Adjective	Noun	Verb	Adverb	
Article	Adjective	Noun	Verb	Adverb	Prepositional Phrase

Write final sentence: _____

Figure 6–8. Simple sentence expansion chart.

Compound Sentence Expansion Chart

Article	Noun	Verb	Conjunction	Article	Noun	Verb

Article	Adjective	Noun	Verb	Conjunc-tion	Article	Adjective	Noun	Verb

Article	Adjective	Noun	Verb	Adverb	Conj.	Article	Adjective	Noun	Verb	Adverb

Write final sentence: _____

_____

Figure 6–9. Compound sentence expansion chart.

1. Write the following headings on a chalk-board: Article, Adjective, Noun, Verb, Adverb, Preposition, Article, Adjective, Noun.

2. Ensure that all students understand what type of word is represented by each of the headings.

3. Have students brainstorm words under each heading. For example:

   Possessive pronoun — *my, our, their, his, her, its, your*
   Adjective — *beautiful, mean, cowardly, enormous*
   Noun — *skyscraper, monster, wishing-well, toothbrush*
   Verb — *crawled, bounced, sang, laughed, hiccupped*
   Adverb — *energetically, noisily, shyly, laughingly*
   Preposition — *under, in, beside, after, above*
   Article — *the, a, one*
   Adverb — *beautiful, gigantic, enormous, stocky, intelligent*
   Noun — *candlestick, dictionary, dog, bottle, grass*

4. Have students construct sentences by choosing one word from each list. Nonsensical sentences are acceptable.

5. Ask students to construct additional sentences that make sense and follow the same pattern.

6. When this sentence pattern has been mastered, teach students to write compound sentences by using conjunctions such as *but, and, although,* and *because.*

Sentence Combining

Several sentence-combining strategies exist whereby a writer is helped to combine several short sentences into one longer sentence. Sentence-combining exercises help students to increase their syntactic maturity (Cooper, 1973; Lawlor, 1983).

To begin, write two or three simple sentences on the chalkboard, and ask students to combine the sentences to form one longer, more elaborate sentence. Discuss all suggestions and write all acceptable sentences produced by students on the board.

Next, take sentences directly from a student's written work. If desired, exercises may focus on a specific aspect of syntax. For example, the focus may be on joining sentences with a variety of conjunctions such as *because*, *but*, and *or*. Emphasis should be placed on instruction in a variety of sentence patterns.

A sentence-combining strategy, adapted from Nutter and Safran (1984), suggests adherence to the following steps:

1. Construct simple sentences in one of two ways:
   a. Compose them from the student's spelling and vocabulary words.
   b. Decombine sentences from the student's textbooks.
2. Teach any unfamiliar words out of context.
3. Provide ample oral practice with the sentences before asking the student to combine them in writing.
4. Be available to guide and provide encouragement when the student attempts written work.
5. Supply any requested spellings.
6. Accept all answers that are grammatically correct.
7. Encourage creativity, not just correctness.
8. Use the strategy several times per week for 5 to 15 minutes.

For further examples refer to Cooper (1973), who presented an outline for developing sentence-combining problems. The outline illustrates many different types of patterns and embeddings.

Sentence Writing Strategy

The Sentence Writing Strategy (Schumaker & Sheldon, 1985) is one of six strategies included in the Expression and Demonstration of Competence Strand of the *Learning Strategies Curriculum* from the University of Kansas. Through this institution, teachers can receive specific training in the use and application of these strategies. This comprehensive strategy is designed to help students learn to write four kinds of sentences. A brief overview is provided:

The sentence types are defined as follows:

Simple. A simple sentence consists of one independent clause or a group of words that makes a complete statement and can stand alone. Four formula types of simple sentences include: (a) single subject and verb, (b) compound subjects and single verb, (c) single subject with compound verbs, and (d) compound subjects and compound verbs.

Examples: *Martha jumped.*
Martha and Bill jumped over the gate.
Martha jumped over the gate and ran.
Martha and Bill jumped over the gate and ran.

Compound. A compound sentence consists of two or more independent clauses that can each stand alone. Seven coordinating conjunctions are presented that may be used to connect the two independent clauses: *for, and, nor, but, or, yet, so.* Two formula types of compound sentences include: independent clauses joined by a coordinating conjunction and independent clauses joined by a semicolon.

Examples: *Martha skipped and jumped.*
Martha was late; she missed the show.

Complex. A complex sentence consists of one independent clause and one or more dependent clause. A dependent clause contains a subject and verb but cannot stand alone. The dependent clause starts with a word that shows the relationship between the two clauses. The related words are called subordinating conjunctions. Two formula types of complex sentences include: independent clause placed before the dependent clause, or the dependent clause preceding the independent clause.

Examples: *Martha had dinner before she went to the show.*

Because she was late, Martha missed the show.

Compound-complex sentences. A compound-complex sentence combines compound and complex sentences and consists of two or more independent clauses and at least one dependent clause (e.g., *Martha had dinner and finished her homework before she went to the show*). Compound-complex sentences with two independent clauses and one dependent clause can be formed in three ways: The dependent clause may be followed by, between, or after the two independent clauses. Formula types of compound-complex sentences include: (a) two where the dependent clause is first, (b) two where the dependent clause is second, and (c) two where the dependent clause comes third.

Examples (a): *Before she went to the show, Martha ate dinner and exercised.*
Before she went to show, Martha ate dinner; it was delicious.
Examples (b): *Martha exercised before she ate, and later she went to the show.*
Martha had dinner; because she exercised, she was late for the show.
Examples (c): *Martha had dinner and exercised, before she went to the show.*
Martha had dinner and exercised; however, she missed the show.

PENS strategy. Another component of the Sentence Writing Strategy is the PENS strategy (Schumaker, Nolan, & Deshler, 1985; Schumaker & Sheldon, 1985). The procedure assumes prior knowledge of: (a) grammatical structure, (b) parts of speech, (c) independent clauses, (d) coordinating conjunctions, (e) compound sentences, and (f) the use of commas and semicolons. The following mnemonic is taught:

P PICK the most appropriate of the 14 different formulas for writing four basic sentence types (simple, compound, compound-complex, and complex sentences). Each formula corresponds to a different sentence structure.
E EXPLORE the different words that fit the chosen formula.

N NOTE the words that have been selected and written down.
S SUBJECT and verb must be present; check the sentences to ensure that they are. Use of this strategy will help students learn to recognize and write different types of sentences.

Macrocloze/Slotting

Two techniques, macrocloze (Whaley, 1981) and slotting (Poteet, 1987), may be used to assist students with sentence expansion. In macrocloze, sentences are deleted from stories and the students are then asked to fill in the missing content. With the slotting technique, blanks are inserted where context can be elaborated in a sentence, and then students brainstorm descriptive words, phrases, and clauses that could be added to make the writing more mature. Students then can select the choices that make the writing most interesting.

Proofreading

Although proofreading and revision are often accomplished in the editing stage of writing, some strategies focus more on the correction of errors in basic skills, whereas others address procedures to facilitate revision of content. Procedures that are more skill-based and used during the editing stage are presented in the following section. Procedures that are more meaning-based and used during the revising stage are presented in Chapter 7.

Strategies

When helping students improve their editing skills, it is often best to limit specific skill instruction to one or two types of error patterns at a time. When teachers focus on only one or two types of errors, such as tense consistency or the use of quotation marks, the mastery of skills becomes manageable for students because the task is finite.

COPS Strategy

The COPS strategy (Schumaker et al., 1981) was designed to help students identify four error types. The mnemonic is used to represent the following steps:

C CAPITALIZATION—check capitalization of first words in sentences and proper nouns

O OVERALL appearance of work—check for neatness, legibility, margins, indentation of paragraphs, and complete sentences.

P PUNCTUATION—check commas and end punctuation.

S SPELLING—check to see if the words are spelled correctly.

Using this strategy, students are encouraged to check their writing independently before submitting their work.

SCOPE Strategy

Bos and Vaughn (1994) described a similar strategy with the acronym of SCOPE. This strategy may be used to help students develop proofreading skills. The strategy consists of the following series of questions that the student applies to writing:

S Is the *spelling* correct?

C Are the first words and proper names and nouns *capitalized*?

O Is the syntax or word *order* correct?

P Are there *punctuation* marks where needed?

E Does the sentence *express* a complete thought? Does the sentence contain a noun and a verb?

Spelling Proofreading Exercises

Poteet (1987) recommended the following procedure for helping students detect spelling errors. The following steps are used:

1. Underline some (or all) of the misspelled words from students' writing samples. Present several words and have students choose the correct spelling. As skill improves, change the activity so that students choose the correct spelling from those offered by either a spell checker in a word processing program or a hand-held spell checker.

2. List the number of misspelled words in a line or sentence. Provide peer, aid, or teacher help in identifying and correcting the errors. As skill improves, encourage students to find and correct the misspellings independently. In addition, list the number of misspellings per paragraph and, ultimately, per assignment.

3. Give students a list of ten words of which they know the spelling of eight. Misspell a number of the words and ask students to identify which words are misspelled and then correct the errors. Initially, tell students how many words are misspelled each time. As skill improves, increase the number of words in the list, do not enumerate the number of errors, and/or require students to correct the errors using a spell checker or dictionary.

4. Provide students with uncorrected writing samples from previous classes. Encourage them to read the samples aloud twice, once for content and once for spelling. Provide the necessary support for the correct identification of errors (e.g., peer help, the number of misspelled words). As skill improves, have students identify the misspelled words. Provide the necessary support in correcting the errors. As skill improves further, expect independent correction of errors.

5. Encourage students to correct writing assignments for spelling by reading the last word first, and ending with the first word. Help them focus on how the words are actually read, not on how they should be read in context. Provide support to correct errors. As skill improves, have students read from front to end in order to check for content and spelling simultaneously. Before reading from the beginning, students must be adept at reading words as they are written.

Corrective Strategy

The following strategy, adapted from Poteet (1987), can be used to help students correct specific errors. The following steps are used:

1. Select one error in a student's writing and point it out.

2. Explain the importance of the skill and the intent of review.

3. Illustrate the correct usage of the skill in the context of the student's paper.

4. Use a colored marker to highlight the skill.

5. Have the student read an example written by the teacher.

6. Have the student demonstrate knowledge of the skill by writing it in an isolated task.
7. Have the student demonstrate knowledge of the skill in the context of a paper.
8. Have the student proofread a paper for the specific skill.
9. Have the student work with a peer to proofread the writing for the specific skill.
10. Have the student write '*Proofread for _____*' on the top of the paper.

Guided Proofreading

Mehlmann and Waters (1985) described a procedure that provides scaffolding for students during the editing process. The following steps are used to help students identify the errors in their papers:

1. Underline all errors in a sentence.
2. Provide clues as to the type of error.
3. Gradually decrease the amount of instructor assistance. For example, the teacher could:
   a. List the errors underneath the sentence in the order they occur (e.g., capital letter, spelling, verb-tense, and spelling).
   b. Present the error clues in random order.
   c. Underline the errors but do not provide clues regarding the type of error.
   d. Provide only the number of errors (e.g., 4).
   e. Have the student locate and correct errors independently.
4. Repeat the method with larger passages of writing (e.g., three sentences, paragraphs).

Editing Errors in Syntax

Tompkins (1994) described several procedures for helping students detect and correct errors in syntax. These procedures help students learn to use a problem-solving approach for editing syntactic errors. Students correct errors only in the editing stage of a process approach. Prior to editing, help students decide which errors to correct through consideration of: (a) audience, (b) function of writing, and (c) composition format. Explain that correct syntax, like correct spelling, is a courtesy to the reader. Keep the explanations of errors brief and do not insist that all errors be corrected. If a student

is not ready to learn the reason for some changes, simply state the necessary changes without explanation.

Use a variety of activities to help students rewrite sentences. For example, you may use sentence-building activities to help students replace overused and nondescript words or help them replace short, simple sentences with more complex ones using sentence-combining activities.

SCAN Strategy

The mnemonic SCAN (Graham & Harris, 1987) can be used to help students clarify sentences. The letters represent the following steps:

S   Does the sentence make *sense*?
C   Is the sentence *connected* to my beliefs?
A   Can more be *added*?
N   Have I *noted* all the errors?

Proofreading Checklist

A proofreading checklist can be used to help students remember what to check in their work. These lists may be individualized or a more generic form may be used with an entire class. The guidelines should gradually become more general with the goal of increasing student independence (Moulton & Bader, 1986). Figure 6–10 illustrates a sample proofreading checklist developed by Weiss and Weiss (1993). This checklist is filled out, checked, and then signed for each written assignment that is taken to the editing stage.

Sentence Proofing Questions/Phrases

This strategy for proofreading questions and phrases, adapted from Bereiter and Scardamalia (1982), helps students to revise sentences within a paragraph during the editing stage. The teacher asks evaluative questions after each sentence. After considering the question, the student decides whether or not the sentence is problematic. If so, the student uses the directive statements to decide how to resolve the problem.

Evaluative questions include:

1. Does the sentence state the topic?
2. Does the sentence add further information to the topic sentence?
3. Does the sentence follow a logical order?

Name: _____

Class: _____

Date: _____

Student's Checklist of Good Proofreading Skills

	1.	I have reread my paper.
	2.	I have begun all sentences with a capital letter.
	3.	I have begun all names of persons or places with a capital letter.
	4.	I have put a period at the end of each sentence.
	5.	I have put a question mark at the end of each direct question.
	6.	I have checked words for misspellings.
	7.	I have reread my sentences aloud to be sure they make sense.
	8.	I have a beginning or introductory sentence.
	9.	I have a concluding sentence, a summary.
	10.	My handwriting is readable (legible), I think.
	11.	I have written on every second line so that I can make changes and corrections.

Signature: _____

Figure 6–10. Sample proofreading checklist.

Note. From *Formulas to Read and Write* (p. 99), by M. S. Weiss and H. G. Weiss, 1993, Avon, CO: Treehouse Associates. Copyright 1993 by Treehouse Associates. Reprinted by permission.

4. Does the sentence say what I really want to say?
5. Does the sentence sound right?
6. Does the sentence show what I really think?
7. Does the information sound credible?
8. Does the sentence summarize what has been said so far?
9. Does the sentence sound like a conclusive comment?
10. Will readers see the importance of the sentence?
11. Will readers be interested in the sentence?
12. Will readers understand what I mean by the sentence?
13. Is the sentence clear and to the point?
14. Is the sentence a good one?
15. Is the sentence connected to the previous one?

Directive phrases include:

1. Change (some of) the wording of the sentence.

2. Expand the sentence to clarify the information.
3. Add further sentences to support the given information.
4. Add further sentences to explain the given information.
5. Delete part of the sentence.
6. Delete the whole sentence.
7. Delete the sentence but rewrite the information another way.
8. Move the sentence to a different place.
9. Use a cohesive tie to connect the sentence with the previous one.
10. Leave the sentence as it is.

Conclusion

Students with learning disabilities face particular challenges related to their need for automaticity in the mechanical aspects of writing (Isaacson, 1994). Although these students often have difficulty expressing their ideas through writing, they experience even more difficulty with the acquisition of basic writing skills. In most instances, when provided with precise feedback and practice, students can develop specific skills within the context of their own writing during the editing stage. Fortunately, many skills become more fluent and automatic as they are practiced (McCutchen et al., 1994).

The difficulty when teaching students with learning disabilities becomes the balancing act of process and product. How can a teacher help a student develop secretarial skills and reinforce the accurate use of skills without discouraging the author? The first step is to involve students in the process through provision of meaningful and interesting writing activities. As students see the purposes and the benefits of writing, their commitment to correcting errors in spelling and usage during the editing stage increases. The important consideration is that teachers, not textbooks, workbooks, or skill sheets, are the key factor to student improvement in basic writing skills (Gaskins, 1982). A supportive, structured, accepting environment in which students feel free to experiment and risk error allows for maximum exploration and development of literacy (Dobson, 1985).

7

WRITTEN EXPRESSION

Beneath the rule of men entirely great,
The pen is mightier than the sword.

—Baron Bulwer-Lytton
in *Richelieu*, Act II, sc.ii

Recent conceptualizations of writing have focused on the cognitive nature of the task and use of strategies to facilitate planning and generation of content (Graham & Harris, 1988). As noted by Strickland (1972): "The quality of what is expressed in writing depends upon the quality of thinking that undergirds it" (p. 498). Many of the methods used to enhance skill in written expression involve the application of strategies. These strategies are designed purposefully to assist students in thinking (cognition) and in thinking about their thinking (metacognition).

This chapter begins with a brief discussion of the relationship between metacognition and strategies for helping students express their ideas. Next, a variety of prewriting activities are presented. Instructional programs for the areas of vocabulary, text structure, and revision are then discussed. Each section begins with a review of general instructional principles and then provides descriptions of specific instructional strategies.

Metacognition and Metalinguistics

Metacognition involves awareness of one's own thinking processes, whereas metalinguistics involves a person's ability to think about language and its uses (Kamhi, 1987). Metacognitive theory has stimulated research in the field of learning disabilities (Borkowski, 1992), particularly in regard to the roles of self-regulation and student motivation (Borkowski, Estrada, Milstead, & Hale, 1989; Graham & Harris, 1993). The teacher helps students

to monitor and control the cognitive processes involved in composing (Graham & Harris, 1988).

The role of the teacher, then, is to hypothesize how a student is processing information. The instructional focus is on each student's learning process and the teacher modifies the teaching strategy to promote both cognitive development and learning (Borkowski, 1992). As noted by Silliman and Wilkinson (1994): "because written language transcends immediate temporal and spatial constraints, it is a potentially powerful metacognitive tool for creating, understanding, and revising ideas about the world" (p. 27). Similarly, metalinguistic analysis places language processing into the conscious realm, allowing for deliberation during production and revision of written language (Hux & Stogsdill, 1993). Translating thoughts into writing allows a student the opportunity to develop and clarify ideas (Dagenais & Beadle, 1984).

Although the impact of metalinguistic deficiencies on writing is not clear, students with learning disabilities are generally inferior in monitoring their written language (Gerber, 1993). Figure 7–1 illustrates an example of poor self-monitoring. Marliss, a sixth-grade student, was asked to write a compare-contrast essay on the major differences between humans and apes. Although she introduced the topic appropriately, she failed to maintain her focus. Fortunately, students can be taught many strategies to help them with self-monitoring.

Principles

Several principles apply to strategy instruction. The following commonalities exist in the majority of the metacognitive intervention strategies (Palinscar & Brown, 1987; Pressley, Borkowski, & O'Sullivan, 1984):

How Humans are like Apes.

Humans and apes are alike in many ways. They look sort of the same and walk on two legs. But they are different to. Humans are more intelligent but not all humans are intelligent because my brother isn't intelligent and he's human at least most of the time. When we were still kids, my brother would do horibal things to me. One day he put a frog in my bed and I screamed and screamed. My mother was mad with my brother. and he had to appollogise to me. But I got him back another day because his friends were going to play basball and I had to tell my brother what time to go and I didn't so he didn't play his game and I thoght it was funny. But I like my brother most of the time.

Figure 7–1. A compare-contrast essay by Marliss, a sixth-grade student.

1. Explicit, elaborate instruction in regard to the goals of the strategies.
2. Explicit, elaborate instruction in regard to how the strategies apply to the task at hand.
3. Feedback in regard to the efficacy of the strategies in aiding task performance.
4. Instruction in monitoring the degree to which the strategies are improving achievement.
5. Identification of the strategies used and explanations as to the reasons for their use.

As a general principle, teachers can facilitate development through guided discussions that help students become aware of the strategies that they use when writing (Englert, Raphael, Anderson, Anthony, & Stevens, 1991). Teacher-student conferences can be used to help students understand how they approach the writing task and to discuss alternative strategies. What the teacher emphasizes will affect how students approach the writing act (Sampson et al., 1991). The following is a transcription of a brief dialogue between Irene and her fourth-grade teacher:

Teacher: Your story writing skill has improved tremendously in the last few months, Irene. How do you select what to write about?

Irene: I sit and think of something that I like or something good that I saw on TV or read in a book. Then I look around the room and in my spelling dictionary to see the words that I can use because I know how to spell them.

Teacher: And then what do you do?

Irene: Then I think out my story but I have to change it sometimes because I can't think of how to spell the words. But I can spell words like "and" and "there" and I couldn't even do that last year.

Teacher: You have so many good ideas but I would rather you were not so concerned about your spelling. Try to get down part of the word you want to write, or just make a blank line and then later when we are editing your story we can put in the correct spelling. You could even draw a little picture of the word if you want.

Irene: That sounds okay because I remember the words that I want to write, I'm just not sure how to spell them. You know I can tell better stories than I can write.

Teacher: You are a good storyteller, but tell me, how else do you get ideas?

Irene: Well, sometimes I get ideas from talking with the other kids in class and other times I look at Brian's paper and see what he's writing about. Sometimes he asks me what I am writing about because he can't think of anything either. Sometimes when I ask him, he helps me with spelling.

Teacher: Maybe next time, before we write, you and Brian could work together and see if you can come up with some ideas that you both would like to write about.

Irene: That would be fun because he can help with spelling and most days I can tell a good story.

Steps in Strategy Instruction

The first step in using metacognitive-oriented strategies is to develop students' sensitivity to and interest in the purpose and communicative functions of writing (Ariel, 1992). When teachers make assignments, they need to provide clear, concise reasons as to why a given writing activity is important so that students view writing as a meaningful activity (Ediger, 1993). Once students are fully involved in the writing activity, specific strategies can be used to help increase skill.

The following general steps apply to teaching all learning strategies (Levy & Rosenberg, 1990):

1. Students are pretrained in the skills necessary for learning and using the specific strategy.
2. Both students and the teacher examine the present level of performance in the selected skill.
3. Students must be aware of, and accept, the importance of skill training. The teacher discusses the rationale for the use of the strategy.
4. The teacher describes the steps and models the strategy.
5. Students memorize the steps of the strategy.
6. Students develop self-instruction in the strategy through practice and corrective feedback

from the teacher. Teacher and students discuss settings and situations in which the strategy can be applied.

7. Students apply the strategy in different circumstances, for different purposes, and without assistance from the teacher.

To become self-regulating, students must be able to see the actions and hear the talk of skilled writers engaged in actual problem solving. Initially, therefore, the teacher models the self-talk and vocabulary, gradually increasing the learners' responsibility to assume whatever aspect of the dialogue they can control (Englert & Mariage, 1991).

Students with writing difficulties require opportunities to manipulate language in order to express complex thoughts. Consequently, methods that encourage language manipulation are an important component of the writing program (Vogel, 1985). These types of activities are easily incorporated into the prewriting stage of the writing process.

Prewriting Strategies

Students write most easily when the topics are related and relevant to their immediate background and environment (Ariel, 1992). As noted by Bereiter and Scardamalia (1982) students often write briefly not because they lack knowledge, but rather because they lack strategies for activating the knowledge that they have. Writers benefit from various activities that help them develop, expand upon, and organize their ideas prior to writing. Prewriting activities can be used for any type of text structure, either narrative or expository.

Readiness for Writing

Some individuals have not developed the following prerequisites for writing (Poteet, 1987): (a) inner language or being able to conceptually associate experiences, things, and people with thoughts and words; (b) ability to communicate ideas through oral expression; (c) ability to interpret pictures, letters, and words; (d) interest in communicating in writing; or (e) ability to sustain attention to the task. A variety of structured techniques can be used to encourage beginning or reluctant writers to compose.

Before creating text, all writers need ideas. Some individuals, particularly those with learning disabil-

ities, often have difficulty generating ideas. Tompkins and Friend (1986) described several procedures that may be used to help students develop ideas prior to writing.

Observation

The following activities were suggested to help students record their observations:

A. Observation (Pictures)
  1. Provide students with an interesting picture with details.
  2. Ask students to name all the things that can be seen in the picture.
  3. List the responses on the chalkboard.
  4. Help students categorize the words.
  5. Have students use the words to write sentences to describe the picture.

B. Observation (Objects)
  1. Gather a collection of common objects such as combs, rocks, and toothbrushes.
  2. Distribute the objects among the students.
  3. Have each student list five observations about his or her object.
  4. Have the students combine the five observations into five sentences, without naming the object.
  5. Collect all the objects and the written descriptions.
  6. Read the descriptions aloud and have the students guess which object is being described.
  7. As skill develops, make the task more difficult by distributing items that are similar.

C. Observation (Events)
  1. Have students observe an event such as a candle burning or a dog eating.
  2. Help students write down words to describe the event.
  3. Help students organize the list of words into a logical sequence.
  4. Ask students to write a description of the event with the help of the organizer.

Giordano (1983a, 1983b, 1984) described the following strategies:

1. Ordered writing. Have students record sequential observations whereby the beginning,

middle, and end of an activity or observation are noted.

2. Incomplete sentence exercises. Provide students with a number of incomplete sentences. Initially, have students choose a response from among controlled selections. As skill improves, have students create their own responses.

3. Paraphrasing. Create different exercises for summarizing material. For example, have students rewrite sentences for different audiences. Or, have students write summaries of lower-grade books that are then attached on the inside cover of the book.

4. Dialogue. Have students create the dialogue for cartoon or fictional characters. Several microcomputer programs are available, or newspaper cartoons with the dialogue deleted may be used.

5. Correspondence. Have students write in a personal notebook. Write a response that emphasizes the communicative aspect of writing and encourage students to reply.

50 Journal Topics

Sometimes students cannot think of anything to write about and need assistance selecting a topic for journal or story writing. The following list, compiled by Wendy Randall Wall, provides possible starters for journal entries.

1. If I could visit any place I would . . .
2. I think life on another planet would be . . .
3. If I had three wishes I would . . .
4. My favorite sport is . . .
5. The last movie I saw is . . .
6. My favorite professional athlete/movie star is . . .
7. I love my pet because . . .
8. A person whom I admire is . . .
9. The best gift I have received is . . .
10. When I was younger I liked to . . .
11. I think an interesting experience would be . . .
12. Something I do well is . . .
13. The most incredible journey I have ever made is . . .
14. The season I like best is . . .

15. If I could be in charge of the world I would . . .
16. My favorite activity is . . .
17. A good book I have read is . . .
18. If I could be locked in a toy store, I would . . .
19. I love my best friend because . . .
20. My family is . . .
21. Something I have always wanted to do is . . .
22. My ideal vacation would be . . .
23. My favorite subject in school is . . .
24. If I could be the teacher I would . . .
25. I felt proud when I . . .
26. When I am older I will . . .
27. If I won the lottery, I would . . .
28. The funniest thing I ever did is . . .
29. What I like most about myself is . . .
30. If I could be the President of the United States, I would . . .
31. Something people don't know about me is . . .
32. After school, I like to . . .
33. The best choice I ever made was . . .
34. If I could be any animal, I would choose to be . . .
35. My favorite place to be is . . .
36. Something I like to do for others is . . .
37. When I go to the mall, I like to . . .
38. One day, I would like to learn to . . .
39. What really drives me crazy is . . .
40. Someone who has really helped me is . . .
41. A country I would like to visit is . . .
42. One of my goals is . . .
43. A fun game to play is . . .
44. A person I would like to meet is . . .
45. I am thankful for . . .
46. If I could fly, I would . . .
47. I was mad/scared/surprised when . . .
48. Something I have always wanted to do is . . .
49. My favorite superhero is . . .
50. If I could change something about myself, it would be . . .

25 Story Starters

Often students like to be provided with the first sentence or two of a narrative. The following list provides 25 story starters. Teachers sometimes may prefer to substitute a name for the word "I" in order to provide variety.

1. One dark, rainy night, as I lay in my bed, I heard . . .
2. I woke up with a start. The room was filled with a bright light, and there in front of me was . . .
3. It was an ordinary Saturday in August. Or so I thought. Everything changed, however, when I went to the store . . .
4. I was reading peacefully when, all of a sudden, my brother ran into the room, screaming . . .
5. I walked into the store and couldn't believe my eyes. There in front of me was the man I had seen on America's Most Wanted . . .
6. At last, I was going to get the chance to play on my school's baseball/soccer team . . .
7. At last, I was going to get the chance to dance/sing in my school concert . . .
8. I was walking to school, minding my own business, when all of a sudden . . .
9. I didn't believe in ghosts. That's why I was happy to stay in the haunted house. Little did I know . . .
10. Once upon a time, a princess was walking in her garden when . . .
11. I thought our trip to the beach would be quite boring, but I was wrong . . .
12. I couldn't believe my ears when my teddy bear/Ninja Turtle/Barbie doll winked at me and said . . .
13. The day was a disaster. Everything went wrong from start to finish . . .
14. The car skidded out of control and . . .
15. I am so excited. I have been waiting for this day to come for what seems like eternity. Tonight is the night that I . . .
16. "Stop," the man shouted, "You cannot go in there." We looked at each other and . . .
17. It could only have happened at Halloween when witches and goblins roamed the streets . . .
18. The doctor spoke with a soft voice, but I saw the evil glint in his eye . . .
19. "That's an odd request," exclaimed my fairy godmother, "but I shall see what I can do . . ."
20. I smiled, thanked my principal for the reward money, and thought back to the events of the day . . .
21. Imagine my surprise when I saw that Santa had left me some magic stardust. What fun I would have that day . . .
22. It was a beautiful, warm day. I was sipping juice in my backyard and listening to the birds when . . .
23. I smiled at my brother/sister and whispered, "Today is going to be the best day of our lives because . . ."
24. I felt myself falling down the deep, smelly hole. I hit the bottom with a thud. With dazed eyes, I looked up and saw . . .
25. I noticed that my teacher looked strange. Suddenly, she leaned forward and . . .

25 Story Enders

As a variation, teachers may sometimes choose to provide students with story enders instead of starters. Many students comment that writing a story with a given ending is more difficult than writing one that has a given beginning. Before using story enders, ensure that students' skill level is sufficient for them to experience success.

1. I opened my eyes and, to my delight, saw that the creature had disappeared.
2. The kangaroo grew to like the zoo and lived there happily for many years.
3. I turned back and glanced at the house, and I knew that I would never return.
4. The magic potion had worked. I had saved the world.
5. Cold sweat was running down my face. I could not believe that it had all been a dream.
6. After cheering me, the villagers returned safely to their homes.
7. I was so happy. My little sister/brother was safe in my mother's arms.
8. The king changed his ways and soon became one of the kindest people in the world.
9. I shall cherish my prize for the rest of my life.
10. The animals took a last look at the cage and ran quickly into the forest.

11. I had had my day with the magic lamp. I wondered who would be the next to discover it.
12. I was in the hospital for 2 weeks and have never forgotten how lucky I was to escape.
13. After the spacecraft left, I wondered if I had dreamt the whole thing.
14. Never again did I look at dinosaur fossils in the same way.
15. The wind blew gently in my hair and the sun warmed my skin. I was free at last.
16. I knew that I would never see anything as beautiful as this again.
17. The giant became friends with the villagers and they all lived happily ever after.
18. I knew that no one would forget April 17th, the day of the flood/fire/earthquake/volcano.
19. They ran into each other's arms and promised that they would never again be parted.
20. Twenty years have passed since then. I wonder if they still remember me.
21. We laughed and danced in the rain.
22. Now I understand why the door must always be kept locked.
23. The noise quieted down slowly and the people left gradually. It was over.
24. It was so long ago. Today, the island is only a memory.
25. It was the happiest day of my life.

Mapping and Graphic Organizers

Cognitive mapping, or webbing, and graphic organizers can help students with writing difficulties develop and organize their thoughts prior to writing. These organizers depict important ideas and their relationships to each other and serve as excellent planning sheets for organizing ideas for writing (Ellis, 1994a, 1994b). Students may list their ideas quickly, and then expand, organize, and structure them. In addition, teacher-constructed graphic organizers can help students begin to perceive relationships among ideas and to recognize common organizational patterns or text structures (e.g., compare/contrast, cause/effect, or sequential) (Ellis, 1994a).

Procedure

The process of developing graphic organizers is similar, no matter which style of map, web, or frame is used. Initially, teacher modeling and cueing are necessary until the student learns to use the strategy independently. Mapping begins with the brainstorming of ideas. The purpose of brainstorming is to increase background knowledge and help students retrieve prior knowledge. During the brainstorming or free association stage, emphasis is placed upon divergent thinking and the rapid production of ideas. No value judgment is made at this stage, as every idea is viewed as pertinent and worthy. The following steps may be used to introduce graphic organizers:

1. During brainstorming, write one- or two-word cues to represent concepts or ideas as they occur.
2. When no more ideas are being generated, return to each cue, elaborating upon the idea within.
3. Color-code ideas that can be grouped or categorized together, and/or:
4. Write the ideas on a graphic organizer developed for the text type (e.g., compare-contrast).
5. Develop paragraphs for each category, expanding upon the ideas already formulated.

As students become more familiar and confident with the use of cognitive mapping and graphic organizers, help them to categorize the ideas as they are generated. At this point, color-coding becomes unnecessary. Once students can construct their own organizers, they are likely to benefit from explaining the organization and their ideas about the topic to others (Ellis, 1994a).

Types

Many different types of cognitive maps and graphic organizers exist. Figures 7–2a and 7–2b illustrate 26 types of graphic organizers with descriptions developed by Hasenstab, Flaherty, and Brown (1994). Three other examples, presented in Figures 7–2c, 7–2d, and 7–2e, include a small version of the graphic in the bottom right-hand corner of the page. Students can fill in the appropriate part of the small visual as they complete the steps on the full-size model. As students' familiarity with graphic organizers increases, they can be encouraged to develop their own models. Figure 7–2f illustrates a graphic organizer developed by Cecilia, a fifth-grade student, who was studying the ocean.

Auditory Plus Visual: Graphic Organizer

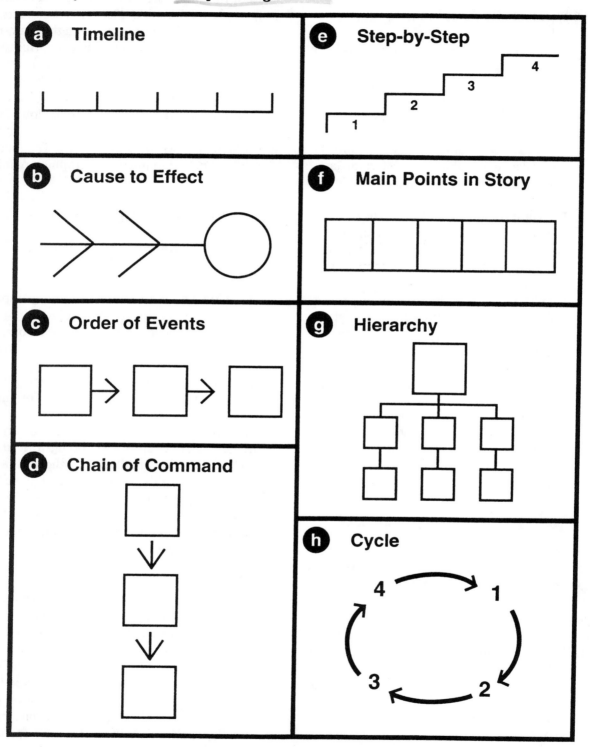

Figure 7–2a. Twenty-six graphic organizers.

Note. From *Teaching Through Learning Channels Participant Manual* (pp. 62–64) by J. K. Hasenstab, G. M. Flaherty and B. E. Brown, 1994. Nevada City, CA: Performance Learning Systems. Copyright 1994 by Performance Learning Systems. Reprinted by permission.

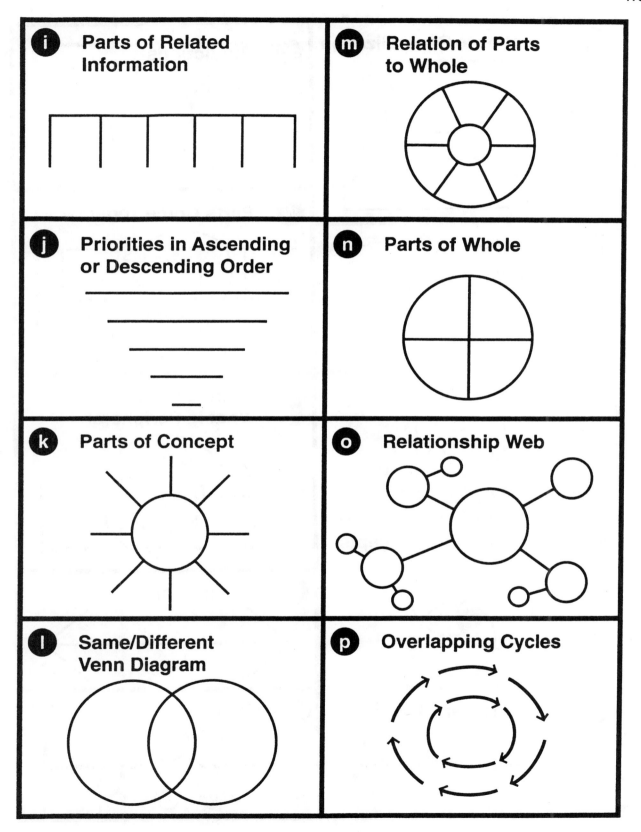

Figure 7–2a (cont.)

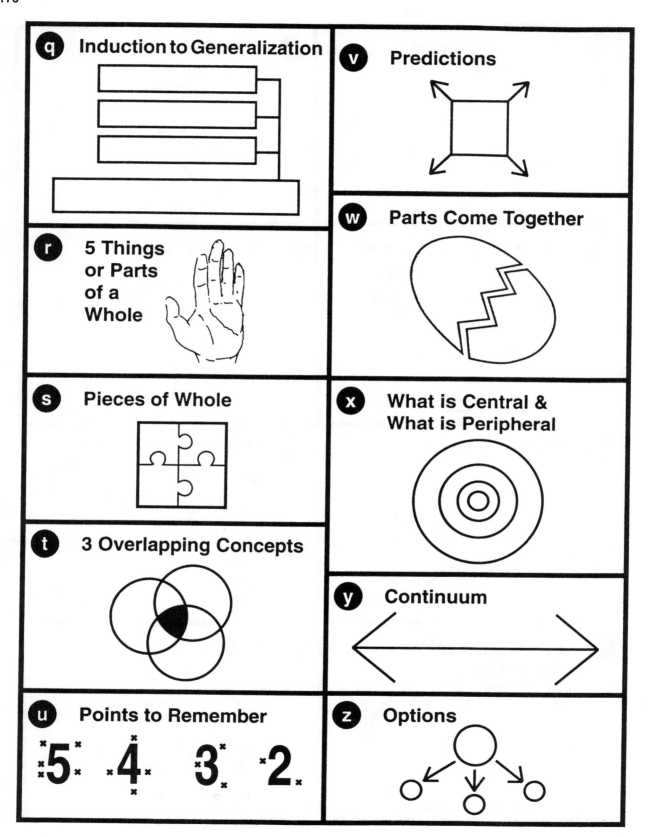

Figure 7–2a (cont.).

[Possible answers: (There could be many more uses for each organizer than the examples given below.)

a. **Timeline.** Could be used to show sequence of historical events. Or it could be used to show things that are going to happen.

b. **Cause to Effect.** Might be used to show steps in a story that lead to a conclusion. Or it could be used to show what might happen as the result of a prediction.

c. **Order of Events.** Could be used to show what happened in a story, what steps lead to war, plans for a class trip, etc.

d. **Chain of Command.** Could be used to show how something is to be carried out. Or it could show order of succession, etc.

e. **Step-by-Step.** Steps toward some conclusion could be given, such as steps taken to complete a project, steps in a story which lead to the conclusion, steps in an experiment, etc.

f. **Main Point of Story.** Used to list the five main points or events in a story, the main ideas in a paragraph, etc. Words could be written in the boxes or cartoons could be drawn in them to represent the concepts or events.

g. **Hierarchy.** Could be used in government classes to show chain of command. It could be used in an analysis of parts, such parts of a member of the plant kingdom, etc.

h. **Cycle.** Any kind of cyclic action that comes back to the beginning and starts over, such as the batting order in baseball, the water cycle, metamorphosis, etc.

i. **Parts of Related Information.** This is a T chart, and related information could be listed in each column. For example, if you wanted students to explore the sensory elements of a meal created in a cooking class you might make a chart that read by column:
"What does it look like?"
"What does it sound like?"
"What does it feel like?"
"What action would you take?"
"What does it smell like?"
"What does it taste like?"
It is used primarily for analysis of parts of a whole viewed from various perspectives.

j. **Priorities in Ascending or Descending Order.** Use when you want students to prioritize from the most to least or least to most important thing to do (or whatever you are prioritizing). Prioritization is symbolized by the shortening of the lines. It could be a descending or ascending order.

k. **Parts of Concept.** This is a basic semantic web used to list parts of the central concept.

l. **Venn Diagram.** Used to show how two concepts overlap. The differences are listed in the outer circles and the similarities are listed in the overlapping area.

m. **Relation of Parts to Whole.** The pie chart is used to show the relationship of parts to a central concept. This graphic is used in this course whenever we discuss Student Compelling Whys. Any number of pie pieces can be created. The concept is written in the center.

n. **Parts to Whole.** Similar to m, this parts-of-a-whole is used when there are four equal parts to a whole, such as earth, air, fire, and water.

o. **Relationship Web.** This is a mind map used to show relationships branching off a core topic.

p. **Overlapping Cycles.** This graphic is used when two cycles are going on at the same time. For example, the outer circle might represent a weather cycle and the inner circle might show what man is doing at the same time in response to the weather cycle.

q. **Induction to Generalization.** The three boxes at the top are three events that occur leading to a generalization. For example, in chemistry a student might try the same experiment three times. The bottom box would list the conclusion he or she came to after trying it three times.

r. **Five Things or Parts of a Whole.** The hand is a great graphic for showing five things to remember written on the fingers. For example, on each finger could be written one of five items students are to remember to bring to school, etc. It might work best with young children.

s. **Pieces of a Whole.** Puzzle pieces indicate parts of a whole. If teachers use the jigsaw group strategy, the group numbers can be shown on the puzzle pieces. The puzzle pieces can be drawn touching each other, as they are in the picture, or separated slightly.

t. **Three Overlapping Concepts.** This diagram is similar to the Venn diagram, except that it shows three overlapping concepts with their own differences, the overlapping of two areas for each circle, and where all three share similarities. You can overlap as many circles as you can draw. You can overlap primary colors in art. You can overlap three concepts.

u. **Points to Remember.** To help students remember the number of points in a concept, steps to remember in a process, or things students need to bring to school, etc., draw a large number on the board. The x's represent points on the number graphic where you would write the items to be recalled. For example, at the four points on the number four you might write items to remember to bring for a field trip, such as lunch, jacket, spending money, and camera. Because it is difficult to recall more than seven items at a time, this type of number graphic should be no higher than the number seven.

v. **Predictions.** In the center of the prediction chart, you could write the situation at the present time. It could be a point in a story, a point in developing a plan for class action, etc. At the end of the arrows different predictions for outcome could be listed.

w. **Parts Come Together.** This is a simple synthesis graphic that looks like the parts of an egg coming together, symbolizing how two parts fit together. For example, one half could represent homework and the other half classwork to form the whole: what it takes for students to learn a concept. Or one half could represent something a teacher does and the other half something students must do to complete a task.

x. **What Is Central and What Is Peripheral.** The circle chart is a way to show a central idea and the ideas that are part of it. The outer rings are things which effect the central core. For example, in the center you could have "The Student" and in the surrounding circles you could have "The Home," "The School," and "The Community." Another way it can be used is to show priorities. The inner circle is the most important and the outer circles become less and less important. For example, you could give students a list of items and they would sort them with the most important (based on criteria) in the middle and the least important in the outermost circle.

y. **Continuum.** Continua are used to show spectrums of opposites, such as high to low, rich to poor, great to small, strong to weak, fast to slow, etc.

z. **Options.** Can be used to get students thinking of optional solutions to a problem. For example, the problem might be "a teenage girl is pregnant" written in the top oval. What are her options? The students would write the options in the lower ovals. Or this organizer could be used to make predictions or state possible outcomes.]

Figure 7–2b. Descriptions of the 26 graphic organizers.

Note. From *Teaching Through Learning Channels Instructor Guide* (pp. 72–74) by J. K. Hasenstab, G. M. Flaherty and B. E. Brown, 1994. Nevada City, CA: Performance Learning Systems. Copyright 1994 by Performance Learning Systems. Reprinted by permission.

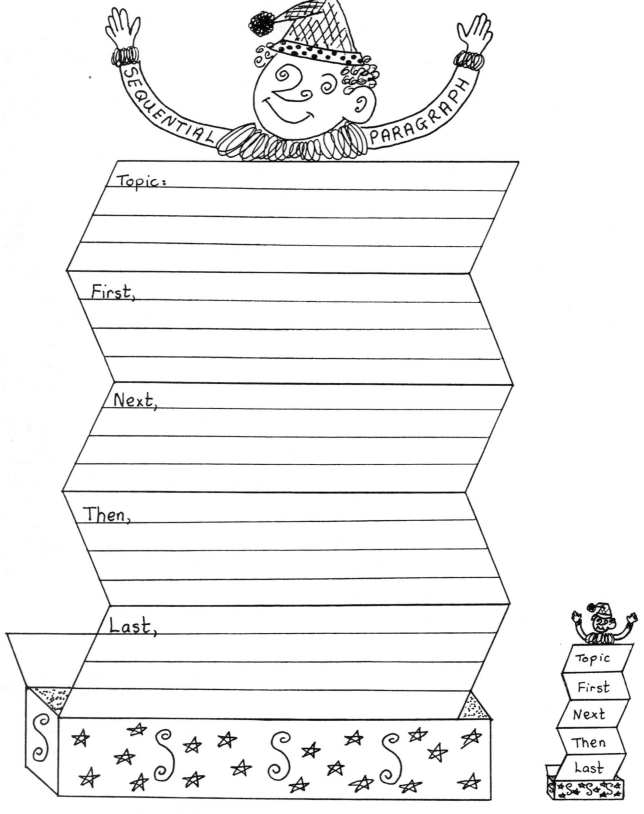

Figure 7–2c. Graphic organizer for a sequential paragraph.

Figure 7–2d. Graphic organizer for a story.

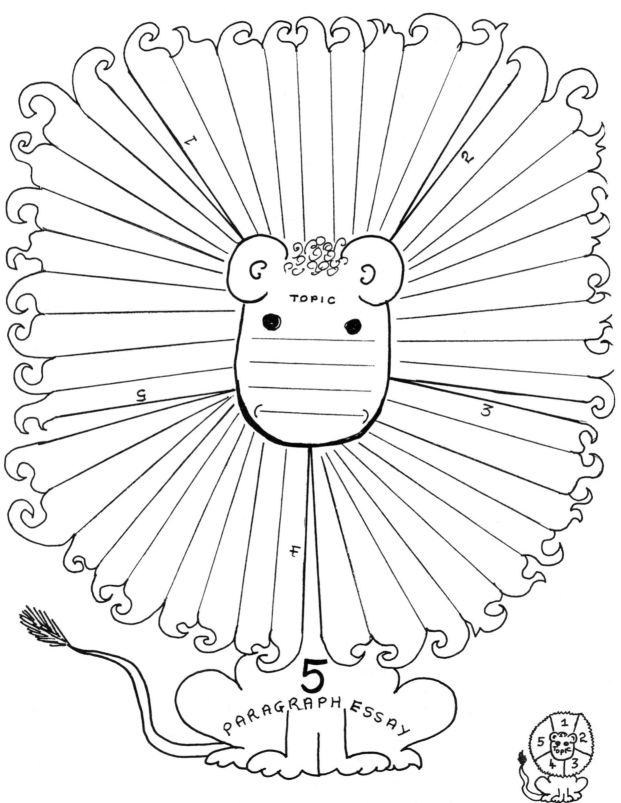

Figure 7–2e. Graphic organizer for a five-paragraph essay.

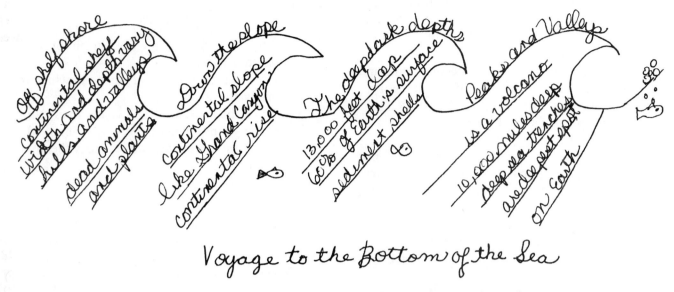

Voyage to the Bottom of the Sea

Figure 7–2f. Graphic organizer by Cecilia, a fifth-grade student.

Vocabulary

Graphic organizers may also be used to help students improve their vocabulary. For example, students can place a word in the center of the map and then generate synonyms or antonyms for the word in the outside circles. A variety of additional techniques may be used to promote vocabulary growth. As with other areas of written language instruction, different methods are selected to meet different educational goals (Carlisle, 1993).

Principles

From a review of several sources, Carlisle (1993) summarized several basic principles of vocabulary instruction. Effective vocabulary instruction:

1. Provides exposure to different definitions.
2. Provides illustrations in natural contexts.
3. Builds a conceptual foundation and semantic relations.
4. Builds links among members of word families.
5. Provides ways to remember basic word meanings.
6. Integrates new information with prior knowledge.
7. Facilitates reexposure to words.
8. Provides opportunities for meaningful use.

9. Assists students' efforts to derive meanings from context (p. 104).

Fortunately, the visual nature of writing provides an excellent opportunity for helping students expand their vocabulary.

Word Retrieval

Training in word-retrieval strategies has been found to be beneficial, resulting in improvement in both oral and written language (Cole & Cole, 1989; McGregor & Leonard, 1989; Wing, 1990). In general, instruction in word usage should help students to: (a) curtail the redundant use of common words, (b) develop synonyms for common words, (c) select precise words, and (d) avoid awkward word combinations (Polloway et al., 1981).

A teacher may encourage vocabulary development by having students brainstorm a variety of words prior to writing. For example, a teacher may have students think of different words for "said" prior to writing (e.g., *shouted, observed, questioned, suggested, spat, drawled, gasped, queried, whispered*) (Leavell & Ioannides, 1993). Ability to classify words can also improve word retrieval by helping a student select more precise vocabulary prior to or during writing. Several prewriting activities adapted from Israel (1984), designed to enhance skill in the ability to classify, rehearse, and recall vocabulary, are presented below.

Classification

1. Association between the category names and the names of members of the category:
   a. An ostrich is a _____
   b. Is an ostrich a bird or a fish?
   c. Ostrich, eagle, and osprey are _____
2. Identification of an item that does not belong in a particular semantic category:
   a. Which does not belong—boy, girl, dog, man?
   b. Why doesn't "cheese" belong in this list—milk, cheese, water, juice?
3. Selection of an item from a heterogeneous list that represents a named category:
   tomato, girl, leg, elephant, rose
   a. Which one is a food? Which one is a flower?
   b. Which one of these is a fruit—potato, apple, or yogurt?
4. Identification of object features to help differentiate between objects:
   a. How are a book and a newspaper alike?
   b. How are a book and a newspaper different?
5. Identification of subcategories within a general classification:
   zebra, dog, cat, elephant, giraffe, rabbit
   a. What is the general classification?
   b. In the above list, what are the two subcategories within the general classification of "animals"?
6. Association of items with some specific shared feature(s):
   a. List/Find all objects that need air to breathe.
7. Visual-imagery of items to help classify and subcategorize:
   a. Close your eyes and imagine you are in a spaceship. Name all of the things you see.

Rehearsal

Rehearsal can improve retention and make words more accessible. Two strategies for rehearsal are provided.

Strategy I

1. Show the student a number of items. The items can be shown either in pictorial or written form.
2. Give the student a brief period in which to study the items.
3. Have the student close his/her eyes while a pre-set number of items are removed.
4. Have the student verbally identify the missing items.

Strategy II

1. Have the student memorize a list of sequenced items that are grouped in sets of three.
2. Have the student repeat each item after the teacher.
3. Have the student repeat each pair of sequenced words after the teacher.
4. Have the student repeat each set of three words after the teacher.
5. Gradually, teach the student to self-monitor the rehearsal and to repeat the words covertly.

Cueing Strategies

When learning words or connected information, instruction in various cueing strategies can help students with word retrieval. Cueing strategies can be most beneficial when learning information for a test or examination. Examples of the most widely used cueing strategies are:

1. Linking the word with its classification (e.g., zebra—animal).
2. Pairing highly associative words with each other (e.g., bread and butter).
3. Using sentence completion or fill-in-the-blank strategies (e.g., Italians eat *pasta*).
4. Using chunking or the recoding of individual items into a superordinate system. As an example, the superordinate structure of animals would include "cows," "horses," and "zebras." Or, students can practice chunking words into semantic categories, regardless of their position in the list (e.g., apple, *tea*, orange, lemon, *coffee*, *juice*, banana, *water*).

5. Using phonemic cueing with the production of the initial sound or syllable (e.g., "ant, peg, herc" for Antigone, Pegasus, Hercules).
6. Forming sentences from the phonemic cues (e.g., "*Richard of York gave battle in vain*" to remember the sequential order of the colors of the rainbow—red, orange, yellow, green, blue, indigo, violet).
7. Using visual-imagery for remembering lists, for first-word cueing, or for remembering important, connected facts (e.g., imagining an *elephant* wearing a *crown* and holding a *noose* to remember the fate of an individual who tried to capture the ruler of Burma).

Morphology

Many students can be taught morphological rules through systematic rule exposure (Hux & Stogsdill, 1993). For example, students can be encouraged to check the endings of words and to note tense markers (such as -*ed*), plural markers (such as -*s*, -*es*), and possessive markers (such as *'s*) (Devine, 1986). The activities described below can help students increase their knowledge of the relationships and meanings of various word forms.

Structural Analysis Maps

Graphic organizers can be used to demonstrate the relationships among prefixes, suffixes, and root words. The root word is written in the middle of the map and then prefixes and suffixes extend from the side. After completing the map as a class activity, students can attempt to write all of the words that can be formed through the addition of various affixes.

Figure 7–3 illustrates several adaptations of this type of procedure. In the first map with the root word "cover," the student can read across from prefix to root word to suffix, creating various derivations of the word. Separate maps can be made for adding prefixes or suffixes. Or, as an alternative, a prefix or suffix can be placed in the center of the map.

Prefixes, Suffixes, and Roots

Additional activities, adapted from Kuchinskas and Radencich (1986), can be used to increase students' understanding of prefixes, suffixes, and/or roots. For the first activity, the following steps are used:

1. Explain that many words consist of prefixes, suffixes, and/or roots.
2. Give examples of some of the common ones and explain their meanings.
3. List common prefixes, suffixes, or roots horizontally along a line.
   e.g., (*UN DIS FRIEND TION LY*)
4. Under the headings, have students list appropriate words.
   (e.g., *unhappy disagree friendless action sadly*)
5. Discuss both appropriate and inappropriate words with the students (e.g., explain why the word *unicorn* does not fit under *un*).
6. Encourage the students to "mix and match" (e.g., *unfriendly, disagreeing*).
7. Have the students brainstorm other prefixes, suffixes, and roots and discuss the meaning of those.
8. Repeat the activity with the new morphemes.
9. Make charts incorporating some of the words suggested for the students to use as a future reference.

The following activity may be used to help students increase their knowledge of the meanings of affixes:

1. Introduce the concept of prefixes, suffixes, and roots to students.
2. Brainstorm examples of prefixes and suffixes.
3. Have students think about and attempt to identify the meaning of each affix.
4. Write the affixes and the meanings on the chalkboard.
5. Stretch students' thinking by asking leading questions (e.g., "Who has ever had a manicure?" "What did it involve?" "So what do you think the prefix 'mani' means?").
6. Have students copy the affixes and meanings onto their papers.
7. Have students combine the prefixes, suffixes, and roots to make multisyllabic words (real or nonsense). For example, the phrase "micropolycephalus monster" (small, many-headed monster) would be an example of a nonsense word.
8. Ask students to draw the person or object they described.

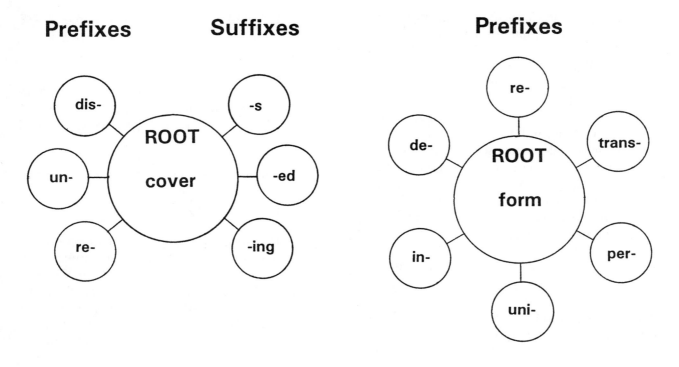

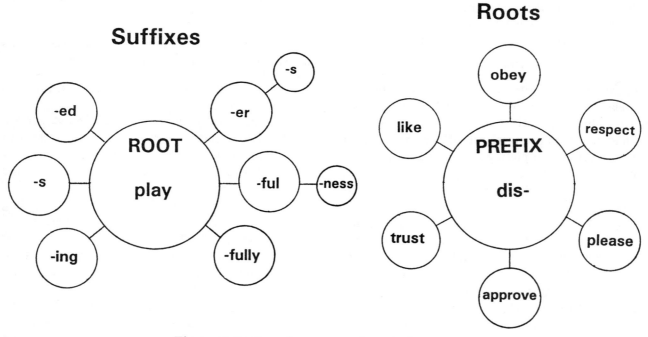

Figure 7–3. Sample structural analysis maps.

9. Have the group try to identify the word from the picture.

Morphological Cloze

The cloze procedure can be used to help draw attention to morphological rules. Prepare a cloze passage where the endings have been deleted from several nouns and verbs within the passage. Ask the student to read the passage and then write in the correct ending.

As an alternative procedure, prepare a cloze passage from the student's own writing. Place a blank where the correct endings were not included and/or use "white-out" to delete endings. Ask the student to reconstruct the passage. Practice with this type of procedure is particularly effective for students who tend to delete word endings in their writing. As Penny, a sixth-grade student, commented: "When I am writing, I just don't notice the endings of words. *Walk* and *walked* look just about the same to me."

Word Knowledge

A variety of strategies can be used to help students increase their breadth and depth of vocabulary. For increasing word knowledge, students appear to benefit from methods that emphasize and depict conceptual relationships (Bos & Anders, 1990a). Although some procedures follow, additional activities for enhancing word knowledge can be found in the prewriting section on graphic organizers and maps.

Five Senses

Tompkins and Friend (1986) described a procedure to help students generate more precise vocabulary. The following steps are used:

1. Draw a large "Five Senses" chart on the chalkboard.
2. Expose the students to some activity such as popping corn.
3. As the event is occurring, have the students contribute words describing the event under each of the "Five Senses" sections.
4. Record the words on the chart.
5. Give the students a follow-up writing activity. Try to vary the task (e.g., a poem, a creative story from the popcorn's point of view, or a newspaper article).

6. Help the students exchange overused words such as *nice* and *pretty* with more descriptive words, such as *tantalizing*.
7. List the overused words in columns opposite the alternative words.
8. Have the students rewrite the assignment using the more descriptive words.

Semantic Feature Analysis

The purpose of Semantic Feature Analysis (Johnson & Pearson, 1984) is to guide students in analyzing the meanings of specific words while integrating the meanings of new words into their vocabularies. This type of activity can help students increase the breadth of their vocabulary knowledge. When introducing this activity, use categories that are concrete and within the experience of the students. Later, progress to less familiar or more abstract categories. The following steps may be used:

1. Select a category and the key words that relate to a topic to be studied or a reading selection.
2. Make a chart with a topic heading at the top, key words down the side, and columns across the page. Head some of the columns with terms that represent features shared by some of the words.
3. Have students place a plus or minus sign in each column depending on whether the word has the feature or not. Have students place a question mark if the relationship is unknown.
4. Have students discuss each word, the reason for selecting a plus or minus, and how the word is similar to or different from the other words.
5. Present a lesson that covers the material (e.g., lecture, reading, video).
6. Based on the information, have students change or complete the signs in the matrix.
7. Guide a discussion about the relationship between the words and features. Present the chart on the board or an overhead. During the discussion, have class members fill in the signs that have attained group consensus.

The following optional steps may be included after steps 3 or 7:

1. Have students add words to the list that fit the category.
2. Have students add shared features in the empty columns.
3. Have students complete the matrix with pluses and minuses.

Mather and Jaffe (1992) presented the following completed example:

Transportation in History

	wheels	*engine*	*computer*	*ticket*
horses	–	–	–	–
bicycle	+	–	–	–
car	+	+	+	+
train	+	+	+	+
airplane	+	+	+	+

When students become familiar with this activity, rather than using pluses and minuses, they may use a 10-point scale to indicate the degree of relationship between words and features (Johnson & Pearson, 1984).

IT FITS Strategy

King-Sears, Mercer, and Sindelar (1992) described a strategy to help students recall difficult terminology, such as new words to be learned for a science or history lecture. The first-letter acronym IT FITS is used with the following steps:

I   *Identify* the term.
T   *Tell* the definition of the term.

F   *Find* a key word.
I   *Imagine* the definition doing something with the key word.
T   *Think* about the definition doing something with the key word.
S   *Study* what you imagined until you know the definition.

The key word may be a rhyming word or a word that evokes specific visual imagery. One may expand this strategy by having the student write several sentences that contain the target word. Fulk (1994) presented several examples of how to use this mnemonic strategy to help students with learning disabilities recall vocabulary and critical content area information.

Active Learning

Kokaska (1994) summarized several teaching tips presented by teachers from community colleges in the state of California. As examples, Patty Schmolze described a procedure for teaching the art of "definitive description." Each student writes a detailed description of a peanut that he or she picks out of a bag. The next day, each student attempts to identify his or her peanut using the written description. The teacher numbers the peanuts so that they can be matched to the paper in case of an unmatched peanut. As another activity, Amy Ulmer recommended the use of a "koosh" ball. Students toss the ball around to class members, reviewing vocabulary words, providing a definition, or using the word in a sentence.

McKeown and Beck (1988) described a classroom activity called "Word Wizard" that would encourage students to extend vocabulary instruction outside of the classroom. Students receive points by reporting the context in which they have seen or heard a word they are studying or for using words in their own speech or writing. These types of active learning games increase student interest and involvement with vocabulary.

Self-Control Strategy

A five-step strategy (Harris & Graham, 1985) may be used to help students expand their vocabulary in their compositions. A certain type of word can be targeted, such as nouns, adjectives, or verbs. To begin, select a picture and present the following five steps to students on a chart:

1. Ask the student to look at the picture and write down a list of the type of targeted word, such as adjectives or describing words.
2. Have the student think of a story that will use the selected words.
3. Ask the student to write a story that makes sense and uses as many of the words as possible.
4. Have the student read the story and ask these questions: Did I write a good story? Did I use the selected words?
5. Have the student edit the story and try to use more of the type of words selected.

Prior to writing, have the student set a goal for the number of describing words to be used in the story. After completion of the story, have the student count the number of targeted words used and chart this number on a graph. Students can also do this type of activity in pairs or small cooperative groups. The additional dialogue with classmates can help students expand their own word knowledge.

Figure 7–4 illustrates the first application of this strategy with Peter, a beginning fourth-grade student. Prior to writing, Peter generated the following adjectives to describe a picture of a peaceful, countryside scene: *fantastic*, *amazing*, *collosal*, *energy-efficient*, *impervious*, *healthy*, and *glorious*. He

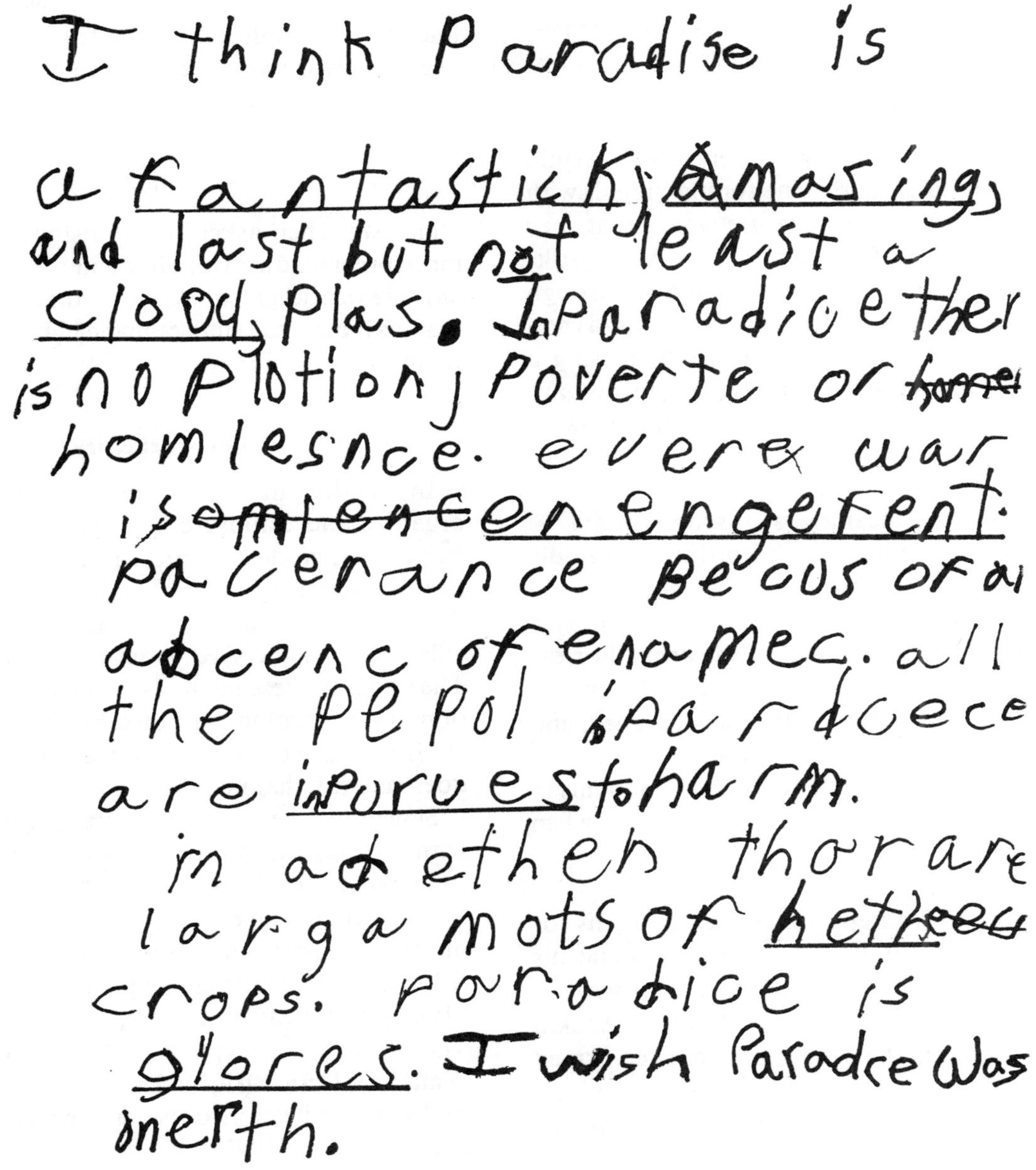

I think Paradise is a fantastick, Amasing, and last but not least a clood plas. In Paradice ther is no plotion, poverte or homlesnce. evere war is often en engerent. pacerance becous of a abcenc of enamec. all the pepol in pardoece are inpruestoharm. in ad ethen thorare larga mots of hethee crops. paradice is glores. I wish Paradce Was onerth.

Translation:

I think Paradise is a fantastic, amazing, and last but not least, a collosal place. In Paradise, there is no pollution, poverty, or homelessness. Everywhere is energy-efficient. Peace reigns because of an absence of enemies. All the people in Paradise are impervious to harm. In addition, there are large amounts of healthy crops. Paradise is glorious. I wish Paradise was on earth.

Figure 7–4. First draft of a story by Peter, a fourth-grade student.

decided that the picture represented Paradise. Upon completion of the first draft, he underlined and counted the adjectives and plotted this number on a chart.

Prior to using this strategy, Peter would not use his extensive vocabulary when writing because of his spelling problems. As a result of the strategy, Peter has started generating and using more complex and descriptive words in his stories.

Synonyms/Antonyms

Many students tend to overrely upon certain words. This is particularly true for individuals with learning disabilities who overuse words that they have written successfully in the past. As a result, students can enlarge their vocabulary through synonym and antonym instruction. Kuchinskas and Radencich (1986) described a procedure using a graphic organizer for teaching synonyms and antonyms. When employing the strategy, the following steps are used:

1. Teach the meaning of a synonym.
2. Have students write a word in the middle of a star graphic.
3. Tell the students to try to write a synonym for the word on each of the arms. For example, for the word *said*, the synonyms *explained*, *whispered*, *questioned*, *argued*, and *suggested* could be written.
4. Encourage students to use the synonyms in writing assignments, and reward them when they do.

Repeat the above steps, replacing antonyms for synonyms. If the central word is *happy*, help students think of words such as *unhappy*, *sad*, *miserable*, *glum*, and *depressed* to record on the arms. As skill improves, provide the students with a ten-armed star, an octopus, or a decagon and have them use a thesaurus to help in filling in the synonyms or antonyms.

For increasing challenge, have students list the words by degree and place them on a graphic organizer that is shaped like a pyramid. For example, *glum, unhappy, sad, miserable*, and *depressed* could be considered to be recorded by gradients of severity. Accept any logical order that the student can explain.

Synonym Cloze

Blachowicz (1977) described a modified cloze procedure to help students be more precise in word choice. Once students have written a story, identify words that are redundant, overused, or imprecise. Delete each word from the line, replace it with a blank, and then write the word below the line. For example, Omar, a fifth-grade student, began his story with the sentence: *It was a nice day*. His teacher rewrote the sentence as:

It was a _____ day.
nice

Omar was then asked to brainstorm and write a more precise adjective. He wrote: *It was a glorious day*. He was delighted with his effort and commented that his improved sentence made him feel like a "real writer."

Text Structure

Instruction in text patterns helps students to organize and elaborate ideas (Horowitz, 1985b). In general, students with learning disabilities appear to benefit from highly structured approaches that are modeled using a student's writing and provide positive and corrective feedback (Moran, 1988). The intent of these methods is to facilitate organization of information. As noted by Vogel and Moran (1982), ability to organize longer pieces of writing does not just happen.

Similar to other areas of written language, students with learning disabilities require direct instruction to increase their knowledge and use of text structure and to improve the cohesion and organization of their compositions (Danoff et al., 1993; Englert & Lichter, 1982; Graves, Montague, & Wong, 1990; Montague & Leavell, 1994; Montague et al., 1990; Thomas et al., 1984; Tindal & Hasbrouck, 1991; Wallace & Bott, 1989; Welch, 1992). Simply asking students to write more does not improve their writing (Sawyer et al., 1992).

Fortunately, many strategies exist to help students improve their knowledge of text structures and increase their ability to organize and sequence ideas logically. As examples, Graves and Montague (1991) found that use of story grammar cue cards or a check-off system for story parts improved the quality of the stories written by students with learning disabilities. Wallace and Bott (1989) found that use of a metacognitive text structure strategy that involved completing a paragraph planning guide improved student skill in paragraph writing. Whatever strategies are selected, they should provide instruction that focuses on making the structures and processes of writing apparent to the students (Englert & Mariage, 1991).

Principles

Stewart (1992) provided the following general guidelines for teaching specific writing skills, including text structure organization:

1. Provide direct instruction in writing by modeling and teaching writing strategies.
2. Emphasize high-level skills that focus on content and organization.
3. Control task difficulty by isolating target objectives.
4. Provide instruction in writing strategies by teaching students to use text structure to plan, generate, and monitor their writing.
5. Have students take control of their writing by teaching them to plan, implement, and monitor their use of strategies.
6. Integrate writing instruction with the curriculum.

As noted, students with learning disabilities often require explicit instruction to master various text structures. Explicit instruction in the use of cohesive ties will help students learn to organize and integrate concepts in writing, whereas explicit instruction in text structure strategies will help students improve both narrative and expository writing.

Cohesion

Instruction in cohesion is aimed at helping students connect the sentences and paragraphs within their compositions. A variety of strategies can be used to help students increase skill in sequencing, organizing, and connecting their thoughts.

Cohesive Ties

Many students can benefit from direct instruction in how to use words that signify a variety of types of semantic relations. Cohesive ties provide

signals as to how a previous clause or statement is related to another. Examples of several types of cohesive ties, described by Wallach and Miller (1988), follow:

Additive: *and, also, in addition*
Amplification: *furthermore, moreover*
Adversative: *but, however, in contrast, nevertheless*
Causal: *if/then, because, due to, as a result*
Conclusion: *therefore, accordingly, consequently*
Temporal: *after, meanwhile, whenever, previously*
Sequence: *first, second, then, lastly, finally*
Spatial: *next to, between, in front of, adjacent to*
Continuative: *after all, again, finally, another*
Likeness: *likewise, similarly*
Example: *for example, as an illustration*
Restatement: *in other words, that is, in summary*
Exception: *except, barring, beside, excluding*

FAN BOYS

As part of the comprehensive Sentence Writing Strategy, Schumaker and Sheldon (1985) described use of the mnemonic FAN BOYS to aid with recall of the seven coordinating conjunctions. These conjunctions are used to write compound and compound-complex sentence patterns. The conjunctions and their meanings are explained as follows:

For: means the same as *because* when used as a conjunction. It differs from the preposition because it is always followed by a subject and a verb.
And: shows that two ideas are equally important and connected.
Nor: used to introduce the second clause of a negative statement and shows that the second clause is also negative. The verb comes before the subject in the second independent clause.
But: shows contrast.
Or: joins two ideas when there is a choice between them.
Yet: shows contrast.
So: shows that the second clause is the result of the first clause.

Transition Device Strategy

The knowledge that good writers use transitions among sentences and between paragraphs is often not sufficient information for many individuals. More scaffolding is needed if they are to use transitions correctly. Judy, a fifth-grade student provides an example. She was asked to use a transition in the following two sentences: *I was told that all kindergarten students loved music. I soon found out that Vic did not.*

After much thought, Judy wrote: *I was told that all kindergarten students loved music. On the other hand, I soon found out that Vic did not.* Judy, like many other students, needs to be taught how to use cohesive ties. Sloan (1983) suggested that students be taught the following seven sentence relationships and the linking words that can be used to express the relationship:

1. Coordination: *and, furthermore, in addition, too, also, again*
2. Observativity: *but, yet, however, on the other hand, although*
3. Causativity: *for*
4. Conclusivity: *so, therefore, thus, for this reason*
5. Alternativity: *or*
6. Inclusivity: (most often expressed with a colon)
7. Sequential: *first, second, third, earlier, later*

Cloze for Cohesive Ties

Thomas (1978) described an adapted cloze procedure for helping students increase their use of cohesive ties in writing. The following steps are used:

1. Delete any cohesive ties that signal the organizational pattern of a passage. Examples of such cohesive ties are:
    a. Words signaling the organizational pattern, such as *first, next,* or *finally.*
    b. Words signaling time order, such as *before, after,* or *when.*
    c. Words signaling a comparison/contrast organizational pattern, such as *however, but, as well as,* or *yet.*
    d. Words signaling a cause/effect organizational pattern, such as *because, therefore,* or *consequently.*
2. If necessary, provide a student with a list of words that may be used to fill in the blanks.

3. Discuss with students the alternatives that could be used in each blank.

    Example:
    When you start to write a paper, _____ research your topic and _____ make an outline or organizational plan. _____, you are ready to begin writing.

Pronoun Referents

Most students seem to learn to use pronoun referents without explicit instruction. Some individuals, however, continue to use pronouns incorrectly. The following procedure, adapted from Baumann (1986), can help students learn to use pronoun referents in their writing:

1. Provide students with a passage in which names and words are repeated rather than being replaced by pronouns or demonstrative articles (e.g., *Mary went on a trip to Africa. Mary had never been to Africa before.*).
2. Show students how the sentence may be rewritten (e.g., *Mary went on a trip to Africa. She had never been there before.*).
3. Provide direct instruction in regard to the meanings of specific pronouns. For example, create a pronoun chart with categories for gender and number of people. Using pictures, if necessary, teach students to whom each of the pronouns refers.
4. Provide students with sentence pairs in which pronouns in the second sentence refer to nouns in the first sentence. Underline the pronouns and draw arrows to their referents.
5. Ask students to replace pronouns with the words they represent.
6. Expand the exercise to include longer passages and have students answer questions regarding pronoun referents.
7. Have students locate pronouns and their referents in passages from their textbooks.
8. Provide students with sentences and passages with redundant words and ask students to replace them with pronouns.

Kerrigan's Method for Connectives

Kerrigan (1979) explained how to teach students to use cohesive ties in essay writing. The goal is to ensure that every sentence is connected with, and makes a clear reference to, the previous sentence. Referencing can be accomplished in one of seven explicit ways:

1. In the second sentence, repeat a word that has been used in the first sentence.
2. In the second sentence, use a synonym of a word used in the first sentence.
3. In the second sentence, use an antonym of a word used in the first sentence.
4. Use a pronoun in the second sentence to refer to an antecedent in the first sentence.
5. Use a word in the second sentence that is commonly paired with a word in the first sentence (e.g., *bacon, eggs*).
6. Repeat a sentence structure.
7. Use a connective in the second sentence to refer to an idea in the first (e.g., *for, therefore, as a result, for example, however, and, but*).

Students may expand upon their knowledge of connectives by studying the four basic connective types:

(1) *Identity connectives.* These indicate that one idea is the same as another. A colon is usually used to punctuate this relationship.
(2) *Opposite connectives.* These indicate something contrary or contradictory to what has previously been asserted. Words used to indicate this opposite relationship are: *but, though, yet, still, however,* and *nevertheless.*
(3) *Equivalent connectives.* These denote parallel ideas with no new ideas being introduced. Words used to indicate this equivalence are: *and, too, also, besides, in addition, moreover, similarly, in the same way, again, furthermore, another, a similar,* and *the same.*
(4) *Cause and effect connectives.* These denote the cause and effect of an incident. Words used to indicate this are: *therefore, so, as a result, as a consequence, thus we see,* and *it follows that.*

At this stage, point out to the student that indefinite connections such as *in fact, indeed,* and *now* can be used, but they do not explicitly point

out the relationship between ideas previously discussed. Inform the student that a guiding rule when writing is to determine the relationship between two consecutive sentences then, if possible, use a connective that indicates the relationship.

Given-New Strategy

Some students need help in understanding how to relate the given information, or information the writer assumes the reader knows, and the new information, or information that needs explanation. In most situations, the given information is usually in the subject position of the sentences, whereas the old information is usually in the predicate (Cooper, 1988). The following procedure, adapted from Cooper, may be used to help students understand the relationship between given-new principles. To begin, students are taught how the concepts presented in sentences often overlap. The following steps are then used:

1. Write two sets of sample sentences, one where the concepts overlap and another where too many new concepts are presented in succession. An example is presented in Figure 7–5.
2. Provide further examples in regard to cohesion using graphic depictions that incorporate overlapping or nonoverlapping boxes. Use overlapping boxes under successive sentences to depict how given information is transformed to slightly new or extended information. Use nonoverlapping boxes under sentences that contain too many new concepts.
3. Have students organize cut-up sentence strips to create a chain of overlapping concepts. Ensure that all the sentence strips pertain to one topic.
4. Have students practice writing the first sentence of a paragraph. Help them to create a chain of overlapping concepts in the sentences that follow. Draw boxes underneath the sentences and label the information as "old" or "new."
5. Demonstrate to students the relationships between paragraphs based on the graphic information given by the boxes. Sentences with overlapping boxes would remain in one

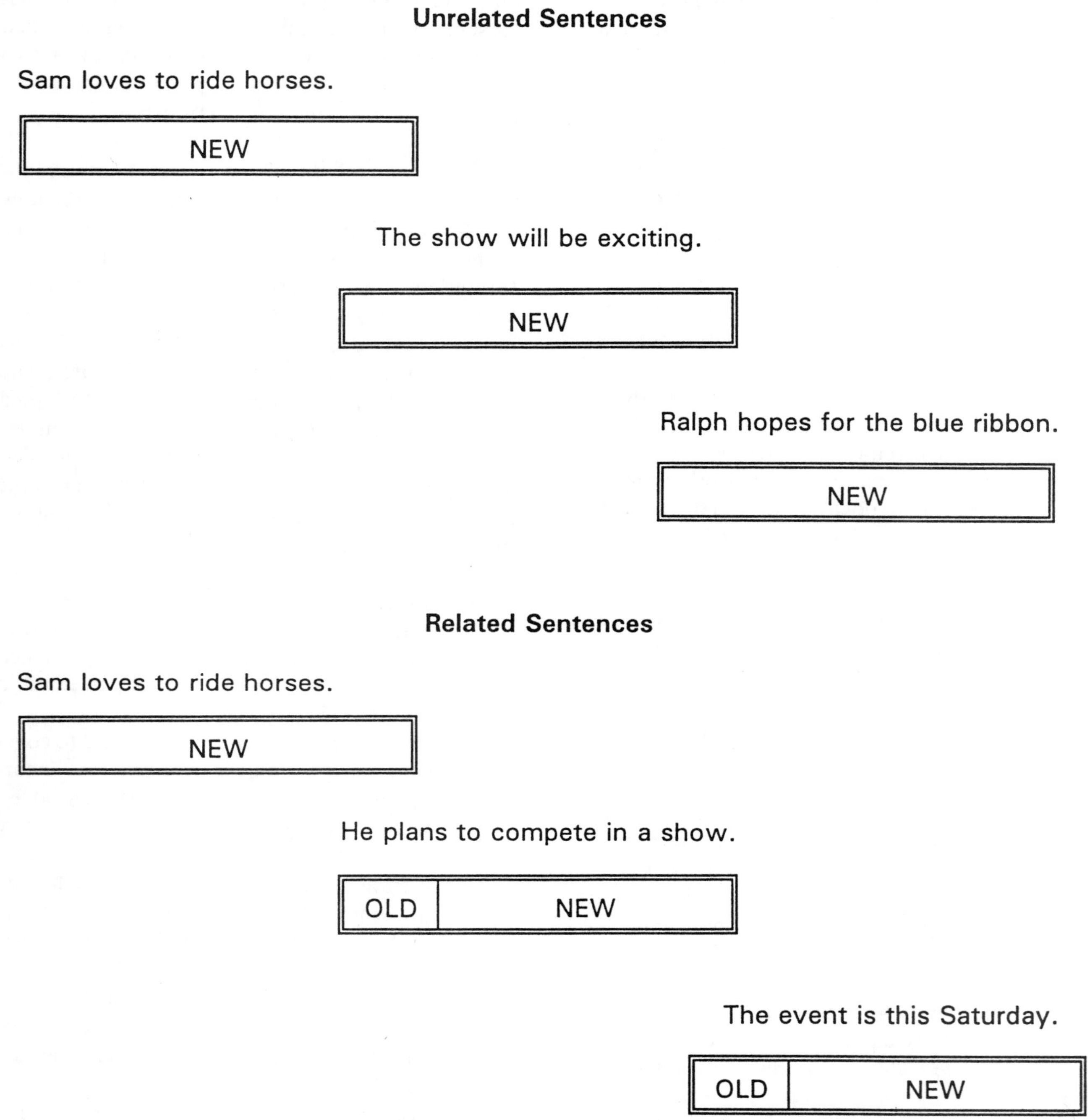

Unrelated Sentences

Sam loves to ride horses.

NEW

The show will be exciting.

NEW

Ralph hopes for the blue ribbon.

NEW

Related Sentences

Sam loves to ride horses.

NEW

He plans to compete in a show.

OLD	NEW

The event is this Saturday.

OLD	NEW

Figure 7–5. Examples of Given-New Principles.

paragraph with a constant topic and linear progression. A sentence with nonoverlapping boxes would be the starting point for a new paragraph.

6. Repeat step 3 using two or three different topics. Explain how the different paragraphs may then be linked together.

7. Continue providing assistance in linking information within and between paragraphs until both local and global cohesion have been achieved.

8. Provide further practice with transitions, linking expressions, and repeated terms, such as the use of pronoun referents.

Narrative/Story Grammar

I keep six honest serving men. (They taught me all I know); Their names are What and Why and When and How and Where and Who.

—Rudyard Kipling

A variety of techniques may be used to assist students in developing their narrative writing skill. Some provide specific instruction in story grammar, whereas others involve special applications of the writing process approach.

Beginning Story Grammars

Teachers may introduce the concept of story grammar as early as kindergarten or first grade. Graphic organizers can be used to relate the concepts. In the early grades, students may be told that every story has three parts: a beginning, a middle, and an end. Three circles can be drawn and connected with arrows to illustrate the progression. Or, a teacher can draw a simple mnemonic with a face representing first (F), then (T), and finally (F), as illustrated in Figure 7–6. Alternatively, a more detailed mnemonic may be drawn for upper-elementary students. An example of this is presented in Figure 7–7.

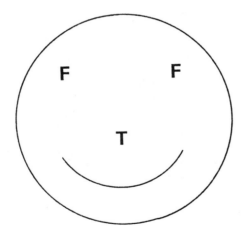

Figure 7–6. First, Then, and Finally Face.

Students can also be given a series of prompts or questions for guiding their writing. A first-grade teacher provided her students with the following prompts for writing: Who? Did What? And then . . .

Another example of a simplified story grammar is based upon the following four questions (Carnine & Kinder, 1985): Who is the story about? What is s/he trying to do? What happens when s/he tries to do it? What happens in the end?

Action Story Schema

Stewart (1992) expanded the simplified story grammar framework presented by Carnine and Kinder (1985). The original four questions are developed into a ten-step strategy. The following steps are used:

1. Teach students to answer four questions when writing an action story:
   a. Who/what is the story about?
   b. What is the main character trying to do?
   c. What happens when the main character tries to do it?
   d. What happens in the end?
2. Read examples of stories that adhere successfully to the above schema.
3. Discuss the successful use of the story frame.
4. Read examples of stories that do not adhere successfully to the above schema.
5. Discuss what is missing from the stories in step 3, and have students suggest how the missing parts could be added.
6. Model how to write a story using the four questions as guides.
7. Have students plan stories on maps, based on the four questions a-d.
8. Have students write one paragraph in answer to each question.
9. Have students read their stories to a partner to see if the listener can answer the four questions.
10. As skill develops, encourage students to expand upon the information, writing more than one paragraph in each section as necessary.

Story Maps

Graphic organizers can also be used to help students develop story maps for writing. Tompkins and Friend (1986) described the following procedure for incorporating maps into narrative writing:

1. Choose an appropriate story map for a writing assignment.
2. Draw the map on the chalkboard.
3. Explain the purpose and benefits of using story maps.

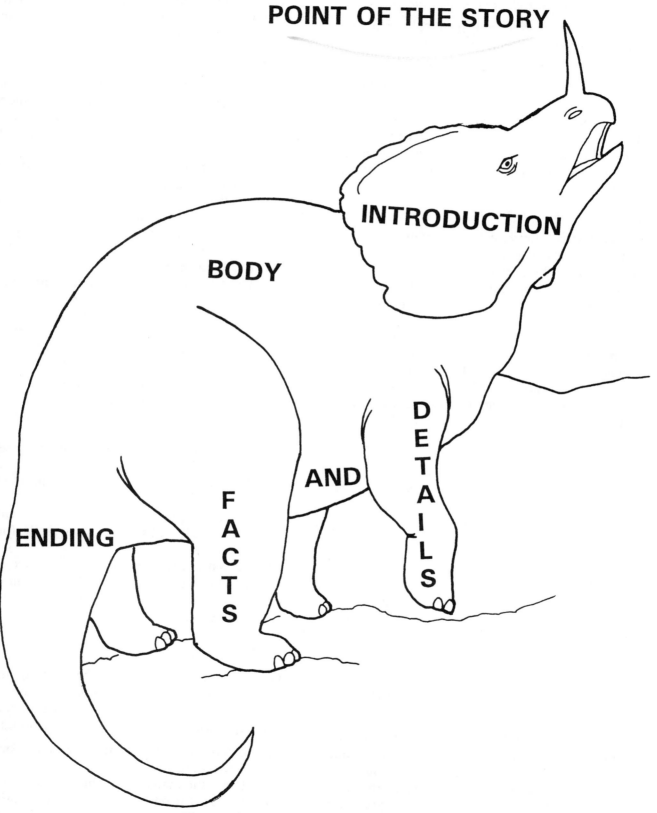

Figure 7-7. Graphic organizer for stories.

4. Brainstorm ideas with students and model how to organize the ideas on the map.
5. Explain how "seeing" information often improves the content of assignments.
6. Give students a blank copy of the map and ask them to copy the information from the chalkboard.
7. Help students synthesize the information into a story.
8. Provide less scaffolding each time maps are used, until students can organize their maps individually.

Adaptations of the Language Experience Approach

The language experience approach (LEA) can be combined with several strategies, such as semantic mapping, in order to improve writing skill. The basic procedure of the LEA involves these steps:

1. Have the student share an experience.
2. Write or type the ideas as the student dictates a story about the experience.
3. Have the student read the story back.

Kaderavek and Mandlebaum (1993) described several teaching strategies that can be used during the oral discussion stage of the LEA. Throughout this process, use modeling techniques and questioning strategies to increase student involvement. The strategies are designed to promote writing skill and include the following steps:

1. Help with construction of a semantic map as students describe an experience.
2. In the middle of the map, write a word central to the experience.
3. Have students suggest different words or ideas that can be arranged in categories around the topic.
4. After the map has been developed, have students dictate a story about the experience into a tape recorder.
5. Have students perform a group evaluation of the taped text. Ask them to evaluate and critique the clarity, organization, and specificity of each part of the story. In addition, students can decide what type of story frame or text structure is best suited to their narrative.

6. Have students discuss the organization of their narrative and then dictate their story a second time.
7. Have the students or a scribe (e.g., teacher, parent) write the dictated story.
8. Have the students read the story aloud.

Story Grammar Framework

Stein and Glenn (1979) suggested that the following elements be included in story grammar instruction:

1. Major setting: introduce the protagonist (main character).
2. Minor setting: describe the time and place of the action.
3. Initiating events: discuss the events that cause the main character to respond.
4. Internal responses: describe the characters' feelings, desires, thoughts, hopes, and/or goals.
5. Attempts: describe what the main character does to try to achieve the goal.
6. Direct consequences: discuss whether the attempt succeeded or failed, and the changes that result from the attempt.
7. Reactions: What are the main character's feelings and thoughts toward the outcome? How are the other characters affected by the outcome?

Story Elements

In a similar strategy, Montague and Graves (1993) suggested that the following seven categories of story elements be taught:

1. Major setting: the main character is introduced.
2. Minor setting: the time and place of the story are described.
3. Initiating event: the atmosphere is changed and the main character responds.
4. Internal response: the character's thoughts, ideas, emotions, and intentions are noted.
5. Attempt: the main character's goal-related actions are represented.
6. Direct consequence: the attainment of the goal is noted; if the goal is not attained, the changes resulting from the attempt are noted.

7. Reaction: the main character's thoughts and feelings in regard to the outcome are specified, along with the effect of the outcome on the character.

Organization Strategy

Initially, some students require increased structure to incorporate elements of story grammar into their writing. Prior to writing, students may benefit from answering specific questions or following specific guidelines pertaining to the setting, episode, and conclusion. The following guidelines and questions are adapted from Stein and Glenn (1979):

1. Discuss the setting:
   Characters
   Who is the main character?
   Who are the other characters?
   Time
   When does the story occur?
   Place
   Where does the story occur?
2. Discuss the episode:
   Event or problem
   What was the initiating event or problem confronting the main character?
   Responses
   What are the responses or goals of the main character for solving the problem?
   What are the responses of the other characters?
   Reaction
   What are the outcomes of the main character's actions?
   What is the reaction to the event or problem?
3. Discuss the conclusion:
   What is the story's conclusion?

C-SPACE

Some students benefit from having a mnemonic to help them remember the steps to follow. The mnemonic *C-SPACE* (MacArthur et al., 1991) may be used as a prewriting strategy. Prior to writing, ask the student to think: (a) for whom the story is being written and (b) what kind of story they want to write. Next, have the student take notes on the story, using the mnemonic:

C—who is the *character*?
S—what is the *setting*?
P—what is the *problem* or *purpose*?
A—what *action* occurs?
C—what is the *conclusion*?
E—what is the *emotion* of the character?

As the final step, have the student write the story by expanding upon the notes.

W-W-W, What = 2, How = 2 Strategy

A similar mnemonic strategy, W-W-W, What = 2, How = 2 (Graham & Harris, 1989b) may be used as a prewriting strategy. Prior to writing, the student answers the following questions:

1. *Who* is the main character? *Who* else is in the story?
2. *When* does the story take place?
3. *Where* does the story take place?
4. *What* does the main character do?
5. *What* happens when he or she tries to do it?
6. *How* does the story end?
7. *How* does the main character feel?

An adaptation of this strategy may be used with a picture stimulus as a basis for writing. Before the student attempts to use the self-instructional strategy, model and demonstrate it while thinking out loud. The steps to be followed are:

1. Instruct students to look at the picture.
2. Tell students to let their minds be free.
3. Have students write down the story-part reminder (W-W-W, What = 2, How = 2).
4. Have students write down ideas to each part.
5. Have students write their stories.
6. Have students read their stories as a group activity.
7. Have the group discuss what elements of the stories are missing and how and where they can be added.
8. Have students add the missing elements.

Provide guidance until students can compose stories independently using the five-step self-instructional statements.

Character Development

In addition to strategies to assist with organization, some students benefit from instruction in character development. Leavell and Ioannides (1993) presented the following questions that may be used to help students expand their descriptions of the physical appearance, the speech and actions, and the thoughts and emotions of the main characters:

1. Physical appearance
   What does the person look like?
2. Speech and actions
   What does the person say?
   What does the person do?
3. Thoughts and emotions
   What does the character think about?
   What emotions does the person display?
   How does the character feel about the outcome?

Before using this strategy, read two paragraphs to students; one where the main character has been developed fully, and one where only minimal information is given. Encourage the students to discuss the differences between the two paragraphs and to note how detailed descriptions can help readers increase their understanding of the characters.

Branching Narratives

Mather and Jaffe (1992) described a procedure for having students write stories to model the "Choose Your Own Adventure" genre. The student begins by writing the opening of the adventure and then stopping at appropriate places in the adventure to write several options that will have different outcomes. For example, after describing the characters entering a haunted house, Jason, a fourth-grade student, writes:

1a. *If you decide to go up the stairs, turn to page* _____.

1b. *If you decide to enter the dining room, turn to page* _____.

Ms. Randall, Jason's teacher, helped him to develop a branching narrative using the following steps:

1. After writing the beginning of the story, Jason decided to write the outcome to 1a. He wrote 1a at the top of a separate page, followed by the opening sentence: *You decide to go up the stairs.* He then proceeded to complete this outcome.

2. After writing the outcome for 1a (which may result in new choices, 2a and 2b, or an ending), Ms. Randall had Jason put a slash through 1a on the first page to show that it had been completed.

3. Jason next wrote the outcome for 1b. He began with the sentence: *You decide to enter the dining room.* He decided to end this branch and wrote: *Bad choice. The chandelier fell on your head and you've never been heard from since. The End.*

The page numbers are added after the book is completed and all the various paths have been resolved.

Figure 7–8 illustrates the first page of the final draft of a branching narrative written by Mike, a third-grade student. His story about Little Dude was 20 pages long.

Shared Writing

Mather and Lachowicz (1992) described a shared writing procedure to help students collaborate on a writing assignment. This technique can be used to motivate reluctant writers. The following steps may be used:

1. Explain to students that they will be writing a story with another person and the goal is to produce a story that sounds like it was written by one person.
2. Have the pairs discuss topic choice.
3. Ask one student to contribute the initial sentence of the story.
4. Ask the other student to read the sentence and then add another sentence to the composition.
5. Ask the pair to take turns contributing sentences and discussing their additions, until they agree that the story is complete. Occasionally, encourage the students to stop and read the entire story before adding a sentence.
6. When the story is completed, have the pair read it together.

Students can share writing by alternating sentences, single words, or paragraphs. When writing sentence-by-sentence, perhaps the least difficult compositional unit, co-authors are required to maintain

There was a poisonous centipede named Little Dude who lived inside a garbage truck. He loved to eat garbage. He had lived in the truck for ten years and even though he loved the food, he was getting tired of the same old place. He wondered if he should leave.
If Little Dude decides to leave, go to page 10.
If Little Dude decides to stay, turn to page 3.

Figure 7–8. First page of a branching narrative by Mike, a third-grade student.

the topic and determine the direction of the story as they take turns adding sentences. Word-by-word composition is a more difficult procedure as it requires greater facility with syntax; partners must adapt word choice with each turn. Creating stories at the paragraph-by-paragraph level requires skill in organization and story cohesion. This type of shared writing may be used with cooperative learning groups for report writing.

Group Writing Strategy

Individual writing skill can be improved through group writing. Participating as a group member can help reduce anxiety and encourage students to participate more fully. A word of caution, however: Try to ensure that all students participate, including those who are shy, quiet, or have difficulty writing. Robin, a fifth-grade student with limited writing skill, became even more discouraged about her writing because in her cooperative learning group, she was always told to just draw the illustrations.

For the majority of students, however, group writing experiences are highly motivating. Poteet (1987) provided a description of an adapted language experience approach that also incorporates mini-lessons in basic skill instruction. The following steps are used:

1. Engage students in some common experience such as a field trip.
2. Have students discuss the experience.
3. Guide students into developing an outline from the discussion.
4. Using the outline, have students dictate the story, which is written on the chalkboard by the teacher.
5. Ensure that most students have made a contribution to the group story.
6. Read the finished story to the class.
7. Discuss how to improve the story:
   —a word or sentence may be changed
   —adjectives, adverbs, or phrases may be added.
8. Use the oral discussion time to introduce new words or skills, thereby teaching them in context.
9. Highlight the new skill or concept (e.g., using capital letters).
10. Have each student copy the group story.
11. Have students read the story as a group, or individually to a partner.
12. As confidence increases, have students write in small groups and, finally, individually.

POWER Strategy

As previously mentioned, many individuals with learning disabilities benefit from the writing process approach. Although all of the above strategies can be integrated into a process approach to writing, some may be used specifically to reinforce story writing as a process.

For example, to help young students remember that writing is a process, Englert et al. (1991) developed the acronym POWER. The letters represent the following steps:

P *Plan*
O *Organize*
W *Write*
E *Edit*
R *Revise*

Writing Process: Scaffolding Activities

Even within the writing process approach, students need guidance and scaffolding. This can be accomplished in many ways. Moulton and Bader (1986) presented the following activities for scaffolding the writing process:

Prewriting:
1. Provide ample time for prewriting activities.
2. Give positive reinforcement for all ideas.
3. Encourage students to jot down *all* ideas they have.
4. Dissuade students from becoming too involved with sequence, spatial organization, spelling, or handwriting at this stage.
5. When no more ideas are forthcoming, have students focus on putting the ideas into some order.
6. Help students organize their ideas. You may:
   a. provide a simple outline that was developed by a student or the group of students.
   b. provide a chart of descriptive words categorized in the way the student or group chose to categorize during the oral discussion.

7. Have students tell the story to a peer.
8. Help students synthesize any appropriate feedback after the oral storytelling.

Planning:
1. Provide a "communication triangle" visual depicting the purpose of writing, the writer's point of view, and the audience perspective.
2. Help students establish a chart, developed from the prewriting activities, to help with sequencing.

Drafting:
1. Request that students write on every other line.
2. Encourage students to focus on ideation, not mechanics.

Revising:
1. Provide ample support throughout this process.
2. Prepare a list of questions and comments about the draft. The questions may include:
   a. How well does the draft adhere to the topic?
   b. How well does the draft adhere to the plan?
   c. Is the information well-organized?
   d. Is the word choice appropriate?
3. Hold individual teacher-student conferences.
4. Have the student read the draft aloud.
5. Provide the student with the questions and comments on a handout.
6. Have the student respond to the questions and comments.
7. Give the student a colored pen for revision purposes during the conference.
8. Let the student take the lead at the conference.
9. Do not focus on all errors. Some will wait until the next assignment and the next conference.

Proofreading:
1. Provide the level of guidance necessary for the individual. Some students will need line-by-line guidance, whereas others will need only a checklist of general reminders.
2. Do not expect students to correct errors that are beyond their current skill level.

3. Remember that improvement and not perfection is the expectation during the proofreading stage.

Final Draft:
1. Provide positive reinforcement.
2. Encourage the student to share writing with others.

Three-Step Process Writing Procedure

Gaskins (1982) described a three-step process that provided guidelines for before writing, during writing, and after writing activities. The following procedures are used:

1. Before writing:
   a. Help students choose a topic for writing based upon their knowledge, interest, and motivation.
   b. Help students gather more information about the topic from numerous sources.
   c. Help students reflect upon the information to ensure understanding of all the material.
   d. Encourage students to select the material appropriate to the writing assignment.
   e. Provide ample time for the information to be organized in a logical order.
   f. Ensure that each student receives enough help during the organization phase.
2. During writing:
   a. Encourage students to write on every other line.
   b. Encourage students to use wide margins for editing purposes.
   c. Circulate throughout the classroom.
   d. Give immediate responses to ideas as they are written.
   e. Emphasize the positive aspects of the student's writing.
   f. On occasion, read a sentence or phrase from a student's work. The sentence may be well written, have good content, or reinforce an important concept.
   g. Do not interrupt students whose train of thought is easily broken. Provide feedback to these students only when requested.

h. Offer unsolicited advice only to those students who are not bothered by interruptions.

i. Provide feedback that focuses only on content and the recording of ideas at this stage.

3. After writing:

a. Have the student share writing with other students.

b. Monitor the feedback given and help the student focus on the appropriate suggestions for improvement.

c. Help the students to consider: (a) thought content, the effectiveness of the ideas and their development; (b) organization, the sequencing, logic, and flow of the ideas; (c) effectiveness, the clarity and power of expression, and vocabulary; and (d) mechanics, capitalization, punctuation, spelling, syntax, etc.

d. Provide encouraging, specific, and objective feedback.

e. Tell the students why a specific comment or suggestion was made and how it will improve the work.

f. From students' written work, note their readiness to learn specific writing skills.

g. Teach the specific skills through a formal and structured program.

h. Hold a teacher-student conference to provide feedback, and to teach necessary skills.

i. Provide the opportunity for students to share their final product.

STORE the Story

STORE the Story (Schlegel & Bos, 1986) is a strategy that incorporates elements of the writing process through the use of a story frame. The following adaptation was presented by Mather and Jaffe (1992):

STORE is an acronym for:
S = *Setting* (Who? What? Where? When?)
T = *Trouble* (What is the trouble or problem?)
O = *Order* of events (What happens?)
R = *Resolution* (What is done to solve the problem?)
E = *End* (How does the story end?)

A. Introduce the Cue STORE:

1. Discuss the meaning of the verb "to store" (save, hold, keep for a while, put away).

2. Discuss the purpose: To help understand and remember (store) any story the students read by recognizing and recalling each part.

3. Explain the parts of a story: Every story has a beginning, middle, and end. Every story also has a SETTING, TROUBLE, ORDER OF EVENTS, RESOLUTION, and ENDING.

B. Demonstration/Modeling:

1. Model the prewriting stage of the writing process approach by thinking aloud the steps of topic selection and brainstorming of ideas. Brainstorm ideas for the story and fill in the STORE cue sheet, crossing out ideas and adding others until satisfied.

2. Read over the cue sheet to make sure that all parts of the story make sense and fit in relation to other parts.

3. Model the writing stage of the writing process approach, and, subsequently, revising, editing, and rewriting. Explain how the use of STORE ensures continuity of the story line.

C. Guided Practice:

1. Guide the students to create a group story using the STORE format.

D. Independent Practice:

1. Have the students create their own stories.

E. Adaptations or Extra Support:

1. Provide picture cards to aid in generating story ideas.

2. If necessary, provide the Setting, Trouble, and some Events. Have the student add some Events and finish the story, or provide the Setting or the Trouble and have the student generate the other parts of the story.

A structured overview of the strategy is presented in Figure 7–9.

Grid Model

The Grid Model, adapted from Crealock (1993), allows students to generate content and develop narrative writing skills within the steps of the writing process. Several record forms for using this procedure are presented in Figures 7–10a, 7–10b, 7–10c,

STORE the Story

Name:_____

Date: _____

Working Title: _____

SETTING

    Who _____

    What _____

    Where _____

    When _____

TROUBLE _____

_____

ORDER OF ACTION

    1. _____

    2. _____

    3. _____

    4. _____

    5. _____

RESOLUTION

    1. _____

    2. _____

    3. _____

    4. _____

    5. _____

ENDING _____

_____

Figure 7–9. A structured overview of the STORE strategy.

7–10d, and 7–10e. There are nine stages to the strategy. All students, regardless of age, complete all of the stages.

Stage 1: Choosing the grid. The first stage can begin at any of four levels and is chosen based on the skill of the students. The teacher selects the appropriate level. The story parts that must be addressed vary among levels:

Level 1:
1. The main character
2. The setting
3. When the story occurs
4. Any animals that will be important to the story
5. Any object, real or imagined, significant to the story

Level 2:
1–5. The elements in level 1
6. A generic plot (e.g., an adventure in Mexico)
7. A specific action, conflict, or problem (e.g., some previously undiscovered pyramids are found near Mexico City)

Level 3:
1–7. The elements of levels 1 and 2 are included.
8. A title is included.
9. Opening and/or closing sentences are noted.
10. Emotions are discussed.
11. A climax is reached.

Level 4:
1–11. The elements of levels 1, 2, and 3 are included.
12. A subplot is planned.
13. The characters are developed in more detail.
14. The style of writing is determined (e.g., fairy tale, second-grade reading book, poem, newspaper article, history text, telegraph).

Stage 2: Grid development. Develop the grid with the students. The structural components (e.g., main character, setting) are listed in horizontal rows. Have the students brainstorm and list ten entries (numbered 0–9) under each component.

Stage 3: Planning. Have each student randomly choose a number for each of the horizontal rows. Thus, 5 random numbers must be chosen if writing at level 1, 7 numbers if writing at level 2, 11 numbers if writing at level 3, and 14 numbers if writing at level 4. The student's specific story components are tabulated by reading the component from the grid that corresponds to each of his or her randomly chosen numbers. A story outline is then written.

Stage 4: First draft. Have students write the first draft, remembering to include all of the components. Ask them to skip lines between sentences so that editing will be easier.

Stage 5: First editing. Have students read their stories to peers and discuss any suggested changes with the group.

Stage 6: Second draft. After deciding which changes would be appropriate, have students incorporate the changes into the second draft.

Stage 7: Cognitive editing. Read the story with the author and discuss further revisions to the content.

Stage 8: Technical editing. Once the content has been edited satisfactorily, the story is proofread sentence by sentence to detect and correct errors in spelling, capitalization, and punctuation. Depending on student skill, technical editing may be performed by the individual, with peers, or with the teacher or aid.

Stage 9: Final draft. When the story is deemed acceptable by both student and teacher, have the student write and share the final draft.

An empty grid is provided for each of the four levels. As the students pass through the nine stages, encourage them to check/color the corresponding square on the graphic at the bottom of their grid. This will help them see that each stage is part of one process.

Expository

Students must be able to communicate subject matter effectively to others in writing (Ediger, 1993). Although instruction in story narratives is often an appropriate place to begin with young writers, instruction in expository structures should be included at all levels (Englert & Mariage, 1991). After being taught a narrative strategy, some students are able to adapt it to expository writing without specific instruction from the teacher, whereas others require direct and assisted practice to accomplish this transfer (Graham & Harris, 1993).

1 **Choose Grid** **(teacher)**	2 **Develop Grid** **(teacher & student)**	3 **Plan Story** **(teacher & student)**
4 **First Draft** **(student)**	5 **First Edit** **(student & peers)**	6 **Second Draft** **(student)**
7 **Cognitive Edit** **(teacher & student)**	8 **Technical Edit** **(teacher & student)**	9 **Final Draft** **(student)**

Figure 7–10a. Stages in grid model.

Poor organization and difficulty with development of ideas are common problems of ineffective writers (Ellis, 1994b). Fortunately, many strategies can be used to help students improve their skills in collecting and organizing the factual information that they wish to include in their paragraph, essay, or report. In general, students benefit from formal instruction that presents organizational models and includes practice in paragraph writing in a variety of modes (Vogel & Moran, 1982).

The most common types of expository text structures are presented in Figure 7–11. This figure provides a brief description of each text structure, a sample sentence as a model for informal evaluation of student writing, and examples of the cohesive ties and key words, most common to each type. Students must acquire several different types

of expository styles to succeed in higher grades (Westby, 1994). These text structures can form the basis for instruction in paragraph and/or essay writing.

Expanding, Interviewing, and Oral Histories

Tompkins and Friend (1986) described three activities for helping students to write paragraphs. Each procedure begins with prewriting activities and progresses to paragraph or essay writing.

Expanding:
1. Select a broad topic (e.g., Things I Have Lost).
2. Have students name several events/objects that the topic brings to mind (e.g., baby teeth, dog, or homework assignment).

	Character(s)	Setting	Time	Animal(s)	Object(s)
0					
1					
2					
3					
4					
5					
6					
7					
8					
9					

Stages:

1	2	3
4	5	6
7	8	9

Figure 7–10b. Grid for Level 1.

	Plot	Action/ Conflict	Character(s)	Setting	Time	Animal(s)	Object(s)
0							
1							
2							
3							
4							
5							
6							
7							
8							
9							

Stages:

1	2	3
4	5	6
7	8	9

Figure 7–10c. Grid for Level 2.

	Title	Opening/ Closing Sentence	Plot	Action/ Conflict	Charac- ter(s)	Setting	Time	Animal(s)	Object(s)	Emotions	Cli- max
0											
1											
2											
3											
4											
5											
6											
7											
8											
9											

Stages:

1	2	3
4	5	6
7	8	9

Figure 7–10d. Grid for Level 3.

	Title	Opening/ Closing Sentence	Plot	Action/ Conflict	Charac- ters	Setting	Time	Animal(s)	Object(s)	Emo- tions	Sub- plot	Dev'mt of char- acter	Style	Cli- max
0														
1														
2														
3														
4														
5														
6														
7														
8														
9														

Stages:

1	2	3
4	5	6
7	8	9

Figure 7–10e. Grid for Level 4.

Text Structures

SEQUENTIAL: A series of events presented in temporal order, that tells how to do or make something.

Cohesive ties and key words:

first	finally	at night
second	in the past	in the fall
third	eventually	during the spring
last	now	at breakfast
then	soon	toward the afternoon
to begin	before	in the morning
next	after	

Sample: "To bake a cake, you have to complete several steps. First, you buy your ingredients ..."

ENUMERATION: A series of facts or details related to a specific topic, listed as points.

Cohesive ties and key words:

in addition	moreover
furthermore	finally
besides	for example
likewise	for instance
of course	in other words
to illustrate	such as
	next

Sample: "Garlic can be used in many ways. For instance, in folk lore garlic was used to ward off vampires. Of course, ..."

DESCRIPTION: A series of attributes and characteristics that tells about the subject. The description may include spatial characteristics, physical attributes, behavioral characteristics, affective characteristics or applications.

Cohesive ties and key words:
refers to
can be explained as
can be defined as
can be described as
is a method for
is a way to

Sample: "The London Bridge is located in Arizona. The bridge spans ..."

Figure 7-11. The most common types of expository text structures.

CAUSE/EFFECT: An explanation of the situation and the reasons for why something happened.

Cohesive ties and key words:

to begin with	because
most important of all	consequently
for one thing	therefore
furthermore	for this reason
as a result	thus

> Sample: "During the past year, physical fitness at our school have increased. These programs have been beneficial in a number of ways ..."

PROBLEM-SOLUTION: The statement of a problem and possible alternative solutions.

Cohesive ties and key words:

last and most important	as a result
in addition	currently

> Sample: "If you're unlucky enough to have a flat tire on the highway, you will need to find ways to cope with the problem."

COMPARE/CONTRAST: Two or more topics compared according to their likenesses and differences along one or more dimensions.

Cohesive ties and key words:

in contrast	even so	although
conversely	otherwise	instead of
on the contrary	still	similarly
however	yet	while
but	whereas	on the other hand

> Sample: "Uganda has a different topography than Kuwait. Uganda is lush and green, whereas Kuwait is arid. The two countries, however, ..."

ARGUMENT/PERSUASION: Statement of a position on an issue with justification.

Cohesive ties and key words:

the first	the major reason
therefore	subsequently
consequently	

> Sample: "The government should spend more money on the prevention of AIDS. The first reason ..."

Figure 7–11 (cont.).

3. Have students brainstorm words that make the experience more vivid in their memories.
4. Have the students write a paragraph in a small group.

Interviewing:

1. Have a group of students work together in choosing a topic (e.g., favorite movie star).
2. Separate students into pairs.
3. Ask each pair to interview approximately eight of their peers, with one of the pair asking the questions and the other recording the answers.
4. On their return, help students synthesize the responses.
5. Have the group write three paragraphs, one on what was done, one on the results, and one on the conclusions.
6. As skill develops, have each pair choose a topic of interest to them. Help the two collaborate and provide support as they write the paragraphs at the conclusion of the study.

Oral Histories:

1. With a group of students, develop a set of questions that will explore an individual's history.
2. Have the students collect data from a family member by asking the questions and recording the answers.
3. Model how to organize the data.
4. Help students organize their data.
5. Model how to integrate the data into a written report.
6. Provide individual support as students write their reports.

Questioning Strategy

Students may also answer a series of questions prior to writing that will increase their awareness of the purpose for writing. For example, before drafting an assignment, have students answer the following questions (Greenberg, 1987):

1. What do I know about the topic?
2. How do I feel about it?
3. What experiences have I had with it?
4. How have these experiences shaped my values and beliefs?

5. What do I want to explain, or show, or prove? If preferred, the questions may be presented in written form and students may jot down a short answer to each. Alternatively, students may answer the questions orally either to the teacher or to a peer. Sharing the answers with others will help students increase their own understanding.

K-W-L Procedure

The K-W-L procedure (Ogle, 1986) can be used as a strategy to help students increase their factual knowledge and participate more actively in the writing process. A strategy worksheet is developed with the following three columns across the top of the paper:

K What I *know*
W What do I *want* to learn
L What I *learned*

Follow these steps in completing the worksheet:

1. In the first column, have students brainstorm and list any information that they already know about the topic.
2. In the second column, have students develop questions about what they want to learn about the topic.
3. In the third column, have students record what they have learned from reading and library research.

Upon completion of the worksheet, ask students to write an expository paragraph that summarizes what they have learned about the topic. A sample worksheet to use with this strategy is provided in Figure 7–12.

K-W-L Plus. Carr and Ogle (1987) described an adaptation of the K-W-L strategy that adds mapping and summarization. They noted that the benefits of this procedure can be enhanced if a writing activity is added. To add the mapping component, students categorize the information listed under *L*. The topic forms the center of the map. For example, if students were learning about the planet Saturn, they would write "Saturn" in the center of the map. Lines are then added to show the relationship between the main topic and the facts that have been learned.

K - W - L

K What we know	W What we want to find out	L What we learned

Figure 7–12. Sample K-W-L strategy sheet.

For the summarization component, students can use the map that depicts the organization of the information. The center of the map becomes the title of the essay and each category is used as the topic for a new paragraph. Supporting details are then added to expand the paragraph or explain the topic further. After practice with this procedure, some students are able to omit the mapping step and write their summaries directly from the K-W-L worksheet.

RAFT Strategy

Many students have problems writing specific and well-focused assignments and fail to describe the topic clearly and completely. Nancy Vandervanter, a teacher who participated in the Montana Writing Project, developed the following strategy to help students structure their assignments in content area classes. This procedure, described by Santa (1988), uses the acronym RAFT to remind the writer of several steps to consider as part of every writing assignment:

R   *R*ole of a writer: Who/What are you? Examples of possible roles are a slave, a blood cell, a cartoonist, or a restaurant.

A   *A*udience: To whom is the assignment written? Possible audiences include a child, an historic figure, a corporation, or a person in the hospital.

F   *F*ormat: What form will the assignment take? Numerous ideas for formats exist, some of which are a letter, an obituary, graffiti, a public notice, a ship's log, a telegram, minutes of a meeting, a news story, a nominating speech, or a prophesy or prediction.

T   *Topic* + strong verb: Set the tone of the assignment by incorporating strong verbs. Example topics include: Persuade a soldier to spare your life or demand equal pay for equal work. Other strong verbs include plead, convince, and clarify.

After introducing the key words, provide instruction in the strategy using the following steps:

1. Explain that the four components represented by the acronym RAFT must be included in every written assignment.
2. Brainstorm topic ideas and list several of those suggested.
3. For each topic, write the acronym on the board and list possible roles, audiences, formats, and strong verbs.
4. Have students decide upon, and write on, one of the topics generated.
5. Use the RAFT strategy at the beginning of a unit to determine background knowledge and/or at the end to summarize concepts and main ideas.

Paragraph Frames

Nichols (1980) described the use of paragraph frames to help students improve their expository writing. Depending upon the genre, these frames contain key words or phrases that provide students with a structure to help them organize their writing (Lewis, Wray, & Rospigliosi, 1994). A frame can be modified and used for all types of different expository writing, such as sequential, chronological order, cause-effect, and comparison-contrast. In general, when constructing these frames, leave spaces for student writing and provide surrounding words that will help the student identify what should be written in the spaces. Although the technique does not produce creative expository writing, the frames can serve as scaffolds for students with limited writing skill who require additional support. Examples of several frames are presented in Figure 7–13.

Question-Answer-Detail (QAD) Method

The purpose of the QAD method (Weiss & Weiss, 1993) is to help students organize paragraphs and reports. Three columns are created across the top of the paper with the headings: Question, Answer, Detail. In the first column, help the students generate several questions that will be answered in the report. In the second column, have the student answer the questions. In the third column, have the student write additional details about the topic.

To write a three-sentence paragraph, the student cuts across the paper including one question, answer, and the related details. The question is then rephrased as an expository statement. As students become more proficient in paragraph writing, a greater amount of detail should be included.

SLOW CaPS

The SLOW CaPS strategy (Schumaker et al., 1985; Schumaker & Sheldon, 1985) may be used for the following four different types of paragraphs: (a) enumerative or descriptive, (b) sequential, (c) compare and/or contrast, and (d) cause and effect. The small "a" in the mnemonic denotes that it is not used as an action reminder.

S   *SHOW* the type of paragraph being used. This must be done in the first sentence.
L   *LIST* the details that will be discussed.
O   *ORDER* the details.
W   *WRITE* the details in complete sentences. In conclusion, CAP the paragraph with:
    C   a *concluding* sentence
    P   a *passing* sentence
or S   a *summary* sentence

PLEASE Strategy

The use of paragraph writing strategies helps students succeed in writing effectively (Englert & Lichter, 1982; Englert et al., 1989; Wallace & Bott, 1989; Welch, 1992). The PLEASE strategy was designed to promote metacognitive problem-solving for both prewriting planning, and composition and paragraph revision (Welch, 1992; Welch & Jensen, 1991). The acronym represents the following steps:

P   *P*ick a topic, the audience, and the appropriate textual format.
L   Using various techniques, such as brainstorming or mapping, *l*ist information about the topic. This information will be used in generating, organizing, and evaluating sentences.

Sample Paragraph Frames

Sequential

In order to _____ a _____ , you must follow

several steps. First _____

_____

Then _____

_____

Next _____

_____

Finally _____

_____

_____

Chronological

At the beginning _____

_____

After that _____

_____

Next _____

_____

The _____ ended when _____

_____

_____

_____

Figure 7–13. Sample paragraph frames.

Enumerative

There were several _____ for _____

_____

First, _____

_____

Second, _____

_____

Finally, _____

_____

_____

Descriptive

The following provides a description of _____

_____

The _____

looks like _____

If you look around you will see _____

_____

You will also see _____

_____

You will also see _____

_____

In general, _____

is very _____

_____

Figure 7–13 (cont.).

Compare - Contrast

_____ and _____

are alike and are different in several ways. First, they are alike

because _____

_____

but they are different because of _____

_____

Secondly, one is _____

while the other is _____

Finally, they are alike because _____

_____

but different because _____

_____

Problem Solution

The problem began when _____

_____

The _____ tried to _____

_____

After that _____

_____

Then _____

_____

The problem was finally solved when _____

_____

Figure 7–13 (cont.)

Cause-Effect

The _____

was caused by _____

As a result, _____

_____

Another consequence was _____

_____

Furthermore, _____

_____

The effects of the _____

_____

are clearly apparent.

Figure 7–13 (cont.)

E   *E*valuate if the list is complete and organize the ideas into a logical order in preparation for sentence generation.
A   *A*ctivate the paragraph idea by writing a short, simple, declarative, topic sentence.
S   *S*upply supportive sentences. The sentences are generated from the list of ideas recorded earlier.
E   *E*nd with a concluding sentence, and *e*valuate the work using an error monitoring strategy such as COPS (Schumaker et al., 1985).

Audience Strategy

Audience considerations are an important part of the writing process. As noted by Blatt (1985): "When he's writing, the writer must take distance. But when he's reading, he must get involved" (p. 366). The AUDIENCE strategy, developed by Mather and Roberts, may be used to remind the writer to consider and identify the needs of the reader prior to and during writing. This type of strategy may help writers attend to the relationship between the information presented in the text and the readers' comprehension of the purpose and meaning. The first-letter mnemonic represents the following steps:

A   sk who the readers are. For example, ask: Who are my readers? What do they already know about the topic?
U   nderstand the readers' needs. For example, ask: What information will be new to my readers?
D   elve into the topic.
I   ntegrate background information with new information.
E   nsure all material makes sense.
N   ote the most important information.
C   onstruct a passage.
E   valuate the passage for clarity by asking questions such as: Is all the information presented clearly? Will any of the sentences confuse the readers? Is there more that I need to explain?

PLANS Strategy

Harris and Graham (1992) described school writing assignments as ill-defined, problem-solving tasks. For example, when asked to write a paper, many students have only a vague idea about how to locate the necessary information. On completion of the assignment, students have a tenuous grasp of how to evaluate their work.

One way of dealing successfully with a writing assignment is to complete a means-end analysis. This involves deciding how the final draft of the assignment will look and selecting the means to attain the end goal.

Goals. The goals can include: (a) general purpose of the paper (e.g., "Write a paper that is fun to read"); (b) completeness of the paper (e.g., "Write a story that has all the basic parts"); (c) length (e.g., "Write a paper that has five paragraphs"); (d) specific attributes (e.g., "Share with the reader four things about the main character"); (e) vocabulary (e.g., "Write a paper containing 15 describing words"); and (f) sentence variety (e.g., "Write a paper in which you use six complex sentences").

Steps. The following strategy involves a means-end analysis and incorporates these steps:

1. Use PLANS
    P   *P*ick goals (from among a number suggested by the teacher).
    L   *L*ist ways to meet the goals.
    A   *A*nd make
    N   *N*otes.
    S   *S*equence notes.
2. Write and say more.
3. Test goals. If the goals have not been met, help the student revise the paper in order to meet the objectives.

Paragraph-Organization Strategy

The paragraph-organization strategy is a highly structured approach for teaching students to write effective formula paragraphs (Moran, 1983). To begin, model writing of different types of paragraphs using the following steps:

1. Discuss with students the development of a topic sentence, supporting statements, and a concluding statement. Write each component on the chalkboard or overhead transparency.
2. Elicit a topic and supporting details from the group to develop a model paragraph.
3. Have students write a practice paragraph and then compare their paragraph to the model paragraph.
4. Discuss with students what revisions are needed to comply with the model.

5. Provide practice with different paragraph types, such as enumerative, sequential, and compare/contrast.

Organizational Charts

Some students may benefit from the use of graphic procedures to aid in organizing materials. Weiss and Weiss (1993) presented a procedure for using an organizational chart, illustrated in Figure 7–14. A student writes a central theme or main idea, and then delineates the major subtopics to be discussed. As a student researches the topic, notes are taken on index cards and filed into the appropriate envelope.

Bos and Anders (1990b) described a similar strategy that can be used with Post-it™ notes. Students write several topics on a paper or poster board and then record and post their notes under the appropriate headings. One nice feature of this type of strategy is that the Post-its™ may be easily moved from category to category as the student attempts to organize and reorganize his or her report.

Writing Wheels

Writing wheels (Rooney, 1990) can also be used to help students organize their essays, paragraphs, compositions, or term papers. The wheels are used to separate the main ideas and details. The first page is a five-circle overview and can be developed using the following strategy:

1. Write the title at the top of the paper.
2. Draw five wheels on the first sheet. In the first wheel write the word START and in the last wheel write the word END or THEREFORE. Write a word or phrase or sentence in the first wheel that identifies the ideas that will be used in the Introduction.
3. Write one main idea inside each of the three middle wheels that will be developed.
4. In the last wheel, marked END, write a word, phrase, or sentence that will be used as the conclusion.

Each wheel is then produced on a separate page. The writer then adds details, ideas, and thoughts in a spoke-like fashion around the wheel. When all the ideas have been recorded, the writer numbers the ideas in the sequence that they will be presented.

Formula for Written Outlining
Helping the Student Structure
Material to Write

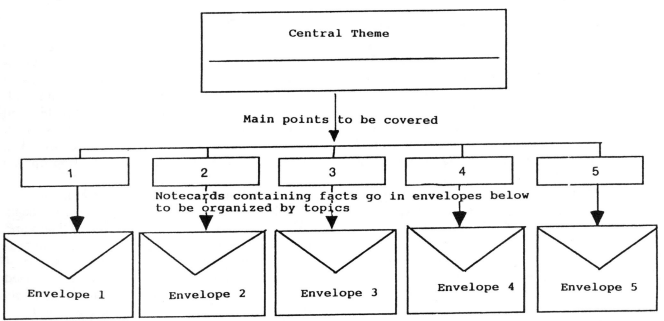

This three dimensional organizational chart is best placed on a large piece of cardboard (oak tag), or in the center of a regular 8 X 11 manila file folder. Envelopes can then be stapled to the file folder. The students places his 3 X 5 notecards in the appropriate envelope according to the way his topics are arranged.

Figure 7–14. An organizational chart.

Note. From *Formulas to Read and Write* (p. 84), by M. S. Weiss and H. G. Weiss, 1993, Avon, CO: Treehouse Associates. Copyright 1993 by Treehouse Associates. Reprinted by permission.

The pages of wheels are then used to write an outline or a rough draft. Figures 7–15a and 7–15b illustrate the first sheet and then the single wheel that may be used for subsequent pages.

Statement-Pie

A strategy that can be used for developing expository paragraphs was described by Hanau (1974). In this strategy, "statement" refers to a topic statement, and "pie" refers to:

P   *proofs*
I   *information*
E   *examples*

Wallace and Bott (1989) described the following adaptation:

1. Give students a completed paragraph guide as a model of the strategy.
2. Explain the meaning of "statement" and "pie".
3. Model the detection and generation of pies.
4. Give students a statement.
5. Have students verbally generate appropriate pies. The planning guide to be used is as follows:
   Statement: topic statement
   Pie: a detail related to the topic statement
   Pie: another detail related to the topic statement
   Pie: another detail related to the topic statement

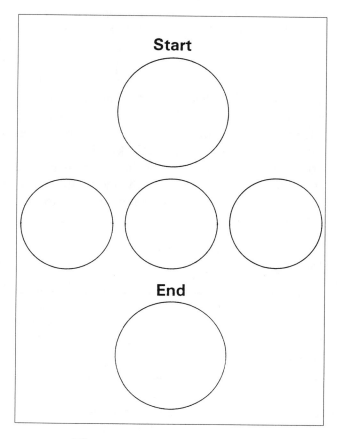

Figure 7–15a. Writing wheels.

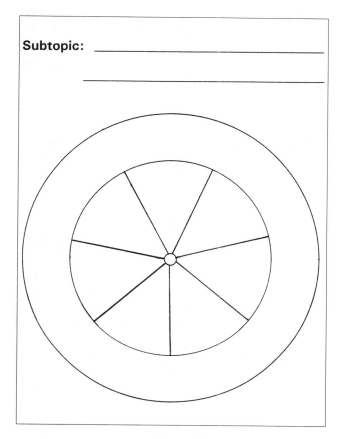

Figure 7–15b. Single wheel for subtopics.

6. Give immediate feedback in regard to the appropriateness of each pie.
7. Give students another statement in an area that is age appropriate and in which students have background knowledge.
8. Have students generate and write appropriate pies to be used as paragraph planning guides on the given topic.
9. Give immediate feedback in regard to the appropriateness of each pie.

Use the following steps for outlining statements and pies in expository paragraphs:

1. Model the outlining of statements and pies in chosen expository paragraphs.
2. Give students paragraphs for guided practice.
3. Circle the statements, and underline the pies.
4. Write the statements and pies in a planning guide such as that noted above.

Writing paragraphs:

1. Model paragraph writing by:
   a. selecting a topic
   b. writing a paragraph planning guide
   c. using the guide to construct sentences
   d. forming the sentences into a paragraph
   e. emphasizing key words and cohesive ties (e.g., *first, next, afterwards, finally*)
2. Have students choose a topic from a list generated by the teacher.
3. Have students generate statement-pie paragraph planning guides.
4. Have students write a paragraph.
5. Provide immediate feedback with regard to the appropriateness of the pies.

Spool Papers

Spool papers (Santa, 1988) provide a system to help students organize information through the use of an introductory paragraph, supporting paragraphs, and a concluding paragraph. Both direct instruction and guided practice are provided to teach this strategy. The following procedure may be used to teach students how to write a paper containing five or more paragraphs:

1. Present the spool diagram on an overhead (see Figure 7-16a) and distribute copies of the diagram to all students. Explain that the procedure is a format for writing an essay with five or more paragraphs.
2. Select a familiar topic. Have students brainstorm ideas related to the topic. Model how to narrow the topic to three major issues or ideas that will be developed into separate paragraphs.
3. Explain that the thesis statement is the controlling idea. Help students to write a clear thesis statement.
4. Draft a spool paper using the generated ideas. Explain the function of the transition words, as illustrated in Figure 7-16b.

5. Provide students with a copy of the essay and the editing checklist, illustrated in Figure 7-16c.

For guided practice assist students in brainstorming and narrowing their ideas, drafting their outlines, and writing their first drafts. Once students have written their first drafts, encourage them to read their drafts to peers for feedback. After revisions are made, have students edit their work using the spool paper editing sheet and then write their final drafts. As skill increases, encourage students to vary the format.

Writing Process Approach Intervention for Essay Writing

Just as with narrative text structures, students benefit from a process approach to expository structures that emphasizes writing and revising. The following procedure has been adapted from Wong et al. (1991):

The spool system is the standard, five-paragraph method of organization. It forces the student to organize his/her writing through use of a thesis sentence that breaks the paper into a logically structured paper with a definite conclusion.

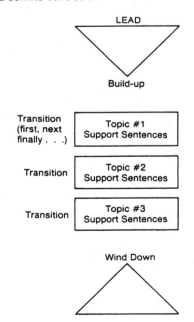

Introductory Paragraph: This starts with a **lead** (question, interesting fact, quote, anecdote) to gain the reader's attention. The last sentence in the introduction is the **thesis,** which is the controlling idea and contains the topics for each paragraph in the body.

LEADS: 1. Asks a question
       2. States an interesting fact
       3. States a quote applying to thesis
       4. States a brief story (anecdote)

The thesis sentence (the last sentence of the introductory paragraph) contains the topics for each paragraph in the body.

Body: This should contain at least three paragraphs. In a paper to convince, the weakest reasons should come first; strongest reason should come last.

Concluding Paragraph: This paragraph starts with a **restatement** of the thesis sentence. **"Clincher"** sentence(s) follow, giving the feeling of business completed. These may relate back to the lead.

Figure 7-16a. Spool System diagram.

Note. From *Content Reading Including Study Systems: Reading, Writing, and Studying Across the Curriculum* (p. 114) by C. M. Santa, 1988, Dubuque, IA: Kendall/Hunt Publishing Company. Copyright 1988 by Kendall/Hunt Publishing Company. Reprinted by permission.

Transition Words Useful in Framed Paragraphs and Spool Papers

Addition

again	in addition
also	last
and	lastly
and then	likewise
besides	moreover
equally important	next
finally	nor
first	secondly
further	thirdly
furthermore	too

Comparison

in like manner
likewise
similarly

Contrast

after all	in contrast to this
although this may be true	nevertheless
and yet	notwithstanding
at the same time	on the other hand
but	on the contrary
for all that	still
however	yet

Place

adjacent to	nearby
beyond	on the opposite side
here	opposite to

Purpose

for this purpose
to this end
with this object

Result

accordingly	therefore
consequently	thereupon
hence	thus
in conclusion	wherefore

Summary, Repetition, Exemplification, Intensification

as has been noted	in sum
as I have said	in brief
for example	in any event
for instance	indeed
in fact	on the whole
in other words	to be sure
in short	to sum up

Time

after a few days	in the meantime
afterward	meanwhile
at length	soon
immediately	

Figure 7–16b. Transition words.

Note. From *Content Reading Including Study Systems: Reading, Writing, and Studying Across the Curriculum* (p. 115) by C. M. Santa, 1988, Dubuque, IA: Kendall/Hunt Publishing Company. Copyright 1988 by Kendall/Hunt Publishing Company. Reprinted by permission.

Spool Paper Editing Sheet

Writer _____   Editor _____

1. Writer is to number lines.

2. Write only on editing sheet.

3. Only the author has the right to change anything on his/her own paper.

4. Steps in editing
   a. Author reads own paper.
   b. Author reads his/her paper to editor.
   c. Editor reads paper back to author.
   d. Complete editing checklist together by writing or summarizing the author's sentences in each position.

   Paragraph 1—Introductory paragraph
   a. opening sentence(s):
   b. thesis statement:

   Paragraph 2
   Thesis or topic sentence:
   a.
   b.
   c.
   Summary or lead

   Paragraph 3
   Thesis or topic sentence:
   a.
   b.
   c.
   Summary:

   Paragraph 4
   Thesis or topic sentence:
   a.
   b.
   c.
   Summary:

   Paragraph 5—Conclusion
   a. restating major point of paper
   b. clincher

Spelling suggestions:

Sentence suggestions:

Figure 7–16c. Spool paper editing sheet.

Note. From *Content Reading Including Study Systems: Reading, Writing, and Studying Across the Curriculum* (p. 116) by C. M. Santa, 1988, Dubuque, IA: Kendall/Hunt Publishing Company. Copyright 1988 by Kendall/Hunt Publishing Company. Reprinted by permission.

1. Teach students that writing is a process involving planning, generating sentences, and revising.

Planning

2. Discuss with students the relevance of planning in real life situations.
3. Elicit from students why planning is useful in writing; to direct them toward a topic and to clarify their writing goals.
4. Select a strategy for the specific essay type to use; narrative, reportive, or compare/contrast.
5. Model the planning strategy.
6. Have students take turns thinking aloud their essay plans.

Writing and revising

7. Have students write a first draft.
8. Read the draft and ask for clarification of unclear sentences in an interactive teaching style, ensuring the student understands why a sentence is unclear.
9. Have each student clarify and expand upon sentences deemed unclear.
10. Work with the student to improve the clarity of the essay.
11. Explain how the revised sentences are better.
12. Have the student rewrite the essay.
13. Repeat steps 8–11 as often as necessary.
14. When message clarity has been attained, work with the student at correcting spelling and grammatical errors.
15. Have the student write the final draft.

TOWER Strategy

Many process-writing strategies have been designed to help students remember and follow steps for essay writing. One such strategy has been developed by Schumaker et al. (1985) and Schumaker and Sheldon (1985). The mnemonic TOWER refers to the following steps:

T   *Think* of the content. Write down:
   (a)   a title
   (b)   major areas for discussion
   (c)   details within each area
O   *Order* the major topic areas and the details under each topic area

W   *Write* a rough draft
E   *Error* monitor the work using an error monitoring strategy such as COPS:
   C   Capitalization
   O   Overall appearance
   P   Punctuation
   S   Spelling
R   *Revise* the rough draft

WRITER Strategy

The acronym WRITER refers to another process-oriented strategy that was developed by Schumaker et al. (1985) and Schumaker and Sheldon (1985). The choice of strategy will depend upon student need and preference. The acronym WRITER represents:

W   *Write* the first draft on every other line of the paper choosing one of the 14 sentence formulas from the PENS strategy (Schumaker & Sheldon, 1985).
R   *Read* for meaning. Inappropriate sentences must be revised.
I   *Interrogate* yourself using the COPS strategy.
   C   Capitalization
   O   Overall appearance
   P   Punctuation
   S   Spelling
T   *Take* the written work to someone else to check if unsure about a potential error.
E   *Execute* a final draft of the work incorporating the corrections made on the first draft and writing as neatly as possible on every line.
R   *Reread* the work and make any necessary final edits.

Compare/Contrast Organization Strategy

Englert and Raphael (1989) described a strategy for helping students write compare/contrast essays. The use of this type of essay format is signaled by key words such as *alike, different from, in contrast to,* and *similar to.* Have the student ask the following questions:

1. What is being compared/contrasted?
2. On what aspect are they being compared/contrasted?
3. How are they alike (mention all similarities)?
4. How are they different (mention all differences)?

Explanation Essay Organization Strategy

A similar procedure was described by Englert, Raphael, and Anderson (1989) for helping students write an explanatory or sequential essay. When using this strategy, have the students ask:

1. What is being explained (e.g., steps involved in making a cup of tea)?
2. What materials are needed to accomplish the task?
3. In what setting is the task to be accomplished?
4. What are the steps involved? — normally, the steps are sequenced (e.g., first, next, third, then, last).

Opinion Essay: TREE Strategy

Some individuals require extra instruction in order to develop the necessary skills. Graham and Harris (1989a) described a strategy to help students improve their skills in writing opinion essays. The student uses the mnemonic TREE as a planning strategy. The following steps are used:

T Generate a *Topic* sentence
R List the *Reasons* supporting the argument
E *Examine* the reasons
E Provide an *Ending*

Power Writing

Power Writing described in *Write for Power* (Sparks, 1982) is a structured program designed to teach students how to subordinate ideas. The powers refer to the following levels of organization:

1st Power: Main idea statements
  2nd Power: Major details or subtopics
    3rd Power: Minor details.

The program progresses from practice in subordinating single words to writing structured essays. Students begin with simple Powergraphs, consisting of one main idea or 1st-power sentence, followed by two 2nd-power sentences. For example, Andrea, a second-grade student, was given the following prompt: *I love to do two things at the beach.* Andrea then wrote two 2nd power sentences: *I love to make sandcastles. I like to jump into the waves.*

Kerrigan's Method

Kerrigan (1979) described a comprehensive procedure for teaching students how to write essays. He presented the following steps for theme organization and composition writing:

1. Have the student write a sentence in which a person or an object is/was something, or does/did something. The sentence must follow seven rules:
    a . Create a sentence about which you can say more.
    b . Concentrate on what the person or object *does*.
    c . Be specific—what *exactly* did the person or object do?
    e . Until you become proficient, keep the sentence short.
    f . Keep the sentence as a *statement*, not a question or command.
    g . Ensure you have only *one* statement.
    h . Do not use a descriptive or narrative sentence.
2. Have the student write three sentences about the original sentence. Encourage the student to use simple, declarative sentences that give information clearly and directly about the original sentence. The information given must pertain to the whole of the original sentence, and not to a piece of it. Help the student not to repeat the same idea in different words, but instead to provide more specific information.
3. Ask the student to write four or five sentences about each of the three sentences in step 2.
4. The sentences in step 3 must be specific and concrete. Encourage the student to go into detail, and use examples. Specify that the goal is to give *more* information about what has already been introduced, thus there must be no new ideas. Sharing short anecdotal stories with the student can be effective during the fourth stage.

At this point, help the student review the content to ensure that the subject has not changed, and that the central idea or theme is obvious from the first paragraph. Have the student focus upon being understood by the prospective audience, not on being entertaining. Encourage the student to use vocabulary that is pertinent to the audience and to concentrate on making the theme clear, real and convincing.

5. Have the student insert a clear, explicit reference to the theme of the preceding paragraph in the first sentence of the following paragraphs.

6. Have the student work to ensure that every

sentence is connected with, and makes a clear reference to, the previous sentence. (See Kerrigan's procedures under Cohesive Ties.)

Use of Kerrigan's (1979) six steps to writing to the point will ensure that the whole theme is thoroughly connected. Figure 7–17 presents the first draft of the Kerrigan procedure written by Jenn, an eighth-grade student.

I like Christmas.

1. Santa Claus comes around.
2. It brings family gatherings.
3. We open presents.

1. Santa Claus comes around.

   a. He comes to different houses & gives presents to children.
   b. When you wake up, there are presents under the tree.
   c. Santa gives mothers & fathers watches, T.V.s and other good gifts.
   d. He always dresses red, black, and white.
   e. After Christmas, Santa goes back to the North Pole.

2. It brings family gatherings.
   a. They sing "Jingle Bells".
   b. They decorate the tree and put lights around the house.
   c. They put presents under the tree.
   d. Everybody eats.

3. We open presents.
   a. We get new things.
   b. We get a gift.
   c. We open them in the morning.
   d. Everybody is happy.

Figure 7–17. First draft of Kerrigan procedure by Jenn, an eighth-grade student.

Kerrigan described additional steps for writing specific types of themes.

Themes of contrast. The following rules apply to themes of contrast:

1. Have the student select important, noticeable differences for discussion.
2. Have the student contrast specifics that can be compared (e.g., shapes with shapes, not shapes with colors).
3. Remind the student to contrast opposite qualities as well as contrasting differences.
4. Remind the student not to include material that does not denote contrast.
5. Have the student sequence the contrasts as they are initially presented (e.g., if contrasting an apple and an orange, in each sentence attributes of the apple must precede those of the orange).
6. Suggest that the student not use the word *contrast* in the theme as a synonym for *difference* as *contrast* is the name of an operation performed. Instead, have the student use words such as *difference, dissimilarity, likeness, similarity,* and *resemblance.*
7. Encourage the student to use the expressions *whereas* and *in contrast.*

Themes of comparison. All rules relevant to themes of contrast can also be applied to themes of comparison, but with likenesses, not contrasts, being discussed. Remember that items described as similar are not identical, but the point of comparing them is to show how they are alike. The following precautions apply to teaching students to write themes of contrast and comparison:

1. Teach the student not to note individual points about A in one paragraph and about B in another. Rather, contrast and compare point by point within each paragraph.
2. Remind the student that the essay must consist of more than a two-paragraph theme. Suggest to the student that if only two major qualities can be used to compare and/or contrast, a third paragraph should be added at the beginning that briefly establishes the similarity or contrasting points, as well as one at the end that states some point about the contrasts or similarities.

Themes of argument. When writing themes of argument, the writer seeks to persuade or convince the reader. The following rules apply:

1. The student must support ideas with reasons, examples and facts that have been researched.
2. The student must choose topics that have two sides; ones that could be supported adequately, regardless of which side is chosen. Remind the student to mention the contrasting views and refute them as expertly as possible.
3. Have the student use connectives so that the reader knows which side of the argument is being discussed (i.e., *true, admittedly, of course, naturally, even now*). Tell the student that *but* may also be used to show when the other side of the argument is about to be presented.

One important point to remember when writing themes of argument is that we argue not to win, but to find the truth.

Themes of expression. Themes of expression may be the most difficult to write as eloquence is required. In this style of writing, the writer seeks to make his or her intention and attitude clearer. Kerrigan (1979) suggests that eloquence may be developed by:

1. Reading every day, some of which being reading aloud.
2. Frequent writing (e.g., letters, journals) in order to practice what has been learned.
3. Observing rules of grammar and taking the time to learn common errors made (both oral and written errors).
4. Increasing one's vocabulary.
5. Being succinct in speech and writing, and eliminating words not contributing to the point.
6. Varying sentence length and form.

Revision

Once students have written their stories, paragraphs, or essays, they should be encouraged to revise and improve their products. Students should not have to revise everything that they write, but rather only the pieces that will be published or shared with others. Ms. Marcus, a third-grade teacher, has her students select one of their writings every 2 weeks to revise for their writing portfolios. Students choose the piece that they wish to include and then complete the stages of revising and editing.

When revising their work, students should be encouraged to focus upon the meaning of the text, not on the detection of errors in basic writing skills. Although some of the revision strategies provide an editing step, the focus of revision activities is upon organization, clarification, and elaboration of content. Many of the strategies for teaching students editing skills involve them in the editing of the writing of other students (Ariel, 1992).

TAG Strategy

Students can provide feedback to each other during the revising stage. Students can use the simple strategy of TAG to help them focus on ideation and guide them in providing constructive feedback to each other. The mnemonic TAG (Clark & Montague, 1993) represents:

T   *Tell* what you liked about the story
A   *Ask* questions for clarification
G   *Give* suggestions for making the story better

Student Editing Strategy

The student editor strategy (MacArthur, 1994; MacArthur et al., 1991) is designed to help students in the writing and revision stages of the writing process. The strategy helps students increase awareness of their audience and the clarity of their writing. Students may write papers on a word processor in order to ease the physical process of revision.

Strategy instruction. Specific teaching guidelines are provided for teaching the strategy. Ideally, strategy instruction is provided to groups of four to six students, although it can also be taught to pairs. First, teach those students who are most likely to learn the strategy easily as, with mastery, they will be able to help teach the strategy to peers.

The model used for strategy instruction was developed by Harris and Graham (1992) and includes seven stages:

1.   Development of necessary preskills. Students should have experience with the process approach to writing and feel comfortable with activities involving planning, writing, revising, and sharing their work.

2.   Initial group conference. Review students' performance level in revision and discuss what revision techniques are currently known. Discuss the importance of revision when writing.

3.   Strategy introduction and discussion. Following the introduction of the strategy, discuss its importance and point out that all professional writers have editors who help them. Help students understand when to use the strategy. Provide direct explanation of the "how," "why," and "when" of the strategy.

4.   Modeling of the strategy. Use an assignment to model the strategy, verbalizing each of the steps and the mental processes involved. Statements that may be beneficial include: Problem definition (e.g., "What do I have to do next?"); self-regulation (e.g., "That's the first two steps completed, now for the third"); self-evaluation (e.g., "I was supposed to add details to the main character. Did I do that?"); and self-reinforcement (e.g., "I think I succeeded in making that description better.").

5.   Mastery of the strategy. Provide a few minutes each session for students to memorize the steps. Continue with this until each student can recite the steps from memory.

6.   Collaborative practice. Have students take turns in being editors for their peers. Provide whatever support is necessary to ensure appropriate strategy use. Fade the support as each pair of students becomes more proficient at using the strategy independently.

7.   Independent performance of strategy. After students have attained mastery, provide periodic feedback and review as necessary. Make specific plans for generalization to other tasks and situations.

Steps. Have students work in pairs and take turns at being the "writer" and "editor." The editor follows these steps:

1.   Listen to the author read the paper, and follow along on a second printed copy of the assignment.

2. Review the content of the paper and tell what part you liked best.

At this stage, the students switch roles and the first two steps are repeated. For the third step, each student works independently on a written copy or a computer printout of their partner's paper.

3. Read your partner's draft and make notes directly on the paper. Look for:
   a. Clarity — is anything difficult to understand?
   b. Details — are there places where more details could be added?
4. Meet with your partner and discuss your queries and suggestions. The discussion should be interactive with the author responding to the editor's comments. Focus upon content and communication, not upon mechanics such as spelling or capitalization errors.
5. On the same day as the conference, each author works separately making revisions to his or her paper.

Step-by-Step Revision Strategy

Cohen (1985) described a strategy that begins with revision activities and progresses to editing strategies. The following steps are used:

1. Have the student complete a free writing assignment and share it with you.
2. Without correcting errors, react to the draft.
3. Upon return, have the student read the assignment aloud to other students in order to detect errors in structure and word usage.
4. Have the student revise and reorganize the assignment, integrating the feedback from peers.
5. Have the student turn in the assignment.
6. Place a check by each line that contains an error. When more than one error exists on a line, write the number of errors by the line in parentheses.
7. Have the student correct the teacher-indicated errors and turn in a third draft.
8. Mark any remaining errors.
9. Have the student incorporate the teacher's corrections into a final draft.
10. Use the approach with numerous writing assignments.

11. Have the student select an assignment for a final paper.

Revision Conferences

In the past, conferences were often ineffective because they were inflexible and teacher-centered (Sampson et al., 1991). Bos and Vaughn (1994) described the following key points to promote in conducting student-centered conferences:

1. Follow the lead of the student and help him or her develop the selected topic.
2. Listen and accept what the student has to say.
3. Ask questions that the student will be able to answer.
4. Ask questions that will teach and provide direction.
5. Conduct frequent, brief (2–3 minutes) conferences.

In many instances, such as when discussing revision of a piece, the teacher will want to write down a few comments and questions for discussion prior to the conference. Teacher feedback during brief conferences can help students revise their drafts.

Through interactive dialogues, the teacher or another student can critique writing for clarity. Wong et al. (1994) describe the following procedure:

1. Identify the student's writing problems in the paper.
2. Discuss the identified problems with the student and explain to the student why they are problematic.
3. Discuss strategies for improving and clarifying the writing.
4. Have the student make revisions.
5. Review and discuss the student's revisions.

Moulton and Bader (1986) described the following procedure for conducting a revision conference:

1. Write a list of comments and questions about the draft and share it with the student. The major questions may include:
   a. To what extent has the topic been covered in the draft?
   b. To what extent does the draft adhere to the prewriting plan?
   c. To what extent has the information been organized for clarity?

d. To what extent has the choice of words been appropriate?

2. Hold a conference and have the student read the draft aloud and respond to the comments and questions.

3. Ask the student to suggest changes to the draft.

4. At the conference, have the student revise the draft using a colored pen.

5. Repeat the process until the student can identify and solve problems independently.

Similarly, Tompkins and Friend (1988) described the following procedure for having small groups of students meet together to read and revise their compositions:

1. Students take turns reading their compositions aloud and listening to feedback from peers.

2. Peers begin by pointing out the strengths of the composition.

3. Writers then ask peers for assistance on trouble spots.

4. Peers ask questions about parts that were unclear to them and make suggestions for revision.

5. Students in the group commit themselves to revising their writing based upon the comments of their peers.

Audience Considerations

As noted in Chapter 3, some students have difficulty considering the needs of the reader. They assume erroneously that their readers have prior knowledge about the topic. Moran (1987) suggested a strategy that can be used to help writers consider audience needs. The following steps are used:

1. Read a student's first draft and then ask the following questions (Moran, 1987):

a. What do you think your audience knows about the topic?

b. What do you want your audience to know?

c. Does your audience need more information and/or description about the topic? If so, where?

d. What more do you know (or can you imagine) about the topic?

e. Is any part of your writing incomplete or confusing?

2. The amended draft can be read to, or given to, some of the student's peers to read for feedback in regard to sections needing further clarification.

Conclusion

A major concern about the writing performance of students with learning disabilities is their lack of improvement across the grades (Houck & Billingsley, 1989). In the past, teachers have failed to integrate written language into the curriculum, both in the public schools and at the teacher training level (Isaacson, 1987; Polloway et al., 1981; Roit & McKenzie, 1985). As a result, many students with learning disabilities have limited writing skill (Poplin et al., 1980; Tomlan, 1986) and fail to construct messages that communicate with clarity (Gerber, 1993).

Presently, many students with learning disabilities are spending the majority, if not all, of their day, in regular classrooms and, like their peers, are being asked to produce clear, coherent writing. These demands necessitate that regular and special education teachers work together to develop effective writing programs (Graham & MacArthur, 1991).

Most important, these students require teachers who can teach them. Clearly, a great deal of work needs to be done to improve the writing achievement of all children (Berninger & Whitaker, 1993). Gabe, an eighth-grade student, wrote a note presented in Figure 7–18 to thank his teacher for sharing his knowledge with the students. We hope, in return, to help students like Gabe improve their writing skill.

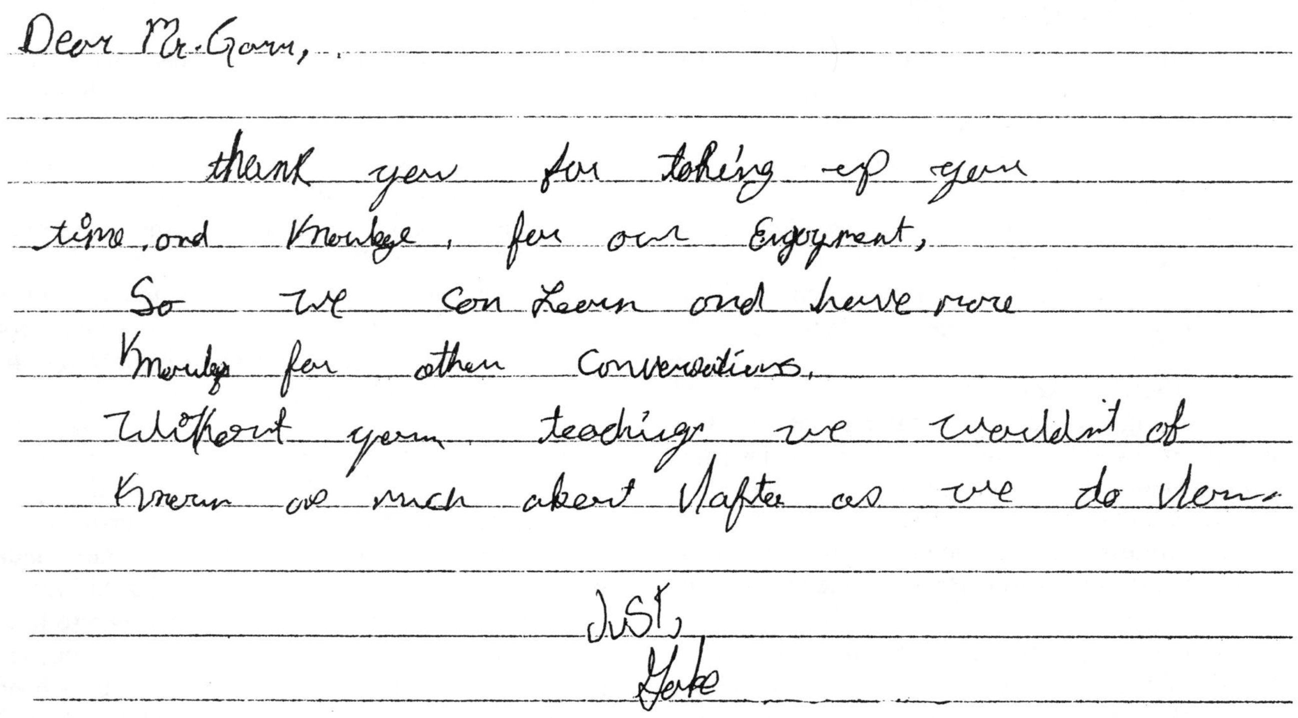

Dear Mr. Gorin,

thank you for taking up your time, and knowledge, for our Enjoyment, So we can Learn and have more knowledge for other conversations. Without your teaching we wouldn't of known as much about it after as we do Now.

JUST,
Gabe

Translation:

Thank you for taking up your time and knowledge for our enjoyment. So we can learn and have more knowledge for other conversations.

Without your teaching we wouldn't of known as much about it after as we do now.

Figure 7–18. A thank you note written by Gabe, an eighth-grade student.

8

ANALYSIS OF WRITING SAMPLES

Research findings document the need for early intervention and comprehensive, systematic instructional programs. Before developing a specific remedial program to correct writing errors, however, one must first conduct a careful and complete assessment of writing ability. The purpose of this assessment is to identify the specific factors affecting writing performance and determine the student's strengths and weaknesses (Phelps-Gunn & Phelps-Terasaki, 1982; Vogel & Moran, 1982).

Tremendous variation exists in the writing skill of students. This variation is evident as early as the kindergarten level and increases with each year. Figure 8–1a provides samples of several beginning kindergarten students writing their names. Although all of the students understand that some type of writing is required, the skill level is extremely varied.

Some students spell their names correctly. Dominic starts his name with an uppercase letter and writes the remaining letters in lowercase. Others have correct spelling, but awkward letter formation. Jenni spells her name correctly, but the letters increase progressively in size, and Kyle makes an uppercase E with four horizontal lines, rather than three. Jana reverses the letter *J* and adds a stick to a circle to form an *a*. Others have learned a few letters in their names. For example, Heather writes her name as *Het*, Sam writes his name as *AS*, and Brian spells his name as *OBD*. Some students understand that their names are composed of a series of letters, but are uncertain as to which ones. For example, Tina writes her name as *Tliibbothu* and Jonathan writes his name as *Em*. Ryan and Sarah produce scribbles or circles, although Ryan understands that some form of discrete symbols is used.

Similarly, Figure 8–1b provides samples of several beginning first-grade students drawing self portraits and writing a sentence about a favorite activity to include in a class directory. Diversity in development of visual-motor skill, as well as writing skill is apparent. Several of the students use invented spellings that are semi-phonetic, whereas a few use prephonetic or phonetic spellings. These initial writings of kindergarten and first-grade students illustrate the tremendous variation that exists in writing skill. This diversity in skill continues across the grades and becomes more pronounced with each year.

This chapter presents 20 samples of writing collected from students in first through eighth grade. The samples are organized by grade and include many different types of writing: journal entries, letters, and narrative and expository text. For each sample, the writing is evaluated in regard to both the student's strengths and instructional needs. Recommendations are then made for instructional programming.

Different types of samples are included to illustrate a variety of writing difficulties. Some of the students have their greatest difficulty with spelling, whereas others have problems with development of ideas. For some students, only one sample is provided. For other students, two or more samples are included to allow for a more in-depth evaluation of writing skill. The majority of samples are students' first drafts of assignments. For a few students, samples are presented from different time periods to illustrate development in writing skill.

Analysis and interpretation of error patterns in writing can often help the practitioner detect and diagnose the factors inhibiting learning. As a caution, the determination of a learning disability would not be made on the analysis of one written language sample. In most instances, this type of diagnosis would be made by a team and would be based upon a multiplicity of factors including classroom performance and teacher observations. In-depth analysis

Figure 8-1a. Kindergarten students writing their names.

Figure 8–1b. First-grade students writing sentences.

of writing samples can, however, provide invaluable information for programmatic decisions and instructional design.

The samples provided in this section may be used for self study or in classes designed to increase diagnostic skill. Prior to reading an analysis, perform a careful error analysis of a student's writing. Attempt to identify both the strengths and weaknesses in writing skill. Next, determine the instructional needs and formulate appropriate educational recommendations. As a final step, read the analysis and note the similarities and differences in the observations.

An index is provided below that includes the students' names, grades, and the major difficulties apparent in the writing. This may assist practitioners in locating a case similar to a student they are evaluating or teaching.

Index

STUDENT	GRADE	AREA(S) OF GREATEST DIFFICULTY
Jose	1st	Handwriting and Spelling
Hannah	2nd	Spelling and Ideation
Julie	2nd	Vocabulary and Ideation
Frankie	3rd	Spelling and Usage
Sam	3rd	Handwriting, Usage, Vocabulary, and Organization
Jennifer	3rd	Spelling
Roger	3rd	Handwriting
Todd	4th	Spelling and Punctuation
Brian	4th	Spelling and Usage
Alan	4th	Handwriting, Usage, and Vocabulary/Ideation
Emily	5th	Spelling and Ideation
Roy	5th	Spelling, Editing, and Expression
Malika	6th	Usage and Organization/Ideation
Wendy	6th	Spelling
Rosa	7th	Organization/Ideation
Felicia	7th	Spelling
Helen	7th	Appearance, Usage, and Organization/Ideation
Tyler	8th	Usage and Organization/Ideation
Jessica	8th	Usage
Tim	8th	Spelling—Accommodations Needed

Student: Jose
Grade: 1st
Assignments: Journal entries

Several samples from mid-year were taken from Jose's journal. Earlier in the year, Jose had been evaluated and accepted in the school's gifted and talented program. Although his teacher was pleased with Jose's ability to express his ideas, she was concerned about the development of handwriting skill.

Analysis

Handwriting

Presently, Jose writes using uppercase letters. He attempts to make his letters fill the space between the lines in his writing journal. The spacing between words is inconsistent. In general, the writing is not pleasing to the eye, but the majority of letters and

Semi-Translations:

Today Mom and Dad came back and I was relieved.
Attention. First day of school. Sam starts kissing me.
Grandma came and Mom and Dad were going to . . . this morning I got up too late.
Scott make me do his work.
My cousins came last night at 10 o'clock.

Figure 8–2. Journal entries by Jose, a first-grade student.

words are recognizable. His human figure drawings are somewhat immature.

Spelling

Jose is using invented spelling successfully. Although he omits a few sounds, he sequences the sounds that he writes accurately (e.g., *grad ma*, for "grandma," and *moning* for "morning!"). Jose appears to be progressing from semi-phonetic to phonetic spelling. As is to be expected with semi-phonetic spelling, he writes the major consonants sounds and omits the vowels in several words (e.g., *frst* for "first," *hs* for "his," *wr* for "were," *strts* for "starts," and *wrk* for "work"). Other spellings are good phonetic equivalents (e.g., *kising* for "kissing," *bak* for "back," and *kusins* for "cousins"). With the exception of two instances (i.e., *re left* for "relieved" and *grad ma* for "grandma"), Jose appears to recognize word boundaries, and he realizes that separations should occur in the phrase: *10 O CLOK*.

Usage

Jose attempts to write in complete sentences. Although several of his periods are too large, he appears to understand the function of a period. Because all of the letters written are capitals, it is unclear as to whether or not Jose knows that sentences begin with uppercase letters. Jose is consistent in verb tense. He uses both present and past tense appropriately in his writing.

Vocabulary

Although unsure of the spelling, Jose attempts to write descriptive words. He notes that when his mom and dad came back, he was "relieved" (*re left*) and that his "cousins" (*kusins*) came.

Organization/Ideation

Jose has ideas that he wants to share through writing. Although letter formation appears to be difficult, he is not reluctant to write.

Recommendations

Handwriting

1. Have Jose work on handwriting daily for short lessons. Provide review and practice of formation of lowercase letters. Show him how to be consistent in the spacing between words. Have him apply the skills that he is learning in context.

2. Teach Jose to write on primary paper that has a clear dotted middle line. Encourage him to form letters properly within these lines.
3. Recognize Jose's effort in trying to write neatly. Give plenty of encouragement as he develops his handwriting skill.
4. As motor skill improves, encourage Jose to reduce the size of his periods.
5. Date all handwriting samples so that Jose can see evidence of his progress.
6. Encourage Jose to engage in a variety of activities to promote fine-motor skill development, such as completing dot-to-dot drawings, solving mazes, or drawing illustrations for his writing. Because Jose is highly motivated to write, explain to him how spending time on fine-motor activities will help make handwriting easier for him.
7. Select a structured handwriting program to use with Jose, such as D'Nealian (Thurber, 1983) or Handwriting without Tears (Olsen, 1994).

Spelling

1. Praise Jose for his logical attempts to spell.
2. Teach Jose that all words contain a vowel. Initially, take some of his semi-phonetic spellings from his writing, and rewrite the words with a blank placed for the missing vowel (e.g., f__rst). Help him determine what vowel belongs in the missing space. Gradually, help him determine where the vowels should be inserted.
3. Introduce and provide practice with common English spelling patterns (e.g., *ck* and *ight*.)

Usage

1. Teach or review with Jose that sentences begin with uppercase letters.
2. Reinforce Jose for his skill in maintaining consistency with verb tense.

Organization/Ideation

1. Provide many opportunities for writing. Discuss with Jose the ideas that he is communicating. Remind him that development of spelling and handwriting skills will improve his ability to communicate ideas to others through writing.

Student: Hannah
Grade: 2nd
Assignments: Letters with illustrations

As part of a Social Studies unit, Hannah was asked to write two letters to a fictional friend and draw illustrations. The samples were written within the same week.

Analysis

Handwriting

On these two samples, the size of Hannah's letters is inconsistent. Formation of a few letters also appears problematic. Her lowercase *a* is sometimes formed like an uppercase *Q*. On several occasions, Hannah substitutes an uppercase *R* for the lowercase letter, and her lowercase *g* does not extend below the line. In addition, the spacing between words

Translation:

Dear Alicia,

It is a Roman soldier that crucified a god on the cross. The red is blood. The black is for when some one dies. The white is purity.

Figure 8–3. Two letters written by Hannah, a second-grade student.

Dear Alicia,
   This is a Fariseo mask and his sticks. The sticks are his so as they can not talk together. They have sign language when speaking.

Figure 8–3 (cont.).

is inconsistent and results in some words being difficult to decipher.

Spelling

Presently, Hannah's sound-symbol correspondence is limited. Although she appears to have knowledge with regard to masks, it is difficult to decipher the words that she is writing.

Usage

Hannah begins both letters with correct capitalization and punctuation. Although Hannah produces several complete sentences, she does not start them with uppercase letters nor end them with periods. She has used present-tense verbs consistently throughout both samples.

Vocabulary

Although the words are difficult to identify, Hannah's choice of words is representative of her good conceptual and topical knowledge. She uses precise vocabulary. Examples include the words: "crucified," "Roman soldier," "Fariseo," "sign language," and "purity."

Organization/Ideation

Hannah has good background knowledge in regard to ceremonial masks. She is motivated to share her ideas and organizes them in a logical way. The ideas are difficult to decipher, however, because of poor spelling.

Recommendations

Handwriting

1. Provide Hannah with primary paper with a dotted middle line to use on all writing assignments.
2. Review and provide practice with formation of the following lowercase letters: *a*, *g*, and *r*. Use a strategy, such as the Fauke Approach (Fauke et al., 1973) or the Self-Guided Symbol Formation Strategy (Graham & Madan, 1981).

Spelling

1. Remind Hannah that the purpose for learning to spell correctly is to enhance her ability to communicate thoughts in writing. Praise her efforts and provide encouragement about skill development. Use an activity such as finger spelling (Stein, 1983) to help Hannah increase her knowledge of sounds within words.
2. As skill develops, encourage Hannah to listen to sounds more carefully as she invents spellings. Ask Hannah to say the word slowly while writing the sounds. Reteach sound-symbol correspondence as needed.
3. Use a spelling flow list to help Hannah master the spelling of words she uses frequently in her writing. Teach only a few

spelling words at a time. Provide daily review and practice until the words are mastered. Review the words weekly to help with retention.

4. Determine an appropriate spelling study strategy for Hannah. One effective approach may be the alternative to the cover-write method suggested by Edgington (1967). Another may be to have Hannah: (a) look carefully at the word, (b) cover the word, (c) write the word while pronouncing it slowly, and (d) check the word against the original. If Hannah has difficulty writing the word from memory, add in a tracing component.
5. Until spelling skill improves, have Hannah read her stories to a scribe immediately after writing. Without this accommodation, the next day Hannah cannot read her writing.

Usage

1. Teach Hannah how to recognize sentence boundaries and include the appropriate ending punctuation marks.
2. In the editing stage, remind Hannah to start sentences with uppercase letters.

Ideation

1. Continue to provide Hannah with frequent, purposeful writing activities.
2. Based upon her interest and talent, provide Hannah with activities that include opportunity for both artistic and written expression. For example, have Hannah illustrate a story that she is writing or write a brief description of a picture she has drawn.
3. For some written assignments, use a modified language experience approach with Hannah. Have her dictate a story to a scribe and then recopy it as a final draft.
4. When evaluating her papers, emphasize the clarity of the message over basic writing skills so that Hannah's interest and willingness to write do not diminish.

Student: Julie
Grade: 2nd
Assignments: Creative writing story
Letter to a friend

For the first assignment, Julie was asked to write a story about an animal. A class discussion occurred prior to writing to help generate ideas. For the second assignment, Julie was asked to write a letter to her friend. The assignments were written within a 2-week period.

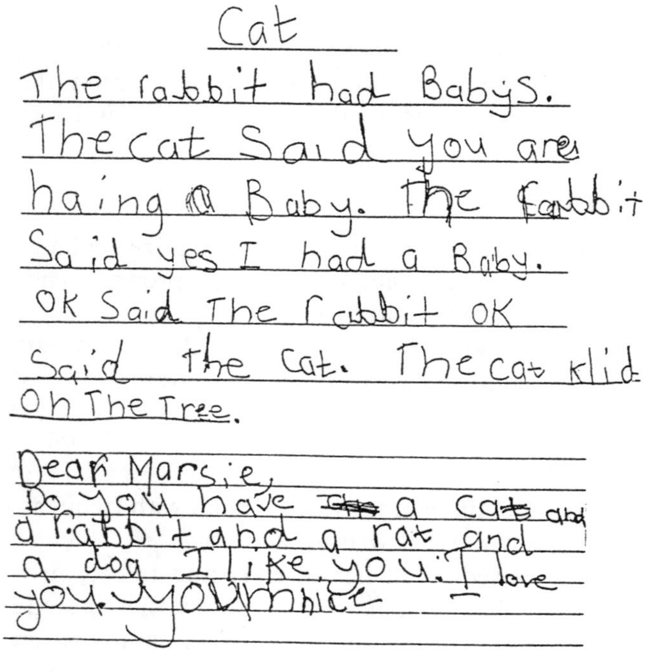
Cat
The rabbit had Babys.
The cat Said you are haing a Baby. The rabbit Said yes I had a Baby. OK Said The rabbit OK Said the Cat. The cat klid On The Tree.

Dear Marsie,
Do you have a Cat and a rabbit and a rat and a dog I like you. I love you. You nice

Figure 8–4. A story and letter written by Julie, a second-grade student.

Analysis

Handwriting

Handwriting on the first sample is adequate for a second-grade student. Julie's handwriting on the second sample, however, is inconsistent and not very pleasing to the eye. Letter formation appears correct with the exception of the lowercase *b*. Julie varies the size of several letters, particularly *y*, *t*, *r*, and *s*. Julie's writing is neater on the wide-line paper than on standard composition paper. The size of her letters on the latter sample increases gradually and appears to be affected adversely by the narrow lines.

Spelling

Julie spells the majority of words correctly. On occasion, she leaves out a sound from less familiar words (e.g., *haing* for "having" and *klid* for "climbed"). She repeats many of the words that she knows how to spell. Out of 66 words, the words "rabbit" and "cat" account for 9 words, or 14% of the text.

Usage

Julie ends sentences with periods and begins most sentences with uppercase letters. She does not use a question mark. She capitalizes the word "I." She consistently but incorrectly writes the word "baby" with an uppercase *B*. Because "baby" is the only word in the samples that starts with *b*, it is unclear whether her confusion is with the word or with the use of an uppercase *b*. In addition, she does not form the plural of the word "baby" correctly.

Julie writes simple sentences that primarily consist of subject-verb-object patterns. Although she uses one prepositional phrase, she probably meant to write "the cat climbed up the tree," rather than "on the tree." She does not use any adjectives.

Vocabulary/Ideation

In these two samples, Julie selects simple words when writing. Both samples lack planning and a clear purpose for writing. The letter written to her friend contains one improbable question (*Do you have a cat and a rabbit and a rat and a dog*). The story does not contain a conflict or problem of interest, but presents a discussion between a rabbit and cat about the rabbit having babies. After the simple discussion, Julie writes: *The cat klid on The Tree.* No reason or explanation is provided for this action.

Recommendations

Handwriting

1. As the size of Julie's letters is inconsistent, provide her with primary writing paper that has a clear top, middle, and bottom line.

2. Teach correct formation of lowercase *b*.

Spelling

1. Encourage Julie to attempt to write words even when she is uncertain of the spelling.
2. In a game format, provide Julie with practice identifying the sequence of sounds in multisyllabic words.

Usage

1. Dictate a few sentences for Julie to write that contain several words beginning with the letter *b*, including the word baby. Based on the results, teach Julie correct usage.
2. Teach Julie how to write more complex sentence patterns, using sentence expansion activities, such as provided in the Phelps Sentence Guide (Phelps-Terasaki & Phelps, 1980). The emphasis in the first part of the guide is on writing sentences based on pictures.

Vocabulary/Ideation

1. Judging from the content of these two samples, Julie's greatest need is in assistance with prewriting activities. Provide a variety of prewriting activities that will help Julie organize and expand upon her ideas prior to writing.
2. Encourage Julie to be more descriptive in her writing. As a prewriting activity, after she has selected a topic, help her create a list of adjectives that she may use when writing.

3. As part of a revision activity, ask Julie questions to elicit more precise descriptions of the characters and events in her stories.
4. Teach Julie a simple story grammar to use for narrative writing. Explain and provide examples of the procedure.
5. Provide a variety of oral language activities that will help Julie develop the characters, plot, and outcome of her stories prior to writing. Use an organizational strategy, such as the one suggested by Stein and Glenn (1979), that emphasizes oral development of the story prior to writing.
6. Encourage Julie to collaborate with peers regarding topic selection and development.
7. Teach Julie how to recognize common, overused words that are present in her writing. Have her underline any words that she believes could be more descriptive. Help her brainstorm alternative words that have a more precise meaning. Provide a variety of examples.
8. Ask Julie to expand orally on a sentence that she has written, adding descriptive words and phrases, additional details or more explicit adjectives. Have her then rewrite the sentence incorporating the new expansions.

Student: Frankie
Grade: 3rd
Assignments: Two creative writing assignments
Two journal entries
Picture with title

For the first assignment, Frankie was asked to write a story entitled "What bad luck." The second and fourth assignments were journal entries, and the third assignment was written in response to the title "What I want to be when I grow up." The picture was drawn to illustrate a movie that Frankie had seen.

what bad loke
A man found a
arplane the man
wit for a rid.
The engin blue up.
The man found a
parshot he jumed.
The parshot had a
holl! There was a
hastach bat there
was a pickfork in the
hastach he mist the
pich fork and mest
the hastach, there
was water bat there
those shacks and
he got on a Ilied.

Odod is seck.
He is he is yes yes
he is. Owknow that
is rite Ow know.
War is he. At the
fet. My mom is
going to get hem.
and he is going
to rest wen he gets
home.

I want to be a baselall
plare wen I grow up.
I well hit it in the crowd
and a cid will cech it.
Then he will cep it intell
he is 90 irs old.
Wen he dis they well bar
it in hes grave.

Translations:

What bad luck. A man found a airplane. The man went for a ride. The engine blew up. The man found a parachute. He jumped. The parachute had a hole! There was a haystack but there was a pitchfork in the haystack. He missed the pitchfork and missed the haystack, there was water but there those sharks and he got on a island.

Hobo is sick. He is. He is. Yes, yes, he is. Oh no. That is right. Oh no. Where is he? At the vet. My mom is going to get him and he is going to rest when he gets home.

I want to be a baseball player when I grow up. I will hit it in the crowd and a kid will catch it. Then he will keep it until he is 90 years old. When he dies they will bury it in his grave.

Figure 8-5a. Several assignments written by Frankie in fourth grade.

Translation:

Know what my brother did on Halloween. When the kids would come up to our house he would jump out and scare the kids. They would run off and drop their candy.

Figure 8–5a (cont.).

Analysis

Handwriting and Appearance

The handwriting on the printed sample is adequate, whereas that on the three cursive samples is good for a third-grade student. The slant is consistent and all the letters are formed correctly but the letters of the last sample are too large. Frankie observes the left margin in all samples. He observes the right margin in all but the third assignment where he begins every sentence on a new line. None of the paragraphs is indented. In addition, only one of the assignments has a title and it is not capitalized.

Spelling

Although Frankie's writing is legible, a number of different spelling errors can be seen in his assignments. Frankie has mastered the spelling of some high-frequency sight words such as *there*, *want*, *the*, *that*, and *was*, but still misspells others such as "when," "went," "him," and "but." Many words are spelled incorrectly. Of the 184 words written, 64 or 35% are either spelled incorrectly or are homonyms to the correct word. Some of the homonyms that Frankie confuses are *know* for "no," *blue* for "blew," *wood* for "would," *there* for "their," and *mist* for "missed."

Frankie appears to have some confusion distinguishing certain sounds in words as illustrated by some of the misspellings such as *well* for "will," *intell* for "until," *wint* for "went," *ceds* for "kids," and *hem* for "him." Perhaps the best example of Frankie's difficulty with sounds is in his writing the well known movie phrase "ET phone home" as *pt foam home.*

Some of Frankie's spellings look very similar although they represent different words. For example, *ceds*, *cech*, and *cep* represent the words "kids," "catch," and "keep," respectively. Frankie also has difficulty with the spelling of medial vowel sounds. The short "e" and "i" sounds seem to be particularly troublesome for Frankie and numerous confusions are evident throughout the writing samples. Frankie sometimes omits sounds from words. He writes *parshot* for "parachute," *shacks* for "sharks," *Ilied* for "island," *bar* for "bury," and *olowen* for "Halloween."

Although Frankie tends to spell phonetically, he has not yet mastered some of the simpler patterns. For example, he sometimes misuses and sometimes omits "ch" in words, as in *hastach* for "haystack" and *pickfork* for "pitchfork." Difficulties with the spelling of other patterns can be seen in Frankie's spelling of *coom* for "come," *dis* for "dies," and *skar* for "scare."

In addition to problems distinguishing sounds, Frankie appears to struggle with visual retention of spelling patterns. This is evidenced by the different spellings of the same word, particularly when the different spellings are in close proximity.

Examples of difficulties with retention can be seen in the first writing sample with *mist* and *mest* for "missed" on consecutive lines, and *bot* and *bat* for "but" only five lines apart.

Usage

Frankie consistently capitalizes the word "I" but is erratic with his capitalization of the first letter in a sentence. He capitalizes the first letter in sentences about 50% of the time in the first sample, 100% of the time in the next two samples, and 0% of the time in the third. In addition, the name "ET" is not capitalized. Frankie's use of periods is also sporadic. In one instance on the first writing sample, he uses a comma instead of a period.

Other usage problems are evident. He uses the article "a," even when the noun begins with a vowel. Most of the sentences are simple and without explanation or elaboration (e.g., "The man went for a ride. The man found a parachute. He jumped."). Also, some problems with pronoun reference can be seen in the second sample when Frankie refers to a ball as "it" throughout.

Vocabulary

On the whole, the vocabulary used is simplistic. The majority of words are one syllable. The words "haystack" and "pitchfork," however, are more complex and demonstrate background knowledge in the area of farming. More advanced words are found in the printed sample. This may indicate that Frankie is able to focus more on vocabulary when not having to concentrate on the mechanics of cursive writing.

Organization/Ideation

Frankie writes information sequentially. Some of his assignments, however, are limited in the information they convey.

Recommendations

Handwriting and Appearance

1. Encourage Frankie to form letters of a consistent size, such as those used in the second sample. Have him keep this or a similarly written assignment in his desk for reference.
2. As Frankie masters the size of letter formation, provide him with wide-ruled paper. Encourage him to skip lines on working drafts and to write on every line only for the final draft.
3. Teach Frankie to indent the first word in each paragraph.
4. Remind Frankie to write to the end of every line rather than begin every sentence on a new line.
5. Encourage the use of titles. Teach Frankie that titles should be centered and each word capitalized.

Spelling

1. During the editing stage, help Frankie listen carefully to words that he is attempting to spell. Have him check his spellings as he pronounces the words slowly. Encourage Frankie to pronounce words syllable by syllable as he checks the spelling.
2. Help Frankie increase his spelling of high-frequency words. Take words from the 1,000 Instant Words List. Use a multisensory technique such as a cover-write method (Edgington, 1967; Kirk & Chalfant, 1984).
3. Teach the spelling of word families around those words taught using the cover-write method. Use a strategy such as chalkboard spelling (Hildreth, 1955; Sisernos & Bullock, 1983).
4. Provide review of spelling words and practice of particular orthographic patterns (e.g., "ch") using the dictation spelling method (Scarrozzo, 1982).
5. Teach the difference between the spellings of homonyms (e.g., *wood* and *would*) in context using sentences to illustrate the difference in meaning.
6. Provide Frankie with a copy of *A Spelling Dictionary for Beginning Writers* (Hurray, 1993) to use at his desk. This reference contains approximately 1,400 of the words most frequently used in writing by children in kindergarten through second grade.

Usage

1. Review the use of capitalization rules with Frankie.
2. Review the use of periods at the end of sentences and help Frankie see the relationship between the use of periods and upper-case letters.

3. Teach Frankie to use an editing strategy such as COPS (Schumaker et al., 1985) for all his assignments.

4. Review the difference between words beginning with vowels and those beginning with consonants. Teach Frankie the rule for when the article *an* is used instead of *a*.

5. Help Frankie write more complex sentences. Use a strategy such as SCAN (Graham & Harris, 1987) or sentence-combining activities.

Vocabulary

1. Reinforce Frankie for using more difficult words and do not penalize him for incorrect spelling. Arrange for a peer editor to work with Frankie on the final draft.

2. Help Frankie create a personalized thesaurus and encourage him to use it when writing an assignment.

Organization and Ideation

1. Work on prewriting strategies with Frankie that will help him present more information. Teach him to use the questioning strategy (Greenberg, 1987) in order to in-

crease his awareness of the purpose for writing.

2. Encourage Frankie to use cognitive mapping to help expand his ideas and sequence them logically.

3. Teach a procedure such as the Given-New strategy proposed by Cooper (1988) to help Frankie consider the needs of the reader as they relate to previous knowledge.

Follow-Up

Frankie received assistance from a special education teacher for 1 year. The major goals were to improve reading and writing skill. A sample of a first draft from a story starter is presented below. Frankie's story is creative, sequenced, and he attempts to offer the reader good advice.

Although his sentence patterns are more complex, he still needs some assistance with identifying sentence boundaries (i.e., where to put a period) and spelling. His spelling has improved greatly, but Frankie continues to misspell some words, writing "will" as *well* and "chocolate" as *choclet*. He does not double the middle consonants in "offer" and "better." Fortunately, spellings of this nature may be corrected easily during the editing stage.

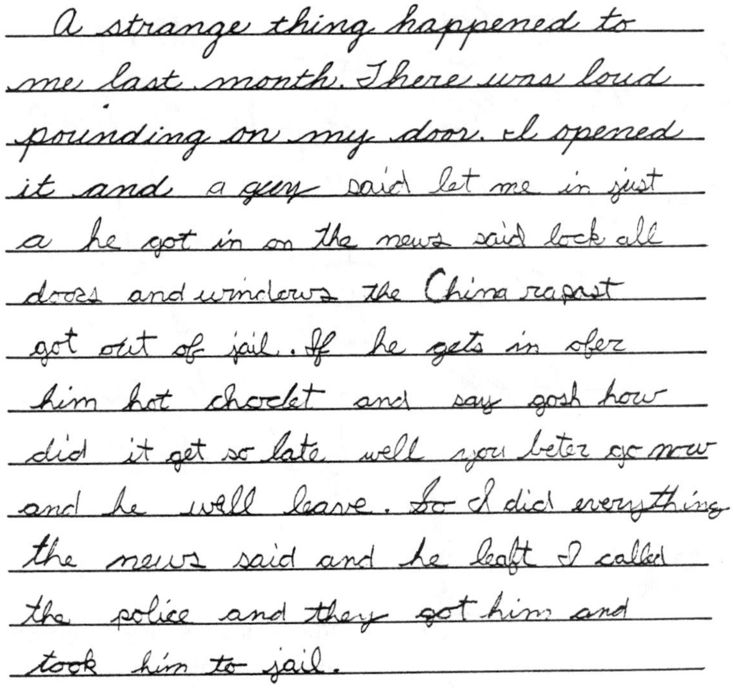

> A strange thing happened to me last month. There was loud pounding on my door. I opened it and a guy said let me in just a he got in on the news said lock all doors and windows the China rapist got out of jail. If he gets in ofer him hot choclet and say gosh how did it get so late well you beter go now and he well leave. So I did everything the news said and he left I called the police and they got him and took him to jail.

Figure 8–5b. Completion of a story starter written by Frankie in sixth grade.

Student: Sam
Grade: 3rd
Assignments: Sentence completion
　　　　　　　 Naming and drawing different
　　　　　　　　　 objects
　　　　　　　 Opinion paper: A person I like

The first two assignments required Sam to write specific information. The third assignment was to write about a favorite person. Although a prewriting discussion was conducted with his teacher, Sam's story does not include the ideas that were generated.

Analysis

Handwriting/Appearance

In first grade, Sam received occupational therapy services because of motor difficulties. Considering his past motor problems, Sam's handwriting is adequate, although his speed of production is very slow. Most of the letters are formed correctly though one *p* and one *h* are reversed and a *g* on the word *syeing* ("swinging") is formed incorrectly. The letter *b* is capitalized regardless of sentence position suggesting that Sam is still uncertain as to the correct orientation of the lowercase letter. The size of his letters is inconsistent.

The free writing sample's appearance is superior to the worksheet appearance. Sam benefits from the provision of ample space. The paragraph, however, is not indented. Although Sam observes the left margin, he appears to have some difficulty observing the right margin.

Spelling

Sam has memorized the spelling of a number of sight words (e.g., "have," "play," and "with"). On the whole, he spells phonetically, writing *catuplr* for "caterpillar," *lernd* for "learned," and *tot* for "taught." Sam has mastered the spelling of some common English orthographic patterns such as "ight" as in *night*, and "ay" as in *play* and *day*.

Some spellings, however, suggest that Sam does not listen carefully or is confused about the sounds in some words (e.g., *syeing* for "swing" and *brifick* and *bifixe* for "breakfast"). In addition, the different spellings of "ice" as *iec* and *ice* and "cream" as *crime* and *crem* on consecutive lines suggest that Sam has trouble remembering how a word looks in order to form it consistently.

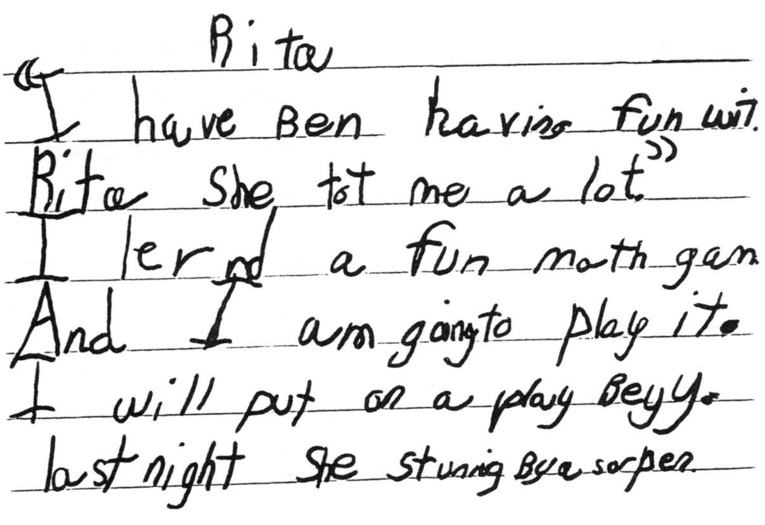

Figure 8–6. Sentence completion, labeled pictures, and an opinion paper by Sam, a third-grade student.

Usage

Although Sam uses periods, he sometimes places them where they do not belong (e.g., *I lernd a fun math game. And I am go to play it*) and at times, he omits them (e.g., in the short story in between "play" and "Bye," and at the end of the last sentence). Quotation marks have been used incorrectly although the marks themselves have been formed correctly and are in the right position on the line.

With regard to capitalization, Sam correctly and consistently capitalizes the word "I." He does not, however, capitalize the first letter of the last sentence in the short story and incorrectly capitalizes the first letter he writes in the sentence completion. In addition, he consistently capitalizes the letter *B* regardless of its position in the sentence.

Sam begins his story on Rita writing in the past tense. He shifts to the future tense and then back again to the past tense.

Vocabulary

Apart from the word "scorpion," the vocabulary used is simplistic and limited. Sam has overused certain words such as "ice cream."

Organization and Ideation

Sam produces limited information on the sentence completion task. His short story contains more information but is poorly organized. The sentences seem unrelated. Having decided to talk about Rita, he says nothing about her except that she has taught him some things. He then mentions a math game and a play that he will perform at school. In the last sentence, he refers back to Rita and assumes that the audience will understand this shift despite his use of the pronoun "she" instead of Rita's name.

Recommendations

Handwriting and Appearance

1. Provide Sam with the opportunity to reinforce his knowledge of the formation of the letters *h*, *g*, *p* and *b*. Use a procedure such as the Progressive Approximation Approach (Hofmeister, 1973). Practice these letters with repeated tracings until the motor pattern becomes automatic.
2. Provide Sam with ample writing space when using worksheets.

3. Provide primary handwriting paper with the top, middle, and bottom lines in order to encourage Sam to be consistent with letter size. If Sam prefers, provide him with thin paper on top and clip handwriting paper underneath the sheet. This will provide Sam with "invisible support."
4. As writing is a slow process for Sam, do not spend the time teaching him how to write in cursive. Instead, begin instruction in keyboarding skills.
5. Encourage Sam to indent the first word in a paragraph.
6. Until his skill improves, place a piece of Scotch tape on the right margin of his papers as a reminder of where to stop. Reinforce Sam for observing right margins.

Spelling

1. Teach word families around the linguistic patterns already mastered by Sam (e.g., as he knows "night," teach "*f*ight," "*fl*ight," "*fr*ight," "*fr*ightened," "*l*ight," "*l*ighter," "*l*ightest," etc.). Use a procedure such as Making Words (Cunningham & Cunningham, 1992).
2. Play games to ensure that Sam can identify all of the phonemes in a word. Use a syllable approach to the teaching of spelling, such as that suggested by Cicci (1980).
3. As Sam experiences some problems with both remembering how a word looks and sounds, combine a syllable approach to the teaching of spelling with a multisensory method such as the Fernald Method for spelling instruction (Fernald, 1943) or a cover-write method (Kirk & Chalfant, 1984; Mather, 1991).
4. Provide Sam with the Spelling for Writing List (Graham et al., 1994) that lists the 300 most commonly used words in alphabetical order. Encourage him to check his spellings against those in the list during the editing stage.

Usage

1. Review the correct placement of periods with Sam and encourage him to edit his work placing periods where needed.

2. When all of the periods are correct, encourage Sam to check that each word following a period begins with an uppercase letter. In addition, reinforce Sam for changing each incorrectly used uppercase *B* to a lowercase *b*.

3. Teach Sam how to use quotation marks in dialogue. During the editing stage, help him learn to include them in the correct places within his stories.

4. Provide practice writing in paragraphs in different verb tenses: present, past, and future. During the editing stage, help Sam maintain consistency with verb tense.

Vocabulary

1. Tape Sam telling a story. Transcribe the story and analyze the vocabulary as compared to that used in his written assignments.

2. If the oral vocabulary is superior to that used in writing, encourage Sam to use his extensive vocabulary in his writing by assuring that he will not be penalized for spelling mistakes, and praising him when he uses more complex vocabulary.

3. Let Sam read and grade paragraphs (written by the teacher or former students) that have overrelied on the use of some words. Have him compare these writings to other paragraphs that have a more extensive vocabulary. Discuss with him the difference between the two paragraphs. Encourage and reinforce Sam for using more extensive vocabulary.

Organization and Ideation

1. Use a process approach to writing. During the editing stage, provide him with assistance from a peer who is a good speller.

2. Explain to Sam why it is necessary to gather and organize information prior to writing. Help him understand how planning prior to drafting will help him structure story content and reports.

3. Although prewriting activities were used, the generated ideas are not reflected in the content. Remind Sam to incorporate his ideas into his first draft. For example, as a prewriting activity Sam could organize his ideas in a graphic organizer shaped like a star. When drafting, he could color in each point of the star after he had written the idea into his story.

4. Teach Sam how to link one sentence to the next using the Given-New strategy (Cooper, 1988). Begin by teaching him how to use pronouns with clear referents. Provide him with a passage in which names and words are repeated rather than being replaced by pronouns (e.g., *Sam went to the play. Sam saw Mark there. Mark waved to Sam.*). Show him how the passage may be rewritten using pronouns (e.g., *Sam went to the play. He saw Mark there. Mark waved to him.*).

5. Provide Sam with sentence pairs in which pronouns in the second sentence provide the meaningful tie with the first sentence. Underline the pronouns and have Sam draw an arrow to the referent.

6. Have Sam generate and then answer a series of questions that will help him organize his writing assignment. Have him answer the questions before writing and then use the answers in his writing.

Student: Jennifer
Grade: 3rd grade
Assignments: Experience stories

On 4 consecutive days, Jennifer was asked to write about a personal experience. Prior to writing, the students in her third-grade classroom discussed the experiences about which they were going to write. After writing, Jennifer read her writings to her teacher.

Analysis

Handwriting/Appearance

Jennifer attempts to form her letters neatly. With the exception of the second sample, the letters are relatively consistent in size within each sample, but they vary among assignments. She observes the left margin, but is inconsistent with the right margin, occasionally writing one or two words on a line.

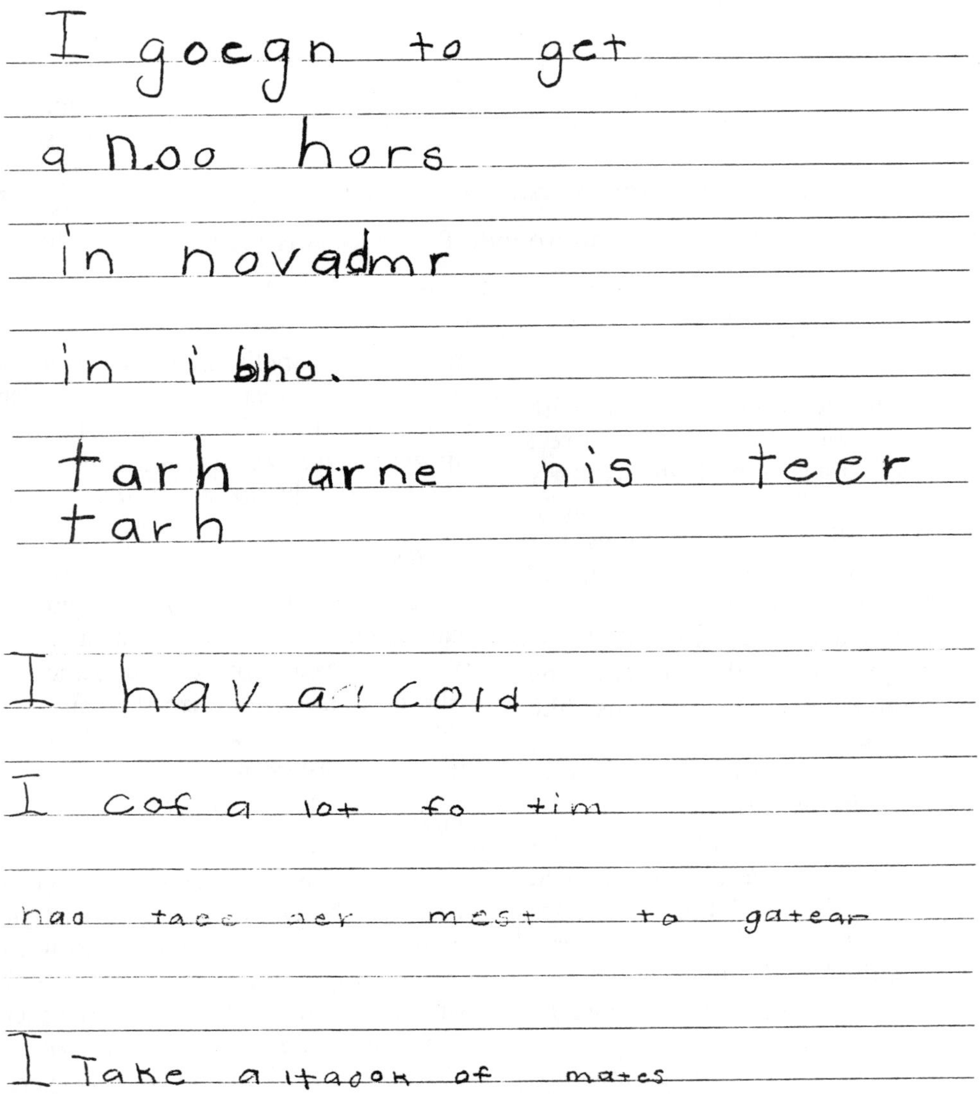

I goegn to get
a noo hors
in novadmr
in i bho.
tarh arne nis teer
tarh

I hav a cold

I cof a lot fo tim

had tacc aer mest to gatear

I Take a itaoon of macs

Translations:

I going to get a new horse in November in Idaho. There are nice trees there.

I have a cold. I cough a lot of times. Now they are messed together. I take a lot of medicine.

Figure 8-7. Language experience stories written by Jennifer, a third-grade student.

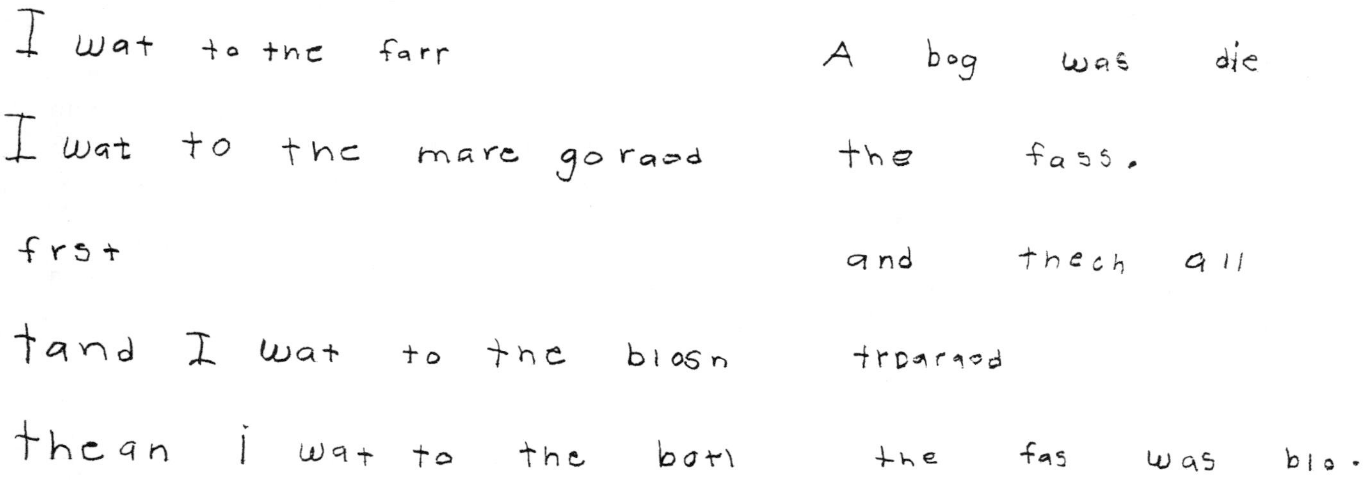

I wat to the farr

I wat to the mare go raod

frst

tand I wat to the blosn

thean i wat to the botl

A bog was die

the fass.

and thech all

trdaraod

the fas was blo.

Translation:

I went to the fair. I went to the merry-go-round first. Then I went to the balloons. Then I went to the bottles. A dog was by the fence and they all turned around. The fence was blue.

Figure 8–7 (cont.).

Spelling

The majority of Jennifer's spellings begin with the correct consonant and end with the correct sound. She has learned to spell a few high-frequency words (e.g., "to," "the," "in," "a," "was," and "all"). Several words are good phonic approximations. For example, she spells the word "new" as *noo*, "horse" as *hors*, and "first" as *frst*. Although Jennifer has developed some knowledge of sound-symbol correspondence, her primary difficulty appears to be with sequencing sounds correctly in spelling. She spells the word "tree" as *teer*, "medicine" as *mates*, "balloons" as *blosn*, and "together" as *to gatear*. On one occassion, Jennifer writes one word as two (*to gatear*). On another occasion, Jennifer combines two words into one, writing *trdaraod* for "turned around." On several spellings, Jennifer reverses the letters *b* and *d* (e.g., *novadmr* for "November," *ibho* for "Idaho," *bog* for "dog," and *die* and "by"). She transposes the letters in a few words (e.g., *fo* for "of" and *aer* for "are").

Jennifer has knowledge that English spellings are invariant. Even though many of her spellings have limited sound-symbol correspondence and some words are spelled in different ways (e.g., *tand* and *thean* for "then"), she attempts to be consistent in her spelling. For example, in the sentence "there are nice trees there" she spells "there" both times as *tarh*. She spells the word "went" four times as *wat*. She also seems to remember some of her incorrect spellings. For example, she spells the "round" in *merry-go-round* as *raod* and the following day, the "round" in *turned around* as *raod*.

Usage

Jennifer begins each assignment with an upper-case letter. She ends several sentences with periods. With one exception, she capitalizes the word "I." She does not capitalize the name of the month (November) or a state (Idaho). Jennifer puts periods at the end of some sentences, but not others.

Organization/Ideation

Jennifer has ideas that she wishes to share through writing. She expresses most of her ideas in complete thoughts. She attempts to use cohesive ties in her paragraph describing her trip to the fair. She writes that "first" she went to the merry-go-round and "then" she went to the balloons.

A few of her statements, however, are difficult to understand. For example, after noting that she has a cold and a cough, she writes that they are all mixed together. In the last paragraph she notes that a dog was by the fence and they all turned around. The referent for the pronoun "they" is unclear.

Recommendations

Handwriting

1. Praise Jennifer for her neat handwriting.
2. Remind Jennifer to write all the way over to the right margin. Explain to her that putting one or two words on a line may confuse the reader.

Spelling

1. Help Jennifer improve her ability to sequence sounds in spelling. Begin instruction with consonant-vowel-consonant words that follow a regular spelling pattern. Using Scrabble tiles or magnetic letters, have Jennifer spell various patterns by rearranging the letters (e.g., *pig, peg, pen, pet,* and *put*).
2. Help Jennifer learn to manipulate sounds in words through expansion of sound sequences. Use the Making Words procedure described by Cunningham and Cunningham (1992). For example, beginning with the word "it," have Jennifer then form with Scrabble tiles or write the words: *pit, spit, split, splint, splinter, splintered, splinters,* and *splintering.*
3. Using Scrabble tiles, help Jennifer recognize the word boundaries that she currently misses. For example, help her recognize that the word "turned" is separate from "around."
4. Treat reversals as spelling mistakes that will be corrected during the editing stage.
5. To reduce reversals of the letters *b* and *d* in writing, have Jennifer say the movement pattern she makes when forming a frequently reversed letter. For example, when writing the letter *b*, she may say: "start high, line down, back up and around." Alter-natively, use the single symbol strategy proposed by Heydorn (1984).
6. Until her spelling skill improves, encourage Jennifer to read her work immediately after its completion so that a translation can be written.

Usage

1. Teach Jennifer capitalization rules sequentially, one rule at a time. Provide practice in a variety of situations (e.g., worksheets, finding the use of the rule in reading, writing sentences and paragraphs, and editing her own work or a peer's).
2. Introduce punctuation and capitalization rules to Jennifer as she needs them for writing. Make sure that she masters one rule before introducing another. For example, remind Jennifer to use a period at the end of a sentence. When this rule is mastered, introduce another rule, such as the use of a question mark.
3. Provide Jennifer with a simple proofreading checklist that she can use in editing that contains the rules that she has learned, such as:
   I started each sentence with an uppercase letter.
   I ended each sentence with a period.

Organization/Ideation

1. Encourage Jennifer to continue to share her ideas through writing. Provide feedback at the prewriting stage.
2. Help Jennifer increase her awareness of audience needs. Explain to her that many people will wish to read what she is saying and that the clearer her writing, the easier it will be for people to understand.

Student: Roger
Grade: 3rd
Assignments: Two journal entries

For both assignments, Roger was asked to write a journal entry. The topics were chosen by Roger, but the teacher spent time discussing the topics with him prior to writing. During the brainstorming sessions, Roger had many good ideas. The assignments, however, are not representative of the ideas he expressed orally. Four weeks elapsed between the writing of the two samples, during which time Roger received instruction in sound-symbol correspondence twice weekly.

Analysis

Handwriting/Appearance

Difficulties with visual-motor skill are evident in both samples. On the first sample, most of the words are on or near the line, but no word boundaries have been recognized. Roger has traced over some letters numerous times. This multiple tracing with a thick-tipped marker pen gives the sample a messy appearance. These problems are not as apparent in the second sample as Roger's writing looks much neater when he uses a fine-line pen. In the second sample, most word boundaries have been observed. Although the paper contained guiding lines, these were not observed and the writing is slanted.

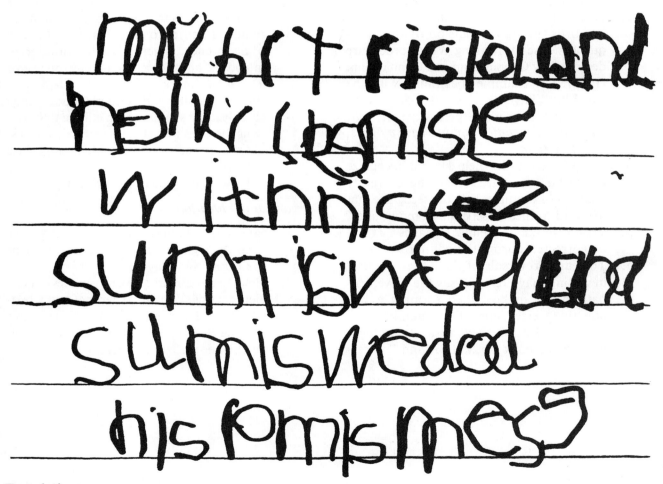

Translations:

My brother is tall and he works nicely with his friends. Sometimes we play and sometimes we don't. His room is messy.

Figure 8–8. Two journal entries by Roger, a third-grade student.

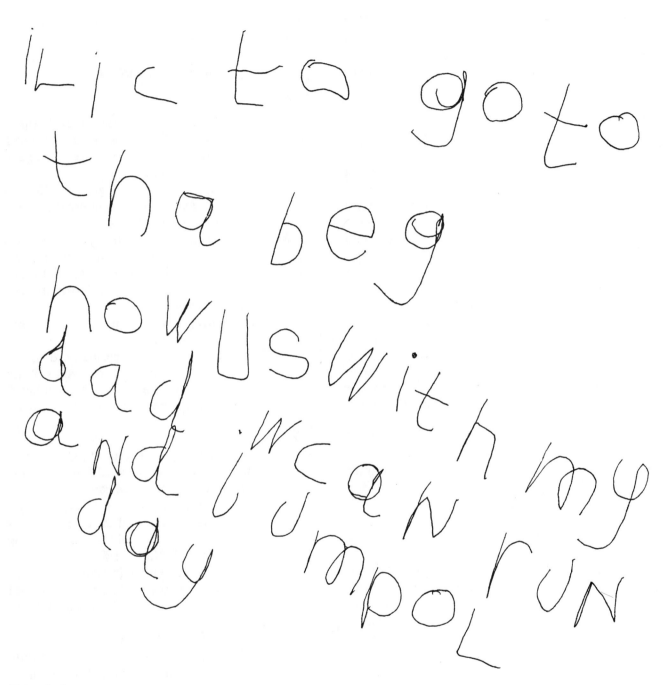

Translation:

I like to go to the big house with my dad. We can run and jump all day.

Figure 8–8 (cont.)

Roger's letter formation is poor. He appears to have the most trouble forming the letters *a* and *g*. Roger has reversed about half the *e*'s in the first sample. Only one *e* was used in the second sample, but it is formed correctly. In his spelling of the word "messy" as *mese*, Roger correctly formed the first *e* then incorrectly formed the *e* two letters later. The letter *j* is reversed in the second sample. Throughout both samples, the letter *l* has been capitalized incorrectly. In addition, the letter *n* has been capitalized throughout the second sample, but written in lowercase throughout the first. Despite some similarities in the samples (e.g., neither has been given a title), much variability exists between the two.

Spelling

Roger has mastered some high-frequency sight words such as "and," "with," and "we," but much of his spelling is semi-phonetic. Analysis of the first sample shows Roger trying to capture what he hears, but without familiarity or retention of common English spelling patterns. For example, "brother" is spelled as *brtr*, "tall" as *tol*, "friends" as *frez*, and "nicely" as *nisle*. On occasion, a sound is omitted. For example, "sometimes" is written as *sumtis* and *sumis*, and "don't" as *dod*.

By the time the second sample was produced, Roger had started learning some common spelling patterns (e.g., "ow," and "ay"), but not others (e.g., "all"). Although incorrect, his spelling of the word "house" as *howus* shows progress toward phonetic spelling. Vowel sounds continue to give Roger some difficulty as can be seen by the spelling of *tha* for "the," and *beg* for "big."

Fewer spelling errors are present in the second sample, but this may be due, at least in part, to the selected words being one syllable and simpler than those in the first sample.

Usage

Roger uses correct sentence structure and syntax. He attempts to write compound sentences (e.g., *My brother is tall and he works nicely with his friends*). Apart from the indiscriminate use of the uppercase letters *L* and *N*, no other uppercase letters are used in either sample. Only one period is used throughout and occurs in the second sample. The period is placed correctly suggesting that Roger may understand the concept of periods, but he forgets to use them.

Vocabulary

The vocabulary is adequate, but is not as complex as the vocabulary Roger suggested during the prewriting brainstorming sessions.

Organization/Ideation

The first journal entry tends to be rather disorganized and it is difficult to follow Roger's train of thought. The second sample is more organized but is limited in ideation.

Recommendations

Handwriting/Appearance

1. Refer Roger to an occupational therapist in order to improve his motor control. Work with the therapist in order to reinforce and generalize the skills taught.
2. Put a triangular pencil grip on Roger's writing implement. Have him use sharp pencils and pens with fine tips.
3. Use a structured handwriting program such as Handwriting without Tears (Olsen, 1994) in order to teach the correct formation of *a* and *g*, and to reinforce the formation of all other letters.
4. Provide Roger with writing paper that has clearly marked lines.
5. Reinforce Roger for recognizing word boundaries and putting spaces between words. When he completes an assignment with neat handwriting, display the sample in the classroom.

Spelling

1. Continue using a structured phonics program. Initially, teach word families using the patterns that Roger already knows (e.g., the "ay" family, teaching "day," "play," "may," "stay," etc.) and the ones he spells incorrectly (e.g., the "all" family, teaching "ball," "small," "fall," etc.).
2. Provide practice with high-frequency words using a multisensory method such as Fernald (1943) or a cover-write method (Kirk & Chalfant, 1984).
3. Do not penalize Roger for incorrect spelling, but reinforce him for attempting to write words even when uncertain of the spelling.

Usage

1. Teach Roger to place periods at the end of every complete thought. Simultaneously, teach him to place an uppercase letter immediately after a period.

Vocabulary

1. Provide Roger with positive feedback when he uses complex or multisyllabic words.

2. During the editing stage, underline two words and help Roger replace these with more interesting synonyms.
3. Use strategies such as Semantic Feature Analysis and graphic organizers to help Roger increase the breadth and depth of his vocabulary.

Organization/Ideation

1. Use a variety of prewriting activities with Roger to help him develop and expand upon his ideas prior to writing.

2. On occasion, provide Roger with a scribe so that his thoughts and ideas will not be hindered by his motor difficulties.
3. Demonstrate to Roger how to sequence his thoughts into a logical order using a story grammar strategy such as the Grid Model (Crealock, 1993).

Student: Todd
Grade: 4th
Assignments: Three short stories

Todd chose the topics for all his stories. The first was entitled: "The Friendly Ghost"; the next two were variations on the theme "If I were a Pilgrim."

Analysis

Handwriting

Overall, the quality of Todd's handwriting is good. His slant is appropriate. The spacing on the page and between words and letters is adequate. A few problems, however, are noted. Todd tends to forget to leave a margin on the right side of the paper, and often writes to the very edge of the page. The writing on the left side of the paper tends to be tightly squeezed, whereas the writing on the right side is larger and more widely spaced. Also, Todd does not leave a large enough space at the end of sentences.

Some problems also exist with letter formation. Specific difficulty is noted with the formation of the letters *t* and *f*. Both of these letters are written smaller than the other letters. Because of this, Todd often accidentally crosses his *i*'s and dots his *t*'s.

Spelling

The percentage of misspelled words in his creative writing stories ranges from 4% to 11%. Analyses of the misspelled words point to several consistent error patterns. The most common types of errors are insertions of unnecessary letters (e.g., *allmost* for "almost," *familay* for "family," *toaday* for "today," *mostley* for "mostly," *barnes* for "barns") and omissions of necessary letters (e.g., *strage* for "strange," *jorney* for "journey," *everbody* for "everybody," *Clombus* for "Columbus," *bankets* for "blankets").

Another type of error pattern is with the accurate sequencing of letters. For example, Todd writes *friut* for "fruit," *eles* for "else," *pulss* for "plus," and *Indains* for "Indians." Compound words are usually written as two words (e.g., *hard ship, every body, leader ship, some where, all ready*). In addition, confusion exists in the spelling of homonyms (e.g., *their* for there, *where* for wear, *hear* for here).

Usage

Todd uses an uppercase letter to begin sentences. He also remembers to capitalize some proper nouns (e.g., *Squanto, Mr. Sour, Massisoit, Clombus, Indians, England*), but not others (e.g., *mayflower, speedwell,* and *english*). Periods are used most of the time, but are omitted on several occasions. For example, in one story of 50 sentences, Todd omitted 9 periods. In addition, run-on sentences are fairly frequent.

Commas are used correctly when writing the date and when listing several items (e.g., *turkey, venison, duck, fish, bread with nuts,* and *succotash*). They are omitted from several sentences, however (e.g., *Yes we finally saved up enough* . . .). Todd uses apostrophes appropriately in possessive nouns (e.g., *Incredible's problem*), and in contractions (e.g., *it's* and *won't*). On most occasions, Todd omits quotation marks (e.g., *Karl said I'd like to see all the musicians* . . .). The one time he uses quotation marks, he forgets to put the ending marks (i.e., *Mr. Sour said, "Try friut, so Incredible tryed some* . . .). He does not use a lot of dialogue in his writing. Todd does, however, use exclamation marks appropriately (e.g., *This is great!*).

Todd's sentence structure is adequate. His sentences have subject-verb agreement, and verb tense is consistent and correct. The use of abbreviations is also correct. Todd uses a variety of sentence types in his writing, including simple, compound, complex, declarative, and exclamatory.

Content/Organization

Cohesive ties are evident in Todd's writing. He uses topic sentences and has logical transitions between paragraphs. His stories include an introduction and appropriate conclusion. The purpose of the writing is clear and the writing is organized to fulfill the purpose of the assignment.

The ideas in all of the samples are expressed in a logical and appropriate sequence. The story "The Friendly Ghost" is organized into paragraphs dealing with a description of the ghost, his favorite things to do, his problem, his response to the problem, and the ending. Todd's understanding of story structure appears to be well developed. He provides titles, an introduction, and supportive information.

The creative writing story titled "If I Were a Pilgrim" is logically sequenced in paragraphs, with

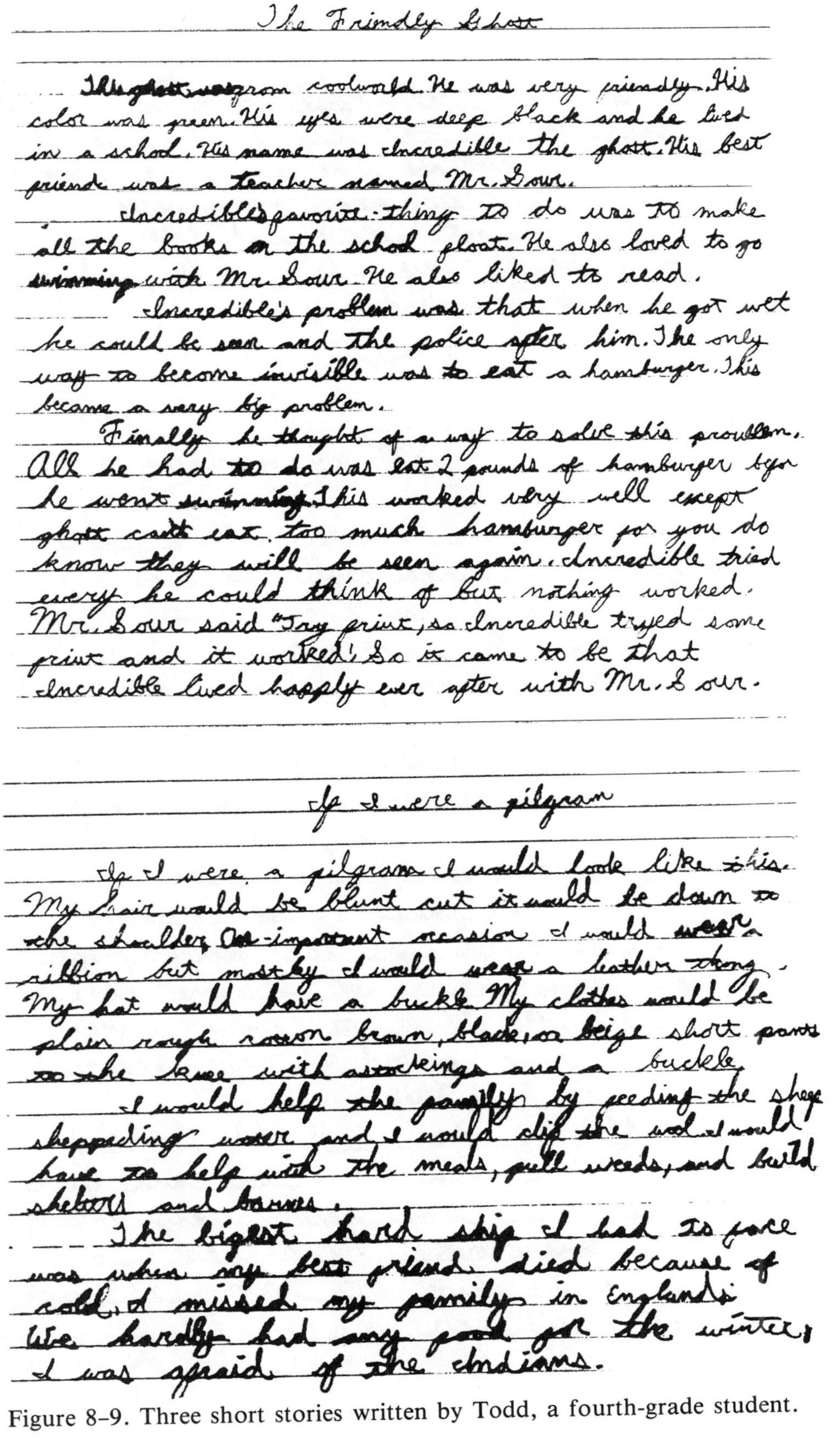

The Friendly Ghost

The ghost was from coolworld. He was very friendly. His color was green. His eyes were deep black and he lived in a school. His name was Incredible the ghost. His best friend was a teacher named Mr. Sour.

Incredible's favorite thing to do was to make all the books in the school float. He also loved to go swimming with Mr. Sour. He also liked to read.

Incredible's problem was that when he got wet he could be seen and the police after him. The only way to become invisible was to eat a hamburger. This became a very big problem.

Finally he thought of a way to solve this problem. All he had to do was eat 2 pounds of hamburger before he went swimming. This worked very well except ghosts can't eat too much hamburger for you do know they will be seen again. Incredible tried every he could think of but nothing worked. Mr. Sour said "Try print, so Incredible tryed some print and it worked! So it came to be that Incredible lived happly ever after with Mr. Sour.

If I were a pilgram

If I were a pilgram I would look like this. My hair would be blunt cut it would be down to the shoulder. On important occasion I would wear a ribbon but mostly I would wear a leather thong. My hat would have a buckle. My clothes would be plain rough rawon brown, black, or beige short pants to the knee with stockings and a buckle.

I would help the family by feeding the sheep sheppading water and I would clip the wool I would have to help with the meals, pull weeds, and build shelters and barnes.

The biggest hard ship I had to face was when my best friend died because of cold. I missed my family in England. We hardly had any food for the winter, I was afraid of the Indians.

Figure 8–9. Three short stories written by Todd, a fourth-grade student.

I was very thankful that my family had survied in the new land and I wanted to celebrate. The feast we planed was incredible. Their was turkey, fish, corn, beans, carrots, sweet potoes, and lots more. I would invite my whole family and my friends pulse the Indains.

If I were a Pilgram

O.K. lets get started when we lived in Holland it was ok I didn't really like their food or their schools. My family wants to go some where eles but we still dont ha enough money. When we do leave I hope my friend comes too.

Yes we finely have saved up enough money to buy a ship it's not new but it's good enough. My griend is comming with us. We leave Des 18, 1620.

We are going to get another ship because their are too many people on the mayflower so we got one called the speedwell. Well its finley time to leave I'm very exsited. We are starting to sail off now. This is great!

Oh no the speedwell is very dripy we are going to stop and leave the speedwell, and have every body on the mayflower. Some people are are gings to leave. We have 102 peopl on the mayflower.

Figure 8–9 (cont.).

We have been in the ocean for a month. It is very hard living. 20 people have all ready died. My friends mom died

We are finely their. its good to see land again 5 men went out toaday. Toaday 12 men went out. They found a good place to start living in the new world.

We have our house built now. I saw some really orange people toaday. We are eating alot of fish because we live near the ocean. Our crops won't grow hear for some reason. Toaday a strange person walked into our village he spoke english! He said his name was Squanto and her learned how too speak english because his familay had been taken by Clombus when he came back his tribe was gone. The next day he brought second person named Massisoit. He spoke english too.

Squanto and Massisoit helped us plant crops that would grow. They called it corn. They also gave us baskets for the winter. It is getting cold. Only 70 of us are left. its winter now and every body is getting sick. My friends dad died now too he lives with use now. Winter is allmost done we are going to celebrate and invite everbody inquliding the strage people.

Their will be wild turkey, venison, goose, duck, fish, joney cake, corn-meal, bread with nuts, and succotash.

It will be great.

Figure 8-9 (cont.).

each paragraph covering a different aspect of Pilgrim life. The first paragraph deals with the pilgrim's appearance, the second with his role within the family, the third with the hardships he faced, and the final paragraph with what he has to be thankful for. Each paragraph has a clear topic sentence.

Todd's productivity, or number of words written, is average for his age. The first creative writing story, "The Friendly Ghost," contained 184 words and 18 sentences, for an Average Sentence Length (ASL) of 10.2. The second story contained 385 words and 50 sentences for an ASL of 7.7. The third story contained 183 words and 15 sentences for an ASL of 12.2. The average sentence length across samples is 10 words.

In general, Todd's expression of his ideas is advanced for his grade. His style is effective in that he uses appropriate tone and selects descriptive words. The samples are written in the first person using a narrative style, and the tone is friendly and informal. Todd's word choice is imaginative and entertaining.

The information given is pertinent to the chosen topic. Original thinking and the ability to assimilate information from class discussions and personal experiences are reflected in all of Todd's samples. In addition, Todd expresses his personal perspective in the stories (e.g., *I didn't really like their food or their schools.*). Todd appears motivated to write and produces entertaining stories.

Recommendations

Handwriting

1. Review with Todd the proper formation of the letters *t* and *f*. Discuss how the formation of these letters affects legibility. Provide opportunities to practice these letters on paper that provides clear top, middle, and bottom lines.
2. Remind Todd not to write all the way to the edge of the paper on final drafts. If necessary, encourage him to place a piece of tape down the right margin as a reminder until the skill is automatic.

Spelling

1. Encourage Todd to pronounce words slowly when spelling. Practice the spelling of multisyllabic words by using a method such as an adapted Glass-Analysis method (Glass, 1973; Mather, 1991), Bannatyne's system (Bannatyne, 1971), a spelling grid, such as described by Wong (1986), or *Corrective Spelling through Morphographs* (Dixon & Engelmann, 1979).
2. Ask Todd to choose the words he wishes to learn to spell. Review the words weekly to ensure retention.
3. Teach Todd to differentiate between homonyms, providing both in-context and out-of-context practice.
4. Teach the spelling patterns of compound words. Praise Todd for using compound words in his written work.
5. Because Todd's handwriting is so small, encourage him to skip lines on first drafts so that editing will be easier.
6. During the editing stage, pair Todd with a peer with good spelling skill. Ideally, the good speller would have difficulty with organization so that both students could benefit from and help the other.

Capitalization/Punctuation

1. Provide direct instruction in the use of periods, commas, quotation marks, and apostrophes.
2. Teach Todd a mnemonic strategy, such as COPS (Schumaker et al., 1981) or SCOPE (Bos & Vaughn, 1994), to remind him of the steps to use in editing his writing.
3. Teach Todd standard proofreading symbols and use them consistently when grading his work.

Content/Organization

1. Reinforce Todd for his ability to organize and logically sequence information.
2. Provide Todd with lots of opportunities to write. Have Todd assist peers with the development and sequencing of ideas.

Student: Brian
Grade: 4th
Assignments: Three journal entries

Brian selected the topics for the writing samples and wrote them in his journal. No brainstorming or prewriting activities had occurred.

Analysis

Handwriting/Appearance

The handwriting in the printed sample is adequate, but that in the cursive samples is better. The spacing between words is inconsistent and, on the whole, too large. With one exception, Brian observes the margins in the samples. The paragraphs, however, are not indented.

Spelling

Spelling is difficult for Brian. He appears to have a significant problem representing the sequence of sounds in words correctly. Numerous examples of poor sound-symbol correspondence exist in the samples, including the spelling of "piece" as *pessne*, "set" as *stunt*, "exciting" as *ininding*, "watch" as *sawsh*, and "mighty" as *mindy*. In addition, Brian appears to have difficulty remembering how words look and, consequently, misspells high-frequency sight words. For example, he spells "went" as *wint*, "house" as *houns*, and "made" as *mand*. The letter "n" is added incorrectly to numerous words such as *rint* for "right," *mand* for "made," *brend* for "bread," *houns* for "house," and *ininding* for "exciting."

Brian tries to spell phonetically. He tends to confuse some common phonic patterns, such as "sh" and "ch" in his spellings of *shire* and *chirsh* for "church," and *sawsh* for "watch." When spelling, not all of the syllables in words are represented. At times, he records fewer syllables than exist, as in the writing of *rocus* for "firecrackers," *chapyn* for "championships," *foull* for "Fort Lowell," and *or* for "over." At other times, Brian writes more syllables than are necessary as demonstrated by his spellings of *pessne* for "piece," *firends* for "friend's," and *besast* for "best." Although able to read his work immediately following writing, Brian is unable to remember what he has written after a short interval.

Usage

Commas were used correctly when used in a list, as can be observed in *fowrd, uafbk, folbk.* Apart from the list, commas are not used. Brian appears not to have mastered the correct usage of periods and uses them in the middle of sentences. Examples of this are *The foull soute out. Is fun and we came in frist plass, . . . I got to drink wind and. We got a lot of fand,* and *. . . I got eta cnandy. At my firends houns.* At times, periods do not occur where necessary as in *I got to go to shire it fin and . . .* In addition, Brian has a tendency to overuse the conjunction "and," as is illustrated in the second sample. In the same sample, Brian correctly uses the conjunction "because." Even though his use of periods is incorrect, Brian consistently remembers to capitalize the first letter after the period. He also consistently capitalizes the word "I."

Although exclamation points are not used in many places, too many have been used in one place in the first sample. Brian also appears to make assumptions with regard to the information that the reader already possesses. For example, he writes that the shootout is fun and "we" came in first place. The reader may infer that the pronoun refers to a team, but has no information with regard to which team. The same problem exists with the pronoun "we" in the next writing sample. It is unclear as to who received the piece of bread.

Although much of the selected vocabulary is simplistic, Brian demonstrates good knowledge and vocabulary pertaining to soccer. He uses words, such as "shootout," "forward," "halfback," "fullback," "championships," and "dog-pile." The majority of the other words are one syllable.

Organization/Ideation

Brian appears to have information that he wants to share. A few organizational problems, however, exist. In the "shootout" sample, Brian introduces the topic and then lists the positions that he can play. Although the intent was not to infer that he played all three positions in the shootout, the placement of the information suggests otherwise. A different organizational problem is evidenced in the third sample when Brian writes about firecrackers, the Mighty Ducks, and church. No explicit connection exists among the activities other than they all pertain to Brian. The activities are not sequenced in any logical way.

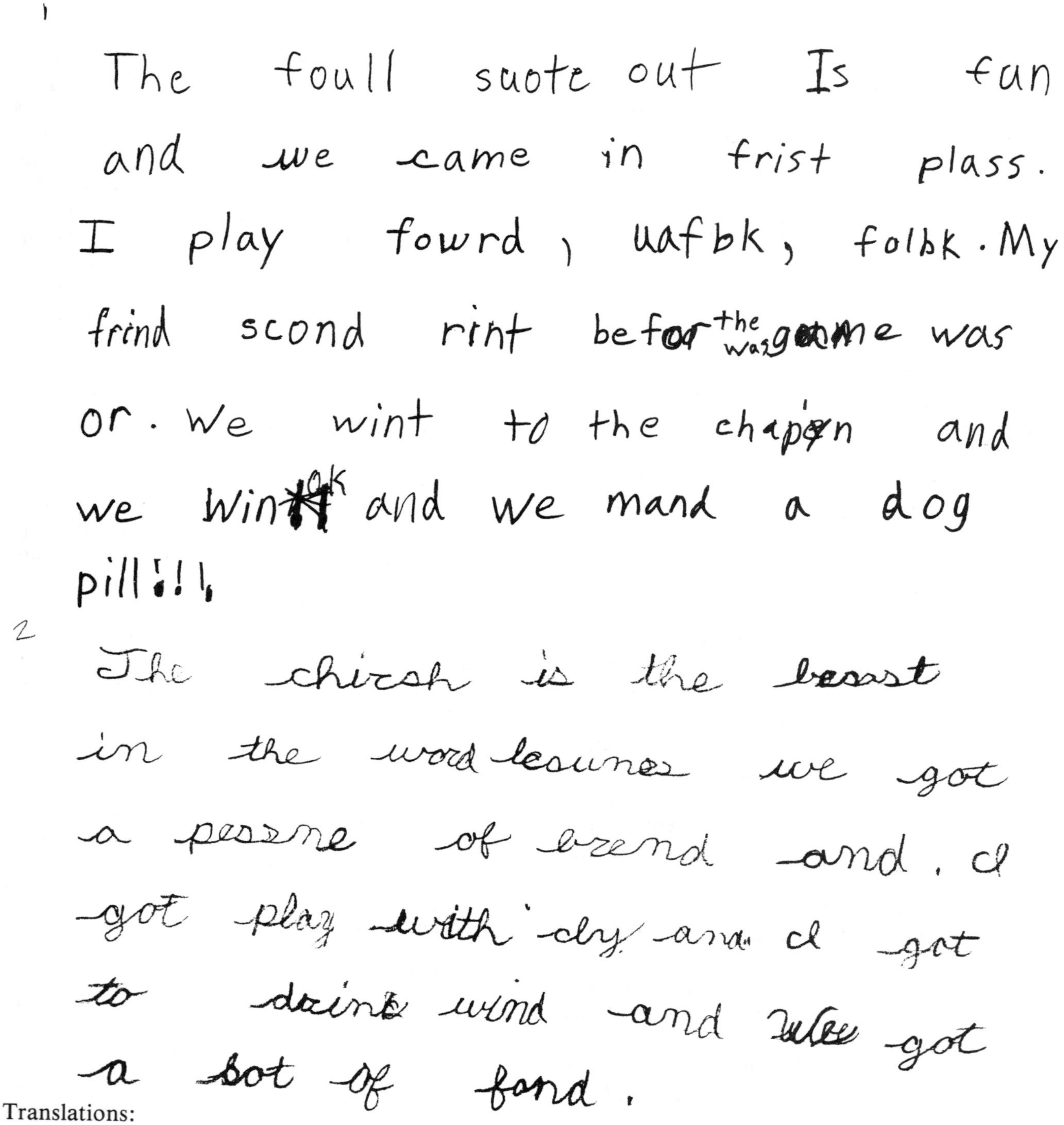

1

The foull suote out Is fun
and we came in frist plass.
I play fowrd, uafbk, folbk. My
frind scond rint befor the was game was
or. We wint to the chapien and
we win ok and we mand a dog
pill!!!

2

The chirsh is the beast
in the word leaunes we got
a pessne of brend and, I
got play with cly and I got
to drink wind and wee got
a bot of fand.

Translations:

The Fort Lowell shoot out is fun and we came in first place. I play forward, halfback, fullback. My friend scored right before the was game was over. We went to the championships and we won and we made a dog-pile.

The church is the best in the world because we got a piece of bread and I got play with clay and I got to drink wine and we got a lot of fun.

Figure 8-10a. Three journal entries by Brian, a fourth-grade student.

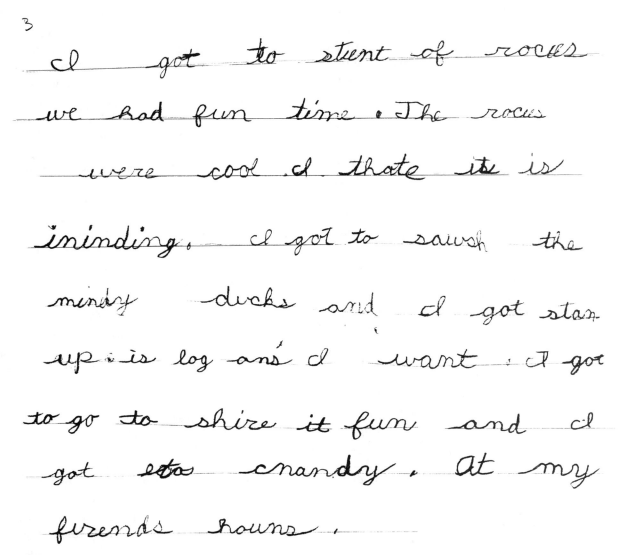

3

I got to stent of rocus we had fun time. The rocus were cool. I thate its is ininding. I got to sawsh the mindy ducks and I got stay up is log ans I want. I got to go to shire it fun and I got etos cnandy. At my firends houns.

Translation:

I got to set off firecrackers. We had fun time. The firecrackers were cool. I thought it is exciting. I got to watch the Mighty Ducks and I got stay up as long as I want. I got to go to church. It fun and I got to eat candy at my friend's house.

Figure 8–10a (cont.)

Recommendations

Handwriting and Appearance

1. Based on its neater appearance, encourage Brian to use cursive writing for all assignments.
2. Review the amount of spacing that should occur between words with Brian. Give him an object such as a small button that he could place between words as he is writing.
3. Reinforce the appearance of the written work regardless of content or spelling.

Spelling

1. Ensure that Brian is not penalized in any situation for his spelling attempts.
2. Encourage Brian to generalize the phonic spelling patterns that he has mastered (e.g., "ay"; he can spell "play" but misspells "clay"). Initially, work with word families using those

structures he knows, then move to new structures. Ask Brian to suggest a word that he would like to spell then teach him both the word and the word family pertaining to it (e.g., if Brian chooses to learn the word "dictionary," also teach "fiction" and "friction").

3. As Brian has difficulty both sequencing sounds in words and picturing words in his mind, use a multisensory spelling approach such as the Gilstrap Method (Gilstrap, 1962). Work with gross-motor movements (e.g., writing in large letters on the chalkboard) before generalizing to fine-motor movements (e.g., writing on lined paper).

4. Provide Brian with a spelling box for storing the words he learns. Encourage him to alphabetize the words in the box.

5. As the number of words in the bank increases, ask Brian to build sentences with the flash cards and then copy them onto paper. This will help generalize out-of-context spelling to in-context use.

6. Help Brian understand the connection between the number of syllables in words and their length. Play games involving clapping or giving counters for each syllable in a word. Ask Brian to "read" his written work by tapping a pen on the table for every syllable.

7. As a fun activity, give Brian a limerick and help him replace a few words, ensuring that the rhythm is kept constant. Point out the regularities in the spelling of the rhyming words. As his skill develops, encourage Brian to write his own limericks.

Usage

1. Teach Brian that a sentence consists of a complete thought and that a period is placed at the end. Provide practice by having him edit assignments written by other students.

2. Encourage Brian to limit use of the conjunction "and." Help Brian edit his work by either replacing "and" with another word or by encouraging him to begin a new sentence.

3. Review the use of pronouns such as "we." Explain to Brian how all pronouns must have clear referents. Provide practice by having Brian write pairs of sentences. The first sentence would include a noun or proper noun. The next sentence would add more information and contain a pronoun.

4. Through questioning in the revision stage, help Brian clarify pronoun referents.

5. Teach Brian the Given-New strategy (Cooper, 1988) in order that he may learn to connect consecutive sentences. Encourage Brian to assume that the reader has no prior knowledge of the topic.

6. Discourage Brian from using too many exclamation points. When they are used, help him understand that one exclamation point is all that is necessary. Remind Brian that writers place only one period at the end of a sentence, not three.

Vocabulary

1. Help Brian to select more precise words to use in his assignments. As a prewriting activity, have him and a peer brainstorm all of the descriptive words they can. Encourage Brian to keep this list in front of him as he writes his first draft. Upon completion, have him count the number of targeted words that he has used.

2. Use a synonym cloze procedure to help Brian increase his writing. After a draft of a story is complete, underline words that could be more descriptive. Delete each word to be changed and then write it under the line. Have him work with a peer to determine other words that would make the writing more interesting.

Organization/Ideation

1. Prior to writing, have Brian engage in discussions about his ideas.

2. Work on prewriting strategies using graphic organizers. Stress the importance of keeping information in an organized order and not including information that does not belong.

3. Help Brian to organize and sequence details. For example, have him list all the information that he thinks is important and then help him think of ways to sequence the points. Teach Brian to use mapping or webbing in order to provide structure to the organization.

Follow-Up

A special education teacher began working with Brian on the above recommendations for 1 hour, twice weekly. During the fourth session, Brian was asked to write a journal entry.

Analysis of the assignment indicates a marked improvement in Brian's writing from 2 weeks prior. The problems discussed in his previous writing still exist but the effectiveness of the specific recommendations can be clearly seen. Brian is encouraged by his improvement and motivated to work at improving his writing further. In addition, to document progress, Brian and his teacher have compared journal entries on a weekly basis. Brian's comment with regard to his latest attempt was "Boy, this is better. My printing isn't good so I should write cursive shouldn't I? But my spelling is so much better. You were right, I *can* write."

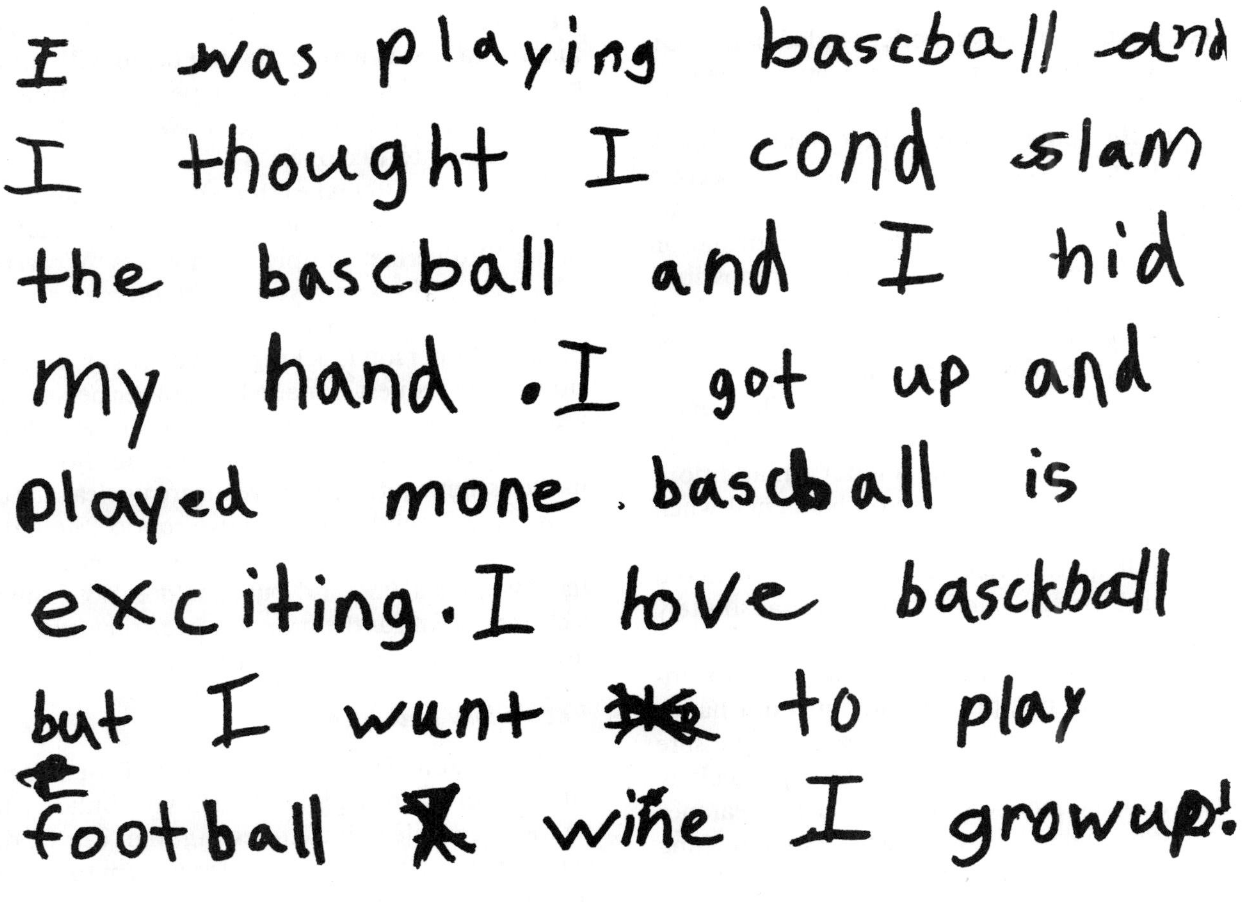

Translation:

I was playing baseball and I thought I could slam the baseball and I hit my hand. I got up and played more. Baseball is exciting. I love baseball but I want to play football when I grow up.

Figure 8–10b. A journal entry written by Brian, a fourth-grade student.

Student: Alan
Grade: 4th
Assignments: Two short stories

The assignment titles were chosen by Alan as no guidance was given in regard to topic selection. No prewriting activities had occurred.

Analysis

Handwriting and Appearance

Alan writes on narrow, college-ruled paper. On the first assignment, his lowercase letters filled the space between two lines with the uppercase letters filling up the space between three lines. A blank line is left in between. The writing in the second assignment begins in the same manner but rapidly changes to every line. The poor letter formation makes the stories hard, and sometimes impossible, to read. The spacing between words is uniform and correct in the "Wolverine" sample but tends to be too small in the "Dinosaur" sample.

Alan positions his letters vertically. The uppercase letter "I" is poorly formed and sometimes appears more like a circle than a letter. In addition, Alan exerts excessive pressure on his pencil when writing. This practice results in the pencil lead becoming dull quite quickly. Alan tends to avoid sharpening his pencil until it becomes absolutely necessary.

Alan observes the left margin but does not indent either beginning paragraph. The poor handwriting and the thick lines from the excessive pressure give the work a messy appearance. This is particularly true in the second sample as the squashed appearance of the writing makes the assignment seem uninviting to the eye. The incorrect formation of the word "I" also adds to the sloppy appearance. Overall, the appearance of Alan's handwriting suggests that he has difficulty with motor control.

Spelling

Alan has learned to spell a number of sight words (e.g., "how," "you," "came," "out," and "cage"). He tries to spell other words phonetically by writing *pepel* for "people," *meeit* for "meat," and *lik* for "like." His spelling of the words "favor" as *faver* and "would" as *wood* suggests that he has mastered

at least some common linguistic patterns. For some of his spellings, Alan spells a part of the word correctly. For example, he writes *rere* for "were," *wacker* for "worker," and *hereding* for "hurting." Alan's spelling difficulties, however, cannot be fully analyzed until his handwriting is more legible or until he has learned to type.

Usage

An uppercase letter is used in the word "I" and perhaps in the name "Wolverine." No other uppercase letters are discernible in the assignments. Although a title is provided for each of the assignments, no words within the title begin with uppercase letters. Alan does not use periods. Some sentences appear to be constructed correctly, but they are difficult to decipher.

Alan appears to make erroneous assumptions with regard to the reader's prior knowledge. For example in the "Wolverine" sample, Alan writes "Wolverine what is it. How would you like to do me a favor," but the reader does not know whether Wolverine or another person is asking for the favor. In addition, if the request is made by another person, the reader has no knowledge of who the person is.

Other examples of erroneous assumptions exist in the assignment. The referents are unclear for *out came his fans* and *he cut the two robots*. Similarly, in the "Dinosaur" sample, the first sentence states that "We had a dinosaur" but Alan does not establish a clear referent for the pronoun "we." The sentences used are simple and limited in description.

Vocabulary and Ideation

The vocabulary used appears simplistic. As not all the words are legible, Alan's vocabulary may be more complex and interesting than can be discerned from the samples. The ideas seem to be adequate, but need elaboration.

Recommendations

Handwriting

1. Alan's writing is basically illegible because of poor handwriting. Consequently, remediation in this area is imperative. Analyze Alan's manuscript and cursive writing, and decide which style is more legible. Provide instruction in that style, using a self-instruc-

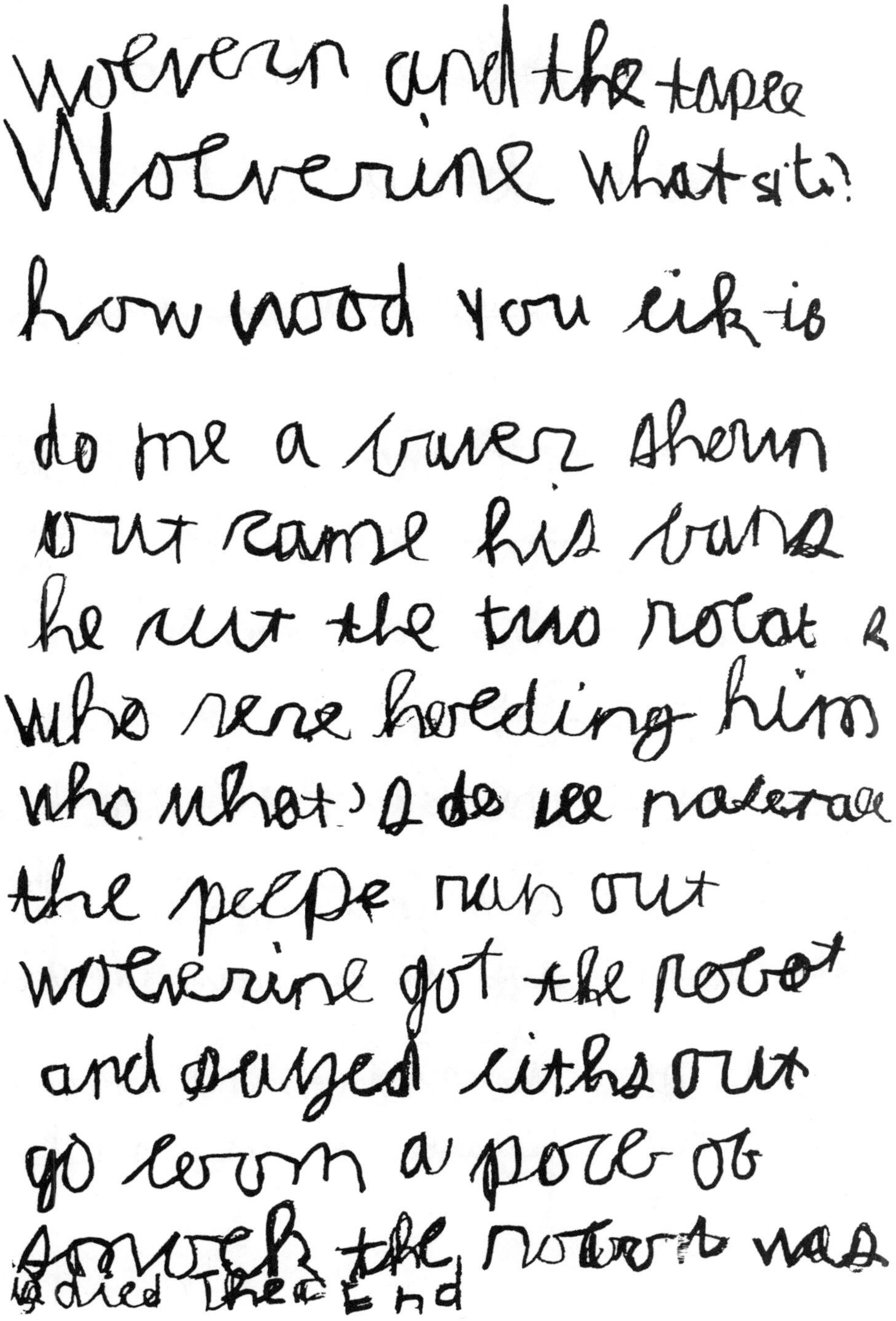

woverin and the tepee
Wolverine what sit?
how wood you eik is

do me a traver sherun
out came his fans
he cut the two robot
who rene hoeding him
who what? a do see naterac
the peepe ran out
woverine got the robot
and sayed ciths out
go boom a puff ob
smoek the robot was
is died thee End

Semi-translations:

Wolverine and the Tepee Wolverine what is it? How would you like is do me a favor. Sure. Out came his fans. He cut the two robots who were holding him who what's do . . . All the people ran out. Wolverine got the robot and said . . . out go boom a puff of smoke the robot was is died.

Figure 8–11. Two short stories by Alan, a fourth-grade student.

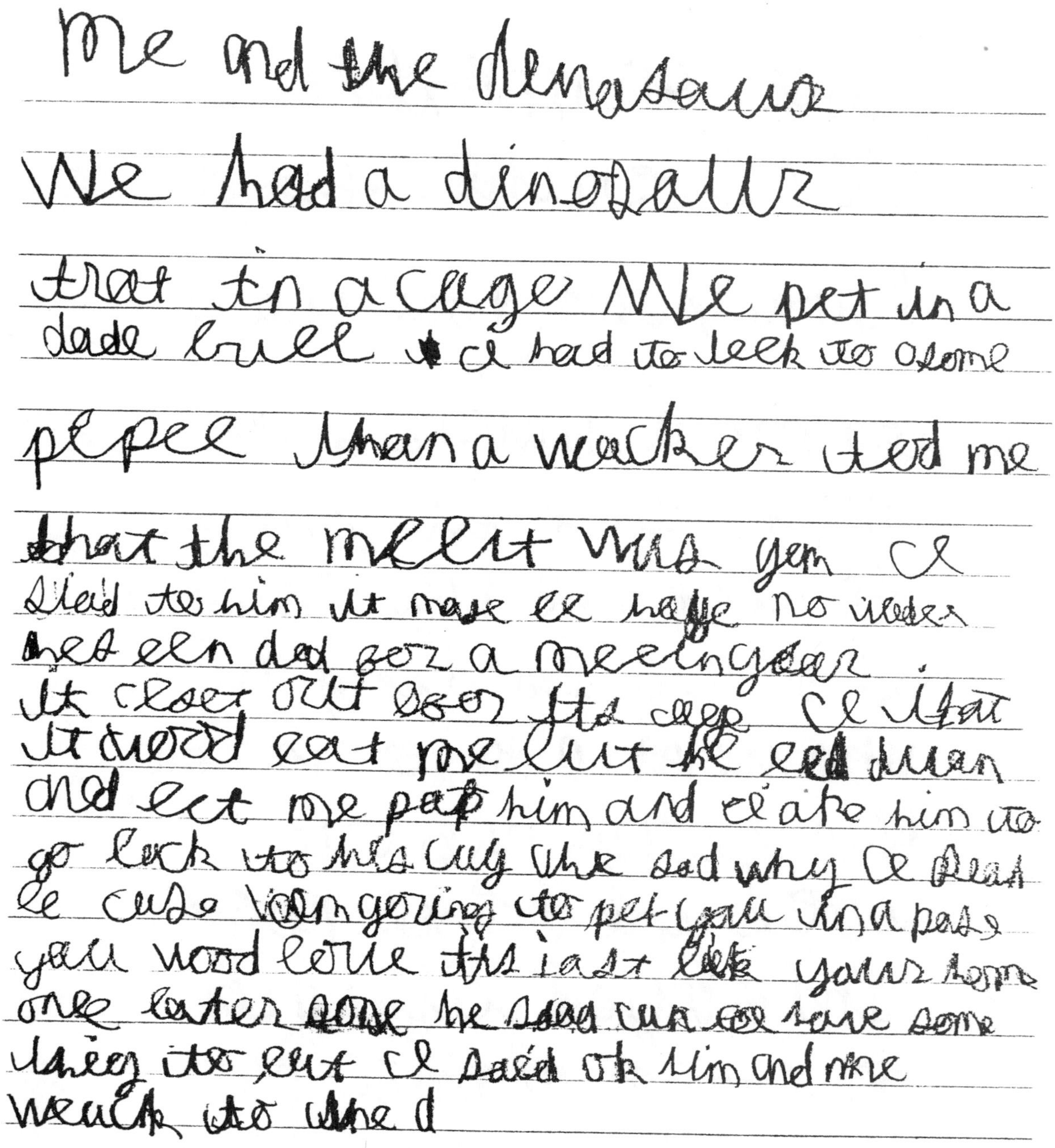

Me and the denasaur

We had a dinosaur

that in a cage We pet in a
dade bull & I had to leek to some

pepel than a wecker ted me

that the meet was gem I
sied to him it may ee haff no idder
net een dad for a meetngear.
It cloer out for its cage I that
it wood eat me but he eet duen
and ect me pat him and I ake him to
go leck to his cag the sed why I Read
ce cuse I am going to pet you in a pass
you wood love this iast lick yaur hom
one later gone he said can I have some
theeg ito eut I said ok him and me
wealk ito whe I

Semi-translation:

Me and the dinosaur We had a dinosaur that in a cage. We put in a dead bull. I had to look to some people. Then a worker told me that the meat was gone. I said to him: it . . . I have no idea. He's in there for a meet and your and it isn't out . . . its . . . I thought it would eat me but he eat . . . and let me pat him and I ask him to go back to his cage. He said why. I said because I am going to put you in a . . . You would love it is just like your home. Only later on he said can I have some thing into eat. I said okay. Him and me walk to . . .

Figure 8–11 (cont.) Two short stories by Alan, a fourth-grade student.

tion strategy such as those suggested by Graham (1983) or Blandford and Lloyd (1987).

2. Teach Alan keyboarding skills. Once he is able to type about eight words per minute, encourage him to type the majority of his assignments.

3. For some assignments, provide Alan with a scribe (teacher, parent, or peer), or allow him to dictate his assignments into a tape. If the latter method is chosen, once Alan has dictated the story, type a copy so that he may feel proud of a neatly presented piece of work.

4. Do not grade Alan in handwriting. Instead, provide many ungraded opportunities for skill to develop.

5. Put modeling clay around the pencil to help Alan develop a more relaxed grip.

6. Help Alan increase his desire to improve his handwriting. Discuss practical reasons for improving legibility.

7. Acknowledge Alan's effort in trying to write neatly. Provide only words of encouragement as his handwriting skill develops.

Spelling

1. Do additional informal analysis of Alan's skill by asking him to spell words orally. Take words from a high-frequency word list, such as 1,000 Instant Words, to determine which words he does and does not know how to spell. Have Alan keep a list of the words that he has mastered.

2. Encourage Alan to write phonetically when uncertain as to how to spell a word. Show him how a spell checker can aid writing and tell him that your goal is to help him learn to spell with enough accuracy that he can use the spell checker independently. Until the goal has been attained, provide Alan with a more knowledgeable other to help him use a spell checker.

3. Build Alan's spelling word bank by using a multisensory approach such as the Fernald method (Fernald, 1943).

Usage

1. Encourage Alan to put periods at the end of sentences. Provide him with practice do-

ing this on a computer with sentences that have been typed for him.

2. Review capitalization rules with Alan. Again, provide the opportunity for practice with sentences that have already been typed on the computer.

3. Praise Alan for his use of story titles and encourage him to capitalize the words within the title.

4. Help Alan become aware of the audience needs. After reading a first draft have him ask the following questions (Moran, 1987):

   a. What do you think your audience knows about the topic?

   b. What do you want your audience to know?

   c. Does your audience need more information and/or description about the topic? If so, where?

   d. What more do you know (or can imagine) about the topic?

   e. Is any part of your writing incomplete or confusing?

5. Encourage Alan to use a variety of different sentence structures. Teach him strategies for elaborating his sentences, such as the slotting strategy recommended by Poteet (1987).

Vocabulary/Ideation

1. Help Alan develop a personalized dictionary of adjectives (e.g., *enormous*, *violent*) and encourage him to use one with any noun he uses in his writing. After becoming competent with adjectives, help Alan focus on the use of adverbs (e.g., *quickly, awkwardly*).

2. Even when Alan's work has been typed by a scribe, encourage him to revise for content and clarify meaning.

3. Use the writing process approach with Alan, providing opportunities for him to either work on a computer or with a peer.

4. So that he does not become discouraged about writing, praise Alan frequently for his effort.

5. Keep a writing portfolio to document Alan's growth in writing.

Student: Emily
Grade: 5th
Assignment: Descriptive paragraph

Emily was asked to write a descriptive paragraph about what she does in the morning before coming to school.

Analysis

Handwriting

In general, Emily's cursive writing is legible. She appears, however, to have some difficulty with the formation of a lowercase *b* when it is joined with the letters, *r* and *u*. In one instance, she reverses an uppercase *I*. The letters below the line extend too far to the left. The spacing between sentences is inconsistent.

Spelling

Emily's greatest difficulty appears to be spelling. Although one may suspect that some of Emily's misspellings are based upon articulation errors (e.g., *griss* for "dress," *bruefis* for "breakfast," and *poll* for "bottle"), these types of sound confusions are not present in her oral language. In general, her spellings indicate poor phonological awareness. She includes unnecessary sounds (e.g., *gent* for "get," *pult* for "put," and *finl* for "fill").

Several of Emily's spellings have limited sound-symbol correspondence but begin with the correct consonant sound. For example, she spells "stuff" as *suth*, "family" as *fomey*, and "fix" as *finck*. Emily does, however, appear to realize that the spelling of words does not vary. As long as the words are close together in the passage, she maintains her invented spelling. For example, she spells the word "get" twice as *gent*, "brush" twice as *brins*, and "wait" three times as *want*.

Usage

Emily begins all sentences with an uppercase letter and ends with a period. Her sentence patterns are relatively simplistic. With the exception of an incomplete sentence beginning with the word "And," she starts each sentence with the word "I." Although verb tense is mostly consistent, Emily has made two errors, writing *dress* instead of *dressed* and *said*

instead of *say*. It is unclear, however, whether these errors are due to problems with spelling or usage.

Organization and Ideation

The activities described contain little detail. In addition, Emily does not introduce her topic or use linking words to order her actions. She does, however, relate her morning activities in an appropriate sequence.

Recommendations

Handwriting

1. Provide Emily with additional practice with letters that require a bridge or handle when joined to other letters (e.g., *b*, *o*, *v*, and *w*).
2. Review with Emily the correct formation of letters that extend below the line, such as *y* and *g*.
3. Remind Emily to leave a space after sentences.

Spelling

1. Provide Emily with an individualized spelling list. Select words that are frequently misspelled in her writing. Initially, select spelling words for Emily that have phonically regular spelling patterns and also teach the families of the chosen spelling words (e.g., alongside "part," teach "cart," "dart," "start" etc.).
2. Help Emily learn to determine the number of syllables that she hears in a word and then the number of sounds. Have her pronounce the word slowly as she pushes out a counter for each sound. Then, have her write the sounds that she hears.
3. Dictate simple spelling words to Emily and have her build the words with magnetic plastic letters or Scrabble tiles. Have her form the word with the letters, then scramble the letters and reconstruct the word from memory.
4. Teach Emily how to spell phonetically by using a strategy such as Bannatyne's System (Bannatyne, 1971). Encourage her to pronounce a word slowly as she writes each sound. This will help Emily sequence letters in the correct order.

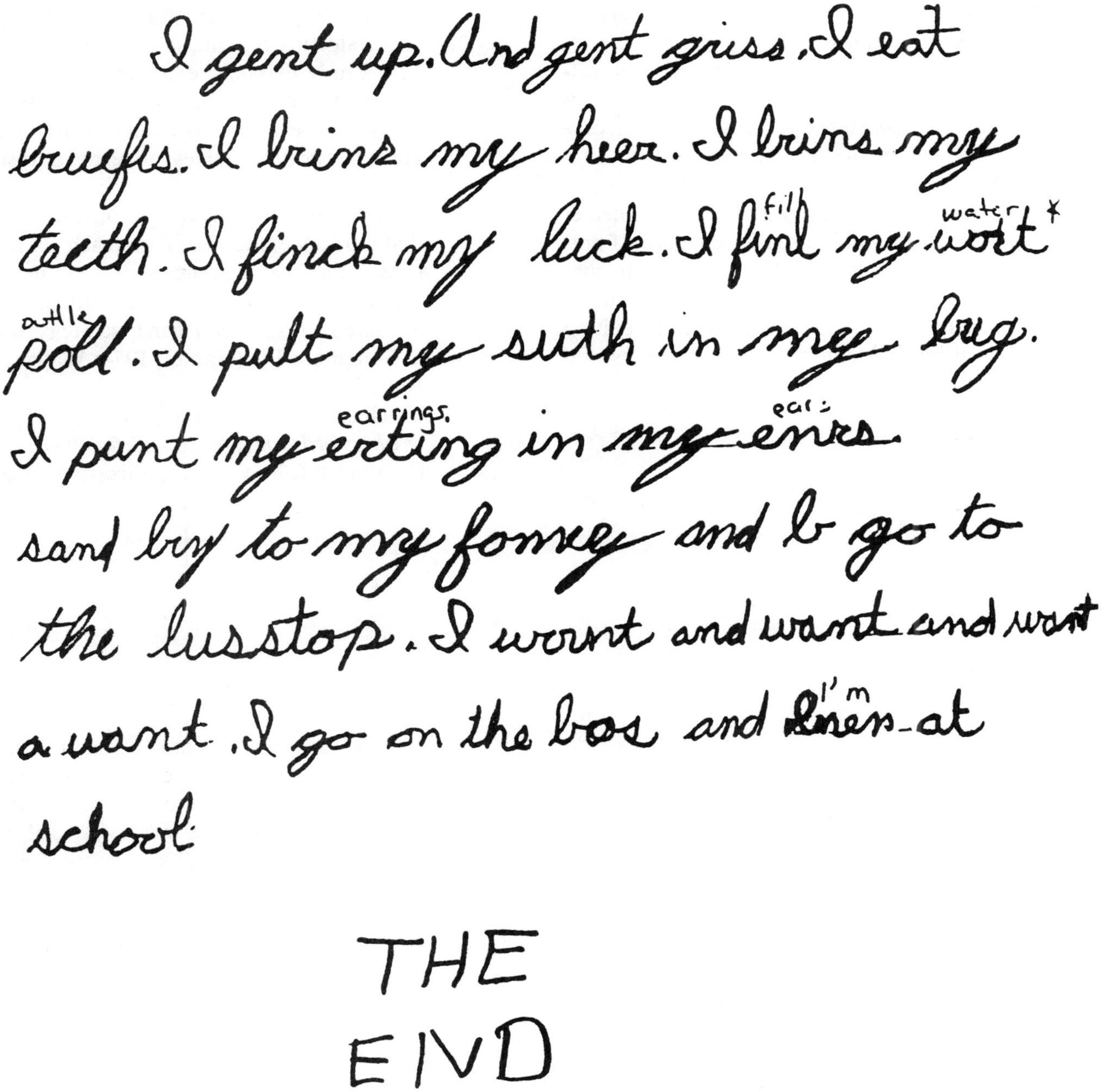

I gent up. And gent giuss. I eat
breefs. I brins my heer. I brins my
teeth. I finck my luck. I finl my wort [water*]
[fill] [ottle] poll. I pult my suth in mee bug.
I punt my erting [earrings] in my enrs [ears].
sand by to my fomry and b go to
the busstop. I wornt and wornt and wort
a wont. I go on the bos and Inen-at [I'm]
school

THE
END

Translation:

I get up. And get dress. I eat breakfast. I brush my hair. I brush my teeth. I fix my lunch. I fill my water bottle. I put my stuff in my bag. I put my earrings in my ears said bye to my family and I go to the bus stop. I wait and wait and wait and wait. I go on the bus and I'm at school.

Figure 8–12. A sequential paragraph written by Emily, a fifth-grade student.

Usage

1. Teach Emily how to write a variety of sentence patterns.
2. Encourage Emily to start sentences in different ways. Suggest that only two sentences may begin with the same word. Reinforce Emily when she attains the goal.
3. Analyze additional writing samples and listen to Emily telling a story to determine whether she is consistent in use of verb tense. If not, provide instruction in how to maintain consistency in verb tense throughout a paragraph. Provide feedback in the editing stage by underlining all of the verbs and helping Emily check them.

Ideation

1. Provide opportunities for daily writing.
2. Use a slotting technique (Poteet, 1987) to help Emily expand her sentences. Take a paragraph that she has written and put in blanks where the sentence can be elaborated. Have her add adjectives, adverbs, phrases, and/or clauses.
3. Teach Emily how to write a topic sentence that introduces the idea. Also teach her how to write a final sentence that summarizes the main idea or provides a transition to a related idea. Teach her a strategy such as Statement-Pie (Hanau, 1974; Wallace & Bott, 1989).
4. Teach Emily to use simple cohesive ties, such as *afterwards*, *then*, *next*, and *finally*, to help the reader follow the organization of her sequential paragraphs.

Student: Roy
Grade: 5th
Assignments: Description of a sporting event
Sailing to the New World

Two first drafts are provided for Roy. The first sample describes a sporting event. The first two pages of his five-page story are included. His second assignment was to write a description of what it would have been like to sail to the New World.

Analysis

Handwriting

The overall quality of Roy's cursive handwriting is adequate. His slant is consistent. The spacing of his letters, words, and sentences is consistent and appropriate. In general, the uppercase letters are clearly taller than the lowercase letters. Although Roy forms most letters correctly, several are reversed or inverted (e.g., *L*, *b*, and *d*). Roy indents the first paragraph of both assignments, but no other indentation is evident. In addition, he leaves too wide a margin on the right side and too wide a space between words.

Spelling

Roy demonstrates good sound-symbol correspondence and correct sound sequence in his spelling. He misspells a number of words, however. Some of his misspellings are caused by letter insertions (e.g., *goail* for "goal," *hundrede* for "hundred," and *whith* for "with"), letter omissions (e.g., *secons* for "seconds," *miunt* for "minute," and *agin* for "again"), and letter reversals (e.g., *dlock dy* for "block by," *bay* for "day," and *calb* for "called"). Other misspellings are due to letter substitutions (e.g., *aroung* for "around" and *shors* for "scores"). Still others are rule-governed errors (e.g., *passis* for "passes" and *calb* for "called"). In addition, Roy has difficulty spelling contractions, writing *I'v* for "I've" and *her's* for "here's."

In some instances, Roy writes two separate words as one (e.g., *afast* for "a fast," *faseoff* for "face off," and *lasanglis* for Los Angeles). Errors are also noted in the spelling of high-frequency words (e.g., *macks* for "makes" and *whith* for "with"). In addition to writing incorrect spellings, Roy is inconsistent in his spellings of some words. For example, he writes *face-off*, *face off*, and *faseoff* for "face off," and *oiles* and *oilers* for "Oilers." Not all errors, however, are inconsistent. Throughout his samples, Roy spells "makes" as *macks* and "goal" as *goail*.

Usage

Roy's use of periods is sporadic and sentence boundaries are not clearly delineated. He capitalizes the first letter of sentences and the word "I." He is inconsistent, however, in his use of uppercase letters in proper nouns (e.g., *lasanglis*, *kelly rudy*, *luke*). Roy demonstrates knowledge of other punctuation marks. He uses commas correctly in lists. He also uses exclamation points, but tends to overuse them in the Stanley Cup sample in an attempt to create excitement. He uses apostrophes correctly in some words, but not others.

In both samples, Roy maintains consistency in his use of verb tense. He uses correctly three conjunctions ("and," "because," and "that") and several prepositions ("with," "in," "of," "to," "on," "for," and "behind"). In general, Roy uses short, simple sentences with many following the subject-verb-object pattern. This may, however, be partially due to the style of the Stanley Cup narration.

Organization and Ideation

Roy's "Stanley Cup" sample is an imaginative and exciting narration of a hockey game. He attempts to build and maintain suspense with regard to the outcome of the game. Although the descriptions are not in-depth, the narrative is well sequenced. The description supports the purpose of his paper and demonstrates excellent use of background information.

In "Sailing to the New World," Roy tends to give information with regard to the ship, crew, passengers, and cargo rather than the journey itself. The story, therefore, is incongruous with the title.

Recommendations

Handwriting

1. Because Roy is aware of his letter reversals in writing, treat them as minor handwriting or spelling errors that will be corrected during the editing stage of writing.

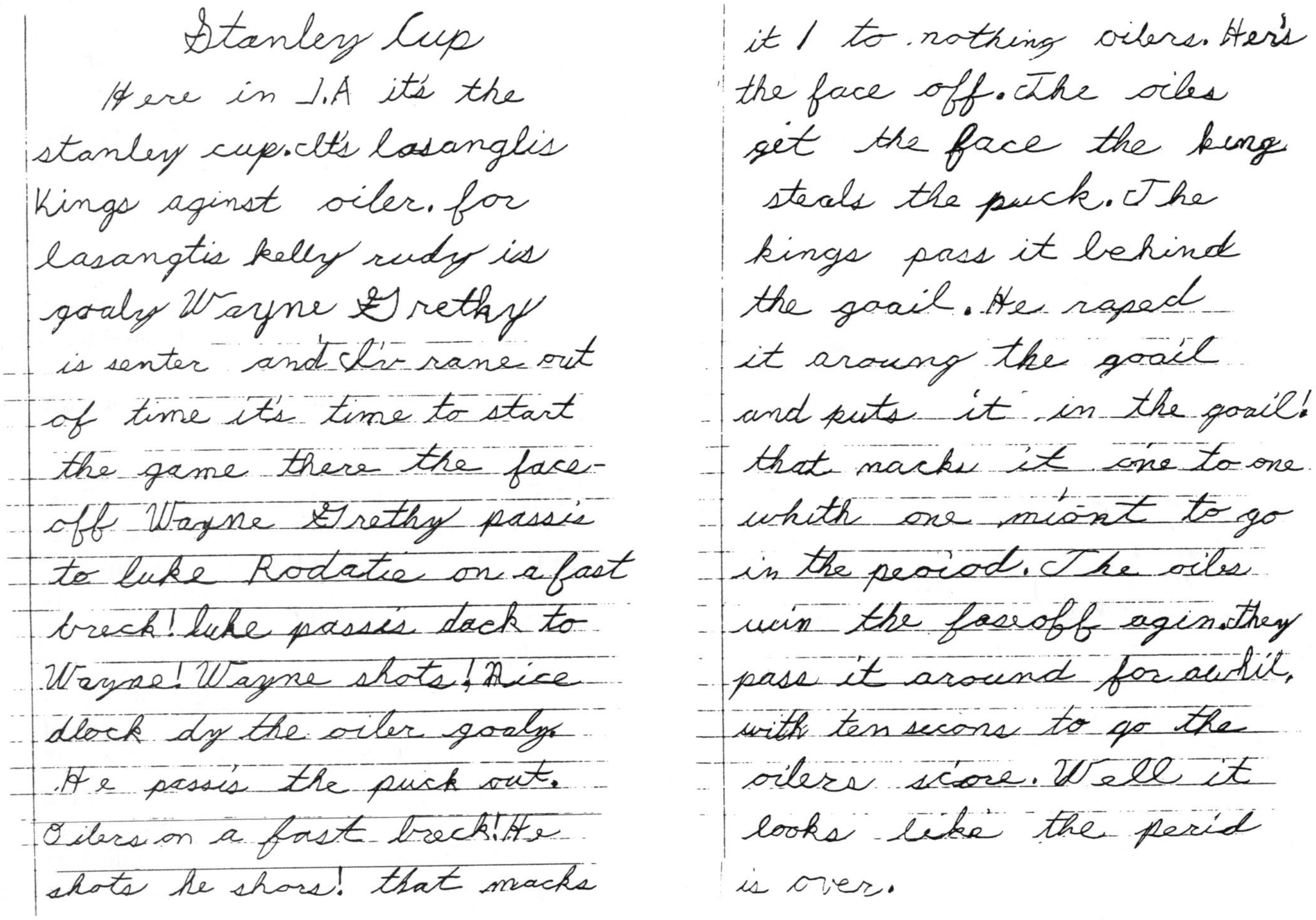

Stanley Cup

Here in L.A it's the stanley cup. It's lasanglis Kings aginst oiler. for lasangtis kelly rudy is goaly Wayne Grethy is senter and his rane out of time it's time to start the game there the face-off Wayne Grethy passis to luke Rodatie on a fast breck! luke passis dack to Wayne! Wayne shots! nice dlock dy the oiler goaly. He passis the puck out. Oibrs on a fast breck! He shots he shors! that macks it 1 to nothing oilers. Her's the face off. The oiles git the face the king steals the puck. The kings pass it behind the goail. He raped it aroung the goail and puts it in the goail! that macks it one to one whith one miant to go in the period. The oiles win the faseoff agin. they pass it around for awhil. with ten secons to go the oilers score. Well it looks like the perid is over.

Figure 8–13. Two compositions by Roy, a fifth-grade student.

2. Teach Roy keyboarding skills. Because the majority of the letters he reverses are lower-case, the uppercase letters on the keyboard will help him resolve this difficulty.

3. When writing his final drafts, encourage Roy to come all the way over to the right margin of the paper and reduce the amount of space between words.

Spelling

1. Do not penalize Roy for misspellings in his written work. Provide assistance as needed (teacher, parent, peer, or spell-checker) for the final draft.

2. Develop an individualized spelling program for Roy using a flow list rather than a fixed spelling list. When using a flow list, provide daily testing and replace each word as mastery is accomplished. Ask Roy to select the words from his writing that he would like to learn to spell.

3. Select a study technique for learning difficult words that has a multisensory emphasis (e.g., the Fernald Method).

3. Encourage Roy to use any of the words that he is learning to spell in his written compositions. Provide positive feedback when he spells the words successfully.

4. On occasion, include assistance with spelling as part of a prewriting activity. For example, prior to writing a paragraph, have Roy brainstorm all the words that he thinks he may need when writing. Write all of the words down so that he can refer to the list when writing his first draft.

5. Have Roy develop a personalized spelling dictionary that is composed of common words that he frequently misspells. En-

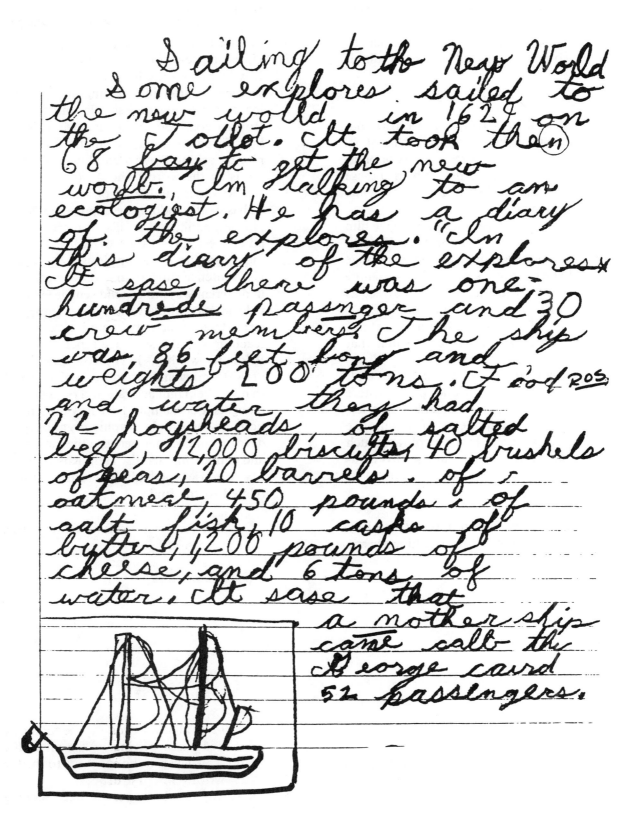

Sailing to the New World

Some explores sailed to the new world in 162 on the Tollot. It took then 68 days to get the new world. I'm talking to an ecologist. He has a diary of the explores. "In this diary" of the explores. It sase there was one hundrede passnger and 30 crew members. The ship was 86 feet long and weights 200 tons. Food and water they had 22 hogsheads of salted beef, 12,000 biscuts, 40 bushels of peas, 20 barrels of oatmeal, 450 pounds of salt fish, 10 casks of butter, 1,200 pounds of cheese, and 6 tons of water. It sase that a nother ship came calt the George caird 52 passengers.

Figure 8-13 (cont.). Two compositions by Roy, a fifth-grade student.

courage Roy to use his personalized spelling dictionary to edit his writing.

6. As skill develops, provide Roy with a pocket-sized, computerized spell checker to edit his work.

Proofreading/Editing

1. Discuss with Roy the types of errors that he frequently makes in writing, such as starting sentences with uppercase letters or omitting endings from words. Prioritize these errors and make a list for Roy to use while editing his work.

2. Before Roy proofreads his paper, give him a list that contains the numbers of spelling, capitalization, punctuation, and usage errors. Have him work with a peer with more advanced skill to identify and correct as many mistakes as they can find.

3. Use the COPS strategy (Schumaker et al., 1985) with Roy to provide a format that will help him with editing.

4. Help Roy recognize where sentences end. Read his story aloud and pause where periods should be placed. In addition, review with Roy the components of a complete sentence. Explain to him why phrases such as *he shoots he scores* comprise two complete sentences.

Expression

1. Have a brief revision conference with Roy before he attempts to rewrite his papers.

Begin by pointing out what he has done well and then provide suggestions for improving the paper.

2. Use sentence-combining techniques to help Roy learn to write longer, more complex sentences. After introducing and practicing the technique, take simple sentences for Roy to combine using his own writing. Specific patterns may be taught, for example, by asking Roy to combine sentences by using the word "who."

3. Ask Roy to expand orally on a sentence that he has written, adding descriptive words and phrases, additional details, or more explicit adjectives. Have Roy rewrite his sentence incorporating his expansions.

4. Use sentence starters to give Roy practice in different ways to expand sentences. Provide practice with a variety of sentence patterns. Use this activity in conjunction with teaching specific sentence types.

5. Prior to writing, have Roy engage in brainstorming and organizational activities that will help him activate and organize his thoughts. For example, have Roy use semantic maps or simple graphic organizers to develop connections between the main idea and supporting details. Help Roy to identify specific vocabulary words that are related to the topic.

Student: Malika
Grade: 6th
Assignments: Two opinion essays

Before the production of the assignments, a prewriting class discussion had occurred. Malika and her peers were then asked to record their personal ideas of "A Perfect Classroom" and "A Perfect Teacher."

Analysis

Handwriting/Appearance

Malika remembered to put a title to the first assignment, but proceeded to place an equal sign after the title turning the assignment into a form of equation. No title was recorded for the second assignment. Malika printed both assignments. Although her handwriting is easy to read and all letters are recognizable, formation of the letter *k* detracts from the overall appearance. She does not indent the paragraphs and seems to have tried to create the appearance of a title from the first sentence in the second assignment. Malika has attempted to observe both left and right margins, but neither is perfect.

Spelling

A number of spelling errors appear in the "Perfect Teacher" sample. As examples, she writes *thout* for "thought," *meen* for "mean," *bloun* for "brown," *samil* for "smile," *hear* for "hair," and *skeeny* for "skinny." Only two errors are made, however, in the "Perfect Classroom" sample (*seting* for "setting and *sets* for "seats"). The words, although incorrectly spelled, have sound-symbol correspondence and are therefore easy to recognize.

Malika shows confusion in her spelling of common homonyms. For example, she spells "no" in the compound words "nobody" and "no one" as *know*. In addition, she spells "by" as *buy*, "their" as *there*, "you're" as *your*, and "sweet" as *suite*.

Usage

Malika's use of periods and uppercase letters is incorrect. Although she capitalizes the first letter in the first sentence of each paragraph, the sentences do not make sense as written (*Is when knom one*

talks and knowbody get out of there sets., and *Who is my perfect teacher is you because your nice sweet prson . . .*). Malika capitalizes the first letter after two of the three periods used. She does not, however, always place periods where needed and has several run-on sentences (e.g., *One tall skeeny has bloun hear one is tall chucky and a suite samil teacher so that how my perfect teacher is.*).

Malika has not yet mastered correct sentence formation. She often writes unfinished sentences and clauses that represent incomplete thoughts (e.g., *and do all there work.*, and *Sometime we can be good I guess we talk it because ever body set by there friends . . .*). Analysis of the syntactic errors suggests that Malika may have expressive language difficulties (e.g., *I thout that when I come to this school . . .* , and *Sometime we can be good I guess we talk it because ever body set . . .*). She tries, however, to write compound sentences connected by the conjunction "because." Malika's use of subject-verb agreement is incorrect after the words "everybody" and "nobody" (e.g., *knowbody get out . . .* , and *ever body set . . .*).

Vocabulary

Although simple, Malika attempts to use colorful and descriptive words, particularly in the "Perfect Teacher" sample. For example, she describes her teachers as being "skinny," "chunky," and having a "sweet smile."

Organization/Ideation

The samples are rather limited in content and lose focus at times. For example, when describing a perfect classroom, Malika discusses when her class is quiet. In the description of the perfect teacher, she mentions three teachers briefly instead of fully describing one.

Recommendations

Handwriting/Appearance

1. Encourage Malika to write a title for every written assignment she attempts.
2. Remind Malika that every paragraph needs to be indented.
3. Remind Malika to observe left and right margins. If she desires, have her place a piece of Scotch tape down the sides of the paper as a reminder to go to the next line.

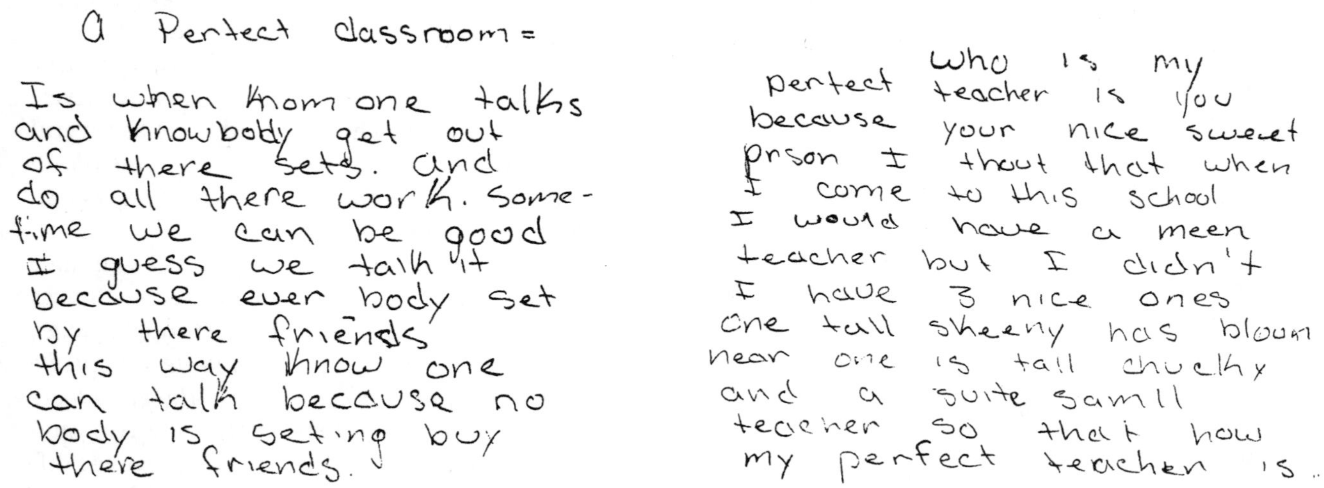

A Perfect classroom =

Is when know one talks and knowbody get out of there sets. and do all there work. Sometime we can be good I guess we talk it because ever body set by there friends this way know one can talk because no body is seting buy there friends. ✓

perfect Who is my teacher is you because your nice sweet prson I thout that when I come to this school I would have a meen teacher but I didn't I have 3 nice ones one tall sheeny has bloun hear one is tall chuchy and a suite samll teacher so that how my perfect teacher is..

Figure 8–14. Two opinion essays written by Malika, a sixth-grade student.

4. Teach Malika the correct formation of lower- and uppercase *k*. Reinforce her for using the correct formation in her written work.

Spelling

1. Help Malika increase the number of high-frequency words that she knows how to spell. Take the words to be taught directly from her writing. Have Malika select additional words that she is interested in learning.

2. Develop an individualized spelling program for Malika using a flow list rather than a fixed spelling list. Test her on the words daily. When a word has been spelled correctly on 3 consecutive days, replace it with a new word from her writing.

3. Show Malika the difference in the spellings of common homonyms, such as "your" and "you're," "no" and "know," "by" and "buy," and "there," "their," and "they're." Teach the homonyms out of context, but reinforce the meaning of the homonyms by providing the opportunity for Malika to use these words in context.

4. When editing her work, provide Malika with a peer who will help her identify and correct any misspelled words.

Usage

1. Review with Malika the correct use of periods. Encourage her to place a period at the end of every complete thought. Discourage her from beginning a new sentence with the word "and."

2. Have Malika place an uppercase letter immediately after a period.

3. Tape Malika telling a story in order to assess whether the syntax and language problems are evident in both her oral and written language. If they are, Malika may benefit from receiving speech/language services. Alternatively, a speech/language consultant may collaborate with the classroom teacher to provide various language activities for Malika.

4. Teach Malika the correct subject-verb agreement with the words "nobody" and "everybody." Extend the lesson to include the words "no one" and "everyone."

5. Teach Malika a variety of sentence structures such as simple statements (declarative), questions (interrogative), and compound sentences. Provide ample opportunity for her to practice using the different sentence patterns.

6. Use the sentence-slotting technique (Poteet, 1987) and sentence-combining exercises to help Malika expand her sentences.

7. Review and provide opportunities to practice the correct use of conjunctions such as "because," "however," and "so."

8. Encourage Malika to edit her work to check for the correct use of periods and uppercase

letters. In addition, encourage Malika to edit for syntax errors by reading the assignment aloud either to herself or to a peer.

Vocabulary

1. Encourage Malika to use more complex vocabulary. Underline two or three words in each of her assignments and ask her to replace the words with more complex or descriptive ones.

2. Before assigning a descriptive paragraph, help Malika generate a number of words in different categories. For example, before writing about a teacher, help her generate five categories (e.g., physical attributes, emotional attributes, likes and dislikes, teaching style, and grading policies). Under each category, the teacher or a peer would help Malika list descriptive words (e.g., under "teaching style," she may list clear voice, steady pace, appropriate use of visuals, etc.).

Organization/Ideation

1. Help Malika develop her sense of audience. Prior to writing, help her identify the reader and encourage her to write to that specific audience.

2. Provide opportunities for the sharing of assignments. Publishing work will help Malika become more sensitive to audience needs. It will also give her a sense of purpose and encourage her to take pride in the work.

3. Although a prewriting discussion had occurred before Malika attempted either assignment, she would benefit from more structured prewriting strategies. Provide her with an appropriate graphic organizer and help her organize her thoughts into a logical order.

4. Provide Malika with the opportunity to read her essays to a peer in order to get feedback with regard to missing elements or those that need expansion. Encourage her to integrate the feedback into her work during the revision process.

5. Use a structured revision conference with Malika, such as the one presented by Moulton and Bader (1986).

Student: Wendy
Grade: 6th
Assignment: A Halloween story

Wendy was asked to write an imaginary story that could have occurred on Halloween night. Other than being provided with the spelling of the word "Halloween," she received no assistance. When asked to read her assignment immediately upon its completion, Wendy was able to capture most of the thoughts that she had written. In contrast, a delayed oral retelling did not match the written transcription but was a vivid, well-sequenced narrative. When reading her story the following day, Wendy pointed along with the text but did not attempt to match her spoken and written words. Wendy is motivated to write and states that she wants to be an author when she grows up. She adds, somewhat shyly, that she hopes to hire a personal secretary.

Analysis

Handwriting/Appearance

Despite an inconsistent slant, Wendy's letter formation and handwriting are adequate. The writing, however, is basically illegible because of poor sound-symbol or grapheme-phoneme correspondence. In addition, the bluntness of the pencil lead makes it difficult to discern some of the letters, particularly *e* and *l*.

Spelling

A few sight words are spelled correctly throughout the story (e.g., *the*, *was*, *which*, *that*, *good*, *doing*, *going*, *night*, and *I*) and a few phrases (e.g., *old man*, *there was now*, *I like to get*, and *I am going to the mall*). Limited knowledge of sound-symbol correspondence is apparent in her spellings of a number of words, such as *chope* for "costume shop," *flitessati* and *feitsstis* for "fantasy candles," *dric* and *dellt* for "dressed," *feull* for "fatal blow," and *fat* for "ballet dancer." Wendy sometimes fails to represent the correct number of syllables in a word (e.g., *prelp* for "purple," *chron* for "children," and *side* for "excited"). She has not yet mastered many orthographic patterns, writing *chot* for "costume," *aing* for "away," and *yohn* for "year." The limited sound-symbol correspondence makes further analysis

difficult. The reader must, to a large extent, rely on Wendy's memory of what she has written because many of the words are unrecognizable.

Usage

Wendy indents her opening paragraph and provides clear margins on both sides of the paper. She does not use any punctuation marks in the sample. With the exception of the word "I," she does not use uppercase letters. Although several syntactic errors were evident in Wendy's first retelling of her story when she was attempting to decipher her writing, no errors occurred in her delayed retelling.

Vocabulary/Organization/Ideation

As evidenced by her oral retellings, Wendy has some ideas to share. She chooses some interesting phrases, such as *green and purple fantasy candles* and *fatal blow* and tries to develop her plot. Until Wendy's written work has improved sufficiently to make it legible, it is impossible to evaluate vocabulary, organization, and ideation.

Recommendations

Accommodations

1. Do not assess Wendy's knowledge through writing. Provide oral projects and examinations. Alternatively, encourage Wendy to work with a peer who has good writing skill but needs help with ideas so that both students will benefit from each other.

Handwriting/Appearance

1. Encourage Wendy to keep her pencil sharpened at all times. Explain to her how a sharp pencil makes her words easier to read and will help the overall appearance of the work. Wendy may benefit from using a pen or mechanical pencil rather than the typical lead pencil.

Spelling

1. Teach Wendy sound-symbol correspondence. Dictate short words and have her write the initial letter.
2. As skill develops, progress to combinations of letters (e.g., blends, digraphs). Stress the spelling of words that follow similar simple

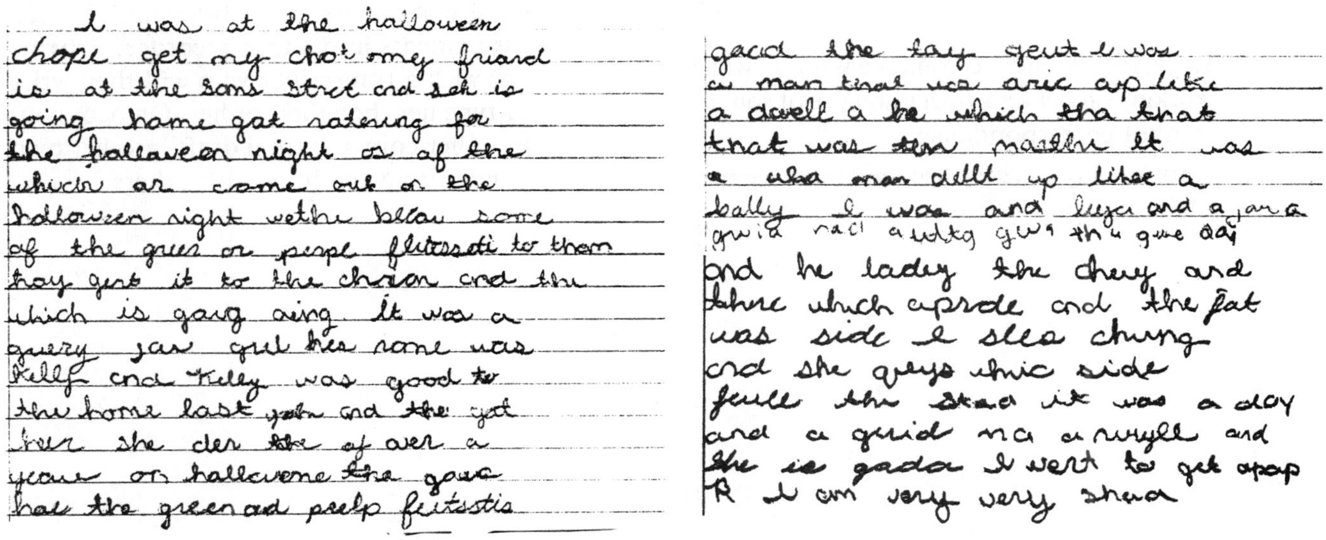

Semi-translation (as read by Wendy immediately after writing):

I was at the Halloween costume shop get my costume. My friend is at the same street and she is going home get something for the Halloween night because of the witch can come out on the Halloween night. Witches blow out some of the green and purple fantasy candles too. Then they give it to the children and the witch is going away. It was a very beautiful girl. Her name was Kelly and Kelly was going to the home last year and they got her. She was captive there for over a year. On Halloween they gave her the green and purple fantasy candles to see who they'd get. It was a man that was dressed up like a devil and the witch thought that that was bad. Magic happened, it was a old men dressed up like a ballet dancer. I was scared and later on the devil gave him a little girl though the girl was a boy and he loaded the firearm and the witch exploded and the ballet dancer was excited. I saved the child and she gave him such a fatal blow the man died. It was next day and a girl had a candle and she is my guardian. I have to get an operation. I am very, very scared.

Figure 8–15. A creative writing assignment written by Wendy, a sixth-grade student.

patterns (e.g., the *at* family) and patterns that she uses in writing (e.g., the *ight* family).

3. Encourage generalization of the spelling patterns to her assignments. Be sure to notice newly learned patterns in Wendy's written work and reinforce her.

4. Through games involving clapping and skipping, teach Wendy that the number of syllables heard in a word relates to word length. Encourage her to place a vowel in every syllable.

5. Teach Wendy a spelling strategy that will help her sequence sounds in words, using a method such as an adaptation of Gillingham and Stillman's Simultaneous Oral Spelling (SOS) (Bradley, 1981, 1983).

6. Once grapheme-phoneme correspondence has improved, teach Wendy common sight words with irregular spelling patterns through a multisensory approach such as the Modified Adapted Fernald Technique (Sutaria, 1984).

7. In conjunction with working on her spelling, teach Wendy beginning keyboarding skills. As her spelling becomes phonetic, encourage Wendy to use the spell checker.

Usage

1. Help Wendy identify where periods belong.

2. Remind Wendy to begin the word following a period with an uppercase letter.

3. Provide help with editing. Use a guided proofreading strategy, such as the procedure described by Mehlmann and Waters (1985), to help her develop independence in editing.

Ideation

1. Encourage Wendy to continue writing, while working on her knowledge and use of sound-symbol correspondence.
2. Until Wendy's writing becomes more legible, have her dictate her stories and written assignments into a tape recorder. Provide her with a transcriber who will then write or type her thoughts for her. On occasion, have her copy the final draft into her own handwriting to share with others.

Student: Rosa
Grade: 7th
Assignment: A story using spelling words

For this assignment, Rosa was asked to write a story using her high-frequency spelling words, some of which were homonyms. The list included the words: *want, think, thing, would, wood, witch, which, there, their, while, were, where, wait, through, war,* and *wore.*

Analysis

Handwriting

Rosa begins her assignment with cursive writing and then, after two words, shifts to manuscript. Throughout the assignment, she intersperses a few words written in cursive. Although most words are legible, her spacing is inconsistent between words and between letters within words.

Spelling

Although the majority of Rosa's assigned words are spelled correctly, she spells additional words incorrectly. For example, she spells "him" as *hem*, "says" as *ses*, and "clothes" as *cloes*. At the end of the passage, Rosa seems to tire of the assignment and so she lists many of the remaining words. She writes one unknown word: *wersht*.

Usage

Rosa writes her name and the lesson period at the top of the paper: *Prod 1*. She begins her story with an uppercase letter. She uses two periods throughout the story: one after the first thought and one after the last sentence. She uses commas correctly when listing her remaining spelling words. Nearly, all of Rosa's sentences are joined by the word "and."

Organization/Ideation

In this sample, Rosa appears to have difficulty expressing her ideas. Her confusion with language is illustrated in the first sentence: *I would be at school today because today is the last day and I want to think that I am here.* Her spelling story evolves into a stream of consciousness where Rosa seems to write whatever thought comes into her mind.

Although several of her spelling words are used semicorrectly in context (i.e., *which cat is it a witch cat*), some are not (i.e., *and I went it at the wood*). Her focus seems to be more on using all of her spelling words than upon generating sensible content.

Rosa's writing lacks clarity of purpose. A topic is not selected or maintained throughout the story. Actions are not presented within a sequence, nor are ideas presented logically. She does not acknowledge or consider her audience. She begins her story with herself as the main character using the personal pronoun "I" and then shifts to the characters of some people and a man and a woman. Over-relying on the words *and, this, to,* the man and the woman seem then to engage in some type of nonsensical dialogue, the purpose of which is to use the remaining spelling words.

Recommendations

Although some problems are evident in all areas, Rosa's greatest difficulty with this particular assignment is in creating logical text.

General

1. Examine additional samples of Rosa's writing. If the quality is similar to this, focus remedial efforts upon the meaningful communication of ideas, rather than upon basic skills.

2. Assuming supportive evidence from additional sources, it appears that Rosa requires a thorough evaluation from a speech-language therapist to assess both general communication abilities and pragmatic language skills. Incorporate the recommendations that evolve from this evaluation into Rosa's educational programming.

Handwriting

1. Find out whether Rosa feels most comfortable with manuscript or cursive handwriting. Encourage her to use her preferred style consistently.

2. Remind Rosa to space letters appropriately within and between words. When writing a final draft, encourage her to leave a consistent space between words.

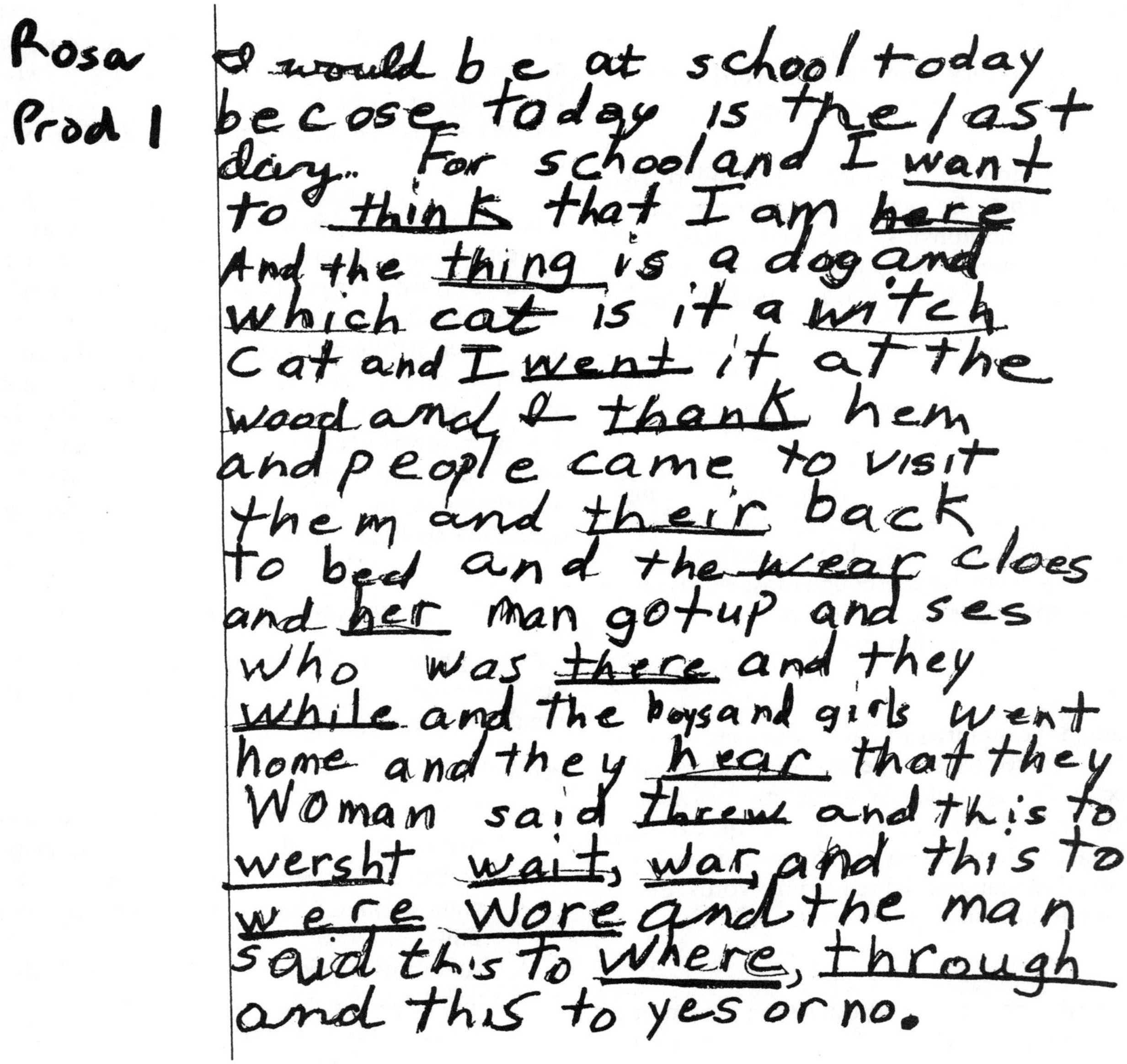

Rosa
Prod 1

I ~~would~~ be at school today becose today is the last day.. For school and I want to ~~think~~ that I am ~~here~~ And the ~~thing~~ is a dog and which cat is it a ~~witch~~ Cat and I ~~went~~ it at the ~~wood~~ and I ~~thank~~ hem and people came to visit them and ~~their~~ back to bed and the ~~wear~~ cloes and ~~her~~ man got up and ses who was ~~there~~ and they ~~while~~ and the boys and girls went home and they ~~hear~~ that they Woman said ~~threw~~ and this to wersht ~~wait~~, war, and this to were ~~Wore~~ and the man said this to ~~Where~~, ~~through~~ and this to yes or no.

Figure 8–16. A story using the week's spelling words by Rosa, a seventh-grade student.

Spelling

1. Provide assistance with spelling in the editing stage.
2. Ensure that Rosa is able to use her spelling words in meaningful contexts.

Usage

1. Teach Rosa how to write simple sentences. Begin with concrete tasks. For example, have her write a sentence that describes what is happening in a picture.

2. Provide Rosa with practice placing periods at the end of short, simple sentences and capitalizing the first word in sentences.
3. Review with Rosa how to write different types of sentence patterns: simple statements (declarative), questions (interrogative), and compound sentences. Begin by having her write declarative sentences that answer simple questions.

Organization/Ideation

1. Provide writing assignments that have a

clear purpose so that Rosa will understand why she is writing. Ensure that she understands what she is doing and why she is doing it. Provide opportunities for her to share her writing with others.

2. Prior to writing, help Rosa identify appropriate topics. Place an emphasis on prewriting activities, such as brainstorming followed by semantic mapping, so that Rosa's ideas will be organized when she writes. Use graphic organizers, semantic mapping, or the K-W-L strategy (Ogle, 1986) to help her organize ideas and clarify the relationships among her ideas. Have Rosa discuss the relationships among the ideas and details before writing.

3. Initially, it may be necessary to pair Rosa with a peer who will help her sequence and organize her ideas during writing.

4. Teach Rosa how to write short paragraphs that follow a narrative sequence. Begin with a series of picture cards that illustrate a sequence of events and have her write a sentence about each card. Further activities are available in the *Phelps Sentence Guide Program* (Phelps-Terasaki & Phelps, 1980).

5. Show Rosa how to use sequence words, such as *first*, *then*, *next*, and *finally*. Use paragraph frames such as those adapted from Nichols (1980). Samples of these frames are provided in Chapter 7.

6. As skill improves, teach Rosa how to organize expository paragraphs by using a strategy such as statement-pie (Hanau, 1974; Wallace & Bott, 1989). Model how to write a main idea statement and then develop several related supporting sentences. Provide systematic practice with multiple examples until she can use this format to write paragraphs.

7. Help Rosa develop her ability to identify and consider the audience when writing. As a prewriting activity, discuss audience considerations. Have her identify who the audience is and what information they will require. During editing, help Rosa clarify any confusing ideas.

Student: Felicia
Grade: 7th
Assignments: Eight first drafts

Eight short samples, written over a 2-month period for her writing portfolio, are included for Felicia. The first three samples present her views on reading and spelling. The fourth was in response to an assignment to write about something she would like to invent. The fifth is a description of how she feels about gum and the sixth is a descriptive paragraph about how the moon looks. The seventh sample is a sequential paragraph on how to make a pumpkin pie. The last sample is an excerpt from a several-page short story entitled "The Rodeo."

Analysis

Handwriting

Felicia's handwriting is inconsistent, with some samples being neater than others. She uses cursive writing on some samples and manuscript on others. In both styles, her slant is inconsistent, as are the sizes of the spaces between words, and the sizes of the letters themselves. In her cursive writing, she tends to extend letters that go underneath the line too far horizontally to the left, particularly the letters *y* and *g*. Felicia's observation of left and right margins is also inconsistent among samples.

Spelling

Felicia's greatest area of difficulty is spelling. In a few instances, she transposes letters or shows confusion regarding letter order (e.g., *brid* for "bird," *tow* for "two," and *firnd* for "friend"). Overall, her spelling is phonetic. On a few words she elongates sounds or makes phonetic overgeneralizations (e.g., *awer* for "our," and *nexcst* for "next"). Analyses of all of her samples indicate limited mastery of high-frequency words. As examples from the last story, she spells the word "was" as *wase*, "from" as *frum*, "what" as *wat*, "said" as *sed*, "were" as *wroe*, and "one" as *won*.

In general, Felicia appears to lack awareness of common English spelling patterns and has difficulty remembering how words look. She misspells high-frequency words, writing "were" as *wore*, "take" as *taeke* and *tacke*, "after" as *aftre*, "said" as *sed*, and "try" as *tiay* and *triy*. Occasionally, she omits entire syllables from words (e.g., *being* for "beginning" and *rill* for "really"). In one instance, Felicia combines two separate words into one word (e.g., *wiptoping* for "whipped topping"), and on two other instances, she separates one word into two (e.g., *all so* for "also" and *all was* for "always"). Inconsistencies in spellings can also be noted across samples. As examples, the word "they" is spelled as *thae* and *thay*, and "were" is spelled as *wroe* and *wore*. Finally, Felicia has written the word *to* on one occasion instead of "too."

Usage

Felicia's use of ending punctuation is inconsistent across samples. On some samples, she punctuates her sentences correctly, whereas on others she expresses her thoughts in complete sentences but does not place a period at the end of the sentence. Although she uses dialogue in her Rodeo story, she does not use quotation marks, but instead encloses the dialogue in parentheses.

Vocabulary

Although the vocabulary is not complex and her descriptions are not detailed, Felicia's choice of words is appropriate for the topics.

Organization and Ideation

Despite significant difficulties with spelling, Felicia is willing to attempt to write her ideas. Several samples reveal a good sense of humor as well as a creative approach to the topic. For example, Felicia writes that after one assembles a pumpkin pie, one should: " . . . put all of the whip topping on it so you can't taste the pie." In another sample, she describes the moon as a "giant trampoline." When asked what she would like to invent, she decides upon a computer that could write great stories by working off of brain waves.

In general, Felicia sequences her ideas appropriately and uses cohesive ties to unify her paragraphs. In describing a picture, she first describes what one of the girls is doing, and then discusses what the other two girls are doing. In writing about the appearance of the moon, she begins by describing the first side and then describing the second side. Similarly, she describes the two things that make her mad. In addition, the action in the Rodeo story is carefully sequenced to build suspense.

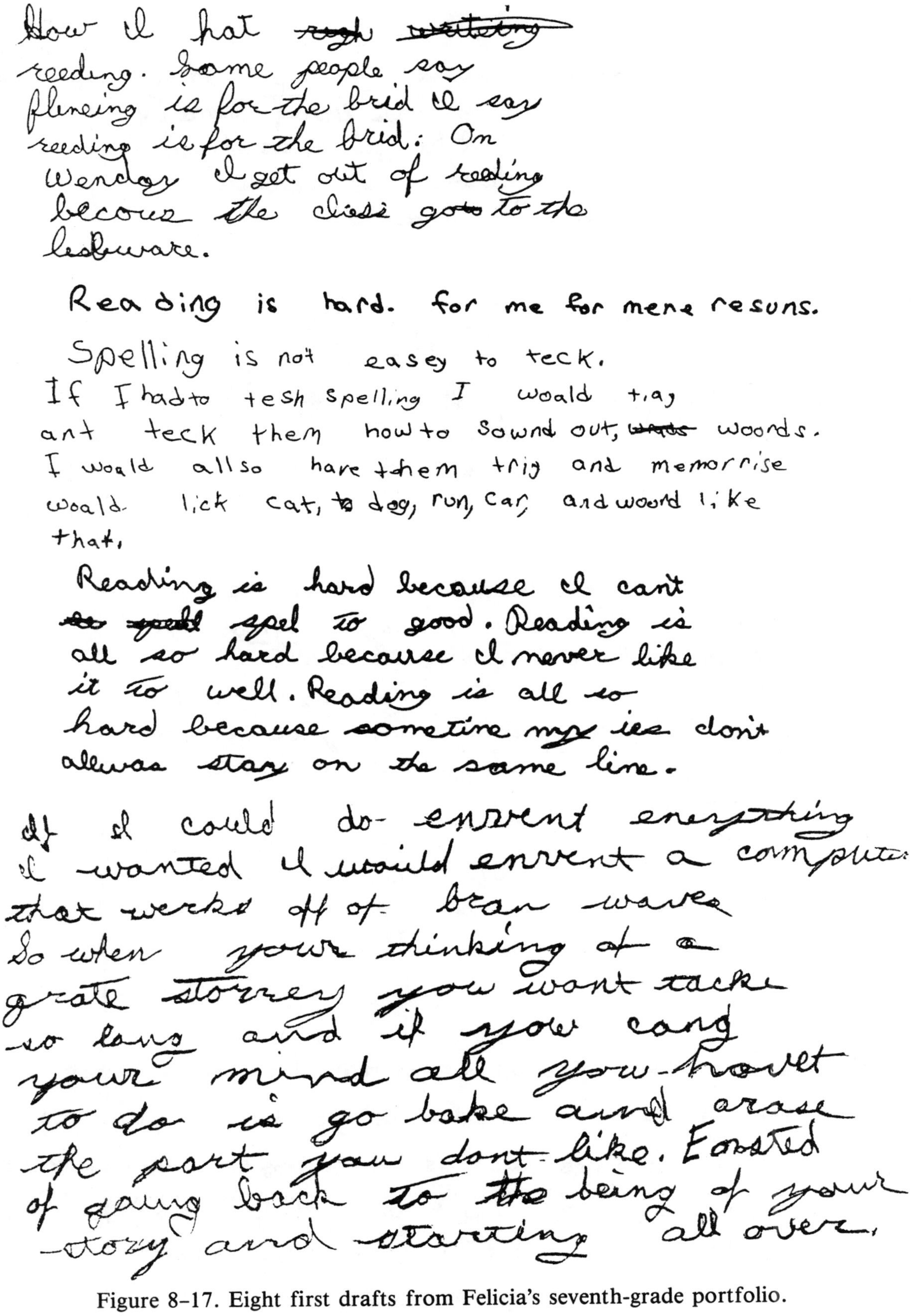

How I hat ~~righ~~ ~~witting~~
reeding. Some people say
flincing is for the brid I say
reeding is for the brid. On
Wendsy I get out of reeding
becouse the class goes to the
lesbware.

Reading is hard. for me for mene resuns.

Spelling is not easey to teck.
If I had to tesh Spelling I woald tiay
ant teck them how to Sownd out, ~~wrds~~ woords.
I woald allso have them trig and memorrise
woald lick cat, ~~to~~ dog, run, car, and woord like
that,

Reading is hard because I can't
~~so~~ ~~spel~~ spel to ~~good~~. Reading is
all so hard because I never like
it ~~to~~ well. Reading is all so
hard because ~~sometine~~ ~~my~~ ies don't
alwas ~~stay~~ on the same line.

If I could do ~~envent~~ enenthing
I wanted I would envent a compute
that werks of of bran waves
So when your thinking of a
grate ~~storrey~~ you want tacke
so lang and if you cang
your mind all you ~~have~~
to do is go bake and arase
the part you dont like. Enstad
of going back ~~to~~ ~~the~~ being of your
~~story~~ and ~~starting~~ all over.

Figure 8–17. Eight first drafts from Felicia's seventh-grade portfolio.

If thar wasnt ensaled thing as
gum most of my frind would
die. I rill like gum and if
I wore a techer I would
let the cid cow gum.

I think the Moon is like
a gient tranpolen. The Moon has
tow side. The first side is all
was facing the sun and the Erth.
the senhent side is all was deke.

Get a Pumpken a pie crest
and a hol lote of wiptopsing.
then Zhen make a holl in
the pumpkin and take ot out
all of the junk and pot it
in the pie crest and then
cookit Cook it. Wem
it is done pot all of the
wipsoping on it so you
cant tae the pie.

SUM won frum the rot was wons no her. He went oven to her
aftre the rase and sed (Woad you Licka god thes
roteow seasoned) wat is it? Riting on awertem wet you
hors we net a good rite and if you woad(oh yes!! ohyes!!)
we praktes oh saturday all be thar.

Figure 8–17 (cont.).

With the exception of the Rodeo story, Felicia's samples are relatively short and lack detail. On a few of the assignments, Felicia does not appear to be motivated to write or does not have much to write about. In her discussion of the story read in class, she notes that she did not like how boring it was and the title sounded stupid. In describing her activities over the weekend, she notes that she did not do much.

Recommendations

General

1. Place emphasis upon encouraging Felicia to write and develop her ideas. Do not penalize her for poor spelling in any of her classes.
2. Encourage Felicia to work with a competent peer editor during the revision and editing stages of writing.

Handwriting

1. Discuss with Felicia ways to improve her legibility. Provide models of correct formation for letters that extend below the line.
2. Encourage Felicia to observe margins. Have her use one of her assignments in which margins have been observed as a model.
3. Teach Felicia keyboarding skills. As her skill improves, encourage Felicia to type all of her assignments.

Spelling

1. Encourage Felicia to master the spelling of high-frequency words. Develop a flow list that contains three to five words for her to practice daily. Begin with words misspelled in her writing.
2. Felicia is likely to benefit from a multisensory whole-word approach to spelling. An example would be the Fernald method (Fernald, 1943) or an adaptation of the Fernald method for spelling. For the latter, use the following steps: (a) write the word to be learned on a card and pronounce it; (b) have Felicia repeat the word and then trace the word with a finger as many times as needed to write the word from memory; (c) remove the word and have Felicia write the word from memory. Have her then check her spelling with the original.
3. Help Felicia develop an individualized list of high-frequency words for easy reference.
4. Encourage Felicia to continue to write approximations of words that she wishes to spell during the drafting phase. Provide Felicia with direct instruction to correct her misspellings during the postwriting phase. Provide feedback in a positive, nonpunitive manner.
5. As spelling skill improves, teach Felicia how to use a spell checker to edit her own work.
6. Provide opportunities for Felicia to write her stories on a word processor so that corrections for the final draft will be easier to make.

Usage

1. Using a story like the Rodeo, determine if Felicia is able to identify sentence boundaries. Have her read the story aloud and mark where each sentence ends. If she is unsuccessful, read the story aloud to her, pausing at the end of each sentence. Have her place in the ending punctuation.
2. Teach Felicia how to use quotation marks for dialogue. Provide practice writing short conversations between two speakers.

Ideation

1. Provide opportunities for Felicia to develop her ideas prior to writing. Remind her that she will not be penalized for spelling and that, when writing, she should attempt to write any word that she wants to use.
2. Encourage Felicia to work on writing assignments for at least one-half hour daily. When evaluating her writing assignments in English classes, place emphasis foremost upon content and increased productivity. Have her continue to keep a portfolio of her work so that she is able to see her progress.

Student: Helen
Grade: 7th
Assignment: Descriptive essay

Instead of writing a descriptive essay entitled *A Person I Shall Never Forget*, Helen wrote a narrative essay. Her introduction was consistent with the assignment, but she quickly veered off track. Apart from being given the title, no prewriting activities were conducted.

Analysis

Handwriting/Appearance

Although Helen tends to have an inconsistent slant in her cursive writing, the words are legible and formed correctly. Some variability exists, however, in her letter size. She leaves a space to create a boundary between each word, but the space tends to be too large. Helen has not indented her paragraph. Although margins have been observed, the appearance of the assignment is marred by overzealous scribbling and the numbering of lines.

Spelling

On this assignment, spelling does not appear to be a problem for Helen. One reason is that the majority of words that she writes are simple and repeated several times. Her spelling of the words "with" as *wiht* and "Chris" as *Chisr* suggests that she may have experienced spelling problems in earlier grades. Helen uses a few words incorrectly, writing *to* instead of "too" and *won't* for "want."

Usage

Helen correctly capitalizes the first letter of her story. She does not use any periods in the 27 carefully counted lines. She remembers to capitalize the first word in the name "Big Boy," and capitalizes the word "I" throughout the story. No commas or quotation marks are used throughout the assignment even though the majority of the story is written as dialogue.

Inconsistencies may be noted in verb tense. Helen begins by writing in the past tense, changes to the present, reverts to the past tense, and then back to the present tense for the dialogue. In addition, subject-verb agreement is incorrect in at least one instance (i.e., *he like me*), and possibly in another (i.e., *he doesn't like me*) where the error could be due to incorrect usage or spelling.

Vocabulary

The vocabulary used is simple and uninteresting. Only four words longer than one syllable are written: *going, Honda, sometime,* and *puppy.*

Organization/Ideation

The assignment is not the requested descriptive essay but, rather, a narrative one. Within the framework of a narrative, the dialogue is somewhat disorganized and uninteresting. The assignment begins with an introduction of Chris, then moves on to someone wanting to hurt him. Chris then appears to become a "cool" person. The discussion then moves to Chris's dog who does not appear to like many people, and from there to the writer's dog. Adding confusion to the story is the lack of a clear reference. Apart from Chris, no other person is introduced though "my friend" is referred to several times.

In addition, some problems with ideation occur. Helen seems to write a lot of words but her story is not well developed. The content is dull and some of the thoughts are difficult to understand (e.g., *he be nice to kid if a boy play*).

Recommendations

Handwriting/Appearance

1. Encourage Helen to indent each paragraph.
2. Discourage numbering of lines. Look over some passages in books with Helen and discuss why authors do not number each written line.
3. Suggest that Helen leave a slightly smaller space in between words.
4. To increase self-monitoring of the appearance of her work, teach Helen the HOW strategy (Archer, 1988).

Spelling

1. Using a visual strategy such as the look-cover-write method (Kirk & Chalfant, 1984), review the spelling of high-frequency words, such as "with." Select words that are misspelled in her writing.

1. There was a man that was

2. be a nerd to my friend

3. his name is chior he is very

4. mean cool to me he was sad I scind said

5. Im going to hurt you you are not

6. yes am going to hurt you ok

7. you won ok I get to hurt you

8. yes you can hurt me ok but I

9. don't wont to fine then I like you

10. you are cool chior do you like cars

11. yes I do good I have a lot

12. of them they are cool hot honds

13. I have a big car to for you

14. to play wiht I have 3 big dog

15. they are cool they are mean

16. to my friend I do not like

Figure 8–18. A descriptive essay written by Helen, a seventh-grade student.

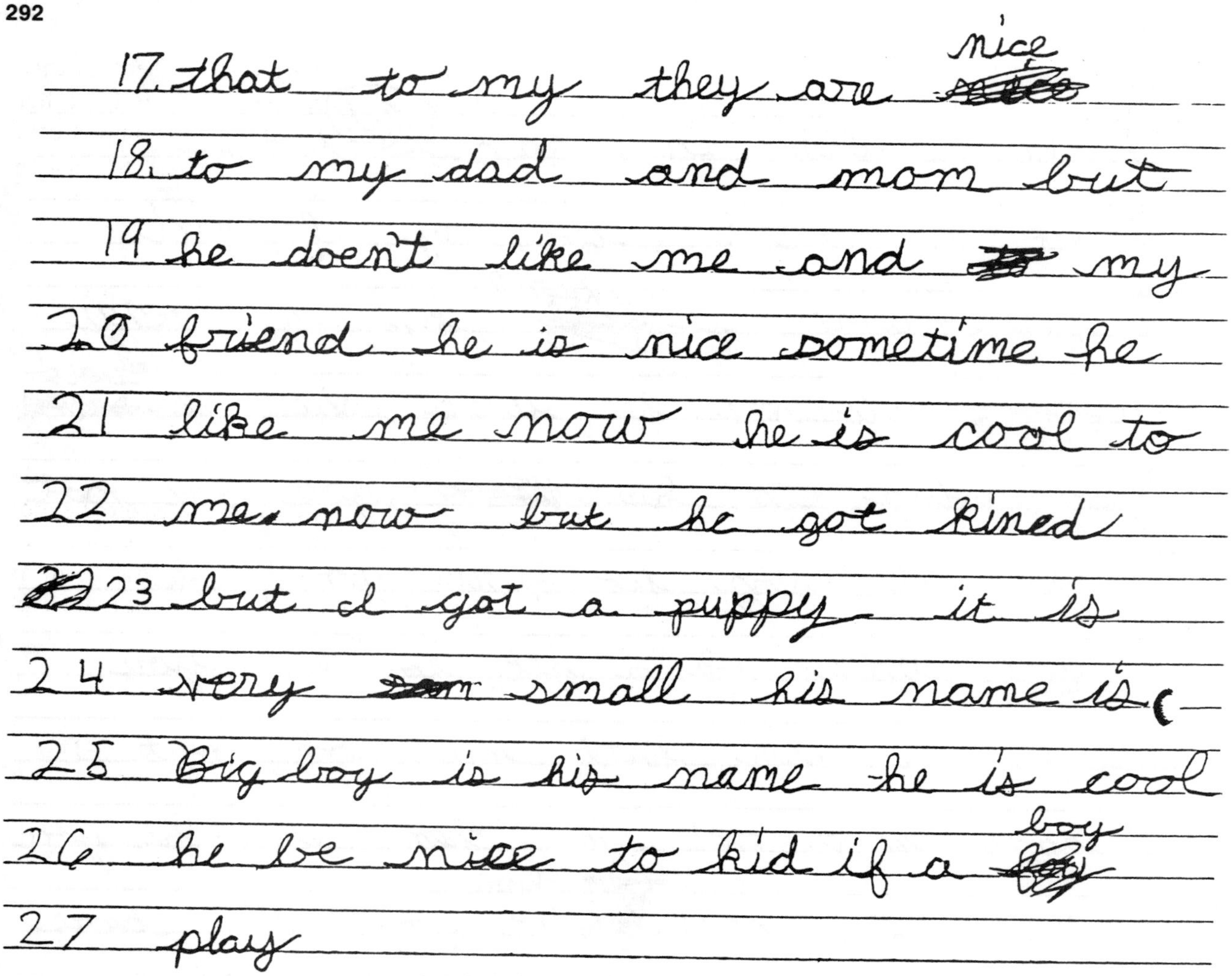

17. that to my they are ~~nice~~ nice

18. to my dad and mom but

19. he doesn't like me and ~~the~~ my

20. friend he is nice sometime he

21. like me now he is cool to

22. me now but he got kined

23. but I got a puppy it is

24. very ~~sam~~ small his name is (

25. Big boy is his name he is cool

26. he be nice to kid if a ~~boy~~ boy

27. play

Figure 8–18 (cont.)

Usage

1. Encourage Helen to place a period after each complete thought. Give her help checking for the correct use of periods in the editing stage.

2. Review the use of uppercase letters. Begin with the use of uppercase letters to start each sentence and in proper nouns.

3. Teach or review all other punctuation marks in the order suggested by Cohen and Plaskon (1980).

4. Review usage rules pertaining to subject-verb agreement and verb tense. Provide Helen with the opportunity to work with the teacher or a peer with advanced writing skill in editing her work.

5. Teach Helen a variety of sentence structures and reinforce her attempt to use them. Use a sentence-slotting strategy (Poteet, 1987) or sentence-combining exercises to help her increase sentence complexity.

6. Show Helen how sentences can be combined together using a variety of conjunctions. Provide her with ample opportunity combining sentences. Reinforce her when she generalizes the skill into her written assignments.

7. Have Helen skip lines when writing her first drafts. Provide Helen with the time and help needed to edit her work. Have her write edits in the space above each line. Have her write the final draft using each line.

8. Teach COPS (Schumaker et al., 1981) or SCOPE (Bos & Vaughn, 1994) as an error-monitoring strategy for use in the editing process.

Vocabulary

1. Help Helen develop a personalized thesaurus and encourage her to use the new words in her written assignments.
2. Use a prewriting strategy to help enhance vocabulary, such as the Self-Control Strategy (Harris & Graham, 1985).
3. In the editing stage, underline a few words and help Helen replace them with synonyms that are more complex and descriptive. Remind Helen to add these words to her thesaurus.
4. Use structural analysis maps to show Helen how the addition of morphemes alters word meaning. Provide practice using the various forms of words within sentences.

Organization/Ideation

1. Have Helen spend a lot of time on prewriting activities. Use different types of graphic organizers to help her sequence her thoughts. Encourage her to use the ideas from her graphic organizers as she writes her story. For example, use an organizer shaped as a star. Have Helen shade in each point of the star after she has included the information in her story or essay.
2. Review the elements in a story (Montague & Graves, 1993).
3. Teach Helen a prewriting strategy, such as C-SPACE (MacArthur et al., 1991).
4. Use a writing process approach intervention, such as the one described by Wong et al. (1991).
5. Teach Helen how to write different types of expository paragraphs. Begin with a sequential paragraph. When this form is mastered, teach her how to write a descriptive paragraph.

Student: Tyler
Grade: 8th
Assignment: Story about a famous mathematician, final draft

Tyler was asked to write a report about a famous mathematician for his eighth-grade Algebra class. He chose Albert Einstein. Prior to writing the first draft, Tyler had engaged in library research and had written notecards. He wrote a first draft and received feedback from his teacher. He recopied his paper, attempting to incorporate the feedback. The following paper is the final draft that he submitted.

Analysis

Handwriting/Appearance

Although not attractive in appearance, Tyler's handwriting is adequate. He indents paragraphs and observes the left margin. Sometimes he writes all the way over to the right side of the paper, but at other times he does not. He tends to leave too much space between words and occasionally does not write on the line.

Spelling

Tyler's spelling is inconsistent and seems more representative of a first draft of a report, rather than the final written product. Although the spellings are nearly correct, Tyler misspells several high-frequency words (e.g., *whith* for "with," *quite* for "quiet," and *sleap* for "sleep"), but then spells several more difficult words correctly (e.g., *charitable, intelligent,* and *distinguish*). He is inconsistent in his application of spelling rules. He does not change the "y" to an "i" when adding an ending (e.g., *discoverys*). Although he usually adds "ed" to form past tense, he simply adds a "d" to a few words (e.g., *faild,* and *learnd*.) He omits a few letters (e.g., *brea down, relitily,* and *daugter*). In addition, Tyler is inconsistent in his spelling of several words. He spells "probably" as *probaly* and *probabaly*. He is unsure of how to spell Einstein's name. Throughout the report, he spells it as: *Eienstien, Einstien, Einsten,* and *Einstein*.

Usage

Many of Tyler's sentences do not end with periods. He rarely capitalizes the first word in a sentence. Tyler does not capitalize several proper nouns (e.g., *abert* [Albert], *germany, jews, isreal, princeton,* and *rosevelt*). On two occasions, he does not include apostrophes to show possession (e.g., *Alberts mother,* and *Einstiens father*) but on another occasion he does (e.g., *Albert's parents)*.

Vocabulary

Although Tyler attempts to make his writing interesting, he seems to have some difficulty selecting specfic words. For example, he writes: *In 1917 a heart breakdown occurred.* He writes that Einstein hated war and . . . *did many charitable causes against it.* A few examples are imprecise and the words are more appropriate for informal oral discourse, rather than written. For example, he notes that Albert was "lousy" at school. In his conclusion, he notes that he discovered that Einstein was more intelligent than he thought, but to the few who think he's a "nerd," this book will probably show them wrong.

Organization/Ideation

Tyler has acquired a lot of information about the life of Albert Einstein. His biographic report is filled with interesting details. He writes an introduction, several paragraphs ordered chronologically, and a concluding paragraph that reiterates his purpose. He begins with Albert's birth and progresses until his death.

Tyler's greatest difficulty seems to come from integrating his own ideas with the ideas that he has gathered through research. As a result, a few of his written thoughts are difficult to comprehend. Although Tyler's intent may be inferred, the words he selects seem to confuse his purpose. For example, he writes: *Albert was quite a child* (a quiet child?). *There was nothing to distinguish him from a future leader.* In the same paragraph, he states: *Einstein was lousy at school who said a teacher "could not make success of anything."* In discussing Albert's first wife, he writes: . . . *she was the only one who failed the final test. No one knew why he married her.* Tyler writes that in 1914, his name crossed the globe: . . . *the last thing he expected "fame."* In describing Einstein's death, he writes: *he died at*

albert was born on twelfth of
March 1879 in Ulm a small Town
in Southern germany Alberts mother
came From a family whith Concider able
welth. Two years before albert
was born his mother helped Herman
Eienstien to set up a small workshop
They helped again when the bisness
Failed a year after abert was born
they moved to a nearby city,
Muvich Einstiens father was well
meaning but did not work
seriously enough.
        Albert's Parents were jews
but not very serious on retigion When
it was time to go to school
for albert went to catolic school
at age five Albert was aquite
child there was nothing to distinquish
him from a future leader.
at age 7 he learned algabra from
his uncle they were very close
Einstien was lousy at school who
Said a teacher could not make sucseed
of any thing"
    In 1903 he married Maleva
maric the daughter of a slav
pesent family she was the
only one who faild the Final test.
one one knew why he married her.

Einsten had two sons,
·Hans albert and Eduard six years
later.

ReBort
180
Math

Figure 8–19. A short story written by Tyler, an eighth-grade student.

later he opend a private lessons
it consisted of three he
probaly opened it for more knowledge
. in 1917 a heart brea down occured
and in 1919 married Elsa his cousin
and devorced his first wife.
by 1914 his hame crosed
the globe the last thing he
expected "Fame"
    Einstien like most people hated
war and did many charitable causes
agianst it.
    He wrote Franklin resevelt that
the atomic bomb coutd be constructed.
einstien warked Hard oh the idea
he thought it would end war.
in 1952 Chaim Weizmann. died
the pres of isreal Albert was
asked and Albert refused.
the end came in 1a55 he
died at age 75 in Prineton
in his sleap. after 2 operations.
it was time to "die, so be it".

Albert Einstein and relitivly showed
me that Einztein was much
more intelligent than I thought
an to the few that think hes a neard
or odd this book will probabaly
Show them wrong. the way I wrote
this is not all about his
discoverys but to Explain his
life and how it was

Figure 8-19 (cont.).

age 75 in Princeton in his sleep after two operations. It was time to die so be it.

Several of the paragraphs contain ideas about Einstein's life and family that are not clearly interrelated. For example, within the second paragraph, Tyler notes that Albert's parents were Jews who were not very serious "on religion" so that when it was time to go to school, Albert went to Catholic school. He goes on to note that Albert learned algebra from his uncle and that they were close.

Tyler makes erroneous assumptions with regard to the background knowledge of the reader. For example, he writes that Albert opened *a private lessons that consisted of three.* It is unclear to the reader, what the private lessons are and how they consisted of three. Near the end of his report, he notes that when the President of Israel died, Albert was asked and he refused. The reader is left to wonder: Was Albert Einstein asked to be President of Israel?

Recommendations

Handwriting/Computer

1. Provide opportunities for Tyler to write on a computer. Help him develop keyboarding skills so that he will be able to use a laptop to take classnotes, draft papers, and prepare final drafts.

Spelling

1. De-emphasize the importance of spelling. Discuss spelling only when Tyler is ready to edit his paper. Provide assistance so that Tyler can correct the majority of his misspellings prior to preparing his final draft.
2. During an editing conference, discuss with Tyler any patterns observed in his spelling. For example, review with Tyler a few common spelling rules (e.g., when a word ending in *y* is made plural, drop the *y* and add *ies*; when adding an ending starting with a vowel, double the final consonant to maintain the short vowel sound).
3. Have Tyler proofread his paper for spelling errors, underlining all words that he thinks are spelled incorrectly. Teach him how to use a pocket-sized, spelling checker to determine the correct spellings. When pro-

ficient with a computer, Tyler can use the spell checker in the word processing program.

Usage

1. Assist Tyler with proofreading his paper for spelling and usage errors. Instead of marking the specific errors on his paper, put a check in the margin by any line that contains an error in spelling, capitalization, or punctuation. If two mistakes occur in the line, place two checks. Have Tyler try to find and correct the errors in each line. Have a peer provide assistance when necessary.
2. Check that Tyler has identified the majority of usage errors prior to writing his final draft.
3. Work on placement of periods at the end of a sentence. Read the draft aloud or ask Tyler to read his piece aloud in order to develop a sense of where periods ought to be placed. When needed, repeat this process to ascertain the placement of commas after introductory clauses.
4. Review the use of an apostrophe to show possession.

Vocabulary

1. Help Tyler learn to recognize ambiguity in his choice of words and provide clarification.
2. Teach Tyler different cohesive ties that can be used in reports organized by chronology (e.g., *first, then, later, finally*). Show him how to write a transition sentence between paragraphs.
3. Encourage Tyler to continue to attempt to use new words in his writing. Have him use a thesaurus to select more precise synonyms.

Organization/Ideation

1. Help Tyler learn how to incorporate research results into his papers. Teach him a system for taking notes and then organizing his notes into a coherent report.
2. Through questioning, help Tyler clarify passages that may confuse his reader. Help him then elaborate points so the purpose is clear.
3. Teach Tyler how to evaluate the organization of his paper. Teach him to review the

style and point of view, the sequence of the ideas, the relevance of the details to the stated purpose, and the clarity of the message. Make suggestions for revisions, as needed.

4. Review with Tyler the major purposes of a topic sentence: introduction of the type of paragraph or essay that is being written and clear specification of what the paragraph or essay will contain. In future sessions, have Tyler develop a variety of topic sentences to introduce different types of paragraphs or essays. Tyler would benefit from activities, such as those provided in *Writing Skills 2* (King, 1993) and *Writing Skills for the Adolescent* (King, 1985).

5. As a prewriting activity, have Tyler develop a graphic organizer that will help him sequence and interrelate the ideas that he wishes to present. Each paragraph would focus on one main topic and the supporting details would extend from the topic. After the information has been gathered, help Tyler determine which facts and details do not fit with the specified topic.

6. Teach Tyler a strategy that will help him provide more detail and structure to his writing. Some examples of techniques that may be used for preplanning an essay or report would be the TREE strategy (Graham & Harris, 1989a), Kerrigan's method of composition (Kerrigan, 1979), or Spool papers (Santa, 1988).

7. Help Tyler learn to differentiate major topics from minor details as he is collecting and organizing facts for a report. Have him list all the important points and then help him think of ways to categorize the major and minor points.

8. Teach Tyler how to incorporate direct quotes from other sources into his writing.

Student: Jessica
Grade: 8th
Assignments: Five descriptive essays

The five assignments represent Jessica's attempts at writing descriptive essays. The assignments were written over a period of 5 weeks.

Analysis

Handwriting/Appearance

Tremendous variation exists in Jessica's handwriting from assignment to assignment. Although her printed samples are quite neat, the writing appears immature. The appearance of the three cursive samples varies from attractive (in the *About Kangaroo* sample) to sloppy (in the *Spring Break* sample). The handwriting in the *Dorm* sample is similar in appearance to the printed stories. All paragraphs are indented. Jessica uses titles in all of her assignments and leaves a space between the title and the body of the assignment. With the exception of the *Spring Break* sample, she centers her writing in the middle of the page, rather than observing the right and left margins.

All of Jessica's letters are formed correctly, and her writing is easy to read even when the overall appearance is sloppy. She leaves adequate space between words, but not quite enough space after a period.

Spelling

Jessica spells most words correctly. She separates a few compound words (e.g., *class room*, *baby sitter*, *Hand writing*, and *after noon*). She mistakenly writes *wishing* instead of "washing," and *dential* for "detail" and on two occasions, she sequences letters incorrectly and writes *Secince* for "Science," and *Sutdy* for "study." On a few occasions, Jessica writes a word that sounds similar to the correct word (e.g., she writes *he's* for "his," *life* for "live," *them* for "then," and *below* for "blow").

Usage

Jessica uses uppercase letters correctly most of the time, both to start new sentences and in proper nouns. On one occasion, however, she capitalizes the word "Dorm" unnecessarily, and on another, she forgets to capitalize the letter beginning a new sentence. She consistently capitalizes the word "I." She capitalizes her titles with the exception of the title: *Spring break*.

Although periods are evident in the samples, they are sometimes omitted (e.g., *Then we came back from jr. high school we go to* . . .). On one occasion, a comma is used instead of a period. Commas are used correctly in the list of school subjects but are not used in other places. No comma appears in Jessica's recording of her birth date.

Jessica's primary difficulties are in the area of usage. In general, her sentences are awkward in construction. As an example, she writes: *In my birth is April 13 I also get my gift in there my mom do the cake and I blow the candle then we eat the cake.* Jessica has not fully mastered English sentence structure and some of her sentences tend to confuse two or more patterns (e.g., *I like to do my work is Language for meaning, Hand-Writing, Math, Secince, S. Sutdy and Creative Writing that I like it,* and *They long about 7 feet long that about men*).

Although correct in her choice of verb tense most of the time, Jessica sometimes chooses the incorrect tense. For example, she writes *Sometime . . . we just sitting around,* . . . *then we came back* . . . , and *He was work at* . . . . At times, the verb is omitted as in *They (are) long, They (live) in the cave,* and . . . *that (is) all.* . . .

On occasion, Jessica uses the incorrect plural, writing *bodys* for "bodies" and *studis* for "studies." Other errors of this type include *35 miles per hours, we visit our sister,* and *wishing clothes and sock.* In one instance, she omits the "t" from "brought." This omission may be a usage rather than a spelling error, as she appears to have a tendency to omit word endings (e.g., *work* for "working" and *sometime* for "sometimes").

Jessica uses prepositions incorrectly in several places. She writes, for example: *I help . . . any people I can help with them., I always help the aids at Dorm,* and *I was over for baby sitter for my brother.* In addition, she has not yet mastered the use of the articles "a" and "the." On occasion, Jessica omits the article (e.g., *at Dorm, They live in Australia and zoo,* and . . . *we go to canteen*). At other times, Jessica misuses the article (e.g., *the Windslow,* and *a shoes*).

Dorm

In the dorm weds the wishing clothes and sock also underwear every we go to canteen and jrhigh school after school are over there then we visit our sister.

Then we came back from jrhigh school we go to dinner room with we came back from the dinner room. We do studis hour about 1 hour then we clean area and dential.

Spring break.

I had a good spring break. for one week. I went to the Yube city I was over for baby sitter for my brother. ~~He came back at Sunday~~
He was work at Yube City at Bashas. also he's wife work at Bashas, I went to the Window I brough a shoes and blouse also pants I life at home so ~~that it that~~ I came back ~~a~~ on Sunday, that all about.

Figure 8-20. Five descriptive essays written by Jessica, an eighth-grade student.

my classroom

In my classroom I do my work. I like to do my work is language for meaning, Hand-Writing, Math, Secince, S. Sutdy and Creative Writing that I like it

In after noon we do lots of work. Sometime we don't do any thing we Just sitting around.

my Self

My Self et do my work and do my thing that way all these year also I always help the cids at Dorm and class room and any people that I can help with them.

In my birth is April 13 et also get my gift in there my mom do the cake and I below the candle them we eat the cake

About Kangaroo

In the pouch the little Kangroo is sitting in it. They live in Australia and zoo and they eat grass and nuts. They run about 35 miles per hours. They long about 7 feet long. that about men. The ladies are small. They in the cave.

Figure 8-20 (cont.).

Vocabulary

The vocabulary used is adequate but, at times, not precise. For example, Jessica writes about doing her work and her "thing," about her mom "doing" her birthday cake, and about herself "doing" the washing and her studies.

Organization/Ideation

Jessica's assignments lack both organization and ideas. Although her ideas are difficult to follow because of poor sentence structure, she maintains the topic in all five samples.

Recommendations

These samples document Jessica's difficulties with the formulation of written language. In this case, the classroom teacher would consult with the speech-language therapist for specific recommendations. The speech-language therapist and the classroom teacher(s) would have ongoing communication in regard to procedures for reinforcing newly developing language skills in the classroom. In general, the selected procedures and techniques would enhance both oral and written formulation.

Handwriting/Appearance

1. Encourage Jessica to observe both the left and right margins in all of her assignments.
2. Encourage the use of cursive writing in all assignments. Provide Jessica the *About Kangaroo* sample, or one similar in appearance, as a model of the neatness expected for final drafts.
3. Using her reading book as a model, review with Jessica the amount of spacing to place after a period.

Spelling

1. Review the spelling of common compound words.
2. Encourage Jessica to listen to the sounds in a word and to try to sequence them correctly when she is uncertain of the spelling. Review the difference between similar sounding words such as "he's," "his"; "life," "live"; "below," "blow"; and "then," "them."

Usage

1. Remind Jessica to capitalize the first word in sentences.
2. Until Jessica's mastery of syntax has improved, provide many opportunities for her to edit her work with a more knowledgeable other (i.e., teacher, parent, or peer).
3. Encourage Jessica to use a variety of sentence patterns. Begin by helping her understand basic sentence structures (e.g., subject-verb-object). Provide extensive practice with these structures. Once she has mastered simple sentence patterns, introduce more complex patterns. Teach her a strategy, such as SCAN (Graham & Harris, 1987).
4. Provide extensive oral practice with sentence-combining exercises. Present Jessica with several clauses or short sentences and have her generate as many sentence patterns as she can using a variety of connecting words. As an alternative activity, provide her with a specific word or words to use in joining clauses or sentences.
5. Help Jessica clarify and expand her written statements through questioning. For example, when she writes a sentence such as *We do lots of work* ask, "What kind of work do you do?"
6. Use a structured program, such as the Phelps Sentence Guide (Phelps-Terasaki & Phelps, 1980) or the sentence expansion procedure described by Tompkins (1994) to help Jessica master simple sentence patterns.
7. Explain the importance of using consistent verb tense. Help Jessica note the errors in her work and encourage her to correct the errors when editing.
8. Provide Jessica with practice using prepositions. Begin by providing examples out of context, and, as skill develops, provide her with practice in context. Help Jessica correct any errors in preposition use in the editing stage of writing.
9. Explain the correct use of articles and help Jessica correct any errors when editing.
10. Review the formation of the plurals of words ending in "y" (e.g., "study" and "baby").
11. Review the difference between "brought" and "bought." Link the verbs to their present

tense forms and point out the "r" in "bring" and "brought."

12. Teach Jessica an editing strategy such as COPS (Schumaker et al., 1981) or SCOPE (Bos & Vaughn, 1994).

13. When grading Jessica's papers, make allowances for language and usage difficulties. For example, overlook grammatical errors in a paper with good conceptual content.

Vocabulary

1. Encourage Jessica to choose more precise vocabulary. Use graphic organizers to help illustrate the relationships between similar words. Reinforce Jessica for using more complex or descriptive words in her writing.

2. Underline one or two words in each assignment that could be clarified or improved upon. Work with Jessica to replace these words with ones that are more complex or more precise.

3. Read stories with Jessica that are slightly above her language level. Discuss any unknown words using pictures or known synonyms. Provide ample practice for her to use the new words in her writing.

Organization/Ideation

1. Use prewriting strategies with Jessica, such as graphic organizers, to help her develop her thoughts.

2. Teach Jessica to consider what information the reader has and what information must be explained. Provide her with practice in identifying the sections in her writing that may confuse a reader.

3. Teach Jessica to introduce and describe what she is discussing in her narratives.

Student: Tim
Grade: 8th
Assignments: Two letters

Two of Tim's letters are presented. One is written to his friend, Annie, and the other is written to his mother and brother. Tim attends a private boarding school for students with severe learning disabilities.

Analysis

Handwriting

In his first letter, Tim combines lowercase and uppercase manuscript letters and cursive letters. In his second letter, he begins writing in cursive and then switches to print. Although neither his manuscript nor cursive writing are attractive in appearance, the major difficulty with legibility is poor spelling rather than letter formation.

Spelling

Although incorrect, several of Tim's spellings are good phonetic approximations (e.g., *mite* for "might," *skrach* for "scratch," *cume* for "come," and *eze* for "easy"). In general, however, Tim's ability to communicate effectively in writing is severely hampered by his extreme spelling difficulties. He has mastered the spelling of very few words. It seems that every time he comes to a word, he has to start again to try and spell it as if for the first time. For example, within the first sample, he spells the word "probably" as *parll* and *prablle*. He misspells many high-frequency words (e.g., *ass* for "as"; *ween*, *win*, and *wew* for "when"; *tray* for "try"; and *wall* for "while"). He confuses word boundaries (e.g., *abager* for "a bagger," *ajob* for "a job," *Newyurk* for "New York," and *Afabter* for Alpha Beta).

With the exception of the correct spelling of "ing" in several words, many of his spellings indicate lack of sensitivity to common English spelling patterns (e.g., *woork* for "work," *dowin* for "down," *monee* for "money," and *wew* for "when"). He also transposes sounds within a few words (e.g., *gart* for "great," *rorg* for Roger, *pells* for "please," and *sifn* for "sniff").

Usage

Tim places a period at the end of most sentences. He expresses his thoughts in complete ideas. He makes three errors in subject-verb agreement (i.e., *. . . my dad dont, Tom call,* and *he get*). It is unclear whether these are spelling or usage errors.

Both letters begin with a salutation and close with a greeting. Tim does not place a comma after his salutation, however, and in the second letter the first sentence is merged with the greeting.

Organization/Ideation

Tim has a lot to say to his friend Annie. His letter is informative and the sequence of his thoughts makes sense. He describes what he plans to do in the summer months. He adds a postscript that reiterates when he will call his friend. Perhaps indicative of other types of sequential difficulties, he writes the dates as *25–24 of Feb*, proceeding backward in time. He also repeats information in one sentence (i.e., "I will probably go to New York this June to work tearing down a building in New York this June").

Recommendations

Tim has a severe spelling problem that is affecting his ability to communicate in writing. Because of the severity of the problem and his age, he will require specific accommodations and modifications to succeed in academic settings.

Accommodations

1. Limit or eliminate copying requirements from both the blackboard and textbooks.
2. Provide tape recordings of the class lectures rather than requiring Tim to take notes.
3. Provide specific instruction in how to use technology as a substitute for writing. For example, teach Tim how to use a tape recorder to complete different types of assignments. Provide practice in taking an oral examination and preparing and giving oral reports, essays, and short stories.
4. Accept tape-recorded assignments as an alternative to written assignments.
5. When necessary, administer content area exams orally. Give exams individually or have Tim dictate responses into a tape recorder for grading at a later time.
6. On some assignments, provide a scribe or typist for Tim. Have him dictate his thoughts to another who will write them or type them

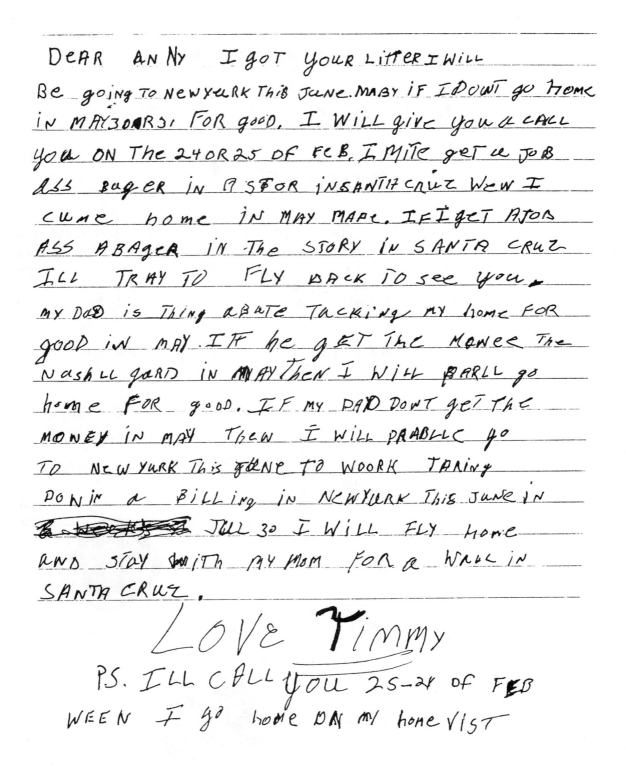

Figure 8-21. Two letters written by Tim, an eighth-grade student.

Figure 8-21 (cont.).

on a word processor. Have Tim then read the printed copy and discuss revisions.

7. Help Tim become an advocate for himself by discussing the possible accommodations that he may require to be successful in both school and vocational settings.

Computer

1. Teach Tim keyboarding skills. Provide practice typing real assignments. Give Tim as much time as is necessary to complete his typewritten assignments.
2. Teach Tim how to write using a word processor. Teach the various functions, such as spell checking, moving and revising text, and saving and printing assignments.
3. Encourage Tim to write his letters and school assignments on a word processor.

Spelling

1. Presently, Tim's level of spelling skill is too low for him to be able to use a spell checker independently. Pair him with a peer who spells phonetically enough to use a spell checker, and provide the time for the two to run a spell check on both students' assignments.
2. Develop a program to teach Tim the spelling of high-frequency words. Because retention has been so poor, Tim is likely to require some type of multisensory method that provides substantial practice and review, such as the Fernald method (Fernald, 1943).

Usage

1. Provide intensive assistance with correcting all usage errors during the editing stage.
2. Review with Tim the format of informal letter writing.

Organization/Ideation

1. Continue to provide real purposes for writing, such as writing letters to communicate with friends and family members.

2. Provide structured strategies to help Tim develop his skill in expository writing. Begin by teaching him how to write paragraphs using a strategy such as SLOW CaPS (Schumaker et al., 1985). Once Tim is able to write different types of expository paragraphs successfully, teach him how to write compare/contrast essays, followed by opinion essays using a technique such as the TREE strategy (Graham & Harris, 1989a).

Conclusion

An in-depth analysis of writing samples can provide invaluable information for programmatic decisions and instructional design. Much information can be gleaned from one sample, providing that the sample is an accurate representation of the individual's ability. A number of samples must be examined, however, to ensure that the errors form a typical pattern.

One single, correct method or strategy for teaching writing does not exist. The approach must be tailored to the specific needs of the individual. The only criterion to be considered in choosing a particular approach is that the method is effective for the student.

The strategies suggested in the analyses are considered methods that may work. Other techniques could be equally effective. Preference or convenience may lead the teacher to choose a different approach from the ones presented. Although tremendous variation will always exist in the writing skill of students, a caring teacher with both an understanding of writing development and a wide range of strategies will be able to help students become more proficient in their writing skill.

9

ADDITIONAL WRITING SAMPLES

This chapter contains 15 writing samples. Guided questions are included for 10 of the samples, whereas the last 5 samples are not analyzed. These samples may be used for in-class discussions, homework assignments, or independent study. An index is provided for both sets of samples that includes: the student's first name, his or her grade, and the type of assignment.

Analysis of the samples includes two stages. Stage one involves determining the strengths and weaknesses in writing skill and identification of the student's specific instructional needs. Stage two involves identifying the types of accommodations and instructional interventions that may help the student become a more competent writer.

When answering the guided questions, try to provide specific examples from the student's writing that illustrate and clarify the points. Following the analysis, suggest instructional strategies and methods for resolving each area of concern. In addition, consider what accommodations the student may need to participate fully in classroom writing activities. Although the process of analysis can be time consuming, the investment is worth the effort. A careful analysis, resulting in appropriate recommendations, can be the key to success for many students. In addition, teachers are rewarded by their students' progress.

Samples with Guided Questions

Index

STUDENT	GRADE	ASSIGNMENT
Rachel	2nd	Reaction to a story; A short story
Darrell	3rd	Social studies essay
Kathy	3rd	A story and a letter
Linda	4th	Two journal entries
Adam	5th	An imaginary story
Owen	5th	A descriptive paragraph
Brad	6th	A story
Tali	7th	Several journal entries
Richard	7th	A short story
Keisha	8th	Three descriptive paragraphs

Student: Rachel
Grade: 2nd
Assignment: Reaction to a story
          Story about helping people

The two assignments were written on the same day and are linked to each other by content. The first is a reaction to a story that was read aloud whereby the hero, Jeff, helped someone. For the second assignment, Rachel was asked to write a story about a time that she had helped someone.

Guided Questions

Handwriting

- Does Rachel form all the letters correctly?
- Is letter size consistent?
- Is the spacing between the letters and words consistent and correct?

Figure 9–1. Two short stories by Rachel, a second-grade student.

- Comment upon Rachel's use of capital and lowercase letters.

Spelling

- Are high-frequency sight words spelled correctly?
- Does Rachel attempt to spell phonetically?
- How well does Rachel associate letters with their sounds?
- Are letter sounds represented correctly in words?

Usage

- Are uppercase letters used correctly throughout the samples?
- Are periods used correctly?
- Does Rachel use conjunctions appropriately?
- Does she write in complete sentences?

Vocabulary

- Comment upon Rachel's vocabulary and suggest a possible reason for her choice of words.

Organization and Ideation

- Is the information presented in the samples elaborate or limited?
- Is the information easy to follow and well organized?
- What factors may be affecting Rachel's written expression?

Supplementary Analyses

- Discuss any additional concerns you may have.
- Is there a need for further analysis?

Instructional Programming

- What accommodations or modifications may be needed to help Rachel succeed on classroom writing tasks?
- What specific instructional strategies may help Rachel improve her writing skill?

Translations:

I liked the story because it was nice and it was what Jeff did.

Because my dad's chest was hurting him really bad and he told me to call people but I phoned my mom to be with us. My mom and dad were surprised.

Student: Darrell
Grade: 3rd
Assignment: Social studies essay

After 4 weeks of learning about the solar system through books, videos, and experiments, Darrell was asked to write an essay about what he had learned from the unit. When handing in his paper, Darrell commented to his teacher: "I know a lot more, but I just can't get it down on paper."

Guided Questions

Handwriting and Appearance

- Is Darrell's handwriting legible?
- Are all the letters formed correctly?
- Are any letter reversals apparent in the sample?
- Are capital letters used correctly?
- Is letter size consistent?
- Is the spacing between letters and words consistent?
- Does Darrell observe word boundaries?

Spelling

- Are the common sight words spelled correctly?
- Are the misspellings phonetic?
- From the types of misspellings, what conclusions can be drawn in regard to Darrell's knowledge of sound-symbol correspondence?
- Are words spelled consistently, even if incorrectly?
- Does Darrell experience difficulties with the spelling of any homonyms?

Usage

- Are paragraphs used and indented?
- Has Darrell included a title and observed right and left margins?
- Are capital letters and periods used correctly within sentences?
- Does Darrell use a variety of sentence patterns?
- Are syntactic rules followed? (e.g., subject-verb agreement, consistent verb tense).
- Are commas used correctly within sentences and lists?

Vocabulary

- Discuss Darrell's choice of words.

Organization and Ideation

- Does Darrell seem well prepared to write about the topic?
- What specific information has Darrell learned from the unit?
- Are the ideas sequenced in a logical manner?
- Does Darrell expand sufficiently upon his ideas?
- Is a difference in ideation apparent between the start and the end of the essay? Give possible reasons.

Supplementary Analyses

- Discuss any additional concerns you may have.
- Is there a need for further analysis?

Instructional Programming

- What accommodations or modifications may be needed to help Darrell succeed on classroom writing tasks?
- What specific instructional strategies may help Darrell improve his writing skill?

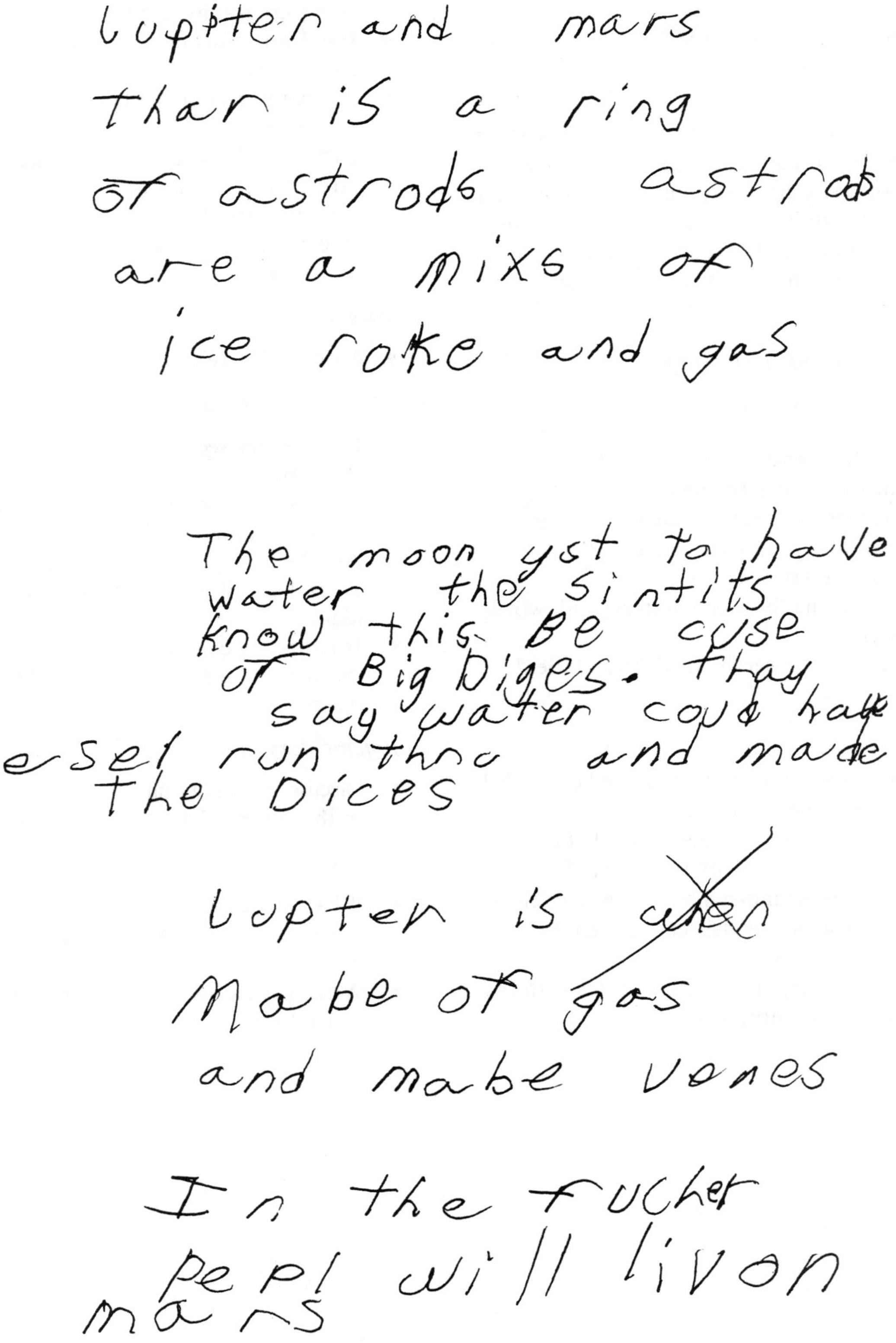

bupiter and mars
than is a ring
of astrods astrod
are a mixs of
ice roke and gas

The moon yst to have
water the sintits
know this Be cyse
of Big biges. thay
say water cou haff
esel run thrn and made
the Dices

bupter is when
Mabe of gas
and mabe vanes

In the fucher
pepl will livon
mars

Figure 9–2. A social studies essay written by Darrell, a third-grade student.

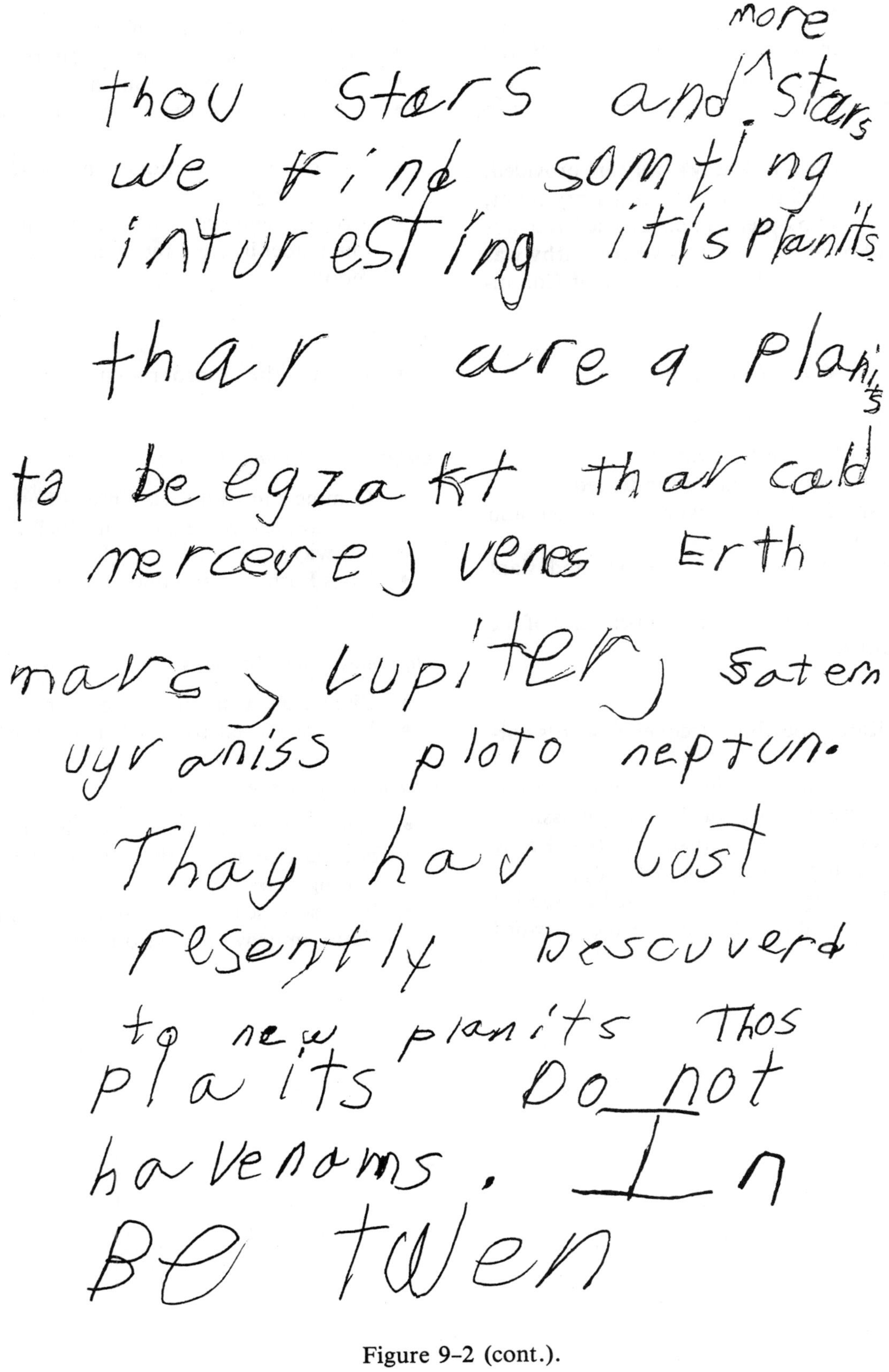

thou stars and ^more^ stars
we find somting
inturesting it is plants

thar are a plants

to be egzakt thar cald
mercere, venes Erth

mars, Lupiter, saten
uyraniss ploto neptun.

Thay hav bast
resently descuverd
to new planits Thos
plaits Do not
have noms. In
Be tWen

Figure 9–2 (cont.).

Student: Kathy
Grade: 3rd
Assignments: Creative story and letter for Social
Studies class

The first two pages of Kathy's story are provided. She had been asked to write about a scary night, but had received no other guidance. The letter was written in a Social Studies class where Kathy was asked to write a letter home from one of Columbus' sailors.

Guided Questions

Handwriting and Appearance

- Does Kathy title her work?
- Are paragraphs used and indented?
- Is the spacing between words consistent and adequate?
- Does Kathy keep her letter size and slant consistent?
- Comment upon the overall appearance of the assignments.

Spelling

- Does Kathy spell high-frequency words correctly?
- Discuss misspellings due to letter insertions.
- Discuss misspellings due to letter omissions.
- What evidence exists to suggest that Kathy is attempting to write phonetically?
- Are all digraphs and blends used correctly?
- Comment upon Kathy's observance of word boundaries.

Usage

- Discuss Kathy's use of periods.
- Discuss her use of capital letters.
- Discuss her use of commas.
- What types of sentence structures does Kathy use?
- Are a variety of conjunctions used? Are they used correctly?
- Are the sentence structures adequate to retain reader interest and create an appropriate mood?

Vocabulary

- Discuss the appropriateness of the word choice.

Organization and Ideation

- Comment upon the relevance of Kathy's ideas.
- Are the ideas represented in a logical, sequential way?
- Does Kathy expand upon and explain the incidents fully?

Supplementary Analyses

- Discuss any additional concerns you may have.
- Is there a need for further analysis?

Instructional Programming

- What accommodations or modifications may be needed to help Kathy succeed on classroom writing tasks?
- What specific instructional strategies may help Kathy improve her writing skill?

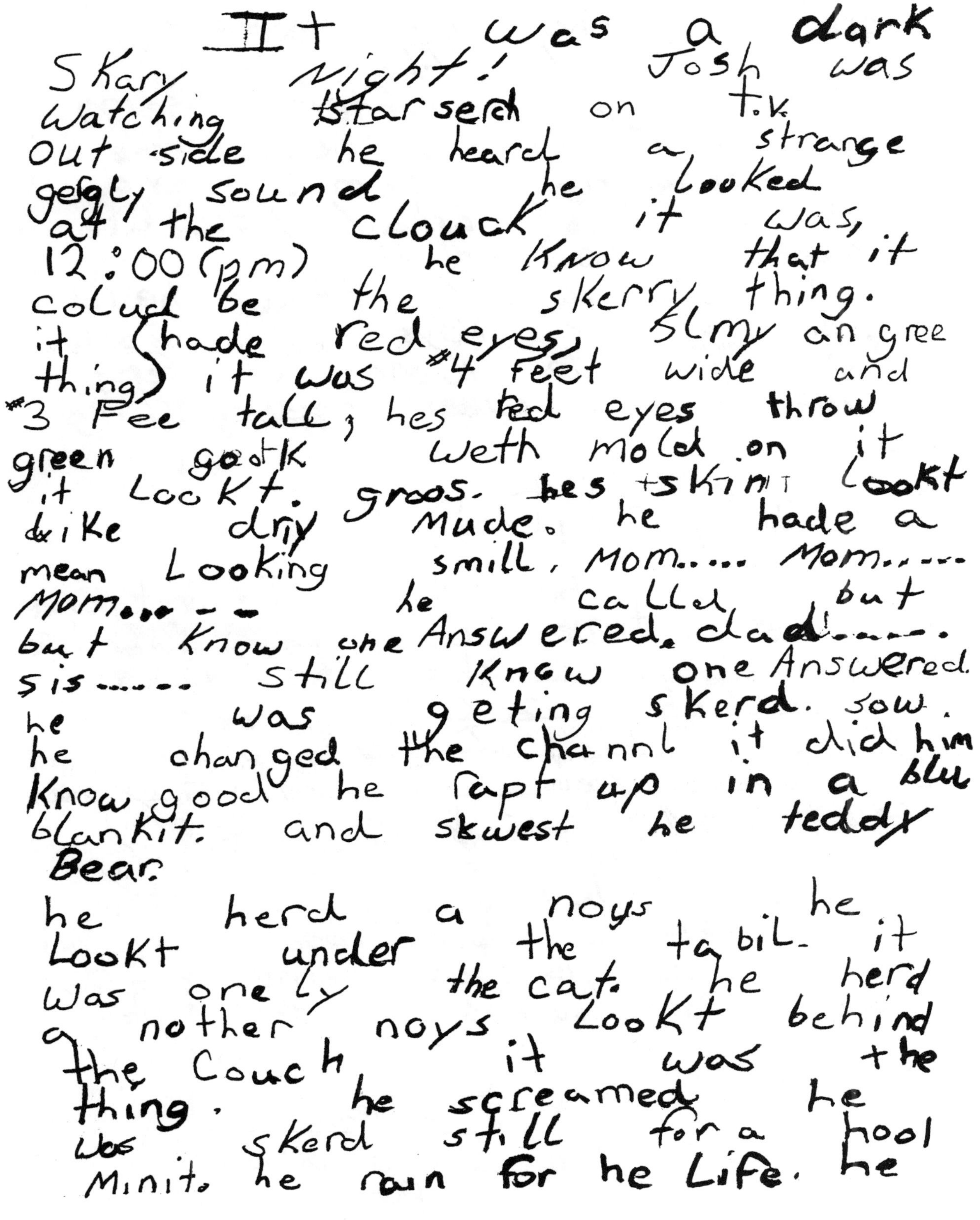

It was a dark skary night! Josh was watching star serch on t.v. out side he heard a strange gegly sound he looked at the clouck it was, 12:00 (pm) he know that it colud be the skerry thing. it shade red eyes, slimy an gree thing) it was #4 feet wide and #3 Fee tall, hes red eyes throw green gook weth mold on it it lookt gross. hes tskint lookt dike driy Mude. he hade a mean Looking smill, Mom..... Mom...... Mom..--- he called but but know one Answered. dad..... sis...... still know one Answered. he was geting skerd. sow. he changed the channl it did him know good he rapt up in a blu blankit. and skwest he teddy Bear.

he herd a noys he Lookt under the tabil. it was one ly the cat. he herd another noys lookt behind the couch it was the thing. he screamed he was skerd still for a hool Minit. he ran for he Life. he

Figure 9–3. Story and letter by Kathy, a third-grade student.

out of the door and to t
Nabeors. weth the thing
come ing after hern
he said the... the.... the..
its come ing come and
doun. tellus what you are
tray ing to say
all asoudeon thay heard
same gergy noys as Josh
did. thay to weer at ferst
thout they weer seeing thing

Dear MoM, and, DaD,
This Mite be the Feairst and
the last time we Communicate
weve alowmest ship recket. whrt
if we ship reck I woont to
tell you this, I Love you and
I alowes weel. I miss you
alowt, and it is vamy skerry
abord ship. I am varry
afarid I Welldround if the
ship seckens The food is Not
Likey ours it is not varny good.
chris teoter cloumbs Is the capteon
he is a grat capeton an a
crazzy man

Love,
Juan de La
Place

Figure 9–3 (cont.).

Student: Linda
Grade: 4th
Assignment: Two journal entries

Linda was requested to record a journal entry on a daily basis. The two samples presented here were written on two consecutive days. No assistance was provided.

Guided Questions

Handwriting and Appearance

- Is the handwriting legible and easy to read?
- Are paragraphs indented and margins observed?

Spelling

- What types of words are spelled correctly?
- Are words spelled correctly consistently?
- Consider Linda's knowledge of sound-symbol correspondence. Which sounds does she seem to know well? Which sounds appear to cause confusion?
- Are words spelled phonetically?
- Address Linda's letter insertions, omissions, and substitutions in words.
- Discuss Linda's spellings of the past tense of verbs. Does she consistently add an *-ed* ending?

Usage

- Are capital letters and periods used correctly?
- What type of sentence constructions does Linda use?

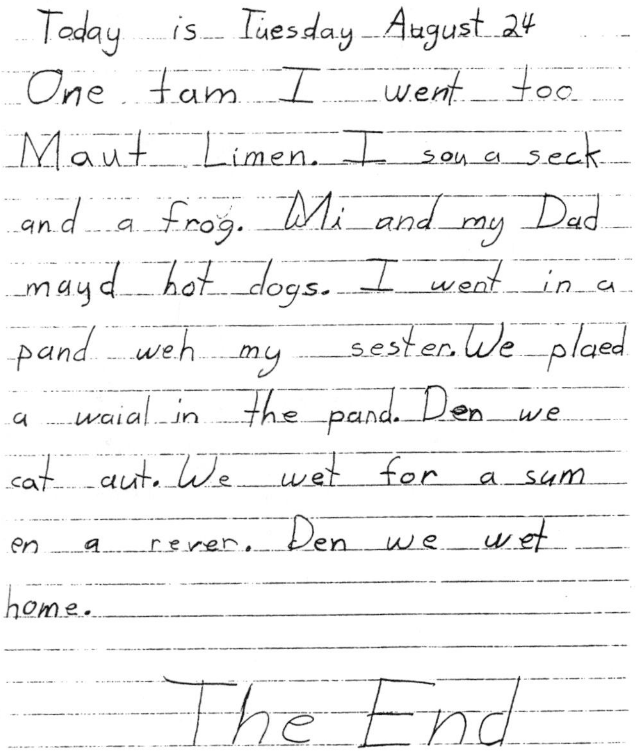

Today is Tuesday August 24
One tam I went too Maut Limen. I sou a seck and a frog. Mi and my Dad mayd hot dogs. I went in a pand weh my sester. We plaed a waial in the pand. Den we cat aut. We wet for a sum en a rever. Den we wet home.

The End

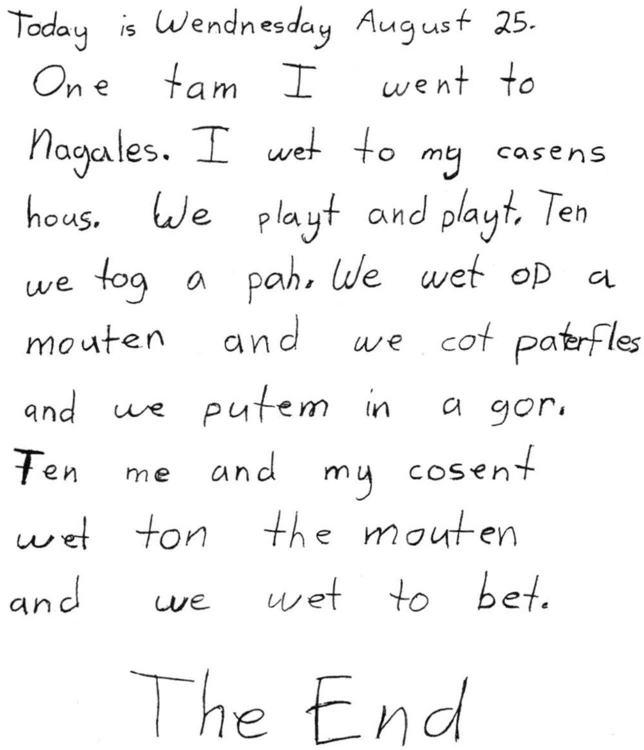

Today is Wendnesday August 25.
One tam I went to Nagales. I wet to my casens hous. We playt and playt. Ten we tog a pah. We wet oṗ a mouten and we cot paterfles and we putem in a gor. Ten me and my cosent wet ton the mouten and we wet to bet.

The End

Translations:

One time I went to Mount Lemon. I saw a stick and a frog. Me and my dad made hot dogs. I went in a pond with my sister. We played a while in the pond. Then we got out. We went for a swim in a river. Then we went home.

One time I went to Nogales. I went to my cousin's house. We played and played. Then we took a path. We went up a mountain and we caught butterflies and we put them in a jar. Then me and my cousin went down the mountain and we went to bed.

Figure 9–4. Two journal entries by Linda, a fourth-grade student.

- Compare and contrast sentence structure between the two paragraphs.
- Discuss the use of conjunctions in the two paragraphs. Compare and contrast the two.

Organization and Ideation

- Has Linda developed her ideas fully?
- Do the journal entries follow a logical sequence?
- Does Linda use cohesive ties?

Supplementary Analyses

- Discuss any additional concerns you may have.
- Is there a need for further analysis?

Instructional Programming

- What accommodations or modifications may be needed to help Linda succeed on classroom writing tasks?
- What specific instructional strategies may help Linda improve her writing skill?

Student: Adam
Grade: 5th
Assignment: An imaginary story

Adam was asked to write a story about wishes. Prior to writing, a class discussion had occurred with respect to the typical wishes of people. Prior to writing, members of the class were encouraged to think about their prospective story-line.

Guided Questions

Handwriting and Appearance

- Has a title been written?
- Does Adam use and indent paragraphs?
- Have the right and left margins been observed?

- Are all the letters formed correctly?
- Do Adam's letters have a consistent slant?

Spelling

- What type of spelling errors can be observed?
- Are word boundaries observed correctly?
- Comment upon Adam's knowledge of sound-symbol correspondence.
- Does Adam have difficulty with the spelling of any homonyms?

Usage

- Discuss Adam's use of periods and capital letters.
- Is the verb tense consistent and correct?
- Analyze the different types of sentence structures that Adam has used.

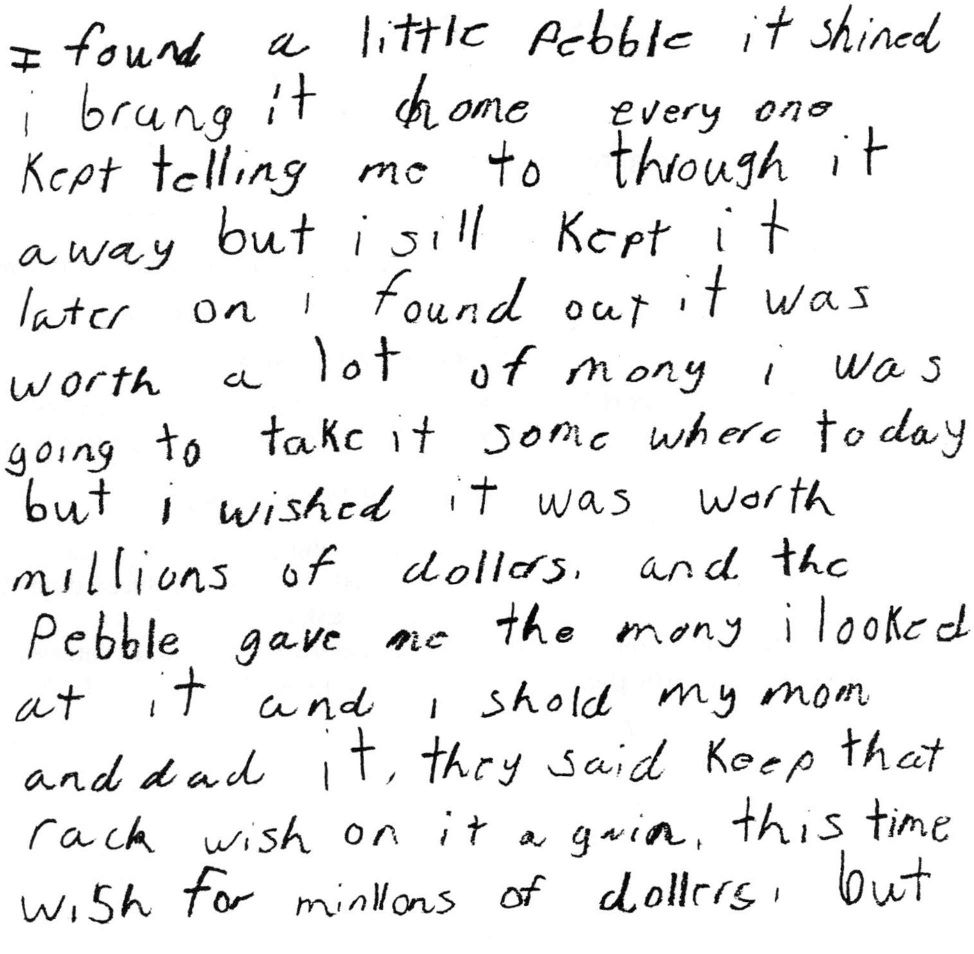

> I found a little Pebble it shined
> i brung it home every one
> Kept telling me to through it
> away but i sill Kept it
> later on i found out it was
> worth a lot of mony i was
> going to take it some where today
> but i wished it was worth
> millions of dollors, and the
> Pebble gave me the mony i looked
> at it and i shold my mom
> and dad it, they said Keep that
> rack wish on it a gvin, this time
> wish for minllons of dollers, but

Figure 9–5. A story by Adam, a fifth-grade student.

i did not work it brung me to
my room and it said to me and
said i will not do it if you
bring me out there wish it in here
ok. i wished it im my room but
we were wishing so much it
said take me some where and
sell me to day and i did, they
said ill give 1,000 dollers for
that rock i thought about it
and i said ok. but we were
rish thout. The end

Figure 9-5 (cont.).

- Discuss Adam's use of dialogue.
- Are conjunctions used correctly?

Vocabulary

- Has Adam chosen words that add to the story?
- Discuss the limited use of multisyllabic words in the assignment.

Organization and Ideation

- Does the story follow a logical order?
- Is the story easy to understand?
- Has Adam explained his ideas adequately?
- Is the quality of the ideas sufficient for the story?

- Is the quantity of the ideas sufficient for the story?

Supplementary Analyses

- Discuss any additional concerns you may have.
- Is there a need for further analysis?

Instructional Programming

- What accommodations or modifications may be needed to help Adam succeed on classroom writing tasks?
- What specific instructional strategies may help Adam improve his writing skill?

Student: Owen
Grade: 5th
Assignment: A descriptive paragraph

Owen was asked to write a descriptive paragraph about his knowledge of basketball. Although Owen was interested in the topic, he did little planning before he began writing. Instead of writing an expository paragraph, he wrote a story about the relationship between Bill and Sandy.

Guided Questions

Handwriting and Appearance

- Are paragraphs used and indented?
- Has Owen provided a title for his story?
- Are left and right margins observed?
- Are all the letters formed correctly?
- Is the letter size consistent and appropriate?
- Does Owen space his letters appropriately within and between words?
- Comment upon the line quality.

Spelling

- What spelling patterns make Owen's writing easy or difficult to decipher?
- Comment upon the misspellings caused by insertions and omissions.
- Is Owen consistent in his misspellings?
- Does Owen have good knowledge of symbol-sound correspondence?
- Comment upon the relationship between observance of word boundaries and the consistency in spacing between words.
- Does Owen have difficulty with the spelling of certain homonyms?

Usage

- Does Owen use periods and uppercase letters appropriately?

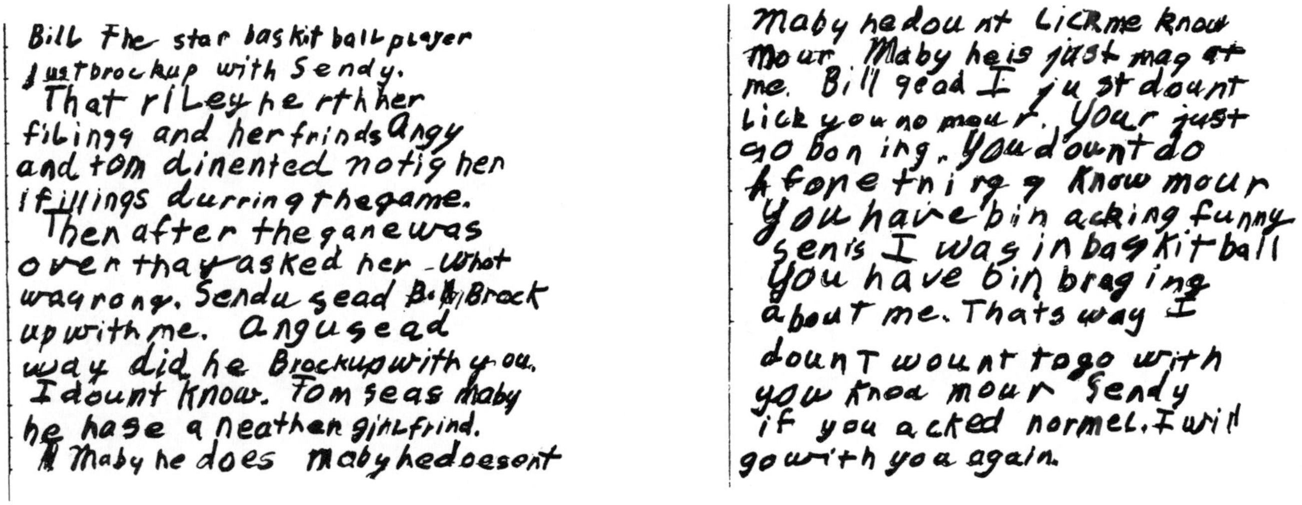
Bill The star baskit ballplayer
justbrockup with Sendy.
That riLeyhe rthher
fiLings and herfrinds Angy
and tom dinented notig her
ifillings durringthegame.
Then after thegane was
over thay asked her what
wagrong. Sendu sead Bill Brock
up with me. angusead
way did he Brockupwith you.
I dount know. Tom seas maby
he hase a neathen girLfrind.
Maby he does mabyhedoesont
maby hedount LicRme know
mour. Maby he is just mag at
me. Bill sead I just dount
Lick you no mour. Your just
go bon ing. You dount do
ffone thing Know mour
You have bin acking funny
senis I was in baskit ball
You have bin braging
about me. Thats way I
dount wount togo with
you knoa mour Sendy
if you acked normel. I will
gowith you again.

Translation:

Bill the star basketball player just broke up with Sandy. That really hurt her feelings and her friends, Angie and Tom didn't notice her feelings during the game. Then, after the game was over, they asked her what was wrong. Sandy said, "Bill broke up with me." Angie said, "Why did he broke up with you?" "I don't know." Tom says, "Maybe he has another girlfriend." "Maybe he does. Maybe he doesn't. Maybe he don't like me no more. Maybe he is just mad at me." Bill said, "I just don't like you no more. You're just so boring. You don't do funny things no more. You have been acting funny since I was in basketball. You have been bragging about me. That's why I don't want to go with you no more. Sandy if you acted normal, I will go with you again.

Figure 9–6. A descriptive paragraph by Owen, a fifth-grade student.

- How well is dialogue used?
- Comment upon the use and adequacy of different sentence structures.
- Are the verb tenses consistent and correct?

Vocabulary

- Does Owen use interesting and appropriate vocabulary?
- Are some words overused?

Organization and Ideation

- Has the story been represented in an easy-to-follow, comprehensive and interesting way?
- Does the story follow a logical sequence?

- Does Owen attempt to use cohesive ties in his writing?
- Has Owen developed the characters?
- To what extent has Owen adhered to the topic?

Supplementary Analyses

- Discuss any additional concerns you may have.
- Is there a need for further analysis?

Instructional Programming

- What accommodations or modifications may be needed to help Owen succeed on classroom writing tasks?
- What specific instructional strategies may help Owen improve his writing skill?

Student: Brad
Grade: 6th
Assignment: A story

Brad was asked to write a story on a topic of his choice. He did not engage in prewriting activities. Although he was not asked to draw a picture, Brad spent more time on that activity than on writing the story.

Guided Questions

Handwriting and Appearance

- Are all the letters formed correctly?
- Has Brad mastered the use of uppercase and lowercase letters?

- Does Brad use consistent letter size?
- Is the slant consistent?
- Is the spacing of letters within and between words appropriate?
- Are left and right margins observed?

Spelling

- Are high-frequency words spelled correctly?
- Why did Brad spell the word "Honda" correctly?
- Are sounds omitted in Brad's spellings?
- Are words spelled consistently, even if incorrectly?

Usage

- Are capital letters and periods used correctly?
- What type of sentence structures are used?
- Comment upon Brad's use of superlatives.

Vocabulary

- To what degree does Brad's choice of vocabulary promote reader interest?
- Comment upon the limited use of multisyllabic words.

Organization and Ideation

- Does Brad fulfill the requirement of writing a story?
- Does Brad elaborate upon his ideas?
- Are the ideas sequenced logically?
- Have cohesive ties been used?
- Discuss the difference between Brad's artistic ability and his writing skill.

Supplementary Analyses

- Discuss any additional concerns you may have.
- Is there a need for further analysis?

Instructional Programming

- What accommodations or modifications may be needed to help Brad succeed on classroom writing tasks?
- What specific instructional strategies may help Brad improve his writing skill?

Translation:

I like to ride my dirt bike. I have a Honda. It is the bestest. I like to do jumps. It is fun to jump. It feels good to jump and go fast.

Figure 9–7. A story by Brad, a sixth-grade student.

Student: Tali
Grade: 7th
Assignments: Entries from her journal

Several excerpts were taken from Tali's journal from her Writing and Literature class. Of interest from these samples are Tali's emotional responses and her acknowledgment that her self-esteem is very low.

Guided Questions

Handwriting and Appearance

- Is Tali's handwriting adequate for journal entries?

Spelling

- What types of misspellings are evident in Tali's writing?
- Are the misspellings recognizable in context? Why?

- Does Tali keep her misspellings consistent?
- Comment upon the sequencing of sounds in multisyllabic words.

Usage

- Does Tali use periods and uppercase letters correctly?
- Comment upon sentence structure.
- Is Tali's writing style appropriate for the task?

Vocabulary

- Comment upon the appropriateness of the word choice.

Ideation

- Given that the journal entries were written over a semester, comment upon the evolution of Tali's self-esteem.
- Is Tali motivated to write?
- Why do you think Tali chooses to write about her feelings?

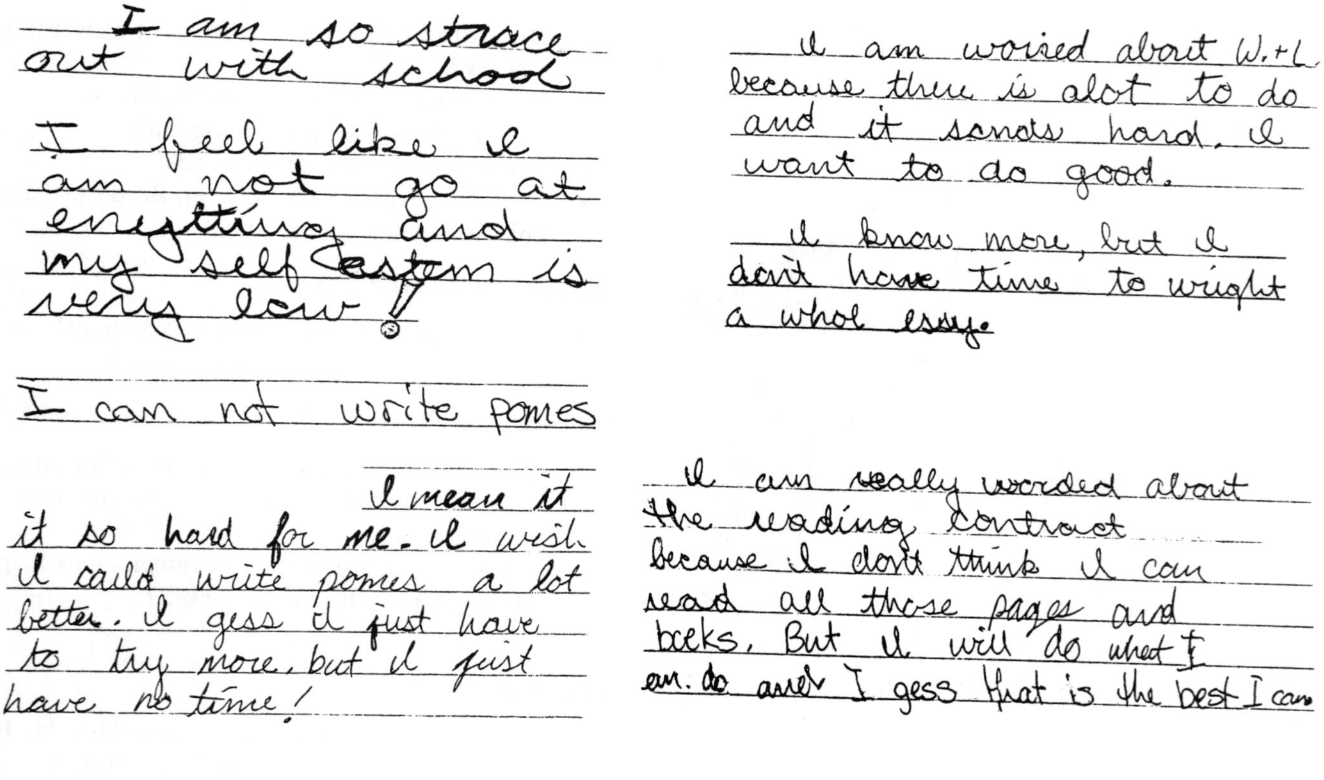

I am so stress out with school

I feel like I am not go at everthing. And my self estem is very low!

I can not write pomes

I mean it it so hard for me. I wish I could write pomes a lot better. I gess I just have to try more, but I just have no time!

I am worried about W.+L. because there is alot to do and it sonds hard. I want to do good.

I know more, but I dont have time to wright a whol essy.

I am really worded about the reading contract because I dont think I can read all these pages and books. But I will do what I an. do and I gess that is the best I can

Figure 9-8. Several journal entries written by Tali, a seventh-grade student.

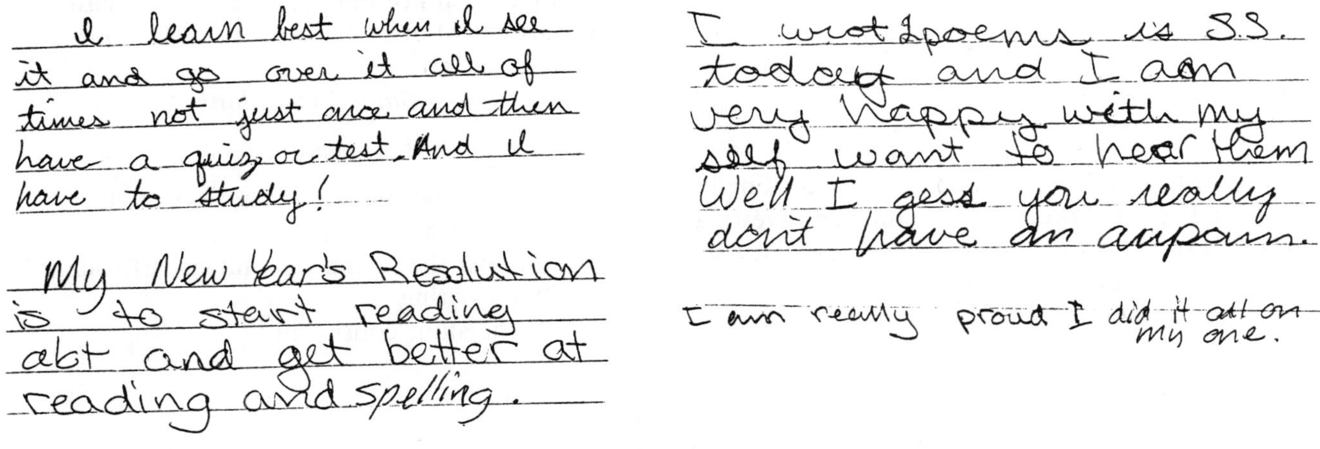

I learn best when I see it and go over it all of times not just once and then have a quiz or test. And I have to study!

My New Year's Resolution is to start reading abt and get better at reading and spelling.

I wrot 2poems is S.S. today and I am very happy with my self want to hear them Well I gess you really don't have an anpans.

I am really proud I did it all on my one.

Figure 9–8 (cont.).

Supplementary Analyses

- Discuss any additional concerns you may have.
- Is there a need for further analysis?

Instructional Programming

- What accommodations or modifications may be needed to help Tali succeed on classroom writing tasks?
- What specific instructional strategies may help Tali improve her writing skill?

Student: Richard
Grade: 7th
Assignment: A short story

Richard was asked to write a story for his English class and selected the topic of a murder investigation in a small town. Prior to writing, he discussed his ideas with his teacher and then a small group of peers. The final story was six pages long. The first three pages of the first draft are included for analysis.

Guided Questions

Handwriting and Appearance

- Are paragraphs used and indented?
- Are left and right margins observed?
- Discuss the formation and size of Richard's handwriting.
- Is the slant consistent?

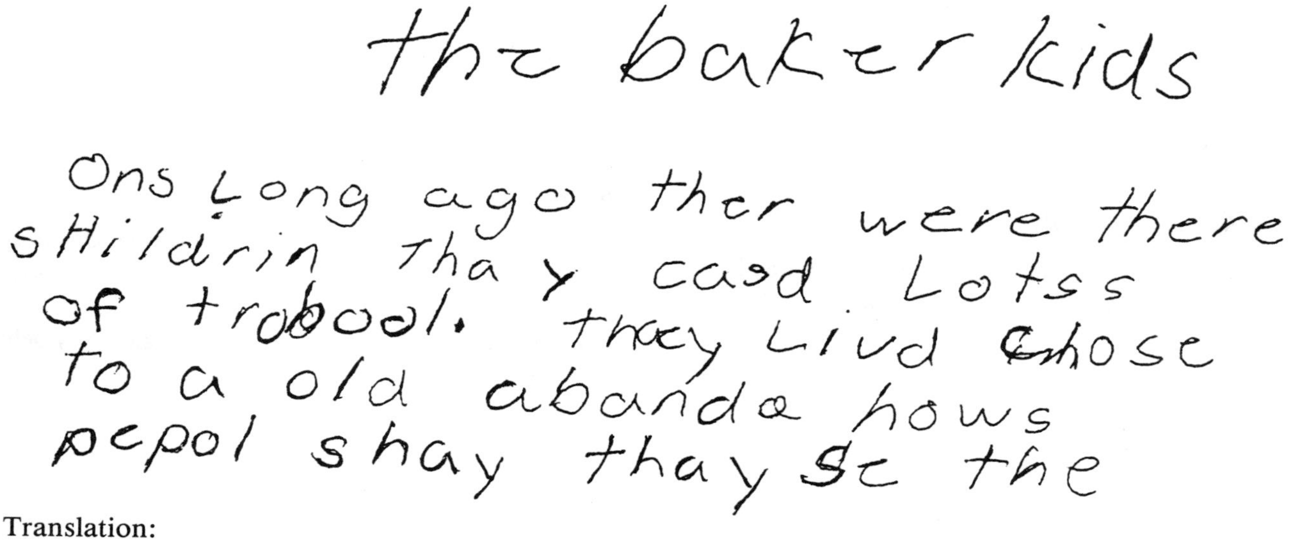

the baker kids

Ons Long ago ther were there sHildrin Thay casd Lotss of trobool. they Livd those to a old abanda hows pepol shay thay se the

Translation:

Once long ago there were three children. They caused lots of trouble. They lived close to a old abandoned house. People say they see the lights flickering on and off. People say it is the Baker kids trying to scare the villagers. But one morning they were missing. Everyone looked for them. They were nowhere in sight. There was only one place they did not look. At the abandoned house on the hill. So the sheriff went to the house. When he got there he claimed he saw the Baker kids on the floor dead. So the sheriff put out an investigation that morning. There were no suspects. People say there used to be an old man living there but he passed away recently. He was a stingy old man that didn't like to be bothered. No one liked him. But people say they see him in the forest sometimes with a shovel. Some people think it was the sheriff when he went up there yesterday. Everyone was scared that there was a killer on the loose. That morning they took them to the mortician. The mortician claimed he found bullets once in each of the kids. The next morning the next day the kids were missing and the mortician was dead. That night a person said he saw the old man with a shovel and a garbage bag walking in the forest. People think there are twins. Everyone gathered their weapons. That morning when they got to the cabin the old man walked out. Bullets rang out everywhere. When people returned to their homes they had a celebration for who they thought was the murderer. Two days later another murder occurred. People were so scared that they left town. People were fed up. People were starting to think there was a ghost in the town. Nothing like this has happened. Can't so much happen to a small community where everyone knows everyone? For one whole week everything was fine until another murder occurred. People started to lock their houses up which they have never done before.

Figure 9–9. A short story by Richard, a seventh-grade student.

Lits flioriy on and off.
pepol say if is the bakerkids
triy to skar the viligers
but wun mong thay wer misig
evry one loot foor them
Thay wer no were in site
ther was only one pase
thay did not Look at toe
abadid hows on the hill
so the sheref went to the
hose wie he got ther he clamd
he soll the baker kids on the
floor ded so the hscrif poot
owt a in westagashin that
moorng. the were no suddspes
pepol shay ther yostod by
an olld man Living thef
but he past away regentley
he was a stegy old man that
dint like to be bothrd

   no wan liked him
but pepol shay thay se Him
in the fori some time s
with a shavol some pepol
think it was the sharif

Figure 9–9 (cont.).

win he wint up ther
yesterdayi evry one wos
skard that ther was a killer
on the loos that mornOning
thay tok them to the morther
tha morthichin clamd he
fown boolit wons in ech
of the kids. tha ~~nickel moning~~
the ppxds day the kids wer
missing and the morthin
was ded that niht a person
sed he soll the old man
with a shuvol and a gardia
bad walking in the forist
pepole think ther are twins
every onz gatherd tere
wepens that moorning
win thay got to the cadin
the old man walki'ed owt
boolits rang owt ery were

wen pepole rethernd to
there homs thay had a scledbashins
for hoo thay that was the murder
tow bays later a nother merder
acherd. pepe were so skard

Figure 9-9 (cont.)

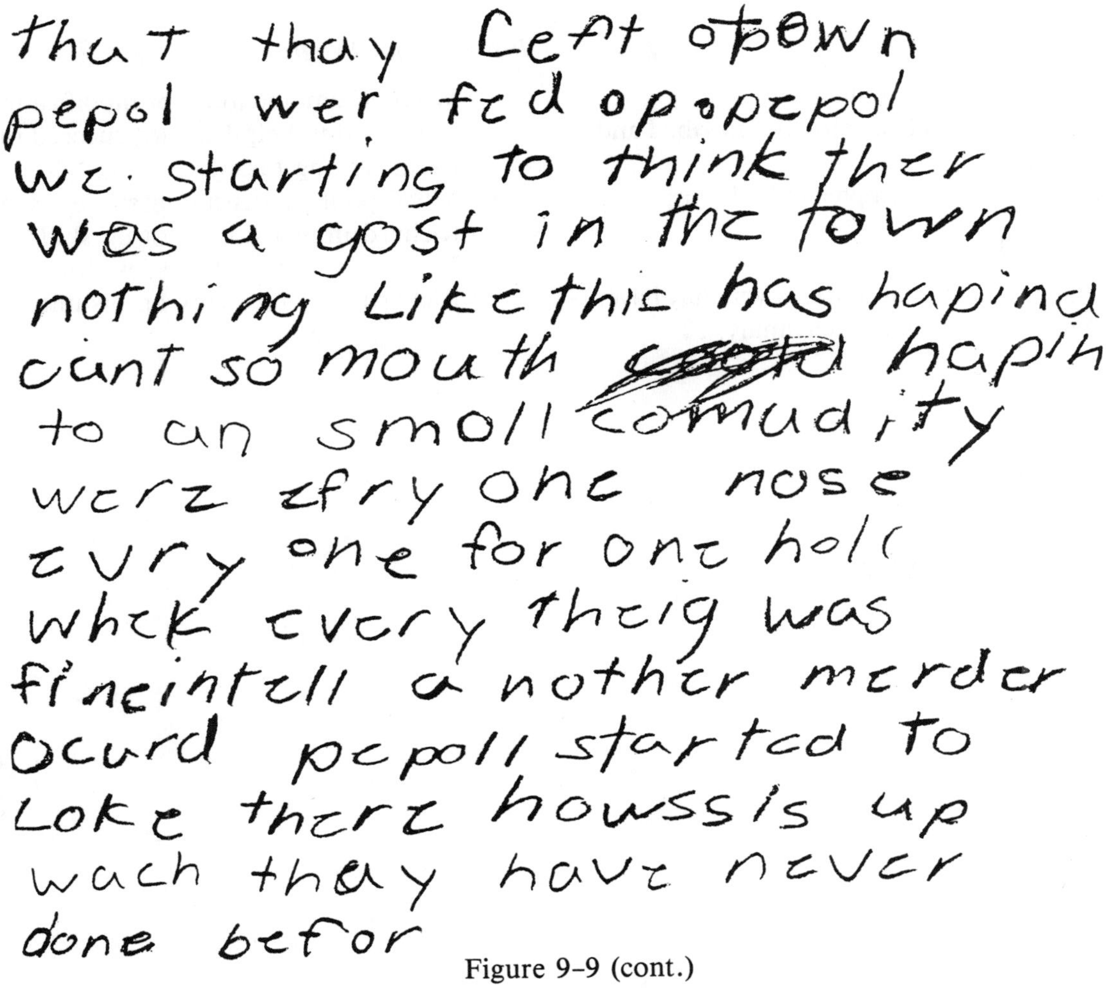

that thay left oßown
pepol wer fed op pepol
we starting to think ther
was a gost in the town
nothing like this has haping
cant so mouth hapin
to an smoll comudity
werz cfry one nose
cvry one for one hol
whek every theig was
fineintell a nother merder
ocurd pepoll started to
loke there howssis up
wach thay have never
done befor

Figure 9-9 (cont.)

- Does Richard use uppercase and lowercase letters correctly?
- Are any letter reversals apparent?

Spelling

- Are high-frequency sight words spelled correctly?
- To what degree does Richard rely on the phonetic spelling of words?
- Do all of the words have good sound-symbol correspondence?
- To what degree does Richard's spelling reflect limited sensitivity to common English spelling patterns?
- Address Richard's difficulties with word boundaries.
- Are any transpositions evidenced in the sample?
- Even if incorrect, does Richard spell words consistently?

- What morphological errors are apparent in the sample?
- Are omissions and additions of letters apparent in Richard's spellings?
- Identify errors in the spellings of homonyms. Why may Richard be making these errors?

Usage

- Are capital letters used correctly?
- Are periods and question marks used consistently and correctly?
- Comment upon Richard's use of articles.
- Is consistency in verb tense maintained?

Vocabulary

- Does Richard use appropriate vocabulary for a narrative about a murder investigation?
- Do Richard's spelling difficulties appear to inhibit his word choice?

Organization and Ideation

- Are the ideas well sequenced?
- Have all the ideas been clearly described and clarified?
- How has Richard attempted to build suspense?

Supplementary Analyses

- Discuss any additional concerns you may have.
- Is there a need for further analysis?

Instructional Programming

- What accommodations or modifications may be needed to help Richard succeed on classroom writing tasks?
- What specific instructional strategies may help Richard improve his writing skill?
- Discuss specific strategies for providing Richard with feedback on his initial drafts.

Student: Keisha
Grade: 8th
Assignments: Three descriptive paragraphs

On three different days within a week, Keisha was asked to write a descriptive paragraph about informative videos that she watched on the Discovery channel in her science class. For the assignments, she was asked to summarize any new information that she had learned from the videos.

Guided Questions

Handwriting and Appearance

- Discuss the overall appearance of the samples. Address headings, indentation, and margins.
- Does Keisha form all the letters correctly?
- Is the slant consistent within and between samples?

Spelling

- Note how Keisha spelled "Science" on the first two paragraphs. To what degree does

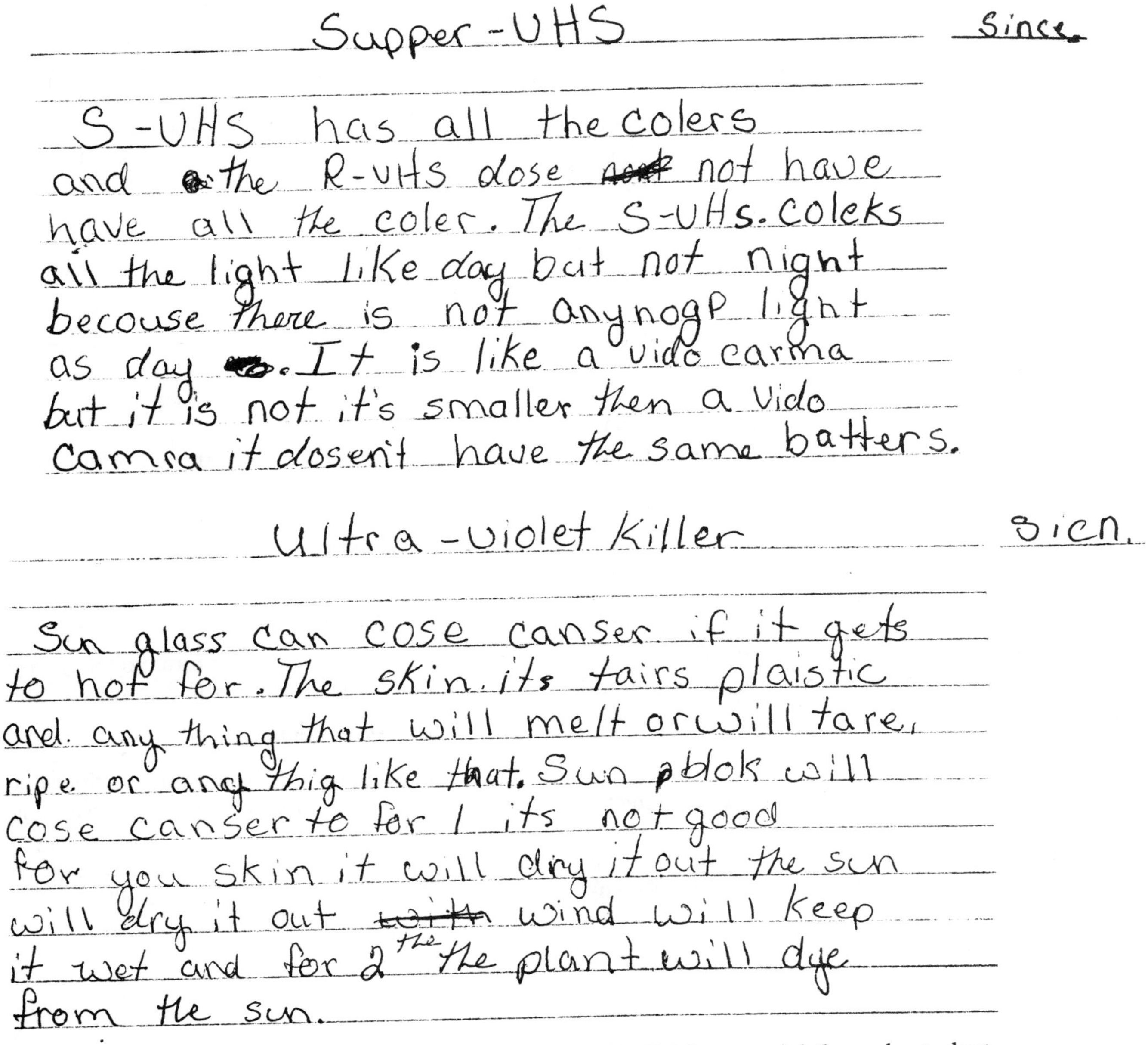

Supper - UHS   Since

S-UHS has all the colers
and the R-UHS dose not have
have all the coler. The S-UHS. coleks
all the light like day but not night
becouse there is not anynogp light
as day. It is like a vido carma
but it is not it's smaller then a vido
Camra it dosen't have the same batters.

Ultra - violet killer   Sicn.

Sun glass can cose canser if it gets
to hot for. The skin. its tairs plaistic
and any thing that will melt or will tare,
ripe or any thig like that. Sun block will
cose canser to for 1 its not good
for you skin it will dry it out the sun
will dry it out with wind will keep
it wet and for 2 the plant will dye
from the sun.

Figure 9–10. Three descriptive paragraphs by Keisha, an eighth-grade student.

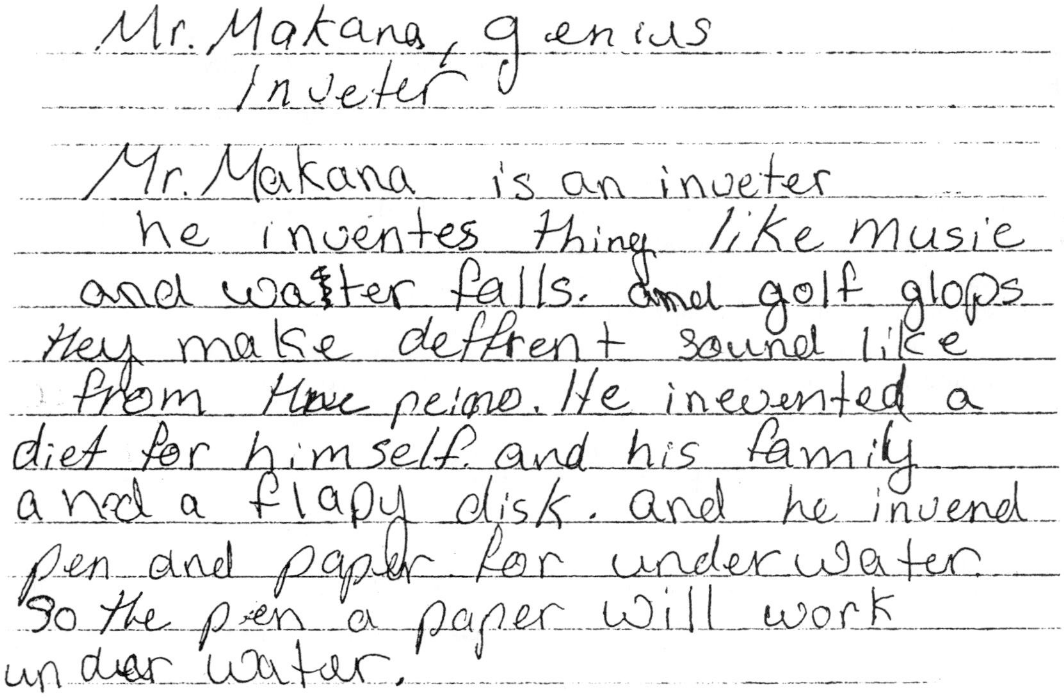

> Mr. Makana, genius
> Inveter
>
> Mr. Makana is an inveter
> he inventes thing like music
> and waiter falls. and golf glops
> they make deffrent sound like
> from the peino. He inevented a
> diet for himself and his family
> and a flapy disk. and he invend
> pen and paper for under water
> So the pen a paper will work
> un der water.

Figure 9–10 (cont.).

Keisha understand that English spelling is invariant?

- How consistent is Keisha in the spelling of a root word when used in different derivations?
- Address Keisha's spelling of words with similar visual patterns.
- Is there evidence of homonym confusion in the samples?
- What may the reasoning be behind the spelling of "enough" as *anyogp*?
- What problems exist with word endings? What type of difficulty may be indicated?
- Does Keisha correctly observe word boundaries?

Usage

- Are periods and capital letters used consistently and correctly?
- Does any evidence exist to suggest that Keisha may not fully understand how to write a complete sentence?
- What type of sentence structures are apparent in the samples?

Organization and Ideation

- Are the ideas presented in a clear and meaningful way?
- Do the ideas follow each other logically?
- Does she use cohesive ties?
- Has Keisha fully expanded upon her ideas?

Supplementary Analyses

- Discuss any additional concerns you may have.
- Is there a need for further analysis?

Instructional Programming

- What accommodations or modifications may be needed to help Keisha succeed on classroom writing tasks?
- What specific instructional strategies may help Keisha improve her writing skill?

The following five samples, listed in the Index below, have not been analyzed. When reviewing the samples, attempt to follow the same pattern of analysis and recommendations as presented in Chapter 8 or write and answer a series of questions.

Two samples are provided for Charlie, one from fourth grade and one from sixth grade. During the 2 years between samples, Charlie received intensive, individualized instruction from a learning disabilities specialist. Although significant progress can be seen, his difficulties with writing are still apparent as is the enduring nature of a learning disability.

Samples Without Guided Questions

Index

STUDENT	GRADE	ASSIGNMENT
Mark	2nd	Description of a field trip
Charlie	4th	Book review, descriptive paragraph, journal entry
	6th	An imaginary story
Babs	5th	A descriptive paragraph
Karen	7th	A journal entry and descriptive paragraph
Andrew	8th	An opinion paper and classnotes

Student: Mark
Grade: 2nd
Assignment: Description of a field trip

Following a field trip to a library and museum, the students in Mark's class were asked to write about their experiences. Prior to writing, an in-depth class discussion occurred. The title *My Field Trip* and the words *library* and *museum* were written on the chalkboard.

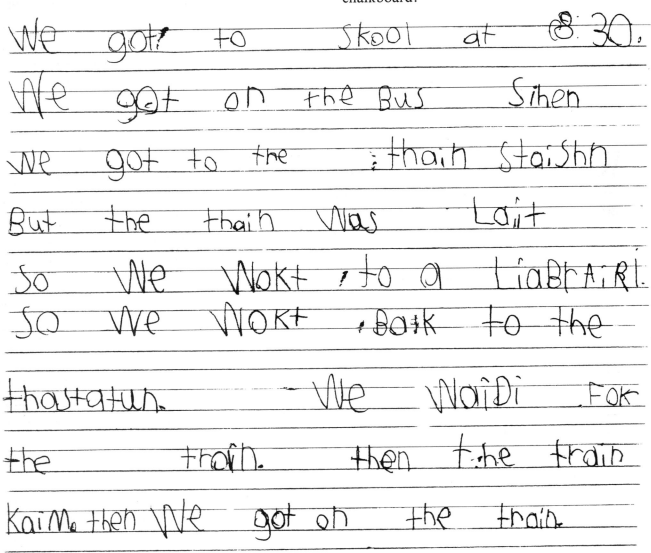

Translation:

We got to school at 8:30. We got on the bus. Then we got to the train station. But the train was late so we walked to a library. So we walked back to the train station. We waited for the train. Then the train came. Then we got on the train. We got our seats. Then the train start moving very slowly. It moved faster. So then we got to . . . Then we went to a picnic place. We ate. We got on the bus. Then we went to the museum. We look around. Then we got on the bus. We went home on the bus. When we were late for the bus so my mom picked me up.

Figure 9–11. Description of a field trip by Mark, a second-grade student.

We got rar Sees. then
the thain sot Mooving vere
Slote. it MooD Foser'r "so
then We got to Bestin.
the,n n: We Wut to a
piki plais. We eait We got
on the Bus. then We Wut
to the Mooseem We Look
a ranD. then We got on the
Bus. We Wut home on
the Bus. Wen We Wer
lait For the Bus. Soi My
MoM pit Me up.

Figure 9–11 (cont.).

Student: Charlie
Grade: 4th
Assignments: Two book reviews, a descriptive paragraph, and a journal entry

---

Charlie was encouraged to write as much as he could for all four assignments. The first and last were book reviews, the titles of which provide information with regard to Charlie's reading level. For the second assignment, the descriptive paragraph, the word *rattlesnake* was written for Charlie to copy. The third assignment, the journal entry, was the longest piece of writing produced by Charlie that year.

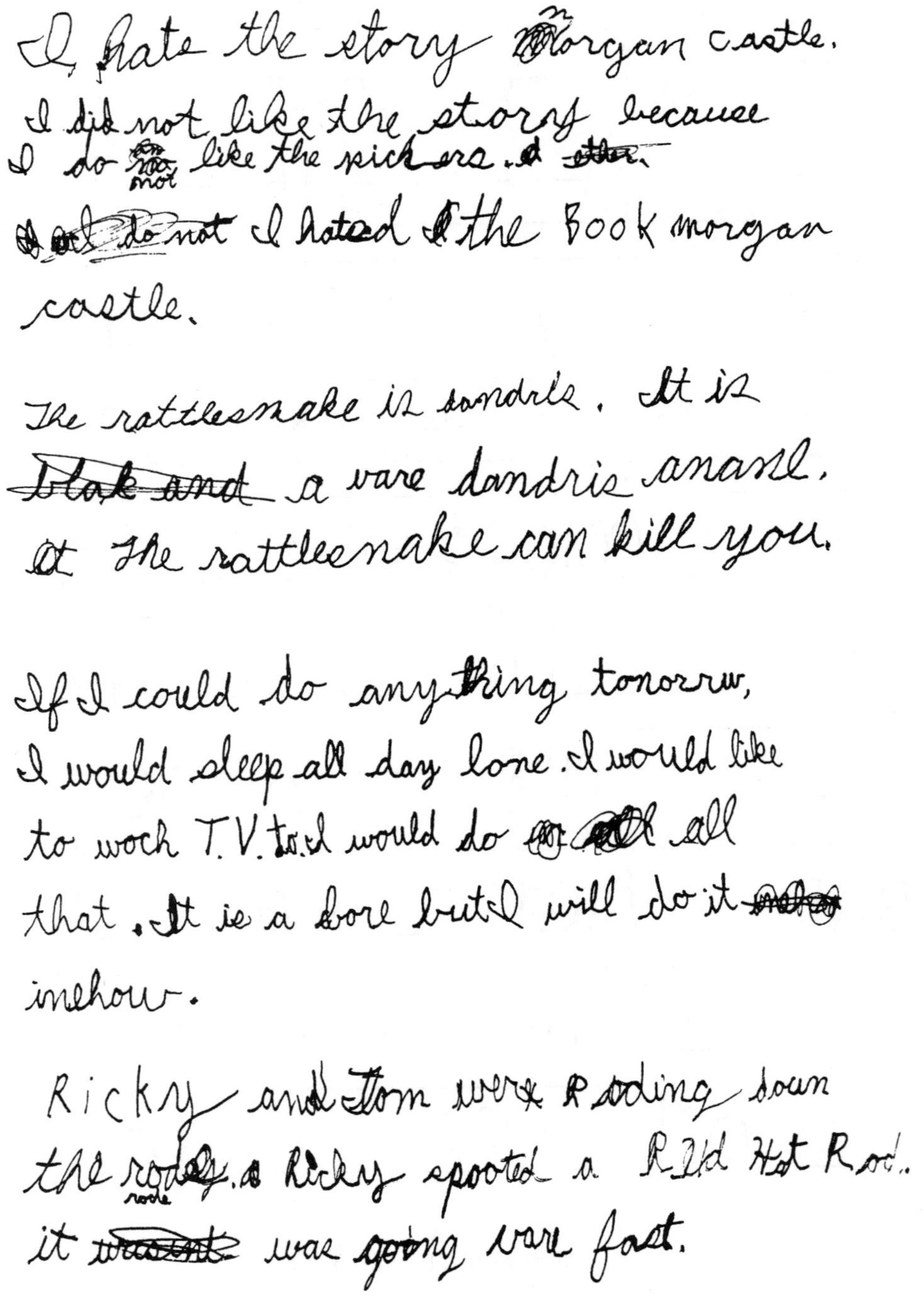

I hate the story morgan castle.
I did not like the story because
I do not like the pickers. ~~I the~~.

~~I at do not~~ I hated the book morgan
castle.

The rattlesnake is sandrls. It is
~~blak and~~ a vare dandris anaml.
at The rattlesnake can kill you.

If I could do anything tonozrw,
I would sleep all day lone. I would like
to woch T.V. to I would do ~~at~~ all
that. It is a bore but I will do it ~~now~~
inehour.

Ricky and ~~Tom~~ were roding down
the ~~road~~. Ricky spooted a Red Hot Rod.
it ~~was~~ was going vare fast.

Figure 9–12a. A page from his journal by Charlie, a fourth-grade student.

Grade: 6th
Assignment: An imaginary story

Charlie was asked to write a story on a topic of his choice. After choosing "The Invasion" as the title of his story, Charlie proceeded to write an unexpected storyline. Prior to writing, he spent a number of minutes thinking about his content and jotted down some notes to help with organization.

The Invasion

One night I was sleeping and my tedy bear became alive. It started to tern green, when it trnd green it started to eat my sheets it spit out one peace at a time. A minut later the spit out sheets started to tern in to green tety Bars, Dren they started to craw on me so I got a nife and stabed the green tety Bears and they disaperd and my tety bear was under the bed.

Figure 9–12b. A story by Charlie written in sixth grade.

Student: Babs
Grade: 5th
Assignment: A descriptive paragraph

Babs was asked to write about her summer vacation. Prior to writing, she was encouraged to draw a semantic map or web to help with organization. After thinking for only a short time, Babs wrote her assignment in less than 10 minutes.

My weekend was good and it was fun. Then I played in the mud. And I got muddy. And me and my brothers played too. And I stomped my feet.

Then I was Eating food. Then I was eating Taco's & rice. Then the next day we ate Pizza. Then at Last for snack we ate Popcorn.

At Last I rode my bike. Then I through the mud. And I went over the hills. And I went in front of the house.

Figure 9-13. A paragraph by Babs, a fifth-grade student.

Student: Karen
Grade: 7th
Assignments: A journal entry and a descriptive
paragraph

The first sample, titled "Kites," was an entry from Karen's journal. The second sample, titled "Esther Island," was written on a topic chosen by Karen and is a final draft. On this assignment, Karen received help from a peer reviewer during the editing stage. Analyze both passages for content and form.

Kits

One day me and my step father wehnt out to fly are Kits. My kit is the same size as his but mine is a different color than his. for Christmas I got lights for my Kit.
       Wen I fly my Kit I half to look up and I get a stif neck. Some times I get pulled away from were I was starding.

Esther Island

Esther Island has the second largest fish hatchery in the world. They raise salmons such as Kings, silvers, dogs, and pinks. Esther does not raise red salmons. Esther gets it's power from the lake and Emergese generators. There are ~~k bought~~ about twenty Eight people in the winter. and about One hundred people in the sumer.
       At Esther Island I go to corespondence with my parents, I study by my self and my teacher corects and grads it all. But my parents are kind of my teachers.

Figure 9–14. A journal entry and a descriptive paragraph by Karen, a seventh-grade student.

Student: Andrew
Grade: 8th
Assignments: An opinion paper and classnotes

Andrew was asked to write an opinion paper for his Science class about his reaction to his lab experience of dissecting a pig. In addition, his classnotes for the lecture that day are provided. What information can you learn about Andrew's writing skill by analyzing these brief assignments?

I think it was egecationel but very boring. It is hard to consentrat with that smell to, I did not like the lab and I had alredy lurned what was in it. Next year I sigjest you get some lisal,

Respiration

1) book lungs — stacked tisow
Spiders

2) gills brething in whater
crostation

3) trakel tubs

Circulation

1) dorsal heart — tube
2) Open circ sistem few arters
and vans

Excretion
1) solid whast — mouth → esofogs —
stomek — intesten — anus
2) liqued whast: eses whater mineges
nitrogen

Figure 9–15. An opinion paragraph and classnotes written by Andrew, an eighth-grade student.

APPENDIX A

COMPUTER SOFTWARE, INSTRUCTIONAL PROGRAMS, AND BOOKS

Computer Software

ACTA. Scottsdale, AZ: Symmetry.

AppleWorks. Santa Clara, CA: Claris.

AppleWorks GS. Santa Clara, CA: Claris.

Bank Street Writer III. New York, NY: Scholastic Software.

Bank Street Writer Plus. Novato, CA: Broderbund Software.

Beamer: Prefixes, Basewords, Suffixes. Kankakee, IL: Data Command.

Big Book Makers. Calabasas, CA: Toucan.

Bilingual Writing Center. Fremond, CA: The Learning Company.

Capitalization (Grades 3–9). Diamondale, MI: Hartley.

Capitalization (Grades 5–12). Big Springs, TX: Gamco.

Cause & Effect. Campton, NM: Troll.

Children's Writing and Publishing Center (English or Spanish). Fremont, CA: The Learning Company.

Complete Spelling Program. Minneapolis, MN: SLED Software.

Create with Garfield. Blacklick, OH: Science Research Associates.

Disney Comic Strip Maker. Northbrook, IL: Mindscape.

Dr. Peet's Talking Text Writer. Diamondale, MI: Hartley Courseware.

Easy Report Writer. State College, PA: Parrot Software.

Easybook. Center Harbor, NH: Chickadee.

English on the Job. Omro, WI: Conover.

Essential Grammar. Big Springs, TX: Gamco.

Essential Punctuation. Big Springs, TX: Gamco.

FrED Writer. Concord, CA: Cue SoftSwap.

Grammar Baseball. Big Springs, TX: Gamco.

Great Beginnings. Gainesville, FL: Teacher Support.

Grolier Writer. Boston, MA: Houghton Mifflin.

Homonyms, Antonyms, and Synonyms. Big Springs, TX: Gamco.

How to Write for Everyday Living. Long Island, NY: Educational Activities.

IBM Process Writing Package. Atlanta, GA: IBM Educational Systems.

Keyboarding Primer. St. Paul, MN: MECC.

Keytalk, Audio Word Processor. Calabasas, CA: PEAL Software.

Kids and Keys. Fairfield, CT: Spinnaker.

Kidworks II. Torrance, CA: Davidson & Associates.

Kidwriter. Fairfield, CT: Spinnaker.

Kidwriter Golden Edition. Fairfield, CT: Spinnaker.

Language Activities Courseware. Boston, MA: Houghton Mifflin.

Language Arts. Boston, MA: Houghton Mifflin.

Language Experience Recorder Plus. Gainesville, FL: Teacher Support.

Little Riddles. Diamondale, MI: Hartley.

Logo Express. Montreal, Canada: Logo Computer Systems.

Logo Writer. Montreal, Canada: Logo Computer Systems.

Lucky Seven Spelling Games. Fairfield, CT: Queue.

Lucky Seven Vocabulary Games. Fairfield, CT: Queue.

MacWrite. Santa Clara, CA: Claris.

MacWrite II. Santa Clara, CA: Claris.

MacWrite Pro. Santa Clara, CA: Claris.

Magic Slate. Pleasantville, NY: Sunburst.

Magic Spells. Fremont, CA: The Learning Company.

Make-A-Book. Gainesville, FL: Teacher Support.

Mavis Deacon Teaches Typing. Chicago, IL: Mindscape.

Microsoft Works. Bellevue, WA: Microsoft.

MicroType: Wonderful World of Paws. Florence, KY: Southwestern.

Mind Reader. Campbell, CA: Brown Bag Software.

Monsters and Make-Believe. Calabasas, CA: Toucan.

Muppet Slate. Pleasantville, NY: Sunburst.

My Own Stories. St. Paul, MN: MECC.

My Words. Diamondale, MI: Hartley Courseware.

New Print Shop. Novato, CA: Broderbund Software.

Newsroom. Fairfield, CT: Spinnaker.

Once Upon a Time. New Haven, CT: CompuTeach.

101 Misused Words. Lake Zurich, IL: Learning Seed.

Outliner. St. Paul, MN: MECC.

Printshop. Novato, CA: Broderbund.

Punctuation Baseball. Big Springs, TX: Gamco.

Punctuation Rules. Norfolk, CT: Optimum Resource.

Read, Write, and Publish Series. Acton, MA: William K. Bradford.

Sensible Grammar. Troy, MI: Sensible Software.

Sensible Speller. Troy, MI: Sensible Software.

Sentence Starters. Gainesville, FL: Teacher Support.

Sound Sentences. Long Island, NY: Educational Activities.

Special Writer Coach. Cambridge, MA: Tom Snyder.

Spell It Plus. Torrance, CA: Davidson & Associates.

Spelling Mastery. Blacklick, OH: Science Research Associates.

Spelling Puzzler. Boston, MA: Houghton Mifflin.

Spelling Puzzles and Tests. Minneapolis, MN: MECC.

Spelling Rules. Norfolk, CT: Optimum Resource.

Spelling Speechware (1-6). Boston, MA: Houghton Mifflin.

Spelling Tutor. Houston, TX: Access Unlimited.

Spelling To Be Somebody. North Billerica, MA: Curriculum Associates.

Spellright Software. North Billerica, MA: Curriculum Associates.

Spider Hunt Spelling. Big Springs, TX: Gamco.

Stickybear Parts of Speech. Norfolk, CT: Optimum Resource.

Stickybear Spellgrabber. Norfolk, CT: Optimum Resource.

Stickybear Typing. Norfolk, CT: Optimum Resource.

Storybook Weaver. St. Paul, MN: MECC.

SuperPrint for the Macintosh-English. Jefferson City, MO: Scholastic.

SuperPrint for the Macintosh-Spanish/Bilingual. Jefferson City, MO: Scholastic.

Talking Text Writer. New York, NY: Scholastic Software.

That's My Story. Chicago, IL: Mindscape.

The Print Shop. Novato, CA: Broderbund Software.

The Student Writing Center for Windows. Fremont, CA: The Learning Company.

Type to Learn. Pleasantville, NY: Sunburst.

Typing Keys. Novato, CA: Academic Therapy.

Typing Tutor. New York, NY: Scholastic Software.

Vocabulary Builders. Big Springs, TX: Gamco.

Vocabulary Challenge. Chicago, IL: Mindscape.

Vocabulary Detective. Pine, AZ: SWEPS Educational Software.

Vocabulary Development. Norfolk, CT: Optimum Resource.

Vocabulary Machine. Gainesville, FL: Teacher Support.

Webster's New Word Spelling Dictionary. Des Moines, IA: Simon and Schuster.

Word Capture. Tulsa, OK: Heartsoft.

Word Launch. Tulsa, OK: Heartsoft.

Word Magic. Chicago, IL: Mindscape.

Write Now. Lakewood, NJ: MacWarehouse.

Write This Way. Katonah, NY: Interactive Learning Materials.

Write This Way-LD. Diamondale, MI: Hartley Courseware.

Writing Adventure. Blacklick, OH: Science Research Associates.

Writing Center. Fremont, CA: The Learning Company.

Writing to Read. Atlanta, GA: IBM Educational Systems.

Writing to Write. Atlanta, GA: IBM Educational Systems.

Writing Workshop. St. Louis, MO: Milliken Publishing Company.

Instructional Programs

Handwriting

A Writing Manual for the Left-Handed. Cambridge, MA: Educators Publishing Service.

Alphabet Mastery (Letters). Novato, CA: Ann Arbor.

Beginning Connected, Cursive Handwriting (Levels 1-3). Cambridge, MA: Educators Publishing Service.

Creative Cursive. Grand Rapids, MI: Instructional Fair.

Cursive Writing (Letters). Novato, CA: Ann Arbor.

Cursive Writing (Words). Novato, CA: Ann Arbor.

Cursive Writing Skills. Cambridge, MA: Educators Publishing Service.

D'Nealian Handwriting (Cursive). Glenview, IL: ScottForesman.

D'Nealian Handwriting (Manuscript). Glenview, IL: ScottForesman.

D'Nealian Home/School Activities (Grades 1–3). Glenview, IL: ScottForesman.

Handwriting: A Fresh Start. North Billerica, MA: Curriculum Associates.

Handwriting with Write and See. Chicago, IL: Lyons and Carnahan.

Handwriting without Tears. Potomac, MD: Olsen.

Learning to Use Cursive Handwriting. Cambridge, MA: Educators Publishing Service.

Learning to Use Manuscript Handwriting. Cambridge, MA: Educators Publishing Service.

Let's Print and Spell. Cambridge, MA: Educators Publishing Service.

Let's Write and Spell. Cambridge, MA: Educators Publishing Service.

Loops and other groups: A kinesthetic writing system. Randolph, NJ: O.T. Ideas.

Manuscript Alphabet. Grand Rapids, MI: Instructional Fair.

Manuscript Writing (Letters). Novato, CA: Ann Arbor.

Manuscript Writing (Words). Novato, CA: Ann Arbor.

Remediation of Reversals: The "Magic Rulers" Program-Revised Edition. Novato, CA: Academic Therapy.

Right Line Paper. Austin, TX: PRO-ED.

Stop-Go Right Line Paper. Austin, TX: PRO-ED.

The Johnson Handwriting Program. (Cursive) Cambridge, MA: Educators Publishing Service.

Transition to Cursive (Books 1, 2). Grand Rapids, MI: Instructional Fair.

Writing Exercises for the Left-Handed. Cambridge, MA: Educators Publishing Service.

Spelling

A Spelling Workbook. Cambridge, MA: Educators Publishing Service.

A Spelling Workbook for Corrective Drill for Elementary Grades. Cambridge, MA: Educators Publishing Service.

A Spelling Workbook for Early Primary Corrective Work. Cambridge, MA: Educators Publishing Service.

Childs Spelling System: The Rules. Cambridge, MA: Educators Publishing Service.

Dr. Spello. St. Louis, MO: Phoenix Learning Resources.

Handbook of English-Spelling. Cambridge, MA: Educators Publishing Service.

How to Spell. Cambridge, MA: Educators Publishing Service.

How to Teach Spelling. Cambridge, MA: Educators Publishing Service.

Instant Spelling Words for Writing. North Billerica, MA: Curriculum Associates.

Language Tool Kit. (reading and spelling). Cambridge, MA: Educators Publishing Service.

Power Over Words (Books 1 and 2). Cambridge, MA: Educators Publishing Service.

Programmed Spelling. Novato, CA: Ann Arbor.

Quick-Word: Handbook for Beginning Writers. North Billerica, MA: Curriculum Associates.

Quick-Word: Handbook for Practical Writing. North Billerica, MA: Curriculum Associates.

Quick-Word: Handbook for Everyday Writers. North Billerica, MA: Curriculum Associates.

Sound Spelling. Cambridge, MA: Educators Publishing Service.

Spell It Out. Columbus, OH: Globe Fearon.

Spellbinding 1, 2. Cambridge, MA: Educators Publishing Service.

Spellbound. Cambridge, MA: Educators Publishing Service.

Spelling and Vocabulary. Boston, MA: Houghton Mifflin.

Spelling Book. St. Louis, MO: Phoenix Learning Resources.

Spelling Makes Sense. Columbus, OH: Globe Fearon.

Spelling Patterns. Cambridge, MA: Educators Publishing Service.

Spelling Power. Providence, RI: Jamestown.

Spelling to Be Somebody. North Billerica, MA: Curriculum Associates.

Speed Spelling 1 and 2. Austin, TX: PRO-ED.

Stetson Spelling Program. Austin, TX: PRO-ED.

The Childs Spelling System: The Rules. Cambridge, MA: Educators Publishing Service.

The Spell of Words. Cambridge, MA: Educators Publishing Services.

Usage

Basic English Composition. Circle Pines, MN: AGS.

Basic English Grammar. Circle Pines, MN: AGS.

Basic Language Principles with Latin Background: A Textbook in Grammar. Cambridge, MA: Educators Publishing Service.

Basic Skills in English. Evanston, IL: McDougall, Littell, & Company.

Basic Skills in Filling out Forms. Churchville, PA: Curriculum Productions.

Basic Writing Skills. Grand Rapids, MI: Instructional Fair.

Basic Writing Skills. Tigard, OR: C.C. Publications.

Beginning English Day by Day. Novato, CA: Academic Therapy.

Beginning Writer's Manual. St. Louis, MO: Phoenix Learning Resources.

Building English Sentences. Silver Spring, MD: Institute of Modern Languages.

Building Language Power. Palo Alto, CA: Dale Seymour.

Capitalization and Punctuation. North Billerica, MA: Curriculum Associates.

Capitalization and Punctuation Makes Sense. Columbus, OH: Globe Fearon.

Caps, Commas, and Other Things. Novato, CA: Academic Therapy.

Elementary Language Skills. St. Louis, MO: Phoenix Learning Resources.

English Day by Day. Novato, CA: Academic Therapy.

English for the World of Work. Circle Pines, MN: American Guidance Service.

English Skills. New York, NY: Harcourt Brace Jovanovich.

English to Use. Circle Pines, MN: AGS.

Essential Writing. Baltimore, MD: Media Materials.

Exercises in English Grammar (Books 1 and 2). Cambridge, MA: Educators Publishing Service.

Fearon's Basic English. Columbus, OH: Globe Fearon.

Fearon's English Composition. Columbus, OH: Globe Fearon.

Fearon's Practical English. Columbus, OH: Globe Fearon.

Fill in the Blanks. Circle Pines, MN: American Guidance Service.

First English Review. Cambridge, MA: Educators Publishing Service.

For the Love of Editing. Palo Alto, CA: Dale Seymour.

Grammar. Grand Rapids, MI: Instructional Fair.

Grammar and Composition for Everyday English. Columbus, OH: Globe Fearon.

Grammar for Teens. East Moline, IL: LinguiSystems.

Grammar for Sentences. Columbus, OH: Globe Fearon.

Grammar Makes Sense. Columbus, OH: Globe Fearon.

Grammar Series (Nouns, Pronouns, Verbs, Adjectives, and Adverbs). Grand Rapids, MI: Instructional Fair.

Grammar Series (Punctuation, Capitals, and Writing Sentences). Grand Rapids, MI: Instructional Fair.

Guidebook to Better English. St. Louis, MO: Phoenix Learning Resources.

Handbook of English. Cambridge, MA: Educators Publishing Service.

Helping Kids Write. Cambridge, MA: Educators Publishing Service.

Houghton Mifflin English. Boston, MA: Houghton Mifflin.

I Can Write. Austin, TX: PRO-ED.

Improving Written Language Expression. Denver, CO: Love.

In Plain English. East Moline, IL: LinguiSystems.

Individual Corrective English, Books 1, 2, 3. San Diego, CA: Coronado.

Junior English Review Exercises (Books 1 and 2). Cambridge, MA: Educators Publishing Service.

Key Ideas in English. Orlando, FL: Harcourt Brace Jovanovich.

Keys to Good Language. St. Louis, MO: Phoenix Learning Resources.

Language for Writing. North Billerica, MA: Curriculum Associates.

Language Handbook for Writers. North Billerica, MA: Curriculum Associates.

Language Skills Series. North Billerica, MA: Curriculum Associates.

Learning Grammar through Writing. Cambridge, MA: Educators Publishing Service.

Lessons in Writing Sentences. North Billerica, MA: Curriculum Associates.

Life Skills English. Circle Pines, MN: American Guidance Service.

Michigan Prescriptive Program in English. Novato, CA: Academic Therapy Publications.

Plurals: Teaching Singular and Plural Noun Forms. Austin, TX: PRO-ED.

Positives, Comparatives, and Superlatives: Teaching Comparative and Superlative Forms of Adjectives. Austin, TX: PRO-ED.

Punctuation, Capitalization, and Spelling. Circle Pines, MN: American Guidance Service.

Punctuation Partners. Santa Barbara, CA: The Learning Works.

Rules of the Game: Grammar through Discovery. Cambridge, MA: Educators Publishing Service.

Scoring High in Language. New York, NY: Random House.

Second English Review. Cambridge, MA: Educators Publishing Service.

Senior English Review Exercises. Cambridge, MA: Educators Publishing Service.

Sentence Mastery: A Sentence-Combining Approach. St. Louis, MO: Phoenix Learning Resources.

The Kim Marshall Series in English. Cambridge, MA: Educators Publishing Service.

The Reading Road to Writing. Columbus, OH: Globe Fearon.

TSA Syntax Program. Beaverton, OR: Dormac.

Using Parts of Speech. Circle Pines, MN: American Guidance Service.

Verbs, Verbs, Verbs. Austin, TX: PRO-ED.

Vocabulary

Blue Ribbon Spelling and Vocabulary. Palo Alto, CA: Dale Seymour.

Building Language Power. Palo Alto, CA: Dale Seymour.

Building Vocabulary Skills. Circle Pines, MN: American Guidance Service.

Lessons in Vocabulary Development. North Billerica, MA: Curriculum Associates.

Monkeying Around with Vocabulary. East Moline, IL: LinguiSystems.

More Vocabulary to Go. East Moline, IL: LinguiSystems.

Stanford Vocabulary. St. Louis, MO: Phoenix Learning Resources.

Survival Vocabularies. Columbus, OH: Globe Fearon.

Syllable Vocabulary Builder. North Billerica, MA: Curriculum Associates.

Teaching Vocabulary Worksheets. East Moline, IL: LinguiSystems.

Vocabulary Booster. St. Louis, MO: Phoenix Learning Resource.

Vocabulary Drills. Providence, RI: Jamestown.

Vocabulary for Achievement. Boston, MA: Houghton Mifflin.

Vocabulary for The Twenty-First Century. North Billerica, MA: Curriculum Associates.

Vocabulary Makes Sense. Columbus, OH: Globe Fearon.

Vocabulary: Meaning and Message. Columbus, OH: Globe Fearon.

Vocabulary to Go. East Moline, IL: LinguiSystems.

The Word Kit. East Moline, IL: LinguiSystems.

Words That Connect. Cambridge, MA: Educators Publishing Service.

Words That Describe. Cambridge, MA: Educators Publishing Service.

Words That Name. Cambridge, MA: Educators Publishing Service.

Words That Tell Action. Cambridge, MA: Educators Publishing Service.

Working with Words. North Billerica, MA: Curriculum Associates.

World of Vocabulary. Columbus, OH: Globe Fearon.

Narrative/Expository

Blank Books. North Billerica, MA: Curriculum Associates.

Clues for Better Writing. North Billerica, MA: Curriculum Associates.

Coming Across: A Structural Approach to Composition. Circle Pines, MN: American Guidance Service.

Complete Writing Lessons. Palo Alto, CA: Dale Seymour.

Composition Book. Cambridge, MA: Educators Publishing Service.

Composition Starters. Cambridge, MA: Educators Publishing Service.

Create-A-Story Series. Palo Alto, CA: Dale Seymour.

Creative Writing Skills. Grand Rapids, MI: Instructional Fair.

Ease into Writing. Bloomington, IN: Phi Delta Kappa.

Globe Writing Program. Columbus, OH: Globe Fearon.

Lessons in Writing Sentences. North Billerica, MA: Curriculum Associates.

Letter Writing. Circle Pines, MN: American Guidance Service.

Lifeskills Writing. New York, NY: Educational Design.

Making the Grade in Writing. North Billerica, MA: Curriculum Associates.

Math and Writing. Cambridge, MA: Educators Publishing Service.

Mindmapping: Your Personal Guide to Exploring Creativity and Problem Solving. Nevada City, CA: PLS Book Store.

Newspaper Workshop. Columbus, OH: Globe Fearon.

Organizing Thinking: Graphic Organizer. Nevada City, CA: PLS Book Store.

Peer Voices: Students Writing for Students. North Billerica, MA: Curriculum Associates.

Preparing the Research Paper. Cambridge, MA: Educators Publishing Service.

Prewriting to Printout. Palo Alto, CA: Dale Seymour.

Process Writing Portfolio Program. Reading, MA: Addison-Wesley.

Reading and Writing on the Job. New York, NY: Scholastic Book Service.

Recipes for Writing. Reading, MA: Addison-Wesley.

Research Reports: Teacher Guide. North Billerica, MA: Curriculum Associates.

Springboards for Writing. Novato, CA: Academic Therapy.

Story Starters. Austin, TX: Steck-Vaughn.

Story Starters (Primary and Intermediate). North Billerica, MA: Curriculum Associates.

Teaching Competence in Written Language. Austin, TX: PRO-ED.

Teaching Creative Writing. Carthage, IL: Good Apple.

Teaching Written Expression-The Phelps Sentence Guide Program. Novato, CA: Academic Therapy.

The Cooperative Think Tank: Graphic Organizers to Teach Thinking in the Cooperative Classroom. Nevada City, CA: PLS Book Store.

The Gift of Words: Writing and Literature in the Elementary Classroom. Reading, MA: Addison-Wesley.

Think and Write. Palo Alto, CA: Dale Seymour.

Think and Write-Composition. Blacklick, OH: Science Research Associates.

Think and Write-Simple Paragraphs. Blacklick, OH: Science Research Associates.

Think and Write-Types of Paragraphs. Blacklick, OH: Science Research Associates.

Thirty Lessons in Note-Taking. North Billerica, MA: Curriculum Associates.

Thirty Lessons in Outlining. North Billerica, MA: Curriculum Associates.

Write Away! Journal. Bloomington, IN: Phi Delta Kappa.

Write for Power. Los Angeles, CA: Communication Associates.

Write More, Learn More. Bloomington, IN: Phi Delta Kappa.

Writers in Training: A Guide to Developing a Composition Program. Palo Alto, CA: Dale Seymour.

Writer's Workshop. Columbus, OH: Globe Fearon.

Writer's Workshop. Palo Alto, CA: Dale Seymour.

Writing: A Fact and Fun Book. Palo Alto, CA: Dale Seymour.

Writing Down the Days. Palo Alto, CA: Dale Seymour.

Writing for A Reason. Columbus, OH: Globe Fearon.

Writing for Your Life. Circle Pines, MN: American Guidance Service.

Writing Makes Sense. Columbus, OH: Globe Fearon.

Writing I: Getting Started. Columbus, OH: Globe Fearon.

Writing Process Transparencies (2-8). Boston, MA: Houghton Mifflin.

Writing Sentences and Paragraphs. Circle Pines, MN: American Guidance Service.

Writing Skills (1 and 2). Cambridge, MA: Educators Publishing Service.

Writing Skills 1-3. Grand Rapids, MI: Insructional Fair.

Writing Skills for the Adolescent. Cambridge, MA: Educators Publishing Service.

Writing to Explain. Palo Alto, CA: Dale Seymour.

Writing to Go. East Moline, IL: LinguiSystems.

Writing to Inform. Palo Alto, CA: Dale Seymour.

Writing to Persuade. Palo Alto, CA: Dale Seymour.

Writing Your Life. Palo Alto, CA: Dale Seymour.

Writing with a Point. Cambridge, MA: Educators Publishing Service.

Books on Writing

Allred, R. A. (1987). *Spelling trends, content, and methods*. Washington, DC: National Education Association.

Adams, K. H., & Adams, J. L. (1991). *Teaching advanced composition*. Upper Montclair, NJ: Boynton/Cook.

Andrasick, K. D. (1990). *Opening texts*. Portsmouth, NH: Heinemann.

Applebee, A. N. (1979). *The child's concept of story: Ages 2 to 17*. Chicago, IL: University of Chicago Press.

Applebee, A. N. (1984). *Contexts for learning to write: Studies of secondary school instruction*. Norwood, NJ: Ablex.

Applebee, A. N., Langer, J. A., & Mullins, I. V. (1986). *The writing report card: Writing achievement in American schools*. Princeton, NJ: Educational Testing Service.

Applebee, A. N., Langer, J. A., Mullins, I. V. S., & Foertsch, M. A. (1990). *Learning to write in our nation's schools*. Princeton, NJ: Educational Testing Service.

Atwell, N. (1987). *In the middle: Writing, reading, and learning with adolescents*. Portsmouth, NH: Heinemann.

Atwell, N. (1990). *Coming to know: Writing to learn in the intermediate grades*. Portsmouth, NH: Heinemann.

Bain, A. M., Bailet, L. L., & Moats, L. C. (1991). *Written language disorders: Theory into practice*. Austin, TX: PRO-ED.

Barbe, W. B., Lucas, V. G., & Wasylyk, T. M. (1984). *Handwriting: Basic skills for effective communication*. Columbus, OH: Zaner-Bloser.

Belanoff, P., & Dickson, M. (1991). *Portfolios*. Upper Montclair, NJ: Boynton/Cook.

Berthoff, A. (1981). *The making of meaning*. Upper Montclair, NJ: Boynton/Cook.

Bishop, W. (1993). *The subject is writing*. Portsmouth, NH: Heinemann.

Bolton, F., & Snowball, D. (1993). *Ideas for spelling*. Portsmouth, NH: Heinemann.

Bolton, F., & Snowball, D. (1993). *Teaching spelling: A practical resource*. Portsmouth, NH: Heinemann.

Bouffler, C. (1993). *Literacy evaluation*. Portsmouth, NH: Heinemann.

Britton, J. (1993). *Language and learning*. Portsmouth, NH: Heinemann.

Buckley, M. H., & Boyle, O. (1981). *The California high school proficiency examination: Evaluating the writing samples-mapping the writing journey*. Berkeley, CA: University of California.

Calkins, L. M. (1983). *Lessons from a child: On the teaching and learning of writing*. Portsmouth, NH: Heinemann.

Calkins, L. M. (1991). *Living between the lines*. Portsmouth, NH: Heinemann.

Calkins, L. M. (1994). *The art of teaching writing* (2nd ed.). Portsmouth, NH: Heinemann.

Capossela, T. L. (1993). *The critical writing workshop*. Upper Montclair, NJ: Boynton/Cook.

Cavey, D. W. (1993). *Dysgraphia: Why Johnny can't write. A handbook for teachers and parents* (2nd ed.). Austin, TX: PRO-ED.

Chapman, G. (1990). *Teaching young playwrights*. Portsmouth, NH: Heinemann.

Cook, G. E., Esposito, M., Gabrielson, T., & Turner, G. (1984). *Spelling for word mastery*. Columbus, OH: Merrill.

Crafton, L. K. (1991). *Whole language: Getting started . . . moving forward*. Katonah, NY: Richard C. Owen.

Daiker, D. A., & Morenberg, M. (1990). *The writing teacher as researcher*. Upper Montclair, NJ: Boynton/Cook.

Daiute, C. (1985). *Writing and computers*. Reading, MA: Addison-Wesley.

Daniels, H., & Zemelman, S. (1985). *A writing project: Training teachers of composition from kindergarten to college*. Portsmouth, NH: Heinemann.

De Fina, A. A. (1992). *Portfolio assessment: Getting started*. New York, NY: Scholastic.

Elbow, P. (1973). *Writing without teachers*. New York: Oxford University Press.

Elbow, P. (1981). *Writing with power*. New York: Oxford University Press.

Fletcher, R. (1993). *What a writer needs*. Portsmouth, NH: Heinemann.

Foster, D. (1992). *A primer for writing teachers*. Upper Montclair, NJ: Boynton/Cook.

Forman, J. (1992). *New visions of collaborative writing*. Upper Montclair, NJ: Boynton/Cook.

Forte, I., & Pangle, M. A. (1985). *Selling spelling to kids: Motivating games and activities to reinforce spelling skills.* Nashville, TN: Incentive Publications.

Fulwiler, T. (1987). *Teaching with writing: An interdisciplinary workshop approach.* Upper Montclair, NJ: Boynton/Cook.

Fulwiler, T. (1987). *The journal book.* Portsmouth, NH: Heinemann.

Fulwiler, T., & Young, A. (1990). *Programs that work.* Portsmouth, NH: Heinemann.

Frank, M. (1979). *If you're trying to teach kids how to write, you've gotta have this book.* Nashville, TN: Incentive Publications.

Fredericksen, C. H., & Dominic, J. F. (1981). *Writing: The nature, development, and teaching of written communication: Vol 2. Process, development, and communication.* Hillsdale, NJ: Lawrence Erlbaum.

Gallo, D. (1992). *Authors' insights: Turning teenagers into readers and writers.* Upper Montclair, NJ: Boynton/Cook.

Gillingham, A., & Stillman, B. W. (1973). *Remedial training for children with specific disability in reading, spelling, and penmanship.* Cambridge, MA: Educators Publishing Service.

Goodman, K. S. (1986). *What's whole in whole language?* Portsmouth, NH: Heinemann.

Goodman, K. S., Goodman, Y. M., & Hood, W. J. (1989). *The whole language evaluation book.* Portsmouth, NH: Heinemann.

Graves, D. (1978). *Balance the basics: Let them write.* New York, NY: Ford Foundation.

Graves, D. (1983). *Writing: Teachers and children at work.* Portsmouth, NH: Heinemann.

Graves, D. S., & Sunstein, B. S. (Eds.). (1992). *Portfolio portraits.* Portsmouth, NH: Heinemann.

Hanna, P. R., Hodges, R. E., & Hanna, J. S. (1971). *Spelling: Structure and strategies.* Boston, MA: Houghton Mifflin.

Hansen, J., Newkirk, T., & Graves, D. (1985). *Breaking ground: Teachers relate reading and writing in the elementary school.* Portsmouth, NH: Heinemann.

Harris, K. R., & Graham, S. (1992). *Helping young writers master the craft: Strategy instruction and self-regulation in the writing process.* Cambridge, MA: Brookline Books.

Harste, J. C., Short, K. G., & Burke, C. (1988). *Creating classrooms for authors: The reading-writing connection.* Portsmouth, NH: Heinemann.

Harwayne, S. (1992). *Lasting impressions.* Portsmouth, NH: Heinemann.

Hawisher, G., & LeBlanc, P. (1992). *Re-imagining computers and composition.* Portsmouth, NH: Boynton/Cook.

Hawisher, G., & Selfe, C. L. (1989). *Critical perspectives on computers and composition instruction.* New York, NY: Teachers College Press.

Henderson, E. H. (1990). *Teaching spelling* (2nd ed.). Boston, MA: Houghton Mifflin.

Hennings, D. G., & Grant, B. M. (1981). *Written expression in the language arts* (2nd ed.). New York, NY: Teachers College Press.

Hildreth, G. (1955). *Teaching spelling.* New York, NY: Henry Holt.

Hodges, R. E. (1977). *Learning to spell: Theory and research into practice.* Urbana, IL: National Council of Teachers of English.

Hoot, J. L., & Silvern, S. B. (1988). *Writing with computers in the early grades.* New York, NY: Teachers College Press.

Hornsby, D., Parry, J., & Sukarna, D. (1993). *Teach on.* Portsmouth, NH: Heinemann.

Irvin, J. L. (1990). *Vocabulary knowledge: Guidelines for instruction.* Washington, DC: National Education Association.

Karelitz, E. B. (1993). *The author's chair and beyond.* Portsmouth, NH: Heinemann.

Kirby, D., & Liner, T. (1988). *Inside out: Developmental strategies for teaching writing.* Portsmouth, NH: Heinemann.

Klein, M. L. (1985). *The development of writing in children: Pre-K through grade 8.* Needham Heights, MA: Allyn & Bacon.

Knapp, L. R. (1986). *The word processor and the writing teacher.* Englewood Cliffs, NJ: Prentice-Hall.

Kutz, E., Groden, S., & Zamel, V. (1993). *The discovery of competence.* Portsmouth, NH: Heinemann.

Lane, B. (1993). *After the end: Teaching and learning creative revision.* Portsmouth, NH: Heinemann.

Larsen, S. C. (1987). *Assessing the writing abilities and instructional needs of students.* Austin, TX: PRO-ED.

Ledoux, D. (1993). *Turning memories into memoirs.* Portsmouth, NH: Heinemann.

Lesmire, T. (1994). *When children write: Critical revisions of the writing workshop.* New York, NY: Teachers College Press.

Lester, M. (1990). *Grammar in the classroom.* New York, NY: Macmillan.

Macrorie, K. (1984). *Searching writing: A context book.* Upper Montclair, NJ: Boynton/Cook.

Macrorie, K. (1985). *Telling writing.* Upper Montclair, NJ: Boynton/Cook.

McGee, L. M., & Richgels, D. J. (1990). *Literacy's beginnings: Supporting young readers and writers.* Needham Heights, MA: Allyn & Bacon.

Mills, H., Clyde, J. A., & Woodward, V. A. (1990). *Portraits of whole language classrooms.* Portsmouth, NH: Heinemann.

Moffett, J. (1992). *Active voice.* Upper Montclair, NJ: Boynton/Cook.

Moffett, J. (1992). *Detecting growth in language.* Upper Montclair, NJ: Boynton/Cook.

Mohr, M. M. (1984). *Revision: The rhythm of meaning.* Upper Montclair, NJ: Boynton/Cook.

Morrow, L. M. (1993). *Literacy development in the early years: Helping children read and write* (2nd ed.). Needham Heights, MA: Allyn & Bacon.

Murphy, S., & Smith, M. A. (1991). *Writing portfolios: A bridge from teaching to assessment.* Portsmouth, NH: Heinemann.

Murray, D. (1982). *Learning by teaching.* Upper Montclair, NJ: Boynton/Cook.

Murray, D. (1985). *A writer teaches writing* (2nd ed.). Boston, MA: Houghton Mifflin.

Murray, D. (1987). *Write to learn.* Boston, MA: Houghton Mifflin.

Murray, D. (1990). *Shoptalk.* Upper Montclair, NJ: Boynton/Cook.

Myklebust, H. R. (1973). *Development and disorders of written language: Studies of normal and exceptional children* (Vol. 2). New York, NY: Grune and Stratton.

Nathan, R. (1991). *Writers in the classroom.* Norwood, MA: Christopher-Gordon.

Newkirk, T. (1993). *Nuts and bolts.* Portsmouth, NH: Heinemann.

Newkirk, T. (1993). *Workshop 5: The writing process revisited.* Portsmouth, NH: Heinemann.

Newkirk, T., & Atwell, N. (1988). *Understanding writing: Ways of observing, learning, and teaching K–8* (2nd ed.). Portsmouth, NH: Heinemann.

Newman, J. (1985). *The craft of children's writing.* Portsmouth, NH: Heinemann.

Newman, J. (1985). *Whole language theory in use.* Portsmouth, NH: Heinemann.

Olsen, J. Z. (1994). *Handwriting without tears.* Potomac, MD: Author.

Olson, J. L. (1992). *Envisioning writing: Toward an integration of drawing and writing.* Portsmouth, NH: Heinemann.

Orton, S. T. (1989). *Reading, writing, and speech problems in children and selected papers.* Austin, TX: PRO-ED.

Parry, J., & Hornsby, D. (1985). *Write on: A conference approach to writing.* Portsmouth, NH: Heinemann.

Parsons, L. (1991). *Writing in the real classroom.* Portsmouth, NH: Heinemann.

Peters, M. L. (1979). *Diagnostic and remedial spelling manual* (rev. ed.). London: Macmillan.

Phelps-Gunn, T., & Phelps-Terasaki, D. (1982). *Written language instruction: Theory and remediation.* Rockville, MD: Aspen.

Power, B. M., & Hubbard, R. (1991). *The Heinemann reader: Literacy in process.* Portsmouth, NH: Heinemann.

Preece, A., Cowden, D., & Mickelson, N. (1993). *Young writers in the making.* Portsmouth, NH: Heinemann.

Rhodes, L. K., & Dudley-Marling, C. (1988). *Readers and writers with a difference: A holistic approach to teaching learning disabled and remedial students.* Portsmouth, NH: Heinemann.

Robinson, J. L. (1990). *Conversations on the written word.* Upper Montclair, NJ: Boynton/Cook.

Romano, T. (1987). *Clearing the way: Working with teenage writers.* Portsmouth, NH: Heinemann.

Routman, R. (1991). *Invitations.* Portsmouth, NH: Heinemann.

Routman, R. (1988). *Transitions.* Portsmouth, NH: Heinemann.

Rule, R., & Wheeler, S. (1992). *Creating the story: Guides for writers.* Portsmouth, NH: Heinemann.

Santa, C. M. (1988). *Content reading including study systems: Reading, writing, and studying across the curriculum.* Dubuque, IA: Kendall/Hunt.

Schwartz, M. (1985). *Writing for many roles.* Upper Montclair, NJ: Boynton/Cook.

Schwartz, M. (1991). *Writer's craft, teacher's art.* Upper Montclair, NJ: Boynton/Cook.

Sheffer, S. (1992). *Writing because we love to.* Upper Montclair, NJ: Boynton/Cook.

Silberman, A. (1991). *Growing up writing*. Portsmouth, NH: Heinemann.

Smith, F. (1988). *Joining the literacy club*. Portsmouth, NH: Heinemann.

Smith, F. (1982). *Writing and the writer*. New York, NY: Holt.

Smith, T. E. C., Polloway, E. A., & Beirne-Smith, M. (1994). *Written language for students with disabilities*. Denver, CO: Love.

Spear, K. (1988). *Sharing writing: Peer response groups in English classes*. Upper Montclair, NJ: Boynton/Cook.

Spear, K. (1993). *Peer response groups in action*. Portsmouth, NH: Heinemann.

Tchudi, S. N., & Huerta, M. C. (1983). *Writing in the content areas: Middle school/junior high*. Washington, DC: NEA.

Tchudi, S. N., & Tchudi, S. J. (1983). *Teaching writing in the content areas: Elementary school*. Washington, DC: NEA.

Tchudi, S. N., & Yates, J. M. (1983). *Teaching writing in the content areas: senior high school*. Washington, DC: NEA.

Temple, C., Nathan, R., Burris, N., & Temple, F. (1988). *The beginnings of writing* (2nd ed.). Needham Heights, MA: Allyn & Bacon.

Templeton, S. (1991). *Teaching the integrated language arts*. Boston, MA: Houghton Mifflin.

Thorn, C. (1991). *A very good place to start*. Upper Montclair, NJ: Boynton/Cook.

Tobin, L. (1993). *Writing relationships*. Portsmouth, NH: Heinemann.

Tompkins, G. E. (1993). *Teaching writing: Balancing process and product* (2nd ed.). New York, NY: Merrill.

Wanner, S. Y. (1994). *On with the story: Adolescents learning through narrative*. Portsmouth, NH: Heinemann.

Watts, I. (1992). *Making stories*. Portsmouth, NH: Heinemann.

Weiss, M. S., & Weiss, H. G. (1993). *Formulas to read and write*. Avon, CO: Treehouse Associates.

Westerman, G. (1971). *Spelling and writing*. San Rafael, CA: Dimensions.

Wilde, J. (1993). *A door opens: Writing in fifth grade*. Portsmouth, NH: Heinemann.

Wrench, W. (1987). *A practical guide to computer uses in the English/language arts classroom*. Englewood Cliffs, NJ: Prentice-Hall.

Yates, J. M. (1987). *Writing in the content areas: Research implications* (2nd ed.). Washington, DC: NEA.

Zebroski, J. T. (1993). *Thinking through theory*. Portsmouth, NH: Heinemann.

Zemelman, S., & Daniels, H. (1988). *A community of writers: Teaching writing in the junior and senior high school*. Portsmouth, NH: Heinemann.

Ziegler, A. (1984). *The writer's workshop I*. New York: Teachers and Writers Collaborative.

Ziegler, A. (1984). *The writer's workshop II*. New York: Teachers and Writers Collaborative.

APPENDIX B

PUBLISHERS

Ablex
355 Chestnut St.
Norwood, NJ 07648

Academic Therapy
20 Commercial Boulevard
Novato, CA 94949-6191
1-800-422-7249

Access Unlimited
3535 Briarpark Dr., Ste. 102
Houston, TX 77042-5235
1-800-848-0311

Addison-Wesley
1 Jacob Way
Reading, MA 01867
1-800-552-2259

Allyn and Bacon
160 Gould St.
Needham Heights, MA 02194
1-800-852-8024

American Guidance Service (AGS)
4201 Woodland Rd.
P.O. Box 99
Circle Pines, MN 55014-1796
1-800-328-2560

Ann Arbor
160 Gould St.
Needham Heights, MA 02192
1-800-852-8024

Aspen Systems Corporation
1600 Research Blvd.
Rockville, MD 20850

Barnell Loft
958 Church Street
Baldwin, NY 11510

Boynton/Cook
P.O. Box 860
52 Upper Montclair Plaza
Upper Montclair, NJ 07043

William K. Bradford
310 School St.
Acton, MA 01720
1-800-421-2009

Broderbund Software
500 Redwood Blvd.,
P.O. Box 6121
Novato, CA 94948-6121
1-800-521-6263

Brown Bag Software
2155 S. Bascom Ave., Ste. 114
Campbell, CA 95008
(408) 559-4545

C.C. Publications
P.O. Box 23699
Tigard, OR 97223

Chicadee Software
R.R.2, Box 79W
Center Harbor, NH 03226
(603) 253-4600

Christopher-Gordon
480 Washington St.
Norwood, MA 02062
1-800-934-8322

Claris
5201 Patrick Henry Drive
P.O. Box 526
Santa Clara, CA 95052-9870
1-800-3CLARIS

Communication Associates
2160 Century Park East, #201 North
Los Angeles, CA 90067

Communication Skill Builders
3830 E. Bellevue
P.O. Box 42050-P92
Tucson, AZ 85733

CompuTeach
78 Olive St.
New Haven, CT 06511
1-800-44-TEACH

Conover
P.O. Box 155
Omro, WI 54963
1-800-933-1933

Coronado
P.O Box 3232
Lawrence, KS 66044

CPPC
4 Conant Square
Brandon, VT 05733
1-800-433-8234

Cue SoftSwap
P.O. Box 271704
Concord, CA 94527-1704
(415) 685-7289

Curriculum Associates
5 Esquire Road
North Billerica, MA 01862
(508) 667-8000

Curriculum Productions
P.O. Box 457
Churchville, PA 18966
(215) 355-0684

Dale Seymour
P.O. Box 10888
Palo Alto, CA 94303
1-800-872-1100

Data Command
P.O. Box 548
Kankakee, IL 60901

Davidson & Associates
19840 Pioneer Ave.
Torrance, CA 90503
1-800-545-7677

Davidson Manors
P.O. Box 548
Valparaiso, IN 46384

Dormac
P.O. Box 752
Beaverton, OR 97075

Educational Activities
P.O. Box 392 Freeport
Long Island, NY 11750
1-800-645-3739

Educational Design
345 Hudson St.
New York, NY 10014
1-800-221-9372

Educators Publishing Service
31 Smith Place
Cambridge, MA 02138

Educational Testing Service
CN 6000
Princeton, NJ 08541-6000

Gamco
P.O. Box 1911
Big Springs, TX 79721

Globe Fearon
4350 Equity Drive
P.O. Box 2649
Columbus, OH 43216
1-800-848-9500

Good Apple
1204 Buchanan St., Box 299
Carhage, IL 62321-0299

Grune & Stratton
111 Fifth Avenue
New York, NY 10003

Harcourt Brace Jovanovich
6277 Sea Harbor Drive
Orlando, FL 32887

Hartley Courseware
P.O. Box 419
Diamondale, MI 48821
1-800-247-1380

Heartsoft
P.O. Box 691381
Tulsa, OK 74169

Heinemann
70 Court St.
Portsmouth, NH 03801
1-800-541-2086

Holt, Rinehart and Winston
301 Commerce St.
Fort Worth, TX 76102

Houghton Mifflin
One Beacon St.
Boston, MA 02107

IBM Educational Systems
P.O. Box 2150
Atlanta, GA 30301-2150
1-800-426-2133

Incentive
Box 12089
Nashville, TN 37212

Institute of Modern Languages
The Language People
2622 Pittman Dr.
Silver Spring, MD 49501

Instructional Fair
2400 Turner Ave.
Grand Rapids, MI 49501
1-800-253-5469

Interactive Learning Materials
150 Croton Lake Rd.
Katonah, NY 10536
(914) 232-4682

International Reading Association
800 Barksdale Road, PO Box 8139
Newark, DE 19714-8139
(302) 731-1600

Jamestown
The Reading People
P.O. Box 9168
Providence, RI 02940
1-800-872-7323

Kendall/Hunt
4050 Westmark Drive
P. O. Box 1840
Dubuque, IA 52004-1840

Learning
6493 Kaiser Dr.
Fremont, CA 94555
1-800-852-2255

Learning Seed
330 Telser Rd.
Lake Zurich, IL 60047

Learning Works
P.O. Box 6187
Santa Barbara, CA 93160

LinguiSystems
3100 Fourth Avenue
P.O. Box 747
East Moline, IL 61244

Logo Computer Systems
3300 Cote Vetu, Ste. 201
Montreal, PQH4R 2B7 Canada
1-800-321-5646

Longman
19 West 44th Street
New York, NY 10036

Love
1777 South Bellaire Street
Denver, CO 80222
(303) 757-2579

Lyons and Carnahan
407 East 25th Street
Chicago, IL 60616

Macmillan College Publishing
866 Third Avenue
New York, NY 10022
1-800-228-7854

MacWarehouse
P.O. Box 3013
1720 Oak St.
Lakewood, NJ 08701-3013
1-800-255-6227

McDougal, Littell & Co.
Box 1667
Evanston, IL 60204

Media Materials
Department 840251
2936 Remington Ave.
Baltimore, MD 21211

Merrill
1300 Alum Creek Drive
Columbus, OH 43216

Microsoft Corporation
One Microsoft Way
Redmond, WA 98052-6399
1-800-426-9400

Milliken
100 Research Boulevard
St. Louis, MO 63132

Mindscape Educational Software
1345 Diversey Parkway
Chicago, IL 60614

Minnesota Educational Computing Consortium
(MECC)
6160 Summit Drive North
Minneapolis, MN 55430-4003
1-800-685-6322

William Morrow
105 Madison Ave.
New York, NY 10016

National Education Association (NEA)
1201 16th Street NW
Washington, DC 20036
1-800-229-4200

Jan Z. Olsen
8802 Quiet Stream Ct.
Potomac, MD 20854
(301) 983-8409

Orton Dyslexia Society
8415 Bellona Lane
Towson, MD 21204

Richard C. Owen
New York, NY

O. T. Ideas
124 Morris Turnpike
Randolph, NJ 07869
(201) 895-3677

Outreach Pre-College Programs
Gallaudet University
Washington, D.C.

Oxford University Press
200 Madison Ave.
New York, NY 10016

Parrot Software
P.O. Box 1139
State College, PA 16804
1-800-PARROT-1

PEAL Software
P.O. Box 8188
Calabasas, CA 91372

Phi Delta Kappa
P.O. Box 789
Bloomington, IN 47402-0789

Phoenix Learning Resources
2349 Chaffee Drive
St. Louis, MO 63146
1-800-822-4636

PLS Book Store
Performance Learning Systems
224 Church St.
Nevada City, CA 95959
1-800-255-8412

Potimum Resource
10 Station Place
Norfolk, CT 06058

Prentice-Hall
Educational Books Division
Englewood Cliffs, NJ 07632

Primary English Teaching Association
P.O. Box 167 Roselle NSW 2039
Australia

PRO-ED
8700 Shoal Creek Blvd.
Austin, TX 78757-6897
(512) 451-3246

Que Software
11711 North College Ave.
Carmel, IN 46032
1-800-992-'0244

Queue
338 Commerce Drive
Fairfield, CT 06430
1-800-232-2224

Random House/Singer School Division
201 East 50th St.
New York, NY 10022

Riverside
8424 Bryn Mawr Avenue
Chicago, IL 60631
1-800-SOS-TEST

Scholastic Book Service
50 West 44th St.
New York, NY 10036

Scholastic
2931 E. McCarty St.
P.O. Box 7502
Jefferson City, MO 65102-9968
1-800-325-6149
1-800-541-5513

Scholastic Software
730 Broadway, Dept. JS
New York, NY 10003
1-800-541-5513

Science Research Associates
P.O. Box 543
Blacklick, OH 43004
1-800-843-8855

ScottForesman
1900 East Lake Avenue
Glenview, IL 60025
(708) 729-3000

Sensible Software
18761 N. Fredrick Ave.
Suite F
Gaithersburg, Troy, MI
1-800-635-8485

Simon & Schuster
P.O. Box 11075
Des Moines, IA 50336-1074
1-800-947-7700

SLED Software
P.O. Box 16322
Minneapolis, MN 55416
(612) 926-5820

Tom Snyder
90 Sherman St.
Cambridge, MA 02140
(617) 876-4463

South Western
7625 Empire Drive
Florence, KY 41042
1-800-354-9706

Spinnaker
Division of Queue
338 Commerce Drive
Fairfield, CT 06430
1-800-323-8088

Steck-Vaughn
807 Brazos
P.O. Box 2028
Austin, TX 78768

Sunburst
1322 Coral Drive W.
Tacoma, WA 98466-5832

Symmetry Software
8603 E. Royal Palm Rd.
Suite 110
Scottsdale, AZ 85258
1-800-899-8603

S.V.E/Mindscape
1345 Diversey Parkway
Chicago, IL 60614

S.W.E.P.S. Educational Software
9 Barker Drive
P.O. Box 1510
Pine, AZ 85544-1510

Teachers and Writers Collaborative
5 Union Square West
New York, NY 10003

Teachers College Press
Teachers College, Columbia University
1234 Amsterdam Avenue
New York, NY 10027

Teacher Support
1035 N.W. 57th Street
Gainesville, FL 32605

Toucan
22711 Sparrow Dell Drive
Calabasas, CA 91302

Treehouse Associates
P. O. Box 1992
Avon, CO 81620

Troll
P.O. Box 960
Campton, NH 03223

University of California
Bay Area Writing Project
Tomlan Hall
Berkeley, CA 94720

University of Chicago Press
5801 Ellis Ave.
Chicago, IL 60637
1-800-621-2736

REFERENCES

Adams, M. J. (1990). *Beginning to read: Thinking and learning about print.* Cambridge, MA: MIT Press.

Adelman, H. S., & Taylor, L. (1990). Intrinsic motivation and school misbehavior: Some intervention implications. *Journal of Learning Disabilities, 23,* 541–550.

Adelman, P. B., & Vogel, S. A. (1990). College graduates with learning disabilities employment attainment and career patterns. *Learning Disability Quarterly, 13,* 154–166.

Alvarez, M. C. (1983). Sustained timed writing as an aid to fluency and creativity. *Teaching Exceptional Children, 15,* 160–162.

Americans with Disabilities Act of 1990, P.L. 101–336.

Anderson, C. W. (1992). The underlining option. *Their World,* 58–59.

Anderson, P. L. (1982). A preliminary study of syntax in the written expression of learning disabled children. *Journal of Learning Disabilities, 15,* 359–364.

Applebee, A. N. (1984). *Contexts for learning to write: Studies of secondary school instruction.* Norwood, NJ: ABLEX.

Applebee, A. N. (1986). Problem in process approaches: Toward a reconceptualization of process instruction. In A. R. Petrosky & D. Bartholomae (Eds.), *The teaching of writing* (pp. 95–113). Chicago, IL: National Society for the Study of Education.

Applebee A. N., & Langer, J. A. (1983). Instructional scaffolding: Reading and writing as natural language activities. *Language Arts, 60,* 168–175.

Applebee, A. N., Langer, J. A., Jenkins, L. B., Mullis, I. V. S., & Foertsch, M. A. (1990). *Learning to write in our nation's schools.* Princeton, NJ: Educational Testing Service.

Archer, A. L. (1988). Strategies for responding to information. *Teaching Exceptional Children, 20*(3), 55–57.

Arena, J. I. (1970). Introduction. In J. I. Arena (Ed.), *Building handwriting skills in dyslexic children* (pp. iii-iv). Novato, CA: Academic Therapy.

Ariel, A. (1992). *Education of children and adolescents with learning disabilities.* New York: Merrill.

Askov, E., Otto, W., & Askov, W. (1970). A decade of research in handwriting: Progress and prospect. *Journal of Educational Research, 64,* 100–111.

Bailet, L. L. (1990). Spelling rule usage among students with learning disabilities and normally achieving students. *Journal of Learning Disabilities, 23,* 121–128.

Bailet, L. L. (1991). Beginning spelling. In A. M. Bain, L. L. Bailet, & L. C. Moats (Eds.), *Written language disorders: Theory into practice* (pp. 1–21). Austin, TX: PRO-ED.

Bailet, L. L., & Lyon, G. R. (1985). Deficient linguistic rule application in a learning disabled speller: A case study. *Journal of Learning Disabilities, 18,* 162–165.

Bain, A. M. (1991). Handwriting disorders. In A. M. Bain, L. L. Bailet, & L. C. Moats (Eds.), *Written language disorders: Theory into practice* (pp. 43–64). Austin, TX: PRO-ED.

Bannatyne, A. D. (1971). *Language, reading and learning disabilities.* Springfield, IL: Charles C. Thomas.

Barbe, W. B., Milone, M. N., & Wasylyk, T. M. (1983). Manuscript is the 'write' start. *Academic Therapy, 18,* 397–405.

Barbe, W. B., Wasylyk, T. M., Hackney, C. S., & Braun, L. A. (1984). *Zaner-Bloser creative growth in handwriting* (Grades K–8). Columbus, OH: Zaner-Bloser.

Barenbaum, E. M., Newcomer, P. L., & Nodine, B. F. (1987). Children's ability to write stories as a function of variation in task, age, and developmental level. *Learning Disability Quarterly, 10*, 175–188.

Baumann, J. (1986). Teaching third-grade students to comprehend anaphoric relationships: The application of a direct instruction model. *Reading Research Quarterly, 21*, 70–90.

Beal, C. R. (1993). Contributions of developmental psychology to understanding revision: Implications for consultation with classroom teachers. *School Psychology Review, 22*, 643–655.

Beck, I. L., Perfetti, C. A., & McKeown, M. G. (1982). Effects on long-term vocabulary instruction in lexical access and reading comprehension. *Journal of Educational Psychology, 74*, 506–521.

Beers, J. W., & Henderson, E. H. (1977). A study of developing orthographic concepts among first graders. *Research in the Teaching of English, 11*, 133–148.

Bereiter, C., & Scardamalia, M. (1982). From conversation to composition: The role of instruction in a developmental process. In R. Glaser (Ed.), *Advances in instructional psychology: Vol.2* (pp. 1–64). Hillsdale, NJ: Erlbaum.

Berninger, V. W., & Hooper, S. R. (1993). Preventing and remediating writing disabilities: Interdisciplinary frameworks for assessment, consultation, and intervention. *School Psychology Review, 2*, 590–594.

Berninger, V. W., & Whitaker, D. (1993). Theory-based branching diagnosis of writing disabilities. *School Psychology Review, 22*, 623–642.

Bernstein, D. K. (1989). Language development: The school years. In D. K. Bernstein & E. Tiegerman (Eds.), *Language and communication disorders* (2nd ed.) (pp. 133–156). Columbus: Merrill.

Big Bend Community College (WA), OCR Region X. (Complaint No. 10-90-2035, 1991).

Blachman, B. A. (1994). Early literacy acquisition: The role of phonological awareness. In G. P. Wallach & K. G. Butler (Eds.), *Language learning disabilities in school-age children and adolescents* (pp. 253–274). New York: Merrill.

Blachowicz, C. (1977). Cloze activities for primary readers. *Reading Teacher, 31*, 300–302.

Blandford, B. J., & Lloyd, J. W. (1987). Effects of a self-instructional procedure on handwriting. *Journal of Learning Disabilities, 20*, 342–346.

Blatt, B. (1985). On writing, reading, and teaching. *Journal of Learning Disabilities, 18*, 366–367.

Borkowski, J. G. (1992). Metacognitive theory: A framework for teaching literacy, writing, and math skills. *Journal of Learning Disabilities, 25*, 253–257.

Borkowski, J. G., Estrada, T. M., Milstead, M., & Hale, C. A. (1989). General problem-solving skills: Relations between metacognitive and strategic processing. *Learning Disability Quarterly, 12*, 57–70.

Bos, C. S. (1988). Process-oriented writing: Instructional implications for mildly handicapped students. *Exceptional Children, 54*, 521–527.

Bos, C. S., & Anders, P. L. (1990a). Effects of interactive vocabulary instruction on the vocabulary learning and reading comprehension of junior-high learning disabled students. *Learning Disability Quarterly, 13*, 31–42.

Bos, C. S., & Anders, P. L. (1990b). Interactive teaching and learning: Instructional practices for teaching content and strategic knowledge. In B. Y. L. Wong & T. E. Scruggs (Eds.), *Intervention research in learning disabilities* (pp. 166–185). New York, NY: Springer-Verlag.

Bos, C. S., & Vaughn, S. (1994). *Strategies for teaching students with learning and behavior problems* (4th ed.). Boston: Allyn and Bacon.

Bradley, L. (1981). The organization of motor patterns for spelling: An effective remedial strategy for backward spellers. *Developmental Medicine and Child Neurology, 23*, 83–91.

Bradley, L. (1983). The organization of visual, phonological, and motor strategies in learning to read and to spell. In U. Kirk (Ed.), *Neuropsychology of language, reading, and spelling* (pp. 235–254). New York: Academic Press.

Brigham, T. A., Graubard, P. S., & Stans, A. (1972). Analysis of the effects of sequential reinforcement contingencies on aspects of composition. *Journal of Applied Behavior Analysis, 5*, 421–429.

Britton, J. N., Burgess, T., Martin, N., McLeod, A., & Rosen, H. (1975). *The development of writing abilities.* London: Macmillan.

Brown, R. (1981). National assessments of writing ability. In C. H. Fredericksen & J. F. Dominic (Eds.), *Writing: The nature, development, and teaching of written communication: Vol 2.*

Process, development, and communication (pp. 31–38). Hillsdale, NJ: Lawrence Erlbaum.

Bruck, M. (1990). Word recognition skills of adults with childhood diagnoses of dyslexia. *Developmental Psychology, 26,* 439–454.

Bruck, M. (1992). Persistence of dyslexics' phonological awareness deficits. *Developmental Psychology, 28,* 874–886.

Bruck, M. (1993). Component spelling skills of college students with childhood diagnoses of dyslexia. *Learning Disability Quarterly, 16,* 171–184.

Bruner, J. (1978). The role of dialogue in language acquisition. In A. Sinclair, R. J. Jarvelle, & W. J. M. Levelt (Eds.), *The child's conception of language* (pp. 241–256). New York: Springer-Verlag.

Calfee, R. C., Lindamood, P., & Lindamood, C. (1973). Acoustic-phonic skills in reading: Kindergarten through twelfth grade. *Journal of Educational Psychology, 64,* 293–298.

California State University-Long Beach, (Complaint No. 09–92–2111-I) (OCR Region IX), 1992.

Calkins, L. M. (1983). *Lessons from a child.* Portsmouth, NH: Heinemann.

Calkins, L. M. (1986). *The art of teaching writing.* Portsmouth, NH: Heinemann.

Campbell, B. J., Brady, M. P., & Linehan, S. (1991). Effects of peer-mediated instruction on the acquisition and generalization of written capitalization skills. *Journal of Learning Disabilities, 24,* 6–14.

Campione, J. C., Rutherford, M., Gordon, A., Walker, J., & Brown, A. L. (1994). Now I'm a real boy: Zones of proximal development for those at risk. In N. C. Jordan & J. Goldsmith-Phillips (Eds.), *Learning disabilities: New directions for assessment and intervention* (pp. 245–274). Boston: Allyn and Bacon.

Carlisle, J. F. (1987). The use of morphological knowledge in spelling derived forms by learning-disabled and normal students. *Annals of Dyslexia, 37,* 90–108.

Carlisle, J. F. (1993). Selecting approaches to vocabulary instruction for the reading disabled. *Learning Disabilities Research & Practice, 8,* 97–105.

Carlisle, J. F. (1994). Morphological awareness, spelling, and story writing. In N. C. Jordan & J. Goldsmith-Phillips (Eds.), *Learning disabilities: New directions for assessment and intervention* (pp. 123–145). Boston: Allyn and Bacon.

Carnine, D., & Kinder, D. (1985). Teaching low-performing students to apply generative and schema strategies to narrative and expository material. *Remedial and Special Education, 6*(1), 20–29.

Carr, E., & Ogle, D. (1987). K-W-L plus: A strategy for comprehension and summarization. *Journal of Reading, 30,* 626–631.

Cazden, C. (1980). Peekaboo as an instructional model: Discourse development at home and at school. *Papers and Reports of Child Language Development, 17,* 1–29.

Chomsky, C. (1971). Write first, read later. *Childhood Education, 47,* 296–299.

Chomsky, N. (1970). Phonology and reading. In H. Levin & J. Williams (Eds.), *Basic studies in reading* (pp. 3–18). New York: Harper & Row.

Cicci, R. (1980). Written language disorders. *Bulletin of the Orton Society, 30,* 240–251.

City University of New York (NY), 3 NDLR 104 (Complaint No. 02–91–2050) (OCR Region II, 1992).

Clark, H. C., & Clark, E. V. (1977). *Psychology and language: An introduction to psycholinguistics.* New York: Harcourt Brace Jovanovich.

Clark, M. L., & Montague, M. (1993). Applying story writing strategies in regular classrooms. *Teaching Exceptional Children,* Summer (Special Edition), 50–51.

Cleary, B. (1993). Jason's story. *Their world: A publication of the National Center for Learning Disabilities.* New York: National Center for Learning Disabilities.

Cohen, B. L. (1985). Writing: A new approach to the revision process. *Academic Therapy, 20,* 587–589.

Cohen, M. W. (1986). Intrinsic motivation in the special education classroom. *Journal of Learning Disabilities, 19,* 258–261.

Cohen, S. B., & Plaskon, S. P. (1980). *Language arts for the mildly handicapped.* Columbus, OH: Merrill.

Cole, M. L., & Cole, J. T. (1989). *Effective intervention with the language impaired child* (2nd ed.). Gaithersburg, MD: Aspen.

Cone, T. E., Wilson, L. R., Bradley, C. M., & Reese, J. H. (1985). Characteristics of LD students in Iowa: An empirical investigation. *Learning Disability Quarterly, 8,* 211–220.

Conway, R. N. F., & Gow, L. (1988). Mainstreaming special class students with mild handicaps through group instruction. *Remedial and Special Education, 9*(5) 34–41.

Cooper, A. (1988). Given-New: Enhancing coherence through cohesiveness. *Written Communication, 5*, 352–367.

Cooper, C. (1973). An outline for writing sentence-combining problems. *English Journal, 62*, 96–102.

Cordoni, B. (1979). Assisting dyslexic college students: An experimental program design at a university. *Bulletin of the Orton Society, 29*, 263–268.

Crealock, C. (1993). The grid model for teaching narrative writing skills. *Teaching Exceptional Children, 25*(3), 33–37.

Cunningham, P. M., & Cunningham, J. W. (1992). Making words: Enhancing the invented spelling-decoding connection. *Reading Teacher, 46*, 106–115.

D'Amico v. New York State Board of Law Examiners, 3 NDLR 291 (1993).

Dagenais, D. J., & Beadle, K. R. (1984). Written language: When and where to begin. *Topics in Language Disorders, 4*(2), 59–85.

Daiute, C., & Dalton, B. (1993). Collaboration between children learning to write: Can novices be masters? *Cognition and Instruction, 10*, 281–333.

Dalke, C. (1988). Woodcock-Johnson Psycho-Educational test battery profiles: A comparative study of college freshmen with and without learning disabilities. *Journal of Learning Disabilities, 21*, 567–570.

Danoff, B., Harris, K. R., & Graham, S. (1993). Incorporating strategy instruction within the writing process in the regular classroom: Effects on the writing of students with and without learning disabilities. *Journal of Reading Behavior, 25*, 295–322.

deCharms, R. (1971). From pawns to origins: Toward self-motivation. In G. Lesser (Ed.), *Psychology and educational practice* (pp. 380–407). Glenview, IL: ScottForesman.

deCharms, R. (1976). *Enhancing motivation. Change in the classroom.* New York: Irvington.

Deci, E. L. (1978). Applications of research on the effects of rewards. In M. R. Lepper & D. Greene (Eds.), *The hidden costs of reward: New perspectives on the psychology of human motivation* (pp. 193–203). Hillsdale, NJ: Lawrence Erlbaum.

DeGroff, L. (1992). Process-writing teachers' responses to fourth-grade writers' first drafts. *Elementary School Journal, 93*, 131–144.

Denckla, M., & Rudel, R. (1976). Naming of object drawings by dyslexic and other learning disabled children. *Brain Language, 3*, 1–16.

Deshler, D. D., Ferrell, W. R., & Kass, C. E. (1978). Monitoring of schoolwork errors by LD adolescents. *Journal of Learning Disabilities, 11*, 10–23.

Devine, T. G. (1986). *Teaching reading comprehension: From theory to practice.* Newton, MA: Allyn and Bacon.

Diamond, J. (June, 1994). Writing right. *Discover*, 107–113.

Digest of Response. OCR rulings, 20 IDELR 134 (1993).

Dinsmore v. Pugh and the Regents at the University of California at Berkeley (settled 1989).

Dixon, R. C. (1991). The application of sameness analysis to spelling. *Journal of Learning Disabilities, 24*, 285–291, 310.

Dixon, R., & Engelmann, S. (1979). *Corrective spelling through morphographs.* Chicago: SRA.

Dobson, L. N. (1985). Learn to read by writing: A practical program for reluctant readers. *Teaching Exceptional Children, 18*(1), 30–36.

Doherty v. Southern College of Optometry. 659 F. Supp. 602 (W.D.Tenn. 1987).

Doherty v. Southern College of Optometry. 862 F. 2nd 570 (6th Cir. 1988).

Donahoe, K., & Zigmond, N. (1990). High school grades of urban LD students and low achieving peers. *Exceptionality, 1*, 17–27.

Donahue, M. (1986). Linguistic and communicative development in learning disabled children. In S. J. Ceci (Ed.), *Handbook of cognitive, social and neuropsychological aspects of learning disabilities* (pp. 263–289). Hillsdale, NJ: Lawrence Erlbaum.

Douglass, B. (1984). Variation on a theme: Writing with the LD adolescent. *Academic Therapy, 19*, 361–363.

Dowis, C. L., & Schloss, P. (1992). The impact of mini-lessons on writing skills. *Remedial and Special Education, 13*(5), 34–42.

Eastern Iowa Community College District (IO), OCR Region VII. (Complaint No. 07-90-2036, 1991).

Edgington, R. (1967). But he spelled them right this morning. *Academic Therapy, 3*, 58–61.

Ediger, M. (1993). Writing and the language arts. *Reading Improvement, 30,* 246–249.

Education for All Handicapped Children Act of 1975, 20 U.S.C. S. 1400–1485, P.L. 94–142.

Ehri, L. C. (1986). Sources of difficulty in learning to read and spell. In M. L. Wolraich & D. Routh (Eds.), *Advances in developmental and behavioral pediatrics* (pp. 121–195). Greenwich, CT: JAI Press.

Ehri, L. C. (1989). The development of spelling knowledge and its role in reading acquisition and reading disability. *Journal of Learning Disabilities, 22,* 356–365.

Ellis, E. S. (1994a). Integrating writing strategy instruction with content-area instruction: Part I — Orienting students to organizational devices. *Intervention in School and Clinic, 29,* 169–179.

Ellis, E. S. (1994b). Integrating writing strategy instruction with content-area instruction: Part II — Writing processes. *Intervention in School and Clinic, 29,* 219–228.

Englert, C. S., & Hiebert, E. H. (1984). Children's developing awareness of text structures in expository materials. *Journal of Educational Psychology, 76,* 65–75.

Englert, C. S., Hiebert, E. H., & Stewart, S. R. (1985). Spelling unfamiliar words by an analogy strategy. *Journal of Special Education, 19,* 291–306.

Englert, C. S., & Lichter, A. (1982). Using statement-pie to teach reading and writing skills. *Teaching Exceptional Children, 14*(5), 164–170.

Englert, C. S., & Mariage, T. V. (1991). Shared understandings: Structuring the writing experience through dialogue. *Journal of Learning Disabilities, 24,* 330–342.

Englert, C. S., & Raphael, T. E. (1989). Developing successful writers through cognitive strategy instruction. In J. Brophy (Ed.), *Advances in research on teaching* (Vol. 1, pp. 105–151). Greenwich, CT: JAI Press.

Englert, C. S., Raphael, T. E., & Anderson, L. M. (1989). *Cognitive strategy instruction in writing project.* East Lansing, MI: Institute for Research on Teaching.

Englert, C. S., Raphael, T. E., Anderson, L. M., Anthony, H. M., Fear, K. L., & Gregg, S. L. (1988). A case for writing intervention: Strategies for writing informational text. *Learning Disabilities Focus, 3,* 98–113.

Englert, C. S., Raphael, T. E., Anderson, L. M., Anthony, H. M., & Stevens, D. D. (1991). Making strategies and self-talk visible: Writing instruction in regular and special education classrooms. *American Educational Research Journal, 23,* 337–372.

Englert, C. S., Raphael, T. E., Anderson, L. M., Gregg, S. L., & Anthony, H. M. (1989). Exposition: Reading, writing, and the metacognitive knowledge of learning disabled students. *Learning Disabilities Research, 5*(1), 5–24.

Englert, C. S., Raphael, T. E., Fear, K. L., & Anderson, L. M. (1988). Students' metacognitive knowledge about how to write informational texts. *Learning Disability Quarterly, 11,* 18–46.

Englert, C. S., & Thomas, C. C. (1987). Sensitivity to text structure in reading and writing; A comparison of learning disabled and nonhandicapped students. *Learning Disability Quarterly, 10,* 93–105.

Enright, M. K., Duran, R., & Peirce, L. P. (1986, April). *Strategies and processes in the solution of GRE analogies.* Paper presented at the American Educational Research Association meeting, San Francisco.

Espin, C. A., & Sindelar, C. A. (1988). Auditory feedback and writing: Learning disabled and non-disabled students. *Exceptional Children, 55,* 45–51.

Fauke, J., Burnett, J., Powers, M., & Sulzer-Azaroff, B. (1973). Improvement of handwriting and letter recognition skills: A behavior modification procedure. *Journal of Learning Disabilities, 6,* 25–29.

Fernald, G. (1943). *Remedial techniques in basic school subjects.* New York: McGraw-Hill.

Fitzgerald, J. (1951). *The teaching of spelling.* Milwaukee, WI: Bruce Publishing.

Fitzgerald, J., & Stamm, C. (1992). Variation in writing conference influence on revision: Two cases. *Journal of Reading Behavior, 24,* 21–50.

Flower, L., & Hayes, J. R. (1980). Writing as problem solving. *Visible Language, 14,* 388–399.

Forte, I., & Pangle, M. A. (1985). *Selling spelling to kids: Motivating games and activities to reinforce spelling skills.* Nashville, TN: Incentive Publications.

Frager, A. M. (1994). Teaching, writing, and identity. *Language Arts, 71,* 274–278.

Frankenberger, W., & Fronzaglio, K. (1991). A review of states' criteria and procedures for identifying children with learning disabilities. *Journal of Learning Disabilities, 24,* 495–500.

Frankenberger, W., & Harper, J. (1987). States' criteria and procedures for identifying learning disabled children. *Journal of Learning Disabilities, 20,* 118–121.

Frith, U. (1980). Unexpected spelling problems. In U. Frith (Ed.), *Cognitive processes in spelling* (pp. 495–515). London: Academic Press.

Fry, E. (1980). The new instant word list. *Reading Teacher, 34,* 286–288.

Fry, E., Polk, J., & Fountoukidis, D. (1984). *The reading teacher's book of lists.* Englewood Cliffs, NJ: Prentice-Hall.

Fulk, B. M. (1994). Mnemonic keyword strategy training for students with learning disabilities. *Learning Disabilities Research & Practice, 9,* 179–185.

Furner, B. (1969). Recommended instructional procedures in a method emphasizing the perceptual-motor nature of learning in handwriting. *Elementary English, 46,* 1021–1030.

Gage, G. T. (1986). Why write? In A. R. Petrosky, & D. Bartholomae (Eds.), *The teaching of writing* (pp. 8–29). Chicago, IL: National Society for the Study of Education.

Gajar, A. H. (1989). A computer analysis of written language variables and a comparison of compositions written by university students with and without learning disabilities. *Journal of Learning Disabilities, 22,* 125–130.

Gamble, B. S. (1993). ADA: Understanding the Americans with Disabilities Act. *Americans with Disabilities Act manual, 2*(4), Part II. Washington, DC: The Bureau of National Affairs.

Garcia, M. W. (1992). *The Arizona student assessment program: Systemic implications.* Phoenix: Arizona Department of Education.

Gaskins, I. W. (1982). A writing program for poor readers and writers and the rest of the class, too. *Language Arts, 59,* 854–861.

Gearheart, B. R., & Gearheart, C. J. (1989). *Learning disabilities educational strategies* (5th ed.). St. Louis, MO: Times Mirror/Mosby College.

Gentry, J. R. (1982a). Developmental spelling: Assessment. *Diagnostique, 8,* 52–61.

Gentry, J. R. (1982b). An analysis of developmental spelling in GNYS AT WRK. *Reading Teacher, 36,* 192–200.

Gentry, J. R. (1984). Developmental aspects of learning to spell. *Academic Therapy, 20,* 11–19.

Gentry, J. R. (1987). *Spel . . . is a four-letter word.* Portsmouth, NH: Heinemann.

Gerber, A. (1993). *Language-related learning disabilities: Their nature and treatment.* Baltimore, MD: Paul H. Brookes.

German, D. N. J. (1979). Word-finding skills in children with learning disabilities. *Journal of Learning Disabilities, 12,* 43–48.

German, D. N. J. (1982). Word-finding substitutions in children with learning disabilities. *Language-Speech-Hearing Services in Schools, 13,* 223–230.

Gettinger, M. (1984). Applying learning principles to remedial spelling instruction. *Academic Therapy, 20*(1), 41–47.

Gillingham, A., & Stillman, B. W. (1973). *Remedial training for children with specific disability in reading, spelling, and penmanship.* Cambridge, MA: Educators Publishing Service.

Gilstrap, R. (1962). Development of independent spelling skills in the intermediate grades. *Elementary English, 39,* 481–483.

Giordano, G. (1982). CATS exercises: Teaching disabled writers to communicate. *Academic Therapy, 18,* 233–237.

Giordano, G. (1983a). Readiness skills for disabled writers. *Academic Therapy, 18,* 315–319.

Giordano, G. (1983b). Integrating remedial writing into reading programs. *Academic Therapy, 18,* 599–607.

Giordano, G. (1984). Analyzing and remediating writing disabilities. *Journal of Learning Disabilities, 17,* 78–83.

Glass, G. G. (1973). *Teaching decoding as separate from reading.* New York: Adelphi University.

Glazzard, P. (1982). A visual spelling approach: It works. *Academic Therapy, 18,* 61–64.

Goodman, L., Casciato, D., & Price, M. (1987). LD students' writing: Analyzing errors. *Academic Therapy, 22,* 453–461.

Gordon, J., Vaughn, S., & Schumm, J. S. (1993). Spelling interventions: A review of literature and implications for students with learning disabilities. *Learning Disabilities Research & Practice, 8,* 175–181.

Gould, B. W. (1991). Curricular strategies for written expression. In A. M. Bain, L. L. Bailet, & L. C. Moats (Eds.), *Written language disorders: Theory into practice* (pp. 129–164). Austin, TX: PRO-ED.

Graham, S. (1983). The effect of self-instructional procedures on LD students' handwriting performance. *Learning Disability Quarterly, 6,* 231–234.

Graham, S. (1986). A review of handwriting scales and factors that contribute to variability in handwriting scores. *Journal of School Psychology, 24,* 63–71.

Graham, S. (1990). The role of production factors in learning disabled students' compositions. *Journal of Educational Psychology, 82,* 781–791.

Graham, S. (1992). Issues in handwriting instruction. *Focus on Exceptional Children, 25* (2), 1–13.

Graham, S., & Freeman, S. (1985). Strategy training and teacher vs. student-controlled study conditions: Effects of LD students' spelling performance. *Learning Disability Quarterly, 8,* 267–274.

Graham, S., & Harris, K. R. (1987). Improving composition skills of inefficient learners with self-instructional strategy training. *Topics in Language Disorders, 7,* 68–77.

Graham, S., & Harris, K. R. (1988). Instructional recommendations for teaching writing to exceptional students. *Exceptional Children, 54,* 506–512.

Graham, S., & Harris, K. (1989a). Improving learning disabled students' skills at composing essays: Self-instructional strategy training. *Exceptional Children, 56,* 201–214.

Graham, S., & Harris, K. R. (1989b). Components analysis of cognitive strategy instruction: Effects on learning disabled students' compositions and self-efficacy. *Journal of Educational Psychology, 81,* 353–361.

Graham, S., & Harris, K. R. (1993). Self-regulated strategy development: Helping students with learning problems develop as writers. *Elementary School Journal, 94,* 169–181.

Graham, S., Harris, K. R., & Loynachan, C. (1994). The Spelling for Writing List. *Journal of Learning Disabilities, 27,* 210–214.

Graham, S., & MacArthur, C. A. (1991). Introduction: Research and practice in writing. *Learning Disabilities Research & Practice, 6,* 200.

Graham, S., & Madan, A. J. (1981). Teaching letter formation. *Academic Therapy, 16,* 389–396.

Graham, S., & Miller, L. (1979). Spelling research and practice: A unified approach. *Focus on Exceptional Children, 12*(2), 1–16.

Graham, S., & Miller, L. (1980). Handwriting research and practice: A unified approach. *Focus on Exceptional Children, 13*(2), 1–16.

Graham, S., Schwartz, S. S., & MacArthur, C. A. (1993). Knowledge of writing and the composing process, attitude toward writing, and self-efficacy for students with and without learning disabilities. *Journal of Learning Disabilities, 26,* 237–249.

Graves, A., & Hauge, R. (1993). Using cues and prompts to improve story writing. *Teaching Exceptional Children, 25*(4), 38–40.

Graves, A., & Montague, M. (1991). Using story grammar cueing to improve the writing of students with learning disabilities. *Learning Disabilities Research & Practice, 6,* 246–250.

Graves, A., Montague, M., & Wong, B. Y. L. (1990). The effects of procedural facilitation on the story composition of learning disabled students. *Learning Disabilities Research, 5,* 88–93.

Graves, D. (1978). *Balance the basics: Let them write.* New York: Ford Foundation.

Graves, D. H. (1983). *Writing: Teachers and children at work.* Exeter, NH: Heinemann Educational Books.

Graves, D. H. (1985). All children can write. *Learning Disabilities Focus, 1,* 36–43.

Greenberg, K. L. (1987). Defining, teaching, and testing basic writing competence. *Topics in Language Disorders, 7,* 31–41.

Gregg, N. (1983). College learning disabled writers: Error patterns and instructional alternatives. *Journal of Learning Disabilities, 16,* 334–338.

Gregg, N. (1985). College learning disabled, normal, and basic writers: A comparison of frequency and accuracy of cohesive ties. *Journal of Psychoeducational Assessment, 3,* 223–231.

Gregg, N. (1991). Disorders of written expression. In A. M. Bain, L. L. Bailet, & L. C. Moats (Eds.), *Written language disorders: Theory into practice* (pp. 65–97). Austin, TX: PRO-ED.

Gregg, N., & Hoy, C. (1989). Coherence: The comprehension and production abilities of college writers who are normally achieving, learning disabled, and underprepared. *Journal of Learning Disabilities, 22,* 370–372.

Grubb, B. (1993). The Americans with Disabilities Act and learning disabilities. *LDA Newsbriefs, 28*(4), 3–4.

Hakola, S. R. (1992). Legal rights of students with attention deficit disorder. *School Psychology Quarterly, 7,* 285–297.

Hammill, D. D. (1990). The many definitions of learning disabilities. *Journal of Learning Disabilities*, 2, 75–80.

Hamstra-Bletz, L. & Blote, A. W. (1993). A longitudinal study on dysgraphic handwriting in primary school. *Journal of Learning Disabilities*, 26, 689–699.

Hanau, L. (1974). *The study game: How to play and win with statement-pie*. New York: Barnes & Noble.

Hanna, P. R., Hodges, R. E., & Hanna, J. S. (1971). *Spelling: Structure and strategies*. Boston: Houghton Mifflin.

Hanover, S. (1983). Handwriting comes naturally? *Academic Therapy*, 18, 407–412.

Harris, K. R., & Graham, S. (1985). Improving learning disabled student's composition skills: A self-control strategy training approach. *Learning Disability Quarterly*, 8, 27–36.

Harris, K. R., & Graham, S. (1992). *Helping young writers master the craft: Strategy instruction and self-regulation in the writing process*. Cambridge, MA: Brookline Books.

Harris, K. R., Graham, S., & Freeman, S. (1988). Effects of strategy training on metamemory among learning disabled students. *Exceptional Children*, 54, 332–338.

Hasbrouck, J. E., Tindal, G., & Parker, R. I. (1994). Objective procedures for scoring students' writing. *Teaching Exceptional Children*, 26(2), 18–22.

Hasenstab, J. K., Flaherty, G. M., & Brown, B. E. (1994). *Teaching through the learning channels instructor guide* (pp. 62–64, 72–74). Nevada City, CA: Performance Learning Systems.

Hebert, B. M., & Murdock, J. Y. (1994). Comparing three computer-aided instruction output modes to teach vocabulary words to students with learning disabilities. *Learning Disabilities Research & Practice*, 9, 136–141.

Hewitt, F. M. (1967). Educational engineering with emotionally disturbed children. *Exceptional Children*, 33, 459–467.

Heydorn, B. L. (1984). Reducing reversals in reading and writing. *Academic Therapy*, 19, 305–308.

Hildreth, G. (1955). *Teaching spelling*. New York: Henry Holt.

Hillocks, G., Jr. (1987). Synthesis of research on teaching writing. *Educational Leadership*, 44(8), 71–76, 78, 80–82.

Hodges, R. E. (1977). *Learning to spell: Theory and research into practice*. Urbana, IL: National Council of Teachers of English.

Hofmeister, A. M. (1973). Let's get it write. Five common instructional errors in teaching writing. *Teaching Exceptional Children*, 6, 30–33.

Horn, E. (1919). Principles of methods in teaching spelling as derived from scientific investigation. in *Eighteenth yearbook: National Society for the study of education*. Bloomington, IN: Public School Publishing.

Horn, E. (1954). *Teaching spelling*. Washington, DC: American Educational Research.

Horowitz, R. (1985a). Text patterns: Part I. *Journal of Reading*, 28, 448–454.

Horowitz, R. (1985b). Text patterns: Part II. *Journal of Reading*, 28, 534–541.

Houck, C. K., & Billingsley, B. S. (1989). Written expression of students with and without learning disabilities: Differences across the grades. *Journal of Learning Disabilities*, 22, 561–567, 572.

Houten, R. V., Morrison, E., Jarvis, R., & MacDonald, M. (1974). The effects of explicit timing and feedback on compositional response rate in elementary school children. *Journal of Applied Behavior Analysis*, 7, 547–555.

Howell, H. (1978). Write on, you sinistrals! *Language Arts*, 55, 852–856.

Hoy, C., & Gregg, N. (1994). *Assessment: The special educator's role*. Pacific Grove, CA: Books/Cole.

Hughes, C. A., & Smith, J. O. (1990). Cognitive and academic performance of college students with learning disabilities: A synthesis of the literature. *Learning Disability Quarterly*, 13, 66–79.

Hughes, C. A., & Suritsky, S. K. (1994). Note-taking skills of university students with and without learning disabilities. *Journal of Learning Disabilities*, 27, 20–24.

Hunt-Berg, M., Rankin, J. L., & Beukelman, D. R. (1994). Ponder the possibilities: Computer-supported writing for struggling writers. *Learning Disabilities Research & Practice*, 9, 169–178.

Hurray, G. (1993). *A spelling dictionary for beginning writers*. Cambridge: Educators Publishing Service.

Hux, K., & Stogsdill, M. (1993). Instruction in the use of morphemes: A case review. *Learning Disabilities Research & Practice*, 8, 182–187.

Individuals with Disabilities Education Act of 1990 (IDEA), P.L. 101–476, 20 U.S.C. S. 1400 et seq.

Individuals with Disabilities Education Act of 1990 Implementing Regulations, 34 CFR Parts 300 et seq. (1992).

Isaacson, S. L. (1987). Effective instruction in written language. *Focus on Exceptional Children, 19*(6), 1-12.

Isaacson, S. (1989). Role of secretary vs. author: Resolving the conflict in writing instruction. *Learning Disability Quarterly, 12*, 209-217.

Isaacson, S. L. (1994). Integrating process, product, and purpose: The role of instruction. *Reading & Writing Quarterly: Overcoming Learning Difficulties, 10*, 39-62.

Israel, L. (1984). Word knowledge and word retrieval: Phonological and semantic strategies. In G. P. Wallach & K. G. Butler (Eds.), *Language learning disabilities in school-age children* (pp. 230-250). Baltimore, MD: Williams & Wilkins.

Jacob-Timm, S., & Hartshorne, T. S. (1994). Section 504 and school psychology. *Psychology in the Schools, 31*, 26-39.

James, S. (1989). Assessing children with language disorders. In D. K. Bernstein & E. Tiegerman (Eds.), *Language and communication disorders* (2nd ed.) (pp. 157-207). Columbus: Merrill.

Jimenez, J. E., & Rumeau, M. A. (1989). Writing disorders and their relationship to reading-writing methods: A longitudinal study. *Journal of Learning Disabilities, 22*, 195-199.

Johnson, D., & Myklebust, H. (1967). *Learning disabilities: Educational principles and practices*. New York: Grune & Stratton.

Johnson, D. D., & Pearson, P. D. (1984). *Teaching reading vocabulary* (2nd ed.). New York: Holt, Rinehart, and Winston.

Johnson, D. J. (1991). Foreword. In A. M. Bain, L. L. Bailet, & L. C. Moats (Eds.), *Written language disorders: Theory into practice* (p. ix). Austin, TX: PRO-ED.

Johnson, D. J. (1993). Relationships between oral and written language. *School Psychology Review, 22*, 595-609.

Jones, N. L. (1991). Essential on the act: A short history and overview. In J. West (Ed.), *The Americans with Disabilities Act: From policy to practice* (pp. 25-54). New York: Milbank Memorial Fund.

Kaderavek, J. N., & Mandlebaum, L. H. (1993). Enhancement of oral language in LEA: Improving the narrative form of children with learning disabilities. *Intervention in School and Clinic, 29*, 18-25.

Kail, R., & Leonard, L. B. (1986). Sources of word-finding problems in language-impaired children. In S. J. Ceci (Ed.), *Handbook of cognitive, social, and neuropsychological aspects of learning disabilities* (Vol. 1, pp. 185-202). Hillsdale, NJ: Erlbaum.

Kameenui, E. J., Carnine, D. W., & Freschi, R. (1982). Effects of text construction and instructional procedures for teaching word meanings on comprehension and recall. *Reading Research Quarterly, 17*, 367-388.

Kamhi, A. G. (1987). Metalinguistic abilities in language-impaired children. *Topics in Language Disorders, 7*(2), 1-12.

Kamhi, A. G., & Catts, H. W. (1986). Toward an understanding of developmental language and reading disorders. *Journal of Speech and Hearing Disorders, 51*, 337-347.

Kamhi, A. G., & Catts, H. W. (1989). Higher-order language processes and reading disabilities. In A. G. Kamhi & H. W. Catts (Eds.), *Reading and disabilities: A developmental language perspective* (pp. 35-66). Boston: Little, Brown.

Kampwirth, T. J. (1983). Reducing reversal tendencies: 25 useful tips. *Academic Therapy, 18*, 469-474.

Katsiyannis, A., & Conderman, G. (1994). Section 504 policies and procedures: An established necessity. *Remedial and Special Education, 15*, 311-318.

Kavale, K. A. (1987). Theoretical issues surrounding severe discrepancy. *Learning Disabilities Research, 3*, 12-20.

Kearney, C. A., & Drabman, R. S. (1993). The write-say method for improving spelling accuracy in children with learning disabilities. *Journal of Learning Disabilities, 26*, 52-56.

Kerchner, L. B., & Kistinger, B. J. (1984). Language processing/word processing: Written expression, computers, and learning disabled students. *Learning Disability Quarterly, 7*, 329-335.

Kerrigan, W. J. (1979). *Writing to the point: Six basic steps* (2nd ed.). New York: Harcourt Brace Jovanovich.

Kincaid, J. M. (1994). *Legal considerations for serving students with learning disabilities in institutions of higher education*. Center Barnstead, NH: Author.

King, D. H. (1985). *Writing skills for the adolescent*. Cambridge, MA: Educators Publishing Service.

King, D. H. (1993). *Writing Skills 2*. Cambridge: Educators Publishing Service.

King-Sears, M. E., Mercer, C. D., & Sindelar, P. T. (1992). Toward independence with keyword mnemonics: A strategy for science and vocabulary instruction. *Remedial and Special Education*, 13(5), 22–33.

Kirk, S. A., & Chalfant, J. C. (1984). *Academic and developmental learning disabilities*. Denver: Love.

Kokaska, S. (1994, Spring). Teaching tips. *CAPED Communique*, 36–37.

Kovitz, V. S. (1982). For btter coppy wrok. *Academic Therapy*, 18, 83–91.

Krashen, S. (1993). How well do people spell? *Reading Improvement*, 30, 9–20.

Kuchinskas, G., & Radencich, M. C. (1986). *The semantic mapper: A cognitive development approach to reading. Teacher's manual*. Gainesville, FL: Teacher Support Software.

Kulberg, J. M. (1993). Afterword: What school psychologists need to know about writing disabilities. *School Psychology Review*, 22, 682–683.

Kurtz, L. A. (1994). Teacher idea exchange: Helpful handwriting tips. *Teaching Exceptional Children*, 27(1), 58–59.

Landsman, J. (1993). Loosening up the uptight student. *Teachers & Writers*, 25(2), 1–5.

Lane, S. E. (1994). Oral and written compositions of students with and without learning disabilities. *Journal of Psychoeducational Assessment*, 12, 142–153.

Langer, J. A. (1984). Literacy instruction in American schools: Problems and perspectives. *American Journal of Education*, 93, 121.

Lapp, D., & Flood, J. (1993). Are there "real" writers living in your classroom? Implementing a writer-centered classroom. *Reading Teacher*, 48, 254–258.

Larsen, S. C. (1987). *Assessing the writing abilities and instructional needs of students*. Austin, TX: PRO-ED.

Laughton, J., & Morris, N. T. (1989). Story grammar knowledge of learning disabled students. *Learning Disabilities Research*, 4(2), 87–95.

Lavoie, R. (1990). *How difficult can this be?* (Videotape). Alexandria, VA: PBS Video.

Lawlor, J. (1983). Sentence combining: A sequence for instruction. *Elementary School Journal*, 84, 53–62.

Leavell, A., & Ioannides, A. (1993). Using character development to improve story writing. *Teaching Exceptional Children, Summer* (Special Edition), 41–45.

Lerner, J. (1993). *Learning disabilities: Theories, diagnosis, and teaching strategies* (6th ed.). Boston: Houghton Mifflin.

Leuenberger, J., & Morris, M. (1990). Analysis of spelling errors by learning disabled and normal college students. *Learning Disabilities Focus*, 5, 103–118.

Levine, M. (1994, February). Regulating deregulated attention during childhood. *Attention Deficit Hyperactivity Disorder in Children and Adolescents—Arizona's Response*. Paper presented at a conference conducted by Developmental Pediatric Education and the Arizona Department of Education Special Education Section.

Levy, N. R., & Rosenberg, M. S. (1990). Strategies for improving the written expression of students with learning disabilities. *LD Forum*, 16, 23–30.

Lewis, M., Wray, D., & Rospigliosi, P. (1994). "And I want it in your own words." *Reading Teacher*, 47, 528–536.

Lewis, R. R. (1993). *Special education technology: Classroom applications*. Pacific Grove, CA: Brooks/Cole.

Lewkowicz, N. K. (1994). The bag game: An activity to heighten phonemic awareness. *Reading Teacher*, 47, 508–509.

Lillie, P. (1992). Your child's IEP: What services can be included? *LDA Newsbriefs*, 27(3), 3.

MacArthur, C. (1988). The impact of computers on the writing process. *Exceptional Children*, 54, 536–542.

MacArthur, C. (1994). Peers + word processing + strategies = A powerful combination for revising student writing. *Teaching Exceptional Children*, 27, 24–29.

MacArthur, C., & Graham, S. (1987). Learning disabled students' composing with three methods: Handwriting, dictation, and word processing. *Journal of Special Education*, 21, 22–42.

MacArthur, C., Graham, S., & Schwartz, S. (1993). Integrating strategy instruction and word processing into a process approach to writing instruction. *School Psychology Review*, 22, 671–681.

MacArthur, C. A., Graham, S., & Skarvoed, J. (1986). *Learning disabled students' composing with three methods: Handwriting, dictation, and word processing*. (Tech. Rep. No. 109). College Park, MD: Institute for the Study of Exceptional Children and Youth.

MacArthur, C. A., Schwartz, S. S., & Graham, S. (1991). A model for writing instruction: Integrating word processing and strategy instruction into a process approach to writing. *Learning Disabilities Practice, 6*, 230–236.

Mandler, J., & Johnson, N. (1977). Remembrance of things parsed: Story structure and recall. *Cognitive Psychology, 9*, 111–151.

Maniet, P. (1986). *Mainstreaming children with learning disabilities*. Bayville, NY: Upward Bound Press.

Margolis, H., & McGettigan, J. (1988). Managing resistance to instructional modifications in mainstreamed environments. *Remedial and Special Education, 9*(4), 15–21.

Martin, M. (1983). Success! Teaching spelling with music. *Academic Therapy, 18*, 505–507.

Martin, R. (1991). *Extraordinary children, ordinary lives: Stories behind special education case law*. Champaign, IL: McNaughton and Gunn.

Martin, R. (1992a). Problems with severe discrepancy formulas. *LDA Newsbriefs, 27*(4), 3, 7.

Martin, R. (1992b). *Continuing challenges in special education law*. Urbana, IL: Carle Media.

Martin, R. (1994). Learning disabilities and the law. *LDA Newsbriefs, 29*(2), 18–19.

Masters, L. F., Mori, B. A., & Mori, A. A. (1993). *Teaching secondary students with mild learning and behavior problems: Methods, materials, strategies*. Austin, TX: PRO-ED.

Mastropieri, M. (1987). Statistical and psychometric issues surrounding severe discrepancy: A discussion. *Learning Disabilities Research, 3*, 29–31.

Mather, N. (1991). *An instructional guide to the Woodcock-Johnson Psycho-Educational Battery—Revised*. Brandon, VT: Clinical Psychology Publishing Co.

Mather, N., & Bos, C. (1994). Educational computing and multimedia. In C. S. Bos & S. Vaughn (Eds.), *Strategies for teaching students with learning and behavior problems* (4th ed.) (pp. 390–417). Boston: Allyn and Bacon.

Mather, N., & Healey, W. C. (1990). Deposing aptitude-achievement discrepancy as the imperial criterion for learning disabilities. *Learning Disabilities: A Multidisciplinary Journal, 1*, 40–48.

Mather, N., & Jaffe, L. (1992). *Woodcock-Johnson Psycho-Educational Battery—Revised: Recommendations and reports*. Brandon, VT: CPPC.

Mather, N., & Lachowicz, B. (1992). Shared writing: An approach for reluctant writers. *Teaching Exceptional Children, 25*(1), 26–30.

McCarney, S. B., & Cummins, K. K. (1988). *The pre-referral intervention manual: The most common learning and behavior problems encountered in the educational environment*. Columbia, MO: Hawthorne Educational Services.

McCarthey, S. J. (1994). Authors, text, and talk: The internalization of dialogue from social interaction during writing. *Reading Research Quarterly, 29*, 201–231.

McCoy, K. M., & Prehm, H. J. (1987). *Teaching mainstreamed students: Methods and techniques*. Denver: Love.

McCutchen, D., Covill, A., Hoyne, S. H., & Mildes, K. (1994). Individual differences in writing: Implications of translating fluency. *Journal of Educational Psychology, 86*, 256–266.

McGregor, K. K., & Leonard, L. B. (1989). Facilitating word-finding skills of language-impaired children. *Journal of Speech and Hearing Disorders, 54*, 141–147.

McKeown, M. G., & Beck, I. L. (1988). Learning vocabulary: Different ways for different goals. *Remedial and Special Education, 9*(1), 42–52.

Meese, R. L. (1994). *Teaching learners with mild disabilities: Integrating research and practice*. Pacific Grove, CA: Brooks/Cole.

Mehlmann, M. A., & Waters, M. K. (1985). From write to right. *Academic Therapy, 20*, 583–586.

Mercer, C. D., & Mercer, A. R. (1993). *Teaching students with learning problems* (4th ed.). Macmillan: New York.

Messerer, J., & Lerner, J. W. (1989). Word processing for learning disabled students. *Learning Disabilities Focus, 5*, 3–17.

Meyer, A., Pisha, B., & Rose, D. (1991). Process and product in writing: Computer as enabler. In A. M. Bain, L. L. Bailet, & L. C. Moats (Eds.), *Written language disorders: Theory into practice* (pp. 99–128). Austin, TX: PRO-ED.

Meyer, B. J. F. (1975). *The organization of prose and its effects on memory*. Amsterdam: North Holland.

Meyer, B. J. F., Brandt, D. H., & Bluth, G. J. (1980). Use of authors' textual schema: Key for ninth-graders' comprehension. *Reading Research Quarterly, 16*, 72–103.

Milone, M. N., Wilhide, J. A., & Wasylyk, T. M. (1984). Spelling and handwriting: Is there a relationship? In W. B. Barbe, V. G. Lucas, & T. M. Wasylyk (Eds.), *Handwriting: Basic skills for effective communication* (pp. 246–250). Columbus, OH: Zaner-Bloser.

Moats, L. C. (1991a). Conclusion. In A. M. Bain, L. L. Bailet, & L. C. Moats (Eds.), *Written language disorders: Theory into practice* (pp. 189–191). Austin, TX: PRO-ED.

Moats, L. C. (1991b). Spelling disability in adolescents and adults. In A. M. Bain, L. L. Bailet, & L. C. Moats (Eds.), *Written language disorders: Theory into practice* (pp. 23–42). Austin, TX: PRO-ED.

Montague, M., & Graves, A. (1993). Improving students' story writing. *Teaching Exceptional Children, 25*(4), 36–37.

Montague, M., Graves, A., & Leavell, A. (1991). Planning, procedural facilitation, and narrative composition of junior high students with learning disabilities. *Learning Disabilities Research & Practice, 6*, 219–224.

Montague, M., & Leavell, A. G. (1994). Improving the narrative writing of students with learning disabilities. *Remedial and Special Education, 15*(1), 21–33.

Montague, M., Maddux, C. D., & Dereshiwsky, M. I. (1990). Story grammar and comprehension and production of narrative prose by students with learning disabilities. *Journal of Learning Disabilities, 23*, 190–197.

Moran, M. R. (1981). Performance of learning disabled and low achieving secondary students on formal features of a paragraph-writing task. *Learning Disability Quarterly, 4*, 271–280.

Moran, M. R. (1983). Learning disabled adolescents' responses to a paragraph-organization strategy. *Pointer, 27*(2), 28–31.

Moran, M. R. (1987). Individualized objectives for writing instruction. *Topics in Language Disorders, 7*, 42–54.

Moran, M. R. (1988). Reading and writing disorders in the learning disabled student. In N. J. Lass, L. V. McReynolds, J. L. Northern, & D. E. Yoder (Eds.), *Handbook of speech-language pathology and audiology* (pp. 835–857). Philadelphia: Brian C. Decker.

Morris, N. T., & Crump, W. D. (1982), Syntactic and vocabulary development in the written language of learning disabled and non-learning disabled students at four age levels. *Learning Disability Quarterly, 5*, 163–172.

Mosenthal, J. H., & Englert, C. S. (1987). The beginning capacity to teach writing. *Remedial and Special Education, 8*(6), 38–47.

Moulton, J. R., & Bader, M. S. (1986). The writing process: A powerful approach for the language-disabled student. *Annals of Dyslexia, 35*, 161–173.

Murray, D. M. (1980). Writing as process: How writing finds its own meaning. In T. R. Donovan & B. W. McClelland (Eds.), *Eight approaches to teaching composition* (pp. 3–20). Urbana, IL: NCTE.

Myklebust, H. R. (1965). *Development and disorders of written language, Vol. 1: Picture Story Language Test.* New York: Grune & Stratton.

Myklebust, H. R. (1973). *Development and disorders of written language: Studies of normal and exceptional children* (Vol. 2). New York: Grune & Stratton.

Nagy, W. E., Diakidoy, I. N., & Anderson, R. C. (1993). The acquisition of morphology: Learning the contribution of suffixes to the meanings of derivatives. *Journal of Reading Behavior, 25*, 155–170.

Newcomer, P. L., & Barenbaum, E. M. (1991). The written composing ability of children with learning disabilities: A review of the literature from 1980 to 1990. *Journal of Learning Disabilities, 24*, 578–593.

Nezworski, T., Stein, N., & Trabasso, T. (1982). Story structure versus content in children's recall. *Journal of Verbal Learning and Verbal Behavior, 21*, 196–206.

Nichols, J. N. (1980). Using paragraph frames to help remedial high school students with written assignments. *Journal of Reading, 24*, 228–231.

Niedermeyer, F. (1973). Kindergartners learn to write. *Elementary School Journal, 74*, 130–135.

Nodine, B. F., Barenbaum, E., & Newcomer, P. (1985). Story composition by learning disabled, reading disabled, and normal children. *Learning Disability Quarterly, 8*, 167–179.

Nutter, N., & Safran, J (1984). Improving writing with sentence combining exercises. *Academic Therapy, 19,* 449–455.

OCR Senior Staff Memorandum, 19 IDELR 894 (OCR 1992).

Ogle, D. M. (1986). K-W-L: A teaching model that develops active reading of expository text. *Reading Teacher, 39,* 564–570.

Olrich, F. (1983). A 'whole person' spelling class. *Academic Therapy, 19,* 73–78.

Olsen, J. Z. (1994). *Handwriting without tears.* Potomac, MD: Author.

Opitz, M. F., & Cooper, D. (1993). Adapting the spelling basal for spelling workshop. *Reading Teacher, 47,* 106–113.

Ormrod, J. E. (1986). A learning strategy for phonetic spellers. *Academic Therapy, 22,* 195–198.

Outhred, L. (1989). Word processing: Its impact on children's writing. *Journal of Learning Disabilities, 22,* 262–264.

Palinscar, A. S., & Brown, D. A. (1987). Enhancing instructional time through attention to metacognition. *Journal of Learning Disabilities, 20,* 66–75.

Perfetti, C. A., & Hogaboam, T. (1975). Relationship between single word decoding and reading comprehension skill. *Journal of Learning Disabilities, 67,* 461–469.

Peters, M. L. (1979). *Diagnostic and remedial spelling manual* (rev. ed.). London: Macmillan Education.

Phelps-Gunn, T., & Phelps-Terasaki, D. (1982). *Written language instruction: Theory and remediation.* Rockville, MD: Aspen.

Phelps-Terasaki, D., & Phelps, T. (1980). *Teaching written expression: The Phelps sentence guide program.* Novato, CA: Academic Therapy.

Polloway, E. A., & Patton, J. R. (1993). *Strategies for teaching learners with special needs.* New York: Merrill.

Polloway, E., Patton, J., & Cohen, S. (1981). Written language for mildly handicapped students. *Focus on Exceptional Children, 14*(3), 1–16.

Polloway, E. A., & Smith, T. E. C. (1992). *Language instruction for students with disabilities* (2nd ed.). Denver, CO: Love.

Poplin, M., Gray, R., Larsen, S., Banikowski, A., & Mehring, T. (1980). A comparison of the components of written expression abilities in learning and non-learning disabled children at three grade levels. *Learning Disability Quarterly, 3*(4), 46–53.

Poteet, J. A. (1978). *Characteristics of written expression of learning disabled and non-learning disabled elementary school students.* Muncie, IN: Ball State University. (ERIC Document Reproduction Service No. ED 159 465)

Poteet, J. A. (1980). Informal assessment of written expression. *Learning Disability Quarterly, 3,* 88–98.

Poteet, J. A. (1987). Written expression. In J. S. Choate, T. Z. Bennett, B. E. Enright, L. J. Miller, J. A. Poteet, & T. A. Rakes (Eds.), *Assessing and programming basic curriculum skills* (pp. 147–176). Boston: Allyn and Bacon.

Pressley, M., Borkowski, J. G., & O'Sullivan, J. T. (1984). Memory strategy instruction is made of this: Metamemory and durable strategy use. *Educational Psychology, 19,* 94–107.

Pressley, M., & Rankin, J. (1994). More about whole language methods of reading instruction for students at risk for early reading failure. *Learning Disabilities Research & Practice, 9,* 157–168.

Raimes, A. (1983). *Techniques in teaching writing.* New York: Oxford University Press.

Read, C. (1986). *Children's creative spelling.* London: Routledge and Kegan Paul.

Reid, D. K. (1988). *Teaching the learning disabled: A cognitive developmental approach.* Boston: Allyn and Bacon.

Reynolds, C. R. (1984–1985). Critical measurement issues in learning disabilities. *Journal of Special Education, 18,* 451–476.

Rhodes, L. K., & Dudley-Marling, C. (1988). *Readers and writers with a difference: A holistic approach to teaching learning disabled and remedial students.* Portsmouth, NH: Heinemann.

Rieth, H. J., Polsgrove, L., & Eckert, R. (1984). A computer-based spelling program. *Academic Therapy, 20,* 59–65.

Roit, M. L., & McKenzie, R. G. (1985). Disorders of written communication: An instructional priority for LD students. *Journal of Learning Disabilities, 18,* 258–260.

Rooney, K. J. (1990). *Independent strategies for efficient study.* Richmond, VA: J. R. Enterprises.

Roth, F. P., & Spekman, N. J. (1989). Higher-order language processes and reading disabilities. In A. G. Kamhi & H. W. Catts (Eds.), *Reading and disabilities: A developmental language perspective* (pp. 159–197). Boston: Little, Brown.

Ruedy, L. R. (1983). Handwriting instruction: It can be part of the high school curriculum. *Academic Therapy*, *18*, 421–429.

Rumsey, I., & Ballard, K. D. (1985). Teaching self-management strategies for independent story writing to children with classroom behavior difficulties. *Educational Psychology*, *5*, 147–157.

Salend, S. J. (1994). *Effective mainstreaming: Creating inclusive classrooms* (2nd ed.). New York: Macmillan.

Sampson, M. R., Van Allen, R., & Sampson, M. B. (1991). *Pathways to literacy*. Fort Worth, TX: Holt, Rinehart, and Winston.

Santa, C. M. (1988). *Content reading including study systems: Reading, writing, and studying across the curriculum*. Dubuque, IA: Kendall/Hunt.

Sawyer, R., Graham, S., & Harris, K. R. (1992). Direct teaching, strategy instruction, and strategy instruction with explicit self-regulation: Effects on learning disabled students' composition skills and self-efficacy. *Journal of Educational Psychology*, *84*, 340–352.

Scardamalia, M., & Bereiter, C. (1986). Research on written composition. In M. Wittrock (Ed.), *Handbook of research on teaching* (pp. 778–803). New York: Macmillan.

Scarrozzo, M. L. (1982). Let's dictate spelling success. *Academic Therapy*, *18*, 213–215.

Scheuermann, B., Jacobs, W. R., McCall, C., & Knies, W. C. (1994). The personal spelling dictionary: An adaptive approach to reducing the spelling hurdle in written language. *Intervention in School and Clinic*, *29*, 292–299.

Schlegel, M., & Bos, C. S. (1986). *STORE the story: Fiction/fantasy reading comprehension and writing strategy*. Unpublished manuscript, University of Arizona, Department of Special Education and Rehabilitation, Tucson.

Schumaker, J. B., Deshler, D. D., Nolan, S., Clark, F. L., Alley, G. R., & Warner, M. M. (1981). *Error monitoring: A learning strategy for improving academic performance of LD adolescents* (Research Report No. 32). Lawrence, KS: University of Kansas Institute for Research in Learning Disabilities.

Schumaker, J., Nolan, S., & Deshler, D. (1985). *The error monitoring strategy*. Lawrence: The University of Kansas.

Schumaker, J., & Sheldon, J. (1985). *The sentence writing strategy*. Lawrence: The University of Kansas.

Schunk, D. H. (1989). Self-efficacy and cognitive achievement: Implications for students with learning problems. *Journal of Learning Disabilities*, *22*, 14–22.

Schunk, D. H. (1991). Goal setting and self-evaluation: A social cognitive perspective on self-regulation. In M. L. Maeher & P. R. Pintrich (Eds.), *Advances in motivation and achievement* (Vol 7., pp. 85–113). Greenwich, CT: JAI Press.

Schunk, D. H., & Swartz, C. W. (1993). Writing strategy instruction with gifted students: Effects of goals and feedback on self-efficacy and skills. *Roeper Review*, *15*, 225–230.

Schwartz, J. (1977). Rewriting or recopying: What are we teaching? *Language Arts*, *54*, 756–759.

Scott, S. S. (1990). Coming to terms with the "otherwise qualified" student with a learning disability. *Journal of Learning Disabilities*, *23*, 398–405.

Scott, S. S. (1994). Determining reasonable academic adjustments for college students with learning disabilities. *Journal of Learning Disabilities*, *27*, 403–412.

Seabaugh, G. O., & Schumaker, J. B. (1981). *The effects of self-regulation training on academic productivity of LD and NLD adolescents* (Research Report No. 37). Lawrence: University of Kansas.

Section 504 of the Rehabilitation Act of 1973, 29 U.S.C. S. 794, P.L. 93–112.

Section 504 of the Rehabilitation Act of 1973, Implementing Regulations, 34 C.F.R. Part 104 (1988).

Seidenberg, P. L. (1989). Understanding learning disabilities. In D. K. Bernstein & E. Tiegerman (Eds.), *Language and communication disorders* (2nd ed.) (pp. 375–416). Columbus: Merrill.

Silliman, E. R., & Wilkinson, L. C. (1994). Discourse scaffolds for classroom intervention. In G. P. Wallach & K. G. Butler (Eds.), *Language learning disabilities in school-age children and adolescents* (pp. 27–52). New York: Merrill.

Silverman, R., Zigmond, N., Zimmerman, J. M., & Vallecorsa, A. (1981). Improving written expression in learning disabled students. *Topics in Language Disorders*, *2*(1), 91–99.

Simmons, D. C., & Kameenui, E. J. (1990). The effect of task alternatives on vocabulary knowledge: A comparison of students with and without learning disabilities. *Journal of Learning Disabilities, 23,* 291–297, 316.

Simms, R. B. (1983). Feedback: A key to effective writing. *Academic Therapy, 19,* 31–36.

Sisernos, K., & Bullock, M. (1983). How do you spell Holiday? *Instructor, 93*(4), 60–61, 160.

Sloan, G. (1983). Transitions: Relationships among T-units. *College Composition and Communication, 34,* 447–453.

Smith, C. R. (1994). *Learning disabilities: The interaction of learner, task, and setting.* Boston: Allyn and Bacon.

Smith, D. D., & Luckasson, R. (1992). *Introduction to special education: Teaching in an age of challenge.* Needham Heights, MA: Allyn and Bacon.

Smith, F. (1982). *Writing and the writer.* New York: Holt, Rinehart, and Winston.

Smith, H. (1975). Teaching spelling. *British Journal of Educational Psychology, 45,* 68–72.

Snyder, I. (1993). The impact of computers on students' writing: A comparative study of the effects of pens and word processors on writing context, process and product. *Australian Journal of Education, 37,* 5–25.

Southeastern Community College v. Davis. 442 U.S. 397 (99 S. Ct. 2361, 1979).

Sparks, J. E. (1982). *Write for power.* Los Angeles: Communication Associates.

Stahl, S. (1983). Differential word knowledge and reading comprehension. *Journal of Reading Behavior, 15,* 33–50.

Stahl, S. A., & Murray, B. A. (1994). Defining phonological awareness and its relationship to early reading. *Journal of Educational Psychology, 86,* 221–234.

Stanovich, K. E. (1982a). Individual differences in the cognitive processes of reading: I. Word decoding. *Journal of Learning Disabilities, 15,* 485–493.

Stanovich, K. E. (1982b). Individual differences in the cognitive processes of reading: II. Text-level processes. *Journal of Learning Disabilities, 15,* 549–554.

State University of New York, (Complaint No. 02-92-2106) (OCR Region II 1993).

Stein, M. (1983). Finger spelling: A kinesthetic aid to phonetic spelling. *Academic Therapy, 18,* 305–313.

Stein, N., & Glenn, C. G. (1979). An analysis of story comprehension in elementary school children. In R. O. Freedle (Ed.), *New directions in discourse processes, Vol. 2* (pp. 53–120). Norwood, NJ: Ablex.

Stein, N. L., & Trabasso, T. (1982). What's in a story?: An approach to comprehension and instruction. In R. Glaser (Ed.), *Advances in instructional psychology* (Vol. 2, pp. 213–267). Hillsdale, NJ: Erlbaum.

Stewart, S. R. (1992). Development of written language proficiency: Methods for teaching text structure. In C. S. Simon (Ed.), *Communication skills and classroom success* (pp. 419–432). Eau Claire, WI: Thinking Publications.

Strickland, R. G. (1972). Evaluating children's composition. In H. Newman (Ed.), *Effective language arts practices in the elementary school: Selected readings* (pp. 496–509). New York: John Wiley.

Strominger, A. Z., & Bashir, A. S. (1977). A nine-year follow-up of language-delayed children. Presented at the Annual Convention of the American Speech-Language and Hearing Association, Chicago.

Struthers, J. P., Bartlamay, H., Bell, S., & McLaughlin, T. F. (1994). An analysis of the add-a-word spelling program and public posting across three categories of children with special needs. *Reading Improvement, 31,* 28–36.

Stubbs, M. (1980). *Language and literacy: The sociology of reading and writing.* London: Routledge & Kegan Paul.

Sutaria, S. (1984). A stitch in time: Adapting Fernald's method. *Academic Therapy, 19*(3), 309–315.

Tangel, D. M., & Blachman, B. A. (1992). Effect of phoneme awareness instruction on kindergarten children's invented spelling. *Journal of Reading Behavior, 24,* 233–258.

Teale, B. (1992). Dear readers. *Language Arts, 69,* 401–402.

Thomas, C. C., Englert, C. S., & Gregg, S. (1987). An analysis of errors and strategies in expository writing of learning disabled students. *Remedial and Special Education, 8*(1), 21–30, 46.

Thomas, C. C., Englert, C. S., & Morsink, C. (1984). Modifying the classroom program in language. In C. V. Morsink (Ed.), *Teaching special needs students in regular classrooms* (pp. 239–276). Boston: Little, Brown.

Thomas, K. (1978). Instructional applications of the cloze technique. *Reading World, 18*, 1–12.

Thurber, D. N. (1983). Write on! With continuous stroke point. *Academic Therapy, 18*, 389–395.

Thurber, D. N. (1988). The D'Nealian pencil grip. *Communication Outlook, 9*(4), 11.

Tindal, G., & Hasbrouck, J. (1991). Analyzing student writing to develop instructional strategies. *Learning Disabilities Research & Practice, 6*, 237–245.

Tomlan, P. S. (1986). *The psycholinguistic analyses of learning disabled adolescents' written language abilities*. Unpublished doctoral dissertation. University of New Mexico, Albuquerque.

Tompkins, G. E. (1994). *Teaching writing: Balancing process and product* (2nd ed.). New York: Macmillan.

Tompkins, G. E., & Friend, M. (1986). On your mark, get set, write! *Teaching Exceptional Children, 18*(2), 82–89.

Tompkins, G. E., & Friend, M. (1988). After your students write: What's next? *Teaching Exceptional Children, 20*(3), 4–9.

Toombs, M. (1990). OCR rulings on handicapped under Section 504. *LDA Newsbriefs, 25*(4), 12,13.

Torgesen, J. (1986). Learning disabilities theory: Its current state and future prospects. *Journal of Learning Disabilities, 19*, 399–407.

Uhry, J. K., & Shepherd, M. J. (1993). Segmentation/spelling instruction as part of a first-grade reading program: Effects on several measures of reading. *Reading Research Quarterly, 28*, 219–233.

Vallecorsa, A., & Garriss, C. (1990). Story composition skills of middle-grade students with learning disabilities. *Exceptional Children, 57*, 48–53.

Van Allen, R. (1976). *Language experiences in communication*. Boston: Houghton Mifflin.

Van Ness, E. (1989, April 9). As easy as 1-3-2. *New York Times, Education Life Supplement*, pp. 47–48.

Vellutino, F. R., Scanlon, D. M., & Tanzman, M. S. (1994). Components of reading ability: Issues and problems in operationalizing word identification, phonological coding, and orthographic coding. In G. R. Lyon (Ed.), *Frames of reference for the assessment of learning disabilities* (pp. 279–329). Baltimore: Paul H. Brookes.

Vogel, S. A. (1974). Syntactic abilities in normal and dyslexic children. *Journal of Learning Disabilities, 7*, 103–109.

Vogel, S. A. (1985). Syntactic complexity in written expression of LD college writers. *Annals of Dyslexia, 35*, 137–157.

Vogel, S. (1987). Issues and concerns in LD college programming. In D. J. Johnson & J. W. Blalock (Eds.), *Adults with learning disabilities* (pp. 239–275). New York: Grune & Stratton.

Vogel, S. (1989). Some special considerations in the development of models for diagnosis of LD adults. In L. Silver (Ed.), *Crisis in education: Diagnosis of learning disabilities in public school* (pp. 111–134). Boston: College-Hill Press.

Vogel, S., & Moran, M. R. (1982). Written language disorders in learning disabled college students: A preliminary report. In W. Cruickshank & J. Lerner (Eds.), *The Best of ACLD 1981: Vol 3. Coming of age* (pp. 211–225). Syracuse: Syracuse University Press.

Vygotsky, L. S. (1962). *Thought and language*. Cambridge, MA: MIT Press.

Vygotsky, L. S. (1978). *Mind in society*. Cambridge, MA: Harvard University Press.

Wallace, G. W., & Bott, D. A. (1989). Statement-pie: A strategy to improve the paragraph writing skills of adolescents with learning disabilities. *Journal of Learning Disabilities, 22*, 541–543, 553.

Wallach, G. P., & Miller, L. (1988). *Language intervention and academic success*. Boston: Little, Brown and Company.

Walmsly, S. A. (1984). Helping the learning disabled child overcome writing difficulties in the classroom. *Topics in Learning and Learning Disabilities, 3*, 81–90.

Weaver, P., & Dickinson, D. (1982). Scratching below the surface structure: Exploring the usefulness of story grammars. *Discourse Processes, 5*, 225–244.

Weiner, S. (1994). Four first graders' descriptions of how they spell. *Elementary School Journal, 94*, 315–332.

Weiss, M. S., & Weiss, H. G. (1993). *Formulas to read and write*. Avon, CO: Treehouse Associates.

Welch, M. (1992). The *PLEASE* strategy: A metacognitive learning strategy for improving the paragraph writing of students with mild learning disabilities. *Learning Disability Quarterly, 15*, 119–128.

Welch, M., & Jensen, J. (1991). Write, PLEASE: A video-assisted strategic intervention to improve written expression. *Remedial and Special Education*, *12*, 37–47.

Westby, C. E. (1994). The effects of culture on genre, structure, and style of oral and written texts. In G. P. Wallach & K. G. Butler (Eds.), *Language learning disabilities in school-age children and adolescents* (pp. 180–218). New York: Merrill.

Westerman, G. (1971). *Spelling and writing.* San Rafael, CA: Dimensions.

Whaley, J. F. (1981). Story grammars and reading instruction. *Reading Teacher*, *34*, 762–771.

White, E. J. (1979). *Dysnomia in the adolescent dyslexic and the developmentally delayed adolescent.* Unpublished doctoral dissertation, Boston University.

Whitt, J., Paul, V. P., & Reynolds, C. J. (1988). Motivate reluctant learning disabled writers. *Teaching Exceptional Children*, *20*(3), 37–39.

Wiig, E. H. (1981). *Language-learning disabilities in school-age children.* Presented at the American Speech-Language-Hearing Northeast Regional conference, Philadelphia.

Wiig, E. H., & Semel, E. M. (1975). Productive language abilities in learning disabled adolescents. *Journal of Learning Disabilities*, *8*, 578–586.

Wiig, E. H., & Semel, E. M. (1984). *Language assessment and intervention for the learning disabled.* Columbus, OH: Merrill.

Wiig, E. H., Semel, E. M., & Nystrom, L. A. (1982). Comparison of rapid naming abilities in learning disabled and academically achieving eight-year olds. *Language, Speech and Hearing Services in Schools*, *13*, 11–23.

Wilde, S. (1990). A proposal for a new spelling curriculum. *Elementary School Journal*, *90*, 275–289.

Willis, M. S. (1993). Deep revision. *Teachers & Writers*, *25*(1), 1–8.

Willows, D. M., & Terepocki, M. (1993). The relation of reversal errors to reading disabilities. In D. M. Willows, R. S. Kruk, & E. Corcos (Eds.), *Visual processes in reading and reading disabilities* (pp. 31–56). Hillsdale, NJ: Lawrence Erlbaum.

Wing, C. S. (1990). A preliminary investigation of generalization to untrained words following two

treatments of children's word-finding problems. *Language, Speech, and Hearing Services in Schools, 21*, 151–156.

Witte, S. P., & Faigley, L. (1981). Coherence, cohesion, and writing ability. *College Composition and Communication*, *32*, 189–204.

Wolf, M. (1986). Rapid alternating stimulus naming in the developmental dyslexias. *Brain and Language*, *27*, 360–379.

Wong, B. Y. L. (1986). A cognitive approach to spelling. *Exceptional Children*, *53*, 169–173.

Wong, B. Y. L., Butler, D. L., Ficzere, S. A., Kuperis, S., Corden, M., & Zelmer, J. (1994). Teaching problem learners revision skills and sensitivity to audience through two instructional modes: Student-teacher versus student-student interactive dialogues. *Learning Disabilities Research & Practice*, *9*, 78–90.

Wong, B., Wong, R., & Blenkinsop, J. (1989). Cognitive and metacognitive aspects of learning disabled adolescents' composing problems. *Learning Disability Quarterly*, *12*, 300–322.

Wong, B. Y. L., Wong, R., Darlington, D., & Jones, W. (1991). Interactive teaching: An effective way to teach revision skills to adolescents with learning disabilities. *Learning Disabilities Research & Practice*, *6*, 117–127.

Wood, J. W. (1993). *Mainstreaming: A practical approach for teachers.* New York: Merrill.

Woodcock, R. W., & Johnson, M. B. (1989). *Woodcock-Johnson Psycho-Educational Battery—Revised.* Chicago, IL: Riverside.

Worden, P. (1986). Prose comprehension and recall in disabled learners. In S. Ceci (Ed.), *Handbook of cognitive, social, and neurological aspects of learning disabilities* (Vol. 1, pp. 241–262). Hillsdale, NJ: Erlbaum.

Wysocki, K., & Jenkins, J. R. (1987). Deriving word meanings through morphological generalization. *Reading Research Quarterly*, *22*, 66–81.

Zaragoza, N., & Vaughn, S. (1992). The effects of process writing instruction on three 2nd-grade students with different achievement profiles. *Learning Disabilities Research & Practice*, *7*, 184–193.

SUBJECT INDEX

AUTHOR INDEX